HENRY ADAMS

AND THE

MAKING OF AMERICA

Henry Adams

AND THE

Making of America

———◆———

Garry Wills

HOUGHTON MIFFLIN COMPANY

BOSTON · NEW YORK

2005

For information about permission to reproduce selections
from this book, write to Permissions, Houghton Mifflin Company,
215 Park Avenue South, New York, New York 10003.

Visit our Web site: www.houghtonmifflinbooks.com.

Library of Congress Cataloging-in-Publication Data
Wills, Garry, date.
Henry Adams and the making of America / Garry Wills.
p.   cm.
Includes bibliographical references and index.
ISBN-10: 0-618-13430-1
ISBN-13: 978-0-618-13430-4
1. Adams, Henry, 1838–1918. History of the United States of
America. 2. United States — Historiography. 3. United States —
History — 1801–1809. 4. United States — History — 1809–1817.
5. Adams, Henry, 1838–1918. 6. Historians—United
States — Biography. I. Title.
E302.1.A2538 2005   973.4'6—dc22
2005040305

Printed in the United States of America

Book design by Robert Overholtzer

QUM 10 9 8 7 6 5 4 3 2 1

TO STUDS TERKEL

national treasure

CONTENTS

Key to Brief Citations   ix

Introduction: Reading Henry Adams Forward   1

Part One: The Making of an Historian

1. Grandmother Louisa and the South   11
2. Boston Historians   33
3. Civil War Politics   49
4. Postwar Politics   72
5. Historical Method   87
6. Historical Artistry   104

Part Two: The Making of a Nation

I. JEFFERSON'S TWO TERMS

1. A People's History: The *History*, Volume One   123
2. Jefferson's Success: The *History*, Volume One   140
3. Reaching Out: The *History*, Volume Two   160
4. Three Foes: The *History*, Volume Three   186
5. Anything but War: The *History*, Volume Four   216

II. MADISON'S TWO TERMS

1. False Dawn: The *History*, Volume Five 249
2. War: The *History*, Volume Six 271
3. Naval History: The *History*, Volume Six 296
4. The War's Second Year: The *History*, Volume Seven 315
5. The War's Third Year: The *History*, Volume Eight 335
6. Shame and Glory: The *History*, Volume Eight 349
7. Peace and Nationalism: The *History*, Volume Nine 366
8. Nation-Making: The *History*, Volume Nine 381

Epilogue 395

Notes 405
Acknowledgments 427
Index 429

KEY TO BRIEF CITATIONS

A   Adams Family Papers, Massachusetts Historical Society

C   Henry and Charles F. Adams, *Chapters of Erie and Other Essays* (Henry Holt, 1877)

DM   Dumas Malone, *Jefferson and His Time,* 6 vols. (Little, Brown, 1948–1981)

E   Henry Adams, *The Education of Henry Adams* (Library of America, 1983)

G   Henry Adams, *The Life of Albert Gallatin* (J. B. Lippincott, 1879)

GS   Henry Adams, *The Great Secession Winter, 1860–61, and Other Essays,* edited by George Hochfield (A. S. Barnes, 1963)

H   Henry Adams, *Historical Essays* (Charles Scribner's Sons, 1891)

J   Henry Adams, *History of the United States of America During the Administrations of Thomas Jefferson* (Library of America, 1986)

JP   *The Papers of Thomas Jefferson,* edited by Julian P. Boyd (Princeton University Press, 1950–)

L   J. C. Levenson et al., editors, *The Letters of Henry Adams* (Harvard University Press, 1982–1988)

M   Henry Adams, *History of the United States During the Administrations of James Madison* (Library of America, 1986)

MHS   Massachusetts Historical Society

NAR   *North American Review*

R   Henry Adams, *John Randolph* (Peter Green, 1969)

S   Ernest Samuels, *Henry Adams,* 3 vols. (Harvard University Press, 1948–1964)

HENRY ADAMS

AND THE

MAKING OF AMERICA

INTRODUCTION

Reading Henry Adams Forward

ENRY ADAMS IS AN AUTHOR deeply esteemed and widely
studied — for what he wrote in the first decade of the twentieth century, when he was in his sixties. But one of the
great mysteries of his life goes all but unnoticed. Why is his
major project so little read, appreciated, or studied? When he was in his
prime, in his forties, he devoted thirteen volumes of historical study to
the first two decades of the nineteenth century in America. His entire
life to that point was a preparation for this epic effort, yet praise for the
work has mainly been perfunctory or misguided. At the core of the
achievement are nine volumes devoted to his country in the years 1800–
1817 — *History of the United States of America During the Administrations of Thomas Jefferson* (four volumes) and *History of the United
States of America During the Administrations of James Madison* (five
volumes). That work is flanked by four volumes dealing with the same
period — *The Writings of Albert Gallatin* (two volumes), *The Life of Albert Gallatin,* and *John Randolph.* He even wrote a fourteenth volume
on the period, a life of Aaron Burr — but he suppressed it. There has
been no complete study of the *History*'s nine volumes, no detailed discussion of what he was saying in those thousands of pages.

Why is this? Is the *History* dull, ill-conceived, poorly executed? Far
from it. I believe it is the non-fiction prose masterpiece of the nineteenth century in America. It is a work that pioneers the new history
coming into existence at the time. It offers archival research on an unprecedented scale in America, and combines it with social and intellec-

tual history, diplomatic and military and economic history. This wealth of material is deployed with wit and a sense of adventure. Adams advances a surprising (almost scandalous) thesis — that the Jeffersonians' four terms at the beginning of the nineteenth century created a national unity and internationalism far in advance of what preceded them. This goes against the announced purpose and subsequent reputation of the Jeffersonians, who claimed to be opposed to such developments. They assumed power to decrease power, to de-centralize the government, to withdraw from international "entanglements."

Adams thinks it is fortunate that they did nothing of the sort. Despite some later changes in his attitude, he was a fervent nationalist and proto-imperialist in the 1880s, cheering on the formation of a trans-sectional politics and an activist federal government. But what is surprising, what gives the volumes their paradoxical flourish, is his contention that *only* the Jeffersonians could have created the national unity they began by deploring. They alone combined the high vision and practical tinkering, the regional ideology and trans-regional organization, the American optimism and sense of destiny, the ambitions for the West, that could bring it all off. It is said of the British that they acquired an empire in a fit of absent-mindedness. Adams suggests that the Jeffersonians acquired a national identity in the same way. All this makes for exciting reading. Nothing occurs as expected. The *History* is as full of historical paradoxes as Tolstoy's *War and Peace*. The shifts and developments in the years covered by Adams call for close and fascinating analysis. Yet the *History* is neglected, even by Adams scholars (who reserve their scholarship for later works), or it is misrepresented, even by leading historians.

A striking example of misrepresentation is offered by the eminent historian Richard Hofstadter. He claims that the misanthropic Adams actually chose a low and vile period of sixteen years to cover in his *History*. Why would he do such a thing? To give a dark view of his own country, in keeping with his own pessimism and doubts about democracy. The time of the Jeffersonians, says Hofstadter, was "regarded by the author himself as dreary and unproductive, as an age of slack and derivative culture, of fumbling and small-minded statecraft, terrible parochial wrangling and treasonous schemes, climaxed by a ludicrous and unnecessary war."[1] Every point Hofstadter raises is manifestly wrong. He describes an Adams critical of the War of 1812 — yet Adams thought that conflict not only necessary but overdue, and he celebrated its feats and heroes with gusto. He sides with Albert Gallatin, who wanted to begin the war during Jefferson's second term.

Hofstadter says that the four presidential terms Adams treats were marked by "small-minded statecraft," though Adams said of the Jefferson-Madison-Gallatin "triumvirate" that "no statesman has ever appeared with the strength to bend their bow" (G 92). In fact, two of the three American leaders Adams admired most (after Washington) were shapers of the period Hofstadter calls "dreary" — Gallatin and John Marshall — and Adams always claimed that "Washington *and Jefferson* doubtless stand pre-eminent as the representatives of what is best in our national character or its aspirations" (G 267, emphasis added). He presents the triumph of Jeffersonians over Hamiltonians as a victory of the American mind, since "everyone admitted that Jefferson's opinions, in one form or another, were shared by a majority of the American people" (J 117). The triumph was a fortunate one: "Mr. Jefferson meant that the American system should be a democracy, and he would rather have let the world perish than that this principle, which to him represented all that man was worth, should fail. Mr. Hamilton considered democracy a fatal curse, and meant to stop its progress" (G 159).

How could an historian of Hofstadter's stature think that this triumph of Jeffersonianism was a sign of "small-minded statecraft"? The answer to that question is one of the true scandals of American historiography, since other well-known historians — including Henry Steele Commager and Merrill Peterson — have said the same thing and they have not been challenged. The answer is that Hofstadter had read the first six chapters of the first volume of the *History* and *accepted that as a description of the whole work*. The opening chapters, often hailed as an early example of "social history," have usually been read in isolation — or even printed in isolation. They survey the state of the country in the year 1800. They give a picture that is, indeed, accurately reported in Hofstadter's claim about the whole work, presenting a country weak and divided, intellectually stunted, bereft of energetic leadership. But he is describing the state of things *before Jefferson's inauguration in the next year* — he is describing the conditions under the presidency of his great-grandfather, John Adams. His point is that things were about to change dramatically.

The proof of this is that the *History*'s last four chapters, coming at the end of the nine volumes, present a vivid contrast to the first four. They praise a nation strong and united, intellectually alert, technologically innovative, religiously tolerant, and looking beyond its borders for prog-

ress. This was accomplished by the Jeffersonians — by Jefferson himself, and Madison, and their key associate (Adams's particular hero)
Albert Gallatin. It is almost unbelievable that a man could present the
opening chapters as Adams's judgment on the whole period and not recognize the pendant at the end. They are bookends, meant to be read in
terms of each other. "Look here upon this picture — and on this." But
Hofstadter is not the worst offender here. Another well-known historian, Noble Cunningham, published a separate book, based on a lecture
series, devoted entirely to the first six chapters of the *History,* presenting
them as an attack on Jefferson — and he too does not even refer to the
final four chapters, on the changes wrought in the course of the sixteen
years covered in the nine volumes of history.[2] He gives us the chrysa-
lis without the butterfly, the windup without the pitch. And, like Hofstadter, he presents the opening picture as typical of the whole work. In
fact, when Adams gives a hint, at the end of his opening chapters, of
better things to come, Cunningham says this is an anomalous note to
be disregarded. He cannot have read the last chapters that fulfill that
prophecy of a bright future.

How could this scandal occur? How could learned men accept so easily that the first chapters were so important that the rest of the series
could be ignored? There are two other factors that contribute to this result. Readers are disposed to think the opening chapters represent the
whole of the *History* because they accept what Hofstadter himself calls
the "family feud" thesis of the *History.*[3] This thesis, held by almost all
who comment on the *History,* is that Adams was out to avenge his own
presidential ancestors by denigrating the man who defeated John Adams and who showed insufficient gratitude to John Quincy Adams for
his support of the Embargo. Adams meant to depict a "decline in statesmanship" from the nobler time of the Federalists.[4] He displayed his "resentment against an old family foe."[5]

But Adams never defended the Federalists. He despised Hamilton,
and he told his Harvard students, "You know, gentlemen, John Adams
was a demagogue" (S 1.216). His attitude toward his grandfather, John
Quincy Adams, was far more caustic — he called him an opportunist in
politics and "demonic" in his family relations.[6] He could not have been
seeking "revenge" for Jefferson's displacement of the Federalists when
he wrote that John Adams's Alien and Sedition Acts proved, in 1800,
that "it was time that opposition should be put in power" (R 35). In the

History itself, he will excoriate the Federalists for their treasonous response to the War of 1812. Henry was so little filiopietistic that he tried to prevent his older brother from publishing a book on their father, Charles Francis Adams, whose achievements he called minor (L 4.467), and he succeeded in quashing his younger brother's book on their grandfather, John Quincy Adams. It is true that he criticizes some of Jefferson's acts in the *History;* but he is never as scathing on them as he is on the Federalists, including his forebears. He thought the Jeffersonians' presidencies highly successful (though in an unintended way) and the Adams presidencies a failure. Yet it is an article of faith in most who refer to the *History* that it is an expression of family animus.

To these first two causes of misunderstanding — taking the first chapters as representative of the whole, and thinking Adams was pursuing a family feud — a third powerful one must be added, perhaps the most influential one — what might be called the *Education* effect. In *The Education of Henry Adams,* privately distributed in 1907 and posthumously published in 1918, Adams does take a world-weary and pessimistic view of the nation and its politics, of the sort read backward into the *History* by way of its dour opening picture of the year 1800. The *Education* is the center of most treatments of Adams. It is the only book of his most people ever read. Since it is mistakenly called an autobiography in its subtitle (an addition by the publisher he would not have approved of), its pessimism is thought to be characteristic of his entire life. This retrojection of later views even leads an eccentric author, Edward Chalfant, to claim that Adams deliberately made the *History* unreadable, its clumsy title hard to cite, so that only an elite — that is, men like Chalfant — could understand it.[7] The author is clearly attributing to the younger man's work what Adams said at the time of the *Education* — that few would understand him, that he did not care, and that "the public is my worst enemy" (L 6.28). Scholars have such a heavy investment in the pessimism of Henry Adams that, for them, an optimistic Adams cannot be the "real" Adams. Yet the mood in which Adams approached his *History,* the mood vindicated in its final chapters, was expressed in 1877 to his best friend, Charles Gaskell:

> As I belong to the class of people who have great faith in this country and who believe that in another century it will be saying in its turn the last word of civilization, I enjoy the expectation of the coming day, and try to imagine

that I am myself, with my fellow *gelehrte* here, the first faint rays of that great light which is to dazzle and set the world on fire hereafter. (L 2.326)

A year before that statement, he had reviewed a German book that called the United States Constitution a failure. Adams argued that it had, on the contrary, conducted the nation toward "real majesty" (GS 287). He said of his nine volumes: "Democracy is the only subject of scientific history" (L 2.563). He worked with incredible energy and concentration through his great project: "I grudge every day which does not show progress in my work. I have but one offspring" (L 2.442). The enthusiasm and engagement of those exciting years are something people will never capture who try to read back into them the lassitude of the *Education*.

The theme of failure that runs through the *Education* bolsters an assumption that Adams is telling the story of a failure when he writes of the Jeffersonians. If the work itself says something else, people are unprepared to hear it. They know what Adams *ought* to be saying, and they make him say it. The spell of the *Education* is all but unbreakable. It is the one Adams book regularly taught in the schools. It is taught by English professors, who dwell on its stylistic ironies and eschatological myths. Adams has become a wholly owned subsidiary of English departments, while he is neglected by history departments. The principal work on Adams was written by an English professor (at my own university), Ernest Samuels, whose three-volume biography traces a rising arc to the summit of a "Major Phase" in the final volume. All else is preparatory to that. All else is read backward from that.

In this book, I mean to reverse the process of reading Adams backward from the *Education*. I will read him forward toward the *History*. It is the trope of the *Education* that Adams repeatedly failed at getting an education. I mean to argue that his studies, his reading of Thucydides and Gibbon, his relations with New England historians, his European travels, his experience in the London legation during the Civil War, his reform activity, his journalism, his teaching, his editing, all equipped him splendidly for the work to which he devoted more years of his life than to any other project. My book has, therefore, two parts, "The Making of an Historian," and "The Making of a Nation." The first part shows how Adams was made the kind of historian who could analyze how the nation was made. The processes of his own development and the nation's are mutually reinforcing. One mirrors the other.

The interaction of intellectual, economic, diplomatic, and military concerns ties Adams's experience of the Civil War to his description of the War of 1812. His acquaintance and work with New England antiquarians taught him to authenticate documents. His work on economic reform after the Civil War affected his understanding of Gallatin's policies. Editing his grandmother's papers introduced him to the mysteries of Washington society and the workings of ambition. Joint projects with his star pupil, Henry Cabot Lodge, re-enacted the dynamics of Federalist–Republican ideological clashes. His own "muckraking" helped him understand the power of journalists like James Callender and William Duane. His efforts to back a reform party showed him the difficulties faced by the Jeffersonians, with their patronage struggles and regional splits. His own resistance to family ties taught him what was dangerous in family cabals like that of the Smiths in Maryland. His insider view of the way Lincoln and Grant formed their cabinets enriched his judgment on Jefferson's and Madison's relations with their advisers. His teaching at Harvard and his visits to European scholars refined his views on historical method. His rides all around Washington inform the topographical detail of his section on the Battle of Bladensburg. Over and over, as one reads the *History,* one can find signs of the extraordinary preparation that fit Adams so precisely for this task. The two parts of my book should be read, as it were, stereoscopically.

There has been a formidable combination of forces making for the neglect or misreading of the *History.* Who, after all, wants to suffer through nine volumes of dreary small-mindedness and failure, of a musty family feud, of a pessimistic attack on democracy and the nation? No wonder there has been no overall treatment of the *History,* much less a volume-by-volume analysis.[8] I shall, in my book's second part, take up each installment to show how Adams shaped the parts of his large structure — the kinds of evidence adduced, the organization of the whole, the narrative ploys used and then adjusted to keep the story moving, the changes in rhetoric called for by the different situations being treated, the judgments (and misjudgments) he made of men and events. I shall indicate the author's weaknesses as well as his many strengths. He was, for instance, too protective of military men in general, too biased in John Marshall's favor, and unfair to Jefferson in the early stages of the Burr conspiracy. He mistakenly thought that war was forced on an unwilling Madison. In fact, his understanding of Madison is considerably less profound than his reading of Jefferson's character. Some who claim to have read the whole nine volumes think there is a falling off in energy or skill in the Madison volumes, but those volumes actually gain new energy in Adams's excitement over the War of 1812, and they glow toward the end in celebration of the Jeffersonians' final achievement. I think some readers may simply be disappointed by the fact that Madison as the central figure is dimmer and less dramatic than Jefferson.

But the full titles of the books have to be kept in mind. This is *a history of the United States of America* during the four presidential terms being treated. And it is a history of the United States in a world setting that did as much to shape the nation as did internal events. Adams is working on a large canvas, where Jefferson shares the spotlight with Napoleon, where Manuel Godoy and Toussaint Louverture had great though unacknowledged influence on America's future. The *History* has a grandeur that suggests his model — Gibbon's *Decline and Fall of the Roman Empire*. Only where Gibbon traced the fall of an empire, Adams traces the rise of a democratic nation (L 2.326). If the Jeffersonians made a nation almost inadvertently, theirs was a comedy of errors, not a tragedy. As Adams wrote: "T. J. is a case for Beaumarchais, he needs the lightest of touches" (L 2.468).

By reading Adams forward toward the *History* rather than backward from the *Education,* one uncovers aspects of the man downplayed or ignored or distorted in many accounts of him — a man optimistic, progressive, and nationalistic, instead of one detached, arch, and pessimistic. Even the prose begins to look different, more energetic, flexible, and engaged, less mannered and self-conscious. I shall quote freely from the *History* to vindicate my claim that it is a prose masterpiece. But anyone can test the thesis simply by opening any page in the nine volumes and reading it through. The first impression is of command and control — command of the evidence, control of the tone and tempo, an easy marshaling of information without strain or obscurity. The general run of language is not uniform, of course. It is more flamboyant at the outset, more caustic or celebratory during the battle scenes of the War of 1812, more hushed in admiration of men like Tecumseh or Toussaint Louverture. But the long-haul performance is a tour de force, an equable flow of words, the best writing he ever did.

PART ONE

❖

THE MAKING OF AN HISTORIAN

1

———◦◆◦———

GRANDMOTHER LOUISA

AND THE SOUTH

On May 20, 1796, Abigail Adams warned her son, John Quincy Adams, against marriage to Louisa Johnson, who was not from New England: "I would hope, for the love I bear my country, that the siren is at least *half blood*." (A 381)

In 1907, Henry Adams wrote of his grandmother, Louisa Johnson Adams: "[I] inherited a quarter taint of Maryland blood." (E 737)

ADAMS COULD NEVER escape the fact that he was a member of *the* Adamses. Yet that does not justify attempts to interpret his whole life as a defense of his family, his region, or his forebears' ideology. In fact, he was determined to escape all three of those things, to be what he called "less Adamsy" (L 6.401). He preferred to be considered a descendant of his Maryland grandmother, Louisa Johnson Adams. His emotional and ideological compass bore due south, from an early age and all through his professional life. Using a genealogical quirk (his grandmother's purported southernness), he sought the South both as symbol and physical location all his life. Except for his six years of teaching at Harvard, Adams preferred Louisa's Washington to Massachusetts, from which he wrote in 1869 that "nothing but sheer poverty shall ever reduce me to passing a whole season here again" (L 2.44).

Most of the men he studied and admired were southerners, and especially Virginians, including his three principal heroes, Washington,

Marshall, and Gallatin (the latter he treated as a Virginian, since Virginia is where Gallatin became an American citizen). The noblest character in his first novel is a Virginian, and the heroine of the tale is the widow of a Virginian. Adams's good friend at Harvard was a Virginian — in fact, the son of Robert E. Lee — and he was visiting the Lee mansion at Arlington the night Lincoln reached Washington for his inauguration.

None of this can cancel the fact that Adams was affected by his own family background. But that was not a simple thing. Those people who claimed that he defended his own family are thinking primarily of the Adamses. But Adams was aware that he was mired in a pretentious muddle of families, of whom the Adamses were the last and least. He was also a Boylston, a Quincy, a Brooks. He wrote his brother Charles: "My own theory of Boylston influence is that you and I have the Boylston strain three times repeated [through their great-grandfather, great-grandmother, and mother]. John Adams had it but once. Which accounts for you and us others being three times as damned a fool as John Adams — which seems hard" (L 6.574).

The Quincy line came from Abigail Adams, and she was very proud of it, unwisely putting its crest on her carriage when she went to New York as the vice president's wife. Henry said that the Quincys were the family's "most aristocratic claim."[1] The Brooks connection was through Henry's own mother, and it made Henry and his siblings the first Adams generation to have inherited wealth. All four of these family lines had ramifying branches dimmed in clouds of in-laws, making Henry live in a forest of cousinhoods. He found this a stifling environment, and came to admire most the one member of his family who had not a drop of Adams, or Boylston, or Quincy, or Brooks blood in her, his grandmother. He exaggerated his blood tie with her, saying it was a "quarter taint" (actually it was an eighth). She had been mistreated by the family, yet she had survived. He meant to do the same. She had been an intruder into the family fold, but she opened a gate through which he could slip free — toward the South.

"The President"

Adams knew his grandmother's husband, John Quincy Adams, during the first ten years of his own life. (His great-grandfather, John Adams, had died twelve years before he was born.) John Quincy stood for the family heritage when Henry was a boy — he was always called "the President" at his Quincy home, where Henry's family spent its summers. The most vivid picture in the first chapter of the *Education* tells how Henry's mother (not otherwise mentioned in the book) could not make her son go to school in the summer, and the president came down from his study to march the boy "near a mile" to school (E 732). Some have taken from this episode an impression that Henry had great respect or affection for the president; but in fact he considered the man incapable of affection, selfish, and cruel. There is no clear evidence when this feeling began; but it was clearly there by his late twenties, when he planned to publish his grandmother's papers.

Later, at the time when he was writing the *Education*, Henry successfully warned his younger brother Brooks not to publish an admiring life he had written of their grandfather. In over eighty pages of scorching commentary on Brooks's manuscript, he said things like this (referring to John Quincy's time as Boylston Lecturer on Rhetoric at Harvard):

> The picture you have drawn of that slovenly German Gelehrte whose highest delight is to lecture boys about a rhetoric of which he never could practice either the style or the action or the voice or the art, and then gloating over his own foolish production in private, instead of rolling on the ground with mortification as his grandchildren would do — this picture grinds the colery [?] into my aesophagus; but it is not so hideous as the picture of his voting for the Embargo under the preposterous and dishonest pretence that it was a measure of resistance, although he knew Jefferson better than anyone else did, and (like Hamilton) knew that Jefferson was a temporizer by nature. Even that is not so bad as his going to caucus to nominate a candidate for the opposition party, an act which scandalized even his admiring mother to hot and just remonstrance. And even this is not so bad as his jumping at the Russian mission and deserting his self-evident duty in Massachusetts at the time of the utmost difficulty and under the hottest kind of fire, avowedly because he wanted to escape attack — my teeth chatter at this exhibition. Yet worse follows! To see him dawdle on in Russia under one pretence or another when his mother and father pray him to come home, and he had ceased to be useful where he is, but during all these years, while the young Americans like Clay are forcing the country to assert some shadow of self respect, I do not see J. Q. A. open his mouth, and his one allusion to the war is to call it a rash act. Finally, I see him find his chief delight in quarreling with foes and friends alike, but still clinging to Europe, until Monroe makes him his tool to break down treacherously the Virginia dynasty which gave Monroe all the credit the idiot ever had.[2]

There is more, much more, of this vituperation.[3] Adams cannot even give J. Q. much credit for his great stand against slavery during his final years in the House of Representatives (which include the ten years when his own life overlapped that of his grandfather):

> Your remark about J. Q. A.'s double nature is as much as you are required to admit, and I think it goes quite as far as I would myself go in public; but the double Puritan nature, with its astonishing faculty of self-deception, was a dart-hole, and when our grandfather upheld Jackson and blinked the Missouri Compromise with its attendant legislation, his critics could not be blamed for charging it on political ambition. Rufus King's record is far better. J. Q. A. deliberately acted as the tool of the slave oligarchy (especially about Florida) and never rebelled until the slave oligarchy contemptuously cut his throat.[4]

These white-hot comments are worth quoting *in extenso,* since they are not in print anywhere else, nor included in the 608 microfilm reels of the Adams Papers:

> I am met by the fact that has always worried us all, and worried his father and mother and wife, that he was abominably selfish or absorbed in self, and incapable of feeling his duty to others. You have pointed at this trait so often that I did not need this last picture of Clay to make me alive to it. His neglect of his father for the sake of his damned weights and measures was almost worse, but his dragging his wife to Europe in 1809 and separating her from her children was demonic.[5]

What can explain such ferocity? The elements for an explanation are in that last sentence, in the earlier references to J. Q.'s stay in Russia, and in the mention of his wife's awareness that he had no "feeling [of] his duty to others." Henry was drawing these judgments from Louisa's papers.

The publication of his grandmother's writings, had he completed it, would have been Henry's first book. He wrote about it to his English friend Charles Gaskell:

> I am myself preparing a volume of Memoirs which may grow to be three volumes if I have patience to toil. It is not an autobiography — *n'ayez pas peur!* An ancient lady of our house has left material for a pleasant story. (L 2.25)

What he calls sardonically a "pleasant story" would show how hard was the fate of an ebullient and delicate woman who married into the iron family of Adamses. His grandmother Louisa is the other vivid presence in the first chapter of the *Education,* which neglects his parents. Henry recalls her as shedding an irresistible grace upon her New England setting. Louisa had been educated in France, spoke French beautifully, and was called by her grandchildren "the Madam":

> He liked her refined figure; her gentle voice and manner; her vague effect of not belonging there, but to Washington or to Europe, like her furniture and writing desk . . . Try as she might, the Madam could never be Bostonian, and it was her cross in life, but to the boy it was her charm. Even at that age he felt drawn to it. (E 735)

After her husband's death, Louisa escaped Quincy by returning to Washington, where her Johnson relatives were, and Henry was charmed all over again when his father took him there at age twelve to visit her.

It is not surprising that the sympathy Henry felt for Louisa would become bitterness toward her husband when he read her account of their relations. The only explanation he could find for the indignities visited on her was that John Quincy had no inner life at all.

> His limitations, too, were astounding. Though he was brought up in Paris, London, and Berlin, he seems to have been indifferent to art. I do not remember that he ever mentions an interest in architecture, sculpture, or painting . . . I half remember that among his books I could never find Goethe or Schiller. I do not think he ever enjoyed Voltaire, and I would give much to be assured that he ever bothered himself to look at the Rembrandts at the Hermitage . . . He must have lived a life of pure void. (L 6.228)

This was opposed to everything Henry knew or supposed about his grandmother, whose aesthetic sensibilities he felt he had inherited.

"The Madam"

Since Henry meant to publish Louisa's papers in three volumes, he went through all her many writings, her two incomplete autobiographies, her Russian diary, her separate account of a trip she took through the battlefields of Europe in 1815, her letters, her plays (or skits), her many poems. One of these writings, and only one, was intended for publication, "Narrative of a Journey from Russia to France, 1815" (1836), and it did not appear in her lifetime. Henry's younger brother Brooks brought it out in *Scribner's Magazine* for 1903. Louisa's first autobiography was

"Record of a Life, or My Story" (1825), which breaks off in 1801, when she was twenty-six. This is less bitter than the second account would be, since it was originally planned for her children's reading. The first title, crossed out, was "Memories of Your Mother."

The second autobiography, "Adventures of a Nobody" (1840), brought her story down to the year 1812. Joan Challinor, who has written the most complete account of Louisa's life, thinks that each biographical fragment was broken off because the memories became too sad for her to continue.[6] The first one ends when Louisa, having just arrived in America, is made to feel that John Quincy had accepted her only because he let his real love, Mary Frazier, get away. The second one ends in Russia, when her infant daughter dies and she wishes to be buried with her in St. Petersburg. Louisa's entire story is disturbing. Her father's financial ruin obviously affected her profoundly. Like many women of her era, she was kept continually pregnant. As Catherine Allgor writes:

> Suffering from the effect of her first pregnancy, Louisa sailed [from England] to Berlin, where he was posted to the Prussian court. Once on shore, she miscarried the child and thus began a death-defying reproductive history that included fourteen pregnancies — nine miscarriages, four live births, and one still-birth.[7]

But Louisa traces her deepest sorrows to a feeling that the Adamses did not consider her worthy of her husband.

Henry began his edition of her writings by conflating and condensing the autobiographies, copying out in his own clear hand nearly two hundred closely packed pages (roughly ninety thousand words). He relies principally on her second autobiography, which is the most critical of John Quincy Adams. This was obviously a very serious project for him, and it is clear that he sides entirely with Louisa and trusts her account. He knew from letters he had not yet begun to copy for publication that Louisa was a victim of the Adamses' ambition.

He did not mean to be such a victim himself. Louisa remained a potent symbolic figure in his imagination. Reflections of her went into the creation of Madeleine Lee, the heroine of his novel *Democracy*, who almost becomes a sacrifice to ambition. And the example of her life would make him especially devoted to another woman whose life was troubled by marriage into an ambitious political family, Elizabeth Sherman Cameron.

Louisa is undergoing a kind of rediscovery, with the help of feminist scholars. She merits a substantial article in *American National Biography* (1999), though she was not included in *Dictionary of American Biography* (1928). Joan Challinor makes extensive use of modern studies of women's education and roles in the nineteenth century. She and other feminists believe that Louisa had ambitions of her own, but that the times as well as the Adamses stifled them. Her writings could reach no public, her political shrewdness was constantly checked or rebuked, in a criticism that she internalized.[8] I believe that Adams anticipated their findings in the use he made of Louisa's life while creating the character of Madeleine Lee. This is just one of the ways in which Adams, in some of his early writings, was a proto-feminist.

To see how important Louisa was to the formation of Henry's attitudes toward family, women, politics, and ambition, the narrative he copied out must be read along with the other writings he intended to put in the second and third volumes of his edition. Though he thought of his grandmother as a southerner, she was born in England, spent her childhood in France, and grew up in London. Her father was from Maryland, but her mother was English. Even after John Quincy Adams married her in England, she did not see the United States for another four years, which she spent in Berlin with her husband on his diplomatic mission. But as soon as she reached America for the first time she sought out her relatives in Washington — in fact, she and her husband would live in the home of her sister and brother-in-law throughout the time when John Quincy was a senator. The South was largely a symbolic reality for her, as it would be for her grandson. The South was all that the Adamses were not — warm and accepting, tainted but forgiving.

Since Louisa was only half "Maryland" and half English, and John Quincy was all New England, it was her son, Charles Francis Adams, who had the "quarter taint" of Louisa's blood. Henry, as the son of Charles Francis, had at most an eighth of his descent from her, though he exaggerated the connection for his own emotional and symbolic purposes. Abigail Adams had met Louisa's family in England when Louisa was only ten or so, and she thought her parents extravagant (as they were). Any child of theirs, she warned her son after he met her in her twentieth year, was unlikely to have the severe code that Adamses required from a spouse. The Johnsons' religion was Anglican, their manners Continental. Louisa's father, Joshua, was a businessman who had become the American consul in London by the time John Quincy met her. Joshua Johnson had a bevy of beautiful daughters, and he was living beyond his means while trying to find them suitable husbands. He went broke almost immediately after Louisa was married. No wonder Abigail thought her son was being trapped by foreign wiles. Louisa would feel the unspoken reproach in Boston, ashamed that her father seemed to promise more in family wealth than was realized.

John Quincy Adams met the Johnson girls in London when he was twenty-eight years old. He had taken a break from his diplomatic duties at The Hague, and the consul's house was a gathering place for Americans. John Quincy worked so hard to contain any sign of emotion that Louisa thought he was interested not in her but in her twenty-one-year-old sister Nancy. When he surprised Louisa by proposing marriage, he was vague about when he would be able to wed her — it would have to wait till the end of his mission in Holland. His mother's letters from home were warning him against marriage, and he seemed partly to heed and partly to defy that counsel.

When Abigail Adams found out, in 1796, that her son was serious about one of the Johnson girls, she wrote on May 20 asking, "Maria, has she no claim?" (A 381). John Quincy had been deeply in love, when setting up his law practice as a young man, with a local charmer, Mary Frazier. Abigail opposed his attempt to marry Miss Frazier, on the grounds that he could not support her in the style provided by her family — Abigail mistrusted those brought up as "fine ladies."[9] Now she was using Maria to fend off Louisa. It was in this same letter that Abigail hoped that Miss Johnson was "at least *half blood.*" After John Quincy became married despite her efforts to prevent it, Abigail wrote on August 16 to his younger brother, Thomas, who was traveling with him, that she hoped he, at least, would remain "free for an American wife" (A 382). Louisa did not know yet that she was caught in this crossfire between mother and son. If she had, she would have understood a lovers' quarrel that made her temporarily break off the engagement. She had complimented John Quincy on his clothes, and he lashed out at her, telling her not to dictate his appearance.[10] She did not know that Abigail had constantly criticized John Quincy for his slovenly dress.

When John Quincy wrote from Holland that he would be going to a new post in Lisbon, he said it would be best that he not marry and take her there. A court life might corrupt her, since she had not yet lived in republican America. He was repeating what his mother had told him. Abigail wrote on August 20 that she was sure Louisa was a fine woman, but "who can answer for her after having been introduced to the dissipations of a foreign court?" John Quincy was passing on other misgivings of his mother, warning Louisa on February 7, 1797, that she was spending too much time on music (a "trivial accomplishment") or novels, instead of improving herself with serious books (A 383). When, in her letters to Holland, Louisa attempted an affectionate nickname for him — "my Adams" — he told her on May 31 that she sounded like one of her sentimental novels (A 384). He suggested that her father take her back to Maryland, where they would be married whenever he returned from Europe. Mr. Johnson said that he could stop off in Holland before going on to America, so the lovers could see each other — but Adams said that it would be better to test their character by not yielding to such desires.[11]

The Johnsons had still not left England when John Quincy returned there to prepare for his trip to Lisbon. He reached the city on the afternoon of July 12, 1797, but did not go to her, or send news of his arrival, that night. And the next day he met with two friends before visiting her. She wrote of her "mortified affection" when he told her of this remarkably insensitive action.[12] He had to prove to her and to himself that he was not driven by passion. He lived by the code espoused in his diary: "If there is a lesson necessary for my peace of mind in this world, it is to form no strong attachment to any person or thing that it contains" (8.382). The last thing that a fiancée wants to know is that her husband fights any strong attachment to her. But he did, in fact, love Louisa, and when his assignment was changed from Lisbon to Berlin, he married her before leaving for Prussia.

In Berlin, the young bride became an instant favorite of the court, where French was the language of the diplomats and her dancing was expert. John Quincy resented or feared her popularity, and tried to instill in her the reserve his mother had imposed on him. When he was ten years old, Abigail wrote him what Joan Challinor calls a "terrible letter," saying that she would rather see him drown when coming back with his father from Europe than that he return "an immoral profligate," and warning him that a slip from virtue would involve him in all the vices of the fall of the Roman Empire — and he was *ten*.[13] When he was seventeen, Abigail had warned him against youthful levity, counseling him not to laugh in public: "I never knew a man of great talent much given to laughter. True contentment is never extremely gay or noisy . . . and I know from experience that sudden and excessive joy will produce tears sooner than laughter."[14] John Adams's sons, she said, must be a credit to him: "Your father's station abroad holds you up to view in a different light from that of a common traveler. And his virtues will render your faults, should you be guilty of any, more conspicuous."[15]

Louisa was now told that she must mold her life to be a credit to her husband. She must indulge none of the feminine wiles his mother had denounced. Abigail found even the Quaker city of Philadelphia full of hussies, who dressed "to seduce the unwary, to create inflammatory passions, and to call forth loose affection by unfolding to every eye what the veil of modesty ought to shield."[16] She had taught John Quincy to be especially censorious about women's makeup. She approved of Holland because, as she said, "Rouge is confined to the stage here."[17] Henry carefully copied out Louisa's account of the cosmetics war she waged with John Quincy.[18] In Berlin, where Louisa underwent a series of miscarriages and illnesses, the Queen of Prussia noticed her pale appearance. She kindly said she would send her a box of her own rouge.

> I answered that Mr. Adams would not let me wear it. She smiled at my simplicity and observed that if she presented me the box he must not refuse it, and told me to tell him so . . . I told Mr. Adams what the Queen said, but he said I must refuse the box as he should never permit me to accept it.

When carnival time came, women dressed in glittery dresses with black hoods, and used compensatory makeup to avoid a mask-like pallor under the hoods. Louisa decided to take the Queen's advice:

> Being more than usually pale, I ventured to put on a little rouge, which I found relieved the black and made me quite beautiful. Wishing to evade Mr. Adams's observation, I hurried through the room telling him to put the lights out and follow me down. This excited his curiosity and he started up and led me to the table and then declared that unless I allowed him to wash my face he would not go. He took a towel and drew me on his knee and all my beauty was clean washed away, and a kiss made a peace, and we drove off.

The cosmetics war was not yet over, but it soon would be. She tried one more time.

> One evening, when I had dressed to go to Court, the everlasting teasing about my pale face induced me to make another trial of a little rouge, and contrary to my first proceeding, I walked boldly forward to meet Mr. Adams. As soon as he saw me, he requested me to wash it off, which I with some temper refused, upon which he ran down and jumped in the car-

riage and left me *planté là,* even to myself appearing like a fool, crying with vexation.

The conflict moved to other issues. Contrary to Abigail's cautions, Louisa was prone to burst into loud laughter at the absurdity of things — at John Quincy's quaint court costume and wig, at her borrowed clothes after landing in a storm, at her own and her sister's prescribed costumes for a royal audience. When an aide to Mr. Adams, who had been driving Louisa around in his carriage, begged her to make the penurious J. Q. buy his own carriage, lest people think she was having an affair with the simpering aide, she could not contain her laughter. Her husband curtailed her attendance at balls, and left her stranded at some they did attend — he played cards for a while, then went home without her. He instructed her not to tell Abigail about events at court, lest his mother think her frivolous — though Abigail was actually curious and asking for details. John Quincy constantly made her aware that she did not meet the "republican" standards of his mother. When Louisa bought her mother-in-law the present of a ring, John Quincy wrote Abigail on January 19, 1798, that he had refused to let her send it, since it was too showy (A 130).

At length, after five miscarriages, Louisa bore her first child, a son who would be her favorite throughout his short life. He was named George Washington Adams, in honor of the president who had appointed John Quincy to his first foreign post, and who had died just sixteen months earlier. Abigail was angry that the family lineage was not more clearly marked by calling him John Adams. She wrote to her son Tom: "I am sure your brother had not any intention of wounding the feelings of his father, but I see he has done it."[19] When Tom called his brother to account on this head, John Quincy wrote a defense of his choice, but he made sure to call his next son John, to placate his mother.[20] (In the next generation, Charles Francis Adams would observe dynastic proprieties by naming his first son after his own father, making him another John Quincy Adams.)

The return to America was made harrowing for Louisa by her husband's warnings against behavior that Abigail would disapprove of. He also told her on the boat about his earlier love for Mary Frazier, an act that depressed her severely. Though it is hard to see how he could do such a thing, I suppose he thought he was preparing her for talk about Mary in Boston, where in fact Louisa would be likely to meet his first inamorata. But the story hardly strengthened her for meeting the formidable Abigail. She was happy in retrospect that her illness when she arrived gave her an excuse for keeping quiet, since she was sure she would have said the wrong things if she had talked freely.

> What shall I say of my first impression of Quincy? Had I stepped into Noah's ark I do not think I could have been more astonished. It was lucky for me that I was so much depressed and so ill, or I should certainly have given mortal offence. Even the church, its forms, the snuffling through the nose, the singers, the dressing and dinner hours, were novelties to me; and the ceremonious parties, the manners, and the hours of [church] meeting (half past four) were equally astounding. In England I had lived in the city of London, in Berlin at court, but the etiquette of court society was not half so burdensome . . . The old gentleman [John Adams] took a fancy to me, but I was literally and without knowing it a "fine lady."[21]

Adams compresses the diary without ellipses to indicate omissions, and here we can see that, even though he retained most of the criticisms of his grandfather, he omitted some of the evidence for mistreatment by others, especially by Abigail. The last sentence quoted above continued, in the diary: "The old gentleman took a fancy to me, *and he was the only one*" (emphasis added). The Adamses, all but John, made her feel "I was an *aparté* in the family . . . it appeared to stamp me with unfitness."[22] Henry also omits the expression of her deepest fear — that the contempt felt for her by his family would become her husband's. "Could it therefore be surprising that I was gazed at with surprise, if not with contempt? — the qualifications necessary to form an accomplished Quincy lady were in direct opposition to the mode of life which I had led, and I soon felt that even my husband would acknowledge my deficiency and that I should lose most of my value in his eyes."[23]

Louisa's husband was sent to the Senate in 1802, and she had become so uncomfortable in Quincy by then that she stayed on in Washington when the Senate was out of session and John Quincy returned to his parents. At the end of his term she had, despite further miscarriages, borne her husband three sons. John Quincy did not like to travel with the children, so he instructed her to leave the two older ones with Abigail in Quincy. Louisa protested against this, but Abigail wrote her on May 21, 1804, that grandparents can be better guides than parents — hardly what a mother wants to hear when being parted from her children:

I have a great opinion of children being early attached to their grandparents. Perhaps it may arise from the bias I formed for mine, and the respect and veneration instilled into my infant mind toward them, so that more of their precepts and maxims remain with me, to this hour, than those of my excellent parents — who were not, however, deficient in theirs. But the superior weight of years, added to the best examples, impressed them more powerfully at the early period when I resided with them. (A 403)

Louisa did not know that a pattern was being established for separating her from her two older sons, including the precious George. At this point, Abigail kept John with her (the one named for her husband), and gave George into the keeping of her nearby sister, Mary Cranch. Later, both boys would be living with the Cranches.

John Quincy was forced to retire some months short of his term's expiration because he had supported the Embargo against the wishes of his constituents. The new president, however, James Madison, rewarded him for this defection from the Federalists by naming him America's first minister to Russia. Louisa, who had not been consulted on going to Russia, was once again not allowed to take her older sons with her. Despite her protests the family decided that John and George should stay with Abigail. John Quincy's brother, Thomas, was deputed to tell Louisa of the decision. Louisa says she was prevented from being alone with her father-in-law, since Abigail feared he would side with her on keeping her sons.[24] Henry omits much of this, but includes Louisa's expression of the basic problem:

My conviction is that, if domestic separation is absolutely necessary, we should cling to the helpless creatures whom God has given to our charge. A man can take care of himself. Nonetheless, not a soul entered into my feelings. My eldest children were left under charge of their grandparents, and we and our youngest child and my sister Catherine sailed on the fourth of August from Boston.[25]

Here we have the source of Henry's comment on the Brooks manuscript: "Dragging his wife to Europe in 1809 and separating her from her children was demonic." It was a separation that would haunt Louisa for the rest of her life, making her feel that the older sons became drunken failures because she had "deserted" them.

In Russia, Louisa and her pretty younger sister, Catherine, became favorites of the Tsar, who caused some scandal by flirting with Catherine.[26] Here, too, French was the court language, and the sisters spoke it not only well but wittily. In Russia, John Quincy performed valuable services at the outset, helping firm up the Tsar's resolve to defy Napoleon by allowing American ships to trade in St. Petersburg. But Adams outstayed any real need for him to be there ("dawdling" for six years, as Henry wrote to Brooks), keeping Louisa from her children while he worked on his hobbies, astronomy and the currency system — self-imposed tasks that could have been performed at home. Henry was voicing the pent-up emotions of Louisa, who was forced to travel alone with her young son (Henry's father) across war-torn Europe in 1815, when John Quincy left her behind to negotiate an end to the War of 1812 at Ghent. (She could not have anticipated, when she set off on her perilous journey, that she would move through the "Hundred Days" mobilization of armies to oppose Napoleon's unexpected breakout from detention at Elba.)

Louisa's letters after the period of her partial autobiographies would have become even more painful reading if Henry had edited them for publication. Louisa was tortured by the fate of her sons. George and John grew up to lead alcoholic and dissolute lives. This repeated a pattern from the earlier generation, when John Adams had left two sons with Abigail (in this case the two younger sons) while he took young John Quincy to Paris with him. Paul Nagle and others find it significant that the two sons and the two grandsons left under Abigail's supervision turned out badly, while only the son and grandson who escaped to Europe with their respective fathers led sober and productive lives. Abigail's constant and detailed grooming of her charges for greatness broke all four of those left with her. The tone of her management is caught in one of her letters to John Quincy: "My anxieties have been and still are great lest the numerous temptations and snares of vice should vitiate your early habits of virtue."[27] Abigail the relentless improver can be glimpsed at the time when she was separated from her own sons during her stay in Paris. She hung up their silhouettes in a place where she could "sometimes speak to [them] as I pass, telling Charles to hold up his head."[28]

Even the boys who escaped Abigail were not entirely free of the emotional damage of her upbringing. John Quincy was severely hampered in his expressions of love and care for Louisa, and Charles Francis blighted his son Charles's life by his cold ways — so Charles himself wrote for the public to read.[29] But at least they had not been total failures, like their siblings. The price of failure in this perfectionist family was high. John Adams refused to see or communicate with his drunkard son Charles, even when he was dying. He said that Charles, who had deserted his wife, was a worse ingrate than Absalom, making his father envy George Washington's childless state. Charles was "a madman possessed of the devil . . . a mere rake, buck, blood, and beast . . . I renounce him."[30]

Her son George was the great loss of Louisa's life. In 1829, when John Quincy had just lost the presidency, the thirty-year-old George set off to meet his parents for their return to Quincy. He was in trouble, in debt, and in drink — the man keeping his illegitimate child (begotten with a chambermaid) was threatening to blackmail him. Traveling by night on the steamer *Benjamin Franklin,* George Washington Adams threw himself overboard and drowned. Henry later told his brother Charles that their uncle George had taken the only course of honor left him: "His blackmail experience was what any other damfool might have had. But his drowning himself showed a tragic quality far above the Adams average" (L 6.574).

Louisa blamed George's death on the family that had taken him away from her for the crucial years of his childhood, this boy she had purchased with so many painful miscarriages. Fearful of what she could have blurted out in her grief when she first learned of George's death, she later drew up a careful demurrer:

> In the awful moment when the hand of the Almighty had smitten us to earth, when my loved George was removed from the face of the earth, my soul was sunk in grief and I felt as if delirium was seizing upon my mind. In this painful state, when my beloved husband's sufferings were beyond control, I was so fearful that my full heart might betray its agony in the language of reproach, and thereby add to his misery, that I think I begged him, whatever I might say in my wanderings, not to believe me. The idea struck me after I became more composed that as human nature is ever prone to think ill, that I might perhaps be thought to have some secret uneasiness that I was fearful of exposing; and this thought has induced me to mark the circumstance and to declare that I hid no terror of conscience or of guilt, but only the apprehension of expressing some *regrets* that might have increased the anguish of us all. So help me God, Louisa [emphasis in original].[31]

Despite this recoil, the Adams papers editor Lyman Butterfield was right to conclude: "To her dying day, Louisa Catherine Adams continued to believe, rationally or irrationally, that her son George was a sacrifice to the political ambitions of the Adams family, particularly those of her husband."[32] Louisa and her son had written poems to each other, and she went on writing dozens to him in her agony. To sample just three:

> 'Twas on the bosom of the wave
> That sparkles high with foam,
> That thou thy suffering corse didst lave.
> He heard thy anguished moan.

> Strew, strew the violet on his breast
> And let his sainted spirit rest.
> In meek humility forbear,
> For life is suffering and care.
> And still the breeze in accent mild
> Shall sigh, alas, My child! My child!

> 'Twas in thy grave I sought to lie,
> My poor, poor boy.
> 'Twas near thy tomb I wished to die,
> My lost, lost joy!

The other son that Louisa had left behind with Abigail — the one named John Adams after Abigail's wishes — was expelled from Harvard for a drunken student prank. He married during his father's term as president, and lived with his wife in the White House, where he caused trouble for the parents who had reluctantly accepted his residence there. Acting as his father's secretary, he inaccurately listed a government source of funds for the White House billiard table he had bought, creating a mini-scandal. Then he publicly insulted a guest in the house and had to be saved from a duel by his father's call on Congress to protect White House staff.[33] He was already on the way to his alcoholic death at thirty-one.

Louisa's time in the White House, capped at the end by George's death, was so trying for her that she reversed herself when John Quincy decided to accept election to the House of Representatives. She who had loved Washington and hated Quincy now refused to go back with her husband to the scene of her recent political ordeal. Charles Francis, Henry's father, was old enough to be caught up in the conflict between his parents. He too had opposed his father's going to Congress. When he feared that he might have influenced his mother's refusal to accompany her husband, Charles Francis asked his brother John to intervene and persuade her to maintain family solidarity. Louisa answered him with what Lyman Butterfield calls "a bitterness almost too painful to read even at this distance in time."[34]

> I look around me in vain for anything like benefit that has resulted to any-one as a reparation for this suffering [in heeding the family wishes] or as a motive for future action. Where is it to be found? Is it in the grave of my lost child? Is it in the very necessity which induces you to claim this sacri-fice? Is it in the advantages resulting to any of our connection of either [Johnson or Adams] side? Or is it to the grasping ambition which is an insatiable passion swallowing and consuming all in its ever devouring maw?[35]

As soon as John Quincy died, Louisa left that house for good, to stay with her Johnson relatives in Washington. When she died there, she was buried in the Congressional Cemetery. But the family, not letting go of her even in death, exhumed the body and moved it to Quincy, where it lies in one of the four granite slabs that totally fill the crypt in the fam-ily church — the two dead presidents and their two wives, Louisa still linked to Abigail, whom she considered the destroyer of her sons.

Some have attributed Henry's early feminist writings to the example of his great-grandmother, Abigail Adams. But the real feminist in the family, and the one whose influence Adams always felt, was his grand-mother. Later, when Louisa and her mother-in-law worked out a truce between them, Louisa read with admiration some of Abigail's letters on women's needs, but she went far beyond Abigail in her denunciation of men who made marriage a "badge of slavery" by denying their wives the right to make decisions for themselves and their children. (It is interest-ing that Henry also said that a wedding ring was not a "badge of slavery" in primitive societies but it became one in the era of the European church — H 35.) Louisa became a follower of the feminists and aboli-tionists Angelina and Sarah Grimké. She read with enthusiasm Sarah Grimké's *On the Equality of the Sexes and the Condition of Women,* and recommended that her son Charles Francis read it, though "I suppose it will not suit your lordly sex."[36] When he lost her copy, she attributed such carelessness to the "harsh and severe" attitude toward women he shared with all his sex.[37] She wrote a fan letter to the book's author, and a warm correspondence was struck up between them. The Grimkés shattered her old southern attitudes toward slavery, convincing her that equality for women and for blacks had to advance together. Sarah Grimké asked Louisa to collaborate with the sisters on a book about the politics of emancipation, and Louisa questioned her Washington acquaintances to supply the sisters with facts on the subject.[38]

The abolitionist Theodore Weld, to whom Angelina Grimké was married, understood from Louisa's correspondence with the sisters that she was unhappy in her marriage. He was surprised, then, when he went to see John Quincy in support of his anti-slavery petitions, to find that the couple seemed on good terms.[39] The battle against slavery helped unite them in their last years. John Quincy came to this battle belatedly — the Grimkés had earlier appealed to him and were disappointed by his rebuff.[40] But Louisa, who had to travel farther from her southern background in a Maryland family, anticipated his arrival at the stance for which his final years became famous. Louisa's cook in Washington was a slave woman rented out by her owner. The slave, named Julia, was saving up to purchase her freedom, but she was two hundred dollars short of the demanded price. Louisa raised the money.[41]

An Honorary Southerner

By his claim through Louisa's blood, but also by temperament, choice, and familial rebellion, Henry Adams felt himself a kind of honorary southerner, admiring and writing about southerners, living in their climate, estranged from the "canting" world he grew up in. From an early age he felt drawn to the South. He notes pointedly that he grew up on Mount Vernon Street, and the real Mount Vernon, early and often visited, became a talismanic place in his life and work, the scene of the most memorable chapter in his first novel, *Democracy*. It was the place where Louisa had gone as soon as she arrived in America. Adams could say of himself what he said of Albert Gallatin, that "he regarded himself as a Virginian" (G 59). It has already been noticed that Adams, who thought the two presidents in his family were failures, always said the only great presidents had been Virginians: "Washington and Jefferson doubtless stand pre-eminent as the representatives of what is best in our national character or its aspirations" (G 267). One of the more striking things about his life is that he resented ever after the support that England had given the Confederacy during the Civil War, but he harbored no hostility toward the South after the war ended. In fact, he would

champion the South against Reconstruction, siding with President Andrew Johnson against the Adams family friend, Charles Sumner. According to him, the North tried to make "serfs" of ex-Confederates (R 71)
like his friend Lucius Lamar (who was nonetheless given amnesty and
became a senator and Supreme Court justice).

As a teacher of American history at Harvard, Adams expounded the
Virginia position and let his graduate student, Henry Cabot Lodge, defend the Federalists of New England. Explaining a planned course to
Harvard's president, Adams wrote: "His [Lodge's] views, being federalist and conservative, have as good a right to expression in the college as
mine, which tend to democracy and radicalism" (L 2.301). As we have
seen, he told students, "You know, gentlemen, John Adams was a demagogue" (S 1.216). Such anti-Federalism was not confined to the class-
room. In his life of Albert Gallatin (1879) — the first book he wrote, as
opposed to edited — he sided, like his subject, with Jefferson against
Hamilton:

> Mr. Jefferson meant that the American system should be a democracy, and
> he would rather have let the world perish than that this principle, which to
> him represented all that man was worth, should fail. Mr. Hamilton consid-
> ered democracy a fatal curse, and meant to stop its progress. The partial
> truce which the first administration of Washington had imposed on both
> parties, although really closed by the retirement of Mr. Jefferson from the
> cabinet, was finally broken only by the arrival of Mr. Jay's treaty. From that
> moment repose was impossible until one party or the other had triumphed
> beyond hope of resistance; and it was easy to see which of the two parties
> must triumph in the end. (G 159)

The Jefferson side had to win because "everyone admitted that Jefferson's opinions, in one form or another, were shared by a majority of the
American people" (J 117).

Those are not the words of a man who, as many claim, wrote the *History* out of some animosity to Jefferson. In fact, Adams was fascinated
by Jefferson, critical of him (as of all politicians but Washington), but
also deeply admiring of him, probing over and over the mystery of the
man:

> Dear old Jefferson! Never was there a more delightful ground for people to
> argue about! We discuss him here by the day together, just as though he
> were alive. We can fight about him as ardently as ever. He is supremely use-

ful still (he and Hamilton) as a sort of bone for students of history to mumble, preparatory to getting their teeth. (L 2.322)

A great part of Adams's fascination with Jefferson came from affinity with him. He resembled him in temperament, and even in his policies. Both men abhorred the national debt, distrusted banks, and were Anglophobic Francophiles. Adams makes fun of Jefferson's proneness to hyperbole — which was one of his own leading traits. Neither man liked the push-and-shove of politics. They preferred to act indirectly and behind the scenes. Adams might have been describing himself when he said that "the rawness of political life was an incessant torture" to Jefferson (J 99):

> He fairly reveled in what he believed to be beautiful, and his writings often betrayed subtle feeling for artistic form — a sure mark of intellectual sensuousness. He shrank from whatever was rough or coarse, and his yearning for sympathy was almost feminine. (J 100)

Neither Jefferson nor Adams was cut out to be a soldier — they were men of the "cabinet," not of the field. They were aesthetes and art collectors, who took care in the construction and decoration of their beautiful homes. Both were fussy about style. Adams wrote to William James that he had the same concern with style as William's brother, Henry James, "but I doubt whether a dozen people in America — except architects or decorators — would know or care" (L 6.118). Jefferson would have known and cared.

Each man thought in north-south (male-female) polarities, and Adams always took the "southern" side of this division, preferring Quincy over Boston, and placing Washington over both of them — just as he favored "female" Chartres over "male" Mont-Saint-Michel. He would have subscribed entirely to Jefferson's geographic chart of character traits. These are Jefferson's words:

IN THE NORTH, THEY ARE	IN THE SOUTH, THEY ARE
cool	fiery
sober	voluptuary
laborious	indolent
persevering	unsteady
independent	independent
jealous of their own liberties, and just to those of others	jealous of their own liberties, but trampling on those of others

interested	generous
chicaning	candid
superstitious and hypocritical in their religion	without attachment or pretensions in any religion but that of the heart[42]

The list explains why Adams felt his cold New England heart open out toward southern warmth when he first reached the city of Washington as a child. He was coming into his spiritual home:

> The May sunshine and shadow had something to do with it; the thickness of foliage and the heavy smells had more; the sense of atmosphere, almost new, had perhaps as much again; and the brooding indolence of a warm climate and a Negro population hung in the atmosphere heavier than the catalpas. The impression was not simple, but the boy liked it; distinctly it remained on his mind as an attraction, almost obscuring Quincy itself. The want of barriers, of pavements, of forms, the looseness, the laziness; the indolent southern drawl; the pigs in the streets; the Negro babies, and their mothers with bandanas; the freedom, openness, swagger of nature and man, soothed his Johnson blood. Most boys would have felt it in the same way, but with him the feeling caught on to an inheritance. The softness of his gentle old [Johnson] grandmother, as she lay in bed and chatted with him, did not come from Boston. His [Johnson] aunt was anything rather than Bostonian. He did not wholly come from Boston himself. (E 760)

When dealing in the north-south polarity, Adams put his Adams relatives — all but his "southern" grandmother, Louisa — at the northern extreme, as cold, calculating, and selfish. He was so convinced of this that when, late in life, he discovered that John Quincy Adams had shown affection for his son, he professed himself shocked. He had thought him incapable of emotion.[43]

Adams's sympathy with Louisa also served him when he came to write the *History*. After she reached America, her husband was sent to the Senate two years after Jefferson took office for his first term as president. Louisa, still new to America, put her vivid impressions of Washington in the diary her grandson copied out so carefully. This is the world and the period of his *History*, brought to life with caustic comments and a woman's shrewd eye. She picked up on the gossip of the time — how the French minister beat his wife, how cold Jefferson kept the White House, how deft Dolley Madison was in social maneuver, how Gallatin's wife kept offstage, how like John Randolph was to a court jester, how illiterate was Henry Dearborn, the secretary of war ("he always spelt Congress with a K"), how flirtatious was Mrs. Merry, the wife of the British minister (she even played coy to the asexual John Randolph). What I have called the stereoscopic effect of Adams's early preparation and his performance in the *History* is nowhere more evident than in the echoes of Louisa in the latter work. He had met all these people he wrote about in Louisa's crackling pages.

2

BOSTON HISTORIANS

Though Adams rebelled against his family ties, he was a typical New Englander in his *furor scribendi*. The place pullulated with writers, and most of them were historians. He skipped law school to do what most New England writers did, to go abroad — and especially to Germany. Adams wrote his brother Charles from there: "Could I write a history, do you think, or a novel, or anything likely to make it worth while for me to try?" (L 1.14). His ambition became more focused when he reached Rome and read how Gibbon had been inspired there (L 1.149). He went to the steps of the Ara Coeli monastery, where Gibbon says he pondered the decline of the Roman Empire. From Rome he wrote to Charles: "Our house needs a historian in this generation" (L 1.149).

Henry knew personally the New England historians — Francis Parkman, George Bancroft, Edward Everett, John Gorham Palfrey, William Hickling Prescott, John Lothrop Motley. He was related to many of them, and friendly with them all. In his early years they had a practical monopoly on the writing of American history, possessing what was, in effect, their own house organ, the most important intellectual quarterly in America during the middle years of the nineteenth century, the *North American Review*. The journal was edited by a series of chroniclers or historians, Jared Sparks, Edward Everett (who taught classical history as well as languages at Harvard), John Gorham Palfrey, Edward Gurney — and Henry Adams.[1] Adams took his place in this line of succession and extended it by training a whole new generation of historians at Harvard — directly in the case of Henry Cabot Lodge, Edward Channing, Henry Osborne Taylor, and Albert Bushnell Hart; and indirectly through his impact on the graduate school of history at the Johns Hopkins University, where his unrelated namesake Henry Baxter Adams used his and his pupils' work as models.[2]

These American historians participated in the larger excitement that came over their discipline in the nineteenth century. In England, Lord Acton hailed a "generation of writers who dug so deep a trench between history as known to our grandfathers and as it appears to us."[3] What caused such a revolution in the status and conduct of historians? The change involved bursting the confines of the preceding period, which had itself been a liberating force when it began. The nineteenth century was marked by the move from philosophical or "conjectural" history to archival research. Medieval history had largely been based on authority, myth, and forgeries. Renaissance scholars, with their sophisticated philological tools, were good at unmasking the forgeries, but they did not quite know how to handle myth. That task was left for the Enlightenment to explore.

The eighteenth century was a period of absolute monarchs and church authorities who kept their records sealed, handed out official versions of events, and censored or outlawed competing versions of the truth. Fenced off from so many original sources, writers like Hume and Gibbon, Voltaire and Montesquieu, had to sift literary accounts, fragmentary and partisan as they were. They tried to correct for partisanship by estimates of the *likelihood* of what was reported. This was Hume's method in his essay on miracles. Firsthand testimony to miracles was abundant, but a mere documentary reproduction of stories would leave untouched the question whether they had verisimilitude. Were such accounts, as Gibbon (Hume's follower) put it, "contradictory to every known principle of the human mind"?[4] Conjecture about accumulated probabilities became the preferred historical method.[5] Gibbon described the historian's task this way:

> The confusion of the times and the scarcity of authentic memorials oppose equal difficulties to the historian who attempts to preserve a clear and unbroken thread of narration. Surrounded with imperfect fragments, always concise, often obscure, and sometimes contradictory, he is reduced to collect, to compare, and to *conjecture;* and though he ought never to place his *conjectures* in the rank of facts, yet the knowledge of human nature, and of the sure operation of its fierce and unrestrained passions, might on some occasions, supply the want of historical materials [emphasis added].[6]

Gibbon entertained the play of possible conjecture, often undermining an official account by a strategic placing of the disjunctive "or":

> The most curious, *or* the most credulous, among the pagans were often persuaded to enter into a society which asserted an actual claim of miraculous powers . . . They felt, *or* they fancied, that on every side they were incessantly assaulted by demons . . . The real *or* imagined prodigies of which they so frequently conceived themselves to be the objects, the instruments, *or* the spectators, very happily disposed them . . . [emphasis added][7]

This method was used not only to question Christian legend but to reveal the mythical foundations of Roman history in Livy.[8] Hume could undermine Roman legend by conjectures on demography, Voltaire could trace the moral history of absolutism, and Chastellux could secularize medieval concepts of happiness. Members of the Scottish Enlightenment created a conjectural sequence of social conditions (the four stages of development).[9]

Eventually, fine-spun hypotheses built on other hypotheses might topple, but the conjecturalists had a long tradition to call upon, including the ancient Greek fondness for arguments from probability (*eikos*). This was a favorite tool of Attic orators. In a culture that could not argue easily from documents (inscriptions were on heavy stone), and where oral testimony was so often contradictory, weighing the different accounts of witnesses often came down to showing which tale represented the more likely account, the *eikoteros logos*. Aristotle lists *eikos* as one of the four sources of proof, and says that it had one advantage, at least, over eyewitness testimony — a witness can be bribed, but you cannot "buy off" an argument drawn from the nature of things.[10] The philosophical historians of the eighteenth century had another source for their reliance on *eikos* — the work of men trying to quantify and test a *calculus* of probabilities (exemplified, for instance, in the work of Thomas Bayes, 1702–1761). Enlightenment figures claimed that probabilistic thinking was a clear advance over medieval arguments from authority and legend.

But toward the end of the Enlightenment, some critics felt that conjecture could create only hypothetical constructs:

> So much of what we know as Enlightenment consisted in the substitution of the probable for the metaphysical that any *philosophe* assault on textual information (i.e., *inscriptions et belles lettres*) as merely probable must be a

debate within Enlightenment in which the *philosophe's* role might prove ambiguous or destructive.[11]

It was with a sense of relief, then, that men greeted the passing of the *ancien régime*, since that opened previously guarded archives, raising the promise at least that previous conjectures could be put to the test of fact. The *philosophes* had claimed that kings or priests *must* have had this or that in mind. Now they could begin to read, slowly at first, what was actually said in previously hidden documents. In the eighteenth century, a Servite priest, Fra Paolo Sarpi, was able to write an honest history of the Council of Trent by interviewing some participants and using their notes; but when the Vatican assigned a Jesuit, Pietro Pallavicino, to refute Sarpi, he was able to draw on Vatican archives closed to Sarpi and everyone else. After Napoleon stole the Vatican archives, revealing new things about the process against Galileo, the absolutists' weapon of secrecy was blunted. Lord Acton said it would no longer be enough to read books in print, as Gibbon or Hume did. One must go to unpublished material and manuscripts.

> The result has been that a lifetime spent in the largest collection of printed books would not suffice to train a real master of modern history. After he had turned from literature to sources, from Burnet to Pocock, from Macaulay to Madame Campana, from Thiers to the interminable correspondence of the Bonapartes, he would still feel instant need of inquiry at Venice or Naples, in the Ossuna library or at the Hermitage.[12]

A new kind of discipline was being born, with all the excitement that attends on novelty and the suggestion of fresh possibilities.

> Even if one agrees that the development of modern historiography should be viewed as a seamless web extending back to the Renaissance, it was not until the late nineteenth century that the cognitive superiority of historical writing based on critical use of source materials, archival research, and a historicist view of human society was able to establish itself.[13]

As we look back on this period, it can seem naïve in its optimism about being able, for the first time, to establish "what really happened" (*wie es eigentlich gewesen*), as Leopold von Ranke put it, in what became a rallying cry at the time — one that Adams took up when he praised work that "is neither a compilation from other books, nor mere ratiocination, but an attempt to ascertain what actually happened" (L 2.492).

The hopefulness incited by the new history was expressed in Acton's prospectus for the Cambridge Modern History:

> Ultimate history we cannot have in this generation; but we can dispose of conventional history, and show the point we have reached on the road from the one to the other, now that all information is within reach, and every problem has become capable of solution.[14]

This promise of new material posed an obvious difficulty. How were historians to take advantage of this flood of unprocessed information? Most archives were not yet organized or catalogued in easily usable ways. They were not tended by trained archivists. There were no grants or fellowships for those wishing to study the untapped materials. Old academies were geared to amateur and antiquarian interests. Universities were just beginning to develop historical research of a professionally systematized sort — Adams would be the first to introduce graduate seminars in history at Harvard, and he was one of the first to do so in this country. He supported his own research from his personal inheritance. This was a common pattern in the early generation of what may be called the gentlemen historians — men like Grote and Acton in England, Adams and Prescott and Parkman in America, Tocqueville and Beaumont in France.

Gentlemen Historians

Though Germany had the rudimentary elements of a system of state-subsidized research programs, other countries (and especially the Anglophone ones) had to rely heavily on men with the leisure and financial independence to explore poorly organized archives. Adams would collect his materials from England, France, Spain, and the American State Department, choosing the items he needed, hiring copyists to provide him with his working papers. Parkman and Prescott, independently wealthy, paid others to search foreign archives and send them copies of any material that might be relevant to their work. Others used diplomatic posts abroad to get access to archives.

Diplomatic appointment was especially useful to American historians. Even Adams's first research abroad, at the British Museum for an article on Pocahontas, was made possible by his appointment as secretary to the American legation in 1861. Though Adams was there at the service of his lawyer father, there was a tradition of sending prominent authors to the Court of St. James's — Washington Irving, John Lothrop Motley, Nathaniel Hawthorne. Because of the absence of a trained diplomatic corps at the time, American administrations often sent literary men to foreign posts, believing that they would be better able to acquire the relevant language if they had not already mastered it, and that they would know something of the history of Europe in general. George Bancroft, who had studied in Germany, was later made the minister to Prussia. Motley, who learned his German from Bancroft at the Round Hill School, was sent as secretary of legation to Russia, where he did research on Peter the Great. Later, he drew on and added to Prescott's collection of unpublished Spanish materials while he was writing his own history of the Dutch rebellion against Philip II.

Prescott was especially good at using diplomats abroad to acquire research material. The American minister in Madrid, and the secretary of legation there, exerted their influence to procure from Spanish experts the documents Prescott needed. So did the consul at Valencia. Edward Everett, serving in Florence, searched the Spanish papers in the Archivo Mediceo and sent what he thought would be useful to Prescott. Bancroft performed similar service for Parkman. Men dealing with foreign governments often got access to papers that, though technically open for research, were hard to penetrate in their disorganized state. They needed the help of local experts, a service not easily obtained without official sanction. Adams's own family ties were very useful to him as he searched foreign archives.

Adams would rely more exclusively on archival sources than did any of his older fellows. But the increasing use of that standard can be seen in the development of the most popular New England historian, George Bancroft. The first volume of his massive history of the United States was drawn almost entirely from secondary literature. But his critics — including Adams, who caught him in a flagrant misuse of the sources on Pocahontas — forced him to base later volumes on archives that he searched diligently, culminating in his final work:

> In 1882, at the age of eighty-two, Bancroft added two volumes on the formation of the Constitution. It was the realization of a very old ambition. To fulfill it he had visited the archives of most of the thirteen states and studied the reports of the ministers of Austria and Holland, France and England.[15]

The German Connection

Besides wealth and diplomatic ties, many of the gentlemen historians shared a third characteristic — study in Germany. That was the source of new rigor not only in history but in disciplines like the classical languages and biblical criticism. New England felt an especial affinity with Germany at this time, and Harvard became a hive of Germanists. Instructors there who had studied at Göttingen alone included Edward Everett, George Bancroft, Joseph Cogswell, George Ticknor — and, of course, Henry Adams. The concept of a Teutonic racial germ of "forest democracy" was the learned fashion of the time. John Lothrop Motley was typical in his glorification of the "Germanic" Netherlands in its revolt against Catholic Spain. Parkman would, in the same way, describe an Anglo-Saxon superiority of the British colonizers over those in "New France." And Bancroft exaggerated the aid, indirect as well as direct, given to the American Revolution by German princes and people — it was important to him that the freedom-loving peoples have the same racial stock.[16] Adams himself would celebrate the Germanic influence as a professor at Harvard, though the nine volumes of his *History* are unaffected by that bias.

Another source of the New Englanders' fascination with Germany — along with the mystical notion of a *Volk* — was the Transcendentalists' interest in the philosophical idealism of Kant and the romantic idealism of Goethe. Bancroft remained a Transcendentalist all his life, a thing reflected in the mystical nationalism of his history. Adams claimed to be immune from Transcendentalism (E 777), but his wife's mother was a Transcendentalist who published her poems in Emerson's journal, and his own later admiration of "Oriental religions" paralleled that of Thoreau. The nature mysticism of his novel *Esther*, and his "Buddhist" poems, shows that Transcendentalism left a deeper mark on him than he would later admit.

The only New England historian who violently rejected Transcendentalism, as well as all things German, was Richard Hildreth, who admired the British Utilitarians, especially Jeremy Bentham.[17] He deliberately fashioned his *History of the United States* as an "Anti-Bancroft."[18] Hildreth is something of a throwback to the conjectural historians. He worked mainly from secondary sources, but brought to them a skepticism about national myths that can be a valuable corrective. His mockery of New England as the "region of set formality and hereditary grimace" led to Harvard's refusing him a professorship; but Charles Sumner, as chairman of the Senate's Foreign Relations Committee, procured him a diplomatic assignment to Trieste during the time Adams was serving in England.[19]

Though Hildreth mocked many things, including New England, his history has a decidedly Federalist bias. Those who think Adams was a defender of Federalism need only read Hildreth to see what shouldering that task would really entail. Adams appreciated Hildreth's jaunty tone (and his low opinion of Bancroft), but he took a very different view of the American past. Nor could he accept Hildreth's anti-Germanism. As editor of the *North American Review*, Adams reviewed and assigned for review the latest products of German scholarship. At Harvard, he directed his students toward German sources.

When he had left his own studies in Germany, it was not to return home and become a lawyer. Instead, despite a guilty feeling about spending his father's money on non-academic projects, he traveled in Europe looking for subjects to write about. He now thought he could build a career on the basis of learned journalism — a very British ambition, based on the work of Acton, Bagehot, Macaulay, and others. He wrote home travel letters for publication in the Boston *Daily Courier*, and won an interview with Garibaldi at the moment of that hero's victory for the Italian Risorgimento. Returned home, supposedly to read law, he went to Washington as his father's secretary in the aftermath of Abraham Lincoln's election in 1860. Thrown into the secession crisis, watching the nation struggle through the interim between Lincoln's election and his inauguration, he was aware that something immense was taking place, and he meant to record it. While writing anonymous newspaper articles for the Boston *Daily Advertiser*, he told his brother Charles to preserve everything he sent him, to be an enduring record of the crisis:

> I fairly confess that I want to have a record of this winter on file, and though I have no ambition nor hope to become a Horace Walpole, I still would like to think that a century or two hence, when everything else about us is forgotten, my letters might still be read and quoted as a memorial of manners and habits at the time of the great secession of 1860. (L 1.204)

This is a close echo of Thucydides' determination, at the beginning of the Peloponnesian War, to write about events as they unfolded:

Thucydides of Athens recorded as it happened the war between the Pelo-
ponnesians and the Athenians, recording the course of its hostilities from
their very onset, in the expectation that this would be a great event, wor-
thier of record than what preceded . . . This is to be a resource for all time,
not a bid for instant popularity.[20]

Adams later made Thucydides a model for his *History*. The ambition he
expressed in 1860 was extraordinary for a young man of twenty-one —
and the main essay he wrote then, "The Great Secession Winter," would
indeed become a valuable source for future historians. Full of bad judgments but also full of inside information, the essay is repeatedly cited in
treatments of the Civil War's onset. Adams was justified in his awareness
of having an important seat at the beginning of a great drama. This out-
did, by a long distance, his report on Garibaldi. And in only two years he
would make an even more "splashy" contribution to history in his first
formal monograph, on Pocahontas. Already in these early days his calling as an historian was clear. He could not have aspired to this but for
the cradle of historians he came from. And that nest could not have been
prepared without the long tradition of record-keeping in his region.

The Antiquarians

If it is asked why American participation in the nineteenth-century history boom was focused in New England, and especially in Boston, we
must remember that an archival urge was not something New Englanders had to import from Germany. They had been out of fashion in the
eighteenth century, while philosophical historians dominated the Enlightenment. They were not "conjectural" historians. They had been avid
collectors of public and private papers from their very arrival on the
American continent. The public nature of private experience in Congregationalist churches led to conversion accounts, captivity narratives,
and community histories that piled up in homes, churches, courthouses,
and government buildings. Since the original settlers believed that providence was guiding their every step, they felt that it was necessary to record each detail of the community's blessings, sins, and repentance.
There could be no conjecture over the probable as these men gave certain testimony to what Cotton Mather called "the great things Christ is
doing in America" (*Magnalia Christi Americana*). Jonathan Edwards,
with an accountant's precision, registered each event that hastened or

delayed the coming of Christ's reign on earth.[21] The New Englanders were such compulsive record-keepers that William Emerson, the father of Ralph Waldo, had to protest against the publication of all this material. The world did not really need to know everything about everyone blessed with a New England birth: "Because there is something peculiar in the history of New England, it is not necessary that every New England man who is capable of putting sentences and paragraphs together should become the historian of his country."[22]

So, after the interval of philosophical history, the New Englanders came into the archival revolution of the nineteenth century with a running start. They already knew how to ransack records and publish them accurately. Later histories of New England, building on this profusion of archival evidence, would not be as certain that Christ could be found there doing great things as were their forebears, but they found new forms of providence — e.g., the rise of the Germanic races, the triumph of Protestantism over Catholicism, the superiority of democracy to absolutism, the fated greatness of America. These themes could be united with archival searches in ways not all that different from the old religious narratives. Even when the subject matter demanded that Catholics be the heroes, they could be exempted from their disabilities by their adversaries. Thus Washington Irving's Columbus was subtly Protestantized by his free-thinking opposition to priestly learning, and even Spanish Catholicism was preferable to Prescott's Aztecs and Incas.

When, therefore, Bancroft or Palfrey or Sparks told again the story of New England's founding, they remained filiopietists. This did not, as some think, prejudice them against the American South. Even those Americans who were not New Englanders fell, after all, on the right side of things, since they were of the same (Anglo-Saxon) racial stock and the same (Protestant) religion. How much these ideological factors affected their truth to sources differed from writer to writer. Jared Sparks was as much an antiquarian as an historian, and a great preserver of original records — but he "improved" the many records he printed to make them more patriotic. Besides, a love for a romanticized past infected the ideal of disinterested study. Many of the nineteenth-century historians had learned their narrative technique from Walter Scott. Adams, too, was deeply affected by Scott in his youth (E 755), especially by his medieval tales, *Ivanhoe* and *Quentin Durward* (L 2.363, 3.469, 4.331, 6.199–200, 623). As late as 1911 he could write: "*Ivanhoe* is an enormous work of instinctive comprehension and genius" (L 6.416). There was a touch of the romantic in the undergraduate courses he taught at Harvard, but it was severely restrained in his graduate course, where he made his students mine the dry documents of land tenure and legal titles. The romantic fires were banked but not extinguished, as one sees from their delayed flaring in *Mont Saint Michel and Chartres*. But in the *History* he takes a cool look at facts, registered in a sober prose, far from the grandiloquence of Bancroft or the gorgeous scenery painting of Parkman.

The way Adams began from, but went beyond, the historical culture that nurtured him can be seen from his first piece of historical research, written when he was only twenty-three, which arose from his relations with the leading Boston antiquarian (Charles Deane) and two Boston historians (Palfrey and Bancroft). He was encouraged by Deane and Palfrey to take up this project, and provoked to complete it by Bancroft. As a result, his first formal effort as an historian changed the entire historiography of his subject — which was John Smith.

Charles Deane and Pocahontas

Adams valued the New England chroniclers — he even said he had "wandered into the pleasant meadows of antiquarianism" himself (E 923). Some, naturally, give a filiopietistic explanation of this. Family papers were a special concern in New England, one that his father and brothers shared. Henry's father built at Quincy the first presidential library, to house his own father's papers. Henry's older brother Charles was a very active president of the Massachusetts Historical Society. He directed the construction of the building that still houses the society.[23] Henry's younger brother Brooks had a fond interest in Adams memorabilia. Henry left this collecting urge to others (L 5.251–52, 6.58–59, 301). As we have seen, he tried to discourage both brothers from writing celebrations of their family — which did not mean that he lacked respect for those antiquarians who supplied authentic history with its materials. He was particularly impressed by Charles Deane (1813–1889), who provided the occasion for his own first historical writing.

Deane was a wealthy businessman who specialized in turning up, authenticating, and publishing historical documents. He released these through the *Proceedings of the Massachusetts Historical Society*, the *Transactions and Collections of the American Antiquarian Society*, and the journals of genealogical and local history societies. His greatest coup was to recover the original manuscript of the most important Pilgrim document, William Bradford's *Of Plymouth Plantation,* which had disappeared during the Revolution and of which no copy had been made. When it was found in London's Fulham Palace, Deane authenticated the handwriting from Bradford's letters, had a copy made, and published it in the 1856 *Proceedings of the Massachusetts Historical Society,* causing what Samuel Eliot Morison called "a literary sensation."[24]

Deane would never score another coup of this magnitude, but he found and edited many other documents of great importance.[25] In 1860, he was the first to publish one of the two first accounts of Virginia's Jamestown settlement. Of these reports, both written in 1608, one, by John Smith, was well known, but the other, by Jamestown's first governor, Edward Wingfield, was unknown until Deane tracked it down — again in London, at the Lambeth Library — and brought it out in the *Transactions and Collections of the American Antiquarian Society.* The publication was controversial because Deane claimed that it demolished the legend of Smith's famous rescue from execution by Pocahontas. Though the rescue is supposed to have occurred just before these two reports were written, *it appears in neither of them.* Deane said that Smith did not write of the supposed event until sixteen years had passed, and he concluded: "No one can doubt that the earlier narrative contains the truer statement," so the rescue story "is one of the few of many embellishments with which Smith, with his strong love of the marvelous, was disposed to garnish the stories of his early adventures, and with which he or his editors were tempted to adorn particularly his later works."[26]

Henry Adams, who got back from Europe in October of 1860, just as this comment appeared, was concentrating on his father's support for the incoming Lincoln administration, and would not have noticed a footnote to an antiquarian document. But John Gorham Palfrey, his father's ally in the anti-slavery politics of Massachusetts, dined with the Adamses early in 1861, before Charles Francis and Henry left for their diplomatic mission to England, and he mentioned the problem of Pocahontas's absence from the first reports of Smith's time with the Indians (L 1.258).[27] Palfrey, the historian of New England, took a special interest in John Smith because of Smith's map of New England and his writings on the region. Palfrey had suspected Smith of exaggerating even before Deane's discovery.[28] But he had not suspected the Pocahontas story, and he was not as sure as Deane that it was an invention. He suggested that editors in England might have altered Smith's manuscript, and wondered if an undoctored manuscript might be found there.

This thought intrigued Adams, and when he had some spare time in London he went to the British Museum and asked a curator of old books and manuscripts what he had by or about John Smith. Two texts convinced him that Smith was telling the truth — Smith's reference in 1612, only five years after the event, to a rescue performed by Pocahontas, and a second reference to it in a letter Smith wrote to Queen Anne in 1616, introducing Pocahontas on her arrival in England after she had married John Rolfe. It seemed clear to Henry that Deane was wrong in saying that Smith did not refer to his rescue from execution until sixteen years later. He wrote to assure Palfrey that Smith could be trusted, at least on the point that Deane had raised, since the 1612 assertion would have been challenged by Smith's many enemies if it had not been true, and the 1616 letter must have been the buzz of King James's court: "Everyone who talked with her (and she talked English) must have mentioned this exploit of hers, and she could have had no motive to keep up the falsehood, if it was one" (L 1.258–59).

Though Adams thought there was no further discovery he could make at this point, he tried to advance Smith scholarship. He learned that the British Museum staff did not know about Deane's discovery of the Wingfield manuscript. He asked Palfrey to get a copy from Deane for presentation to the British Museum (L 1.259). When that was done, the museum's board of directors voted to thank Deane (L 1.280–81). Adams then began corresponding directly with Deane, supplying him with a copy of Smith's will, which they both took to be authentic (L 1.514). When Deane came to London after the Civil War, Adams helped him find Smith's grave, which again they took to be authentic.[29]

But before Adams opened communication with Deane, Palfrey had relayed to him his own and Deane's criticism of Adams's first conclusions about the 1612 and 1616 mentions of Pocahontas. The two older researchers pointed out to him that the 1612 text referred to a different rescue already reported in the 1608 *True Relation of Virginia* — how, after Smith's release from captivity, Pocahontas came to the settlement to warn the British of her father's intention of attacking them. As for Smith's letter to the Queen, it was first printed in his *General History* of 1624. No mention of it occurred earlier, reflecting what Adams called the buzz of the court. There was nothing but Smith's later word to indicate that it was actually sent in 1616, and his word was the thing at issue. Adams confessed his errors, and went back to the British Museum to search manuscripts and state papers (L 1.280, 287).

After gathering every early account of the Jamestown settlement, Adams came to agree with Deane that there was no mention of the rescue from execution prior to Smith's *General History* of 1624 — and there was every reason why there should have been such a mention if the rescue had in fact occurred. He wrote up this "chain of evidence" in 1862 (L 1.287). He had no present intention of publishing it, but he sent it to Palfrey for his and Deane's criticism (L 1.340). Not till after the war, when he was preparing several essays for publication, did he ask Palfrey to send the manuscript back. He would now have to acknowledge the new edition of Smith's *True Relation* that Deane brought out in 1866. He also asked Palfrey for the latest edition of Bancroft's *History of the United States,* volume one, containing the Pocahontas story. Adams had found that Bancroft gave a flowery version of the story, which he claimed to be deriving from the 1608 *True Relation,* where it does not occur. After Deane's edition of Wingfield appeared in 1860, Bancroft added a footnote naming the 1616 letter to Queen Anne as his source. Adams wanted to know if Bancroft had made any further changes, since he meant to use his version as an example of "the tyrannical sway still exercised by Smith over the intelligence of the country."[30]

Adams told Palfrey he meant to change his essay into a review article of Deane's two editions, and Palfrey mentioned it to the editor of the *North American Review,* who expressed interest in it. Adams then sent two essays, of which he was at the moment more interested in the second, "British Finance in 1816," since it was part of a series on finance he wanted to publish in America and Scotland (L 1.509). But the *Review* ran "Captain John Smith" as the first thirty pages of its January, 1867, issue.[31] It made an instant sensation. Three responses were published in the South, and the president of the Maryland Historical Society planned a debate over it (L 1.560). Adams encouraged Deane to join that debate, but he was about to go from London to Italy, and he took no further part in the argument.

Yet he was proud of the essay. He reprinted it with revisions in both his own collections of his essays, *Chapters of Erie* (1871) and *Historical Essays* (1891). Judged simply in terms of impact, this first historical work of Adams was his most successful one. It changed the whole Smith historiography. Until Adams wrote there had been no real challenge to the Pocahontas story. For a century afterward, though the Pocahontas myth lived in popular legend, learned opinion was with Adams. And Smith's whole body of writings was subjected to a new skepticism. Not many historians have published a paper while still in their twenties (and written at the age of twenty-three) that alters a scholarly field. (Frederick Jackson Turner was thirty-two when he produced his even more revolutionary paper on the frontier.)

But a reaction was probably inevitable. What is surprising is that it was so long in coming. Come it did, however, beginning in the 1960s, when a group of men started defending Smith's veracity across the whole range of his writings. That Adams's view was the orthodox one can be seen from the fact that these new defenders of Smith were called "revisionists." A harbinger of their work had appeared in 1953 — Bradford Smith's psychobiography of Smith, which claimed that, because of his mother's remarriage, Smith constructed "an idealized mother" image that "haunted him the rest of his life."[32] To avoid besmirching this image, Smith did not tell the Pocahontas story to his fellow Jamestown settlers. "The men would make leering remarks about his relations with the girl. Sex-starved themselves, they would never let the subject alone."[33] This does not explain why Smith did not send the tale to England for publication, where (presumably) not all readers were sex-starved.

The Smith revisionists resort to a similarly tortured logic to explain why Smith omitted the role of Pocahontas in the first account of his captivity. Inevitably, some claim that Adams was just writing out of family pride, trying to besmirch John Randolph, an Adams foe who claimed descent from Pocahontas. But Adams's essay is very respectful to Pocahontas. Doubting Smith's word reflects no dishonor on her. It is true that Adams jokingly wrote Palfrey that discrediting Smith's story "would make John Randolph turn green" (L 1.287). But his own life of Randolph does not defend the Adamses (as we shall see). Others claim that Adams was writing anti-southern propaganda during the Civil War, though he published it after the war, and he was so pro-southern during Reconstruction that he accused old friends like Charles Sumner of treating ex-Confederates like serfs (R 71). He advocated pardons for southern leaders like Lucius Lamar.

The reasons given by the revisionists for omitting Pocahontas from Smith's 1608 work are multiplied out of desperation. One says that Smith was rescued so often by Pocahontas that omitting one example hardly mattered.[34] It is true that Smith later wrote, "In the utmost of *many* extremities, that blessed Pocahontas, the great king's daughter of Virginia, *oft* saved my life" (emphasis added).[35] But the first time she is supposed to have done this should have taken pride of place. In 1608,

Smith could not know that she would help him out again and again. Others say that the rescue is omitted because it would make his fellows so jealous that they would kill him.[36] Or it was omitted to spare Smith, proud of his self-reliance, from the embarrassment of depending on a mere girl for his life.[37] But then why tell the story later, and add to it many rescues by women, at home and abroad? Smith wrote:

> Even in foreign parts, I have felt relief from that sex. The beauteous lady Tragabigzanda, when I was a slave to the Turks, did all she could to secure me. When I overcame the Bashaw of Nalbrits in Tartaria, the charitable Callamata supplied my necessity. In the utmost of many extremities, that blessed Pocahontas, the great king's daughter of Virginia, oft saved my life. When I escaped the cruelty of pirates and most furious storms, a long time alone in a small boat at sea and driven ashore in France, the good lady Madam Chanoyes bountifully assisted me.[38]

The prize excuse offered by the revisionists was made up by Philip Barbour, who says Smith did not include the Pocahontas story because Smith was not in danger of execution — he was witnessing his own adoption ceremony.[39] If so, why did he later present it as an execution, after he had many occasions to learn that it was not that at all? The desperation of all these attempts to save Smith's credibility is suggested by J. A. Leo Lemay's terminal case of perhapsing:

> *Perhaps* Powhatan promised to free Smith but changed his mind. Or *perhaps* Powhatan intended from the first to adopt Smith after an initiation ceremony in which Pocahontas would sponsor him. Or *perhaps* at the trial the tribal leaders surprised Powhatan by arguing that the prisoner should be killed, and he tentatively agreed, only to have the pleadings of Pocahontas confirm his former decision. I concede, however, that it seems suspicious that Smith dropped Powhatan's early promise when retelling the story in *The General Historie* [emphasis added].[40]

Or "Smith may also simply have omitted the anecdote for no special reason."[41] All these attempts to save an account for which there is only Smith's (delayed) word cannot cancel the plain facts that Adams marshaled in his brilliant first work of history. With the help of Deane the champion archivist and Palfrey the New England historian, the men who found and studied the Wingfield manuscript, Adams learned from the outset the importance of working from original sources. He had found his métier.

3

―――――▶◆◀―――――

CIVIL WAR POLITICS

F OR ADAMS TO BECOME a knowledgeable political, diplomatic,
economic, cultural, and military historian, it was not enough
for him to know how to find and evaluate documents. He
needed an intimate acquaintance with the way people act,
plan, react, provoke, or right themselves again, under the pressure of
crises. There could have been no better training in all these areas than
the domestic and foreign activities Adams was plunged into during his
early twenties. He was partly an agent himself, partly an observer, partly
a spy, as the nation unraveled at home and alliances were frayed abroad.
The anonymous journalism he wrote from Washington in 1860 and 1861
seemed to be coming from a person far older and more experienced than
he was. He had access to information denied to other journalists.

He was writing propaganda, of course; but so were most newspaper
reporters of the time. His judgments were often wrong, but the process
of making them proved instructive to him, then and later. He was striving to make sense of inscrutable or duplicitous men — of Lincoln not
tipping his hand on how he would form or use his wartime cabinet, of an
old friend like Charles Sumner playing new roles, of a new friend like
William Seward hiding his plans in plain view.

Then, when Adams went to London as his father's secretary-assistant,
he had to read the deliberately or inadvertently confusing signals emit-
ted by British statesmen, Confederate representatives, and commercial agents. He did not fight the Civil War in the field like his brother
Charles, but he learned a great deal about the logistics of war, the economics of war, the provision and maintenance of military equipment,

and the international-law implications of hostility. He helped his father find, expose, and denounce the secret construction of Confederate warships in England. He helped spell out the legal rights and wrongs of the search for and capture of warring ships at sea. He collected information on the economic conditions of England and the way they made British merchants favor their former cotton suppliers in America. He learned from Seward's traveling emissary in England, Thurlow Weed, how public relations campaigns are mounted. With his instinct for history, he went back to study British economic conditions as they affected the War of 1812, which would be the culminating event of his later *History*.

In the *Education*, Adams presented his situation in Washington and London as paired psychomachies, two struggles of the spirit, in which he stood with his father as they tried to assess contending claims. In Washington, the conflicting claims on Adams's loyalty were made by Charles Sumner and William Seward. In London, the claims on his trust were made by Lord Palmerston and Earl Russell. Which was the friend and which the foe — or were both men both things, interchangeably but on staggered timetables? Adams will deliberately mystify both these psychomachies in the *Education*, saying they were unsolvable mysteries. They did not look like that at the time because they were not like that. He drew very different conclusions from his experience in the *History*, which better reflects what he learned while preparing for it.

Adams liked to say in later life that he came back from Europe, at twenty-two, to cast his first presidential vote for Abraham Lincoln (E 809). But while still traveling abroad he had been deeply upset when he learned that Lincoln won the Republican nomination in Chicago. He was a supporter of William Henry Seward, as were his father and brothers at home. Going into the election year 1860, Henry wrote from Dresden: "The day that I hear that Seward is quietly elected President of the United States will be a great relief to me, for I honestly believe that that and only that can carry us through, if even that can" (L 1.67). He and some American friends in Dresden determined to do anything possible to elect Seward (L 1.76), and he wrote to Brooks:

> You just mark what Seward says; he's the man of the age and the nation; he knows more in politics than a heap; he's a far-sighted man and yet he's got eyes for what's near, too. I aspire to know him some day. Pray tell him so if you ever lack matter of conversation. Keep him allied with papa, the

closer the better. If he comes in as president, in that case we shall see fun. (L 1.91–92)

When Seward, having lost the nomination, agreed to campaign for the Republican ticket in the general election, he was plotting how he could manipulate Lincoln after his election. The Adams family joined in this endeavor. Henry's brother Charles went out on a campaign swing with Seward, and the two met Lincoln for the first time at Springfield.

But when this Seward *apparat* went to Washington after Lincoln's election, a longtime friend of the Adamses, Senator Charles Sumner, stood in opposition to Seward. Which side would the Adamses take? The contest swayed back and forth. Sumner prevailed over Seward on the first point at issue, how far to compromise with the South in order to prevent further secessions. But when Seward, as secretary of state, seemed to have the upper hand in dealing with other nations during the war, Sumner said, in effect, "Not so fast." As chairman of the Senate Committee on Foreign Relations, he was in a position to fight Seward. Henry and his father would feel the repercussions of this struggle while they served in London. And Henry found himself still torn between Sumner and Seward when he went to Washington as a journalist after the war. Sumner the dreamy loner and Seward the gregarious fixer were opposite types, and Henry, who had all but idolized each in his time, tried to reconcile their appeals.

Sumner

Sumner had the earlier claim on Adams's loyalty. In fact, Henry had a kind of proprietary feeling about Sumner's entry into the Senate. Sumner had worked with Henry's father in setting up the Free Soil party in the 1840s, at a time when Sumner was often at the Adams home and Henry conceived a great fondness for him. He tells us that he admired Sumner more than his own father (who was roughly Sumner's age):

> The boy Henry worshiped him, and if he ever regarded any older man as a personal friend, it was Mr. Sumner. The relation of Mr. Sumner in the household was far closer than any relation of blood. None of the uncles approached such intimacy. Sumner was the boy's ideal of greatness; the highest product of nature and art. The only fault of such a model was its superi-

ority, which defied imitation. To the twelve-year-old boy, his father, Dr. Palfrey, Mr. Dana, were men, more or less like what he himself might become; but Mr. Sumner was of a different order. (E 748)

It is not surprising that Sumner, who was both lonely and vain, should welcome the hero worship of a precocious teenager. He was a man of strong but baffled emotions, of aspiring but limited intellect. On the emotional side, he was a romantic, one who felt poetry deeply and wanted to compose it. His closest lifelong friend was the poet Longfellow, and he moved in the circle of Transcendentalists around Emerson. On the intellectual side, he was a pupil of the legal scholar and Supreme Court justice Joseph Story. From being Story's student at Harvard Law School, he went on to become his assistant, teaching courses for him when Story was detained in Washington. But Sumner never became a legal theorist himself, any more than he became a poet. His oratory, with which he first made his name, was a labored blend of the would-be poet and the would-be jurist.

After Sumner spent two and a half years in Europe acquiring languages and polishing his style, he returned to Boston with a zeal for philanthropy and social projects. With no family of his own, he warmed himself at the beneficent fires of prison reform, school improvement, abolition, and pacifism. As war with Mexico loomed, he made a sensation with a Fourth of July oration denouncing war. A strapping and handsome man, he yearned for companionship, but seemed to have no interest in women.[1] (A late attempt at marriage failed almost immediately.) When his weekday reform efforts left him adrift on weekends, he divided his time between visits to the Wordsworths in Cambridge and the Adamses in Quincy — where his abolition work had made him a favorite of John Quincy Adams in his last days. During the week, however, he was most often at the Beacon Hill home of Charles Francis Adams, planning anti-slavery efforts like the Free Soil party.

The hold of the southern Democrats on their northern party members was weakening in the 1840s. But Whig efforts to forge a national alternative suffered the divisions of the anti-slavery movement. Abolitionism took many forms. Some were "immediatist" abolitionists, some gradualists, some anti-expansionists, some colonizers, some compromisers between two or more of the above. Small parties rose and disintegrated — Anti-Masons, Native Americans, Free Soilers. After the failure of the Free Soilers in 1848, on whose ticket Henry's father ran as vice president, the fight became again a struggle for control of the Whig party. Daniel Webster led the "Cotton Whigs," who tried to use commercial leverage to compromise with the plantation owners over new territory. The "Conscience Whigs" considered Webster a traitor because he supported the Compromise of 1850, including the fugitive slave law.

One leader of the Conscience Whigs, Joseph Wilson, thought the way to circumvent Webster was to form a coalition of the Conscience Whigs with anti-slavery Democrats. Wilson's former colleagues doubted the sincerity of Democratic opposition to slavery, and thought he was selling out simply to defeat Webster. Henry's father, without condemning those who went with Wilson, considered it unworthy for an *Adams* to do so. He wrote in his diary (November 14, 1850) that for one "who is rising in the world, a little abrasion of this sort will do no harm, whilst to me who am constantly contrasted with my predecessors, it would be discreditable." Sumner, who had set the bar high for purity and principle, was expected to be just as opposed to compromise. But he made no grand renunciation. He left his options open as the Massachusetts legislature tried to muster the votes to choose state and national offices. A deadlock prevailed for three months between divided Whig and divided Democratic factions. No interparty or intraparty combination could break the deadlock. While Sumner professed reluctance to be part of any deal, his name for senator was used as a bargaining chip by Democrats who wanted the governor's office for themselves.

Finally, on April 23, Sumner was announced the winner of the Senate seat on the twenty-second ballot. But there was some doubt even then. Sumner was staying at the Adams home, and Charles Francis sent his twelve-year-old son Henry to run up the street to the statehouse and confirm the outcome. Henry had to report back that one vote had been contested, voiding the election. Not till the next day, after four more ballots, was Sumner's election confirmed. Henry, who by then was waiting around for the outcome, ran home with the good news: "He enjoyed the glory of telling Sumner that he was elected; it was probably the proudest moment in the life of either" (E 766).

In the *Education* Adams does not recount the complicated three-month effort to find some way out of an electoral impasse. He does not say he had been sent earlier by his father to check the outcome. He misremembers his age, advancing it from twelve to "near fifteen," and then says his joy in Sumner's election made him part of the dirty bargain with Democrats that his father was too good for.

Thus before he was fifteen years old, he had managed to get himself into a state of moral confusion from which he never escaped. As a politician, he was already corrupt, and he never could see how any practical politician could be less corrupt than himself. (E 76)

Where on earth did that language come from? He tells us where, in letters he wrote about his composition of the *Education.* His model was the *Confessions* of Saint Augustine: "Never have I seen so outrageous an [autobiographical] ambition attempted, except by Saint Augustine, from whom I deliberately stole it, knowing that no one would now know enough to detect the theft" (L 6.221).

Saint Augustine derives his entry into a world of sin from an apparently trivial thing that happened in his sixteenth year, when he gratuitously stole some pears he did not even want. Adams, dramatizing his own folly in order to attack the world's when he was writing the *Education,* has entirely distorted what really occurred. His father did not think Sumner a traitor to his principles, and his career in the Senate would show no temporizing with slavery. But Henry, in the darkened mood of the *Education,* wants to dramatize the degradation involved in all political activity.

Contrary to the suggestion that Sumner had sold his soul, with the connivance of his twelve-year-old coadjutor, he became the fiercest opponent of the expansion of slavery into Kansas in 1856, and he paid dearly for this stand on principle. In a book-length speech, "The Crime Against Kansas," delivered over the course of two days, Sumner was so strident that Stephen Douglas, pacing restlessly in the rear of the chamber on the first day, muttered, "That damn fool will get himself killed by some other damn fool."[2] On the second day, Douglas responded to the speech by asking, "Is it his object to provoke some of us to kick him as we would a dog in the street, that he may get sympathy upon the just chastisement?" Sumner turned on the short, rotund, and bibulous Douglas, and said that "no person with the upright form of man can be allowed" — he paused, and Douglas goaded him on: "Say it." Sumner did: "The noisome, squat, and nameless animal to which I now refer is not the proper model for an American senator. Will the senator from Illinois take notice?" "I will," Douglas answered, "and therefore will not imitate you, sir."[3]

But the part of Sumner's speech that drew the most attention was his personal slur against Senator Andrew Butler of South Carolina. Butler had a lisp, and Sumner mocked "the loose expectoration of his speech" in favor of slavery. This maddened a cousin of Butler, Preston Brooks, who served in the other chamber. The thirty-six-year-old Brooks waited outside the Senate to attack the forty-five-year-old Sumner. Horsewhips were the proper weapon for southerners who considered their opponent too low to meet in a duel, but Butler said he thought the older Sumner might wrest the whip from him, so he brought a thick cane. When Sumner did not leave the Senate chamber after the session ended, Brooks went inside and struck his head half a dozen times while Sumner was pinioned behind his desk. Only by wrenching the desk from the floor, to which it was firmly bolted, could the bleeding Sumner rise, and then, as he staggered about, Brooks rained more blows on him till the cane broke, after which he continued beating him with the thick end of it.

Brooks later boasted: "Every lick went where I intended . . . [I] gave him about thirty first-rate stripes. Towards the last he bellowed like a calf. I wore my cane out completely but saved the head, which is gold."[4] People rushed to the sound of Sumner's screams. Brooks did not stop till Congressman Ambrose Murray grabbed his arm. Senator John Crittenden ran up, crying, "Don't kill him," but Congressman Lawrence Keitt, who had come with Brooks, knowing and approving of his attack, raised his cane against Crittenden, shouting, "Let them alone, God damn you." Senator Robert Toombs of Georgia warned Keitt not to strike Crittenden, but let the beating of Sumner go on ("I approved of it"). Finally Murray and Congressman Edwin Morgan separated Sumner from his assailant, who went off with his friend Keitt.

Brooks became an instant hero in the South, where townships gave him votes of thanks, and presented him with canes to be used on others who insult the South. The Senate appointed a committee to investigate the incident, but it had not a single Republican on it, and it reported that the Senate could do nothing to punish a member of the other chamber. A House committee recommended expulsion, but the motion failed for lack of the required two-thirds vote. Brooks took the initiative by resigning his seat, standing for re-election, and returning by a large majority. There were passionate expressions of rage in the North.[5] The newspapers reported continually on Sumner's state. He lay for weeks feverish and racked with pain. His head wounds were healing, but brain damage was feared. It would be three years before he was healthy enough to return to his seat. The Massachusetts legislature held it open, as a symbol of reproach, until he was ready. Since Sumner had been liable to psychosomatic disturbances even before he was beaten, some suspected that his martyrdom was spun out; but Sumner underwent painful therapies in Europe, which hardly suggest malingering.

Naturally, Henry Adams was stunned by the news of what had happened to his hero. He was still a student at Harvard in 1856, but when he went to Berlin he found that Sumner was in France still seeking health cures in 1858. Henry instantly offered his services to help Sumner recover: "I will leave German, law, Latin and all and go with you and take care of you, and see that you don't speak a word of politics or receive a letter or a newspaper for the next two years. And then I believe you would be as well as any man on this earth" (L 1.12). Implicit in this offer was Henry's belief that Sumner should give up the idea of going back to "that bar-room of a Congress" and let some other fill the empty Massachusetts seat. But Sumner was back in the Senate when Henry went to Washington to join his father in 1860. Charles Francis Adams in the House and Sumner in the Senate worked closely in efforts to stave off disunion. This was during the four-month interval between Lincoln's election and his inauguration. Sumner was once again a regular at the Adams dinner table in Washington, where Henry's old hero had now to compete with his new one, William Henry Seward.

Seward

Though Seward had his own house on Lafayette Square in Washington, he too visited the Adamses night after night. He had a wife and four children back in New York, but he was really married to politics, under the guidance of the New York political boss Thurlow Weed. Though Seward and Sumner were in many ways opposite types, they had some things in common. They had made their early fame as reformers of prisons and schools, Seward as governor of New York from 1839 to 1843. They were both outspoken foes of slavery. Seward entered the Senate two years before Sumner, where they both opposed the Kansas-Nebraska bill in 1856. Seward had moved for the Senate to investigate Brooks after the attack on Sumner.

But Seward did not yearn ineffectually toward poetry and the law, like Sumner. With Weed at his side, he lived and breathed for power, and had his eyes on the presidency from early in his life. He could probably have had the Republican nomination in 1856, but Weed thought it was not the party's year. He advised his man to wait till 1860, meanwhile making his name better known nationally. This he accomplished with an 1858 speech calling the clash between slave and non-slave states an "irrepressible conflict." The speech went too far, and probably cost him the nomination he had long been working for. Lincoln, despite his own "House Divided" speech, was seen as more flexible on sectional matters. That is ironic, since Seward would be the man, in the winter of 1860–61, trying to strike a compromise with the South.

Once Lincoln was elected, Weed told him that he would need the far-better-known and better-connected Seward to form a strong government. Weed went to Springfield to make this case, arguing for a cabinet approved by Seward. Seward expected to be made secretary of state, but Weed insinuated that he might not accept the post unless his wishes for other cabinet members were honored. Lincoln kept his own counsel, and let Seward lead efforts in Washington to prevent the border states from seceding. Seward came up with a series of last-minute deals. With the help of Charles Francis Adams, he promoted an offer suggested by Maryland congressman Wilson Davis — to admit New Mexico as a slave state. Seward also organized a closed-door peace conference with southern representatives.

Henry Adams, writing anonymously in the Boston *Daily Advertiser,* enthusiastically backed all of Seward's initiatives. He was as smitten with Seward now, in his early twenties, as he had been with Sumner in his early teens. "From the first sight, he loved the Governor [Seward], who, though sixty years old, had the youth of his sympathies" (E 814). After Seward's first appearance at the Adams home, Henry wrote Charles:

> I sat and watched the old fellow with his big nose and his wire hair and grizzly eyebrows and miserable dress, and listened to him rolling out his grand, broad ideas that would inspire a cow with statesmanship, if she understood our language. There is no shake in him. He talks square up to the mark and something beyond it. (L 1.204)

Henry was flattered by Seward's confidences in him, as he had been by Sumner's: "The old file [rascal] has taken a great shine to my cigars and we smoke our good papa perfectly dry after dinner" (L 1.215). The most cited physical description of Seward is Adams's from the *Education* — "a head like a wise macaw" and so on (E 814). But a more vivid one is in his letter to Charles:

I have excited immense delight among some young ladies here by a very brilliant proposition which I made to dye the old sinner's hair bright crimson, paint his face the most brilliant green and his nose yellow, and then to make an exhibition of him as the sage parrot; a bird he wonderfully resembles in manner and profile. If I had a knack at drawing, I would make some such sketch for *Vanity Fair*. (L 1.223)

The Adamses shared with Seward an impression that Lincoln had surrendered the management of things to Seward's better-skilled hands. Henry told his brother that Seward was "the virtual ruler of this country" (L 1.223). "Lincoln is all right" because he is following Seward's lead (L 1.209). Seward "has arranged or is arranging things through Thurlow Weed" (L 1.218). One of the things he was supposed to be arranging was the appointment of Charles Francis Adams as secretary of the treasury.

While the evenings with Seward glowed ever more brightly, those with Sumner grew chillier. A first reunion went smoothly enough: "Sumner dined here yesterday and was grand as usual" (L 1.210) — though Henry thought Sumner was dreaming when he said that he (not Seward) would be secretary of state. Things got stickier at later meals, as Sumner opposed the compromises of Seward and Henry's father. Henry looked on with approval as Charles Francis rebuked Sumner for his "stiff-necked obstinacy" toward the South: "Egad, it would have done you good to see how papa faced round on him and hit in, one, two, three, quick as lightning" (L 1.222). "Sumner was up here again yesterday when pa rapped him again over the knuckles" (L 1.223).

When Sumner opposed the peace conference with southern representatives, Henry wrote that he was making a fool of himself, and probably working to destroy Charles Francis's standing with the abolitionists (L 1.228). Sumner stopped coming to dinner, though Henry urgently invited him back. He knew the cause of the rift: Sumner opposed the men he called "compromisers," and "our irascible papa got into a passion with him" (L 1.232). Sumner, though he was never personally hostile, made no secret of his disagreement with Charles Francis's course.[6] In fact, the report of this disagreement reached Boston, so that Henry blatantly denied the truth of it in an anonymous article for the Boston *Advertiser* (S 1.87).

In the *Education*, this whole sequence is badly misrepresented. Adams says there that he was "thunderstruck" that his old friend could criticize his father and cut him. Why should that have surprised him? He had watched the rift opening at his own dinner table, and cheered his father on as he hit Sumner, one, two, three. Adams is using the incident to stage once again the *Education*'s scenario of failure and betrayal:

> The shock opened a chasm in his life that never closed, and as long as life lasted, he found himself invariably taking for granted, as a political instinct, without waiting further experiment — as he took it for granted that arsenic poisoned — the rule that a friend in power is a friend lost. (E 818)

The absurdity of that is striking. Sumner was more a friend when he had more power, before he was caned. And Seward was the one coming into power, not Sumner. The friendship of Seward was being won, not lost. Besides, Henry was later a friend to many in power, including his closest friend, John Hay, while Hay was secretary of state.

As if to top himself, Henry goes on to compare Sumner's "defection," based on his opposition to the South, with the desertions *of* the South: "Not one rebel defection — not even Robert E. Lee's — cost young Adams a personal pang; but Sumner's struck home" (E 818). Adams vastly overplays his own break with Sumner. His letters at the time say Sumner "is very cordial when we meet," though he does not come to the house (L 1.232), and Henry was soon writing him for advice on approaching London newspapers (L 1.234). Because of the distortions in this part of the *Education*, Adams has to contrive a kind of later reconciliation where none was needed (E 949–50).

The essay that Adams wrote at this time, "The Great Secession Winter," is effusive in its praise of Seward, but it blames Lincoln for not explicitly coming to the support of Seward's compromises:

> Mr. Seward, Mr. Winter Davis, and the southern Whigs, Mr. Adams, Mr. Sherman and a large share of the best ability of the party, exhausted their influence in advocating these measures, and still the mass of the party hesitated, and turned for the decisive word to the final authority at Springfield. The word did not come. In its stead came doubtful rumors tending to distract public opinion still more. In spite of the assertions of newspapers, and to the surprise of the country, it became more and more evident that there was no concerted action between the president-elect and the Republicans at Washington, and that Mr. Seward had acted all winter on his own responsibilities. The effect of this discovery was soon evident in the gradual destruction of party discipline in Congress, where every man began to follow an independent course, or commit himself against the measures proposed, from an idea that the president was against them. (GS 25–26)[7]

Henry at this time thought that Lincoln had sabotaged the heroic efforts of Seward to save the Union. His father would continue to think that for the rest of his life. As late as his eulogy to Seward, delivered in 1873, Charles Francis was still rebuking Lincoln for not lending aid to Seward's efforts at compromise.

> His mind had not even opened to the nature of the crisis. From his secluded abode in the heart of Illinois, he was only taking the measure of geographical relations and party services, and beginning his operations where others commonly leave off.[8]

His father's continuing hostility to Lincoln was embarrassing to Henry, who came to know Lincoln better from his friend John Hay, Lincoln's secretary, who wrote his biography. In the *Education,* he shows his embarrassment over the past by denying the conflict between Lincoln and Seward, making them act in a concert that did not exist at the time:

> Rightly or wrongly the new president and his chief advisers in Washington decided that, before they could administer the government, they must make sure of a government to administer, and that this chance depended on the action of Virginia. The whole ascendancy of the winter wavered between the effort of the cotton states to drag Virginia out, and the effort of the new president to keep Virginia in . . . As far as a private secretary knew, the party united on its tactics. (E 815–16)

This is one of the more blatant distortions of the record in a book that is full of them. Henry's changed attitude toward Lincoln can be seen from the fact that he says: "Had young Adams been told that his life was to hang on the correctness of his estimate of the new president, he would have lost" (E 817).

Despite some youthful misjudgments reached in the swirl of events, Adams gained much by his observation of the incoming administration. The fiercest struggle between Lincoln and Seward was over the formation of a cabinet. If Seward had prevailed, the cabinet would have been his creature, not Lincoln's. That is just the maneuver that Senator Ratcliffe uses in Henry's novel *Democracy;* but where Seward failed, Ratcliffe (with far different purposes) succeeds. Adams himself would lend aid to people trying to affect Ulysses S. Grant's choice of his first cabinet. He would also give Jefferson high marks in the *History* for the cabinet he formed, while Madison scores low marks on the same count. The importance of cabinet choices was a lasting lesson he learned from

Lincoln's way of thwarting the Weed-Seward challenge to his early days as president.

Another effect of this first exposure to national politics in America was that it made Adams always favor a strong executive. As he watched President Buchanan dither, while Congress proved itself incapable of compensating for his weakness, he agreed with Seward that the new executive would have to be a strong one (Seward thought it would be under his guidance). Some believe that Lincoln would take on too many powers during the war, but Adams claimed, at the end of the conflict, that the executive was still too weak. In the *History,* he will not criticize Jefferson for making the executive too strong (though he tweaks him for acting against his own theory that it should be weak). He felt Jefferson did not take strong enough steps — in his response to the *Chesapeake* affair, for instance, or his neglect of the navy.

Adams was still early in the process of sifting his political experience for its historical usefulness. But he was learning. And he was, after all, only twenty-two years old.

London

Seward wanted to make Charles Francis Adams secretary of the treasury, insuring that he would have a docile ally there. When Lincoln appointed Salmon P. Chase instead, Seward resigned; but Lincoln quietly ignored him back onto the team. Seward insisted, however, that some reward was coming to the man who had helped hold the country together in the House of Representatives. How about minister to England? Lincoln agreed to that, and Charles Francis accepted. But when Charles Francis went to thank Lincoln, he was expecting serious conversation about his duties. He did not realize that Seward had taken him into Lincoln's office, unexpected and unannounced, during a conversation Lincoln was having with an Illinois congressman about an appointment in his state. This confirmed Charles Francis's opinion that Lincoln was interested in nothing but grubby patronage aspects of the presidency.[9]

This was not an auspicious beginning for the Adams mission, and Charles Francis made things worse by delaying his departure for six weeks. His oldest son John was getting married in four weeks, and Charles Francis, instead of leaving his wife to attend that ceremony, waited around himself. He did not know, though he might have guessed, that the seceded states had already sent three emissaries to London, who held meetings with the prime minister (Lord Palmerston) and members of Parliament. Those agents did not get all they hoped (diplomatic recognition as a separate government), but they got an important first step — a Queen's proclamation of neutrality. This recognized the South as a belligerent, not simply as a refractory part of the Union. The position Charles Francis had to maintain was that the seceders were not at war with his government but were criminals within that government, disobeying it. The Queen's proclamation came out the very day Charles Francis arrived, May 13, 1861. He was behind before he began, and he could not, for all his effort, get that first action rescinded. He had to keep working hard to prevent the next step, full diplomatic recognition.

As secretary to his father in England, Henry wrote anonymous dispatches to the New York *Times,* hiding the fact that he was riding an emotional roller coaster. The ups and downs are revealed in long and frequent letters to his brother Charles. One day he would call the prospect favorable (L 1.238). A few days later he would drop into despair. The Adamses had left America with no trust in Lincoln, but with great confidence in Seward as secretary of state. Yet less than a month after their arrival, Seward sent minister Adams an instruction, Dispatch No. 10, which Henry and his father considered mad. Charles Francis was to convey to the British this message: If Great Britain recognizes the South as belligerents, accepts diplomatic emissaries from the Confederacy, or fails to honor the North's blockade of the South, the United States will "become once more, as we have twice before been forced to be, enemies of Great Britain."[10] What had happened to Seward, Henry's hero? He wrote to his brother:

> A dispatch arrived yesterday from Seward, so arrogant in tone and so extraordinary and unparalleled in its demands that it leaves no doubt in my mind that our government wishes to force a war with Europe ... I have said already that I thought such a policy shallow madness, whether it comes from Seward or from any one else. It is not only a crime, it's a blunder. (L 1.239)

Henry's father could not believe that Seward would invent a scheme so foolish. He wrote in his diary (June 10, 1861) that demented men in the cabinet must have forced it on the "calm and wise" secretary of state.

The Adamses in London did not realize that this was just one link in a series of erratic acts tumbling out of Seward after the inauguration of

Lincoln. After months when Seward thought that he and he alone could save the nation, he refused to assume the subordinate place Lincoln had assigned him. Seward strove to maintain his policy of conciliation toward the South. He said that Fort Sumter, in Charleston harbor, should be abandoned, since it was a provocation to the South. When Lincoln overruled him, Seward tried to sabotage the flotilla being sent to resupply the fort — he not only leaked details of the mission to the press, but redirected the lead ship to a different objective.[11]

On the same day this last ploy was attempted, he sent Lincoln "Some Thoughts for the Consideration of the President," arguing that the nation was adrift — there was no policy; the conflict over slavery was irresolvable — and therefore Lincoln should "CHANGE THE QUESTION" (his capital letters). He must demand an assurance from the European powers that they are not interfering in the American hemisphere, and — should that not be forthcoming — must "convene Congress and declare war against them." This would reunite the North and the South, which would be fighting a common enemy — and forgetting, in the process, the subject of slavery.

Seward explained that this course would have to be pursued full-time by one man, and since the president had other duties to keep him from such concentration, "I neither seek to evade nor assume responsibility" for doing it. He was asking to be made a war czar. The document is so mad that it is known to historians by its date, the April Fool's Letter. Henry would not have been so puzzled by Dispatch No. 10 if he had known of these preambles to it. His brother Charles, who had not yet gone into the army, watched incredulously what Seward was doing in Washington. Like all the family, he had revered Seward — he campaigned with him, remember, the year before. But drawing on his diary notes from 1867, he later wrote: "Seward lost his head. He found himself fairly beyond his depth, and he plunged! The foreign-war panacea took possession of him."[12]

Lincoln had softened Dispatch No. 10 before he let Seward send it. The president offered it only for the minister's consideration, not for presentation to the British. Charles Francis accordingly muted and disguised its message when dealing with the British Foreign Office. But rumors of this and other aberrations of Seward were relayed to London by the British minister in Washington, Lord Lyons. To them were added speeches in which Seward had talked of the inevitability of Canada's someday becoming part of the United States — which was interpreted, along with his other bellicosities, to mean he wanted war with England in order to gain Canada. Charles Francis Adams had to cope with a belief (which even his son shared) that Seward was maneuvering toward a foreign war.

Because Henry now suspected Seward of wanting to provoke war, he thought the *Trent* affair was an aggression authorized by Washington, and therefore despaired of his father's task in keeping England from an alliance with the South. The *Trent* affair was this: James Mason and John Slidell, former senators in the Union but now Confederate emissaries, were known to be commissioned for England, where they would seek recognition of their government. Union ships had been alerted to intercept them if they were on ships under Confederate control. But when they were caught, it was on a British mail ship, the *Trent*. The Union ship *San Jacinto* fired a shot across the bow of the unarmed vessel, boarded it, and took the Confederate agents off to an American prison. The public in England was outraged, and Henry desponded:

> I consider we are dished, and that our position is hopeless . . . It is our ruin . . . Now all the fat's in the fire, and I feel like going off and taking up my old German life again as a permanency. It is devilish disagreeable to act the part of Sisyphus, especially when it is our own friends who are trying to crush us under the rock . . . This nation [England] means to make war. Do not doubt. What Seward means is more than I can guess. But if he means war also, or to run as close as he can without touching, then I say that Mr. Seward is the greatest criminal we've had yet. (L 1.263–64)

Henry described the British anger over the capture of Mason and Slidell: "The phlegmatic and dogmatic Englishman has been dragged into a state of literal madness, and though not actually riotous, he has lost all his power of self-control" (S 1.109). That passion on one side of the Atlantic was matched with an equal frenzy on the other side. American crowds rejoiced at the imprisonment of Mason and Slidell, and wanted them tried for treason — or not, at any rate, released with an apology. The British and American governments tried to control these emotions, vacillating between compromise and ultimatum. The negotiations went on for three months.

At last, Lincoln's cabinet agreed to an offer that Seward relayed to Charles Francis Adams. The Confederate agents would be released, but not because taking them was wrong in itself. The boat they were on could have been seized legally, but only if taken to an admiralty court for judgment. This let everyone off the hook. The Confederates had their men back. The British had the admission of an error in procedure. Lincoln's constituents had the assurance that this was not really an apology. Henry had his faith in Seward restored, praising his brilliant solution to the problem (L 1.272). He did not realize that his recent hero had been bailed out by his former hero, Charles Sumner. And when he came to learn of this, he did not put it in the *Education*. Lincoln had used Sumner to check Seward.

Dumbfounded earlier by Seward's "Thoughts" on making himself a war czar, Lincoln called in the chairman of the Senate Committee on Foreign Relations, and quietly made him a consultant, his own confidential anti-Seward. Having read Seward's April Fool's Letter, Sumner backed Lincoln's softening of it, and warned Lincoln against letting such gasconading get out of hand. David Donald claims that, as a result, "Lincoln gave Sumner a virtual veto over foreign policy."[13] Sumner and Seward thus performed a neat *dos à dos*. In the secession winter, Sumner had been intransigent toward the South while Seward was yielding. Now, dealing with England, Seward was the hard-liner and Sumner the accommodator. Sumner did not hide his new access, which made him the rallying point for all anti-Seward sentiment, especially in the diplomatic corps.

> When it became known that Sumner was, in effect, setting up his own State Department at the opposite end of Pennsylvania Avenue, his presence at diplomatic dinners and soirees became as indispensable as that of Seward. Visiting foreigners in Washington, like Prince Napoleon, a cousin of Napoleon III, naturally enough sought out Sumner, because he was the only senator who spoke fluent French, because he had such a wide acquaintance abroad, and because he exercised power.[14]

Sumner was on very good terms with the British minister in Washington, Lord Lyons, and he assured him that Seward's hard line should not be taken as the policy of the whole government. This message, sent back to England, only partially eased misgivings there, since Seward was still seen as hostile. But Lyons could at least convey the impression that Lincoln had room to maneuver between Seward and Sumner. Meanwhile, Sumner used his English friends to warn the president against intransigence over the *Trent*. During his time in London, Sumner had become close to the liberal reformers John Bright and Richard Cobden, letters from whom he showed to Lincoln, confiding that retention of Mason and Slidell would surely lead to war. Bright recommended submission of the problem to mediators. Lincoln seriously considered this recommendation, backed by Sumner.[15] Having established that as a working option in the cabinet, he then moved beyond it by deciding that the mediation process would take too long — a quicker way of releasing the men should be found. The idea of invoking a procedural error was actually suggested by Charles Francis Adams in a letter to Seward.[16]

No wonder Henry thought Seward's resulting paper brilliant (L 1.273). He and his father still thought Lincoln incapable of real statesmanship — at one point Henry growled at "the incompetence of Lincoln" (L 1.260) — and the Adamses were not yet aware of Sumner's role in the matter. So they attributed the outcome to "Mr. Seward's good sense" (E 930). They undoubtedly heard something of Sumner's intervention from his friends Cobden and Bright, who were the Adamses' own London allies in promoting American interests (E 824), but they thought that Sumner, when writing to the British reformers, was just expressing his personal jealousy of Seward. Thurlow Weed, Seward's political manager, wrote to confirm their suspicions of Sumner.[17]

Weed had learned of the British distrust of Seward, and he suggested that Seward send him as a personal emissary to England. Normally, American diplomats on the scene would resent an intruder, especially if it were known that the newcomer had closer personal ties with the secretary of state than did the minister. Nor did it help matters that Weed's reputation as a party boss had preceded him to England. But the Adamses welcomed Weed, and watched him work his political magic even on the British (L 1.268, 275). As a newspaper editor himself, Weed was able to deal with British journalists and convince at least some of them that they had misjudged his close friend Seward. Henry, still in his hero-worshiping days, even conceived a "sympathy and affection" for the old political fixer and followed him around "much like a little dog" (E 853). The more Seward was accepted, the Adamses felt, the easier would their task become. But Weed promoted Seward by attacking Sumner, deepening the Adamses' disaffection with the latter.

The Confederate Navy

Aside from the *Trent* matter, Charles Francis Adams had three major objects of concern in London, and all three — like the *Trent* case — involved relations at sea. These were the Declaration of Paris, the Confederate ship *Alabama,* and the building of two iron-clad ramming ships for southern use. The Declaration of Paris was important enough to Henry that he wrote a little treatise on it at the time (though it was not published until 1891, in *Historical Essays*).[18] Charles Francis had instructions to join the European countries subscribing to the Declaration. It had been drawn up after the Crimean War to set rules for belligerents' activity at sea. It outlawed privateering, protected all private property on ships except contraband, and outlawed "paper blockades" (those without actual ships sufficient to close off a territory). The United States was invited to join the accord in 1854, but the Franklin Pierce administration did not want to outlaw privateering. In 1861, the anti-privateering proviso suddenly became the Lincoln administration's favorite one. Confederate President Jefferson Davis, lacking a navy, had swiftly issued "letters of marque" to privately owned ships that would serve the South's interests. The North denied the validity of these letters, since issuing them is a prerogative of governments, and it did not accept that the South had a government. In the North's eyes, the crews of these ships were outlaws, and the law of the sea should treat them as pirates. But if England did not agree that they were pirates, calling them instead privateers, then the Declaration of Paris would, after ratification, outlaw them anyway.

When Adams had his first audience with the British foreign minister, Lord (soon to become Earl) John Russell, he declared America willing to sign the Declaration of Paris. Russell said that Her Majesty's government had already authorized its minister in Washington, Lord Lyons, to reach an accord on the matter. He observed that a simple notice would suffice to secure allegiance to the agreement, since that is how the European powers had subscribed. Adams knew that this would not be adequate in America, where the Senate would require confirmation of the pact as a treaty. He hoped things would be concluded in Washington. Yet Lord Lyons had no treaty to propose there.

When Adams said that a treaty was necessary, Russell used that news to delay things — he would have to consult the other subscribers to the Declaration if it were to be something so formal (H 256–57). When at last Russell offered a formal convention drawn up by his government, it contained all the terms of the Declaration, including the ban on privateers — but Russell added that the Queen had made one exception to the convention: nothing in it "shall have any bearing, direct or indirect, on the internal differences now prevailing in the United States," thus denying the Americans the principal advantage they had been seeking (H 264). Adams said that his government could not accept an agreement with such a loophole in it. Although Charles Francis had begun these negotiations with a sense that Russell was sincerely trying to reach an agreement, he soon came to think he was being deceived. The British consul in Charleston had approached the Confederate government with an offer to let *it* subscribe to the Declaration (L 1.250).[19] By granting the South such a prerogative of legitimate government, Britain would have removed the designation of privateers from its ships. Henry was convinced that Russell was angling all along to recognize the South.

Since the United States could not subscribe to the Declaration of Paris with its humiliating codicil, there would be no set rules of the game for maritime intercourse during the war. Crisis after crisis had to be dealt with on an ad hoc basis, redefining rights and then fighting for the new definitions. The principal points of dispute now became Confederate attempts to build a navy. The South had long-established ties, amicable and remunerative, with British shippers, factory owners, and trade officials. These ties had been cultivated as part of the South's economic base — the exporting of cotton, mainly to England's flourishing mills. The first three Confederate commissioners who rushed to England were able to extract a neutrality proclamation with such celerity because they knew just whom to see and how to appeal to them. They were followed by a swarm of men who acquired ships to take munitions and other goods to the South. Ship after ship ran the North's blockade on these errands — the *Bermuda,* the *Thomas Watson,* the *Fingal,* the *Gladiator.*[20]

A more daring project was undertaken by James Bulloch of Georgia (whose sister was the mother of Theodore Roosevelt). He ran the blockade himself in the *Fingal,* and used his trip to scout locations for reconfiguring, refueling, and repairing the warships he meant to build in England. Bulloch's ships would become the terror of Union trade — the *Florida* captured 38 vessels, the *Alabama* captured 66, the *Shenandoah* captured 36.[21] Most of the Union ships taken were scuttled or burnt. Naturally, Charles Francis protested Bulloch's activity to British authorities, but the clever Georgian had provided the government with a fig leaf, covering his actions with phony European contracts. He did not put guns or armor on the ships until they had left Liverpool and gone to the Azores. The British philosophy of laissez faire forbade interference in what posed as a commercial endeavor.

Only when Bulloch began building what were unmistakably warships — iron-clad vessels with rams at their prow — did Adams finally succeed in thwarting him. Under heavy pressure from Charles Francis, the British bought the two completed rams from Bulloch and added them to their own navy. The indefatigable Bulloch went to France and began building new ram ships there — he got one as far as Havana, but the war ended before it could be used. In the *Education,* Adams treats the thwarting of the rams project as his father's finest hour. In a final protest over letting the rams go to the South, Charles Francis resorted to an ultimate threat: "It would be superfluous in me to point out to your Lordship that this is war" (E 878). Henry knew by the time he wrote the *Education* that Earl Russell had decided to stop Bulloch before he received this threatening missive, but he allows his father his moment of courage. After all, it was Charles Francis's earlier persistence in complaint (along with some British legal opinions) that helped bring about Russell's submission.

In his treatise on the Declaration of Paris, Henry concludes that Earl Russell meant all along to recognize the South. All denials of this he treats as lies (H 276). In the *Education* he says that his father was gullible in believing, at least part of the time, that Russell's intentions were good (E 843, 857–58). This is simplistic. Russell was no doubt exploring all kinds of options as the uncertain situation unfolded in America, and he had clashing constituencies at home to mollify, reward, or redirect. His relations with the other principal player in the government, Lord Palmerston, were touchy, and their responses to the American situation, though coordinated, did not mesh perfectly. The two British statesmen had a long history of weaving in and out of shifting ministries, one sometimes ranking above the other, sometimes under.[22]

Neither in his correspondence nor in the *Education* does Adams ask what the two men's histories had to do with their different responses, though he would undoubtedly have learned all he could from English friends and fellow diplomats about their past — that was just part of his duties to his father's mission. The closest he comes to hinting at a prior history lies in references to their age. He calls Palmerston an octogenarian (E 843), though he was a septuagenarian (seventy-seven in 1862). He says that Russell was "verging on senility" (E 871), but adds that "Russell's generation were mostly senile from youth" (E 873). In fact, Russell was seventy in 1862. Neither of these shrewd veterans was acing from the kind of narrow ideological agenda Adams assigns them. They were adaptable men, and had to be, to have survived so many ministry battles.

Palmerston had the reputation of being hostile to America, and Russell of being favorable, and the Adamses began with that assumption. In the *Education,* Henry presents his father's whole diplomatic task as a matter of choosing which of the two men to believe, and he criticizes the choice of Russell as the more trustworthy. But then, in the kind of *bouleversement* Henry likes to contrive in the *Education,* he says that Russell fooled the father by being worse than Charles Francis thought, while Palmerston fooled the son by being better than Henry thought. After reading Russell's posthumously published correspondence in 1889, Henry learned that at one point (September, 1862) Russell said that the time had come to recognize the South, but it was Palmerston who favored delay: "The roles were reversed. Russell wrote what was expected from Palmerston, or even more violently; while Palmerston wrote what was expected from Russell, or even more temperately" (E 860).

From this revelation, Adams solves his problem of whom to trust, Palmerston or Russell. You could trust neither. In fact, "if one could not trust a dozen of the most respected private characters in the world, composing the Queen's ministry, one could trust no mortal man" (E 857). This conclusion fits Adams's design in the *Education,* to draw no lessons from anything — except the lesson that one can draw no lessons. But it does this by presenting a false quandary. Diplomacy is not based on personal trust. Denying the very possibility of morality in politics because diplomats fail to speak the whole truth is something only the most naïve or the most ignorant can do — and Adams was neither. He is, here as elsewhere in the *Education,* forcing a nihilistic scheme on events. If there is such a thing as cheap optimism, the *Education* proves that there can also be a cheap pessimism.

Henry in fact drew very important lessons from his diplomatic experience. The results can be seen in the *History,* where any reduction of diplomacy to personal trust is mocked, where complex factors in the forming of policy are sifted and weighed, where deceptions are played off against each other, yet where morals — especially the morality of war and the use of force — are also analyzed. The puzzlement Adams felt in his twenties while trying to read the motives of Palmerston or Russell would prove a great preparation for the effort, in his forties, to discern the motives of Napoleon. And his readings on the law of the sea, or on the economics of financing a war, would come back to prove useful in his treatment of the War of 1812. The problems posed by the northern blockade of the 1860s would arise again when he dealt with the British blockade of Napoleon's continent in the 1810s.

Perhaps most important, he was acquiring by hard experience a feel for the interplay of personality and politics. The elusiveness of British statesmen like Palmerston or Russell made him alert, in the *History*, to actions their predecessors, Canning or Castlereagh, would take. Reading the years of preparation and the *History* stereoscopically, one finds many situations mirrored in both. The bafflement of Henry between Sumner and Seward suggests the quandary of Gallatin, caught between his old friend Burr and his later ally Jefferson. The intransigence in the House under Thaddeus Stevens resembles that in the Senate under William Branch Giles. But for the Civil War, Adams would not have seen as well as he did the shape of the War of 1812.

4

POSTWAR POLITICS

WHEN ADAMS SUBMITTED two articles to the *North American Review* in 1867, why was he less interested in seeing the John Smith piece appear than in his other item, "British Finance in 1816"? It may seem surprising now, but he considered the latter work more urgent and timely. He came back from London convinced that the problem of restoring government after the war offered a special opportunity to reform America's financial system. He wanted to follow the example of England's free trade liberals, Cobden and Bright, who held that economic policy was the key to every other reform. Adams used England's emergence from the Napoleonic Wars (and the War of 1812) as an example of the wrong way to move from a war footing to a peace economy. In 1816, Chancellor of the Exchequer Nicholas Vansittart clung to outmoded policies of taxation, protection, and soft money:

> Mr. Vansittart was not a man gifted with the blind Toryism of Lord Sidmouth, or the narrow-minded perverseness of Lord Eldon. He was simply a thoroughly incompetent man. It would scarcely be worth the while to dwell upon his qualities at any length, if it were not that he was almost a perfect representative of the old school of financiers — the school of Perceval and Addington — a school which had sprung from Mr. Pitt's side when his better days had passed, and which lent the influence of narrow minds to encourage and aggravate the mistakes of a great man. (C 294–95)

Adams followed this article with a longer one that went farther back in British history, to analyze the system that Vansittart had inherited from William Pitt, who suspended specie payment in the wars with

France. This piece, "The Bank of England Restriction," appeared in the October, 1867, *North American Review*. Pitt's action was being used as a precedent to justify the issue of paper money in the Civil War. Adams argued that the British suspension, risky though it was, did not parallel the dangers of American "greenbacks" — the British were just borrowing from the Bank of England, and the notes involved were convertible to specie on demand. "Thus the Bank was throughout a mere channel of credit" (C 238). Adams's essay, which has the appearance of an academic exercise, had a polemical purpose, to promote the contraction of paper money in the postwar economy of America; but it seemed to be sneaking up on the subject in a roundabout way. Adams knew he had to be more direct if he were to promote his whole economic program — free trade, low tariffs and taxes, hard money, the prevention of manipulated markets by reform of the patronage and grant-distribution system.

It would be hard to make Americans focus on such economic issues in the wake of the Civil War. People were more concerned with Reconstruction in the South, development of the West, and a return to prewar patterns of life. He saw the problem clearly:

> Slavery, the war, and the conditions of peace were the issues on which members [of Congress] had appealed to their constituents, until the popular humor leaned decidedly towards a contempt for matters of mere administration as of trifling importance compared with those overruling interests. Good government, however, is a condition of national success, no matter how important other issues may be; and the day when a nation's politics turn exclusively on questions of fidelity to great moral abstractions is a disastrous day for good government. The leaders of Congress, brought up as they had been to study moral abstractions alone, carried, as heads of committees and framers of bills, the wildest financial theories into practical effect.[1]

Adams was, therefore, facing a situation quite different from the one Cobden and Bright had dealt with in their pamphleteering for the Anti-Corn-Law League. The British knew then that their problems were economic, and pressure to bring down the price of food by lowering grain ("corn") tariffs was met with popular support. In postwar America, by contrast, Adams would first have to get the national attention before he could preach his economic doctrine.

Though the odds against doing this seemed long, Adams was quick to fall in with a nucleus of men in Washington who shared his reform concerns. His rapid entry into the councils of government came from his friendship with William Evarts, Andrew Johnson's attorney general. They had met in England when President Lincoln sent Evarts to give legal support to Charles Francis Adams in the dispute over Confederate ships being built in Liverpool. Evarts was a brilliant lawyer, whom Henry praised to his brother Charles: "Mr. Evarts is grand in these trials" (L 1.372). His friendship with the older man was sealed on a tour of Cambridge they made together (L 1.356). Evarts became another of those older men whom Henry cultivated as father figures — Sumner, Seward, Weed, Evarts, and Salmon P. Chase.

Thus when Henry came to Washington in 1868, Attorney General Evarts urged him to stay at his house till he found quarters of his own. Evarts had defended Andrew Johnson in his impeachment trial (L 2.5), and he took Henry to meet the beleaguered president, who impressed Adams as no later president did. As a hard-money man, Evarts was preparing the case against the Legal Tender Act which he meant to plead before the Supreme Court. He discussed the arguments he would be using with Adams and introduced him to allies in the government — principally Hugh McCullough, secretary of the treasury, and David Wells, special commissioner of the revenues. These men supplied Adams with statistics on matters vital to economic reform, which he reviewed in a lengthy article for the *Edinburgh Review,* "American Finances, 1865–1869."[2] Adams, Evarts, McCullough, and Wells felt that their economic program was the only thing that could bring order to the extravagance, speculation, and corrupt influence of what would soon be known as the Gilded Age. Adams's description of the situation foreshadowed what he would use, a decade later, as a backdrop to his novel *Democracy:*

There is much reason to regret that every voter in the United States cannot be compelled, at some period of his life, to visit Washington, for the purpose of obtaining the passage through the various stages of legislation of some little bill, interesting only to himself and perhaps having "a little money in it." The lesson would be a useful one. As the visitor cast from the lobby a momentary glance through the swinging doors of the House, and was bewildered by the crash and war of jealous and hostile interests within — as he felt how his own just and proper request was the sport of a thousand accidents — as he appreciated the difficulties in the way of getting a committee to report his bill at all, and the still greater difficulty of putting it on its passage, and as he then watched it float here and there in the eddying current of legislation, he would be better able for the future to understand one of the greatest difficulties of government. Within the walls of two rooms are forced together in close contact the jealousies of thirty-five millions of people — jealousies between individuals, between cliques, between industries, between parties, between branches of the government, between sections of the country, between the nation and its neighbors. As years pass on, the noise and confusion, the vehemence of this scramble for power or for plunder, the shouting of reckless adventurers, of wearied partisans, and of red-hot zealots in new issues — the boiling and bubbling of this witches' caldron, into which we have thrown eye of newt and toe of frog, and all the venomous ingredients of corruption, and from which is expected to issue the future and more perfect republic — in short, the conflict and riot of interests, grows more and more overwhelming; the power of obstructionists grows more and more decisive in the same proportion as the business to be done increases in volume; the effort required to accomplish necessary legislation becomes more and more serious; the machine groans and labors under the burden, and its action becomes spasmodic and inefficient.[3]

How was Adams's little reform team to take on this hydra? They were all sympathetic to Andrew Johnson. They would like to strengthen the president against the Senate that was opposing him over Reconstruction. Adams, like his father, was opposed to slavery but not free from racism when it came to black suffrage. They supported the Thirteenth Amendment (freeing the slaves) but not the Fourteenth and Fifteenth. Henry wrote that the Fourteenth was too punitive to the South (R 71) and denied the constitutional role of the states:

> The powers originally reserved by the Constitution to the states are in future to be held by them only on good behavior and at the sufferance of Congress; they may be suspended or assumed by Congress; their original basis and sanction no longer exist; and if they ever offered any real protection against the assumption of supreme and uncontrolled power by the central government, that protection is at an end. (H 385)

The Fifteenth Amendment labored under the same difficulties (NAR 108.613) and expected too much of the black freedmen. "The new [Fifteenth] amendment seems to have this inevitable result, of swelling the blind, unreasoning vote which follows mechanically a party standard, and thus encourages and protects party corruption" (NAR 108.618). This view of black incapacity would remain with Adams.

> The one great boon the sensible Negro at the South should pray for would be to be let alone by his "protectors" in Washington — to be allowed to as-

sume, as quietly and speedily as he can, those natural relations to which, in spite of everything, he must at last come with the community in which his lot is cast. (NAR 123.435–36)

Though Adams admired Andrew Johnson for his "look of a true president" (E 945), he realized that a hostile Congress made him powerless for any reform action. Again, as in the runup to the war, he principally blamed an overweening Senate, which "has always been, as it always must be, the furnace of intrigue and aggressions" (H 393). He saw no hope of checking the Senate under the paralyzed Johnson. The reformers were therefore happy to see Johnson go, despite their fondness for him. The president elected in 1868, Ulysses Grant, had no entanglement with the political past, with cabals or "rings" — he could bring a breath of fresh air to jaded Washington. Adams hoped he would be another George Washington, a military man above petty politics.

> The new president had unbounded popular confidence. He was tied to no party. He was under no pledges. He had the inestimable advantage of a military training, which, unlike a political training, was calculated to encourage the moral distinction between right and wrong. (H 370)

Adams hoped that Grant would keep McCullough as secretary of the treasury, the position he considered the most important in government (H 375), and would afford the secretary powers that a weakened Johnson could not.

Readers of the *Education* may take as overblown Adams's reaction to Grant's choice of a cabinet: "Within five minutes, [it] changed his intended future into an absurdity" (E 959). But for once that book is not exaggerating, even though there were some good choices in the cabinet — Adams would, in fact, work closely with the new attorney general, E. Rockwood Hoar (a cousin to Evarts, his predecessor), in opposing the Legal Tender Act. But none of that counted, in Adams's eyes, compared with what he took to be Grant's tragic choice of George Boutwell to be secretary of the treasury. Though Boutwell was coming in with a new Republican administration, he had been the Democrat chosen as Massachusetts governor in 1850. In other words, he was part of the bargain that sent Sumner to the Senate "for balance" — the very transaction Adams later represented as the "original sin" of his own twelfth year.

Boutwell, "fresh from Congress, and trained in a partisan school," would do nothing to control the legislature.[4] On the contrary, he had been active in the House of Representatives to bring about what Adams considered the most irresponsible act of Congress, its impeachment of President Johnson. Boutwell was an easy-money man, mocked as such in Twain's *The Gilded Age,* in which the "greenbacker" Colonel Sellers tells his friend President Grant: "Boutwell's got the right notion, but he lacks courage. I should like to run the treasury department about six months."[5] Boutwell stood for everything Adams opposed. Adams called for a return to the gold standard, but Boutwell's view of the matter was that of Colonel Sellers: "What we want is more money. I've told Boutwell so. Talk about basing the currency on gold; you might as well base it on pork. Gold is only one product. Base it on everything! . . . Grant's got the idea."[6] Adams was for civil service standards, but Boutwell fostered Grant's patronage abuses.

Adams began his attack on Grant just a month after his inauguration. In the first of what he intended to be a series of annual reports on legislation, based on a British series that covered each session of Parliament, he said that "General Grant has placed himself in isolation" by his bad cabinet choices.[7] He predicted, accurately, that Grant would therefore be unable to break the power of the financial combines ("rings"): "A network of rings controls Congress, and forms a hedge which marks the limit within which arguments and reason may prevail" (NAR 108.616). Grant did nothing to reduce what Adams called "senatorial government" (NAR 108.625). Against Grant's patronage practices Adams issued a pamphlet, *Civil Service Reform,* that he had published first as an article in the *North American Review* (October, 1869), in which he advocated appointments on merit (including some from the former Confederacy) and an insistence on professionalism in the choice of ambassadors (NAR 109.452, 461).

With Congress corrupt and the executive feckless, Adams next turned his hopes toward the Supreme Court. If Boutwell would not take the lead in returning the currency to a gold standard, then perhaps the Court could declare the Legal Tender Act of 1862 unconstitutional. Prima facie that seemed unlikely, since the chief justice of the Supreme Court, Salmon P. Chase, was the secretary of the treasury in 1862, and he administered the act. But Chase was now an opponent of soft money, and Adams, after cultivating his friendship, wrote an article claiming that Congress had forced the act on Chase despite his misgivings. Adams laid the blame especially on Senator Thaddeus Stevens, who showed "contempt for financial knowledge" (H 283), and Senator Elbridge G. Spaulding, whose former experience had been in "shaving notes at a country bank" (H 286). Going over the congressional records of the 1862 debates, Adams praised James Gallatin, a banker who testified against the Legal Tender Act (H 290, 293) — a remote first brush with the Gallatin family that would mean so much to his later life. James Gallatin was the older son of the great treasury secretary Albert Gallatin, whose papers Adams would edit.[8]

When the Legal Tender Act was brought before the Supreme Court, Chief Justice Chase cast the deciding vote in a four-to-three decision overthrowing the act (*Hepburn v. Griswold,* 1870). But Grant immediately put two justices in the empty seats on the Court, and the decision was speedily reversed (*Knox v. Lee,* 1871). Adams claimed that Grant's two judges, confirmed by the Senate with an assignment to rescue the Legal Tender Act, "would establish beyond dispute a precedent for packing the Court whenever it suited Congress to do so, and destroying the independence of the judiciary as a co-ordinate branch of the American government" (H 394). Now blocked in his efforts with all three branches of the government, Adams turned to public agitation as the sole tool left for reform.

> The true policy of reformers is to trust neither to presidents nor to senators, but appeal directly to the people . . . To effect this there is no way but to attack corruption in all its holes, to drag it before the public eye, to dissect it and hold the diseased members up to popular disgust, to give the nation's conscience no rest nor peace until mere vehemence of passion overcomes the sluggish self-complacency of the public mind.[9]

To put this program into effect, Adams teamed up with his brother Charles to attack the most famous corrupters of the polity, Jay Gould (who "had not a conception of a moral principle") and Jim Fisk (who "was not yet forty years of age, and had the instincts of fifteen"). In paired articles for the *North American Review,* Charles traced the corruption involved in taking over the Erie Railroad, and Henry traced the attempt to corner the gold market.[10]

This was a new form of journalism in America, anticipating by thirty years the later sensation caused by the "muckrakers" who attacked corporate graft (Ida Tarbell, Lincoln Steffens, and Ray Stannard Baker). The difference between them is that the muckrakers wrote for the middlebrow magazine *McClure's,* while the Adams brothers were roughhousing in the most genteel American journal. In this respect they partly resembled such conservative radicals as Ruskin and Carlyle in

England. But here, too, there was a difference. Ruskin and Carlyle were attacking Manchester liberalism, while the Adamses were espousing it. Perhaps the closest thing to the Adamses' attack (apart from the Cobden and Bright pamphlets of the 1830s) was the graphic satire of Thomas Nast, who published in a journal halfway between *McClure's* and the *North American Review* — *Harper's* — and combined a European visual style with American irreverence.

In "The New York Gold Conspiracy," Henry argues that the controllers of the Erie Railroad wanted to manipulate gold prices so that freight carried on their line would sell on good terms to the European market, which accepted only gold payments (H 335–36). This allowed the financiers to pose as friends of the farm states, whose price for grain would rise. But the two men could not be sure of controlling prices unless they knew when and if the Treasury meant to lower demand by releasing gold from the national reserve. They hoped to get warnings from Grant about any such price fluctuations, approaching him through Abel Corbin, the New York businessman who was married to Grant's favorite sister, Virginia. Whenever Grant stayed with his sister and her husband while passing through New York, Fisk and Gould were also invited by Corbin (whom they were greasing with gold certificates).

Grant was entertained by these operators at restaurants, in private rail cars, and on yachts, but the president foiled their schemes with naïveté. They did not think he could be so innocent as not to understand how he had been compromised, but the president's modern biographers think the innocence was genuine: "Grant rarely met a businessman he did not trust."[11] Adams, too, believed in Grant's innocence, though he admitted it took a stretch of the imagination to do so. The gullibility of the inexperienced leader would show up again in the unnamed president of Adams's novel *Democracy,* and in his description of Grant in the *Education* (E 961–63). The limits of politicians' intelligence were borne in on him with indelible force after his two crowded years of reform effort in Washington.

The *North American Review*

The indispensable basis for Adams's reform efforts was the *North American Review,* whose editor, Ephraim Gurney, gave him great freedom in what he wrote, making him the editorial voice of the magazine. But Gurney, who was overworked between editing the journal and teaching history at Harvard, wanted to give up the journal. Adams himself had already turned down an offer from Harvard's president to teach history (L 2.72), but when that was coupled with the editorial post at the *Review*, he felt he had to accept the double assignment. Henry did not want to leave Washington to go back to the Boston area — just the year before he had written that he would never again live in Massachusetts (L 2.44). But he could not count on another editor to give him the freedom Gurney had. By taking over himself, he would not only have total access to the journal's pages for his own work, he could choose contributors, subjects, and books for review that advanced his reform agenda. He sent letters to his Washington allies in reform, asking them to think of the *Review* as their organ (L 2.85–88, 107–9).

Adams's two years of amazingly energetic pamphleteering and lobbying in Washington had run up against the unyielding obstacles of Grant, Congress, and the Supreme Court. He decided that reform had to be a long-term project of altering public perception and starting new party organizations. He hoped to direct others' energies into this. During his first semester at Harvard, he helped organize a meeting in New York of reform-minded newspaper editors (L 2.90–92). In the *Review*, he did his best to promote the careers of men he admired at the time — Carl Schurz (L 2.86), James Garfield (L 2.185), Samuel Tilden (L 2.120), Lucius Lamar (NAR 123.249–50), Salmon P. Chase (NAR 122.246–53).

Of course, the *North American Review* was not just a political opinion journal. It covered a broad spectrum of cultural concerns — historical, anthropological, philological, aesthetic, economic. Adams's wide circle of acquaintance, at home and abroad, enabled him to draw on many kinds of expertise. Adams brought a new depth and focus to its articles and reviews, laying special emphasis on foreign books. James Russell Lowell said that he turned the review from a teakettle to a steam engine (S 1.221). Adams's letters to contributors show how closely he edited their pieces. He was ruthless in turning down friends when he thought they were not right for an article or review they asked to contribute. He also ran reviews that criticized his fellow Boston historians. (See the letter to Bancroft at L 2.220.)

There was a yearlong hiatus in Adams's reform work, as well as in his teaching and editing, while he used a honeymoon tour of Europe (1872–1873) to prepare his graduate seminar in medieval history. But his endeavors quickened as the election of 1876 approached, with the prospect of Grant's departure. In January of 1875, he took part in a mass rally against the Grant administration at Fanueil Hall (L 2.217). Now he felt that he needed a more immediate organ of agitation than his genteel quarterly. He tried to buy a newspaper — first the Boston *Daily Advertiser* and then the Boston *Post*. He hoped Carl Schurz might edit the first (L 2.215) or Horace White the second (L 2.259).

His aim was to create a "third force" of independent voters. He did not want to call this force a separate party. It should play the parties off against each other, then unite with the one that accepted its views in order to get its support (L 2.226). But when Rutherford Hayes and Samuel Tilden were chosen as the candidates, Henry's independents could not agree on the one more likely to accept their program. To Henry's disgust, Carl Schurz went with Hayes while he and his brother Charles supported Tilden, thus frittering away the combined force they were aiming at. As if fed up by this, the brothers wrote the most openly partisan article the *Review* had run, in which they indirectly endorsed Tilden a month before the election.[12]

The owner of the *Review*, James Osgood, thought that Adams had gone too far with this article, and let it run only with a disclaimer that announced Adams's severance from the enterprise after that issue (S 1.286–87). Adams was having troubles with Osgood anyway, since the owner thought he paid his writers too much and Adams was ashamed to pay them any less (L 2.224). He had already decided to make his sixth year as editor his last.[13] He clearly meant to end with a bang.

The Centennial Issue

Not only was 1876 an election year. It was also the centenary of the Declaration of Independence. Adams had begun the year with a special issue devoted to a survey of the first one hundred years of the republic. This issue, the one he was most proud of, is of great importance to any study of the *History*, since it anticipates the survey of the state of the nation in 1800 with which Adams begins his nine-volume series. Moreover, themes treated in the centennial issue would be echoed in various parts of the *History*, especially at the end of it. Adams asked experts on various aspects of the century under review for thoughtful treatments of six subjects, and hoped they would each fill forty pages in the *Review*.[14] The authors stuck fairly close to their page assignments, as one can see from the final layout:

"Religion in America, 1776–1876," pages 1–47
"Politics in America, 1776–1876," pages 47–87
"Abstract Science in America, 1776–1876," pages 88–123
"Economic Science in America, 1776–1876," pages 124–54
"Law in America, 1776–1876," pages 154–91
"Education in America, 1776–1876," pages 191–228

It was a 228-page rumination on where the country had been, where it stood, and what its prospects for the future were. His instruction to contributors went like this one:

> The object is to ascertain whether and to what degree Americans should feel satisfaction or disappointment at the result of a century's activity . . . I leave the treatment to you. Of course it is no mere catalogue of names I want, but a classification of thought . . . Without self-glorification or fault-finding, a short analysis of our methods and our station in the world ought to be valuable. (L 2.231–32)

The national report card was a mixed one. It is revealing to see the quality of the authors Adams felt capable of producing this ambitious set of essays:

1. On religion, Jeremiah Diman — an historian at Brown University and a prized contributor to the *Review* (L 2.202–6) — found a remarkable series of changes, all based on the motion from established religion in the colonies to the secular state, for which Jefferson is given the principal credit. The proliferation of sects had not caused religious strife, Diman concludes, because the sects cluster in denominational types and share a moderate Reformed Protestantism.

Dogmatic conflict was muted as the religious ethos moved from a theological concern, through an ethical one, to an emotional one (a thesis Adams will make his own in the concluding chapters of his *History*). A key factor in the transition from dogma to emotion was the popularity of what Diman takes to be the representative American sect, Methodism. Of Catholics he notes their "war on public education," which has led to the large acquisition of real estate for parochial schools.[15] In the census of 1870, Catholics stood fourth in the number of their parishes, but second in church property — which raises, for Diman, the issue of tax exemption of churches, an inequity he thought should not be continued.

2. The man chosen to cover politics was William Graham Sumner, the famous Yale sociologist who reputedly "had a wider following than any other teacher in Yale's history."[16] He was also the leading exponent of

Social Darwinism, which injected another form of racism into the mix of nineteenth-century thought. Since competition, in Sumner's scheme, must lead to inequality, he was anti-egalitarian, and his account of the century before 1876 begins with a lament for the fall of the Federalists. Jefferson, who was the hero of Diman's essay, is something of a villain in Sumner's. "Jefferson, in fact, was no thinker. He was a good specimen of the a priori political philosopher. He did not reason or deduce; he dogmatized on the widest and most rash assumptions, which were laid down as self-evident truths."[17] Post-Jeffersonian politics display "the great democratic tide which flows through and forms our political history" — a trend Sumner deplores:

> This movement has been in favor of equality. It has borne down and obliterated all the traditions and prejudices which were inherited from the Old World. It has eliminated from our history almost all the recollection of the old Federal party, with its ideas of social and political leadership. It has crushed out the prestige of wealth and education in politics. It has restrained the respect and authority due to office, by narrow tenures, and by cutting away all terms of language and ceremonial observances tending to mark official rank.[18]

That sounds like what some people claim is said of Jefferson in Adams's *History* — though it is not said there. What Adams found valuable in Sumner at this stage — Adams was by now thirty-eight, and Sumner was thirty-six, and both men had their major work before them — was not his Federalism but the economic program he shared, favoring hard money, free trade, low taxes.

3. The nation gets an F on its report card in the third (scientific) essay, written by Simon Newcomb, an astronomer at the United States Naval Observatory. Adams called this essay "Abstract Science in America," to distinguish it from practical sciences like medicine, agronomy, and others for which he had no room. The only practical science he gives a separate essay to is "Economic Science," though jurisprudence would have justified his calling the fifth essay "Legal Science" rather than, simply, "Law." Newcomb argues that different nations show different scientific skills, less because of any national talent than because of different organizations of resources. He takes different nations' reactions to Darwin as a touchstone of their scientific aptitude in the nineteenth century.

> One disposed to study what we might call the intellectual natural history of nations would find an instructive subject of investigation in the different

view of Darwinism prevalent in the four great intellectual nations of the world. In the land of its origin, it is a subject of fierce controversy between the religious world on the one side and the scientific one on the other; in Germany, received with universal applause as one of the great philosophic triumphs of the century; in France, so utterly groundless a piece of specula-tion as to be unworthy of the attention of a biologist; in America, received by naturalists, but viewed by the public as something on which it is quite incompetent to pass judgment.[19]

Newcomb complained that America had lacked a scientific *commu-nity* for most of the preceding century. Academies and universities were sluggish in forming scientific enterprises. Government sponsorship set up the army Signal Corps station, and the coastal and territorial surveys, but profound scholars were not enlisted in their activities. Adams's own later interest in the work of Clarence King for the U.S. Geological Survey was no doubt sharpened by his editorial dealings with Newcomb.

4. The fourth essay, on economic theory, was written by Charles Franklin Dunbar, professor of political economy at Harvard, whose book on the subject had been reviewed in the *North American Review* a year earlier (January, 1875). Dunbar finds some practical economists in American history — Franklin, Hamilton, Gallatin — but no theorists of any depth. Part of the blame for this he traces to the American habit of turning debate on economics into debate on politics. Americans, for instance, concentrated on questions of constitutionality when dealing with the Bank of the United States, or paper money, or tariffs and taxes. They kept asking, that is, whether government had the *power* to act on these measures, rather than whether the measures made good economic sense.

5. The fifth essay, on jurisprudence, was written by George Tucker Bispham, a scholar-lawyer who wrote *The Principles of Equity* (1874). Here the nation gets good marks. The author shows how questions treated by the common law in England had been more satisfactorily handled here — everything from women's property rights (a subject that especially interested Adams) to riparian and land-use law to penal re-form. Bispham thinks America's jurisprudential excellence comes from its use of written constitutions in the states and the federal government.

6. The last article was written by Daniel Coit Gilman, whose reputa-tion would in time prove more solid than that of William Graham Sum-ner. Gilman had, just a year before, been chosen as president of a new university in Baltimore, the Johns Hopkins, which became the most in-

fluential model for American graduate education on the German ideal. Gilman had been called to Baltimore after his leading role in shaping the Sheffield School of Science at Yale and after a brief term as president of the University of California at Berkeley. He knew and respected and learned from Adams's experiments at Harvard, and he would ask Adams to join the Hopkins faculty, or — failing that — to address its members on teaching methods, or to serve as an examiner of its doctoral candidates (L 2.327, 350, 613).

Gilman was as knowledgeable as anyone in America about the subject assigned him. He systematically looked at every level of education. The nation had succeeded in adopting widespread primary education, but the "grade schools" were weakened by being treated too often as the final stage of education. This undermined the secondary schools, which had not been developed on a scale complementary to the primary level. Colleges had mushroomed to serve sectarian religious purposes, producing hundreds of colleges with poor standards, faculty, and libraries. Gilman, though he was just taking up the presidency of a private university, recommended the strengthening of state universities, for their secular emphasis on excellence as opposed to religious orthodoxy. He also argued that public schools, both primary and secondary, should become secular to prevent the divisive growth of a separate Catholic school system for immigrants. This essay chimed, therefore, with Diman's in praising the separation of church and state.

E. L. Godkin, in a generally favorable review of the centennial issue in *The Nation*, felt that it was too harsh on "the practical American," who would not be patient enough to learn from it "the depths of his own ignorance" (S 1.275–76). The report card was in fact more favorable, overall, than harsh — though it does not single out for praise the spurt of progress Adams would find in the first sixteen years of the nineteenth century. What we learn from it is how carefully Adams was trying to sift the various ways of evaluating a culture. He agreed with most of what was said (which is not surprising, since he chose the authors), but disagreed sharply as well. It should be remembered that he greeted the centennial year with what he called his own "centennial oration" — a review of H. von Holst's *History of the United States* in which Adams rejected Holst's judgment that the Constitution had been a failure.

> We have a right to claim and we do claim that the Constitution has done its
> work. It has made a nation. It has thoroughly vindicated the good sense

and practical statesmanship of its framers. And more than this, in spite of the many shortcomings and petty drawbacks which are so well catalogued in this book, the people of the United States, as they pass further and further from the vital struggles which characterize this first period of their national history, are quite right in believing that, above all the details of human weakness and corruption, there will appear in more and more symmetry the real majesty and *force of the national movement* [emphasis added].[20]

Those last five words express the agenda of the *History* he would soon be writing. To his own question for contributors — should Americans feel satisfaction in their history so far — his own answer was a resounding yes. The pessimist of later years is not to be found here.

5

◆◦◆

HISTORICAL METHOD

THOUGH HIS TIME as editor helped make Adams an historian, far more central to that formation was his simultaneous work at Harvard, where he learned about historical method by teaching it. No one knew better than he that he began with deficiencies he would have to overcome. At age thirty-two, without a higher degree of any sort, and more specifically without formal historical training, he was expected to teach medieval history. That was less shocking then than it would be now, since the study of history was still in a pre-professional stage. Adams would be starting from scratch, but so had his older contemporary, William Stubbs, considered a founder of medieval studies in England.

> His formal education had been in classics and mathematics; indeed, he took his degree before modern history had entered the curriculum as a subject of study of the B.A. Hence, as a scholar he was self-taught, while as Regius Professor [at Oxford] his efforts to build a school of history were unprecedented.[1]

The very materials for study were just being opened up, and would not be effectively used till the end of the century.[2] Stubbs was part of a team that became known as the Oxford School of medievalists, men who did pioneer work in their period, all of whom Adams came to know as he visited England to prepare his graduate course. The best-known men, besides Stubbs, were Edward A. Freeman and John Richard Green. By joint effort they were turning the university into a scholarly center, relying less upon tutors and more upon professors — men now expected to do original research, not simply to teach the old curriculum.[3] The clubbiness of the team is suggested by a mocking couplet of the time:

Ladling butter from alternate tubs,
Stubbs butters Freeman, Freeman butters Stubbs.[4]

These scholars were trying to give a more serious foundation to the romantic medievalism made popular by Walter Scott or John Ruskin in England, by Johann von Goethe or Richard Wagner in Germany. They made the Anglo-Saxon language a gateway to serious study of the period, as they tried to familiarize the world with terms like *gemot, maegth, maegburh, mund, sacu, socn, soen, wed, weotuma, wergelt,* and *witan*.[5] Because of their efforts, graduate students in English departments would be doomed for many decades to begin their courses with the Anglo-Saxon poets. Enthusiasts wanted to move everyday language in an Anglo-Saxon direction — substituting, for instance, "bodeful" for "ominous."[6] One medieval historian, Frederic Maitland, named his daughter Fredegonde.[7] Adams himself said that the movement went too far when it insisted on spelling King Alfred as "Aelfred."[8]

Even before his appointment to teach at Harvard, Adams knew something of this movement from his time in England during the Civil War. One of his best friends there was the son of the recently deceased Francis Palgrave, the deputy keeper of records, who began the publication of ancient documents.[9] Palgrave's son, Francis Jr., the "Frank" of Adams's heavy correspondence with him, was active in advancing his father's work, and he had constant dealings with other medieval historians at the time when Adams was in London. An even closer British friend of Adams — in fact, his closest friend for many years, until John Hay assumed that post — was Charles Milnes Gaskell, whose country home was a confiscated monastic complex (Wenlock Priory), which became a magic place for Adams. His interest in its background was intense from the outset, colored as it was by Carlyle's account of the monastic foundation, Bury St. Edmund's, in *Past and Present* (1843).

We tend to think of Adams's teaching stint at Harvard in terms of its permanent monument, the publication of his doctoral students' dry-as-dust dissertations (*Essays in Anglo-Saxon Law*). But his first year of purely undergraduate teaching had a much broader scope, in keeping with his knowledge at that stage, which included a strong element of medieval architecture (a forecast of *Mont Saint Michel and Chartres*) and other aesthetic issues. Adams wrote Gaskell during his first year of teaching that he was reading Ruskin and Viollet-le-Duc on medieval fortresses and cathedrals (L 2.103), and the next year Gaskell gave him a complete set of Viollet-le-Duc's works as a wedding present (L 2.137).

The picturesque side of the Middle Ages had a deep impact on one student, Henry Cabot Lodge, who took Adams's undergraduate course during his first year of teaching it (1870–1871). But for that course, said Lodge, he would have left Harvard with no real learning experience.

In all my four years, I never really studied anything, never had my mind roused to any exertion or to anything resembling active thought until in my senior year I stumbled into the course in medieval history given by Henry Adams, who had then just come to Harvard. How I came to choose that course I do not exactly know. I was fond of history, liked to read it, and had a vague curiosity as to the Middle Ages, of which I knew nothing. I think there was no more intelligent reason than this for my selection. But I builded better than I knew. I found myself caught by strong interest, I began to think about the subject, Mr. Adams roused the spirit of inquiry and controversy in me, and I was fascinated by the stormy careers of the great German emperors, by the virtues, the abilities, the dark crimes of the popes, and by the tremendous conflict between church and empire in which emperors and popes were antagonists. In just what way Mr. Adams aroused my slumbering faculties I am at a loss to say, but there can be no doubt of the fact. Mr. Adams has told me many times that he began his course in total ignorance of his own subject, and I have no doubt that the fact that he, too, was learning helped his students. But there was more than this. He had the power not only of exciting interest, but he awakened opposition to his own views, and this is one great secret of success in teaching. In any event, I worked hard in that course because it gave me pleasure. I took the highest marks, for which I cared, as I found, singularly little, because marks were not my object, and for the first time I got a glimpse of what education might be and really learned something. I have never lost my interest in the Othos, the Henrys and the Fredericks, or in the towering figure of Hildebrand. They have always remained vital and full of meaning to me, and a few years ago I made a pilgrimage to Salerno with Adams himself to see the burial place of the greatest of the popes, who had brought an empire to his feet and had died a beaten exile. Yet it was not what I learned but the fact that I learned something, that I discovered that it was the keenest of pleasures to use one's mind, a new sensation, and one which made Mr. Adams's course in the history of the Middle Ages so memorable to me.[10]

After his graduation Lodge entered Harvard Law School; but his interest in history had been so stimulated that he went on to take a doctorate in history under Adams's tutelage. He became Adams's teaching assistant, and when Adams left Harvard in 1877, Lodge stayed on for two years teaching his mentor's courses. When Lodge entered politics and became a senator, he and his wife became members of Adams's Washington salon. The families traveled together (most notably to Mont-Saint-Michel), and Lodge's son, the poet George ("Bay") Cabot Lodge, looked on Adams as a second father. When Bay died young, Adams wrote his biography.

Adams kept up with some of his other students. Perry Belmont, the son of sportsman-philanthropist August Belmont, became another regular at the Adams home in Washington after he entered Congress. One of the characters in Adams's novel *Democracy* is modeled on Belmont. Another student who became a friend for life was Charles Franklin Thwing, later the president of Western Reserve University, to which Adams donated many of his own books. But some students would not, presumably, have wanted to prolong their acquaintance with Adams, including President Grant's son, Ulysses Jr., who took one of his courses and got the lowest mark in it.[11]

In the *Education,* of course, Adams calls his teaching career a failure. As soon as the book appeared in 1918, a number of his students published denials, saying they did not recognize what they had undergone in his account — an account, one asseverated, "which I know from experience to be *entirely* wrong."[12] Some called him not only their best teacher at Harvard but the best teacher in their lives. Typical statements include: "He was the most alive man of all my teachers." Or: "He had a remarkable mind and had a talent, quite unusual, for stimulating and compelling the students to think for themselves." Another student gathered his own testimonies: "He was the greatest teacher I ever had except Experience." Or: "My own intellectual debt to him is untold . . . I shall end, as I began, his profoundly grateful pupil."[13] Charles Thwing devoted to Adams a chapter of his book *Guides, Philosophers, Friends* (1927).

Adams taught about three hundred men in his six years at Harvard.[14] The roster of them includes two college presidents, a line of distinguished lawyers, and four professional historians. His reputation as a teacher was such that President Gilman tried to bring him in as head of the department at the Johns Hopkins University. Failing that, he asked

Adams to supply the Hopkins faculty with advice on teaching. Adams answered: "Teaching is and always must be experimental, if not empirical, in order to be successful . . . My only advice to my scholars who succeeded me in my branches of instruction was, 'Whatever else you do, never neglect trying a new experiment every year'" (L 2.351).

Adams's years at Harvard were not only a pedagogical success but made a real contribution to scholarship, through the pioneering graduate seminar he taught during his last three years there and the book that seminar produced, *Essays in Anglo-Saxon Law.*[15] Even in his undergraduate classes, we are told: "The general purpose of all Mr. Adams's courses seems to have been to indicate a method and not to teach facts."[16] But he knew that he needed a deeper immersion in the best of modern scholarship before he could teach a graduate course. So he took a year to visit leading scholars in Europe — in Germany, Theodor Mommsen, Ernst Curtius, Rudolf von Gneist, George H. Pertz, and Heinrich von Sybel; in England, William Stubbs, Henry Maine, and his friend from Civil War days, John Richard Green; in Italy, Ernst Grzanowski (S 1.238–39) — collecting the latest books and articles, asking for guidance. Then, on his honeymoon cruise of the Nile, he studied the books he had acquired and taught himself the Anglo-Saxon language (L 2.136).

His own scholarly standards were spelled out at this time in the letters he wrote to Henry Cabot Lodge, who was at law school but wondering if he should become a professional historian. "Learn to appreciate and to use the German historical *method,* and your *style* can be elaborated at leisure" (L 2.139). Lodge's aim should be "to master the scientific method, and to adopt the right principle of subordinating everything to perfect thoroughness of study" (L 2.154). "It matters very little what line you take, provided you can catch the tail of an idea to develop it with solid reasoning and thorough knowledge" (L 2.156). Adams tells him to perfect his German (L 2.155). Medieval documents must be read in their original languages, "French, Latin, and Anglo-Saxon" (L 2.173). His advice to him at a later stage is much the same as at the outset:

I thought and still think that you were trying to cover too wide a field of mere fact. For the present I was much less inclined to trouble myself about the amount you learned than about the method you were learning. I have, no doubt, more respect for knowledge even where knowledge is useless and worthless, than for mere style, even where style is good; but unless one learns beforehand to be logically accurate and habitually thorough, mere knowledge is worth very little. At best it never can be more than relative ignorance, at least in the study of history. (L 2.172)

The course Adams worked out as he wrote to Lodge, his prospective student, was followed when he returned to Harvard. He taught English law from original Anglo-Saxon documents, translating, comparing, debating, assigning to each student a special angle from which to consider the field — property law, family law, judicial courts, and so on. The students read other treatments of these documents — in the Oxford historians, in German scholars like Rudolph Sohm and Paul Roth. Each person wrote a doctoral dissertation on his specialty. Harvard then awarded its first doctorates in history to the students of a man who had no doctorate himself.

Meanwhile, Adams had arranged for the publication of three dissertations, with an introductory essay of his own, as *Essays in Anglo-Saxon Law* (Little, Brown, 1876). He appended his own translations of key Anglo-Saxon documents (after checking his translations with other scholars — L 2.263). The volume had no commercial appeal — he joked with his English friend Charles Gaskell when he sent him a copy: "The book is fearfully learned. You cannot read it, and I advise you not to open it" (L 2.275). Adams could get it published only at his own expense — paying $2,000 for it, the equal of his annual salary as a professor (S 1.248). With his love of the physical beauty of books, he did not stint on the costs of publication. He wanted it to be an impressive item on the résumés of his scholars: "Their success is mine, and I made the investment for them, expecting to draw my profit from their success" (L 2.275).

Teutonism

Adams's emphasis on scientific German method did not free him from Germanic myths. Though the Oxford School wanted to dispel the false romanticism of Walter Scott, it substituted what it considered a *real* romantic story. The historians gave scholarly validation to what has been called the "Teutonism" of the time. This was a view that had been formulated in the eighteenth century and adhered to by many people, including Thomas Jefferson — the belief that the Germanic peoples possessed from the outset a primitive democracy, exercised through a communal body (*witan*) and organized by "hundreds." These free institutions were later corrupted by Roman law and practices. For England, this meant that the freedom-loving Saxons lost their institutions when the Norman Conquest brought feudal structures over from a Rome-influenced continent. Jefferson presented the American Revolution as a recovery of Saxon freedoms from the Norman-corrupted England. For the obverse of the national seal he proposed the figures of the Saxon chiefs Hengist and Horsa (JP 1.493). When he planned the division of Virginia into self-governing school districts, he called them by the medieval term "hundreds" (JP 1.327). As he later wrote to an English friend, these districts "answer to the hundreds of your Saxon Alfred."[17] For the curriculum at his University of Virginia he strongly recommended the study of the Anglo-Saxon language, to provide "a full understanding of our ancient common law, on which as a stock our whole system of law is engrafted."[18]

When Adams was beginning his seminar, the best scholars, both in Germany and in England, subscribed to some form of the Teutonic thesis. They were attacking Whig historians like Macaulay, who saw foreign intervention as liberating — whether at the Norman Conquest in 1066 or the Glorious Revolution of 1688. In the *Education,* astonishingly, Adams would claim that he never accepted the Teutonic thesis, though his writings and those of his students prove that this is false.[19] Adams would not reject the "beer-swilling Saxon boors" (E 1095) until he came to glorify the Norman architecture at Mont-Saint-Michel. His view at Harvard was quite different, as one can see from his treatment of Edward the Confessor:

> His acts, not merely in reference to jurisdiction but throughout his career, show that he was not an Anglo-Saxon but a Norman king. It was he who introduced the worst maxims of government into England; and whatever abuses may have existed from his time in the practice of judicial administration, it was he and his advisers who revolutionized the law.[20]

It is true that Adams was sometimes critical of the Oxford School historians in his *North American Review* book notices, but he was critical of details in almost all his book reviews. Hans Rudolf Guggisberg argues that Adams made crucial distinctions in his use of the Teutonic thesis without jettisoning it.[21] In fact, sometimes Adams rebukes the English for not being *thoroughgoing enough* in their Anglo-Saxonism. He criticized Stubbs, for instance, when he claimed that the township, not the hundred, was the early unit of law.

> If the clue offered by the hundred is once lost, or even if it is loosely held, the entire history of the English judicial constitution becomes a confused jumble of words. The one permanent Germanic institution was the hundred. The one code of Germanic law was hundred-law, much of which is now the common law of England. The hundred and its law survived all the storms which wrecked dynasties.[22]

Adams became so enthusiastic for the primitive liberties of the Anglo-Saxons that he took a leap most English historians were too wise to attempt. He asserted that communal democracy was original not only to the Germanic peoples, *but to all free peoples:*

> From these [Anglo-Saxon] laws and this society, not from Roman laws or William the Conqueror's brain, England, with her common law and constitutional system developed . . . as every society which is based on the principle of contract always has and always must have developed.[23]

At this point, Adams became almost absurdly Jeffersonian, claiming that kings and priests are a later intrusion on a primitive popular assembly "which embraced every free man, rich or poor, and in theory at least allowed equal rights to all."[24] All societies at their origin resemble the Germanic by exhibiting "not a trace of religious or priestly influence," as opposed to "civil" (Romanized, corrupted) societies like the "Aryan" (Norse) ones: "The Aryans are the creators of civil law" (L 2.312).

Adams, like Jefferson, believed that American Indians had preserved the primitive equality. He tried to verify this thesis with a scholar of Native American culture who did not accept Parkman's view of the debased Indians (L 2.264–65). When he did not elicit full agreement from his chosen scholar, he tried to make at least one point:

> I see you state that their [Indians'] marriage permitted separation at will of either party. This implies that the wife remained after marriage under the general protection of her own family, and was not a member of her husband's family [as in Roman law]. (L 2.271)

This point was important to Adams, since he was trying to counter Sir Henry Maine's view that patriarchy was the original state, from which liberties had to be developed. In reviewing Maine's *Lectures on the Early History of Institutions,* Adams proclaimed his own Teutonism:

> The late investigations into the earliest known forms of Teutonic law seem to have rendered one conclusion probable which was hardly to have been expected. They show that the German society, when it first emerged into the view of the civilized world, was not founded on a tribal system . . . The German *magenschaft,* or kindred, was a loose organization, without a patriarchal head and without a common property. It included the mother's as well as the father's relations.[25]

Adams worked especially closely with his student Ernest Young to argue that the original equality of families in the hundred implied an equality of men and women. There were three products of this partnership between professor and student: (1) Young's dissertation, "The Anglo-Saxon Family Law," (2) Young's Harvard commencement address, "The Patriarchal Theory" (L 2.280–81), and (3) Adams's own Lowell Institute lecture (the only one he ever gave) on "The Primitive Rights of Women" (H 1–41). All three of these were made public in 1876, as the culmination of Adams's teaching career, in which he had fulfilled his boast to Harvard's president that he was a radical and a socialist.

Adams and Young both argued that the wife, under Anglo-Saxon law, remained free in marriage, the controller of her own property, able to divorce her husband, to control inheritance, and to dispose of joint property: "Generally the wife was the acting, and the husband the consenting, partner" in alienation of goods.[26] Young, going further, doubted the very possibility of patriarchy in primitive society.[27] Adams, going further still, argued that a primitive communism in all societies gave the woman more power than the man, since descent could be traced only through her. For Young and Adams, the subjugation of women was a later development, caused in the West by Roman and church law. Despotism in state and family were the product of "the manifest injustice toward women which the church had either stimulated or permitted."[28] Though Adams was not arguing directly from the treatment his grandmother Louisa received at the hands of the puritanical Adamses, her example could not have been far from his mind. He was able to express here what he had felt, only eight years earlier, when he tried to publish her own testimony to the repression of women. It is significant that he felt strongly enough about his lecture on women's rights to republish it twenty-three years later in *Historical Essays.*[29]

American Documents

Beginning in 1874, Adams added to his undergraduate courses in medieval history some courses on American history — in which, as one student remembered, "Adams did not in the least spare the reputation of his great-grandfather, John Adams."[30] Henry Cabot Lodge later assisted him in this work, and the two men were reading early American documents in the Massachusetts Historical Society. Both, for instance, read there the papers of Timothy Pickering (L 2.291), since Lodge was preparing to write a biography of his grandfather, George Cabot, an ally of Pickering, and Adams decided to publish a suppressed book by his grandfather, who was a Pickering foe. John Quincy Adams had attacked both Cabot and Pickering as members of an "Essex Junto," called that because they came from Essex County, where Salem was the center.[31] Lodge proved that Cabot had turned down Pickering's overtures to lead a secession of New England from the Union — though that was what John Quincy had claimed.

During the presidential campaign of 1826, which deprived John Quincy of his presidency after one term, he was unwise enough to answer a charge against him with a public letter that dragged in an attack on the Essex Junto, which he accused of trying to break up the Union during Jefferson's presidency.[32] Descendants of the men President Adams named as belonging to the Junto indignantly disputed his letter. After losing the election, Adams wrote a lengthy book against those descendants — it was this that Henry Cabot Lodge would dispute in his life of George Cabot. Cooler afterthought made John Quincy set aside the completed work. When Adams and Lodge looked it over, Adams thought enough time had passed to make it part of the historical record, along with the charges that prompted it and the correspondence of the men involved. The result was his first book, *Documents Related to New-England Federalism, 1800–1815* (Little, Brown, 1877).

This book has suffered the same fate that all his early writing did. It was taken as a defense of his grandfather (though we know what his opinion of him was). In fact, though Adams believed that Pickering was a secessionist, he knew that his grandfather was wrong in claiming that Cabot was — Adams felt that Cabot was too anti-democratic to believe the republic redeemable, even by secession (J 413–14). But all this is beside the point, since John Quincy spent most of his book defending the support he gave to Jefferson's Embargo, which Henry always thought a hideous mistake. So it is nonsense to treat Lodge's and Adams's books as "dueling" defenses of their respective grandparents. They considered them a joint enterprise. Adams sent Lodge's book with this recommendation to the southern historian Hugh Blair Grigsby: "Mr. Lodge is, or was, one of my scholars, and took under me the degree of Ph.D. at Cambridge last year. His book was written under my eye" (L 2.239). To Lodge himself he wrote: "The two volumes ought to sell each other" (L 2.238). As if to guarantee this, each man wrote a favorable (anonymous) review of the other in *The Nation*.[33] They pay credit to each other's scrupulous editing of the documents, which is hardly surprising — they had just been working over authenticated medieval documents.

While he was finishing his work on the documents available to him in Boston, Adams was pining toward the richer storehouse in Washington when a lucky offer sped him in that direction. He was asked to edit and publish the papers of Albert Gallatin, secretary of the treasury under both Jefferson and Madison. Nothing could have opened the documentary way into his chosen period so swiftly and effectively. Living with the thoughts of Gallatin gave Adams a perfect vantage from which to view the "triumvirate" of Jefferson, Madison, and Gallatin that was at the heart of the four presidential terms in his *History*. Adams found Gallatin — cosmopolitan, urbane, balanced — particularly sympathetic. He already agreed with many of his views — especially his opposition to Hamilton, debt, and the British. Through the prism of Gallatin's papers, Adams would be able to give a fair reading to everything the Jeffersonians did. His admiration for Gallatin is unmistakable. He wrote to Samuel Tilden, a modern politician he admired:

> To do justice to Gallatin was a labor of love. After long study of the prominent figures in our history, I am more than ever convinced that, for combination of ability, integrity, knowledge, unselfishness, and social fitness, Mr. Gallatin has no equal. He was the most fully and perfectly equipped statesman we can show. Other men, as I take hold of them, are soft in some spots and rough in others. Gallatin never gave way in my hand or seemed unfinished. That he made mistakes I can see, but even in his blunders he was respectable. (L 2.491)

Even if he had not enjoyed the company of Gallatin so much, the opening of such a treasure would have been irresistible. Familiarizing himself with all the papers would naturally lead to a biography of Gallatin (L 2.311), and doing research for the biography would lead him to many other sources — the few people alive who remembered Gallatin, relatives of Gallatin's wife in New York, descendants of those who had received letters from Gallatin. For Gallatin's early career, he needed to consult archives in Virginia and Pennsylvania. In the national archives at Washington, he had to go through all the Jefferson papers to trace the interaction between the president and his secretary of the treasury. The work on the papers and the biography would give him, in effect, a first run-through of the years he would be covering in his *History*. As he notes, he would get no pay for this project (though Gallatin's son under-wrote all expenses): "I get all my own objects in acquaintance with the papers" (L 2.311). While he worked on the Gallatin project, he had scribes copying materials on Jefferson for later use (L 2.333).

Since Adams was especially interested in Gallatin's early Virginia years, he recruited the help of Hugh Blair Grigsby in tracking down the papers of John Randolph, Patrick Henry, William Branch Giles, Wilson Cary Nicholas, Nathaniel Macon, and William H. Crawford (L 2.315, 317). He also wrote directly to the heirs of Randolph and Henry (L 2.319–21). He knew that Grigsby might be suspicious of an Adams, ex-pecting to find in him an ancestral enemy of Virginia, so he wrote: "I cannot treat Mr. Jefferson roughly in a life of Gallatin" (L 2.322). As he continued his search for Virginia documents, he told Grigsby: "I have unearthed much private correspondence of that time, including masses of John Randolph's and Macon's letters. I fear that they will not give our generation any extravagant opinions of their predecessors" (L 2.339).

Adams turned to Lewis Henry Morgan, the *Review*'s expert on Ameri-can Indians, for advice on Gallatin's ethnological writings (L 2.341). He applied to John Russell Bartlett, who had published his reminiscences of Gallatin, for any little items he might have left out of the printed ac-count: "Probably you have many traits of his character which you did not care to print, but which would throw light on my path. If so, I would be greatly obliged by such assistance" (L 2.347). Adams was obviously giving much thought to the nature of biography, which was a new genre for him:

> The comments of a great man on his own career — especially on his own faults and character — are invaluable to a biographer. A word — some-times, even, a look, or a moment of mere silence — may tell more than all the printed volumes. I beg that you will ransack your memory of these slight touches of character. (L 2.348)

Unfortunately, Adams did not follow his own hints on the way to write a biography. Work with his graduate students had perhaps made him much more an archivist than an historian at this point. Perhaps under pressure from the Gallatin family, he followed Victorian decorum in the "life and letters" format of his book, preserving a great formality, in the vein that Lytton Strachey would make fun of in his *Eminent Victorians*. The book's subject is always "Mr. Gallatin," never simply "Gallatin." And so with "Mrs. Gallatin" and all other characters in the story. The narrative is carried in great part by long quotations from Gallatin's letters. Correspondence related to Gallatin's Genevan origins is quoted without translation, since "it is always a little impertinent to suggest that one's readers are ignorant of French" (L 2.330). Since some letters to the Gallatins came from Voltaire, Adams had a supporting reason for just printing the original: "I have my doubts whether the man who thinks he can translate him is not a little of a fool" (L 2.330).

The biography exposed Adams to a veiled assault from his own brother Charles, who resented the criticism it contains of their great-grandfather and grandfather. Charles wrote an anonymous two-part attack in *The Nation*, having persuaded the magazine's editor, E. L. Godkin, that it would be a good joke to publish this unsigned attack by one brother on another.[34] Then, when Henry expressed resentment, they would spring the surprise on him. But Henry spoiled their game by ignoring the review. He knew, of course, who had written it, but he did not want to give his brother the satisfaction of any response at all. Charles's clumsy jocularity, the references to literature known to them both, his branding of Henry as "German," along with the defense of John Quincy, were all dead giveaways. Knowing that Charles wrote the hostile review no doubt intensified the profound dislike Henry's wife, Marion ("Clover"), felt for Charles.

Godkin may well have hesitated, when the review was turned in, at the ferocity of its opening paragraph: "With its superficial makeup this volume falls little short of being an outrage both on Albert Gallatin and on everyone who wishes to know anything about him." When Henry did not condescend to notice the review, Godkin got the uncomfortable feeling that he had been drawn into some family intrigue. He kept asking Henry if he did not want to know something about the review, hinting at mysteries, saying he was not the originator of the piece, that he should not be blamed, and so on. Henry dismissed the matter whenever Godkin tried to explain, and finally had to tell him to quit pestering him.

Suppose me to be walking down Broadway thinking kindly of all creation when I meet you, and you address me much as follows, with a very awkward air:

Godkin. My dear Adams, I hope you are not offended at my pulling your nose the other day.

I. But Godkin, you didn't pull my nose. What do you mean?

Godkin. Yes, I did indeed! Lots of people saw me do it, and said you would have to resent it. But the fact is, it was not my fault; it was a man round the corner who made me do it, because he said it would do you good.

I. (Much perplexed and unwilling) But my dear fellow, don't you see that if you really did pull my nose, it is you and not the man round the corner whom I must hold responsible for it? What on earth can I do if you, with your airs of mystery, not to say of conspiracy, insist upon goading me into resentment which I don't feel? (L 2.410–11)

Charles was right to see that Henry was on Gallatin's side when the latter attacked John Adams, denouncing his economic program, his Alien and Sedition Acts, his "midnight appointments." Gallatin wrote of Adams: "You can have no idea of the meanness, indecency, almost insanity, of his conduct, specially of late" (G 265). Charles was most upset by Henry's claim that Gallatin had to save the peace delegation at Ghent from the bumbling of John Quincy Adams. Henry also shared Gallatin's hostility toward Hamilton.[35] We have already seen how he makes Gallatin what he felt himself to be — an honorary Virginian. Gallatin became a United States citizen in Virginia, acquired his first circle of friendly sponsors there (including John Marshall and Patrick Henry), and settled on what was the western fringe of that state. "He regarded himself as a Virginian" (G 59).

Gallatin, Adams's fellow Virginian, also had the endorsement of a third southerner, Adams's grandmother Louisa. She wrote of Gallatin in the autobiography Adams copied out for publication:

I have since known him intimately, and found him one of the most charming and gifted men I ever knew in any country, shrewd, subtle, and penetrating. Few could cope with him, and many of the prudent in society thought it was necessary to be on their guard when brought into contact with him.

Gallatin was driven out of his original farm in Virginia by the threat of Indian harassment, but he moved only slightly north into Pennsylvania, where he would make his political career, first in the state legislature, then as Madison's coadjutor in the House of Representatives, where his ties with the Virginians led to his appointment as Jefferson's and Madison's secretary of the treasury.

By studying Gallatin, Adams entered into the inner councils of the Jeffersonians. But he was acutely aware of the limits of this approach. He was looking not only through the eyes of one man, but from the shores of one country. He felt that the American story could not be told only from the American viewpoint. As soon as he finished his Gallatin project he set off on an ambitious hunt for previously unexplored documents in London, Paris, Madrid, and Seville. This campaign in three countries was a difficult one. Even with his connections, and with the aid of American ministers to each country, he had to struggle for access to records that seemed tantalizingly close yet closed. In England, he had to get a law suspended that sealed all documents after 1802 (L 2.364, 375). In France, the premier promised his help but did nothing (L 2.384).

Frustrated, Adams left Paris for Madrid, where his former colleague on the Harvard faculty, James Russell Lowell, was the American minister. But Lowell, whose wife was dying, was too distracted to be much help (L 2.378–80). After striking off on his own to Seville, where he found a scholar willing to help him in that city's records, Adams returned to Madrid and gained access, now, through the grandson of the Marqués de Casa Yrujo, the Spanish minister in Washington during Jefferson's presidency, who would play a large role in the *History* (L 2.391).

Going back to Paris, Adams found scholars to sponsor his request — including the editor of the *Revue Historique,* whose work he had published in the *North American Review* (L 2.391). He helped seal the bargain through his friendship with William Evarts, the American secretary of state, arranging reciprocal rights of access for French scholars to study the archives in Washington (L 2.394–97). Then it was back to London, to spend seven-hour days reading the newspapers of the time in the British Museum — where his historical work had begun for the Pocahontas essay (L 2.292). He worked at a feverish pace, accumulating mountains of material. There was a heart-stopping moment when he heard in London that his list of materials to be copied had disappeared, along with the vast quantity of paper he had provided for this. He said that the copyist must then look at his paper marks in the volumes he had studied, and if doubtful what part of a document was needed, to copy it all (L 2.395–96). These sources were precious to him. As he wrote from England:

> I have finished with the Record Office, completed my search through the newspapers, collected the greater part of my pamphlets, and sounded all the wells of private collections I could find. In Paris and Madrid copyists are at work for me and ought soon to send their copy. I foresee a good history if I have health and leisure the next five years [it would be ten], and if nothing happens to my collections of material. My belief is that I can make something permanent of it. (L 2.399)

Archival history in America was about to make a great leap forward.

Adams was not only heroically persistent in overcoming the difficulties posed in getting at the archives he wanted. Once he reached them, he was scrupulous and thorough in sifting them for relevant material. One can see that in the extracts taken from state papers, which now reside in the Library of Congress. He had his materials copied onto sheets of paper of uniform size, so he could bind them in thick volumes arranged chronologically. There are over a thousand items contained in twenty volumes, with a big box for the items not of uniform size — these are filed in a large box. Working in the correspondence of the British Foreign Office, he did not confine himself to the years actually covered in the *History*. He began a decade earlier, to get a feel for the diplomatic context of the years that followed. Nor did he study only the dispatches from Washington. He also covered the correspondence with the British ministers in Canada — and not only for the years of the War of 1812, but for the years leading up to that conflict. This means that the British materials are arranged this way:

Volume I: 1789–1792
Volume II: 1793–1794
Volume III: 1795–1796
Volume IV: 1800–1801
Volume V: 1798–1806 (Toussaint, Louisiana material)
Volume VI: 1808–1814 (War of 1812)
Volume VII: 1789–1798 (Canadian correspondence)
Volume VIII: 1794–1795 (Canadian correspondence)
Volume IX: 1796–1798
Volume X: 1798–1799

The box of papers not uniformly bound is drawn mainly from the Admiralty Office, with valuable information on the dealings with Toussaint, copied out by Adams himself.

Besides this, there are nine volumes from the French archives, with their invaluable material on Napoleon, Talleyrand, the Spanish relations, and Louisiana. These, too, begin before 1800 (specifically, in 1787), and are chronologically arranged. The Spanish material is in one bound volume, dealing with Godoy, Louisiana, and the Burr affair. The Massachusetts Historical Society has a one-hundred-page notebook in which Adams copied notes and lists of British pamphlets and newspaper articles for the period of Madison's presidency.[36] There was presumably a companion notebook for the Jefferson years, but it has not been found.

No wonder Adams returned from Europe with a miser's delight in the treasures he had acquired.

6

HISTORICAL ARTISTRY

ENRY ADAMS WAS AN ARTIST, though he forgot that fact while writing the shapeless *Gallatin*. He was an aesthete, sensitive to line and tone and proportion, a collector proud of his Turner watercolors and Blake prints. He was highly conscious of form in writing his prose masterpieces. But in 1878 he lined up document after document in his Gallatin biography, then trudged dutifully alongside them in chronological order. He could not get high enough above his material to shape it meaningfully. He was, at this point, more a chronicler than an historian. He had spent six years grading student papers, reading documents with his graduate students, editing articles by other authors, and then spent two years sifting Gallatin archives. He was too mired in these numbing tasks to take control of his first book as an author rather than an editor.

He meant to remedy that fault in the history he was about to undertake. It is natural, therefore, that he should experiment in various prose forms during the preparation and early stages of that project. He was commissioned to write two brief biographies, of John Randolph and Aaron Burr, and he undertook two novels on his own, one published anonymously in 1880 (*Democracy*), the other published pseudonymously in 1884 (*Esther*).[1] The biographies were especially tempting, since they dealt with two figures who would be important in his *History*, and he was able to treat them in a manner as far from the Gallatin book as possible — as vivid sketches, not mechanically inclusive records. Adams had read lively descriptions of both Randolph and Burr in his grandmother's diary of her first year in Washington (1804), and for Randolph, at least, he got an important tip from her.

John Randolph

The *Randolph* is an economical portrait, vivid but balanced; the *Burr* was considered to be even better by those who read it, but it was rejected by the publisher — on political grounds, not literary ones. After toying with the idea of taking the *Burr* to a different publisher, Adams put it aside and then suppressed it. The fate of the two books has been scrambled in later accounts, and the surviving one has been heavily misrepresented for a familiar reason — as a thing written to defend the Adams family. Even the man who commissioned the book in 1881 came, many years later, to hold that view of it. The man in question is John T. Morse, who edited the "American Statesmen" series for the Houghton, Mifflin publishing house — books written by learned men for a popular audience. Morse, a friend of Adams, consulted him on the matching of authors with subjects (L 2.425, 452, 473), and many of the books were written by members of the Adams circle — but Morse claimed that *Randolph* was the only assignment he regretted having made. He was speaking half a century after the event, and he confused and forgot many things.[2] He could not even remember having heard of the Burr biography, and he transfers the bad feelings from that forgotten commission to the *Randolph*, which he praised at the time of its appearance (L 2.479).

By 1930, Morse had picked up the tired commonplace that Adams wrote only to avenge his family. The same view is expressed in modern introductions to the *Randolph*. Milton Cantor, in the "American Lives" series of 1969, says that Adams accepted the offer to write the book from "an irresistible opportunity to give expression to a personal and sectional animus," and that he produced "a wicked, debunking study which consistently violated the canons of objective history."[3] Robert McColley, in the "American History Through Literature" series, says (ludicrously) that the book expressed "the distilled bitterness of four generations of political Adamses."[4] Robert Dawidoff calls the book a "partisan, retributive biography."[5]

Can these people not read? Adams finds things wrong with Randolph (who could not?), but he says that Randolph's opposition to John Adams was a *duty:*

When hostilities with France broke out, and under their cover the Alien and Sedition laws were passed, backed by a large army, with the scarcely concealed object of overawing threatened resistance from Virginia, it was time that the opposition *should* be put in power [emphasis added]. (R 34)[6]

Another thing that has created a prejudiced readership of the Randolph biography is Adams's normal self-deprecation in letters to intimates. He told Morse, who had praised the book, that he winced at its acidity, absorbed from its subject: "The rule of a writer should be that of a salad-maker; let the vinegar be put in by a miser, the oil by a spendthrift. In this case however the tone was really decided by the subject, and the excess of acid is his" (L 2.479). Actually, the book is not written with bitterness but with brio. Adams rejoiced in his release from the authorized formality of his *Gallatin.* The least appropriate thing to say about the *Randolph* is that it has an "unrelieved gloom."[7] It is important to dispel this misconception, since Adams follows here the lead given him by his grandmother, a lead that will in turn lead to many sparkling pages of the *History.* Louisa had written that Randolph "was to Congress what Shakespeare's fools were to a court. He kept Congress awake 'with his quips and cranks'" (A 269). Randolph will be a tormented but truth-telling jester in the *History.*

The fact that the book is not vindictive can be readily established. If Adams merely wanted to punish Randolph, he could have used material he explicitly renounced, though he knew it well.[8] That material concerned a family scandal to which Randolph reacted with a mad vengefulness, and the physical malady that exposed him to ridicule. The scandal could not be omitted in more recent (less Victorian) biographies, since it involved the whole Virginia establishment — John Marshall, Patrick Henry, Thomas Jefferson and his daughter, and much of the thickly ramifying Randolph connection. The story is lurid. It has been called "the greatest scandal that ever touched this proud [Randolph] family" (DM 3.173) and "Virginia's most famous eighteenth-century criminal proceeding."[9]

First, the scandal. On October 1, 1792, when John Randolph was nineteen, his beloved older brother Richard was accused of a sexual affair with his beautiful sister-in-law and cousin, Nancy Randolph. He apparently covered up Nancy's miscarriage and disposed of the evidence of it.[10] Richard Randolph, with the help of a stellar team of lawyers (John Marshall, Patrick Henry, Alexander Campbell) got the charges dismissed, though Jefferson's daughter Martha, a friend of Nancy, said that the public did not accept the whitewash (JP 26.53). John Marshall's biographer says that he "may not have had any other case that required quite as adroit and persuasive an interpretation of the known facts."[11]

So far the scandal had not touched John Randolph, though he gave misleading information to defend his brother at the hearing. But he disgraced himself horribly two decades later. He convinced himself that Nancy had not only ruined but ended his brother's life (he died three years after the scandal). Now he set out to destroy her and her marriage to Gouverneur Morris, the revolutionary financier of New York. Morris had wed Nancy in 1809, after asking John Marshall if there was anything he should fear from the old scandal (Marshall answered no). When Richard's son visited Morris's home, the thought of his brother's offspring under Nancy's roof drove Randolph into a frenzy. He sent a long letter to Nancy, addressed to Morris with instructions that he read it before delivering it to her.

The letter claimed that Nancy secretly buried her illegitimate child, since it had a black father, her slave Billy Ellis, though she told Richard that the father was his brother Theodorick (who died, conveniently, eight months before the birth). After bearing and killing the baby, she got Richard to hide it in a woodpile, out of pity for her — and she repaid him, three years later, by poisoning him. Randolph warns Morris that she may be planning to poison him. She is "a vampire that, after sucking the best blood of my race, has flitted off to the North and stuck her harpy fangs into an infirm old man."[12] Adams says in the biography that Randolph was unhinged at times. That is evident from many things Randolph said and did. Adams did not have to adduce this episode to prove it. But his only reference to the scandal and Randolph's response to it is this:

> Richard's last years had been embittered by a strange and terrible scandal, resulting in a family feud, which John, with his usual vehemence, made his own. These complications would have been trying to any man, but to one of his peculiar temper they were a source of infinite depression and despair. (32)

John Randolph passionately missed his brother, whose manliness he admired, since Richard seems to have accepted him as a full and equal partner, despite his physical impediments. John's voice never changed, his beard never grew. He was abnormally tall and thin, but with a child's appearance. Some blame this on a disease (scarlet fever, syphilis, or other) contracted when he was nineteen; but if his voice had not changed by then, it seems unlikely that it would have, even in the absence of any disease. The odd configuration of his body, which looked emaciated and bony, suggests there was some congenital problem in his makeup. Once again, Adams draws a veil over this mischance, making only two slight references to it:

> He seems to have been suffering under a complication of trials, the mystery of which his biographers had best not attempt to penetrate. (32)

> From the first, some private trouble weighed on his mind, and since he chose to make a mystery of its cause, a biographer is bound to respect his wish. (165)

A modern biographer would probably think this reticence does Randolph no favor, since knowing his affliction can help explain his personal imbalance and excess. It can elicit our sympathy. Not that Adams fails to show sympathy for Randolph in his misery, even without spelling out its causes:

> Of all his eccentricities, the most pitiful and yet the most absurd were not those which sprang from his lower but from his higher instincts. The better part of his nature made a spasmodic struggle against the passions and appetites that degraded it. Half his rudeness and savagery was due to pride which would allow no one to see the full extent of his weakness. (175)

Adams does not traduce Randolph when he notices his emotional instability. Even a sympathetic recent treatment calls Randolph an example of "the degenerate weirdness of the gothic south."[13] Adams tries to understand what threads of continuity run through all the divagations — Randolph's consistency to his southern creed, his proud scorn of compromise, his aspirations toward noble conduct. Of Randolph's youth Adams says only that there was little in his upbringing to restrain him from headstrong waywardness. His childhood was what a year-round Quincy would have been for Adams, "a boy's paradise of indulgence" (22). This was tempered, in Randolph's case, only by his mother's piety and his stepfather's refinement. His father had died when he was two, and his mother married the great jurist from Bermuda, St. George Tucker, who joined his wife and her three sons on the Randolph plantation, Matoax.

John raced horses skillfully, and argued forcibly in his treble voice. Impatient of schooling, he flitted from Columbia to Princeton. He was at

Columbia when Washington's inauguration occurred in New York. The coachmen of Vice President John Adams's carriage, which was "emblazoned with a scutcheon," snapped a whip at Randolph's brother for being in the way (29). Though Adams does not say it here, he knew that the blazonry was one of Abigail's sillier ideas, which her husband abjured.[14]

When the government moved to Philadelphia, Randolph went there for some desultory study of law with his cousin Edmund Randolph, President Washington's attorney general. He was already defying ridicule by a rush toward the center of attention. Visiting in Charleston, he was remembered by a bookseller as "a tall, gawky-looking, flaxen-haired stripling, apparently of the age from sixteen to eighteen [he was actually twenty-three], with a complexion of a good parchment color, beardless chin, and as much assumed self-confidence as any two-footed animal I ever saw" (31).

His first foray into politics was to flay the old Republican purist Patrick Henry, for defending the Federalists during the crisis over the Alien and Sedition Acts. The ailing Henry had come out of retirement in response to President Washington's plea that he hold the Union together, at this divisive time, by running for Congress. Adams calls this Henry's touching sacrifice for a Union he had often opposed (35), but Randolph, with the principled intransigence of youth, challenged him for the seat, and when Henry died during the campaign, Randolph was elected to the House at the barely constitutional age of twenty-six. In that chamber, with his quick mind and tongue, his aggressive bearing, and even his freakish appearance, with the high voice of an angel thundering soprano dooms, he seemed like some vessel of sublimated idealism. The Speaker of the House, Nathaniel Macon, fell under his spell, and made him chairman of Gallatin's old creation, the Ways and Means Committee, where Randolph, still in his twenties, became the most powerful figure in what was then the most powerful chamber.

Randolph, working closely with Gallatin, did more than anyone in Congress to advance Jefferson's programs at the outset of his term. Adams calls his chapter for this period "In Harness." This was Randolph at the height of his youthful power and influence, the man Henry's grandmother Louisa observed in 1804:

In Congress, John Randolph was the lion of the day. Full of all the attributes which form great men, his temperament was irritable and sensitive almost to madness. Ever in extremes, he was at times a delightful companion or an insolent bully. He appeared to be a great man of his day, for he ruled the timid and amused the weak. He kept Congress awake and made the ladies smile.[15]

Following Jefferson's strong lead made Randolph compromise some of his anti-federal ideology, especially in authorizing the Louisiana Purchase. Yet even when working for the administration, Randolph had to indulge a contrarian streak. Adams repeatedly compares him to Don Quixote. He was a walking exception, and his instinct was to emphasize this as a way of turning his disadvantages into a strength.

He went along with Jefferson's assault on the judiciary, but wrested into his own hands the impeachment of Supreme Court justice Samuel Chase, working without the legal counsel that he so badly needed, fashioning an idiosyncratic rationale for impeachment (74–76). He introduced, as one count, a departure from legal procedure — which would have imperiled every judge alive. Used to dominating the House with his daring pre-emptive moves, he badly underestimated his power in the different arena of a Senate trial:

> Even though he had all the resources of his party in the House to draw upon, including Joseph H. Nicholson and Caesar A. Rodney, both fair lawyers, yet at the bar before him he saw not only Justice Chase, keen, vigorous, with long experience and ample learning, but also, at Chase's side, counsel such as neither Senate nor House could command, at whose head, most formidable of American advocates, was the rollicking, witty, audacious attorney-general of Maryland; boon companion of Chase and the whole bar; drunken, generous, slovenly, grand; bulldog of Federalism, as Mr. Jefferson called him; shouting with a schoolboy's fun at the idea of tearing Randolph's indictment to pieces and teaching the Virginian democrats some law — the notorious reprobate genius, Luther Martin. (99)

That sentence is a good example of the flexible instrument Adams's prose was becoming. It applies thirteen adjectives to Luther Martin, but in such clever variations of structure — reflecting Martin's own legal sinuosities — that they give no effect of dull repetition.

Randolph was humiliated by the trial. But Adams, observing chronology, inserts between Chase's House impeachment and his Senate trial a more serious cause of Randolph's estrangement from almost all his former allies — the Yazoo issue. Randolph was feeling a need to reassert states' rights, and Yazoo gave him the occasion. It was a matter that could only embarrass his own party, and especially the secretary of state, James Madison. In 1795, the legislature of the state of Georgia, as a result of wholesale bribing of its members, had sold Indian lands to speculators (many from the North). Disgust at this procedure made Georgia's voters throw the state legislators out and cancel their fraudulent sale. The purchasers of the land took their right to ownership into various courts and put pressure on Jefferson's administration, when he took office, to enforce their contracts. Since Jefferson needed to increase and hold the extension of his party into the North, and many of the speculators were part of the nascent Republican party there (including his own postmaster general), he appointed a committee to work out a compromise, with his most trusted associates as its members — Madison, Gallatin, and Attorney General Levi Lincoln.

The committee, as such bodies do, fashioned a compromise: the federal government would take over the disputed land, pay Georgia an indemnity, parcel out the land, recognize some claims on a reduced scale, dismiss others. As Adams says, this was a pragmatic way out of an impasse. It seriously harmed few, and benefited many, especially the Republicans:

> The compromise suggested would cost nothing to Georgia, for she had given the lands to the United States, and would cost nothing to the United States, for they held the lands as a gift from Georgia. A refusal to compromise would throw the whole matter into the courts, with the result of retarding settlement, multiplying expense, and probably getting in the end an adverse decision. It would create serious political ill-feeling in the party, and on the other hand, what possible object could be gained by it? (78)

The committee had struck a typical political deal — responding to party interests, favoring cronies and constituents. But Randolph stood on principle. What right had the federal government to tell a state it could not rescind its own act? How could federal officers solve their own problem by seizing the property of a state? Washington had no business intruding into the internal affairs of Georgia. While recognizing the utter impracticality of Randolph's position, Adams admires idealism, and expresses his sympathy by comparing it to his own anti-corruption campaign against the railroads in the 1860s: "Were a state legislature today bribed by a great railroad company to confer a grant of exclusive privileges fatal to the public interest, for a nominal consideration, it would be dangerous to the public safety to affirm that the people could never free themselves from this servitude" (80).

Once he got this bone in his teeth, Randolph never let it go. Anyone who had any part in the deal was forever after "a Yazoo man," to be denounced by Randolph year after year in Congress. From being the great implementer of Jefferson's policies, he became a constant carper against them, railing like Thersites, sometimes with cause but with decreasing effect, as he attacked both good and bad initiatives of the executive. When Jefferson's cat's-paw General James Wilkinson came to Richmond to testify against Aaron Burr for his western separatism, Randolph, serving on the grand jury, tried to get Wilkinson indicted. He had earlier expressed admiration for Burr in his conflict with Hamilton — Adams quotes his attacks on Hamilton with obvious pleasure (83–84) — and by now he preferred Burr to Jefferson.

But the principal Yazoo man in Randolph's eyes was Madison. He tried to prevent him from becoming president in 1808 by pitting Monroe against his candidacy. When Madison won, Randolph opposed his designs on the Floridas, his War of 1812, and Gallatin's attempt to save the Bank of the United States. Randolph became a weird Jeremiah figure in the chamber, bewailing the loss of all republican virtue. Opposition to the War of 1812 brought Randolph briefly into alliance with New England's critics of "Mr. Madison's war," and his district deprived him, for the first and last time, of his House seat in 1814, but let him retake it in 1816.

Though he had backed Monroe against Madison in 1808 — or, rather, *because* he had — Randolph felt that Monroe betrayed pure Republicanism, and affronted Randolph personally, when he consented to become Madison's secretary of state. When Monroe in turn became president, Randolph maintained his record of opposing his own state's men in the executive office. And if he had resisted men from his own state, he was not likely to be any kinder to a man from New England when John Quincy Adams became president:

> The warfare which Randolph at once declared against the administration of J. Q. Adams was not only inevitable; it was, from many points of view, praiseworthy, for it cannot be expected that anyone who has sympathy with Mr. Jefferson's theories of government in 1801, unfashionable though they are now, will applaud the theories of J. Q. Adams in 1825. The two doctrines were, in outward appearance, diametrically opposite; and although that of Mr. Adams, in sound accord with the practice if not with the theo-

ries of Mr. Jefferson, seems to have won the day, and though the powers of the general government have been expanded beyond his utmost views, it is not the business of a historian to deny that there was, and still is, great force in the opposite argument. (186)

When John Quincy entered the White House in 1825, Randolph had a new perch from which to attack the northern president — the Senate. He was elected to fill out the last two years of a vacated Virginia seat — but only because the popular favorite, his younger half-brother, Henry St. George Tucker, withdrew out of deference to him. When the two years were up, however, Randolph lost his bid for re-election. Not even his own state supported him now — though his own district loyally returned him to the House.

As a senator, Randolph launched his most famous insult at J. Q. Adams, in conjunction with his secretary of state, Henry Clay. It was the latter man Randolph resented most, as a slaveholder from Kentucky who was serving the northern president. To characterize the two of them, Randolph drew on Henry Fielding, his favorite author after Shakespeare. In Fielding's *Tom Jones,* Blifil is a whiny preacher and Black George a blustering rogue. In 1826, he opposed sending American representatives to a congress called by Latin American countries. When the vote went against him, he lamented: "I was defeated, horse, foot, and dragoons — cut up and clean broke down — by the coalition of Blifil and Black George, by the combination, unheard of till then, of the Puritan and the blackleg" (188). ("Blackleg" meant swindler at the time.) Adams does not give the reason for Randolph's emotional resistance to the Latin American congress. Randolph's sympathetic biographer reveals it: "Randolph had no mind to see the United States represented in a congress where its delegates were as likely to find themselves seated beside mulatto generals and statesmen as white men."[16]

The defense of slavery shows why, after he had lost his own state, Randolph still had power in the House, based on his appeal to the cotton states of the Deep South. As a champion of the slavemaster, he enthralled them, as Calhoun would entrance them afterward. This was no longer simply a matter of states' rights, as Adams shrewdly notes. In doing so, he comes up with a concept that would serve him well in the *History*. It is the most original part of the Randolph book, and it comes in the later sections that have been dismissed as perfunctory.

It is customary to say that the Jeffersonians opposed federal power until it came into their hands, when they embraced it from a natural effect that power has on those who hold it. Adams's view is subtler. He thinks there was a structural, not merely a psychological, reason why the southerners had to aggrandize the central authority. Though Randolph associated states' rights with the protection of slavery, the real protection of the institution had to come from the federal government:

> Between the slave power and states' rights there was no necessary connection. The slave power, when in control, was a centralizing influence, and all the most considerable encroachments on states' rights were its acts. The acquisition and admission of Louisiana; the Embargo; the War of 1812; the annexation of Texas "by joint resolution" [rather than treaty]; the war with Mexico, declared by the mere announcement of President Polk; the Fugitive Slave Law; the Dred Scott decision — all triumphs of the slave power — did far more than either tariffs or internal improvements, which in their origin were also southern measures, to destroy the very memory of states' rights as they existed in 1789. Whenever a question arose of extending or protecting slavery, the slaveholders became friends of centralized power, and used that dangerous weapon with a kind of frenzy. Slavery in fact required centralization in order to maintain and protect itself, but it required to control the centralized machine; it needed despotic principles of government, but it needed them exclusively for its own use. Thus, in truth, states' rights were the protection of the free states, and as a matter of fact, during the domination of the slave power, Massachusetts appealed to this protecting principle as often and almost as loudly as South Carolina. (178–79)

There is nothing more crushing for a man of principle than to be undone by his own principles. Randolph thought he could protect slavery by asserting states' rights, while in fact the former undermined the latter. The breakdown of Randolph's physical and mental constitution, coinciding with the collapse of his early view of the states' role, had a kind of tragic inevitability. Adams's description of Randolph's disintegration is not more vivid, though it is more pathetic, than that of anyone looking at the record. William Cabell Bruce describes the effects of frequent illnesses, heavy use of laudanum and alcohol, and isolation leading to paranoia. Alone on his dilapidating plantation, Randolph felt that his slaves were robbing him, his family deserting him. He renounced his kindly stepfather, St. George Tucker. It is Bruce, not Adams, who writes: "He at times exhibited angry and vindictive feelings against almost all persons with whom he had had any intercourse, with a few exceptions, and occasionally he was possessed by the sheer desire to kill of a maniac."[17]

Randolph's worst torture must have been the at least intermittent realization of what was happening to him. He labeled his laudanum "Poison," and kept open the option of using enough to commit suicide. But then he reproached himself:

> I am fast sinking into an opium-eating sot; but, please God, I will shake off the incubus yet before I die; for whatever differences of opinion may exist on the subject of suicide, there can be none as to "rushing into the presence of our Creator" in a state of drunkenness, whether produced by opium or brandy.[18]

Adams used none of these details, though he knew of them — the last quotation comes from the Garland biography he had open before him as he wrote. I do not understand how people can call Adams's book bitter or malicious. In the late picture Adams creates — of Randolph raving unregarded through the halls of Congress he had dominated in his shining youth — Don Quixote has turned into King Lear:

> During these last years Randolph was like a jockey, thrown early out of the race, who rides on, with antics and gesticulations, amid the jeers and wonder of the crowd, toward that winning-post which his old rivals have long since passed. He despised the gaping clowns who applauded him, even while he enjoyed amusing them. He despised himself, perhaps, more than all the rest. Not once or twice only, but day after day, and especially during his short senatorial term, he would take the floor, and, leaning or lolling against the railing which in the old Senate chamber surrounded the outer row of desks, he would talk two or three hours at a time, with no perceptible reference to the business in hand, while Mr. Calhoun sat like a statue in the vice-president's chair, until the senators one by one retired, leaving the Senate to adjourn without a quorum, a thing till then unknown to its courteous habits; and the gallery looked down with titters or open laughter at this exhibition of a half-insane, half-intoxicated man, talking a dreary monologue, broken at long intervals by passages beautiful in their construction, direct in their purpose, and not the less amusing from their occasional virulence. These long speeches, if speeches they could be called, were never reported. The reporters broke down in attempting to cope with the rapid utterance, the discursiveness and interminable length, the innumerable "Yes, sirs" and "No, sirs." Mr. Niles printed in his Register for 1826 one specimen verbatim report, merely to show why no more was attempted. In the same volume, Mr. Niles gave an account of a visit he made to the Senate

gallery on May 2, 1826, when Randolph was talking. Lolling against the rail, stopping occasionally to rest himself and think what next to talk about, he rambled on with careless ease in conversational tones, while the Senate chamber was nearly empty and the imperturbable Calhoun patiently listened from his throne. (194–95)

Aaron Burr

When John Morse asked Adams to write the biography of Randolph, Adams responded: "If I find Randolph easy, I don't know but what I will volunteer for Burr" (L 2.424). Adams was used to suggesting subjects to Morse and having them accepted. He had a special reason for wanting to do the Burr biography. He had uncovered a great deal of fresh evidence about Burr's conspiracy in his tour of the foreign archives, and like most researchers he did not like to sit on explosive new material. He could give a teasing foretaste of what was coming in the *History*. He told John Hay that the book would serve as an "outrider for my first two volumes of history" (L 2.488). He said, "I knew it would make a sensation" (L 2.513), and Hay, who read it, agreed, predicting it would make "a great popular success . . . very saleable."[19] Adams's wife, Clover, wrote her father: "I'm glad you like Henry's Randolph; the Burr is much better."[20]

But when Adams turned the manuscript in to Morse, he was told that Henry Houghton, the series publisher, would not print it in the "Statesmen" series because Burr was no statesman. Adams wrote Hay:

> Houghton declines to print Aaron Burr because Aaron wasn't a "statesman." Not bad, that, for a damned bookseller! He should live awhile at Washington and know our real statesmen. I am glad to get out of Houghton's hands. (L 2.475)

Adams was not mad at Morse but at Houghton, with whom he had already clashed when Houghton was publisher of the *North American Review* (L 2.224). Houghton, the model for the title character in William Dean Howells's *The Rise of Silas Lapham*, was not a man Adams would naturally respect. But his relations with Morse would continue friendly until his death. His response to the book's rejection did not interfere with their cooperation in assigning other volumes for the series.

> I want you to understand that my offer to write Burr was an offer to you, not to Houghton, to help you out in your editing. I should not choose Houghton for my publisher, and for many reasons prefer to publish in New

York or Philadelphia. So long as it looked like going back on you, I would not back out of my offer, but I confess, if you will release me, I shall be glad of it; and you have only to tell Houghton that I have withdrawn my offer. (L 2.472–73)

In 1930, twelve years after Adams's death, this passage was published in Worthington Ford's early edition of Adams's letters.[21] Morse, who was still alive at the time, read it and took offense, thinking it was a slur on him rather than on Houghton. He took his objection to the Massachusetts Historical Society, which he had been asked to address. There he claimed that what Adams was describing never happened. "I had never heard of any such undertaking by Mr. Adams."[22] The contemporary correspondence shows that memory had failed the old man, and his friction with Adams over this book was transferred to his skewed memory of another one, the *Randolph*. In 1882, Morse not only had heard of the Burr, but tried to get it into print with someone else after Houghton turned it down, prompting an offer from James Osgood, who had become the publisher of the *North American Review* (L 2.513). Adams, however, was considering a New York publisher (L 2.475). He did not follow up on this idea — perhaps because the book was conceived in a brief-lives format, and he could neither present it as a full-scale biography nor expand it without anticipating too much of his *History*. Hay regretted the lack of publication. "I want to read it once again before I die."[23]

It is a pity the book never appeared. Burr is the most uni-dimensional person in the *History*, perhaps because the detailing of his conspiracy takes up too much space for Adams to bring in the man's other aspects, as war hero, as organizer of the Republican party in New York, or as wit and charmer, things he would have had to advert to in the biography. He knew of Burr's genius for friendship from Gallatin's warm bond with him. He knew of Burr's charm from his grandmother's vivid memories of him. Louisa, like so many others, had been horrified at Burr's "murder" of Hamilton (something that would not upset Henry very much, given his view of Hamilton). But when she saw him presiding as vice president over the Senate, she could hardly connect his dignity with his infamy. From her place in the Senate gallery, she saw:

> Mr. Burr was vice president, and there has never been such a president of the Senate since his day. He presided with dignity yet with firm, urbane politeness. The force of manner was illustrated in this little man, for independent of his known gallantry with the ladies, he kept them [the senators]

under the most perfect and judicious control during the daily sessions at which they attend, and the little hammer in his graceful little hand would startle them into silence at the instant application.

Of Burr's farewell to the Senate, she wrote:

> On the third of March Mr. Burr took his leave of the Senate in a most elegant and even pathetic address, delivered in the most graceful and touching manner; and Mr. Adams, who has never liked him, came home quite affected by his manner, appearance, and sentiment.

She still did not want to be in the man's company, and was afraid she could not avoid it when told that Burr would depart from Washington in the same coach the Adamses were taking. She was relieved when he did not appear, but the reprieve was only temporary. In Baltimore, Burr boarded the packet boat with them:

> I was formally introduced to the vice president. He was a small man, quite handsome, his manners strikingly prepossessing, and in spite of myself I was pleased with him. He appeared to fascinate everyone on the boat, down to the lowest sailor, and knew everybody's history by the time we left. He was politely attentive to me, devoted to my sister. At table he assisted me to help the children, with so much ease and good nature that I was perfectly confounded. At about midnight we landed, and it was diverting to see Mr. Burr with my youngest child in his arms, a bundle in his hand, and I leaning on his other arm to walk from the wharf; yet it was done with so little parade, and with such entire good breeding, that it made one forget he was doing anything out of the way. He talked and laughed so that we were quite intimate by the time we got to Philadelphia where he called to see us. And this was the first and last occasion which I ever met the celebrated man.

If Adams had imported some of that firsthand experience of Burr into his biography, it would have rounded out the rather villainous presentation of him in the *History*. Apparently, he was too disappointed with the fate of his brief biography to import more of it into the third of his nine volumes than was necessary for tracing the complex conspiracy — and once that third volume appeared, bringing out the book that was supposed to be its forerunner must have seemed otiose. He destroyed it. But perhaps the exercise of writing it was worthwhile. If Hay and his wife were right about its "sensational" aspect, then he was moving even farther from the artlessness of the Gallatin to a compelling narrative strategy. The fruits would show up in the *History*.

PART TWO

❖

THE MAKING OF

A NATION

I. Jefferson's Two Terms

1

A PEOPLE'S HISTORY

The *History*, Volume One

ADAMS BEGINS the first volume of the *History* with six chapters describing the condition of the United States in 1800. The chapters anticipate a kind of history about to become fashionable, known as "people's history." In the nineteenth century, there was a shift of attention from aristocrats' lives to the condition of "ordinary folk." This led to "realist" novels, Wordsworthian poetry, *verismo* opera. It went with a focus on social conditions rather than on dynastic and military leaders — on the *Volk*, on national ethos, on racial type, on *Kulturgeschichte*, on economic conditions. A confluence of these concerns resulted in the first great success of the new style, John Richard Green's best-selling *Short History of the English People* (1875). This was followed in America by works of John Bach McMaster, John Fiske, and Edward Eggleston.[1] Adams, a friend of Green, was ahead of the curve in American reaction to the *Short History*'s great success. His survey of economic and cultural conditions for the centennial edition of the *North American Review* was in preparation while Green's work was appearing, and the first six chapters of his *History* had already been distributed to friends when McMaster published what is called the initial people's history on this side of the Atlantic (L 2.507).

The first chapters of Adams's *History* are often called an anticipation of twentieth-century efforts to write history from the bottom up rather than the top down. But they are separated from the rest of the *History*, which some call old history, especially old diplomatic history. The trouble with this, as has already been noticed, is that the six chapters are not viewed in conjunction with the four concluding chapters of the entire *History*. Adams means for the tension between these two "bookends" to be felt throughout, and he offers in the body of the *History* frequent pointers to the motion from the opening chapters to the concluding ones. But for the moment let me follow the bad custom of considering separately the first six chapters. Just how new were they, and why were they new? Like most new things, they had a close connection with older things — in Adams's case a lucky reliance on one of the key books he taught at Harvard as a proponent of the Teutonic school of history.

The Teutonists honored as their founding text the only work of an-thropological sociology to have survived from classical antiquity, *The Germans' Rise and Territory* (c. 98 C.E.) by Senator Cornelius Tacitus, a book commonly known as the *Germania*.[2] Describing a people basically different from his own, Tacitus collected everything he could find out about the Germans' religion, education, family conditions, and what in-fluence those conditions had on political and military affairs. He had certain Greek models for this, but those models are all lost (except for part of Herodotus' history).

> It is incomparably the fullest and most valuable monograph of its kind that has come down to us from antiquity. Thanks to it, we know more of the Germans of the first century A.D. than of any other people outside the Ro-man Empire and, indeed, of many within it.[3]

The Germanists looked to the book for its methodological procedures, teaching them to "probe the soul of a people."[4] But they also found in Tacitus a confirmation of their own substantive position, since the peo-ple he described possessed the traits they would attribute to the whole Germanic *Volk:* they were self-ruling, egalitarian, mystical yet practi-cal. The ancient Germans had a "forest mysticism" bound to delight nineteenth-century Wordsworthians — "they make holy the forests and groves, and give their mystery the names of gods visible only to their in-ner awe (*Germania* 9).

Naturally, Adams taught from this text in his Teutonic courses at Har-vard.[5] He clearly drew on it for his lecture about the primitive equality of women. According to Tacitus, men gave dowries to women they married (18). Equal living conditions made women have the same physical stat-ure as men (20). They married at the same age. And women, though not trained to fight, accompanied their men into battle to inspire them. Adams also found in Tacitus the "hundreds" as units of political life. The Germans elected their leaders — from ancient families for civil affairs, from the bravest for military affairs. "The leaders can settle trivial matters, but serious questions are decided by the whole community" (11). Adams was learning as he taught others how Tacitus could weave together geographic, economic, religious, military, and cultural factors to give an integrated sense of a community's identity. He was learning, that is, how to edit the centennial issue of the *North American Review*, and the opening and closing chapters of the *History*.

Of course, there were limits to the usefulness of Tacitus in Adams's survey of America in 1800. The study of foreign peoples, especially exotic ones, differs from the attempt to analyze one's own society in a scientific way. Adams's contemporaries had engaged in a kind of cultural anthropology when they described the morals and manners of distant peoples — Parkman describing American Indians' way of life, Prescott doing the same for the Incas and Aztecs. Motley and Irving treated the Catholicism of sixteenth-century Spain in much the same way. That kind of distant view taken by outsiders to the culture does, indeed, resemble Tacitus's work on the "primitive" Germans. But Adams sought to view his own society from the inside. Though he was looking back to the beginning of the century he lived in, what he saw had its living remnants around him as he spoke. He needed a closer model for this kind of study, and he found it in Thomas Babington Macaulay, a forerunner of the people's histories being written later in his century.

Macaulay

Macaulay wrote about his own nation and people, though he looked farther back than Adams would. From the first half of the nineteenth century, he described conditions at the end of the seventeenth century. This was accomplished in the famous third chapter of his *History of England*, "The State of England in 1685." Macaulay surprised and delighted his contemporaries by the vivid way he made their own past come alive for them. The book sold more copies worldwide than any work of history that had appeared to that point. Henry's brother Charles says that it was an epoch in the family's history when his father brought home Macaulay's first volume in the revised edition of 1848, when Charles was twelve. Charles derived from that event his own intellectual awakening, and the ten-year-old Henry, who still looked up to his older brother for guidance, clearly shared in the intellectual excitement. Henry generally spoke well of Macaulay, giving him and Sainte-Beuve as models of style (L 2.97) and taking his example when it came to including his own social history in the first volume of his work (L 3.161). His own Teutonism warned him off from Macaulay's Whig politics, but he saw all that he could learn from his predecessor's analysis of conditions in a single pivotal year.

Adams's description of 1800 resembles Macaulay's of 1685 down to such details as length, intention, range of sources, and order of presentation. The two surveys are of almost uniform size — Macaulay's 48,000 words filling 145 pages of the 1900 Houghton, Mifflin edition, and Adams's 47,000 words compressed into 117 of the more densely printed pages of the 1980 Library of America edition.[6] Both men found their work growing under their hand, so that Macaulay covers only four years in his five volumes, while Adams covers sixteen in his nine volumes.[7] Macaulay clearly intended to pair his chapter three with a contrasting description of England at the end of the great changes that came in with the Glorious Revolution — but he never reached the end proposed. Adams was able to accomplish what Macaulay only hoped to do, and his use of the paired descriptions had the same motive Macaulay was working from — to give a before-and-after picture of a society drastically changed in the course of the period chosen for study. Macaulay meant to show how liberty came to England, and Adams to show how nationhood came to America.

What set Macaulay apart at the time of his writing was his range up and down the social scale, using previously neglected sources such as newspapers, popular ballads, and fictional depictions of ordinary life. It was a hesitating early stride toward history from below. He was also strong on the material bases of national life — food supply, state of the currency, workers' wages, the economics of literary and other cultural production. In this he reflects the economic and sociological work done by the writers of the Scottish Enlightenment, and especially by David Hume. In fact, Hume was as much a source for him as the Greek ethnographers had been for Tacitus.

In the later parts of his *History of England,* Hume marked the end of each monarch's reign with what he called "a general survey of the age, so far as regards manners, finances, arms, commerce, arts and science."[8]

Though these surveys are briefer than Macaulay's would be, the elements of what Macaulay did are in Hume's book. Indeed, since Hume finished his work at the year 1688, and Macaulay began his at 1685, the end of the one overlapped the beginning of the other. Macaulay, it is true, was able to take advantage of newer disciplines — especially the statistics of William Petty's "political arithmetic," which were still being worked out in Hume's lifetime. Nonetheless, he draws some details as well as much inspiration from Hume. He had to ignore, of course, Hume's disparagement of the Whig myth that was taking shape already by the time Hume wrote — a myth that "proved destructive to the truth of history" (in Hume's words).[9]

Despite their differences, the two men handle some topics in nearly identical ways — such matters as national revenue, taxation, commerce, the militia, the navy, foreign relations, religion, literature, and science. Hume does not tell us much in the 1688 survey about social manners, but in earlier summary chapters he had broached these, marking for instance the first appearance of sedan chairs in England, and the abolition of bear baiting.[10] He also tells us: "The first mention of tea, coffee, and chocolate, is about 1660. Asparagus, artichokes, cauliflower, and a variety of salads were about the same time introduced into England."[11]

Both men agree on the licentiousness of literature under the Stuarts, and the important advances made by science — they are equally contemptuous of Dryden, and equally impressed by Newton. Hume attacks Dryden's "loose productions, the refuse of our language," and Macaulay his "swaggering licentiousness, at once inelegant and inhuman."[12] But Macaulay, not surprisingly, is more upset by Dryden's politics than by his prurience: "The spirit by which Dryden and several of his compeers were at this time animated against the Whigs deserves to be called fiendish."[13] For Hume, Newton is "the greatest and rarest genius that ever arose to be the ornament and instruction of the species," while Macaulay said, "In no other mind have the demonstrative faculty and the inductive faculty coexisted in such supreme excellence and perfect harmony."[14]

Since Macaulay meant to exhibit the happy developments following on the Revolution of 1688, his description of the time before those developments is a fairly dark one. Adams would, from a similar motive, portray the America of 1800 as backward and little fitted for the tasks it would be performing. For both men, the most important obstacle to progress was the sad state of transportation and communication. Macaulay says:

> Of all inventions, the alphabet and the printing press alone excepted, those inventions which abridge distance have done most for the civilization of our species. Every improvement of the means of locomotion benefits mankind morally and intellectually as well as materially, and not only facilitates the interchange of the various productions of nature and art, but tends to remove national and provincial antipathies, and to bind together all the branches of the great human family. In the seventeenth century, the inhabitants of London were, for almost every practical purpose, farther from Reading than they now are from Edinburgh, and farther from Edinburgh than they now are from Vienna.[15]

He accordingly castigates the shortsightedness of a government that would not provide highways, bridges, and canals — which, indeed, obliged the intervening rural areas to maintain roads between major cities, with the foreseeable result that they were not maintained.[16] He also notes that the possibility of steam travel had been suggested by the Marquis of Worcester's "fire waterwork," which was ignored by the academies of the time, as well as by governmental departments.[17]

Adams has an even harsher picture to draw, of canals not built (J 9–11), of steam engines of a more advanced kind being neglected (J 7–53), of roads so lacking that "between Baltimore and the new city of Washington, it [the road] meandered through forests" (J 11).

> In the southern states the difficulties and perils of travel were so great as to form a barrier almost insuperable. Even Virginia was no exception to this rule. At each interval of a few miles the horseman found himself stopped by a river liable to sudden freshets and rarely bridged. Jefferson, in his frequent journeys between Monticello and Washington, was happy to reach the end of the hundred miles without some vexatious delay. "Of eight rivers between here and Washington," he wrote to his attorney general in 1801, "five have neither bridges nor boats." (J 13)

Americans' reluctance to submit to any requisitions on their own money made them put up with the terrible costs of bad roads or no roads rather than submit to paying turnpikes (J 46).

But difficult as was north-south travel along the eastern coast, it was dwarfed by the problem of bridging the mountain chains that divided the mass of America's inhabitants, whose population center was near

Baltimore, from the one-fifth of the population that had crossed the mountains and looked to the Mississippi as its vent to the world. "Nowhere did eastern settlements touch the western. At least one hundred miles of mountainous country held the two regions everywhere apart" (J 6). For many years this distance would threaten the union of the states, and little had been done to close the gap.

One of the worst byproducts of slow transportation was the cost and delay involved in posting mail and dispatches, slowing the whole society's thinking process. In England, improvements in the post were fought by conservative keepers of the old methods.[18] In America, the mails of 1800 amounted to an average of one letter per year for "every grown inhabitant" (J 45).

Like Macaulay, Adams takes a geographic tour, over the slow roads of the time, of the major cities his book will treat.[19] Macaulay's trip reaches a climax in London:

> In the days of Charles the Second, the population of London was more than seventeen times the population of Bristol or of Norwich. It may be doubted whether any other instance can be mentioned of a great kingdom in which the first city was more than seven times as large as the second.[20]

Adams's swing through the cities, moving down from New England, peters out as he arrives at the less urban states of the South, where even the advantages of Charleston in South Carolina could not overcome the burden of a three-to-one ratio of slaves to citizens (J 17–30).

Macaulay presented the landed aristocracy as mired in the past — a trend for which there was no parallel in Adams's non-aristocratic world.[21] But both men claimed there was a falling off of religious devotion in their respective eras, and they attributed this to similar reasons — ill-educated or ill-supported clergy, and the survival of old forms without the infusion of fresh thinking. Macaulay found the established church still reeling from the Puritan Revolution, though he distinguished the better preachers of court and city from the poor and ignorant parsons of the countryside. Adams had a more variegated picture of religion to consider, with differences between northern Puritans and southern Anglicans, with Quakers and Catholics (among other sects) in the middle states. He finds decay most pronounced in the South, with the North moving in the same direction, while the middle states, with the least established religions, retained some of their reforming vigor. An impediment to religious learning, as to all learning, was the thin supply of books and libraries, deplored by each man.

Adams was well served by one of Macaulay's devices, the garnering of evidence from newspapers. In part this move was forced on Macaulay by the lack of access to official records, which meant that he had to puzzle out policy from the monarch's managed newspapers, the *Observator* and the *Gazette*.[22] Adams not only used the newspapers of America; he pored over the London journals of the past in the British Museum. Later in his narrative, he would show how naïve were Americans' expectations of a British response to their protests over trade and impressments. The London papers portrayed Jefferson and Madison as lackeys to Napoleon, stiffening British resistance to both presidents.

The great difference between Macaulay and Adams is that Macaulay came too early to profit by the archival revolution of the century. The idea of uniting documents in the Rolls Court and the Court of Records, and of making the new range of sources available to scholars, had just broken through old inhibitions when Macaulay completed his work. Macaulay was also unable to search American archives for trade policy and statistics. Adams, by contrast, could read governmental materials in England, France, and Spain, as well as in American sources. But he was only completing what Macaulay (and Hume) had begun.

From Multiplicity to Unity

Early in the twentieth century Adams presented his *Education* as a sequel to his book on medieval art, *Mont Saint Michel and Chartres*. He was charting a decline, from medieval unity to modern multiplicity, since he had come to believe in historical entropy, the fission of things no longer able to cohere. Those who go backward to the *History* from the *Education* look for some similar decline — from an age of Federalist statesmen, say, to the courting of separate clienteles, from the Revolution's impulse to the growth of partisan politics. In short, from Adams to Jefferson. But the *History* tells exactly the reverse of that story. It moves from a fragmented country, its regions out of touch with each other and stalled in tired traditions, to a nation pulling itself together in terms of geography, communication, technology, and common purpose. The end of the story is foreshadowed in chapter six of the first volume. But the completion of the changes is fully expressed only in the last four chapters of volume nine. He begins with this condition: "Each group of states

lived a life apart" (J 11).[23] Three such separate cultures are described —
in New England, in the middle states, and in the South.

1. *New England.* Adams argues that no region was more moribund in
1800 than the one he came from, dead at both its centers, Boston and
New Haven. Boston's strength in the past had been a strong and sincere
bond formed by a sense of religious mission and discipline. That had
given way to external observance and insincere profession. How does
one measure such a thing? Adams uses a number of tests, demographic,
legal, and literary. Harvard College, the great training ground of Boston's religious leaders, was producing fewer graduates in 1800 than in
the past, and of those graduates far fewer were going into the ministry
— down by about a half over the last half-century (55). Not as many
men, and those of lesser talent, felt that religious service was the highest
vocation. Religious books were no longer produced in the same number
or with the intellectual force manifested in the works of Jonathan Edwards or Samuel Hopkins (58). The authority of the clergy had not been
enough to sustain the ban on theaters, and even the laws against Sunday
travel were widely evaded and about to fall (64).

Leaders like Fisher Ames now upheld the church for its social usefulness, without showing any interest in its doctrinal authenticity. The
church could be used against political enemies, in particular the Jeffersonians, who were denounced as unbelievers. In fact, this instrumental
use of religion was at once the last source of strength for the establishment and a fatal sign of its weakness. Only religion could keep down, for
a time, the rising tide of Republicanism — but it did so by cheapening
and undermining itself:

> Nothing tended so directly to make respectability conservative, and con-
> servatism a fetish of respectability, as this union of bench and pulpit. The
> democrat had no caste; he was not respectable; he was a Jacobin — and no
> such character was admitted into a Federalist house. (57)

Adams's method for testing spiritual authenticity was used at just this
time for his novel *Esther*, in which the heroine, partly modeled on his
wife, Clover, sees through the pretensions of the minister who woos her.
His church is more a social gathering, his sermons more indulgent than
exigent, than what she conceives true belief would entail. Using his
north-south typology, with its general favoring of the southern alternative, Adams calls the New England Federalists "sons of granite and ice"
(61) who lacked the hearth of a genuine religion to thaw them out.

The college [Harvard] resembled a priesthood which had lost the secret of its mysteries, and patiently stood holding the flickering torch before cold altars, until God should vouchsafe a new dispensation of sunlight. (55)

Since "only the shell of orthodoxy was left" (63), the society desperately held on to other outer casements, already obsolete but not recognized as such — from its eighteenth-century styles of dress (64), of dance (no waltz, just minuets), and of poetry (Augustan formalism resisting Romantic innovation): "They strained prose through their sieves of versification" (70).

At the other center of New England thought, New Haven, Adams engages in a withering literary criticism of the poets called the Connecticut Wits, exempting only Joel Barlow because he had the sense later to become a Republican and to embrace science in the form of the steam engine. Barlow would eventually "patronize Fulton and employ Smirke, counsel Jefferson and contend with Napoleon" (72). Thus Adams, who is supposed to be the enemy of Jeffersonian Republicanism, finds that one of the few rays of light in New England is derived from just that quarter.

2. *The Middle States.* The two centers in this region were New York and Philadelphia. To emphasize the contrast between New England and these middle states, Adams used a striking but faulty analogy: in 1800, he claimed, New England was to New York and Pennsylvania as Scotland was to England. In the North, a rigid kirk and a conservative establishment, where even the disbelievers outwardly conformed. Southward, old landed families and urban sharpies in New York, quietly dissenting sects and secular improvement in Pennsylvania. But one should not treat Adams's parallels as anything more than a provocative opening hint, not to be followed into detail. The differences were at least as great as the similarities. The snoozy Harvard of Adams's description could not rank with the four Scottish universities still vibrating with the energies of the Scottish Enlightenment; and the Tories of England had far greater staying power than the patroons of the Hudson Valley.

But the contrast between the regions, whatever symbols one might use for it, was real. The Anglican establishment of New York was subsiding into irrelevance more precipitately than was Puritanism in Massachusetts. Some New Yorkers were reaching out of their own region, welcoming electoral alliance with the Jeffersonians. New York had already adopted and was perfecting the blatant electioneering that was still frowned on (though guiltily practiced) in Massachusetts and Virginia. Scientific studies, though inchoate, were going forward more rapidly in New York City than in Boston, with two distinguished men at the otherwise undermanned Columbia College (77–78). Family rivalries prompted innovations that would have been considered improper (if not immoral) in New England. Charming rogues had a clearer field in New York, as Aaron Burr and the nascent Tammany organization suggested (79–80). In this rough-and-tumble region the refinements of literature were coming, but had not yet arrived. Washington Irving, James Fenimore Cooper, William Cullen Bryant were still in their childhood or adolescence in 1800 (77).

The scene was far otherwise in Pennsylvania. It is the region Adams knew very well from his work on Gallatin's frontier experience on his farms and his later political life in Harrisburg and Philadelphia. Adams had stressed Gallatin's Virginia connections in his biography of the man, but in the *History* Gallatin exemplifies the strengths, the steadiness, the enlightenment of Pennsylvania. (Once again, those who think he was a defender of New England have simply not read him.)

> The only true democratic community then existing in the eastern states, Pennsylvania, was neither picturesque nor troublesome. The state contained no hierarchy like that of New England; no great families like those of New York; no oligarchy like the planters of Virginia and South Carolina . . . With twenty different religious creeds, its practice could not be narrow, and a strong Quaker element made it humane . . . They indulged in endless factiousness over offices, but they never attempted to govern [the nation], and after one brief experience they never rebelled. (80–81)

The "brief experience" referred to was the Whiskey Rebellion, expressive of unrest in the state but not of separation from the Union — which the South flirted with in 1798 and the North in 1804. Adams, with his hatred of the very idea of secession (a hatred instilled by the Civil War), praises Pennsylvania for its firm commitment to the nation.

> The value of Pennsylvania to the Union lay not so much in the democratic spirit of society as in the rapidity with which it turned to national objects. Partly for this reason the state made an insignificant figure in politics. As the nation grew, less and less was said in Pennsylvania of interests distinct from those of the Union. Too thoroughly democratic to fear democracy, and

too much nationalized to dread nationality, Pennsylvania became the ideal American state, easy, tolerant, and contented. (80)

Of course not all was sweetness and light in Pennsylvania, as Adams knew from his account of Gallatin's enemies there. The state had the liveliest (most libelous) press in the nation, beginning with William Cobbett's *Porcupine's Gazette*, and continuing with William Duane's *Aurora* and Joseph Dennie's *Portfolio*. The state also lagged in providing education, outside the religious schools of the different sects (89).

But humanitarian causes were a trademark of the state. It was famous for its anti-slavery societies, its experimental prison system, its homes for the treatment of the insane, its hospitals in a medical community whose standards had been raised by John Morgan, William Shippen, Caspar Wistar, Philip Syng Physick, and Benjamin Rush (88). Urban hygiene, lighting, and amenities had been developed from Franklin's pioneer work. The city's refinement was not inhibited by a Puritan fear of "luxury." It fostered a desirable commercial energy (81–82). In Pennsylvania, too, the American West was given its first authentic voice, in the *Modern Chivalry* of Hugh Henry Brackenridge (Gallatin's ally in trying to contain the Whiskey Rebellion). Adams contrasts this book's fresh and truly American style with the tired Augustan imitations of the Connecticut Wits (86–87). Pennsylvania also had the first American novelist of any stature, Charles Brockden Brown (85–86). The literary scene, with many minor figures, was described by the visiting British poet Tom Moore (84–85) — with whom Adams's grandmother Louisa had sung Moore's own songs in Washington.

Adams's vision of the future for America was foreshadowed in Pennsylvania — its pluralism and tolerance, its social mixture of great variety without extremes of class hierarchy, its encouragement of scientific, intellectual, and literary creativity, and especially its drive toward the West.

3. *The South.* Pennsylvania should by geography have been part of the Chesapeake Bay and Delaware Bay water systems.

Any part of Chesapeake Bay, or of the streams which flowed into it, was more easily accessible to Baltimore than any part of Massachusetts or Pennsylvania to New York. Every geographical reason argued that the Susquehanna, the Potomac, and the James should support one homogeneous people; yet the intellectual difference between Pennsylvania and Virginia was already more sharply marked than that between New England and the middle states. (91)

The difference had one clear cause: slavery. Traveler after traveler noted the shock of moving from an area of free farms and neat cities into fields where slovenly shacks were not tended by the owners of human property. This had struck Adams himself when he first traveled, when he was twelve, into slave territory:

> The railroad, about the size and character of a modern tram, rambles through unfenced fields and woods, or through village streets, among a haphazard variety of pigs, cows, and Negro babies, who might all have used the cabins for pens and styes, had the southern pig required styes, but who never showed a sign of care. This was the boy's impression of what slavery caused and, for him, was all it taught. (E 719)

Yet Adams admires the things that drew him toward the South — the rural simplicity, the courteous code of the owning class, the leisurely pace, the feebleness of open commercial ambition. He quotes the northern churchman William Ellery Channing on the superior manners of the South: *"They love money less than we do"* (92, emphasis in original). Adams pays generous tribute to the character and integrity of the leading men of Virginia — the incomparable George Washington, the astute John Marshall, the universally esteemed George Wythe, the "ideal republican" George Mason (with the "severe beauty" of his Virginia Bill of Rights), the work of Thomas Jefferson and James Madison for religious freedom (92–93). He has no such praise for any galaxy of New Englanders.

Yet this region, too, was backward at the time. Its celebration of "agrarian virtue" could be a cover for ignorance. The church was led by drunken priests, and the Anglican college (William and Mary) was a haven of idleness (94). This general lassitude resulted in a hypertrophy of the political intellect.

> Debarred from manufactures, possessed of no shipping, and enjoying no domestic market, Virginian energies necessarily knew no other resource than agriculture. Without church, university, schools, or literature in any form that required or fostered intellectual life, the Virginians concentrated their thought almost exclusively upon politics, and in this concentration produced a result so distinct and lasting, and in character so respectable,

that American history would lose no small part of its interest in losing the Virginia school. (95–96)

Washington and others knew that slavery was a burden, economic as well as moral (93), and hoped vaguely that something could someday bring it to an end; but the state (and every other southern state) was quick to resent and resist any outside pressure to change the whole infrastructure of southern life. The southern leaders who ratified the Constitution, over a stout resistance, were "influenced by pure patriotism as far as any political influence could be called pure," but the popular majority was still hostile to the Union, and certainly remained hostile to the exercise of its powers (96). It was this restive majority that Jefferson and Madison could count on in their appeal to resist the federal government in 1798, when Virginia moved further toward secession than Massachusetts would in 1804 (97–98). Washington's massive influence was constantly needed to keep his state in line with the Union.

Jefferson was clearly the leading thinker of Virginia, and Adams writes here the first in a series of character sketches of the man that will be a running feature of the *History*. Jefferson, he says, is a living contradiction — a democratic theorist with an aristocratic temperament, a cosmopolitan with a primary attachment to his own state ("my country"), a party organizer who was reclusive and shied from public performance.

> After all deductions on which his enemies might choose to insist, his character could not be denied elevation, versatility, breadth, insight, and delicacy; but neither as a politician nor as a political philosopher did he seem at ease in the atmosphere which surrounded him [the point grandmother Louisa had made in her diary] . . . During the last thirty years of his life he was not seen in a northern city, even during his presidency; nor indeed was he seen at all except on horseback, or by his friends and visitors in his own house. With manners apparently popular and informal, he led a life of his own, and allowed few persons to share it. His tastes were for that day excessively refined. His instincts were those of a liberal European nobleman like the Duc de Liancourt, and he built for himself at Monticello a chateau above contact with man. The rawness of political life was an incessant torture to him, and personal attacks made him keenly unhappy. His true delight was in an intellectual life of science and art. To read, write, speculate in new lines of thought, to keep abreast of the intellect of Europe, and to feed upon Homer and Horace, were pleasures more to his mind than any to be found in a public assembly . . . His writings often betrayed subtle

feelings for artistic form — a sure mark of intellectual sensuousness. He shrank from whatever was rough or coarse, and his yearning for sympathy was almost feminine. That such a man should have ventured upon the stormy ocean of politics was surprising, the more because he was no orator, and owed nothing to any magnetic influence of voice or person. Never effective in debate, for seventeen years before his presidency he had not appeared in a legislative body except in the chair of the Senate. (99–100)

These very contradictions would open the way to progress under Jefferson. The Federalists were consistent, and imprisoned in their consistency. Jefferson, by contrast, was a localist in theory, the leader of resistance to the Union in 1798, but a cosmopolitan by inclination. Conservative and cramped in his views on what government could do, he was "prone to innovation" and grand projects that only government could advance.

His mind shared little in common with the provincialism on which the Virginia and Kentucky Resolutions were founded. His instincts led him to widen rather than to narrow the bounds of every intellectual exercise; and if vested with political authority, he could no more resist the temptation to stretch his powers than he could abstain from using his mind on any subject merely because he might be drawn upon ground supposed to be dangerous . . . He wished to begin a new era . . . He set himself to the task of governing with this golden age in view. (100–101)

Adams has so far chosen two states as typical from each of his three regions, showing some division within the regions. But nowhere was the division more marked than in the South. In New England, Connecticut proved even more doctrinaire and self-righteous than Boston. In the middle states, New York combined extremes of Dutch stiffness and Tammany earthiness, setting it off from the more civilized Pennsylvania. But the greatest gap within a region set the Deep South off from the upper South. Virginians were rural, expansive, generous, idle, and they could take religion or leave it alone. But South Carolinians — or at least Charlestonians — were disciplined, hardworking, urbane, and pious. They had prominent families — the Middletons, Pinckneys, Rutledges, and Loundeses — that affected English manners but voted with the Francophile Jefferson. In 1800 the leading South Carolinian of the future, John C. Calhoun, was eighteen and still getting the education that would make him alternate radicalisms, theoretical and practical — the populist and the anti-democrat.

Adams said that Charleston seemed to be poised in 1800 to become the first city of the South, or even of the East. Virginia's soil had been depleted by crop after crop of mineral-leaching tobacco; but the cotton harvests of South Carolina were already supplying the mills of Liverpool.

> The exports of South Carolina were nearly equal to those of Massachusetts or Pennsylvania; the imports were equally large. Charleston might reasonably expect to rival Boston, New York, Philadelphia, and Baltimore . . . Neither Boston nor Baltimore saw about them a vaster region to supply, or so profitable a staple to export . . . Not even New York seemed more clearly marked for prosperity than this solitary southern city, which already possessed banking capital in abundance, intelligence, enterprise, the traditions of high culture and aristocratic ambition, all supported by slave labor, which could be indefinitely increased by the African slave trade. (28–29)

Yet it was the slave system that made South Carolinians stubbornly defy the world, with a romantic rigidity that Calhoun would embody. North Carolina was caught somewhere between these poles.

> Neither aristocratic like Virginia and South Carolina, nor turbulent like Georgia, not troubled by a sense of social importance, but above all thoroughly democratic, North Carolina tolerated more freedom of political action and showed less family and social influence, fewer vested rights in political power, and less tyranny of slaveholding interests and terrors, than were common elsewhere in the South. Neither cultivated nor brilliant in intellect, not great in thought, industry, energy, or organization, North Carolina was still interesting and respectable. The best qualities of the state were typified in its favorite representative, Nathaniel Macon. (102)

The picture of America in 1800 is indeed "dreary," as Hofstadter said. But in the final chapter of this opening section Adams points to the future with hope. If America could learn little from its institutions, neither was it bound down by them. It did not have the oppressive legacies of Europe — the stratified classes, the feudal hierarchies, the absolutism of church and monarch. America was conservative in 1800, but not as the Old World was: "In Europe, the conservative habit of mind was fortified behind power" (1190). All America needed in 1800 was a call to become itself.

> American society might be both sober and sad, but except for Negro slavery it was sound and healthy in every part. Stripped for the hardest work, every muscle firm and elastic, every ounce of brain ready for use, and not a trace

of superfluous flesh on his nervous and supple body, the American stood in the world a new order of man. Compared with its lithe young figure, Europe was actually in decrepitude. Mere class distinctions, the *patois* or dialect of the peasantry, the fixity of residence, the local costumes and habits marking a history that lost itself in the renewal of identical generations, raised from birth barriers which paralyzed half the population. Upon this mass of inert matter rested the church and state, holding down activity of thought. (1109)

What this "new order of man" needed was a new kind of leadership — not the plump and gaitered figure of a John Adams, but the lean visionary whose inauguration is the subject of Adams's very next chapter.

2

———◼◆◼———

JEFFERSON'S SUCCESS

The *History*, Volume One

DAMS BEGINS his narrative proper, at chapter seven of volume one, with the inauguration of Jefferson in March of 1801. Though Adams has just described the conditions of 1800, he does not cover the heated election of that year — or its aftermath in the early months of 1801, when the House narrowly broke the electoral tie between Jefferson and Burr. He gives Jefferson, as it were, a clean slate to write on. One reason is that he means to articulate the political calendar with inaugurations, sessions of Congress, annual addresses to Congress, and elections. He had already used one such unit in his two articles on "The Session," punctuating the year by its congressional gatherings. The model for this framework was Thucydides (5.20), who divided his history by military seasons — Adams was carefully reading Thucydides at this time (L 2.464, 469), and he meant to mark time by political seasons.

Though Adams does not bring up the rancors of the election that preceded Jefferson's inauguration, he sees in the men at the center of that ceremony the promise of future conflict:

> Thus when the doors of the Senate chamber were thrown open and the new president of the United States appeared on the threshold; when the vice president rose from the chair, and Jefferson sat down in it, with Aaron Burr on his right hand and John Marshall on his left, the assembled senators looked up at three men who profoundly disliked and distrusted each other. (133)

Given such potential for conflict, Jefferson did what any good politician would, trying to assuage misgivings and offer a hand of reconciliation.

Inaugural Address

In his justly famous speech (inaudibly delivered) Jefferson said that the turmoil of the past had been resolved: "We are all Republicans, we are all Federalists" (136). It would be hard to justify that as a piece of political analysis. "A revolution had taken place, but the new president seemed anxious to prove that there had been no revolution at all" (141). Actually, "in representing that he was in any sense a Federalist, he did himself a wrong" (136). Yet this was a shrewd thing to assert, casting those who would continue conflict as outside the new consensus. In other words, it was good politics for Jefferson to say that, but did he really believe it?

Adams argues that he did. Because of Jefferson's general belief in the goodness of men, he thought Federalist followers had good hearts — they had simply been deceived by scheming leaders. Now that those leaders were repudiated, "we shall completely consolidate the nation in a short time" (211). Less than a year after his inauguration, he wrote: "I am satisfied that within one year from this time, were an election to take place between two candidates merely Republican and Federal, where no personal opposition existed against either, the Federal candidate would not get the vote of a single elector in the United States" (209). "The candid Federalists acknowledge that their party can never more raise its head" (240). It was a strength of Jefferson that he could support a position marked for its utility by holding it with a robust sincerity.

But that paradox leads to another, that optimism should itself breed suspicion. The optimist, who thinks that all things will turn out well, has to resort to conspiracy theories when they do not. Some evil force must be interrupting the natural course of events.

> The inveteracy of their quondam leaders has been able to check the effect in some small degree until they shall be exposed . . . They are marked, like the Jews, with such a perversity of character as to constitute, from that circumstance, the natural divisions of our parties. (210)

He is attacking, here, the northern "priests" who called him an infidel:

> From the clergy I expect no mercy. They crucified their Savior, who preached that their kingdom was not of this world, and all who practise on

that precept must expect the extreme of their wrath . . . I wish nothing but their eternal hatred. (214, 217)

Adams recognizes that Jefferson believed in both his bright expectations and his dark premonitions.

> In any other man such contradictions would have argued dishonesty. In Jefferson they prove only that he took New England to be like Virginia — ruled by a petty oligarchy which had no sympathies with the people and whose artificial power, once broken, would vanish like that of the Virginia church . . . When he said that all were Republicans and all Federalists, he meant that the churches and prejudices of New England were, in his opinion, already so much weakened as not to be taken into account. (218)

But Jefferson was also saying that he would call off his own side's animosity in the clash between Anglophile Federalists and Francophile Republicans. He attributed that conflict to the French Revolution, which had receded from importance, taking with it the passions it aroused (including his own):

> During the throes and convulsions of the ancient world, during the agonizing spasm of infuriated man, seeking through blood and slaughter his long-lost liberty, it was not wonderful that the agitation of the billows should reach even this distant and peaceful shore; that this should be more felt and feared by some than by others; that this should divide opinions as to measures of safety. But every difference of opinion is not a difference of principle. (136)

That Jefferson was sincere in wanting to call off ideological partnerships with other countries he proved by his early acts as president. He sent a special message to Talleyrand, the French foreign minister, to say: "As to the government of France, we know too little of the state of things there to understand what it is, and have no inclination to meddle in their settlement. Whatever government they establish, we wish to be well with it" (278). And he invited the Federalists to give up their engagement in the wars of England with France. As Adams concludes from Jefferson's correspondence: "Convinced that the quarrels of America with France had been artificially created by the monarchical Federalists, he believed that a policy of open confidence would prevent such dangers in the future" (272). In this spirit, Jefferson coined the second most famous phrase in his inaugural speech, renouncing "entangling alliances" (138) — a phrase often attributed to Washington's Farewell Address, but in fact first used here. The renunciation of such alliances was wise if it could be maintained, since the United States was encircled by foreign powers — England in Canada, Spain in Louisiana and the Floridas, France along with others in the Caribbean and the Indian territories. How did Jefferson mean to fend off these challenges from all sides? By force? One passage seemed to hint at that:

> Would the honest patriot, in the full tide of successful experiment, abandon a government which has so far kept us free and firm, on the theoretical and visionary fear that the government, the world's best hope, may by possibility want energy to preserve itself? I trust not. I believe this, on the contrary, the strongest government on earth. (136)

That passage, Adams says, wants considering:

> Clearly Jefferson credited government with the strength which belonged to society; and if he meant to practice upon this idea, by taking the tone of "the strongest government on earth" in the face of Bonaparte and Pitt, whose governments were strong in a different sense, he might properly have developed this idea at more length, for it was likely to prove deeply interesting. (137)

But Jefferson had a new concept of power, which was largely the power to ignore threats away. If the government would only deprive itself of the means of aggression, it would have no need for instruments of defense. He had put it this way in the preceding year:

> Only let our affairs be disentangled from those of all other nations, except as to commerce, which the merchants will manage the better the more they are left free to manage for themselves, and our general government may be reduced to a very simple organization, and a very unexpensive one. (145)

To avoid "entanglement," he meant to recall all foreign ministries but three, to put the entire navy in drydock, and to reduce the army to a peacekeeping force on the frontiers. Adams grants that this was, indeed, "a new experiment in government" (141). The nine volumes opened here will trace its working out.

Jefferson's first task was to assemble his cabinet — a process that had fascinated Adams ever since he watched in dismay as President Grant assembled his government, and a process he had just described in his novel *Democracy*. John Adams's cabinet had been divided and disloyal. Jefferson wanted unity and cooperation, and would by and large get it. He had to act rapidly if he hoped to get confirmation for any nominees before the Senate adjourned. President Adams had kept the Senate in emergency session after the House resolved the election dispute in February, so that Jefferson would have an opportunity to use it for appointments if he wanted to. Gallatin thought this was a trap, since the outgoing (Sixth) Congress still had a Federalist majority, and could cause trouble if Jefferson put himself at its mercy for confirmation of his nominees. But George Washington had done the same thing for Adams, at their transition, and in fact the outgoing Senate quickly confirmed the three men Jefferson submitted to it — James Madison for secretary of state, Henry Dearborn for secretary of war, and Levi Lincoln for attorney general.

The list was short, at this stage, because Jefferson could not submit one name and he did not want to submit another. He could submit no name for the post of secretary of the navy, since several men had already turned it down — it was clear to them that Jefferson disliked the navy. The new president did not want to submit the name of Gallatin for secretary of the treasury, since he was not sure this Senate would confirm him. Gallatin's opponents alleged a problem with his foreign birth, but Federalists actually resented his dogged opposition to Hamilton when Gallatin was in the House of Representatives and Hamilton was secretary of the treasury. After the Senate adjourned, Jefferson gave Gallatin a recess appointment, confident that the new Senate, with its Republican majority, would confirm him — especially since he would be the acting secretary for almost nine months before the Seventh Congress (in that leisurely time of legislation) convened.

Patronage

Jefferson's inaugural address had called for starving government back into its proper insignificance. That program must have seemed a simple thing to accomplish in 1801, since Congress would not return until December, and Supreme Court sessions would be suspended by act of Congress for the whole of his second year in office. The executive was the only game in town, and he controlled that. But he was drawn into a series of acts he had not wanted or foreseen, as the price of forging a national party. It was part of his republican ideology that filling "places" with executive appointees was the cause of constitutional corruption. That is what had been said of royal patronage in England and of the power of colonial governors to name officials before the Revolution.[1]

Madison warned in 1789 that a president's "wanton removal of meritorious officers would subject him to impeachment and removal from his own high trust" (452). At first, accordingly, Jefferson said he would not remove many officers, "probably not twenty" (152).

But pragmatic new recruits to Republicanism in New York, Connecticut, and Pennsylvania had little patience with country ideology, "agrarian virtue," or individual honor. There was a clamor for rewards, especially where the Republicans were making inroads into Federalist strongholds. Gideon Granger (soon to be chosen postmaster general) and Levi Lincoln (newly appointed attorney general) wanted rewards to be distributed to challengers of the religious establishment in Connecticut. George Clinton and his rival Aaron Burr were fighting each other for dispensing favors in New York. Governor McKean and the newspaper editor William Duane had their own lists for Pennsylvania. Jefferson began to back off from his first assurance that removals would be few, gradual, and only for incompetence or "malfeasance," not for party views.

The problem with that first position, that only incompetence or malfeasance was cause for removal, is that it made each dismissal an assault on the character of the man losing his job — he was, by Jefferson's professed standard, either unable or unwilling to give faithful service. When Jefferson, yielding to the demands of Gideon Granger and Levi Lincoln, removed Elizur Goodrich from the lucrative post of collector to the port of New Haven, the body of Connecticut merchants protested that the man was neither incompetent nor malfeasant — so how could he be fired? Jefferson had to spell out a new set of rules in his public answer to the merchants, saying that equity demanded a restoration of balance between Republicans and Federalists, after the Federalists had monopolized appointments. But he would only make substitutions until Republicans filled half the total number of posts (153). He would soon be changing that number to two-thirds of the positions for Republicans, reflecting what he said was their majority in the nation. So now, contrary to the first criteria he announced, he was appointing according to party views. Dumas Malone does not hide the fact that Jefferson soon came to know the real importance of patronage as a weapon against the Federalists: "He wanted to destroy them politically" (DM 4.74).

Gallatin, with the vast patronage of his department, had taken Jefferson's first (purist) stance as his own. He drew up a statement of policy that rejected any ideological test in hiring and firing. Jefferson persuaded him not to issue the statement until such time as certain party demands had been satisfied — a time that never came. Jefferson had not realized that his victory, as the first one for an organized party at the presidential level, would bring unexpected demands for party payoffs. "He could not follow his true instincts; for the pressure upon him, although trifling when compared with what he thus helped to bring on his successors, was more than he could bear" (159). Gallatin, however, continued to act on the principles of his unissued policy statement, as did Madison (160).

William Duane, the powerful editor of the Philadelphia *Aurora*, was angered when his pressure for the appointment of friends was resisted by Madison and Gallatin. The irritable Duane, who rarely forgot and never forgave, began a long campaign of criticism against the two cabinet officers, a campaign that paid off when Madison, after his election as president, was prevented from making Gallatin his secretary of state — Duane had sown too much resentment and distrust of Gallatin for him to be in a position to deal with other nations. Madison had to keep Gallatin at Treasury, where he would not need Senate confirmation for an office he already held. Gallatin described the situation: "Duane, intoxicated by the persuasion that he alone had overthrown Federalism, thought himself neither sufficiently rewarded nor respected; and possessed of an engine which gives him an irresistible control over public opinion, he easily gained the victory for his friends" (432).

Here Jefferson faced another of the requirements for a national party. He had to keep Pennsylvania on his side — which meant that he kept buttering Duane while the latter kept battering Gallatin (and, to a lesser degree, Madison): "His [Jefferson's] political strength depended on the popular vote [in Pennsylvania], which followed Duane and [his ally Michael] Leib . . . At length he temporized, became neutral, and left Gallatin and [his ally Alexander] Dallas to their own resources" (434).[2] Duane constantly boasted that he was voicing Jefferson's views, and Jefferson would not contradict him: "He was forced to endure Duane's attachment, and to feel that Madison and Gallatin were sacrificed to his own safety" (436).

The most venomous patronage war was fought not where Republicans were replacing Federalists, but in New York, where rival Republican factions — those of Governor Clinton and of Vice President Burr — were competing to be the conduit of party influence. Burr seemed to have the right of greater contribution to the party's success. By skillfully choosing candidates for the state assembly, which would choose New York's presidential electors, he gave Jefferson the twelve votes that made him president. But Burr alienated Jeffersonians during the runoff in the House of Representatives, and Clinton used that fact to muscle Burr aside for New York appointments. This was another patronage battle that scarred Gallatin, as Burr's longtime friend.

Gallatin, while continuing his opposition to patronage, argued that if appointments *had* to be made to Republicans in New York, they should go to supporters of Burr, who was less selfish than the Clintons or Livingstons (156). The ostracism of Burr at this point led indirectly to his duel with Hamilton and his schemes in the West, all of which had thus been influenced by the patronage battles of Jefferson's early days in office. This was a process Adams would have described in more detail in his biography of Burr, from which the following powerful passage in the *History* may survive:

> Never in the history of the United States did so powerful a combination of rival politicians unite to break down a single man as that which arrayed itself against Burr; for as the hostile circle gathered about him, he could plainly see not only Jefferson, Madison, and the whole Virginia legion, with Duane and his *Aurora* at their heels; not only De Witt Clinton and his whole family interest, with Cheetham and his *Watchtower* by their side; but — strangest of companions — Alexander Hamilton himself joining hands with his own bitterest enemies to complete the ring. (226)

Making a national party was Jefferson's first step toward making a nation; and to make a party you must break some eggs. As became the custom when Jefferson overruled Gallatin, the president ignored his appeals.

While Jefferson was nationalizing politics by patronage, he planned to get rid of Hamilton's nationalizing instrument, the public debt. During these early days of an empty Washington, Gallatin drew up elaborate plans for a "sinking fund" to eliminate the debt. His task was made difficult by the fact that Jefferson forswore all excise taxes. It is true that Gallatin had opposed Hamilton's excise on grain alcohol, which sparked the Whiskey Rebellion; but total elimination of taxes would make customs duties the sole source of government income. This meant that the Virginians would be tied to, and would have to support, things they distrusted — commerce and trade, with its corollaries of interest and banking. So, by a roundabout circle, the de-nationalizing fiscal policy promoted a nationalizing trade structure.

The anomalies in this situation would soon reveal themselves, when Jefferson had to protect American trade from the tribute demands of Tripoli. The navy he meant to put in drydock had to be sent off to battle, and a new generation of commodores was created for war purposes (they would come into their own during the War of 1812). To keep financing the war, Gallatin was forced by 1803 to create a new layer of duties known as the Mediterranean Fund. A government dependent on duties had to collect extra duties in order to maintain its first stake in them. Once again, Jefferson was forced into a nationalizing act. "No reproach henceforward roused more ill temper among Republicans than the common charge that their elaborate financial precautions and formalities were a deception, and that the Mediterranean Fund was meant to conceal a change of principle and a return to Federalist practices" (397).

"Midnight Judges"

Jefferson feared that his "second revolution" could not be completed so long as Federalists were entrenched in the judiciary branch of the government, where they could wage war on the popular branches that had been won by the Republicans. "They have retired into the Judiciary as a stronghold. There the remains of Federalism are to be preserved and fed from the treasury; and from that battery all the works of Republicanism are to be beaten down and erased" (175). He was especially incensed that Congress had created a new system of district courts, which President Adams filled with judges of his preference before leaving office. These "midnight appointees" must go, though the Constitution put obstacles in the way. Judges could not have their pay reduced during the term — and Jefferson was about to reduce the new judges' pay to zero, by dismissing them. More important, judges could be removed only by impeachment for high crimes and misdemeanors. These judges had not had time to commit even low crimes.

Adams argues that Jefferson should have called for a constitutional amendment to make judges recallable by joint action of the other two branches. That would have expressed his real concept of democracy, and he had a Congress willing to work with him in radical ways. "A word from Jefferson would have decided the action of his party" (176). Some of the Republicans, like William Branch Giles, were more intent on smashing the judiciary than Jefferson himself was. But Adams is being unrealistic here. The amendment process could be drawn out, as it went to the states, and it might fail. If the process were prolonged, the judges would have time to make rulings that must be upheld. They would be part of the system. Jefferson saw that they must be killed at once or not at all.

So he resorted to subterfuge. Shouldering aside the constitutional questions, he presented the elimination of the district courts as part of his plan for government economy. The courts were too expensive, filled no need, and would be a senseless drain on the Treasury (175). He submitted documents to support these claims that supporters like Dumas Malone call misleading (DM 4.120–21). John Randolph, while voting for the cancellation, admitted that the financial argument was "paltry" (201). In fact, the courts were needed.[3] Malone himself writes that they "corrected genuine defects in the organization of the federal judicial system which many responsible leaders had recognized for years" (DM 4.113). Some of Jefferson's future troubles would come from the way he eliminated these courts. Jefferson prevailed, but he gave ammunition to those who considered him devious.

Foreign Affairs

Jefferson initially meant to disengage his country from the world, closing diplomatic missions, leaving commerce to the merchants, putting the navy in storage. He told the French minister Louis-André Pichon, "I have ever considered diplomacy as the pest of the peace of the world" (DM 4.386). That may be why he did not consider it a drawback to appoint, in Madison, a secretary of state who had never been out of the country. Gallatin, of course, had grown up in Europe, but his Swiss background and French accent made some in Congress distrust him, so Jefferson had to be careful about using him to speak on foreign policy. That left Jefferson as the only professional diplomat on the team — he had been minister to France and secretary of state.

But his own record in this area was uneven. He had been carried away in France by the early stages of the Revolution. As secretary of state he had been naïve in his initial support of Citizen Genêt and had protested the neutrality policy he now embraced. Of the men in the triumvirate, he was the least "diplomatic" in the common usage — the least careful and conciliatory in his speech. He was the one who said he would "reduce Toussaint to starvation" (DM 4.252) or would "marry the British fleet" (277) or would "throw away the scabbard" against France (DM 4.292), leaving Madison to tone down his extravagances — what Malone calls his "diplomatic indiscretions" (DM 4.255) and Adams calls his "flighty talk" (904) — while Gallatin removed from Jefferson's annual messages things like attacks on commerce.[4]

Jefferson and his coadjutors were certainly intelligent and able. But Adams, more than most American historians, realizes that they were up against an extraordinary set of opponents — men like Napoleon and Talleyrand in France, Canning and Pitt in England, and Manuel Godoy ("the Prince of Peace") in Spain. These were wily, experienced, ruthless adversaries, and they had Europe in their bones. They knew each other, distrusted each other, outmaneuvered each other — and for the highest stakes. The American triumvirate stumbled into one of the most dramatically charged and fateful periods of international conflict, a clash of giants. As Hamlet says (5.2.60–62):

> 'Tis dangerous when the baser nature comes
> Between the pass and fell incensed points
> Of mighty opposites.

The wonder is that they walked through the diplomatic killing grounds relatively unscathed. Shakespeare is again relevant, this time from *Julius Caesar* (4.3.67–69):

> For I am arm'd so strong in honesty
> That they pass by me as the idle wind,
> Which I respect not.

Only because the United States did not suffer the disaster it seemed to deserve could Adams treat the whole drama with a constant play of humor, irony, and satire. The story called, as he said, for the light touch of a Beaumarchais. The European principals were so busy undoing each other that the Jeffersonians kept benefiting from transactions they were barely aware of. They wandered, like Little Nemo, through a surreal landscape, magically unscathed.

Madison knew neither France nor England; but his opponent, Talleyrand, knew England and America. He visited both countries in 1794, during a period when he was out of favor at home, and he took the measure of both countries' politics. In America, for instance, he sized up one of the men he met by saying, "Hamilton has intuited (*avait diviné*) Europe" (238). Madison neither knew nor intuited Europe. Adams puts the whole comedy in one of his characteristically cumulative sentences, one that drops abruptly into bathos at the end. He is describing Napoleon:

> Ambition that ground its heel into every obstacle, restlessness that often defied common sense; selfishness that eat [ate] like a cancer into his reasoning faculties; energy such as had never before been combined with equal genius and resources; ignorance that would have amused a schoolboy; and a moral sense which regarded truth and falsehood as equally useful modes of expression — an unprovoked war or secret assassination as equally natural forms of activity — such a combination of qualities as Europe had forgotten since the Middle Ages, and could realize only by reviving the Eccelinos and Alaberics of the thirteenth century, had to be faced and overawed by the gentle optimism of President Jefferson and his Secretary of State. (227)

By reference to the long European history of perfidy, Adams makes this sentence re-enact in little one of his friend Henry James's novels on American innocence exposed to the depths of European experience. Adams makes even the structure of his sentence a mystery, in order to convey a mystery. A grim list of traits must be dealt with — but how? The scale of the challenge appears not only in the introductory piling up of lurid qualities but in the suspense of not knowing how this list will fit into the sentence. Finally, the long catalogue of challenges comes up against its countering agent. It is faced by — "gentle optimism." The sentence shows by its movement the descent of a fearsome lion on innocent victims.

It was bad enough having to deal with Napoleon. But he had to be approached through Talleyrand, a Minotaur to guard the labyrinth:

> If Talleyrand was an enigma to be understood only by those who lived in his confidence, Bonaparte was a freak of nature such as the world had seen too rarely to comprehend. His character was misconceived even by Talleyrand at this early period; and where the keenest of observers failed to see through a mind he had helped to form, how were men like Jefferson and Madison, three thousand miles away, and receiving at best only such information as Chancellor Livingston could collect and send them every month or six weeks — how were they, in their isolation and ignorance, to solve a riddle that depended on the influence which Talleyrand could main-

tain over Bonaparte, and the despotism which Bonaparte could establish over Talleyrand? (228)

Talleyrand's tactics he described himself: "To announce too much of what one means to do is the way not to do it at all" (238), a sentence that is itself all simple surface over depths.

Talleyrand had designs on the American hemisphere, linked with his master's designs on England. Talleyrand had decided, while visiting America, that the English language, traits, religion, and commerce were too strong in the United States for it to be trusted in any conflict France might have with England. He would prevent the Anglophone nations joining hands by placing a menace in the rear of America, tugging the nation off from Britain to protect the Mississippi. This meant getting back the Louisiana Territory west of the Mississippi, which France had ceded to Spain in the Treaty of Paris at the end of the Seven Years War. Talleyrand had argued in 1798 that Spain should cede back (retrocede) the previously French holdings, since Spain was too overextended to protect that territory from an aggressive United States. He sent this message to King Carlos IV in Madrid:

> There are no other means of putting an end to the ambition of the Americans than that of shutting them up within the limits which Nature seems to have traced for them; but Spain is not in a condition to do this great work alone. She cannot, therefore, hasten too quickly to engage the aid of a preponderating Power, yielding to it a small part of her immense domains in order to preserve the rest . . . Let the Court of Madrid cede these districts [Louisiana and the Floridas] to France, and from that moment the power of America is bounded by the limit which it may suit the interests and the tranquility of France and Spain to assign her. The French Republic, mistress of these two provinces, will be a wall of brass forever impenetrable to the combined efforts of England and America. (241)

France had already made such a proposal to Spain in 1795, when the Directorate was in power; but the shrewd Spanish foreign minister, Manuel Godoy, beat it aside. When Talleyrand renewed it in 1798, Godoy was temporarily out of favor, and Talleyrand did not realize that he too would be ousted from his position in 1799. In 1800, however, he assisted Napoleon in the coup of 18th Brumaire. Back in power under Bonaparte as First Consul, Talleyrand was sure he could get Louisiana this time. He also renewed the bribe earlier offered to Queen Luisa of

Spain — a Tuscan kingdom for her beloved daughter (along with her husband).

The authorities in Washington knew nothing of this secret plot against them. They were convinced that France was showing great friendliness to America. John Adams had, in the last year of his presidency, sent negotiators to end the Quasi War with France in the Caribbean. When France signed the Treaty of Morfontaine in September, 1800, it seemed that Jefferson would reap the benefits of Adams's initiative, which had cost him some of his Federalist support and therefore the presidency. The Quasi War had ended before Jefferson took office; John Adams's treaty was being ratified by the Senate while the House decided between Jefferson and Burr; Napoleon returned his ratification of the Treaty of Morfontaine during Jefferson's first summer as president. The international situation looked almost comatosely sunny from American shores.

But during this deceptively peaceful-looking interval, a parallel and polar-opposite treaty process was going on in secret. The Treaty of Morfontaine was signed on September 30.

> The next day, October 1, Berthier signed at San Ildefonso the treaty of retrocession [of Louisiana to France], which was equivalent to a rupture of the relations established four-and-twenty hours earlier. Talleyrand was aware that one of these treaties undid the work of the other. The secrecy in which he enveloped the treaty of retrocession, and the pertinacity with which he denied its existence, showed his belief that Bonaparte had won a double diplomatic triumph over the United States. (25)

There, as traced in detail by Adams, we have the plot against the United States that was outside Jefferson's awareness or control. And if he were not to control it, who or what would?

Napoleon was thwarted, primarily, by two men — Manuel Godoy and Toussaint Louverture. Godoy was recalled to power by King Carlos IV to oversee the implementation of the secret accord on Louisiana. The King feared that Napoleon would not get the assurances from other powers that would make the Spanish kingdom in Tuscany an international reality (269). Napoleon, meanwhile, since the process was being prolonged, tried to get new concessions for himself while granting some to Carlos. He wanted the Floridas to be thrown in along with Louisiana (270). Godoy brought the English into the secret, alerting them that Jamaica would not be safe if Napoleon held the Floridas (272). Godoy could now innocently act as if *he* were willing to give away the Floridas, while telling Talleyrand that *England* would not let him do it.

Napoleon made the mistake of sending his brother Lucien, venal and vainglorious, to deal with Godoy, a virtuoso of flattery and bribes. "Supple and tenacious as any Corsican," says Adams, "Godoy was well suited to deal with Lucien. He was more subtle, and not less corrupt" (251–52). The stalling tactics of Godoy led to an important further concession by Napoleon: Talleyrand promised that if Spain retroceded Louisiana, France would never alienate it to a third country (269). Spain, of course, worried that this prize property would somehow end up in American hands — though Talleyrand had said the whole point of the retrocession was to deny westward expansion to the United States. Godoy delayed any agreement on Florida for a year, while Napoleon tried to satisfy Carlos that he was making good his side of the bargain. Godoy thus gave Jefferson an unrecognized if temporary reprieve against an unrecognized danger.

That year of delay was a crucial one for Napoleon, since problems were accumulating for France in Saint Domingue, where Napoleon had sent an army, under the talented general Victor-Emmanuel Leclerc (married to Napoleon's beautiful sister Paulina), to put down the rebellion of the black general Toussaint Louverture. Napoleon needed a secure base in Saint Domingue, since it was the richest and most powerful French colony in the Caribbean, the destined center of all his operations in the New World, operations which Talleyrand was urging upon him. Jefferson, convinced of the peaceful intentions signaled by the French in the Treaty of Morfontaine, had at first (July, 1801) told Napoleon's agent in America that he would help the French "reduce Toussaint to starvation."[5] At this point, Jefferson had heard rumors of the transfer of Louisiana to France, but still could not believe Napoleon was deceiving him. Even after Rufus King sent from England a copy of the retrocession, on November 29, 1801 (274), Talleyrand denied its existence to Robert Livingston, the American minister in Paris. "President Jefferson received at the same instant Talleyrand's explicit denial and the explicit proof that Talleyrand was trying to deceive him" (276).

As the scale of the threat France now posed sank into Jefferson's consciousness, he changed his attitude entirely. Now he wanted Napoleon to fail in Saint Domingue (279). Toussaint had become the second hidden check, after Godoy, against Napoleon's hidden designs. Jefferson was angry at being duped by the French and panicky about the consequences (276). His benign neutrality began to look like a weak isolation from all the great powers. He reacted impulsively, against his whole past history of Anglophobia, pledging to "marry ourselves to the British fleet and nation." This was part of a special message Jefferson gave to his friend Dupont de Nemours, who took it to Paris for delivery of its contents to Talleyrand. Thus rapidly had the policy of disengagement failed. The pacific Jefferson was now roaring like the British lion:

> This [Louisiana] measure will cost France, and perhaps not very long hence, a war which will annihilate her on the ocean, and place that element under the despotism of two nations — which I am not reconciled to the more because my own would be one of them . . . The day that France takes possession of New Orleans fixes the sentence which is to restrain her forever within her low-water mark. It seals the union of two nations, who in conjunction can maintain exclusive possession of the ocean. From that moment we must marry ourselves to the British fleet and nation. (277)

It struck even the messenger, Dupont, that threatening Napoleon might not be the most useful form of diplomacy (278–79).

But while Jefferson was strutting before Napoleon, he was, in the same message, groveling before Talleyrand. One of the reasons for Talleyrand's temporary fall from favor in 1799 had been that he was caught using agents (the famous "X, Y, and Z") to suborn bribes from American emissaries. Jefferson now told Talleyrand that the Republicans always knew that story was an invention of the Federalists, and the American people had punished them for telling the fib: "The nation has done him [Talleyrand] justice by dismissing them [the Federalists]; those in power are precisely those who disbelieved that story, and saw in it nothing but an attempt to deceive our country. We entertain toward him personally the most friendly dispositions" (278). Can one wonder that Adams saw his tale as a comic one? He remarks: "Talleyrand must have known enough of the American character to feel that a Republican president could not seriously mean to represent his own election as an act of national justice to a venal French politician" (278).

Through the summer of 1802, Jefferson kept his new fears hidden. Congress was out of session, and he was still hoping that Leclerc's Saint Domingue expedition would fail (as it eventually did, with the help of a yellow fever epidemic). But a firestorm of anger among his western constituents made it impossible for him to suppress international concerns after October 18, 1802. That is when the Spanish intendant (local magistrate) of New Orleans, Don Juan Ventura Morales, closed American shipping deposits at his city (282). Before that, American goods came down the Mississippi on barges and were stored, with warehouse costs but without duties, while waiting to be loaded onto oceangoing vessels. This was a right of "deposit" granted for three years in a 1795 treaty with Spain. After three years, according to the treaty's terms, the Spanish had a right to demand duties and/or move the entrepôt to some other Mississippi site. They had never exercised that option. Now that the three-year grace period was long past, the intendant declared, it was legal to deny storage rights.

Since it was known by now that France was the owner of Louisiana, though it had not yet taken delivery, the intendant was thought to be responding to French authority, though he denied this (282). Spanish officials said he had acted on his own, not on their instruction, though it is likely that Godoy was behind the move. He was certainly trying in other ways to provoke American resistance to Napoleon's takeover, and in this case he succeeded. The West had always been fierce in protection of navigation rights to the Mississippi. This had been a prominent demand in the treaty that ended the Revolution. When the Jay-Gardoqui Treaty was drafted offering Spain control of the river in 1786, parts of the West threatened to secede if the treaty were ratified (it was not). Under the new provocation of the closure of New Orleans in 1802, the legislatures of Kentucky and Tennessee called for forcible resistance (290). When Congress reassembled on December 7, there was a war party from the West being egged on by the Federalists, who said Jefferson was failing to respond to the retrocession and the closure because of his old favoritism toward France.

Jefferson was hoping for a change in the international situation whenever war should be resumed (as was expected) between France and England. Since that might offer him better options than he could find at present, he told friends he must "palliate and endure" whatever France was up to (293). To tamp down the war fever, he called in the help of the Spanish representative in America, Don Carlos Martínez Yrujo — who was married to the daughter of Republican governor McKean of Pennsylvania — to convince Congress that the intendant had acted on his own, and would soon reopen New Orleans (286–87).

Congress agreed to accept that assertion for the present (290), but it wanted to know what Jefferson was doing to "palliate" as well as "endure" what France was doing. He decided to send a special mission to France, entrusted to a man the West admired, James Monroe. (Monroe had been passionate in objection to the danger offered the Mississippi by the Jay-Gardoqui Treaty.) But what could Monroe do there that was not already being done by the regular representative, Livingston? Jefferson's supporters in the House called another secret session to authorize the expenditure of two million dollars for an unspecified "expense" of the mission — which the representatives knew would be spent in an effort to purchase New Orleans and West Florida from Napoleon. Jefferson had written Dupont that this would be a "palliation" for France's taking the whole Louisiana Territory.

Since this opened the final act of the process that resulted in the Louisiana Purchase, it is important to realize that the negotiation was based on a misunderstanding from the outset. When the retrocession was just a rumor, it had been assumed that Spain was giving to Napoleon both Louisiana (which it had got from France) *and* the Floridas (which it had got from England). Napoleon knew this was not the case, as he proved by continuing to press Carlos IV — unsuccessfully, thanks to Godoy — to obtain the Floridas *after* the act of retrocession had been signed. (Transfer of the Floridas would not be a *retro*cession, since France had never owned them.) But as early as September, 1801, when the rumors were still unsubstantiated, Madison had instructed Livingston, *if* he found that the rumors were true, to explore the idea of buying West Florida — from France, which did not own it — as the price of American submission to French occupation of Louisiana (DM 4.250). Napoleon and Talleyrand, while refusing to confirm the transfer, did not disturb the misconception that if there were a deal, the Floridas would be part of it.

The Monroe mission was meant to follow up on Livingston's initiative with a concrete cash offer. A modern college student may wonder, on first reading of the Louisiana Purchase, why Jefferson could think that West Florida (which did not include what is now the whole state of Florida) would be a compensation for France's taking all of the Louisiana Territory. Well, it was a "palliation," not a real compensation. The price for Louisiana would have been considered beyond American means if Napoleon were really bargaining for it. His precipitate rush to be rid of it, once Toussaint had thwarted his movements in the Americas, could not be foreseen (even Talleyrand had not foreseen it). More concretely, possession of West Florida would have eased the immediate fears of southwesterners, since the rivers debouching at Mobile and Pensacola were fed by branches from the Mississippi, and they would keep open western trade.

West Florida — what is now the coastal area of Mississippi and Alabama — had been a constant irritant to Georgians and Carolinians, since Indian raiders crossed its borders into asylum. Furthermore, land disputes (especially over the Yazoo purchases) could be eased by seizure of the Spanish territory in Florida. If Jefferson could get West Florida, he might ease southwestern war pressure while he pondered whether, in fact, he had no alternative but to marry the British fleet. The importance of the Floridas would be an issue throughout both Jefferson's and Madison's presidencies, with the southern pressure to seize them as unremitting as was French coyness on whether to cooperate with those efforts or block them. Only the momentous nature of the Louisiana Purchase has tended to obscure how persistent and irritating was the Florida problem throughout the first quarter of the nineteenth century. But at the end of Jefferson's first term, with so much riding on Monroe's mission, Florida was at the center of foreign affairs, while Louisiana was being pushed into the background by Jefferson. He hoped that the former would make people forget, for a while, the latter. But then Napoleon, always unpredictable, threw Louisiana onto the table, at a bargain price.

> Bonaparte's hatred of Godoy and determination to crush him were among the reasons why Louisiana fell at a sudden and unexpected moment into the hands of Jefferson, and no picture of American history could be complete which did not show in the background the figures of Bonaparte and Godoy, locked in struggle over Don Carlos IV. (254)

Godoy has not had a good reputation, despite Goya's heroic painting of him, but Adams argues that his many faults did not prevent him from giving America an unintended but important service. Even his affair with Queen Luisa aided his efforts. Adams describes him at the time of the affair:

> A young man, barely thirty years old, on whose head fortune rained favors, in an atmosphere of corruption, was certainly no saint; yet this creature, Manuel Godoy, reeking with vice, epitome of the decrepitude and incompetence of Spanish royalty, was a mild, enlightened, and intelligent minister so far as the United States were concerned, capable of generosity and of courage, quite the equal of Pitt or Talleyrand in diplomacy and their superior in resource. (236)

Adams was the first American historian to give full credit to the other figure holding Napoleon off from America, Toussaint. Adams writes of him, dying in captivity far from Saint Domingue:

Toussaint never knew that St. Domingo had successfully resisted the whole power of France, and that had he been truer to himself and his color he might have worn the crown that became the plaything of Christophe and Dessalines; but even when shivering in the frosts of the Jura, his last moments would have glowed with gratified revenge, had he known that at the same instant Bonaparte was turning into a path which the Negroes of St. Domingo had forced him to take, and which was to lead him to parallel at St. Helena the fate of Toussaint himself at the Chateaux de Joux. In these days of passion, men and women had little time for thought; and the last subject on which Bonaparte thereafter cared to fix his mind was the fate of Toussaint and Leclerc. That the "miserable Negro," as Bonaparte called him, should have been forgotten so soon was not surprising; but the prejudice of race alone blinded the American people to the debt they owed to the desperate courage of the five hundred thousand Haitian Negroes who would not be enslaved. (316)

While Jefferson was running up a string of victories at home — on patronage, on the judiciary, on the debt — events were being prepared for him abroad that would bring him his greatest triumph of all: Louisiana.

3

—————◦◆◦—————

REACHING OUT

The *History*, Volume Two

JEFFERSON'S FIRST TERM, which began with a principled withdrawal from the world's entanglements, ended with a reach outward to new realms of American influence — in Louisiana, in the
Floridas, and in the Mediterranean (through the Tripolitan War).
Meanwhile, in domestic politics, the nationalizing tendency that began
with the patronage appointments continued with passage of the Twelfth
Amendment. The Jeffersonians promoted the amendment, creating a
single ticket of presidential and vice presidential candidates, to prevent
the separate votes for each office that led to the Burr-Jefferson tie in
1800. But the inevitable result of the amendment was to cause regional
balancing on the ticket, helping to bind together the party and the nation.

> Slight as this change might appear, it tended toward centralizing powers
> hitherto jealously guarded. It swept away one of the checks on which the
> framers had counted to resist majority rule by the great states. Lessening
> the influence of the small states, and exaggerating the office of president by
> lowering the dignity of vice president, it made the processes of election and
> government smoother and more efficient — a gain to politicians, but a re-
> sult most feared by the states' rights school. The change was such as Penn-
> sylvania or New York might naturally want; but it ran counter to the theo-
> ries of Virginia Republicans, whose jealousy of executive influence had
> been extreme. (391)

This was one of many indications that party-building would involve na-tion-building. More spectacular was the way territorial designs on land and at sea would create a national feeling. The Tripolitan War made a new set of national heroes — men not fighting for one state but for them all — and expressed the military pride and professionalism that Presi-dent Adams had begun to foster in the Quasi War. Naturally the most important development was the huge increase in *national* land by the Louisiana Purchase.

Louisiana

Finally breaking through the delays Godoy had imposed upon him, Napoleon readied his fleet in the summer of 1802 to take over the retroceded Louisiana. His instructions to the captain-general of the ex-pedition, which Adams found in the French naval archives, would have terrified Americans if they had known of it. "My intention is to *take pos-session of Louisiana* with the shortest delay, and that this expedition be made *in the utmost secrecy, under the appearance of being directed on St. Domingo*" (269, emphasis added). That is, indeed, enough to justify marrying the British fleet. The French captain-general, Marshal Victor, was to establish himself all along the west bank of the Mississippi, "to take the place in these colonies of the American commerce" (307). Trou-ble was to be anticipated on the opposite (eastern) bank, to be dealt with by an infiltration of spies and of agents provocateurs among the Ameri-cans there:

> A little local experience will soon enable you to discern the sentiments of the western provinces of the Federal government. It will be well to main-tain sources of intelligence in that country, whose numerous, warlike, and sober population may present you a redoubtable enemy. The inhabitants of Kentucky especially should fix the attention of the Captain-General . . . He must also fortify himself against them by alliance with the Indian nations scattered to the east of the river [i.e., in American territory]. (308)

As for New Orleans, "it is clear that the republic of France, being master of both banks at the mouth of the Mississippi, holds the key to its navi-gation" (308–9).

The French troops and artillery were dispatched from Dunkirk to take up armed positions on the Mississippi (305). But only seven months after these troops were scheduled to sail, Napoleon was practically forcing Louisiana upon the United States (for a fee). What had happened? "The explosion of April," as Adams calls it, happened (315). Napoleon, impatient with failure, had seen his Louisiana scheme falling apart, component by component, in places as far apart as Madrid, Tuscany, and Port-au-Prince. Thanks to Godoy's maneuvering, Bonaparte could not count on Spanish support in the New World, and he was not yet ready for war with Carlos IV (though that would come). Tossing about for compensatory projects elsewhere, he found his treasury drained by his incessant campaigns. His troops for Louisiana were being diverted to Haiti, where the quagmire created by Toussaint Louverture had combined with yellow fever to kill fifty thousand men. It was getting harder to send men off, away from his own inspiring presence, to almost certain death by tropical disease.

Napoleon's efficient brother-in-law, General Leclerc, had died of the fever in January, and his replacement in Saint Domingue, General Rochambeau, an incompetent son of the Rochambeau who fought with Washington at Yorktown, was floundering:

> At St. Domingo, horror followed fast on horror. Rochambeau, shut in Port au Prince — drunken, reckless, surrounded by worthless men and by women more abandoned still, wallowing in the dregs of the former English occupation and of a half-civilized Negro empire — waged as he best could a guerrilla war, hanging, shooting, drowning, burning all the Negroes he could catch; hunting them with fifteen hundred bloodhounds bought in Jamaica for something more than one hundred dollars each; wasting money, squandering men, while Dessalines and Christophe massacred every white being within their reach. (315)

At this point James Monroe arrived in Paris with promises of money for West Florida (316). Napoleon was exasperated with Talleyrand, who had led him into the Caribbean cul-de-sac, and with two of his brothers, who tried to keep him in the cul-de-sac — they were taking bribes to prevent their brother's going to war with England (DM 4.295). The most dramatic explosion of that explosive month took place when Napoleon was confronted by his brothers (Joseph and Lucien) while he was bathing. According to Lucien's memoir, he told Bonaparte that, if he meant to alienate Louisiana, he would have to ask the permission of the legislature of the republic. Otherwise his act would be unconstitutional.

Napoleon, referring to the way Lucien had abetted his coup of 18th Brumaire, replied, "Unconstitutional is droll from you" (327).

The offer of Louisiana, then, not only took by surprise the American negotiators, Livingston and Monroe. It dumbfounded Napoleon's own closest associates. Talleyrand regretted the loss of his Spanish and American projects, but he was also pained by the way Napoleon openly broke the pledge Talleyrand had personally given to the Spanish King — that Louisiana would not be alienated to any third country. (After all, Spain had surrendered the territory precisely to keep it out of American hands.) It was not that Talleyrand was above perfidy, but it was his style to lie under cover of good manners. Bonaparte just gave the pledge a brutal disregard — which was *his* style.

The explosion of April left burning resentments behind it. Adams points out that it was a trebly illegal act on Napoleon's part, violating two parts of his agreement with Spain and flouting the French constitution (339). Adams probably exaggerates, but not by much, when he writes: "The sale of Louisiana was the turning point in Napoleon's career; no true Frenchman forgave it. A second betrayal of France, it announced to his fellow conspirators that henceforward he alone was to profit by the treason of the 18th Brumaire" (328). At any rate, Talleyrand's relations with Napoleon would never be the same:

[Talleyrand was] obliged to sell Louisiana, turn his back on the traditions of France, and shut up his far-reaching mind within the limits of his master's artillery politics. Day by day he saw more clearly that soldiership, and not statecraft, was to guide the destinies of France, and that the new regime was but revolution without ideas. He had probably begun already to feel that the presence of his coldly silent face was becoming irksome to a will which revolted at the memory of a remonstrance. Talleyrand was corrupt — perhaps he thought himself more corrupt than he was; but his political instincts were sounder than his private morality. He was incarnate conservatism; but he was wider-minded and more elevated in purpose than Napoleon. (510–11)

Napoleon had mocked his brothers, saying they presented the sale as an act of "Louisianicide" (327). The joke may have been on him.

The sale caused resentment among some Americans, too, starting with the principal American negotiator of the deal, Edward Livingston. He realized that Monroe, arriving at just the moment of the April explosion, would get all or most of the credit for what he had long been patiently angling for. In order to get back as much credit as he could, he personally handled the claims part of the treaty, and botched it. A fourth of the money the United States paid was to go to American citizens, in settlement of outstanding claims against the French government for depredations on their commerce. Livingston in his haste badly calculated the sums involved, and too roughly sketched the manner of distributing them to claimants, which led to endless later legal problems (333–34).

But such problems could not dim the joy of the nation when news of the Purchase reached the United States on July 3, 1803. Jefferson and Congress were eager to ratify the treaty. Jefferson had constitutional qualms about the power to buy a foreign land and its citizens; but his own party in Congress was not ready to hear such objections. So, just as with his qualms about patronage, he let the party decide for him: "Jefferson did not lead the way, but he allowed his friends to drag him in the path they chose" (363). Those friends had to drag themselves out of their own deeply entrenched bunkers of states' rights and strict construction if they were to give Jefferson the authority he needed for the Purchase. Adams is amused by this precipitate tumbling of men out from their own bastions. The two who had presented the Kentucky and Virginia Resolutions to their respective legislatures — John Breckinridge in the first state, John Taylor of Caroline in the second — now favored the broadest grants of power to the federal government on this matter: "If Breckinridge had expressed these ideas in his Kentucky Resolutions, American history would have contained less dispute as to the meaning of states-rights and the power of the central government; but Breckinridge himself would have then led the Federalist, not the Republican party" (376).

The most heated debate in Congress was not over acquiring the territory of Louisiana, but over making states of the land and citizens of its inhabitants. Should the Spanish, French, and other residents be treated as a colonized people, a bought people, a conquered people? Did they have the right to any say in their own destiny? Adams credits Madison with the draconian plan that the administration put in Breckinridge's mouth; but modern scholars make Jefferson the author of it (DM 4.351). Adams quotes the objection of Thomas Hart Benton:

> It was a startling bill, continuing the existing Spanish government; putting the president in the place of the king of Spain; putting all the territorial of-

ficers in the place of the king's officers; and placing the appointment of
these officers in the president alone, without reference to the Senate. Nothing could be more incompatible with the Constitution than such a government — a mere emanation of Spanish despotism, in which all powers, civil
and military, legislative, executive, and judicial, were in the Intendant General, representing the king, and where the people, far from possessing political rights, were punishable arbitrarily for presuming to meddle with political subjects. (382)

The bitterness felt over this system in New Orleans would provide some
of the troubled waters in which Aaron Burr would soon be fishing. There
was deep resentment of the officials Jefferson appointed to rule there.
The civil power was committed to well-intentioned but ill-equipped
William Claiborne, and the military power to corrupt James Wilkinson.
The retiring French prefect in the city, Pierre-Clément de Laussat, described the two:

> The first, with estimable private qualities, has little capacity and much
> awkwardness, and is extremely beneath his place; the second, already long
> known here in a bad way, is a flighty, rattle-headed fellow, often drunk, who
> has committed a hundred impertinent follies. Neither the one nor the
> other understands a word of French or Spanish. They have on all occasions,
> and without delicacy, shocked the habits, the [Catholic] prejudices, the
> character of the population. (807–8)

Within a year of the Purchase, the French-speaking (Creole) remains of
the old order sent a three-man delegation to Washington to beg for
some elements of self-government:

> They saw Claiborne, who knew nothing of their society and law, abolish
> their language, establish American judges who knew only American law,
> while he himself sat as a court of last resort, without even an attorney to ad-
> vise him as to the meaning of the Spanish law he administered. At the same
> time that as a judge he could hang his subjects, as Intendant he could tax
> them, and as governor he could shoot the disobedient. (808)

In a chapter called "Conspiracy," Adams treats again the attempt of
Pickering to provoke a northern secession over Louisiana — considered
earlier in connection with his *Documents Related to New-England Federalism*. He disagrees with John Quincy Adams and agrees with Henry
Cabot Lodge that Timothy Pickering could not get men like George
Cabot to join him because they had despaired of democracy (412) and
did not have Pickering's "sanguine mind" (411), his "tough sense and

democratic instincts" (414). Adams shows no concern that the Purchase extended slavery into a vast new area.

The Floridas

For some Americans, and especially for southern Americans, the purchase of Louisiana was incomplete if it did not include what was first aimed at, West Florida and its seaports.

> From the Potomac to the Mississippi, every Southern man expected and required that by peace or war Florida should be annexed to the Union; and the annexation of Louisiana made that of Florida seem easy. Neither Monroe, Madison, nor Jefferson could resist the impulse to seize it. (467)

That impulse first took the shape of saying that Florida was included in the Purchase. Livingston, in Paris, asked Talleyrand if that were not so, and was given an equivocal answer. So Livingston decided, unilaterally, that if he went to Paris in order to obtain Florida, then he must have obtained it. He reasoned thus: Louisiana had been ceded to Spain in 1763 (by France), and the Floridas had been ceded to Spain in 1783 (by England), so they could be considered a package — buy one, buy both. Adams satirizes the claim:

> He did not assert that Spain intended to retrocede Florida to France, or that France had claimed it as included in the retrocession. He knew the contrary . . . [so] he was forced at last to maintain that Spain had retroceded West Florida to France without knowing it, that France had sold it to the United States without suspecting it, that the United States had bought it without paying for it, and that neither France nor Spain, although the original contracting parties, were competent to decide the meaning of their own contract. (468)

The amazing thing about this argument is that Livingston convinced Monroe of its truth, and Monroe convinced Madison and Jefferson. For the next twenty years, these men would try to demonstrate to France and Spain that Spain had given Florida to France, and France had sold it to America. Nothing could convince them that this was not the case. Napoleon's instructions for the captain-general of Louisiana had included the flat statement: "Florida belongs to Spain" (307). But Madison said that the failure to turn over the Floridas at the time of the Louisiana Purchase did not weaken the American case, since "a delivery of a part, particularly of the seat of government [in New Orleans], was a virtual delivery of the whole" (475). He tried to make his case that the three provinces were one during a conversation with France's minister in America, General Louis-Marie Turreau, who reported the exchange to Talleyrand. Madison said, "But General! We have a map which persuasively carries to the Perdido the eastern limit of Louisiana." Turreau replied: "I should be curious to see it, Sir; the more because I have one which includes Tennessee and Kentucky in Louisiana. You will agree that maps are not titles" (480).

Though the United States had made no formal protest when the Floridas were not handed over to France along with Louisiana, the materials on the treaty that Jefferson sent to Congress contained the assertion that the three areas were one. So Congress, in passing the legislation for the new territory, made provision for customs collection at Mobile. This bill, known as the Mobile Act, was passed. It received the president's signature (475). Understandably, this infuriated Godoy. After keeping the Floridas out of Napoleon's grasp by many twisty maneuvers, he was not going to let them slide easily under American dominion by a piece of legislation. He joined Talleyrand in a united front on the meaning of the Purchase as exclusive of Florida, and Talleyrand was happy to cooperate, since Napoleon was now courting Spain for help in his war with England (489).

Godoy also had his minister in America, Don Carlos Martínez Yrujo, speak in very hard terms about the Mobile Act. Yrujo needed no lessons in using hard terms. He had already expressed his own as well as his government's anger at the delivery of Louisiana before terms for it were completed; at the assertion that Florida was part of the Purchase; and at demands for spoliation payments from Spain. The Mobile Act made him storm into Madison's office and make insulting accusations. But he also sent the government a note "so severe as to require punishment, and so able as to admit of none" (477). By signing the Mobile Act, Jefferson had let legislation run ahead of diplomacy in an embarrassing way. "Madison could neither maintain the law nor annul it; he could not even explain it" (478). Yrujo was soon planting anti-government articles in American newspapers (481), an act reminiscent of Citizen Genêt's offenses during the Washington administration, and Madison asked Spain to recall him. But Yrujo was not so easily expelled from the country, since he was married to the daughter of Jefferson's ally in Pennsylvania, the Republican governor Thomas McKean.

In Madrid, meanwhile, the American minister, Charles Pinckney, was making Yrujo look like a silken whisperer by contrast with his own bluster. He had been negotiating claims for Spanish maritime spoliations when news of the Mobile Act reached Godoy. Pinckney said that to link objections to the two matters — claims and the act — would violate Spanish honor (490). When the government refused to consider the claims until the Mobile Act was rescinded, Pinckney instituted a move that normally signals the onset of hostilities. He sent a circular letter to all consuls in Spanish ports telling them to be ready to depart "should things end as I now expect" (491). This "created a panic in the Mediterranean" (490), what Adams calls Pinckney's quasi-war (494).

Monroe was still in Europe as a special agent. He was supposed to have gone to Spain after signing the Purchase treaty in Paris, leaving Livingston there as regular minister. But Talleyrand convinced him that the Spaniards were still smarting from the sale of Louisiana, after Napoleon had promised to alienate it to no third country. He told Monroe that it would be better for him to postpone his trip to Spain. Since Monroe was an envoy extraordinary not assigned to any one country, he went to England, where he filled in the interim between Rufus King's departure as the American representative there and the arrival of Robert Livingston. The crisis of the Mobile Act sent him back to Paris, since that is where Godoy had now centered the action. He conferred again with Livingston, and with John Armstrong, who had just arrived to replace Livingston. The three of them drew up a document asking Talleyrand for help in acquiring the Floridas. But Talleyrand would respond only to the kinds of bribes that had been turned down when President Adams's representatives were in Paris. Livingston had already caught on to this and, a little more slowly, so did Monroe:

> Monroe, though honest as any man in public life, and more courageous in great emergencies than some of his friends or rivals, was commonly not quick at catching an idea, nor did he see it at last from a great elevation; but in this instance the idea was thrust so persistently into his face, that had he been blind he could not have missed it. (508)

Determined not to pay again for what he thought he had already bought, Monroe did not even wait for Talleyrand's reply to their joint request (which was suavely dismissive), but went straight to Spain to negotiate on his own — that is what envoys extraordinary have as their mission. What awaited him there is a tale that belongs to Jefferson's

second administration. Suffice it here to say that the Floridas problem would still be unresolved when Monroe became president himself
in 1817.

Impeachments

Having dismissed President Adams's "midnight judges" by repeal of the
Judiciary Act of 1801, Congress feared that the Supreme Court would
declare its repeal unconstitutional (since it was). It therefore canceled
the next two sessions of the Court. By the time the Court reconvened,
the district courts would have been dissolved. Justice Samuel Chase of
the Supreme Court tried to persuade his fellows not to go back on circuit, replacing the justices dismissed by the repeal; but Chief Justice
Marshall defeated that effort. He was saving his ammunition for a more
tricky maneuver. But Chase was now marked by Jefferson's men as a target for impeachment.

When the Court reconvened in the spring of 1803, war between the
Republicans and the federal judiciary began in full earnest. Jefferson
fired the first shot when he sent a letter to Congress on February 4 suggesting that federal justice John Pickering of New Hampshire should be
impeached for aberrant behavior. But before the impeachment could
take place, Chief Justice Marshall stung the administration with the
Marbury v. Madison decision (February 24, 1903). Marshall, as we have
seen, was the Virginian Henry Adams admired second only to Washington:

> The Chief Justice, a man who in grasp of mind and steadiness of purpose
> had no superior . . . was of all aristocrats the most democratic in man-
> ners and appearance . . . Simple as American life was, his habits were re-
> markable for modest plainness; and only the character of his mind, which
> seemed to have no flaw, made his influence irresistible upon all who were
> brought within its reach. (131)

Adams saw that Marshall was fighting at a tremendous disadvantage
in 1803. Jefferson had the executive and the people with him. He had
the Congress, as that body's suspension of Court sessions proved. Marshall knew better than to take on the new president in a head-to-head
confrontation, as Chase did. He had to choose his occasion and his
instruments — and that is what he did in *Marbury*. He put the very
weapon that had been turned against him — Congress's suspension of

the Court's 1801–1802 sessions — to his own use. Before that suspension, William Marbury, a justice of the peace who was one of John Adams's "midnight appointments," had appealed to the Court because Madison, the new secretary of state, had refused to deliver his commission, though Congress approved it and President Adams signed it. In taking up that case, after the long hiatus when the Court was not sitting, Marshall was speaking on a subject no longer alive — Marbury was not interested anymore in the minor office denied him so long ago. Just to make sure there would be no fuss on that point, Marshall found a way (beyond the lapse of time) to bury the case even deeper in oblivion — Marbury, he ruled, had no right of direct appeal before the Court, which could hear him only on an appellate basis, after earlier adjudication.

Marshall seemed to be taking on a matter that would put him in a bind. If he tried to put Marbury in office, the executive would just laugh him off. But if he did not support Marbury, that would seem to be a preemptive capitulation to the executive's assault on the courts.

> If the Court were to order Madison to produce Marbury's commission, or a copy thereof, Madison would, on Jefferson's instruction, simply disregard the order, thereby confirming, for all to see, the powerlessness of the highest court in the land.[1]

The proof that Congress could bully the Court was obvious to Marshall — it was made clear in the dissolution of the district courts, the suspension of the Court's sessions, the impeachment move on Judge Pickering, and Senator Giles's brazen threats to Marshall himself. Marshall seemed to be in a no-win situation; yet it was a situation of his own choosing. Why did he choose it?

Because he knew a way to turn Marbury down while planting a Parthian dart as he fled. Marbury's lawyers had claimed they could come to the Court for a ruling, without going through appellate preliminaries, because Congress in 1789 gave the Court the power to issue a mandamus (order of action) on direct address. Marshall said that the 1789 Congress had no authority to extend the Court's reach beyond what the Constitution had given it. He thus "lost" the power to speak on Marbury *while quietly asserting the power of the Court to declare a congressional statute unconstitutional.* He planted his dynamite in this odd little corner of the ruling, where Jefferson would have looked picky in finding it out and denouncing it.[2] Who was going to go back and defend the 1789 Congress?

Marshall knew that there were people like Giles who might call this an impeachable decision. But he wound his way into it so circuitously, and kept it so without immediate application, that it was hard to make the decision one to which people could rally in protest.

Marshall had planted a time bomb under the President's House, one that would explode only later. Adams is awed by his cleverness. He had used "language too guarded to furnish grounds for impeachment" (401). Though Giles did not realize what he had done, Jefferson did, and fumed at what he would later call Marshall's "twistifications." In fact, Marshall's actions all through this tense time of testing against the president were brilliant: "Had Marshall been a man of less calm and certain judgment, a single mistake by him might easily have prostrated the Judiciary at the feet of partisans" (454). He had defended the Court when it seemed that he could not do that, and had at the same time defended himself. Adams is right: it was a work of genius.

Though *Marbury* was a check on Jefferson's attempt to make the judiciary submit to popular control, Jefferson's own time bomb, planted two weeks before the *Marbury* decision, was ticking away even as Marshall gave his ruling. The House of Representatives was pursuing his suggestion that the Federalist judge John Pickering of New Hampshire should be impeached for aberrant actions on the bench. Pickering was a distinguished man who had become alcoholic and senile. If the Judiciary Act had not been repealed, his caseload could have been shifted to one of the new courts set up by the Adams administration. But now the only way to get rid of him was by impeachment. That raised constitutional problems, but the Republicans, smarting at *Marbury*, were prepared to brazen them out.

The Constitution furnished no grounds for impeachment but "high crimes or misdemeanors." Was craziness a crime? The Senate could not bring itself to say so, even in its verdict. It called him "guilty as charged," not "guilty of high crimes and misdemeanors," the formula that would deliberately be restored in the Chase trial. At the end of the trial, two senators refused to vote and three others "tacitly protested by absenting themselves" (408):

> In a Senate of thirty-four members only twenty-six voted, and only nineteen voted for conviction. So confused, contradictory, and irregular were these proceedings that Pickering's trial was never considered a sound pre-

cedent. That an insane man could be guilty of crime, and could be punished on *ex parte* evidence, without a hearing, with not even an attorney to act in his behalf, seemed such a perversion of justice that the precedent fell dead on the spot. (408)

Adams thinks that the consideration tipping the minds of just enough senators to convict was that "acquittal of Pickering would probably be fatal to the impeachment of Chase" (407). This was the first move in a campaign to get at the Supreme Court.

The Republicans now moved to unseat the most vulnerable member of the Supreme Court, Samuel Chase. Jefferson had a great stake in the conviction of Chase. He had initiated the impeachment. He was often a secret mover behind the scenes, but this time he did not leave it to a subordinate to make the first move. Referring to a polemical charge Chase had given a jury in Maryland, he wrote Joseph Nicholson in the House, saying: "Ought this seditious and official attack on the principles of our Constitution and on the proceedings of a state to go unpunished, and to whom so pointedly as yourself will the public look for the necessary measures? I ask these questions for your consideration; for myself, it is better that I should not interfere" (403). Adams is amused at that final comment:

> "Non-intervention," according to Talleyrand, "is a word used in politics and metaphysics, which means very nearly the same thing as intervention." The event proved that non-intervention was wise policy, but Jefferson was somewhat apt to say that it was better he should not interfere in the same breath with which he interfered . . . The success of any attack upon Chase would be a gain to him, and he was so ordering [it] as to make failure a loss only to those who undertook it. (403)

Dumas Malone says that Jefferson did *not* interfere by "passing the problem on to Congress," because judging judges was not "within Executive cognizance" (DM 4.460, 462). But Adams believed, and so have most historians after him, that Jefferson did try to influence the outcome of the trial. Presiding over it would be Aaron Burr, fresh from his duel with Hamilton. The president, who had driven Burr out of the party's favor and cut off all his patronage in New York, suddenly became fond of Burr's company at dinner. Could this be because he killed Hamilton, Jefferson's foe and the Federalists' hero? Surely not. If anything, Jefferson would have continued his cold treatment of the man to avoid that suspicion. What he was up to is confirmed by other actions undertaken at the same time, not only by Jefferson but by Madison and Gallatin:

> They made efforts to conciliate Burr, whose opposition to the impeachment [of Chase] was most feared. Jefferson appointed J. B. Prevost of New York, Burr's stepson, a judge of the Supreme Court at New Orleans; James Brown, who married Mrs. Burr's sister, was made secretary to the Louisiana Territory, and sent to govern St. Louis, solely on Burr's recommendation; James Wilkinson, one of Burr's intimate friends and general-in-chief of the army, was made governor of the Louisiana Territory. (450)[3]

Malone argues that all these appointees had merit, so they may have been appointed without any attempt to influence Burr (DM 5.215–16). But the men Burr wanted appointed in New York had merit, and a connection with him had doomed them. Obviously, a connection with him had different value as his importance to the Chase trial became clear.

Burr had the Senate chamber reconfigured and redecorated for the trial, adding galleries, arranging the senators on either side of his raised chair, providing opposed boxes for counsel. Many have attributed this to his innate theatricality; but Adams rightly saw the rationale for it — Burr was reshaping the chamber to make it resemble the British House of Lords when it tried the impeachment of Warren Hastings ten years before the Chase trial (454). That was *the* impeachment of the age, and the famous speeches of Edmund Burke for the prosecution had become instant and widely read classics. Burr presided over the trial with great dignity and fairness. Some Federalists thought he might have succumbed to the president's blandishments, but Burr's critics praised his evenhandedness by the end of the trial.

The outcome of the trial did not depend on rulings from the bench, but on arguments from the floor, between the House managers presenting the articles of impeachment and the skilled defense team assembled by Chase. It was Jefferson's bad luck that John Randolph led the House managers. He was hasty and undisciplined at the best of times. Adams, who had supplied one of his pen portraits earlier, when Randolph first entered the *History* (182), gives him another "close-up" to identify the flaws hampering him in this difficult affair. Adams's sentences poke, as it were, into this and that cubbyhole or back corridor of the man's strange mind:

> Randolph was no lawyer; but this defect was a trifling objection compared with his greater unfitness in other respects. Ill-balanced, impatient of ob-

stacles, incapable of sustained labor or of methodical arrangement, illogical to excess, and egotistic to the verge of madness, he was sparkling and
formidable in debate or on the hustings, where he could follow the wayward impulse of his fancy running in the accustomed channels of his
thought; but the qualities which helped him in debate were fatal to him at
the bar. (404)

With these strikes against him to begin with, Randolph added heavy
new burdens as he was going into the trial. He had just finished his long
and exhausting denunciation of the Yazoo Lands Commission. His frenzied pursuit of "Yazoo men" had left him not only fatigued, but with a
backlash of hatred from the Republicans he had savaged in the process
— the very men whose votes he had to solicit in the Chase trial. Furthermore, he became ill as the trial began, and did not have sense enough to
yield the direction of it to other hands. Randolph's summing up was an
excruciating spectacle:

> Randolph's tall, thin figure, his penetrating eyes and shrill voice, were fa
> miliar to the society of Washington [as Louisa had attested], and his vio
> lence of manner in the House only a short time before, in denouncing
> Granger and the Yazoo men, had prepared his audience for some eccentric
> outburst; but no one expected to see him, "with much distortion of face and
> contortion of body, tears, groans, and sobs, break down in the middle of his
> self-appointed task, and congratulate the Senate that this was 'the last day
> of my sufferings and of yours.'" (461)[4]

The necessary two-thirds majority to convict was not reached on any of
the eight counts. Chase was acquitted and served on the Court until his
death seven years later.

The outcome might have been the same even if Randolph had not
blown the prosecution. Chase's team of lawyers was good enough to save
him against a more formidable adversary. They used the Republicans'
own arguments against the Sedition Act to defend free speech. They ridiculed the way impeachable offenses had been reduced to absurdity in
the Pickering trial. They admitted that Chase was highhanded and domineering; but many judges would be in peril if these were enough to remove them. Besides, some of his accusers were highhanded, too. Bad as
Chase may have been, he was himself a great lawyer, and he had only
great lawyers standing up for him. Adams quotes from the arguments of
all of them but one. The argument of Luther Martin, who would later

defend the man presiding over this trial, Aaron Burr, was so brilliant that Adams will not wrong it by partial citation.

> Rough and coarse in manner and expression, verbose, often ungrammatical, commonly more or less drunk, passionate, vituperative, gross, he still had a mastery of legal principles and a memory that overbalanced his faults, an audacity and humor that conquered ill-will. In the practice of his profession he had learned to curb his passions until his ample knowledge had time to give the utmost weight to his assaults. His argument at Chase's trial was the climax of his career; but such an argument cannot be condensed in a paragraph. Its length and variety defied analysis within the limits of a page, though its force made other efforts seem unsubstantial. (456)

Pêle-Mêle Diplomacy

Though Jefferson felt a lifelong antipathy toward England (he liked nothing about the English but their gardens), he assumed the presidency with a determination to be evenhanded toward all nations. There was good reason to be fair where England was concerned. With the Federalists out of power, their alleged yearning back to British monarchy was, Jefferson declared, a thing of the past. Now the South meant to foster good relations with England:

> Southern Republicans had nothing to gain from a quarrel with England; they neither wished for Canada, nor aspired to create shipping or manufactures; their chief antagonist was not England, but Spain. The only power which could seriously injure them was Great Britain; and the only injury they could inflict in return was by conquering Canada for the benefit of Northern influence, or by building up manufactures which they disliked, or by cutting off their own markets for tobacco and cotton. Nothing warranted a belief that men like Jefferson, Madison, and Gallatin would ever seek a quarrel with England. (534)

The first year of Jefferson's presidency had been a good time for détente between the old adversaries of the Revolution. Britain's prime minister at the time, Edward Addington, was better disposed to the old colonies than any prime minister except Charles James Fox, whose future tenure was brief and too distracted for him to give the United States much of his time. Addington followed the fierce William Pitt and preceded the fiercer George Canning. In this interval, America's representative in London, Rufus King, was given respectful attention, and Edward Thornton, the British chargé in Washington, found Jefferson warmly attentive to him. This was the moment when Jefferson feared a sudden descent of Bonaparte upon Louisiana. He was forced to entertain the idea of marrying the British fleet as the only way to escape the French threat. And so the man who was feared by Federalists for his Francophile leanings surprised them by becoming cozy with King George's emissary:

> At Washington, Thornton's intimacy at the White House roused the jealousy and alarm of Pichon [the French chargé]. As Bonaparte's projects against Louisiana disclosed themselves, and as Leclerc's first successes at St. Domingo opened the French path to New Orleans, Jefferson began to pay sudden and almost eager court to Thornton, who was a little embarrassed by the freedom with which the President denounced the First Consul. (536)

So amicable had relations become that Thornton's successor, when he was sent out in 1802, was elevated from Thornton's status of chargé to that of full minister. The appointment had been made in deference to Rufus King, who did not like the first man suggested for the post (546). But the resulting choice, Anthony Merry, found a Washington awaiting him very different from the one in which Thornton had been cosseted. Jefferson was again hoping to get Florida from Napoleon. The First Consul, whom Jefferson had vilified in conversations with Thornton, was being wooed and mollified. Jefferson had not been truly evenhanded during Thornton's time in America — he had, instead, favored England against his natural inclination, acting under the humiliating pressure of fear. Now he meant to right the balance, by a compensatory tipping away from his former indulgence — and Merry would pay the price.

Merry, a vain man, had several shocks in store for him when he arrived. The first came when he was formally received by a very informal president. Jefferson's shabby clothes were the first thing that many people noticed about him when they went to the President's House, as Adams knew from his grandmother's diary on her White House visits. Senator William Plumer of New Hampshire, on entering the residence, mistook Jefferson for one of the servants (550). The Federalists were the first to make much of the worn attire, indicating that he lacked respect for the office of president, that he was making a veiled criticism of the formality of Washington's and Adams's court. But Republicans tried to make their own capital of the matter. For them, the shabbiness demonstrated that Jefferson was, improbably, just a plain man of the people. Louisa rightly considered him an aristocrat pretending to be a democrat, noting that he presided in plain clothes over a gourmet's meal tended by liveried servants, all to the standards, as she said, of a European court.

She was wrong to think Jefferson's attire affected. Or, better, it was not a private affectation but one of his class. He was not hiding his aristocratic style but exhibiting it. The aristocrat is often negligent of appearances, to show he is above relying on them. It is the nervous middle-class striver who is anxious about his dignity. The country gentleman, from Squire Weston to Lord Emsworth, often putters about in old clothes, proving that he has nothing to prove. The Virginia style was apparent in John Randolph, who went onto the floor of the House in muddied riding clothes, high boots on his thin stork legs. Even George III in England liked to call himself a farmer, as Carlos IV in Spain called himself a worker:

> Don Carlos was a kind of Spanish George . . . the gunsmiths, joiners, turn-
> ers, and cabinet-makers went with him from Madrid to Aranjuez, and from
> Aranjuez to La Granja. Among them he was at his ease; taking off his coat
> and rolling his shirt-sleeves up to the shoulder, he worked at a dozen differ-
> ent trades within the hour, in manner and speech as simple and easy as the
> workmen themselves. (232)

That was an aristocrat's style, not a genuine workman's. So was Jefferson's an aristocratic style. Adams catches this class pose, along with its weakness, in the story he tells of Philip II of Spain, who rebuked an official for making a fuss over mere ceremony — to which the man replied: "But Your Majesty's self is but a ceremony!" (548)

The problem at Merry's reception was not how Jefferson was dressed, but how Merry was. In all the governments of Europe, a diplomat's first meeting with the ruler of a country required formal dress, as a sign of respect for the nation represented by the ruler. Adams knew this not only from his own service with his father in England, but from Louisa's diary, which has much fun with all the formality expected of her in Prussia and Russia. John Quincy Adams had to buy a formal sword to wear with his gaiters. Louisa and her sister had to buy elaborate gowns for their receptions. Jefferson himself had dressed like a court dandy in Europe, as we know from the first portrait of him, by Mather Brown, in which he wears a wig and frilly lace in the highest French fashion.

Merry, therefore, appeared in full diplomatic splendor at the President's House, only to be made the fool for wearing fancy attire before a man who was saying, with his own dress, that attire is meaningless. Adams goes to the real point:

> No law of the United States or treaty stipulation forbade Jefferson to receive Merry in heelless slippers, or for that matter in bare feet, if he thought proper to do so. Yet Virginia gentlemen did not intentionally mortify their guests; and perhaps Madison would have done better to relieve the President of such a suspicion by notifying Merry beforehand that he would not be expected to wear full dress. In that case the British minister might have complimented Jefferson by himself appearing in slippers without heels. (550–51)

This was only the first penalty to be exacted from Merry in return for Jefferson's regretted gushiness toward his predecessor. The next installment came at the first dinner he was invited to by Jefferson. It was customary for such a dinner to honor a recently arrived minister from abroad (an honor, of course, to the country he represented). It was also the custom not to invite to the same dinner representatives of warring countries. Jefferson, of all people, should have recognized the courtesy of this, since he did not even invite Federalists and Republicans to eat at the same table, lest an air of hostility mar the good company (DM 4.380). At this time, England was at war with France. Yet Jefferson not only invited the French chargé, despite his inferior rank and hostile status, but urged him especially to return to Washington from Baltimore to be present at the dinner (552). That Frenchman, Louis-André Pichon, reported this with amusement to Talleyrand, saying Jefferson expressly told him what was up (*ce qui en était*) and that he looked forward to seeing how it would turn out (*connaître ce qui se passerait* — 552). Merry was being made the victim of a cruel experiment. This puzzles even Dumas Malone, the diligent Jefferson apologist.

> Since there was some deliberation in it, this cannot be viewed merely as an instance of thoughtlessness on the part of an elderly man who had no vigilant wife to forewarn him [excuses Malone has used for other informalities], though unquestionably he needed one. It may perhaps be regarded as

an act of bravado [what does this mean?] or as a deliberate attempt to cut a pompous diplomat down to size. (DM 4.380)

But Jefferson had no way of knowing yet that the newly arrived diplomat was pompous. Besides, it is the man's country that is "cut down to size" by such slights. Adams's comments are more appropriate than Malone's:

> Of all American hospitality none was so justly famous as that of Virginia. In this state there was probably not a white man, or even a Negro slave, but would have resented the charge that he was capable of asking a stranger, a foreigner, a woman, under his roof, with the knowledge that he was about to inflict what the guest would feel as a humiliation. Still less would he have selected his guest's only enemy, and urged him to be present for the purpose of witnessing the slight. (557)

Pichon's presence was not the only slight involved in Merry's first dinner at the President's House. In diplomatic circles, the host conducted the wife of the guest of honor to the table and seated her at his right hand. Instead, Jefferson gave his arm, not to Mrs. Merry, but to Dolley Madison, seating her at his right, while the wife of Yrujo, the Spanish chargé, sat on his left. Merry's wife was left to shift for herself. Yrujo reported gleefully to his government that the president discomfited Merry by paying his (Yrujo's) wife more attention than the Englishman's (553).

The random seating was not a new thing at this meal, though the pointed snubbing was. Once again, Jefferson's equality at the dinner table was the mark of a Virginia aristocrat. At Monticello, the assumption was that all one's guests were part of the same plantation elite or that elite's guests (no one else would be there). But the formal relations between nations were not best signified by the rules of Monticello. When Merry complained to other diplomats about his wife's treatment, and got a sympathetic hearing from them, Jefferson turned his table into an ideological statement of republicanism, something mandated by the Constitution itself, since it was meant to "obliterate any germs of a distinction of ranks, forbidden by our Constitution" (DM 4.500). That is what Jefferson wrote in an editorial to be placed by Duane in the *Aurora*.

Jefferson, at this point, did some homework on the etiquette at foreign courts, soliciting a report on the subject from Rufus King in London, before issuing what was in effect a manifesto of republican social norms, his "Canons of Etiquette to Be Observed by the Executive" (549).

Merry rightly said that it would have been more considerate to issue this before he and others were misled (568). But even before the canons were adopted, Madison went out of his way to complete Merry's humiliation. Invited to his first dinner with the secretary of state, Merry sought assurances that he and his wife would not be insulted again. Other members of the diplomatic corps told him that Dolley Madison, like all other cabinet members' wives, had always followed the accepted norms of precedence at dinner. But the Merry dinner became the first at which Madison changed the rules, to correspond with Jefferson's ideological informality. Yrujo told his government that "on this day the secretary of state too altered his custom without informing us beforehand" (553). It was another pointed snub, as Pichon reported to Paris:

> There is no doubt that Mr. Madison in this instance wished to establish in his house the same informality as at the president's, in order to make Mr. Merry feel more keenly the scandal he had made [by his complaints]; but this incident increased it. (554)

Seeing his wife in danger of being stranded all alone, Merry took her hand himself and proceeded to the table.

Republican senators now joined in the attack on Merry by denying him the diplomatic access normally given to a foreign minister (551). And Jefferson used even the man's gallantry against him. When Merry protested the treatment of his wife, Jefferson blamed the "virago" herself:

> I should be sorry to lose him as long as there remains a possibility of reclaiming him to the exercise of his own dispositions. If his wife perseveres she must eat her soup at home, and we shall endeavor to draw him into society as if she did not exist. (557)

In accord with this policy of rescuing Mr. Merry from his dominatrix, Jefferson invited him and Yrujo to dinner without their wives. Both men declined the invitation (556). Their wives also boycotted the New Year's reception at the President's House which, as Louisa Adams noted in her diary, *everyone* attended (555). Yrujo's wife, it should be remembered, was an American, the daughter of Jefferson's Pennsylvania ally, Thomas McKean. Jefferson wanted everyone to be seen as equal? All right, said Merry in effect, then a snub given him could be returned on equal terms — even to a president.

In his rush to defend his actions in terms of high principle, Jefferson was not able to achieve consistency. Since he had taken the wife of the secretary of state into the dinner Merry attended, Madison at first explained the act to Merry as based on a principle — that Jefferson always took a cabinet member's wife on his arm, though there may be foreigners present. But then Jefferson issued his formal canons, which said there was no precedence at all. Everything was random — *pêle-mêle*, as he put the democratic rule in his aristocratic French. Merry noted, however, that when Napoleon's brother Jérôme brought his American-born bride to dinner with the president, she was taken by Jefferson and placed at his right hand (555–56).

Malone thought that too much was made of these snubs (DM 4.384).[5] But Adams rightly notes that it can be politically damaging to ignore diplomatic protocol, which is meant to keep uniform rules of civility in times of international stress. Jefferson's canons deliberately set themselves against all foreign usage in an invidious way, and divested normal procedures of that predictability that is meant to afford a cushion to encounters. Without a symbolic language to reward favors, or to warn of possible trouble, diplomacy would fumble in the dark. The ranking of states by the degree of honor afforded their representatives is itself a continual way of feeling out the attitudes of the other country, where ambiguity can lead to dangerous misunderstandings. Jefferson had won an expression of foreign regard when the British post was upgraded from chargé to minister — and he threw this regard back into England's face with less courtesy than he showed to any correspondent who addressed him out of the blue.

By forswearing the symbolic language of diplomacy, therefore, he was not simply saying nothing, he was saying something rude, the last thing one would expect of him. It is a measure of his self-revulsion at having used blandishments on England. Adams notes that there was only one other major head of state in Jefferson's time, Napoleon, who dismissed formal courtesies. Jefferson said that he detested diplomats, but Napoleon gave a more vigorous expression of his opinion when he called Talleyrand "a silk stocking stuffed with filth" (513). Napoleon could get away with disregard for forms because he relied on brute strength, on his million men in arms. That was not quite Jefferson's situation: "His soldiers were three thousand in number and his own training had not been that of a successful general; he had seven frigates, and was eager to lay them up in a single dry-dock" (558). If he were not going to rely on war, he had better learn to use whatever weapons diplomacy could give him.

Jefferson seems to have learned this lesson. With a change in the international situation, with France once more a threat, and with the mild Addington replaced by Pitt in England, Madison decided that it would be helpful to court Merry after all (645–47). And Jefferson violated what he thought constitutional norms by changing his dress habits. Senator Plumer, who mistook him for a servant in 1803, was able to record a change by the end of 1804: "He has improved much in the article of dress; he has laid aside the old slippers, red waistcoat, and soiled corduroy small-clothes, and was dressed all in black, with clean linen, and powdered hair" (577–78). Jefferson had at first said that Merry was cutting himself off from useful diplomatic exchanges. "The consequence will be that Mr. and Mrs. Merry will put themselves into coventry, and that he will lose the best half of his usefulness to his nation" (557). But Jefferson, too, was being cut off from useful information, as Madison showed by trying to repair past damage.

The damage, however, had been done. Far from putting himself in coventry, Merry found much sympathy in the diplomatic corps, and became popular with all those opposed to Jefferson's policies. "The first serious evil was an alliance between Merry and Yrujo, the two men whom Jefferson had most interest in keeping apart" (554–55). Yrujo had been the only full minister in Washington before Merry arrived, but they were soon joined in that rank by Turreau from France — and all three disapproved of the way Jefferson dealt with them socially. For one thing, they did not like the fact that mere secretaries of legations were treated as the equals of ministers under the president's roof. Adams himself, while in England during the Civil War, had been received at court as his father's secretary; but he would have resented the indignity to his father if he had been placed on a par with him. For a time, the Yrujos and the Merrys turned down invitations to cabinet dinners unless they were assured that their wives would be given formal treatment (555). Yrujo and Merry "concerted reprisals," as Pichon said, agreeing "that whenever they should entertain the [cabinet] secretaries and their wives, they should take none of them to table, but should give their hands to their own wives" (555).

The French minister, Turreau, while agreeing with Yrujo's grievances, tried to dispel the personal animosity between him and Madison; but he failed, he said, because of "the fault of the latter" (Madison), whom he called dry and spiteful (486). Jefferson could talk of Merry's isolating himself while the president, in his first term, remained the social center of Washington. But as his troubles multiplied upon him in his second term, General Turreau could report to Paris "the drawing off of a part of his friends, and even of the diplomatic corps, who, with the exception of the French minister [himself], no longer visit the president" (745).

The real cost of Jefferson's treatment of Merry was that soon every man with a plot or a grievance against Jefferson ended up on the British minister's doorstep. Timothy Pickering and Roger Griswold were there, with their separatist schemes. Burr was there. So were the Creole delegates from New Orleans, protesting their treatment under the despotic rule imposed on them by the Louisiana Government Act. Merry described to London how he became the resort of such people:

> The deputies [from New Orleans] above mentioned, who while they had any hopes of obtaining the redress of their grievances, had carefully avoided giving any umbrage or jealousy to the government by visiting or holding any intercourse with the agents of foreign powers at this place, when they found that their fate was decided, although the law had not yet passed, no longer abstained from communicating with those agents, nor from expressing very publicly the great dissatisfaction which the law would occasion among their constituents — going even so far as to say that it would not be tolerated, and that they would be obliged to seek redress from some other quarter. (575)

Talk of appealing to other powers was the currency of the Merry household. It became the center of an information network, the resort of those wanting to scheme or hear of schemes. "Merry entered the path of secret conspiracy; he became the confidant of all the intriguers in Washington, and gave to their intrigues the support of his official influence" (567–68). That was the high price Jefferson paid for the gratification of shocking with worn slippers a man wearing full diplomatic gear.

Tripoli

Despite the diplomatic wrangles around Merry, Jefferson's first term had been a great success, which made his re-election easy. Adams rightly thinks his account of this administration should end on a note of triumph, "the brilliant close of his only war" (591). Another foreign concern permeating the first administration was the Tripolitan War, which was nearing its end as Jefferson completed his first term. Adams, who did not share the modern aversion to war, saves for a climax to volume two "the brilliant close of his [Jefferson's] only war" (591). The action in the Mediterranean was bracketed between two feats of military heroism, by Stephen Decatur at the outset and by William Eaton at the end.

The American frigates built by Joshua Humphreys were marvels of nautical architecture, the finest and fastest ships of their class in the world. For one of them to fall into enemy hands was like the loss of a high-tech modern airplane with all its secrets of design and equipment. Thus when the frigate *Philadelphia* was captured by the Tripolitans, it became important to destroy it before the enemy could learn its uses and turn it against the Americans. The *Philadelphia* had been trapped on a reef in the Tripoli harbor, and a raid into the harbor was called for. Captain Edward Preble of the flagship USS *Constitution*

> ordered Stephen Decatur, a young lieutenant in command of the *Enterprise*, to take a captured Tripolitan craft renamed the *Intrepid*, and with a crew of seventy-five men to sail from Syracuse, enter the harbor of Tripoli by night, board the *Philadelphia*, and then burn her under the castle guns . . . Decatur ran into the harbor at ten-o'clock in the night of Feb. 16, 1804, boarded the frigate within half gunshot, set the ship on fire, remained alongside until the flames were beyond control, and then withdrew without losing a man, while the Tripolitan gunboats and batteries fired on him as rapidly as want of discipline and training would allow. (395–96)

The war ended with an even more spectacular feat. The *Constitution*, the greatest of the Humphreys ships, sailed five times into the harbor of Tripoli and battered its walls without forcing the Pasha to capitulate. But meanwhile an American adventurer, William Eaton, recruited the Pasha's rival for the throne, his older brother, to march with him from Egypt across the desert toward the capital in Tripoli.

> So motley a horde of Americans, Greeks, Tripolitans, and Arab cameldrivers had never before been seen on the soil of Egypt. Without discipline, cohesion, or sources of supply, even without water for days, their march of five hundred miles was a sort of miracle. Eaton's indomitable obstinacy barely escaped ending in his massacre by the Arabs, or by their desertion in a mass with Hamet [the brother] at their head, yet in about six weeks they succeeded. (595–96)

At Derne, they rendezvoused with three American cruisers and captured one of the Pasha's key cities. Eaton was still seven hundred miles from Tripoli, but his dogged advance, now supported by American ships along the coast, made the Pasha surrender his demands for tribute and sign a treaty that left no further room for bribes. The frigates had created new legends, heroes, and sources of communal morale. They interacted with all the other things that were knitting together a nation.

4

———◀◆▶———

THREE FOES

The *History,* Volume Three

FOLLOWING HIS TRIUMPHANT first term, Jefferson had a progressively difficult second term. It began with trouble coming from three foes, two abroad (Talleyrand and Pitt) and one at home (Marshall).

The First Foe: Talleyrand

Engagement in Paris with Talleyrand had been broken off, for a time, by Monroe. Fed up with French attempts to make a "job" of negotiations for Florida, Monroe decided that he could, as a special emissary, leave Paris and make his demands for Florida directly to Spain. But he began in Madrid with a great disadvantage, the presence there of the regular minister, Charles Pinckney, whose bluster had amused as much as offended the court. Instead of making things better, Monroe brought things to an abrupt halt by refusing to discuss the separate points at issue with Spain (618). He said all of five demands must be met together — (1) surrender of Texas as part of "Louisiana," (2) surrender of Florida as part of "Louisiana," (3) recompense for spoliations incurred by the closing of New Orleans, (4) return of ships and goods seized by Spain, and (5) return of ships and goods seized by France and taken to Spanish harbors. He was exasperated that "for nearly a year past the French and Spanish governments had combined to entrap and humiliate him" (622). He and Pinckney encouraged each other to think that threats of force were the only expedient left them.

In this spirit, Monroe urged Armstrong in Paris to threaten American action if France did not join in pressuring Spain to yield what he was asking. As Adams puts it, "He undertook to terrify Napoleon" (622). A harsh response from the French government convinced Monroe that he could do no more in Madrid than in Paris.

> To escape from Madrid without suffering some personal mortification was his best hope, and fortunately Godoy took no pleasure in personalities. The Spaniard was willing to let Monroe escape as soon as his defeat should be fairly recorded. (624)

In this mood Monroe went to England, which still lacked an American in the minister's post. But he fared no better there. In Spain his demands had at least been turned down courteously (if tediously); in England they were rudely rebuffed when not ignored:

> Monroe had felt the indifference or contempt of Lord Harrowby, Talleyrand, and Cevallos: that of Lord Mulgrave was but one more variety of a wide experience. The rough treatment of Monroe by the Englishman was a repetition of that which he had accepted or challenged [provoked] at the hands of the Frenchman and Spaniard. Lord Mulgrave showed no wish to trouble himself in any way about the United States. (624)

Monroe was dealing not only with a new foreign minister but a new prime minister as well. William Pitt had replaced the accommodating Addington, and he had a new weapon in his arsenal for use against America. The famous judge of Admiralty Court Sir William Scott decided the *Essex* case in July, 1805, invalidating the former "broken voyage" rule for neutral trade — that a ship could take goods from the Caribbean to Europe if it stopped on the way in a United States port, unloaded there, paid customs, and put the merchandise on a new ship. Now such trade must terminate in America (632). With this ruling, the British fleet began capturing American merchant ships that had observed the old broken voyage rule. Monroe could do nothing but protest, and Pitt would do nothing but point to the ruling. Monroe in his frustration saw no recourse for America but to "threaten war upon France, Spain, and England at once" (534). Adams sees a sadly comic side to Monroe's travail, rejected in court after court, like a silent-movie actor who opens a series of doors and gets a pie in the face every time:

> During a century of American diplomatic history, a minister of the United States has seldom if ever within six months suffered, at two great courts

[French and Spanish], such contemptuous treatment as had then fallen to Monroe's lot . . . and he could no longer avoid another defeat [in England] more serious, and even more public, than the two which had already disturbed his temper. (631)

The frustration was mounting at home as well. Through the summer and fall of 1805, the Washington triumvirate tried to assess the damage registered in the reports from all three major powers, France, England, and Spain. Negotiation was at a dead end in all three places. Monroe had trod a weary round of rejection. What was left to do? What plan could be put before Congress at the end of the year? On Florida, Jefferson could not understand Spain's attitude. As he told the new minister being sent to Madrid, James Bowdoin, "We want nothing of hers" — nothing, Adams wryly notes, but Baton Rouge, Mobile, Pensacola, East Florida, and Texas (642). But the president felt that for now he could demand little more than navigation rights on the Mobile River (639). Madison agreed, and said that a new mission should be created to propose this — which prompts Adams's first severe criticism of the man whose presidency he will later be studying: "Madison, after enduring one 'refusal of all our overtures in a haughty tone,' suggested that another be invited" (42).

Jefferson was meanwhile reverting to his idea of marrying the British fleet in order to defy France and Spain by seizing Florida and Texas. In August, he wrote to Madison, who was in Philadelphia (where his wife was being treated by the eminent doctor Philip Syng Physick):

> Whatever ill humor may at times have been expressed against us by individuals of that country, the first wish of every Englishman's heart is to see us once more fighting by their side against France; nor could the King or his ministers do an act so popular [with their subjects] as to enter into an alliance with us . . . England should receive an overture as early as possible. (646)

Did Jefferson really think that the British had been hugging sentimental memories of the French and Indian War for nearly half a century ("the Spirit of '63")? Adams noted a little earlier that "Jefferson had the faculty, peculiar to certain temperaments, of seeing what he wished to see, and of believing what he wished to believe" (641).

Jefferson agreed with Madison's proposal for sending Bowdoin on the mission to Spain, a mission to secure the status quo, but only as a cover for his real response to this crisis: "We should take into consideration whether we ought not immediately to propose to England an eventual treaty of alliance, to come into force whenever (within __ years) a war shall take place with Spain and France" (544). That was written less than a month after the *Essex* decision, when Jefferson could not know that the British fleet was already seizing American commercial vessels for violation of it. Madison, too, was ignorant of the decision when he said that he would improve relations with Merry, to see if England might be open to an alliance — though he warned against giving too many benefits in return (645–47).

Gallatin, writing from Washington to Madison in Philadelphia and Jefferson in Monticello, threw cold water on all the options being entertained — negotiation, war, or some combination of the two. He did not share his fellows' belief that Florida belonged to the United States. The negotiations with Spain had failed because of the "unpardonable oversight or indifference" of Livingston and Monroe in not making the boundaries of the Purchase clear before signing the treaty (648) and because "the demands from Spain were too hard to have expected, even independent of French interference, any success from the negotiation" (DM 5.51–52). As for war, "We again run the risk of lowering the national importance by pretensions which our strength may not at this moment permit us to support" (647).

The physical separation of these three men during such a crucial discussion gives us in their letters a hint of what may have gone on in their Washington meetings. It is an interesting dynamic — Jefferson's high-flying optimism, Madison's cautious stalling, and Gallatin's realistic concentration on what could actually be done. In this case, he advised renewed negotiations with England and Spain, with fewer demands, while preparing for eventual war. Congress should be asked to build ships of the line — not gunboats, and not even frigates, but the Flying Fortresses of their day. Much as Gallatin hated the idea and expense of a navy, if the United States were going to have one, it should be a real one.

Madison, while still warning that a bargain with England might ask of the United States more than it could give, agreed that it would be a good idea to make gestures in that direction, to put the French "under apprehensions of an eventual connection between the United States and Great Britain" (651). Adams is scathing on this plan:

To leave Bonaparte "under apprehensions" was to be the object of Madison's diplomacy at Paris — a task which several European governments were then employing half a million armed men to accomplish, hitherto without success, but which Madison hoped to effect by civilities to Merry. (651)

Jefferson could not come up with any better plan. Overtures to the British as war partners "would correct the dangerous error that we are a people whom no injuries can provoke to war," but he shrank from the hated step, just as he had during the closing of the entrepôt at New Orleans. "He shrank from war except under the shield of England, and yet he feared England for an ally even more than Spain for an enemy" (652). What Jefferson meant by using England for a shield was made clear in his report on a cabinet meeting after he had returned to Washington. He wrote Madison, who was still in Philadelphia, that the cabinet considered "whether we shall enter into a provisional alliance with England to come into force only in the event that *during the present* war we become engaged in war *with France,* leaving the declaration of the *casus foederis* [activation of the alliance] ultimately with us" (652, emphasis in original).

The idea that this arrangement would appeal to William Pitt is perhaps even more comic than an appeal to the Spirit of '63. There is a poignancy in reading this correspondence and reflecting that these men were engaged in conflict with people as shrewd and tricky as Pitt, Napoleon, Talleyrand, and Godoy. At the very time of this writing, "Pitt's great collaboration with Russia and Austria against Napoleon took the field" (653). Napoleon was moving on toward his victories at Ulm and Austerlitz — yet Madison hoped to put him "under apprehensions" that the United States, without an army, might someday, somehow, do what the troops of Russia and Austria were actually doing.

Only against the backdrop of the irresolute resolutions the triumvirate came up with in the summer and fall of 1805 can one understand what was decided in November, less than three weeks before the reassembling of Congress, when some plan had to be presented. In September, Talleyrand sent an intermediary to deliver a letter, in his hand but unsigned, to Armstrong in Paris. The Emperor was still willing to offer his services for the acquisition of Florida if the United States would pay Spain ten million dollars. Armstrong rejected the idea out of hand, but the intermediary came back with a lowered price — only seven million. It was clear that France would pocket all or most of the money, and force Spain to do its will. When Talleyrand was jobbing, says Adams, "Spain was always the party to suffer, and France was always the party to profit by Spanish sacrifices" (629).

Madison had written in the very month when this letter was delivered that the United States would refuse "every hope of turning our controversy with Spain into a French job" (651). Yet when the letter reached Jefferson, such was his extremity that he was already considering some such measure. Talleyrand would get the money? No matter. It was time for a new effort, he told Madison in late October:

> Where should this be done? Not at Madrid, certainly. At Paris! through Armstrong, or Armstrong and Monroe as negotiators, France as the intermediary, the price of the Floridas as the means. We need not care who gets that, and an enlargement of the sum we thought of may be the bait to France." (954–55)

The triumvirate was ready to bargain — but it would offer only five million, with two million put down as an advance payment. Now all the triumvirate had to do was get the two million from Congress, which would be harder than they imagined.

Since Adams is scornful of the plan the triumvirate finally came up with (or had thrust upon them), it is worth asking what he thought should have been done. Monroe and Armstrong, convinced by the futility of their negotiations that they would never achieve what was wanted, urged Jefferson to seize Texas by force. The Mexican army was not large on that frontier, and it would take time for Spain to supply extra troops. Adams — who thinks Texas, unlike Florida, *was* a part of the Purchase — agrees with the two ministers:

> Spain might then [after the seizure of Texas] have declared war; but had Godoy taken this extreme measure, he could have had no other motive than to embarrass Napoleon by dragging France into a war with the United States, and had this policy succeeded, President Jefferson's difficulties would have vanished in an instant. He might then have seized Florida; his controversies with England about neutral trade, blockade, and impressment would have fallen to the ground; and had war with France continued two years, until Spain threw off the yoke of Napoleon and once more raised in Europe the standard of popular liberty, Jefferson might perhaps have effected some agreement with the Spanish patriots, and would then have stood at the head of the coming popular [anti-Bonapartist] movement throughout the world — the movement which he and his party were destined to resist. (658)

Jefferson, by continually deferring to Napoleon, hoping to get Florida from him, had helped crush freedom in Haiti, handicapped England in its effort to rally Europe against the Emperor, and made it harder for Spain to slip out from under his yoke. Even Dumas Malone agrees on what (ideally) should have been done in suppressing Napoleon:

> In the light of subsequent events it can be argued that Jefferson would have run relatively little risk and have saved much later trouble if he had followed the recommendation of his representatives abroad that he employ force at this juncture. Had he been a Napoleon Bonaparte, or even an Alexander Hamilton or Aaron Burr, conceivably he might have taken military steps as a result of which his country would have gained speedy possession of territories it was destined to acquire later by means which were not wholly diplomatic. By ranging the United States, in effect, on the side of Great Britain in the international conflict, he might have greatly reduced, though he could hardly have wholly obviated, later commercial difficulties with that country. He might have prevented the War of 1812 and hastened the downfall of Napoleon, whom he actually detested. Unlike the historian, however, he was unable to take a retrospective view. (DM 5.55)

Instead, Jefferson chose a course that did not work and one that was morally sordid, one that would rely on Napoleon, not oppose him. As Jefferson told the Anglophobe editor of the *Aurora:* "We were not disposed to join with Britain under any belief that she is fighting for the liberties of mankind" (DM 5.108–9). But in fact, she was. The course Jefferson chose had only an outside chance of working (and it did not work), and it involved unsavory means — used, as John Randolph put it when shown the plan, to "excite one nation by money to bully another nation out of its property" (695).

To pursue his scheme, Jefferson first needed to get the money he would be offering Talleyrand. He had to approach Congress in a way that would not arouse public opposition to buying what Jefferson said had already been bought. Secrecy was important, as Talleyrand knew. Jefferson decided to use a two-track approach, one for the American public and one for those with what would later be called "security clearance." To throw the public off, he used his inaugural address to inveigh heavily against Spanish aggressions in the vicinity of New Orleans, as if there were no longer any hope of negotiation with that country. This, he told Gallatin, would have the extra benefit of putting pressure on France to settle the Florida question without war. "He played a game of finesse hardly safe in the face of men like Godoy, Talleyrand, and Napoleon, whose finesse was chiefly used to cover force" (682).

While requesting funds for fortifications and naval expansion, Jefferson said he would be sending a message to Congress for its confidential consideration. Adams thinks that the martial language of the address made members of Congress expect war plans to be laid before them. Instead, Jefferson's message assured the members that there was now great promise of successful negotiation and that he would need two million dollars as "expenses" for this unspecified plan. Gallatin criticized the message as too vague — the two million was to be a down payment on a larger sum, but Congress might think it was the whole amount required.

Jefferson also asked Congress to join him in deception of the public. He actually sent Congress two messages, "double messages breathing war and peace" (684), and asked that Congress make a public answer only to the bellicose one while secretly voting the money asked for in the other one. John Randolph wanted neither the secrecy nor the grant of money. Randolph, whose hatred for Madison over the Yazoo settlement had become a fixation, was now trying to promote Monroe for president, and he remembered how Monroe had left Paris in high dudgeon rather than "grease the fists of Napoleon with American gold" (DM 5.75). Randolph lost this battle. The Two Million Act was passed, though there was a rancorous dispute over the choice of an emissary to offer Talleyrand the money.

John Armstrong was chosen as the emissary to work with James Bowdoin, the minister already in Paris. The two submitted their bid to Napoleon, but when no reply was forthcoming they floundered in the uncertain world of Talleyrand's agents and money managers. At length Napoleon told Talleyrand he was not willing to take Florida for the Americans — Adams thinks because his designs on Spain made it desirable that hostility exist between that country and America (860–69). Talleyrand lost his bribe money, and the Americans again lost the Florida they claimed they already had. It is a trying thing to put one's soul up for sale and find no buyer.

The Second Foe: Pitt

In the fall of 1805, while the seizure of American ships after the *Essex* decision was ravaging the neutral trade of the United States, two books on that trade appeared simultaneously, one in America, one in England. The first book, published anonymously, defended the neutral trade; but it was unreadable and had no measurable impact. The other one, an attack on that trade, was not only highly readable; it became one of those rare books that effect a change in world politics. The first was written by James Madison. A copy of it was placed on the desk of every senator and representative, but few read it. Senator Plumer said that it went on too long (DM 5.100), like its title — *An Examination of the British Doctrine Which Subjects to Capture a Neutral Trade Not Open in Time of Peace.* Madison argued that the *Essex* decision had no basis in international law. The argument, says Adams, however fine, was not likely to convince William Pitt. "That Pitt could occasionally be convinced of his mistakes was certain; but no reasoner except Napoleon and Moreau [in battle] had ever effectually convinced him" (679).

The other book — *War in Disguise, or The Frauds of the Neutral Flags* — was written by James Stephen, a member of the well-known family of religious dissenters (635). *War in Disguise* confirmed and inflamed British opinion that the *Essex* decision had not gone far enough to incapacitate American shipping: "Sir William Scott [by the *Essex* decision] had merely required an additional proof of its [the trade's] honesty; England with one voice demanded that, honest or not, it should be stopped" (635). Stephen, without benefit of Madison's learned research into the legists (Grotius, Pufendorf, and the rest), had a simple thesis: the neutral trade was not neutral. Its real effect was to support the war efforts of France. It was an arm of Bonaparte, deployed in support of his despotism. France and Spain did not have commercial fleets able to supply their troops and colonies, and what ships they did have were forced to struggle through the dragnet of the widely deployed British navy. But they did not need ships of their own if American vessels could with impunity carry goods to them through that British network. The "neutral" trade was, from the British standpoint, an enemy trade, more hateful for its pretense of impartiality. The British public, therefore, stirred and lashed by Stephen's book, wanted William Pitt to reciprocate bellicosities with the Americans and their "war in disguise." Pitt was willing to play along.

Stephen's argument had great force. Jefferson claimed that a perfectly neutral trade favored no single nation and should therefore be impeded by no nation. But that was never a part of the real world, and he knew it.

American shipping expanded greatly during the wars between England and France, and it was not because all nations were benefiting by it, and certainly not benefiting equally. Jefferson was cultivating good relations with Napoleon because he hoped that American trade with France would bring Napoleon to take sides with the United States over Florida. The more Napoleon profited from that trade, the more likely he was to give Jefferson what he so clearly wanted. This situation led to what John Quincy Adams called the administration's "unqualified submission to France" (DM 5.95).

As the Ninth Congress convened in 1805 — the first of Jefferson's second term, and the first deeply contentious one he experienced — the "cabinet vacillations" that Adams described over Spanish policy were paralleled by indecision over what to do in response to Pitt's war on shipping. The British were not only seizing ships at sea but blockading ports to prevent neutral ships from sailing, and they were intensifying impressments — the searching of American ships for deserting British seamen and "pressing" them back into service. This latter practice, though of long standing, was particularly galling in a time of increased activity, because it often mistook the nationality of seamen and swept Americans aboard British ships, where they received the harsh treatment given "deserters." In 1805 the rate of pressings reached a thousand men a year.

One might think that pressing would in itself be a *casus belli*, and no one should have been more ardent for retaliation than the merchants whose ships were stopped and whose crews were in danger of mistaken arrest. But the merchants, while grumbling, faced impressments with equanimity. Maritime insurance rates, which shot up when the *Essex* decision exposed ships to confiscation, had never been much affected by impressments. There was a good reason for that. Though the British got 1,000 men back in 1805, they actually lost 2,500 deserters in the same period (668). "Both the mercantile and the national marine of the United States were largely manned by British seamen and could not dispense with them" (667). The temptation to desert the harsh conditions traditional in the British navy, increased by all the risks of wartime service, made British seamen prompt to jump to the expanding American commercial fleet, with its need for experienced seamen. The merchants were willing to let impressments go on when they got over two British crewmen for every one that was taken back, and their ships sailed on free after being stopped and searched. Only the prevention of that continued course by the *Essex* decision provoked the merchants to use pressing as an emotional issue to force the government to protect neutral trade.

But how to do that? The cabinet was as unclear on this, when Congress met, as it had been in the summer about the Florida negotiations. John Randolph had complained that Jefferson offered dictation "by backstairs influence," not public guidance, with the Two Million Act (713). But now Jefferson sent no message at all on what to do about British depredations at sea. Left to its own devices, Congress came up with three resolutions — one declaring the British assault on neutral trade a violation of international law, a second "demanding" that the president do something about this, and a third calling for restrictions on the import of British products.

All parts of this program offended John Randolph. He was one of the Old South men who patterned themselves on English squires, riding to hounds. These men used to send their sons abroad to study at the Inns of Court in London. They tended (like Randolph) to quote Shakespeare or Fielding as a mark of their culture. Randolph said the British navy was too proud an institution to be intimidated by a refusal to buy British trinkets. If this country wanted to exert commercial pressure, it should call in all its ships — then, should the British truly be desperate for our products, they would invite us back onto the ocean. (This was a weird early recommendation for what became the Embargo.)

> I will never consent to go to war for that [shipping] which I cannot protect. I deem it no sacrifice of dignity to say to the Leviathan of the deep: "We are unable to contend with you in your own element" . . . Shall the great mammoth of the American forest leave his native element and plunge into the water in a mad contest with the shark? (712)

Besides, at this moment the "Leviathan" was fighting the Corsican despot in the cause of freedom. England, in Randolph's eyes, was "the sole bulwark of the human race against universal domination" (713–14).

The resolution that the president should demand recognition of American rights was coupled, by those who presented it to Jefferson at his residence, with a call for special commissioners to carry this demand to England. Senator Samuel Smith was the man urging this course, and he hoped to lead the delegation, replacing Monroe in London. Randolph, who was promoting Monroe for president, felt this was a plot to support Madison against his man. As luck would have it, action to implement the next stage of the Yazoo settlement came up in this session. The confluence of all these things — the bribe to be paid for Florida, the secrecy surrounding that bribe, the commercial restriction bill, the Yazoo Lands Act, the campaign to replace Monroe — struck Randolph as a concatenation of many elements undoing the Constitution, and he went into a pyrotechnical rage against the administration. Since he was an admirer of Gallatin and cautious about striking at the king himself, the only member of the triumvirate he could vilify at this point was Madison. It was not hard for him to think of the secretary of state as a backstairs schemer, since Madison was indeed a brilliant committee-man, one who preferred quiet compromise to public gesture.

> No one who knew the man, or who had followed the course of President Jefferson's first administration, could feel surprise that Madison's character should act on John Randolph as an irritant. Madison was cautious, if not timid; Randolph was always in extremes. Madison was apt to be on both sides of the same question, as when he wrote *The Federalist* and the Virginia Resolutions of 1798; Randolph pardoned dalliance with Federalism in no one but himself. Madison was in person small, retiring, modest, with quiet malice in his humor, and with a marked taste for closet politics and delicate management. Randolph was tall in stature, abrupt in manner, self-asserting in temper, sarcastic, with a pronounced taste for publicity, and a vehement contempt for those silent influences which more practical politicians called legitimate and necessary, but which Randolph, when he could not control them, called corrupt. (679–80)

Adams argues that Randolph, for all his frothing oratory, made some valid points. The attempt to buy Talleyrand *was* ineffectual as well as demeaning. The attempt to undermine Monroe was, on the part of Samuel Smith, a naked power play (though not inspired, as Randolph charged, by Madison). The Non-Importation Act was a pinprick on the tough sides of "the great Leviathan of the ocean." The indulgence in war talk was mere emotional venting. "The so-called resistance to England, like the resistance to Spain, was sham" (715). England was the last bastion against Napoleonic aggression. Beneath all the vituperation, in fact, Randolph was calling for what both Adams and Malone agree would have been the best course to take. America should have cast its lot with England. The harassment of neutral trade would no longer take place if it were "neutral" on England's side. "Nothing was needed but that Randolph should keep his temper in order to win a triumph" (715). In England, the hard Pitt line was about to be softened by his death, with

Charles James Fox, a friend to America, taking over the Foreign Office. Now was the time to reach an accommodation of the two nations — not quite marrying the British fleet but taking the British side sufficiently to win British support.

Adams is drawing the same lesson here that he had in Toussaint's case. If Toussaint had awaited events, harboring his strength, using his guerrilla advantages rather than engaging in showdown battles, he would have prevailed — yellow fever was about to come to his aid. But he could not restrain his desire to settle things *now*. In the same way, Randolph could not wait for Napoleon's increasing menace to make his foes coalesce, creating a partnership to which America would have been welcomed. Randolph could have helped America make that transition with the rest of the world if he had possessed a temperament capable of supporting his policies. But he threw all his advantages away in his blind desire to get at Madison.

> The entire situation had changed, an entirely new policy must be invented, and this could hardly fail to follow Randolph's ideas. He had only to wait; but meanwhile he was consumed by a fever of rage and arrogance. Thinking that the time had come to destroy the secretary of state, he set himself vigorously to the task. Day after day he occupied the floor, attacking Madison with more and more virulence. (715)

Though Randolph was attacking Madison, he was actually challenging Jefferson, and Jefferson was not an adversary to be defeated by Randolph's rough methods: "He had not the self-control that was needed in the face of an opponent so pliant and conciliatory as Jefferson. Randolph took pleasure in making enemies, while Jefferson never made one enemy except to gain two friends" (712).

Most commentators on Adams's biography of Randolph assumed that the author was simply contemptuous of his subject. He was, rather, regretful at the waste caused by Randolph's lack of discipline — waste of opportunity, of talent, of service to his country. Randolph could have been what he thought he was, the conscience of the South, the man to keep Jefferson true to his best self, the scourge of cant in all its forms. In Adams's *History*, which is mainly a comedy in the Beaumarchais vein, Randolph is, along with Toussaint and Tecumseh, the only figure of genuine tragedy — and that, for Adams, was very good company.

The post of special commissioner that Samuel Smith wanted went, instead, to William Pinkney, who was sent to London to cooperate with

Monroe in extracting concessions from the Board of Trade by brandishing the Non-Importation Act. Monroe was now in the position of Livingston when he (Monroe) was sent to supplant the minister for purchasing Louisiana. Pinkney was coming to supplant Monroe — acting, that is, as "Monroe's Monroe." But neither of the two, nor both together, could repeat the triumph of the Louisiana negotiation. They labored under the same kind of unbending instructions that Monroe had taken to Spain. This was a mission that had been forced on Jefferson by Congress's three resolutions, and he did not want for it to jeopardize the good relations that were being cultivated with Napoleon in order to get Florida. Randolph wrote Monroe that Madison meant for him to fail and be eliminated from the presidential race.

> Monroe knew that Jefferson had ever strongly opposed any commercial treaty with Great Britain, and that he never spoke of Jay's treaty except with disgust and something like abhorrence . . . Pinkney could add that Jefferson, as everyone in Washington was aware, had been unwillingly driven into the present negotiation by the Senate, and that as the measure was not his its success would hardly be within his expectation; that it would embarrass his relations with Napoleon, endanger if not ruin the simultaneous negotiation for Florida, and exalt Monroe, the candidate of Randolph, at the expense of Madison. (879)

Jefferson was not in the mood for bargaining with England now, but for threatening it. Once he had fancied a marriage with the British fleet, to keep Napoleon out of Louisiana. Now he fancied using France and Spain to create an American fleet greater than England's. He wrote to Madison:

> England may by petty-larceny thwartings check us on that element [the sea] a little; but nothing she can do will retard us there one year's growth. We shall be supported there by other nations, and thrown in their scale to make a par of the great counterpoise to her navy . . . We have the seamen and material for fifty ships of the line and half that number of frigates; and were France to give us the money and England the dispositions to equip them, they would give to England serious proofs of the stock from which they are sprung, and the school in which they have been taught, and added to the efforts of the immensity of seacoast lately united under one power would leave the state of the ocean no longer problematical. (881)

That passage is almost enough to make one wonder if Jefferson really, as we have been told, drank no alcohol but light wines.

It was in this spirit, then, that Monroe was instructed to issue three ultimatums to the British (878–79) — to cease all impressments, leave neutral trade unharassed, and pay restitution for ships seized after the *Essex* decision. Monroe might as well have asked the British to sink all their ships at once:

> No harder task could well have been imposed than was laid upon Monroe. Not even when he had been sent to Madrid in defiance of Talleyrand and Godoy, to impose his own terms on two of the greatest powers in the world, had his chance of success been smaller than when his government required him to obtain from England, after the battle of Trafalgar, concessions which England had steadily refused when she was supposed to be drawing almost her last gasp. For a British ministry to abandon the Rule of 1746 was to challenge [provoke] opposition; to throw open the colonial trade was to invite defeat; but to surrender the so-called right of impressment was to rush upon destruction. No minister that had ever ruled over the House of Commons could at such a moment have made such a treaty without losing his place or his head. (880)

Even without the anti-impressment condition, the treaty Monroe was laying on the table was less an offer than an insult. The Non-Importation Act, presented by the Americans as an aid to negotiation, was a bar to it. "Two thirds of the British people understood the Non-Importation Act as a threat — as though the Americans said, 'Surrender to us your commerce and your shipping, or surrender your liberties to France'" (875). It became clear to Monroe that he and Pinkney could not begin to get a hearing on this basis. "The difficulty of obtaining favors was increased by the attempt at compulsion" (877). So the Americans in London decided that if they could not get a treaty on the terms set by their superiors, they would get the only treaty that was gettable. Monroe had failed often enough by following instructions. If he were going to fail again, it would not be for lack of reaching any agreement at all. Monroe and Pinkney could see the fear that Napoleon was instilling in the British at this critical juncture, and they thought it was time to join England in its moment of peril, even if that meant abandoning all three of their ultimatums.

All three of them were abandoned, even though the two men received a last-minute message from Madison saying that any treaty that did not end impressment would not be ratified. When the treaty was brought to Jefferson, he had not even read it through before he refused to submit it to the Senate. Samuel Smith, who had led the forces pressing on Jefferson the mission to England, resented the fact that the Senate would not get a chance to see the product of its effort.

> A treaty was effected. It arrives. It is well known that he was coerced by the Senate to the measure; and he refuses to submit it to their approbation. What a responsibility he takes! By sending it back he disgraces his ministers, *and Monroe is one* [emphasis in original]. (901)

Jefferson liked to say, on other occasions, that republican theory left decisions on war and peace with the Congress. But not this time.

The Third Foe: Marshall

Jefferson had won the initial battles with the courts — repeal of the Judiciary Act, conviction and removal of Judge Pickering. He had suffered a threatened check in the *Marbury* decision, and a loss in the escape of Justice Chase. But his real showdown with John Marshall came in the trial of Aaron Burr, which made Jefferson renew his fantasies of impeaching the chief justice. Adams devotes six of his nineteen chapters in this volume to the Burr conspiracy and trial. Based on the fresh evidence he had found in English, French, and Spanish archives, he believed that it was a threat more real than many imagined. Not only did correspondence in those archives prove that Burr claimed he would dismember the Union. What is more surprising, all three of the major foreign diplomats in America not only knew of Burr's schemes at a time when Jefferson professed ignorance of them, but *all three thought Burr had a solid chance of success.*

The British representative, Anthony Merry, at whose house so much plotting took place, wrote on November 25, 1805, that he had "every reason to believe" Burr's representation of the western sections' readiness to break away from the Union (762). He had heard of Burr's scheme by August 4, 1805, and only feared that it was becoming too widely known (758–59). He reported Burr's request for British aid "with as much approval as he dared give it" (763).

The French representative, Louis-Marie Turreau, wrote his government on February 11, 1806, about "the project of effecting a separation between the Western and the Atlantic states."

> [Burr] has set off again for the South, after having had several conferences with the British minister. It seems to me that the government does not pen-

etrate Burr's views, and that the difficult circumstances in which it finds itself, and where it has placed itself, force it to dissimulate. This division of the confederate states appears to me inevitable, and perhaps less remote than is commonly supposed. (759)

Most surprising of all were the dispatches from the Spanish representative, Don Carlos Martínez Yrujo, who had better knowledge of America in general and of the West in particular than most of the diplomats in Washington, and he alone knew that General Wilkinson was taking bribes from the Spanish government. He wrote on New Year's Day, 1806:

> For one who does not know the country, its constitution, and above all certain localities, this plan would appear almost insane; but I confess, for my part, that in view of all the circumstances it seems to me easy to execute . . . It is beyond question that there exists in this country an infinite number of adventurers, without property, full of ambition, and ready to unite at once under the standard of a revolution which promises to better their lot. Equally certain is it that Burr and his friends, without discovering [revealing] their true object, have succeeded in getting the good will of these men, and inspiring the greatest confidence among them in favor of Burr. (767)

Four months later he was just as sanguine: "The principal [Burr] has opened himself to me; and the communications I have had with him confirm in me the idea, not only of the probability, but even of the facility, of his success, under certain circumstances" (773). One of the circumstances was financial aid from Spain and England. Why would Spain assist Burr, who would later say that he was raising troops to aid in a United States assault on Mexico? Because General James Wilkinson was at the center of the plot, and Yrujo was certain that "Wilkinson is entirely devoted to us. He enjoys a considerable pension from the King" (838). Yrujo felt that Wilkinson's aim was to divide America, not invade Mexico.

What was Adams to make of his discovery? Were these foreigners in Washington just giving rosy visions to their governments, which would like to see the United States humbled? Had they indulged in wishful thinking? The discoverer of new material is always tempted to exaggerate its importance. On the other hand, Adams's experience in the American legation in London had given him a good feel for what was deceptive and what indicative in embassy gossip. In this case, he decided that so much smoke signified a certain amount of fire. Contrary to former conjectures, there *was* a chance that Burr could have succeeded, at least in creating a serious uprising — which might have been crushed if Jefferson resorted to the means Washington had used to crush the Whiskey Rebellion. Jefferson had not approved of that earlier exertion of federal power, and he would have been reluctant to use it himself — though he would probably have been forced to do so had Burr entrenched himself in New Orleans, as Adams is convinced he meant to do.

In the social-history chapters with which he opened the *History*, Adams had stressed the difficult communications between the West and the East in the early days of the nineteenth century. Westerners' vent to the outside world was through the Mississippi and New Orleans rather than over the mountains toward the East. When that vent was imperiled by the Jay-Gardoqui Treaty in 1786, there was a western effort to withdraw from the Union, which aborted the treaty. In 1797, United States Senator William Blount, the former territorial governor for Tennessee and a close ally of Andrew Jackson, conspired with England to withdraw his state from the Union. When President Adams learned of this, he turned an incriminating letter from Blount over to the Senate, which expelled Blount and tried to impeach him (though the Constitution does not authorize impeachment against members of the legislative branch). Burr knew of this plot, since agents of it had sounded him out, and Andrew Jackson not only knew of it but remained loyal to Blount after he was exposed.[1]

Spain kept exploring the possibility that others might lure the West away from the Atlantic states. It bribed Wilkinson precisely to keep informed of such activity. It dangled old land grants before people willing to ignore the new government imposed by Jefferson. Gallatin wrote on February 12, 1806, that Wilkinson "must be closely watched, and he has now united himself with every man in Louisiana who has received or claims large grants under the Spanish government" (DM 5.224). Burr was especially interested in the delegates from New Orleans who had visited Washington to protest the rule of Jefferson's appointees over them (574–77). Burr was not deranged in his expectation of setting up a counter-government on the basis of this record, especially if he were working with General Wilkinson, who held all the military power in the region.

Why, if Burr had a genuine chance of succeeding, has his scheme been dismissed as moonshine? Adams argues that Wilkinson was able to destroy the evidence when he imposed martial law on New Orleans, seizing some minor figures in the plot and collaborating with more important ones in a silence that saved the local establishment (824). Wilkinson had played along with Burr to see how far the plan could go, and what he could make from it, while keeping his options open in other directions — to Spain for money, to New Orleans as a local base, to Washington for troops and power. When he decided that Burr was not bringing as much to the deal as he had hoped, Wilkinson had to cover his tracks.

Burr, realizing this, knew that Wilkinson would silence him if he got the opportunity: "If Burr went on [with his flotilla], he would fall into the hands of Wilkinson, who had every motive to order him to be court-martialed and shot" (627). So Burr surrendered himself to the acting governor of Mississippi, Cowles Meade. But then the local grand jury freed him (the third time this had happened): "The very militia who stopped him were half inclined to join his expedition" (827). Escaping in disguise, Burr remained at liberty for nearly a month, aware of his varied dangers. "If he fell into Wilkinson's hands, he risked a fate of which he openly expressed fear" (827).

This is a lurid tale, but it is as plausible as any other reading of the evidence, and more plausible than most. It clears up at least some of the many mysteries surrounding the affair. John Randolph, who serves here, as in other parts of the *History*, as the mad truth-teller, saw through Wilkinson's cooking of the evidence and wanted to indict him as Burr's co-conspirator, but Jefferson had many motives for upholding Wilkinson's innocence and shifting all the blame to Burr. He could not admit that his government of Louisiana had given cause for rebelliousness, or that he had been remiss in appointing Wilkinson in the first place and supporting his questionable activities afterward.

Some of the leading men accused in the conspiracy were Republicans, including his old ally and the presenter of the Kentucky Resolutions for resisting federal authority, John Breckinridge. The most ardent denouncers of the plot were Federalists, including the main accuser, Joseph Daveiss, who was not only a Federalist, but had been appointed attorney general in Kentucky by President Adams, had founded an anti-Jefferson newspaper, and — worst of all in Jefferson's eyes — had married the sister of John Marshall. All these considerations help us in assessing what is otherwise not easily understood, the urgency of Jefferson to see Wilkinson vindicated and Burr hanged — an urgency that has been heavily criticized by Leonard Levy:

Having convicted Burr before the bar of public opinion prior to his appre-
hension, the first magistrate proceeded relentlessly to mobilize executive
resources to prove the preconceived guilt. Jefferson did not turn the case
over to the United States attorney, but acted himself as prosecutor, super-
intending the gathering of evidence, locating witnesses, taking depositions,
directing trial tactics, and shaping public opinion as if judge and juror of
the nation. The object was not to secure justice by having Burr's guilt — or
innocence — fairly determined, but to secure a conviction, no matter how,
on the charge of high treason.[2]

Since Adams found in the foreign archives the evidence that Burr's
schemes were the subject of Washington gossip as early as the summer of 1805, he wondered why Jefferson was so slow to suspect those
schemes and to do something about them. He began to raise, in effect,
the same questions asked during impeachment hearings of a later president, Richard Nixon: "What did the president know and when did he
know it?" John Randolph was the person asking those questions on January 16, 1807, and Jefferson gave a straightforward answer on January
22: "Some time in the latter part of September [1806] I received intima-
tions that designs were in agitation in the western country, unlawful and
unfriendly to the peace of the Union, and that the prime mover in these
was Aaron Burr" (835). Adams is not satisfied with that answer: "He had
received such intimation many times, and long before the month of September." He is referring to what he calls "the reiterated warnings of
Eaton, Truxton, Morgan, Daveiss, and even to the hints of Wilkinson
himself" (830). Adams uses the very constitutional proviso that was
used against Nixon — that he failed to observe the injunction of Article
II, Section 3, obliging the president to "take care that the laws be faith-
fully executed."

Though Adams is not as harsh on Jefferson as Leonard Levy, I think
this is the first place in the *History* where he is provably unfair to his
subject. There was evidence of Burr's conspiracy that Jefferson disregarded. But these were like warnings of a sneak attack before Pearl Harbor, clear in retrospect but lost in a static of hard-to-weigh indications
beforehand. In the case of Burr, the information that reached Jefferson
looked unspecific or tainted or contradictory, and reaction to it could
have been more panicky than reasoned. Some of the warnings came in
anonymous letters, of which a president receives many and which he
would be foolish to heed.

Adams says that the non-anonymous warnings before September

1806 came from "Eaton, Truxton, Morgan, Daveiss" (830). There is something faulty in each of these supposed warnings. That is clearest in the case of Colonel George Morgan. He did not warn Jefferson prior to September, 1806, but on that date — it is his letter that Jefferson cites as the beginning of his own knowledge of the plot (DM 5.239). William Eaton did make his charge before that date — he went to see Jefferson on March 6, 1806, but he had already made accusations to members of Congress and been dismissed as a perennial complainer (770).

Eaton, the hero of the march to Derne in the Tripolitan War, felt he had not received the proper rewards for his feat, and had lapsed into a dissolute life of drinking, gambling, and whoring. When he went to Jefferson, it was with the recommendation that Jefferson should send Burr out of the country as a dangerous man. "The President asked where he should send him. I said to England or Madrid" (770). He was asking Jefferson to act as if the Alien Act were still in force, and Jefferson had become a supporter of it. (770). Eaton's later testimony at Burr's trial would be disregarded because of his character. It would have been imprudent for Jefferson to follow his wild recommendation.

Thomas Truxton was another of the military men Burr hoped to enlist in his project. As one of six captains given command of the Humphreys frigates built by Washington, he won the great victory of the *Constellation* over the *Insergente* in the Quasi War, but he had always quarreled with his naval superiors, and Jefferson was glad to accept his complaints as a form of resignation. His supposed part in the plot was not made known to Jefferson until Wilkinson sent his letter to Jefferson in January 18, 1807, long after the September date the president gave for his realization that there was some kind of conspiracy.

Perhaps Adams's worst distortion of this whole episode is his treatment of Joseph Daveiss, the federal attorney general in Kentucky. Adams inexcusably omits the fact that Daveiss was John Marshall's brother-in-law. He also fails to give full descriptions of the kinds of warnings Daveiss sent Jefferson. The first warning from Daveiss (received January 10, 1806) did not name Burr, but said that General Wilkinson, a Jefferson appointee, was a pensioner of Spain prepared to plot against the United States. Jefferson showed the letter to Gallatin, who affirmed Wilkinson's loyalty. The president then asked Daveiss (in a letter of February 15, 1806) to send more details. Even before that response was received, Daveiss sent a second letter calling Burr's western trip suspicious, and then a third letter listing ten people, all Republicans, as parts of a western plot. Wilkinson was third on the list, and Burr was ninth (DM 5.224–25).

The other names included Henry Clay and John Breckinridge. The last name was enough to discredit the whole list. Breckinridge was such a supporter of Jefferson's Louisiana government that he had introduced the Senate bill to authorize it. Jefferson was bound to think Daveiss a partisan who was smearing Republicans with a broad brush. When Daveiss brought Burr before two Kentucky grand juries, both of them dismissed the charges. Jefferson removed Daveiss from his post as attorney general in Kentucky. Jefferson was wrong to trust Wilkinson, but Daveiss had not brought supportable charges against him or Burr. On the question of what Jefferson knew and when he knew it, Adams does not provide a convincing account of what happened. He is better on what Jefferson did after he found out that Burr was indeed plotting — something or other.

On October 22, 1806, Jefferson told his cabinet that he had heard of more reports from Eaton and was sending an emissary (John Graham) to investigate Burr's activities (795–97). Then, on November 25, Wilkinson's own letter accusing Burr arrived in Washington. Jefferson immediately issued a proclamation (November 17, 1806) informing the public that there was illegal activity occurring in the West, but not naming Burr — though he quietly dispatched military forces to apprehend Burr (798–99). So far Jefferson was beyond reasonable reproach. But after that his desire to be in charge of the investigation led him into a series of indiscretions.

Wilkinson had imposed martial law and was covering his own past actions in a flurry of repressive measures against the vague plot he now claimed to have uncovered. He made military arrests of civilians and defied court orders to recognize their right of habeas corpus. He did not want full investigations on the spot. Instead, he sent the captives, Dr. Eric Bollman and Samuel Swartwout, who had been illegally detained, under guard to Jefferson in Washington. He also sent an edited but incriminating letter from Burr, trying to convince Jefferson that his extralegal activities were justified by the conspiracy he was facing (822–23). Jefferson received this letter on January 18, 1807, after Wilkinson had already used it in New Orleans to justify his acts. Jefferson sent the letter to Congress on January 22, asserting "of his [Burr's] guilt there can be no doubt." That phrase would come back to bedevil Jefferson when Luther Martin, at Burr's trial, said that Jefferson had pronounced his client guilty before he was convicted, violating the presumption of innocence for arrested men.[3] Martin orated:

> The President has undertaken to prejudge my client by declaring that "of his guilt there can be no doubt." He has assumed the knowledge of the Supreme Being himself, and pretended to search the heart of my highly respected friend. He has proclaimed him a traitor in the face of that country which has rewarded him [with the vice presidency]. (912)

When Bollman and Swartwout, the prisoners Wilkinson had illegally apprehended, arrived in Washington, they were finally arraigned on charges of treason. The Senate passed a bill retroactively exonerating Wilkinson for defying habeas corpus proceedings by suspending that right during the Burr crisis. The House refused to go along with this, and John Randolph introduced a measure to make such suspensions impossible. He criticized the author of the letter submitted to Congress — General Wilkinson — and the man who was trusting Wilkinson's word, the president. Jefferson summoned one of Wilkinson's prisoners, Bollman, for personal questioning. He asked Bollman to supply signed answers to his questions, giving "his word of honor that they shall never be used against himself, and that the paper shall never go out of his hand." This pledge of honor was broken in both its parts — Jefferson sent the letter to Richmond for his attorney general there to use against Bollman in pre-trial depositions.[4]

Attorneys for Bollman and Swartwout applied for a dismissal of the charges against them, and Justice Marshall granted it, since no overt act had been established as a basis for the treason charge (817). Burr's trial was taking place in Richmond, since Blennerhassett's Island, the site of the alleged overt act of marshaling troops, was then in Virginia. If Jefferson had not repealed the Judiciary Act, a district judge would have conducted the trial. But as it was, the Supreme Court judge for that circuit had to conduct the trial — which meant that Jefferson's foe, the Chief Justice himself, was in charge.

Marshall first convened a grand jury and appointed John Randolph its foreman. Jefferson rightly suspected that there would be little sympathy for him in this tribunal.

> What seemed to be the indictment and trial of Burr became, in a political point of view, the trial of Wilkinson, with John Randolph acting as accuser and President Jefferson as counsel for the defense, while Chief Justice Marshall presided in judgment. No more unpleasant attitude could be readily

imagined for a man of Jefferson's high position and pure character than to plead before his two most formidable and unforgiving enemies as the patron and protector of a client so far beneath respect. (88)

When Jefferson's attorney general for the district, George Hay, made a motion to commit Burr to prison awaiting trial, he brought two charges as probable cause — treason (for trying to sunder the Union) and misdemeanor (for preparing to invade Mexico). At this preliminary hearing, Marshall would not admit the treason allegation for want of sufficient evidence to establish "probable cause," but admitted the misdemeanor charge, since the bar is lower for that than for treason, the only crime defined — and narrowly defined — in the Constitution. Burr was granted bail on the misdemeanor charge, and he became, while free, a favorite of Richmond society. Marshall himself attended a dinner where Burr was present — a fact Adams does not report (DM 5.302).[5] When, after indictment for treason, Burr was imprisoned pending his trial, he was treated so deferentially that William Duane called him "the emperor of the penitentiary" (DM 5.331).

Jefferson was furious over Marshall's refusal to admit the charge of treason at the commitment hearing. Senator Giles again talked of impeaching Marshall, and Jefferson wrote to him, egging him on: "All the principles of law are to be perverted which would bear on the favorite offenders who endeavor to overturn this odious republic!" Jefferson's only hope was that the people would amend the Constitution to take away judicial independence, since it is "the error in our Constitution which makes any branch independent of the nation . . . If their protection of Burr produces this amendment, it will do more good than his condemnation" (911). Adams does not cite from this letter to Giles the charge that his Federalist opponents were "mortified only that he [Burr] did not separate the Union or overturn the government" (DM 5.304).

Burr knew just how to irritate Jefferson. He asked Marshall to issue a subpoena *duces tecum* (evidence to be brought in person) served on the president of the United States. This move had a plausible excuse. As Burr's local lawyer, the former attorney general of the United States Edmund Randolph, explained, he wanted Wilkinson's letters, to confront him with them and disqualify his testimony.[6] Marshall ruled as a matter of principle that the president is not above the law, and issued the subpoena. Burr said that he would not require the president's actual appearance, but Jefferson had already expressed his indignation that the court aimed, in his words, to "bandy him from pillar to post, keep him constantly trudging from north to south and east to west, and withdraw him entirely from his executive duties" (913). He took his anger out on Luther Martin, who was one of the lawyers arguing for issuance of the subpoena. Jefferson had heard of a rumor against Martin spoken by a Maryland man named Graybell, and he wrote to Hay, who was handling the prosecution in Richmond:

> Shall we move to commit Luther Martin as *particeps criminis* with Burr? Graybell will fix upon him misprision of treason at least. And at any rate his evidence will put down this unprincipled and impudent Federal bulldog, and add another proof that the most clamorous defenders of Burr are all his accomplices. (915)

Adams says that Jefferson defied the subpoena. Malone denied this. Presidential defiance of the Supreme Court was a touchy issue when Malone's volume dealing with the Burr trial appeared in 1974. President Nixon had only months before appealed to what he called "the Jefferson rule," saying the Court could not force him to turn over White House tapes to a judge presiding at the trial of Nixon's subordinates. A column by Malone appeared in the New York *Times* on November 26, 1973, contradicting Nixon and asserting that Jefferson "cannot be rightly said to have rejected it [the subpoena]." Jefferson, he says, offered to comply in part, sending what he thought material to the case, and Marshall accepted this, extending what Malone called "a kind of privilege" to the president.

Malone is right in saying that Jefferson did not outright defy the subpoena. He certainly wanted to do that — and at first signaled that he would. He wrote Hay saying:

> Reserving the necessary right of the President of the U.S. to decide independently of all other authority, what papers, coming to him as president, the public interests permit to be communicated, and to whom, I assure you of my readiness, under that restriction, voluntarily to furnish on all occasions whatever the purposes of justice may require. (DM 5.320)

In other words, he would comply only so far as he decided to, not as the Court directed. But he quickly followed this up with letters saying that he had already turned over what the subpoena demanded to the attorney general, Caesar Rodney, who had (he believed) sent the material to the federal prosecutor in Richmond, George Hay. The documents should be sought there. Thus far Malone is right. Jefferson had threatened non-compliance but did not act on the threat.

The action then moved to Hay, who, after identifying the documents called for, offered to let the court and Burr's attorneys, but not Burr himself, look at them. Hay alleged national security concerns for this reservation. Burr nonetheless insisted on seeing the Wilkinson letter, and procured a subpoena served on Hay for this purpose.[7] Hay refused to turn the letter over for Burr's perusal, and Justice Marshall said he could refuse only if the president himself said there were urgent reasons for not letting Burr (as opposed to the court) see the letter. This was the only "privilege" Marshall seemed to grant the President; but even this was based not on personal prerogative but on the nature of the national security threat that would be posed by letting Burr see the letter. Marshall was clear on the basis of his action: "The propriety of introducing any paper into a case as testimony must depend on the character of the paper, not on the character of the person who holds it."[8]

Jefferson was being asked, in effect, to testify as an expert witness on national security issues in the letter. The nature of the document was at issue, and Jefferson was the best witness for identifying material to be excluded because of *its* nature. There was no presidential privilege involved. Burr did not press his demands further. What President Nixon called "the Jefferson rule" was never accepted by Marshall, nor was Malone's "kind of" privilege extended to the president. Burr's legal team let the demand on Hay lapse — it was no longer needed to discredit Wilkinson. No rule or privilege can be established from this sequence of refusals to push the matter to a showdown. Jefferson backed off by releasing the material to Hay, Hay did so by offering the evidence to the court, Burr did so by not continuing his demand to see the evidence, and Marshall did so by saying the president could testify on the need to restrict the viewing of the evidence.

This unwillingness to push toward an extreme reflects the sense of danger attending the trial. To hang a former vice president for treason would be momentous in its consequences. But to defy a president who so clearly wanted that hanging was also a tremendous thing. Jefferson convinced himself that the chief justice's enmity was so great he might send a marshal to arrest him and force his testimony — Jefferson told Hay to order federal marshals not to comply with such an order.[9] The chief justice, for his part, knew that some were watching his every move to find an occasion for impeaching him. Hay even hinted at that in the court, by referring to the impeachment of Supreme Court justice Samuel Chase:

> His arbitrary and irregular conduct at the trial [of John Fries] . . . was one of the principal causes for which he was afterward impeached. He attempted to wrest the decision from the jury, and prejudge the case before hearing all the evidence in it — the identical thing which this court is now called on by these gentlemen [Burr's lawyers] to do. (924)

Hay was clumsy, and not only in this veiled threat. Jefferson's direction was not helpful to him. By raising fears of persecution from the bench, it prevented clear legal thinking. Hay was as outclassed by lawyers on the other side as John Randolph had been at the Chase trial. In fact, the key defense figure at both trials was the same man — Luther Martin of Maryland. His final speech was a masterpiece:

> On Friday, August 28, Luther Martin rose to speak for the defense. He spoke for two days and his speech covers 118 pages, or almost one tenth of the entire Richmond proceedings. His points were cogent, well organized, and effective. His presentation was one of the great courtroom speeches by a lawyer in the history of American law.[10]

At the end of Burr's trial, Marshall gave an instruction to the jury that seemed at odds with his ruling on Bollman and Swartwout, Wilkinson's two prisoners. In the earlier decision, Marshall said that the men could be convicted of conspiracy to commit treason even if they were not at the scene of the overt act where war was being waged on the United States. In his charge to the Burr jury, he seemed to be saying that Burr could not be convicted if he were not present at the overt act. To find an inconsistency here, however, one must ignore the force of one small word — *if* — in the Bollman ruling:

> *If* war be actually levied, that is, if a body of men be actually assembled for the purpose of effecting by force a treasonable purpose, all those who *perform any part*, however minute or however remote from the scene of action, and who are actually leagued in the general conspiracy, are to be considered as traitors [emphasis added].[11]

In his instruction to the Burr jury, ruling on the admissibility of evidence, Marshall said that the levying of war (at Blennerhassett's Island) had not met the constitutional test of two witnesses' testimony, which made it impossible to say that Burr had *performed a part* in an unproved act. The jury, in other words, had to find Burr innocent.

For Jefferson, this was one of what he called Marshall's "twistifications" of the law.[12] Adams realizes that others might feel that way:

> An uneasy doubt could not fail to suggest itself that the Chief Justice, with an equal effort of ingenuity, might have produced equal conviction in a directly opposite result. On the other hand, the intent of the Constitution was clear. The men who framed that instrument remembered the crimes that had been perpetrated under the pretence of justice; for the most part, they had been traitors themselves, and having risked their necks under the law, they feared despotism and arbitrary power more than they feared treason. No one could doubt that their sympathies, at least in 1788, when the Constitution was framed, would have been on the side of Marshall's decision. If Jefferson, since 1788, had changed his point of view, the Chief Justice was not under obligations to imitate him. (925)

Here Adams is anticipating the view of some modern scholars, that Marshall actually did Jefferson a favor in this ruling. He prevented a president from hounding a personal enemy to the gallows on the basis of a broad construction of treason, relying on evidence scrambled and discredited by the scoundrel who brought it, James Wilkinson: "It was probably fortunate for Jefferson's reputation as America's champion of human rights that Marshall spared Aaron Burr from the gallows."[13] Jefferson's own prosecutor, George Hay, came to see what his superior never did, that any evidence deriving from Wilkinson was worthless (927–28). Jefferson's attachment to Wilkinson was an eerie thing:

> The world often loved and cherished its worst rogues — the Falstaffs, Macheaths, and Burrs — and Jefferson was not exempt from such weakness; but that his respect and esteem for Wilkinson should require him to retain a pensioned Spanish spy and a confederate with Burr and Dayton as the head of the United States Army during several years of extreme public danger, was a costly consequence to the people whose confidence Jefferson claimed and held. John Randolph saw this point at once, and his bloodhound instinct detected and followed, without hesitation, the trail that led to the White House. Whether the Chief Justice intended it or not, he never struck Jefferson a blow so mischievous as when he directed the clerk to place John Randolph as foreman of the grand jury. Randolph's nature revolted from Wilkinson, and if the President and the General could be gibbeted together, Randolph was the man to do it. (917)

Jefferson did not give up when Burr was acquitted. He ordered Hay to bring a new trial before Marshall. (The completed one was for the treason charge. The new one would be for misdemeanor — the plan to invade Mexico.) He had no hope of winning again from Marshall, but he hoped Marshall would make mistakes, exposing him to impeachment. Jefferson had instructed Hay to keep a complete record of the trial from its outset, to get witnesses' depositions before they left Richmond, and to pursue every legal claim before Marshall.

> These whole proceedings will be laid before Congress, that they may decide whether the defect has been in the evidence of guilt, or in the law, or in the application of the law, and that they may provide the proper remedy for the past and the future. (927)

Senator Giles would pursue Jefferson's purpose in the Senate, offering an amendment to make judges removable by the president on a joint petition from both houses of the Congress. Short of that, Jefferson believed, the nation would continue to exist under a judicial tyranny:

> The scenes which have been acting at Richmond are sufficient to fill us with alarm. We had supposed we possessed fixed laws to guard us equally against treason and oppression. But it now appears we have no law but the will of the judge. Never will chicanery have a more difficult task than has been now accomplished to warp the text of the law to the will of him who is to construe it. (DM 5.354)

Giles, in the next session of Congress, went further in his war on Marshall's treatment of Burr. He offered an amendment to redefine treason, making any resistance to a law treasonous — a return to the Sedition Act, this time coming from Jefferson's camp (1069). And some states began the ratification of an amendment for removing judges even before that amendment had passed through Congress (1068). The defeat of these moves showed that Marshall had won: "If, in the full tide of Jefferson's power, Marshall had repeatedly thwarted or defied him with impunity, the chance was small that another president would meet a happier fate" (1070).

Jefferson was still defending Wilkinson in 1810. After granting that Wilkinson broke the law by seizing men, denying them trial, and sending them out of the territory, he exonerates him because the men seized were "notorious conspirators," and danger rendered the law irrelevant.

> A strict observance of the written law is doubtless one of the high duties of a good citizen; but it is not the highest. The laws of necessity, of self-preservation, of saving our country when in danger, are of higher obligation. To

lose our country by a scrupulous adherence to written law, would be to lose the law itself, with life, liberty, property, and all those who are enjoying them with us, thus absurdly sacrificing the end to the means.[14]

To another correspondent Jefferson went further, arguing for a temporary dictatorship:

> Under the maxim of the law itself, that *inter arma silent leges* [laws fall silent when guns speak], that in an encampment expecting daily attack from a powerful enemy, self-preservation is paramount to all law, I expected that instead of invoking the forms of the law to cover traitors, all good citizens would have concurred in securing them. Should we have ever gained our Revolution if we had bound our hands by manacles of the law, not only in the beginning but in any part of the revolutionary conflict? There are extreme cases where the laws become inadequate even to their own preservation, and where the universal resource is a dictator or martial law.[15]

The villainy of Wilkinson, which Jefferson stubbornly denied, was obvious to the jurors and audience in Richmond, and was commonly talked of in Congress — as by William Plumer:

> Wilkinson has done more to destroy our little feeble military establishment than its bitterest enemies have been able for years to effect. The President ought instantly to remove him from his two offices of gov. of upper Louisiana and commander of the army. If he does not do it, Wilkinson will damn him and his administration. Thomas M. Randolph told me he thought Wilkinson must be removed or his father-in-law's administration would fall. The public indignation seems now to be transferred from Burr to Wilkinson . . . It is now very apparent Wilkinson himself has created much of the alarm, and has greatly exaggerated the force and importance of Burr.[16]

Though Wilkinson did not cause Jefferson's administration to fall, Jefferson's retention of him as the highest officer in the army would undermine that army, threaten Madison's administration, and interfere with the conduct of the War of 1812. Jefferson's vendetta was a costly one. It is hard to weigh which thing was more costly, Jefferson's enmity toward Burr or his amity with Wilkinson. In any case, he delivered himself over, by the confluence of those two things, into the hands of John Marshall, where Adams felt that he got the treatment he deserved.

5

ANYTHING BUT WAR

The *History*, Volume Four

O
N JUNE 22, 1807, while the Burr grand jury was at work in Richmond, the British navy offered what many people, including Albert Gallatin, considered an occasion of war. Adams, agreeing with his favorite in the administration, thought the occasion should have been taken. But Jefferson was willing to try any expedient but war. He was not a pacifist from humanitarian concerns. He thought war centralized and increased the powers of the state, violating his small-government principles. "War, which every other nation in history had looked upon as the first duty of a state, was in America a subject for dread, not so much because of possible defeat as of probable success" (1072). Ironically, the means Jefferson chose to avoid war, the Embargo, would give sweeping and arbitrary powers to the state, and especially to the executive, accomplishing what war would have — thus helping to make the nation, which is Adams's theme.

USS *Chesapeake*

The occasion for war was provided near the mouth of Chesapeake Bay, where the British frigate *Leopard* poured a fusillade of cannon shot into the American frigate *Chesapeake*, before the latter had time to service its guns. Shortly before that, an officer from the *Leopard* had been received on the *Chesapeake*, sent there to demand deserters from named British ships. He was acting on an order from George Berkeley, the admiral of the whole British fleet in American waters. James Barron, the captain of the *Chesapeake*, assured the emissary that none of his crew came from the listed ships (though he did not add that there were men from other ships). As soon as the British boarder returned to the *Leopard*, it sent three unanswered, unanswerable broadsides into the American vessel, killing three men and wounding eighteen others. One of those wounded was Captain Barron, who had to strike his flag and offer the *Chesapeake* as prize to his assailants. The captain of the *Leopard*, after taking four deserters off the crippled vessel — including three Americans who had joined and then left British service — refused to accept the prize, and made an offer, which was rejected, of his own surgeon's assistance to the wounded.

Adams says that it was only a matter of time before such an incident occurred — in fact, it was surprising that it had not happened before. He blames the incident on Jefferson, for the contradictions in his policy. The president did not want the frigates to be at sea in the first place. He had planned to drydock them all until the Barbary pirates made him keep some of them out. The president's lack of interest in the military, and his trust in a mediocre naval secretary (Robert Smith), led to lackadaisical upkeep of the Eastern Branch naval yard, which sent the *Chesapeake* to its embarkation point at Norfolk in less than ready condition. Since Jefferson said the reason for keeping the ships off the sea was that they were a provocation to war, Secretary Smith's instructions to Captain James Barron were that he "should cautiously avoid whatever may have a tendency to bring us into collision with any other power" (943). In other words, a warship should not act like a warship.

Captain Barron used those orders to explain why he did not call his crew to the guns as soon as he was presented with the demand. He was still unaware of danger. The British regularly searched commercial ships, but they had taken the assurances of officers on American warships that they had no deserters. For the *Leopard* to act so swiftly with deadly force had no precedent.[1] But a warship in the presence of another country's warship should not take for granted its pacific intent, especially when it maneuvers, as the *Leopard* had, for the wind advantage. Adams has to admit: "If Barron had wished to invite an attack, he could have done nothing more to the purpose than by receiving Berkeley's orders without a movement of self-defense" (937). But Barron argued that to prepare for action would have contravened his orders "to avoid whatever may have a *tendency* to bring us into collision." He did not act like a warrior, it is true. But his president did not want him to act like a warrior.

Despite Barron's honorable prior service, a court-martial sentenced him to five years' suspension without pay.

> The president and the secretary of the navy could alone say whether Barron had understood their orders correctly, and whether his plea, founded on the secretary's instructions, was sound. In the light of Jefferson's diplomacy, Barron's course accorded with his instructions; and perhaps, had the president claimed his own share in the *Chesapeake*'s disaster, he would have refused to degrade a faithful, able, and gallant seaman for obeying the spirit and letter of his orders. Unfortunately, such an interference would have ruined the navy; and so it happened that what Jefferson had so long foreseen took place. He had maintained that the frigates were a mere invitation to attack; they created the dangers they were built to resist, and tempted the aggressions of Great Britain, which would, but for these ships, find no object to covet; and when the prediction turned true, he was still obliged to maintain the character of the service. He approved the sentence of the court martial. (944)

George Bancroft, in the margin of the preliminary printing of the *History* that Adams sent him, objected to this "speculative" passage (944). Adams, in a gesture to him, slightly modified it, removing the phrase "should have come to the support of his officers" from its place before "and would have refused to degrade." He also changed "stood in exact agreement with those instructions" to "accorded with his instructions."[2] But the stand he took was essentially unaltered. Was it fair to Jefferson?

Adams says that the equivocal leadership that led up to the affair was continued in Jefferson's conduct after it. Gallatin advised the president that Congress should be called back into session immediately, to consider the provocation. Jefferson agreed only to move the convening date up from November to October — four months after the attack. Jefferson was responding from Monticello, in accord with his policy of avoiding Washington as unhealthy during the summer. But the British and French ministers were able to bear the Washington heat, and they read the refusal to take emergency measures as proof that Jefferson would not even consider war as a response. Turreau assured Talleyrand "that the president does not want war, and that Mr. Madison dreads it still more" (952). David Erskine, who had by now replaced Anthony Merry as King George's representative, said that there was a popular outcry for war after the *Chesapeake* attack, but that a British apology for this one incident "would make it impossible for the Congress to bring on a war upon the other points of difference between His Majesty and the United States" (953).

Jefferson said that he did not rule out war as an option, but that only Congress could declare it, and that Congress could not do that until the British were given a chance to defend the *Leopard*'s action or to make an apology and reparations. Meanwhile, he banned all British ships of war from American ports and sent a protest to London. Gallatin said that Congress could not declare war when it met unless war preparations had been made. Such preparations should be undertaken immediately, simply to preserve the option Jefferson had not ruled out. Before one can threaten with a sword, one must forge it. War would destroy Gallatin's cherished economic plans, but he was prepared to sacrifice them, as he wrote to his wife:

> Having considered from the first moment war was a necessary result, and the preliminaries appearing to me but matters of form, my faculties have been exclusively applied to the preparations necessary to meet the time . . . We will be the poorer both as a nation and as a government, our debt and taxes will increase, and our progress in every respect be interrupted; but all these evils are not only not to be put in competition with the independence and honor of the nation, they are moreover temporary, and a very few years of peace will obliterate their effects. Nor do I know whether the awakening of nobler feelings and habits than avarice and luxury might not be necessary to prevent our degenerating, like the Hollanders, into a nation of mere calculators. (950)

While leaving the nation in an unready state for stronger action, Jefferson made exigent demands in his protest to the British, to be delivered by Monroe. In London, Monroe was still smarting from Jefferson's rejection of the treaty he had negotiated, and now he was told to submit peremptory demands to the British foreign minister, George Canning. As soon as the attack had been reported in London, Canning sent Monroe a note saying that he regretted it and would be ready to make amends "if the British officer should prove to have been culpable" (955). Monroe agreed that this immediate issue should be addressed, taking priority over all other grievances, since "it is improper to mingle them with the present more serious cause of complaint" (956). That was the obvious diplomatic procedure — to isolate, stigmatize, and resolve a concrete matter where England was ready to admit having committed some wrong, and then build further negotiations from that base:

> That the attack on the *Chesapeake* should be disavowed, that the men who had been seized should be restored, that punctilious exactness of form should mark the apology and retribution — was matter of course; but that this special outrage, which stood on special ground, should be kept apart, and that its atonement should precede the consideration of every other disputed point, was the natural method of dealing with it if either party was serious in wishing for peace. Such a wound, left open to fester and smart, was certain to make war in the end inevitable. (955)

In line with these considerations, England did in fact offer to apologize for the attack, to admit that the *Leopard* was acting beyond instructions, to suspend Admiral Berkeley, to return the three Americans taken off the ship, and to pay reparations to the widows and children of the dead, as well as to those who were wounded.

Monroe wanted to make arrangements on that basis, but his principals would not let him: "Both the president and Madison wanted peace; yet their instructions to Monroe made a settlement of the *Chesapeake* outrage impracticable by binding it to a settlement of the wider dispute as to impressments from merchant vessels" (954). Monroe, having had his treaty rejected for not following instructions on impressments, could not defy them a second time. Canning slyly commiserated with his plight:

> If your instructions leave you no discretion, I cannot press you to act in contradiction to them. In that case there can be no advantage in pursuing a discussion which you are not authorized to conclude, and I shall have only the regret that the disposition of His Majesty to terminate that difference amicably and satisfactorily is for the present considered unavailable. (960)

Monroe could not add a fifth humiliation to the unbroken string of them that had followed on the successful purchase of Louisiana. Adams wonders that Jefferson "should have thought such a policy of accumulating unsettled causes for war consistent with his policy of peace" (954). But Jefferson, as often before, saw signs of hope in any trouble with England — it was bound to make France better disposed to settling the Florida matter. The French minister Turreau, reporting to Talleyrand, quoted Jefferson's words from a long conversation held with him at this time: "If the English do not give us the satisfaction we demand, we will take Canada, which wants to enter the Union; and when, together with

Canada, we shall have the Floridas, we shall no longer have any difficulties with our neighbors . . . I expected that the Emperor would return sooner to Paris — and then this affair of the Floridas would be ended" (952).

American historians of the *Chesapeake* affair stress the outrage felt by the American citizenry. They rarely reflect an even more feverish and venomous outburst that followed in England. If some Americans wanted war, more wanted it in England, where the means of waging it were vastly greater. The newspaper that spoke for the government (the *Morning Post*) trumpeted: "A war [with America] of a very few months, without creating to us the expense of a single additional ship, would be sufficient to convince her of her folly by a necessary chastisement of her insolence and audacity" (976). Monroe tried to make clear to Jefferson and Madison how the British, fearing Napoleon, took any demand from America as a message relayed from Bonaparte himself. But Monroe's superiors, feeling he gave in too easily to British pressure, never understood the explosive situation he was experiencing. The British populace took a savage joy in the assault on the *Chesapeake*. Canning would be harshly criticized for offering any apology and recalling Admiral Berkeley — "for a time Canning seemed likely to be devoured by his own hounds" (980).

British hostility had been inflamed by James Stephen's attack on "neutral" trade as disguised war. What, the outraged readers asked, was the government doing against this war? Stephen's friends were in the new government. The Duke of Portland was prime minister, but the chief figures were Canning at the Foreign Office and Spencer Perceval in the Exchequer (967, 984). Supporters of this ministry felt that the Americans were trying to make England surrender to Napoleon. Even a pamphlet that was sympathetic to some aspects of the American position admitted: "Hatred of America seems a prevailing sentiment in this country . . . The fact is undeniable that the bulk of the people would fain be at war with them" (977).

George Canning understood the uses of hate. He was a radical conservative who took pleasure in Napoleon's coup of the 18th Brumaire, since it gave England a clearly despotic enemy to arouse its combative juices — "he held that Napoleon's course had absolved England from ordinary rules of morals" (970). Adams describes the paradox of such a radical conservative: "It was impossible to say what time-honored monument he might overthrow in defending [it]" (968). But Canning was a minute calibrator of the degree of hatred that was useful. He defied his own extremists in offering an apology over the *Chesapeake,* since he knew that America had so few warships it was not worth asserting a right to search them. He saved his arguments for continuing searches of the huge American commercial fleet (981). It was, in his eyes, uneconomical to go to war with America if he could stop its merchants from helping Napoleon without the expense or trouble of war. He was certain he could accomplish this, since America had suffered endless assaults on its commercial ships without making any war preparations.

In a fascinating debate conducted within the Portland ministry, superbly tracked by Adams (985–98), the way America was helping Napoleon received a precise definition. It was not by supplying Europe with its wares. England had to do that as well, since all countries on the Continent were not to be starved because Napoleon had conquered or was threatening them. Besides, England, as an overproducing island in need of imports, had to support its war with its trade. America's menace was that it could, by free trading on the markets in Caribbean islands and European ports, undercut British prices and deprive England of the money needed for its struggle with Bonaparte. The *Essex* decision of July 23, 1805, had reduced that threat by inhibiting free trade in and out of the Caribbean. The Orders in Council of January 7, 1807, drew the noose tighter by banning free trade from one port to another in Europe. A further tightening was achieved by the Orders in Council of November 11, 1807 (five months after the *Chesapeake* attack), requiring that all American trade with Europe go through British ports and customs, where American prices could be held down. As Perceval put it, the Americans "will have no trade, or they must be content to accept it through us" (995).

These last steps by England were responsive to Napoleon's Berlin Decree of November 21, 1806, which ordered that no goods coming from England would be received in ports under his control (which included all the European coasts except those of Denmark and Portugal). Napoleon, still stringing Jefferson along on Florida, did not at first enforce this decree against American vessels. Indeed, Perceval said that one reason England had to impose its ban on American neutral trade was that Napoleon had exempted America from the Berlin Decree (986–87). But, in the fall of 1807, after a year of non-enforcement, Napoleon began his campaigns against Denmark and Portugal by saying they must enforce the Berlin Decree, even against the United States (1000–1002). A double bind thus pinched off American trade to Europe. England said that no ship could land there unless it came by way of England, and Napoleon said that no ship could land there if it did come by way of England.

Thus, step by step, American trade was being crowded off the sea. The Europeans at first thought that a nation thus pinned down would fight back. But Jefferson's rhetoric had convinced them that the United States would never do that (1024–26). Napoleon believed that Americans were cowards (1020), and his minister in Washington agreed:

> France has, and will ever have, nothing to hope from the dispositions of a people that conceives no idea of glory, of grandeur, of justice; that shows itself the constant enemy of liberal principles; and that is disposed to suffer every kind of humiliation. (1023)

Embargo

Congress convened on October 26, 1807, its first meeting since the *Chesapeake* was fired on. Jefferson was still waiting for a response to the protest he sent to England. Meanwhile, his proclamation banning British warships from American ports was still in force, but some stronger action seemed called for, so Jefferson proposed a non-importation bill on British products, which was passed on December 14 (1040). A mere three days later news came of a further British offense, the reaffirmation of its right to impressment — a rejection of the main point in Jefferson's *Chesapeake* protest. In this drumbeat of bad news, rumor also arrived of the more stringent Orders in Council, making all American trade move through British ports.

Adams wrote that these aggressions called for a "vindictive" response (1040). Adams's brother Charles objected to this adjective in the margin of the private copy of this volume Henry had circulated, and it was changed to "energetic." But what would a more energetic measure be? There were not many arrows left in Jefferson's quiver. Escalation was moving inexorably up to the point where no response short of war was left — except, perhaps, an embargo on all trade. If the British wanted to interdict American shipping, the United States would engage in preemptive interdiction, imposing a ban on itself. Jefferson drew up an embargo bill, using the new Orders in Council as one motive for it. But the Orders had not officially been delivered to America, so Madison rewrote the bill omitting that as a reason (1043). The Embargo Act was signed by Jefferson on December 22, with all three readings completed in the Senate on a Friday, and the House acting as swiftly on the following Monday (1045–49).

The bill was pushed through even though the arrival of George Rose, a British commissioner sent to treat of *Chesapeake* reparations, was expected momentarily — he reached Norfolk four days after the Embargo Act was signed. The only slight delay in passage of the act occurred when, in the House, amendments were proposed to give a time limit to it. That was customary with embargoes, which usually had two aims — protective (to call ships back out of danger) and procrastinating (to create a delay while war could be prepared). In either case, the Embargo was seen as temporary, a means to one or other or both of the customary ends. Embargoes had not ordinarily been used to create commercial pressure on a nation. Non-intercourse was the instrument for that.

But Madison had long espoused the idea that embargoes could be used as a form of "peaceful coercion" on other nations. Some in Congress would later complain that they had voted for the Embargo under the impression that it was defensive in purpose, not offensive, and temporary in its operation, not open-ended. Gallatin saw such problems lurking in the bill, which was ambiguous, hasty, and based on sketchy knowledge of recent British moves. As he told the president:

> An embargo for a limited time will at this moment be preferable in itself and less objectionable in Congress. In every point of view — privations, sufferings, revenue, effect on the enemy, politics at home, etc. — I prefer war to a permanent embargo. Governmental prohibitions do always more mischief than had been calculated, and it is not without much hesitation that a statesman should hazard to regulate the concerns of individuals, as if he could do it better than themselves. The measure being of a doubtful policy, and hastily adopted on the first view of our foreign intelligence, I think that we had better recommend it with modifications, and at first for such a limited time as will afford us all time for reconsideration and, if we think proper, for an alteration in our course without appearing to retract. As to the hope it may have effect on the negotiations with Mr. Rose, or induce England to treat us better, I think it entirely groundless. (1044)

That was a statement prescient in every way, but it was rejected by Jefferson and Madison. The ironic thing is that Gallatin — as the superior of port officials — would have to enforce the Embargo he disapproved of.

Gallatin, who hoped that war was not entirely or indefinitely excluded by the Embargo, asked Congress for taxes to increase the army and build ships for the navy. But on the latter point he could get no support from Jefferson, who opposed the very idea of a seagoing navy. He preferred a system of gunboats deployable at harbor entrances, mere movable platforms for cannon, not fit for action away from shore. He believed these were cheap to build, did not demand permanent crews, and could be easily stored when not in actual use. He convinced enough members of Congress of their usefulness that they voted to build 188 more gunboats, bringing the total number of the force to 254. Jefferson was pleased that the frigates, whose provocative nature he deplored, could now be used simply to serve the gunboats, ferrying crews to them as needed: "It is considered that in case of war these frigates would serve as receptacles for enlisting seamen to fill the gunboats occasionally" (1036).

Gallatin knew that gunboats were almost entirely useless. Left unmanned, they quickly rotted. They were unstable, uncomfortable, and inefficient. Professional seamen did not want to serve on them, and amateurs could not manage them. Their only use was to prevent the creation of real ships for use by a real navy. Gallatin tried to appeal to Jefferson's hatred of expenditures by noting that the gunboats "will inevitably decay in a given number of years, and will be a perpetual bill of costs for repairs and maintenance" (G 353). But as Adams noted of Jefferson: "When he fairly mounted a hobby-horse, he rode it over all opposition, and of all hobby-horses gunboats happened at this time to be his favorite" (G 353).

The Rose Mission

It has already been noticed that the George Rose mission was known in America before his actual arrival. Rose was instructed to make a settlement of *Chesapeake* claims but also to issue a set of British demands. To show that the United States had to meet *his* terms, he refused to leave his ship until given explicit assurance that the proclamation banning armed British vessels did not apply to it. He knew that ships on diplomatic errands were not covered by the proclamation — but he was taking the opportunity to underline British displeasure with the proclamation. His instruction was to demand that it be lifted for all ships before discussing reparations (1049).

On the *Chesapeake,* the British repeated their offer to suspend Admiral Berkeley, to return Americans captured by the *Leopard,* and to pay reparations to relatives of the *Chesapeake*'s killed and wounded. But Rose said Admiral Berkeley would not be dismissed from service (as America had asked), because the *Leopard* had been provoked by the captain of the *Chesapeake*, who had on his ship a British seaman "seduced" into American service. Captain Barron of the *Chesapeake*, already suspended, should be asked to disavow his conduct, and the American government should promise to hide no other British seamen on their warships.

This was a settlement that did not appeal to any Americans but high Federalists like Timothy Pickering, who quickly became a personal friend to Rose. Madison knew that the impressments issue would prevent any real agreement with Rose, but he had the diplomatic imperative to keep talks going. The main obstacle to that was the demand that the proclamation be lifted *prior* to negotiation. No nation likes to submit to such an ultimatum, so Madison tried to work out a formula that would *simultaneously* lift the proclamation and discuss the *Chesapeake* settlement. At this point, Robert Smith at the Navy Department tried to lend Madison a bumbling hand, telling Rose that the president could not sustain his popularity if Rose did not yield on the prior requirement. Adams thinks that Smith was authorized to make this appeal, and quotes Rose's report back to England:

> He [Smith] avowed to me that what had passed was with the knowledge of the President, whose difficulty arose from the sacrifice of public opinion which he apprehended must follow from the abandonment of the Proclamation. He said I must be aware how dear to Mr. Jefferson his popularity must be, and especially at the close of his political career, and that this consideration must be held particularly in view by him; and he pressed me earnestly to take such steps as would conciliate the President's wish to give His Majesty satisfaction on the point in question, and yet to maintain what was pre-eminently valuable to him. (1056–57)

Adams, believing Smith when he says he was authorized by Jefferson to make this plea, grimaces at the notion that "in 1808 — for the first and probably the last time in history — a president of the United States begged for mercy from a British minister" (1058). But Smith was the loose cannon in this cabinet, and trusting his word is not something the skeptical Adams should so readily have done.

While Rose was still in his first month of dealing with Madison, news came that Napoleon's Berlin Decree (banning all trade that went through British ports) was finally being enforced against the United States. Rose was delighted at this, since he thought it would force America to deal with England (1061). Madison did indeed try to show that he would be more accommodating, telling Rose that British subjects would be banned from service on American warships (but not from commercial vessels). Yet the administration still refused to lift the proclamation prior to dealing with the *Chesapeake*. Rose's optimism soon faded. From Gallatin, whom he considered "by far the ablest and best informed member" of the government, he heard that the Orders in Council would lead to war unless they were revoked — which "went far beyond any threat ever made before by President Jefferson" (1062–63). Rose departed, his mission a failure, as it was bound to be under the instructions he carried. He left behind his friend Pickering of Massachusetts, to defend England and attack the Embargo — in a public letter of February that made a sensation and was, according to Adams, "stamped by a touch of genius" (1091).

New England Resists the Embargo

The success of Pickering's best-selling letter could not have occurred, less than three months after passage of the Embargo Act, if that act were not already resented and defied (1093). The lax compliance with it had called, almost instantly, for supplementary acts meant to stop the holes in its observance. A First Embargo Supplementary Act (January 8, 1808) banned coastal and fishing trade — ships that put out to trade down the eastern coast of America too easily claimed that winds had swept them to sea and forced a landing on foreign shores (1099). A Second Embargo Supplementary Act (March 12) banned trade by land — people were moving their products over the Canada or Florida border without recourse to sea vessels.

The act was so unpopular in New England that when John Quincy Adams answered Pickering's letter, defending the Embargo, the Massachusetts legislature chose his successor half a year early, issued instructions that its senators must vote against the Embargo, and forced Adams's resignation. With Adams's resignation and Pickering's triumphant re-election to the Senate, the Republican party that had taken over Massachusetts under Governor James Sullivan was beaten back: "All, and more than all, that Jefferson's political labors had gained, his Embargo in a few weeks wasted" (1094).

When Congress left town after its spring session, it could no longer issue supplementary acts, though defiance of the Embargo was spreading like wildfire. The president had to use his executive authority — first in a proclamation that there was an insurgency at the Canadian border, to be put down by federal troops; then in a circular letter to governors, telling them to limit the interstate trade in grains (1100–1101). To Gallatin he issued directives calling for detention of all goods suspected of departure abroad. He called detention "the panacea," and urged Gallatin to use it freely, "that we may by a fair experiment know the power of this great weapon, the Embargo . . . Where you are doubtful, consider me as voting for detention" (1100). He instructed the governors:

> It would be well to recommend to every collector to consider every shipment of provisions, lumber, flaxseed, tar, cotton, tobacco, etc. — enumerating the articles — as sufficiently suspicious for detention and reference here . . . to consider every vessel as suspicious which has on board any article of domestic produce in demand at foreign markets, and most especially provisions. (1101)

Governor James Sullivan, the man who had built the Republican party in Massachusetts by appealing to the merchants of that state, felt he had to issue certificates of trade to this base of his party; but Jefferson threatened him with military reprisal if he did not stop issuing the certificates. Sullivan answered defiantly. He knew how support of the Embargo had already ended the Senate career of John Quincy Adams. He told Jefferson, six months into the operation of the Embargo:

> You may depend upon it that three weeks after these certificates shall be refused, an artificial and actual scarcity will involve this state in mobs, riots, and convulsions, pretendedly [professedly] on account of the Embargo. Your enemies will have an additional triumph, and your friends suffer new mortifications. (1103)

Sullivan said that even those Massachusetts Republicans who had supported the Embargo initially were now convinced that it should be ended.

> They do not perceive any of the effects from it that the nation expected; they do not perceive foreign powers influenced by it, as they anticipated. They are convinced, as they say, that the people of this state must soon be reduced to suffering and poverty . . . These men consider the Embargo as operating very forcibly to the subversion of the Republican interest here.

Should the measure be much longer continued, and then fail of producing any important public good, I imagine it will be a decisive blow against the Republican interest now supported in this commonwealth. (1103–4)

Jefferson responded by instructing his secretary of war, himself from Massachusetts, to have troops ready to move into that state:

The collector of Sullivan is on the totter. The Tories of Boston openly threaten insurrection if their importation of flour is stopped. The next post will stop it. I fear your governor is not up to the tone of these parricides, and I hope on the first symptom of an open opposition of the law by force, you will fly to the scene and aid in suppressing any commotion. (1104)

As the Embargo was more openly defied, Jefferson said that a presumption of guilt, not of innocence, should prevail in areas known for resistance:

A general disobedience to the laws in any place must have weight toward refusing to give them any facilities to evade. In such a case, we may fairly require positively that the individual of a town tainted with a general spirit of disobedience has never said or done anything himself to countenance that spirit. (1105)

Jefferson federalized the militia of New York and ordered its governor, Daniel Tomkins, to lead it in person against the towns trading with Canada (1105). Secretary of the Navy Smith was told to deploy gunboats in the harbors where smuggling was occurring. Smith protested to Gallatin: "Upon it [the Embargo] there will in some of the states, in the course of the next two months, assuredly be engendered monsters" (1107).

Gallatin tried to convince the president that the only way to enforce the Embargo would be to turn the United States into a police state, employing "a little army along the Lakes," telling Congress to "invest the executive with the most arbitrary powers," authorizing collectors "with the general power of seizing property anywhere," even though "such arbitrary powers are equally dangerous and odious" (1107–8). Gallatin was trying to get Jefferson to prepare for war — the only use he saw in the Embargo; but Jefferson replied that everything and anything must be done to enforce the Embargo (1108). Jefferson by this time had only one member of his cabinet still committed to his course — Madison, who had created its rationale. Gallatin was trying to wake Jefferson to what he was doing. Adams in effect joins in that effort, devoting a whole chapter (twelve) to the effects of the Embargo, indulging a persuasive hyperbole as if he were at Gallatin's side rubbing Jefferson's face in the evidence. He describes the spread of a blight on the nation, as Thucydides (2.47–55) described the way plague came to Athens. The description is like a cinematic panning shot over a vast scene:

> At a moment's notice, without avowing his true reasons, President Jefferson bade foreign commerce to cease. As the order was carried along the seacoast, every artisan dropped his tools, every merchant closed his doors, every ship was dismantled. American produce — wheat, timber, cotton, tobacco, rice — dropped in value or became unsalable; every imported article rose in price; wages stopped; swarms of debtors became bankrupt; thousands of sailors hung idle round the wharves trying to find employment on coasters and escape to the West Indies or Nova Scotia. A reign of idleness began; and the men who were not already ruined felt that their ruin was only a matter of time. (1118–19)

That Jefferson could effect all this was, in a sense, a tribute to his skill as a leader, to the trust he had built up in his ideals:

> Thus the Embargo was imposed; and of all President Jefferson's feats of political management, this was probably the most dexterous. On his mere recommendation, without warning, discussion, or publicity, and in silence as to his true reasons and motives, he succeeded in fixing upon the country, beyond recall, the experiment of peaceable coercion. (1048)

Adams concedes that "the Embargo was an experiment in politics well worth making" (115). But he thought Jefferson should have seen at some earlier point that the experiment had failed, that it was not worth the infringements of liberty that it progressively entailed. Congress, which had passed the Embargo Act, was turning against it. John Randolph, of course, objected to the federal government's assuming unparalleled powers — he said that the Constitution gave a right to regulate commerce, but not to destroy it, not to prohibit it entirely (1109). He added that not a single state would have ratified the Constitution if that power had been contained in it. "With all John Randolph's waywardness and extravagance, he alone shone among this mass of mediocrities, and like the water snakes in Coleridge's silent ocean, his every track was a flash of golden fire" (1188). Adams itemizes the costs of the Embargo, legal, economic, moral, and political (1116–20). But the great opportunity lost was to put America on the right side in the major struggle of the time, against Napoleonic despotism.

War for Liberty

At a moment when America was four months into the Embargo, it was not very concerned with an event that attracted attention elsewhere. Even today, the term "Dos de Maio" is known to some Americans only for Goya's *El Dos de Maio* and *El Tres de Maio*, the most famous paintings of war atrocities before Picasso's *Guernica.* Goya's works are devoted to the Napoleonic army's brutal suppression of Spanish civilians in Madrid on May 2, 1808, and the execution of prisoners on May 3. It is one of the many merits of Adams's *History* to break through the provincialism of American history and place events in their world context. He argues that Dos de Maio was a pivotal event in the history of America — important for what Jefferson did *not* do.

Napoleon had planned the acquisition of Spain over the years. Now he had plunged into what would be known as the Peninsular War against the army of Spain, and of England fighting alongside Spain. At such a moment Napoleon had to fear what Talleyrand had always warned him against, that the United States would ultimately join with England against him — that the ancestral, linguistic, and commercial ties between the "Anglo-Saxon nations" would have this result. But Napoleon possessed what he considered a preventive tool against that happening. After long teasing on the subject, he at last made an outright offer of both Floridas to Jefferson — on one or both of two conditions: alliance with him, or declared war on England (1130). John Armstrong, the United States minister, replied that "the United States are at the moment on the eve of a war with Great Britain," but that France had by the Berlin Decree made itself no ally in that war (1130). He sent the Emperor's offer to Washington with this interpretation of it: "With one hand they offer us the blessings of equal alliance against Great Britain; with the other they menace us with war if we do not accept this kindness; and with both they pick our pockets with all imaginable diligence, dexterity, and impudence" (1121).

On February 12, nine days after his offer of the Floridas, Napoleon commanded General Murat to occupy Madrid, ostensibly to support an uprising against King Carlos by his treacherous son Fernando, actually to end the Bourbon rule. The King, his Queen, his son, and Godoy were summoned to the Emperor's presence in Bayonne, where Napoleon looked them over as toys he had acquired, remarking that "the Queen carries her heart and history on her face" (1133). The Bourbons were held in exile, and Napoleon's brother Joseph was put on the Spanish throne. The uprising of the populace against this foreign rule led to the brutal repression of the second of May. This date became, for liberal forces of the time, a magic number, like 1776 for America or 1789 for France, a third modern revolution against tyranny, equating the Emperor Napoleon with two kings, George III of England and Louis XVI of France.

> Each of the other anniversaries — that of July 4, 1776, and of July 14, 1789 — had been followed by a long and bloody convulsion which ravaged large portions of the world, and the extent and violence of the convulsion which was to ravage the Spanish empire could be measured only by the vastness of Spanish dominion. So strangely had political forces been entangled by Napoleon's hand that the explosion at Madrid roused the most incongruous interests into active sympathy and strange companionship. The Spaniards themselves, the least progressive people in Europe, became by necessity democratic; not only the people, but even the governments of Austria and Germany felt the movement and yielded to it; the Tories of England joined with the Whigs and Democrats in cheering a revolution which could not but shake the foundations of Tory principles. (1134)

Napoleon had created an international liberal sentiment that would not be paralleled until the 1820s, when the freedom of Greece was championed against Ottoman rule. But there was one standout from this international crusade. Jefferson actually welcomed the idea of Spain's overthrow, which put not only the Floridas but all of Spain's New World holdings up for grabs: "On hearing the earlier reports of Spanish resistance, his first thought was selfish: 'I am glad to see that Spain is likely to give Bonaparte employment. *Tant mieux pour nous*'" (1160). Jefferson, ready for the disintegration of the Spanish Empire, sent a message to Mexico and Cuba that if they wanted assistance after the fall of Spain, America could be helpful: "No allusion to Florida was made in this outline of a new policy, and none was needed, for Florida would obviously fall to the United States" (1161). Jefferson wrote Monroe:

> Bonaparte, having Spain at his feet, will look immediately to the Spanish colonies, and think our neutrality cheaply purchased by a repeal of the illegal parts of his decrees [of Berlin, etc.], with perhaps the Floridas thrown into the bargain. (1162)

By standing apart from the struggle, Jefferson forfeited the chance to join an international war for liberty. "While all Europe, except France, joined hands in active or passive support of Spanish freedom, America, the stronghold of free government, drew back and threw her weight on the opposite side" (1134). Earlier I noticed how Malone himself agreed with Adams that the United States would have done better to use English support in seizing Texas and the Floridas. Malone noted that this would probably have obviated the War of 1812. That move made even more sense in the wake of the Dos de Maio. The United States could have struck a bargain with England in terms of principle, as an ally in the fight for Spanish (and all European) freedom. Instead, American inaction gave quiet support to Napoleon.

> The Embargo, in its effects upon Spain and her colonies, was a powerful weapon to aid Napoleon in his assault on Spanish liberty and in his effort to gain mastery of the ocean. In an instant England appeared as the champion of human liberty, and America as an accomplice of despotism. Jefferson, in his pursuit of Florida, lost what was a thousand times more valuable to him than territory — the moral leadership which belonged to the head of democracy. The New England Federalists seized their advantage, and proclaimed themselves the friends of Spain and freedom. Their press rang with denunciations of Napoleon, and of Jefferson his tool. (1160)

John Marshall agreed with northerners that Jefferson had made himself Napoleon's collaborator (1166).

Once before, Jefferson had betrayed the cause of liberty abroad — in opposing the revolution of Toussaint Louverture — and that time, too, he had been collaborating with Napoleon and angling for the Floridas. The pattern repeated itself in 1808. Yet Jefferson received no reward from Bonaparte for his refusal to join the international crusade against him. Since the United States had turned down his offer of alliance, Napoleon issued a new decree from Bayonne (where, as we have seen, he was toying with the ousted Bourbons). This decree said that since any United States ship at sea was breaking its own country's law (the Embargo), he was just enforcing the laws of America if he seized it (1136).

The response of Madison was servile. On May 2, the Dos de Maio on his side of the ocean, he instructed Armstrong to protest in the gentlest of terms, "taking care, as your discretion will doubtless suggest, that while you make that government sensible of the offensive tone employed [in the Bayonne Decree], you leave the way open for friendly and respectful explanations, if there be a disposition to offer them, and for a decision here on any reply which may be of a different character" (1137).

Jefferson took a similarly cajoling tone with Napoleon's representative in Washington, Turreau. Though it was the official pretense of his government that the Embargo was a neutral proposal, not favoring any nation over another, Jefferson told the French minister: "The Embargo, which seems to strike at France and Great Britain equally, is in fact more prejudicial to the latter than to the former, by reason of the greater number of colonies which England possesses, and their inferiority in local resources" (1149).

But Napoleon was not to be swayed by sweet talk. Having offered Florida as a bribe, he snatched it away again when all his conditions were not met. He told an American diplomat visiting Bayonne that his new decree would be enforced by the destruction of any American ships found at sea:

> England has made them tributary to her. This I will not suffer. Tell the President from me when you see him in America that if he can make a treaty with England, preserving his maritime rights, it will be agreeable to me; but that I will make war upon the universe should it support her [England's] pretensions. I will not abandon any part of my system. (1142)

Napoleon did acknowledge that the Embargo favored him. He was not, however, going to reward Jefferson with anything other than ironic praise for his courage in pitting the Embargo against England. In a public statement of September 1, 1808, he wrote:

> The Americans — this people who placed their fortune, their prosperity, and almost their existence in commerce — have given the example of a great and courageous sacrifice. By a general embargo they have interdicted all commerce, all exchange, rather than shamefully submit to that tribute which the English pretend to impose on the shipping of all nations. (1142)

While Bonaparte praised the Embargo for hurting England, the English were discovering that it hurt America more than it hurt them. Lord Castlereagh said:

> I think it better to leave them with the full measure of their own difficulties to lower and degrade them in the estimation of the American people. The continuance of the Embargo for some time is the best chance of their being destroyed as a party, and I should prefer exposing them to the disgrace of rescinding their own measure at the demand of their own people than furnish them with any creditable pretext for doing so. I look upon the Em-

bargo as operating at present more forcibly in our favor than any measure of hostility we could call forth were war actually declared. (1150)

In other words, with the Embargo Jefferson was wielding a sword, but he had mistaken the ends of it, pointing the blade at himself and offering the handle to his enemies. Castlereagh thought this too rich an opportunity to be wasted: "The Embargo in America seems to be working so well for us, without our interference, that on that ground alone I confess I could wish that no new steps should be taken" (1151).

In one respect the British did relax their Orders in Council. To encourage smugglers to take provisions to Sweden and the West Indies, the British would not force ships with those as their destination to move through their customs. This move exasperated Madison, who said, "A more extraordinary experiment is perhaps not to be found in the annals of modern transactions" (1152). Adams finds that response unreasonable:

> Certainly governments did not commonly invite citizens of friendly countries to violate their own laws; but one avowed object of the Embargo was to distress the British people into resisting their government, and news that the Negroes of Jamaica and the artisans of Yorkshire had broken into acts of lawless violence would have been grateful to the ears of Jefferson. (1152)

In other words: "Each government had tried to overthrow the other; but that of England was for the moment the more successful" (1154).

At this point Madison renewed an offer to end the Embargo, so far as it affected England, if the Orders in Council were lifted. This overture reached England just as news arrived of Wellesley's victory over Napoleon's troops in Portugal. Canning, the British foreign minister, flung Madison's offer back in his face. He said this was no time to give credit to a country that "did not come in aid of the [British] blockade of the European continent." With hypocritical regret, Canning added that he would have liked to see the Embargo end, not for any advantage to England, but to facilitate "its removal as a measure of inconvenient restriction upon the American people" (1157–58). Jefferson had missed the chance to join the crusade, and now the victors were jeering him. As Jefferson told the British minister, referring to this letter, it "was written in the high ropes [disdainfully, *OED*], and would be stinging to every American breast" (1169).

Jefferson had tried to get rid of the Embargo on the only terms that seemed to save some honor, and he had been unable to. What course was left him? He was stranded outside the world coalition fighting for Spanish freedom. Napoleon was not listening to his overtures for Florida. Discontent with the Embargo had spread among Republicans as well as Federalists. The second session of the Tenth Congress would begin in November. What action could he recommend to it?

Jefferson found what other presidents have, that it is easier to get into a rash commitment than out of it. Rufus King made a comment that would be repeated when America tried to disentangle itself from Vietnam: "The longer it [the Embargo] is continued, the deeper our disgrace when it is raised" (1167). John Marshall wrote privately: "Nothing can be more completely demonstrated than the inefficacy of the Embargo; yet the demonstration seems to be of no avail" (1166). These views were perhaps expectable from Federalists. But Jefferson's friends were gently trying to break the news to him as well. Wilson Cary Nicholas, Jefferson's neighbor at Monticello whom the president had urged to re-enter the House, tried to warn him. Nicholas knew what he was writing about, since he had been a collector of customs in Norfolk during the interim between his House terms. He wrote:

> If the Embargo could be executed, and the people would submit to it, I have no doubt it is our wisest course; but if the complete execution of it and the support of the people cannot be counted upon, it will neither answer our purpose nor will it be practicable to retain it. (1164)

Jefferson was deaf to such arguments. As one of John Quincy Adams's correspondents wrote at the time, he "was inclined to hug the Embargo and die in its embrace."

It was in this time of disillusionment with the Embargo that Madison was elected to succeed Jefferson. Adams asks how, with the administration's Embargo causing such opposition, Madison won the election. First of all, he notes, the opposition to him was divided, with Randolph supporting Monroe but unable to break into the congressional caucus that chose the nominee, and with the Federalists unable to break out of their regional base. Thus "neither George Clinton nor James Monroe could control the whole body of opponents to the Embargo" (1123). De-Witt Clinton's challenge to the Embargo from within the Republican party collapsed under the weight of his own inconsistencies (1122). Besides, the Electoral College lagged behind events:

The state legislatures had been chosen chiefly in the spring or summer, when the Embargo was still comparatively popular; and in most cases, but particularly in New York, the legislature still chose presidential electors. The people expressed no direct opinion in national politics, except in regard to congressmen. State after state deserted to the Federalists without affecting the general election. (1123)

Thus "the Republican party by a supreme effort kept itself in office" (1125). Even so, Madison received forty fewer electoral votes than Jefferson had in the previous election, and the Federalists doubled their numbers in Congress.

Paralysis

When the outgoing Congress met after the election, Jefferson had no new defense of the Embargo to offer it, and no willingness to listen to others' plans for ending it. His passivity alarmed the other two members of his triumvirate. Gallatin was still trying to make him realize the gravity of the situation:

> Both Mr. Madison and myself concur in the opinion that considering the temper of the legislature, it would be eligible [desirable] to point out to them some precise and distinct course. As to what that should be, we may not all perfectly agree, and perhaps the knowledge of the various feelings of the members [of Congress], and of the apparent public opinion, may on consideration induce a revision of our own [opinion on the Embargo]. I feel myself nearly as undetermined between enforcing the Embargo or war [the option Gallatin kept raising and Jefferson kept refusing to consider] as I was at our last meeting. But I think that we must, or rather you must, decide the question absolutely, so that we may point out a decisive course either way to our friends. Mr. Madison, being unwell, proposed that I should call on you, and suggest our wish that we might, with the other gentlemen, be called by you on that subject. Should you think that course proper, the sooner the better. (1171)

Jefferson did not want to discuss the Embargo, even with his own cabinet. He sensed that its members were slipping away from him, and he withdrew into himself. As his admiring biographer Merrill Peterson says, "He virtually surrendered his leadership when the electoral result became known in November."[3]

Jefferson offered the excuse that he did not want to do to Madison what Adams had done to him — make decisions in the interim between a November election and a March inauguration that would bind his successor. Two days before he received Gallatin's plea to summon the cabinet and make decisions, he wrote to Levi Lincoln: "On this occasion, I think it is fair to leave to those who are to act on them the decisions they prefer, being to be myself but a spectator. I should not feel justified in directing measures which those who are to execute them would disapprove" (1171). As Noble Cunningham remarks, "This was inadequate justification for his premature retirement from leadership."[4]

Jefferson would not, after all, be making midnight appointments that Madison would oppose. In 1800 Jefferson came into office from a party, and with a set of policies, at odds with those of his predecessor. Madison was not only of the same party but of the same administration as Jefferson. He was a colleague who wanted Jefferson to keep the executive functioning while he still held its legal powers. Jefferson, by refusing to discuss the Embargo, made it impossible for Madison or Gallatin on his own to reverse course on the subject. Jefferson's virtuous profession of regard for his successor went against that successor's earnest wish that he steer the drifting bark.

The torpor of Jefferson's last four months in office has puzzled historians. Adams was harsher on him in his biography of Gallatin than he is in the *History*. There he wrote: "So cowed was he as to do what no president had ever done before, or has ever done since, and what no president has a constitutional right to do: he abdicated the duties of his office, and no entreaty could induce him to resume them" (G 377). Jefferson's defender Dumas Malone thinks he was just tired by the end of his term (DM 5.633–26). But Jefferson was a healthy sixty-five-year-old who would live, and live energetically, for another eighteen years. He had, besides, spent two or three months of every year at his plantation. Franklin Roosevelt, it is true, was fatigued and ill at the end of his presidency, and he was only sixty-three — but he was a disabled man, a smoker and drinker, who had spent over twelve years as president during a harrowing depression and war, and he did not relinquish his duties until death forced him to. No other president has complained at the end of eight years that he was too tired to perform his duties.

Besides, Malone's explanation of fatigue as the reason for Jefferson's withdrawal does not cover earlier and similar withdrawals when Jefferson felt he had lost power. As Virginia's governor during the Revolution, when he felt unable to defend the state, he pleaded with Washington to bring the Continental Army to his rescue — though Washington could not ignore the rest of the nation to save his own state (JP 6.33). Then, when Jefferson was driven from Monticello by British troops, he went to his western plantation, Poplar Forest, far from the troubled scene, and did nothing to help the incoming governor — conduct that led to an investigation for possible impeachment (JP 6.106–7). Later, as secretary of state, when he felt frustrated with Hamilton, he resigned his office, though Washington said that he needed him for balance in the administration (JP 26.627–30). When he felt powerless, Jefferson walked away.

Some scholars seek deep psychological explanations for his withdrawal at the end of his second term. Leonard White thinks that he was paralyzed by a massive loss of self-confidence — his certainty that the Embargo was a noble experiment had disintegrated as he came to use unconstitutional means to enforce it.[5] Robert Johnstone argues that he felt incapable of resolving the conflicts he faced:

> A psychological explanation may be the most satisfactory under the circumstances. His surrender of policy initiative at this time may have been related in a larger sense to his desire to escape from conflict. One of the recognized methods among political actors of the resolution of conflict is illness or resignation. One form of "resignation" might well be a psychological abdication of power.[6]

Adams's explanation of the funk is both simpler and subtler than it was in the *Gallatin*. He stresses in the *History* how important to Jefferson was popularity. Losing it was like losing oxygen: "He was sensitive, affectionate, and, in his own eyes, heroic. He yearned for love and praise as no other great American ever did" (220). "Loss of popularity was his bitterest trial. He who longed like a sensitive child for sympathy and love left office as strongly and almost as generally disliked as the least popular president who preceded or followed him" (1239). This explanation for his lassitude sounds simple — too simple — if it means only that Jefferson was vain. But Adams means something more profound. Popular support mattered so much to Jefferson because he felt he had a kind of mystical union with the people, with their goodness, and optimism, and basic sense. Not unreasonably he felt that he voiced their aspirations. In great measure he did. Adams himself, as we have seen, said: "Everyone admitted that Jefferson's opinions, in one form or another, were shared by a majority of the American people" (117), and those opinions had to prevail in the end (G 159).

In the past, Jefferson felt that those who opposed him (and therefore opposed the people) were either malicious plotters or their dupes. But that became a difficult thing to maintain during the Embargo crisis. Even Republicans, even friends, even cabinet members questioned a policy he thought so obvious that opposition to it was literally inexplicable to him. As Joseph Story, a Republican congressman arriving late for the fall session of Congress, noticed:

> I found that as a measure of retaliation the system had not only failed, but that Mr. Jefferson, from pride of opinion as well as from that visionary course of speculation which often misled his judgments, was absolutely bent upon maintaining it at all hazards. He professed a firm belief that Great Britain would abandon her Orders in Council if we persisted in the Embargo; and having no other scheme to offer in case of the failure of this, he maintained in private conversation the indispensable necessity of closing the session of Congress without any attempt to limit the duration of the system. (1173)

Though in 1808 he could not explain to others or to himself the lack of support for the Embargo, his need to fabricate some conspiratorial explanation showed itself after he got back to Monticello and constructed retrospective defenses for his actions. He decided that this very freshman congressman, Joseph Story, doomed the Embargo by deluding his fellows in the House. This is more than unlikely; it is ludicrous. Story was not a Federalist, but he came from Salem, which Jefferson considered the hotbed of Pickering-style "monocrats." Story was also a turncoat. He had supported the Embargo before he got to Congress. Story's biographer claims that he had supported the Embargo only when he thought it a temporary means of preparing for war, since he had opposed in 1805 any permanent or "absolute non-intercourse."[7]

Story was a protégé of the staunchly Republican Crowninshield family of Salem, and when Jacob Crowninshield was dying in 1808, the twenty-nine-year-old Story filled out the last months of his term in the House of Representatives. His fellow member from Massachusetts, Ezekiel Bacon, was his guide in Washington. Story expressed opposition to the Embargo in the House but left before the final vote on its termination. From this sequence of events Jefferson would invent in 1810 a tale of conspiracy, treachery and single-handed seduction:

> The Federalists during their short-lived ascendancy [after the congressional election influenced by the Embargo] have nevertheless, by forcing us from the Embargo, inflicted a wound on our interests which can never be

cured, and on our affections which will require time to cicatrize. I ascribe all this to one pseudo-Republican — Story. He came on in place of Crowninshield, I believe, and stayed only a few days — long enough, however, to get complete hold of Bacon, who, giving in to his representations, became panic-struck, and communicated the panic to his colleagues, and they to a majority of the sound members of Congress. They believed in the alternative of repeal or civil war, and produced the fatal measure of repeal. This is the immediate parent of all our present evils, and has reduced us to a low standing in the eyes of the world ... I have ever been anxious to avoid a war with England unless forced by a situation more losing than war itself; but I did believe we could coerce her to justice by peaceable means; and the Embargo, evaded as it was, proved it would have coerced her had it been honestly executed. The proof she [England] exhibited on that occasion that she can exercise such an influence in the country as to control the will of its government and three fourths of its people is to me the most mortifying circumstance which has occurred since the establishment of our government. (1245)

Jefferson has reverted to his belief that nothing could go wrong in America without a British plot behind it. In this case, Story was just a tool of the British Empire.

Jefferson maintained till his death that the Embargo would have worked if it were just given more time. England would have caved in, making the War of 1812 unnecessary. In 1825 he called the Embargo "a measure which, persevered in a little longer, we had subsequent and satisfactory assurance would have effected its object completely" (1246). He was like those who said later on that if the United States had just stayed in Vietnam longer, it would have "won" (whatever that means). Story would later write:

I learned the whole policy of Mr. Jefferson, and was surprised as well as grieved to find that in the face of the clearest proofs of the failure of his plan, he continued to hope against facts ... The very eagerness with which the repeal was supported by a majority of the Republican party ought to have taught Mr. Jefferson that it was already considered by them as a miserable and mischievous failure.[8]

Even Jefferson's warm defenders now know better than to defend the Embargo. Noble Cunningham voices the judgment of history:

Some of them [the provisions of the Enforcement Act] clearly violated guarantees of personal liberty (the searches and seizures clause of the Fourth Amendment, for instance) and overall, so vast was the concentration of power in the president and in minor functionaries, the measure mocked every principle Jefferson held except the one principle, that of the Embargo itself . . . Justifying the Embargo to himself, Jefferson closed his eyes to the faults of the policy . . . The nation plunged from unparalleled prosperity into an economic decline from which it would not fully recover for a quarter of a century.[9]

Jefferson remained obsessed with Story, and Madison showed great courage and independence when he nominated Story for the Supreme Court (at the age of thirty-two) over Jefferson's objections. His friend wrote from Monticello: "Story and Bacon are exactly the men who deserted us on that [Embargo] measure and carried off the majority."[10]

During the interim when Jefferson had abdicated his office without leaving it, the direction of government was left to rumor and speculation. Nathaniel Macon, until recently the Speaker of the House, who should have been an intimate of the administration, was left in the dark:

It is said that the president gives no opinion as to the measure that ought to be adopted. It is not known whether he be for war or peace. It is reported that Mr. Madison is for the plan I have submitted [armed non-intercourse], with the addition of high protective duties . . . I am as much against war as Gallatin is in favor of it. Thus I have continued in Congress till there is no one of my old fellow laborers that agrees with me in opinion. (1180)

Congressional debate on the Embargo began with Josiah Quincy of Massachusetts declaring that God had given New Englanders the ocean, and the government could not take it away from them:

[Are] the people of New England, after eleven months' deprivation of the ocean, to be commanded still longer to abandon it? For an undefined period to hold their unalienable right at the tenure of the will of Britain or of Bonaparte? . . . This Embargo must be repealed. You cannot enforce it for any important period of time longer. When I speak of your inability to enforce this law, let not gentlemen misunderstand me. I mean not to intimate insurrection or open defiance of them, although it is impossible to foresee with what acts that oppression will finally terminate which, we are told, makes wise men mad. (1183)

Quincy, like Gallatin, preferred war to continuance of the Embargo: "I shall be told this may lead to war. I ask, Are we now at peace? Certainly not, unless retiring from insult be peace, unless shrinking under the lash be peace" (1184).

Yet Congress still shrank from war — illogically, in Adams's eyes:

> The worst military disaster that could happen would be a bombardment [from sea] or temporary occupation of some seaboard city; the most terrible punishment within the range of possibility was the burning of a few small wooden towns, which could be rebuilt in three months, and whose destruction implied no necessary loss of life. Neither England nor France had armies to spare for permanent conquest in America; but so thoroughly had the theory of peaceable coercion taken possession of the national character that men of courage appealed to motives such as, in a private dispute, they would have thought degrading. (1185)

The opening discussions of Congress proved that its distaste for the Embargo was matched or surpassed by its fear of war (1182–89). In this case, what was Gallatin to do? Jefferson had no new ideas on how to maintain the Embargo. Gallatin therefore presented still another supplementary Embargo bill, the harshest one proposed so far. Why? He was against the Embargo. Adams offers a striking explanation for his action, one he can legitimately entertain after the years he spent with Gallatin's papers. "If he meant to break down the Embargo, he chose the best means; if he meant to enforce it, he chose the worst" (1202). He meant to break it down.

Gallatin had so far been acting on the executive orders of Jefferson. He wanted to supply a legislative warrant for what he had been doing. In the process, he would show the Congress what its passage of the Embargo really entailed. Revealing the extent of what was going on, he would reduce it to absurdity. The ploy worked. Though Congress passed the Enforcement Act on December 21, 1808, it soon recoiled in horror from what it had done. Town after town in New England rebelled at the prospect of a police state, and demanded instant repeal of the Embargo (1208–15). They threatened interposition by their states or nullification of the oppressive law — a northern version of the Kentucky and Virginia Resolutions that Jefferson and Madison had written a decade before (1215). Jefferson later recalled, "I felt the foundations of the government shaken under my feet by the New England townships" (1230). Congress, stunned, voted itself an extra session to debate a response to this outburst (1219). Among the first responses to the crisis was one Gallatin did not want. The Senate voted to rehabilitate and man all the idle gunboats. For Gallatin this meant that Congress would "throw into the ocean all the money reserved to support the first year of hostilities" when war was declared (1220). This idea was backed by Gallatin's old scourge, the incompetent secretary of the navy, Robert Smith. But Gallatin was able to defeat the Senate's bill. This further envenomed Gallatin's critics.

Within weeks of passage of the Enforcement Act, the pressing question in Congress had become whether to repeal the Embargo immediately or leave that to the extra session voted for May.

> Jefferson asked only to be spared the indignity of signing with his own hand the unconditional repeal of the Embargo, while the single point on which Story, Bacon, Pickering, and Canning were agreed was that the repeal should be the act of the man who made the law (1225).

Madison asked that the cut-off date be in June. A committee of the House voted 70–0 to end it on March 4, the date Jefferson would leave office (1228). He must take away the loathed thing with him. The full House responded to an objection that merchants and sailors could not be so swiftly notified of the change — it delayed enforcement, but only to March 15. But Congress sent the bill of repeal to Jefferson on the last day of February, and Jefferson was forced to sign the document of his own defeat on March 1, three days before leaving office.

The Senate added an insult that Jefferson felt very deeply. He had made an executive appointment when the Congress was out of session, sending his friend William Short as the first minister to Russia. In his last formal communication with Congress, he asked the Senate to confirm the appointment. Without consulting him on the need for such representation, the Senate refused. Jefferson had to write in embarrassment to Short:

> We took for granted, if any hesitation should arise, that the Senate would take time, and that our friends in that body would make inquiries of us and give us the opportunity of explaining and removing objections; but to our great surprise, and with an unexampled precipitancy, they rejected it at once. This reception of the last of my official communications to them could not be unfelt. (1248)

Jefferson's departure from the executive mansion was unlike his arrival there.

> He had undertaken to create a government which should interfere in no way with private action, and he had created one which interfered directly in the concerns of every private citizen in the land. He had come into power

as the champion of states' rights, and had driven states to the verge of armed resistance. He had begun by claiming credit for stern economy, and ended by exceeding the expenditure of his predecessors. (1239)

The interesting thing is that Adams does not consider these developments bad for the nation. No matter how it was brought on, stronger authority and central control were necessary steps to making a nation. Madison would add what Adams thought the proper agent for progress toward such national unity.

II. Madison's Two Terms

1

FALSE DAWN

The *History,* Volume Five

JEFFERSON'S INAUGURAL ADDRESSES were inaudible but ele-
gant. Madison's were just inaudible. Neither man was an orator.
Admittedly, Madison was speaking in the new House chamber
designed by Benjamin Latrobe, whose acoustics were notoriously
bad, and the grand room no doubt dwarfed Madison, our shortest president. But that does not explain the dull nature of Madison's text. He was
one of the most important writers of the founding era, but that is not
manifest in his presidential papers. Adams claims:

> If Madison's fame as a statesman rested on what he wrote as President, he
> would be thought not only among the weakest of executives, but also
> among the dullest of men, whose liveliest sally of feeling exhausted itself in
> an epithet, and whose keenest sympathy centered in the tobacco crop; but
> no statesman suffered more than Madison from the constraints of official
> dress. (125)[1]

This judgment is confirmed by anthologists of Madison's papers. A
three-volume collection of his papers, published in 1849, included nothing he wrote during his eight years as president.[2] The Library of America collection of his writings (1999) devotes only 40 of its 864 pages to
those years.[3]

Why was Madison so tongue-tied as a president? A clue is given by
Adams when he says that the best paper he composed while in office was
issued over the name of his secretary of state, Robert Smith, "perhaps
the best and keenest paper Madison ever wrote" (91). Most of the writ-

ings for which he is now famous appeared without a profession of authorship — his Numbers in *The Federalist,* his notes on the Constitutional Convention, his *Memorial and Remonstrance* defending religious liberty, the Virginia Resolutions and the *Report* defending them, his anonymous speeches for Washington, and his pseudonymous essays for Jefferson. The converse of this secret eloquence was a kind of overt blandness when he did sign his own handiwork. Madison was a superb committeeman, an orchestrator of compromise, a source of others' arguments, a backstairs operator. Adams says, "Madison's resemblance to a cardinal was not wholly imaginary" (11), with a reference to Senator Mills of Massachusetts, who had described him that way (J 128). Madison liked to work behind cover.

This is not always the best trait for an executive. Madison accommodated. He put off confrontation. He was more deferential than are most men in power. He assembled and failed to discipline a contentious cabinet throughout his first term. "From the outset, Madison's cabinet was the least satisfactory that any president had known" (12).

> Madison was often at odds with at least one of his colleagues — who were also at odds with each other — and he had developed as a consequence the habit of tolerating, usually by recourse to ambiguity, personal differences of opinion rather than trying to settle them . . . Consequently, the president dealt with many serious problems only when he could no longer avoid the difficulties his own methods had created.[4]

This trouble had begun before Madison's inauguration. The enemies of Gallatin, knowing that Madison meant to move him from his post as secretary of the treasury into his own former office as secretary of state, organized to prevent Gallatin's confirmation. Since the Republican coalition had been unraveling under the pressure of the Embargo, Madison felt he could not antagonize the anti-Gallatin faction, which had remained (however uneasily) loyal to Jefferson. This group — which hated Gallatin while it only distrusted Madison — was led by Michael Leib and William Duane in Pennsylvania, Samuel and William Smith in Maryland, and Wilson Cary Nicholas (whose family was interrelated with that of the Smiths) and William Branch Giles (who thought he should himself be secretary of state) in Virginia.

So, with New England forfeited for a while to the anti-Embargo Federalists, Madison felt that he could not afford to defy Gallatin's enemies. Instead, he would buy them off. He offered to move Robert Smith from the Navy Department to the Treasury, if in return Samuel Smith would procure the confirmation of Gallatin at the State Department (11). But Gallatin, who had told Madison how corrupt the Smiths were in profiteering from the navy (13), refused to see them given richer pickings in the Treasury. Madison claimed that Gallatin could do the real work of both departments, with Smith as a mere figurehead, but Gallatin knew better. He had been frustrated by conflict with Smith even in Jefferson's comparatively harmonious cabinet.

Madison still thought of Robert Smith as the solution to his problem, as the key to assuaging the opponents of Gallatin. He could not get enough support to keep Gallatin at Treasury unless he provided his enemies with a sop, and Smith was the only one available. So he made the incompetent and corrupt Smith his secretary of state, reasoning that he could do most of the actual work himself. In fact, he would write and rewrite papers issued in Smith's name. But he underestimated the mischief Smith could do, and the rancor he would cause in cabinet meetings. As time went on, Madison was forced to hold fewer cabinet meetings, to keep Smith out of play — which caused more resentment on Smith's part, and more trouble emanating from him.

Smith was not the only weak member of the administration. Smith's replacement as secretary of the navy was Paul Hamilton, a drunkard. The secretary of the army was William Eustis, whose only military experience was as a field surgeon during the Revolution (12). Whatever his talents, Eustis could not exert control over the army as long as Wilkinson was retained as its highest officer. Meanwhile, Madison's vice president, George Clinton, was being manipulated by his nephew DeWitt Clinton for the advancement of New York Republicans. The Clintons wished to displace the Virginia dynasty at the head of the Republican party and of the nation. Vice President Clinton, presiding over the Senate, would in time cast the deciding vote against Gallatin's attempt to renew the charter of the Bank of the United States (234).

Despite his troubles with the governing team he had assembled, Madison began his term with an unexpected blessing. The confusion caused by those acting for him was set against the consolation caused by things happening to him. The repeal of the Embargo, which he had so strenuously resisted, drew the fangs of the extreme Federalists. More moderate counsels prevailed. "Success had sobered them; the repeal of the Embargo seemed so great a triumph that they were almost tempted into good humor" (15). They were cheered by the resumption of legal traffic, opening markets for their increased production. In the year of the Embargo, the cotton mills of Rhode Island had grown from eight thousand spindles to eighty thousand (16–17). The Embargo that bruised merchants had blessed manufacturers:

> At no time could such industries have been established without the stimulus of a handsome profit; but when Virginia compelled Massachusetts and the northern states to accept a monopoly of the American market, the Yankee manufacturer must have expected to get, and actually got, great profit for his cottons and woolens, his hats, shoes, soap and nails. As though this were not more than enough, Virginia gave the northern ship owners the whole freight on southern produce, two thirds of which in one form or another went into the hands of New England shipbuilders, shippers, and merchants. Slowly the specie capital of the Union drifted towards the banks of Boston and New Haven, until, as the story will show, the steady drain of specie eastward bankrupted the other states, and the national government. Never, before or since, was the country so racked to create and support monopolies as in 1808, 1809, and 1810, under southern rule, and under the system of the president who began his career by declaring that if he could prevent the government from wasting the labors of the people under the pretence of protecting them, they must become happy. The navy and army of the United States were employed, and were paid millions of dollars, during these years in order to shut out foreign competition, and compel New England at the cannon's mouth to accept these enormous bribes . . . American manufacturers owed more to Jefferson and Virginians, who disliked them, than to northern statesmen, who merely encouraged them after they were established. (18–19)

Tricked by Canning

If the lifting of the Embargo restored domestic calm in America, it angered Napoleon, who had hoped its extension would provoke a war between the United States and England. His representative, Turreau, wrote from Washington (28) that opposition to the Embargo "terrified Congress to such a degree [that] the dominant party became divided, and the feebleness of Mr. Jefferson sanctioned the last and the most shameful act of his administration [the canceling of the Embargo]." In England, however, the foreign secretary, George Canning, welcomed repeal, since he wanted to funnel American grain toward his new ally, Spain, by canceling duties on American ships going there (33). Besides, Canning was under pressure to bring American trade back to England.

The Tory cabinet was as factious as Madison's, with Canning maneuvering against the secretary of war, Lord Castlereagh (43).

In this circumstance, Canning sent new instructions to America — ones that would satisfy his critics that he was trying to reopen trade, but that would not surrender any points he considered essential. There was some ambiguity about the freedom of negotiation that would be left to his minister in America, David Erskine (42). Erskine was known in England to be sympathetic to the United States (he was married to an American), and using him seemed to signal a wish for good relations. He was authorized to renew the offer of reparations for the *Chesapeake,* if the Americans would give up their demand for the dismissal of Admiral Berkeley. Further, Canning said the Orders in Council would be rescinded if Madison modified non-intercourse so that it applied only to France. That was a step Madison might well have balked at, since he agreed with Jefferson that Napoleon was the key to their hopes for Florida. Another condition — that the United States be limited in wartime trading to countries it had traded with in peace — was a possible deal breaker. But the third condition was the real deal breaker — that England be authorized to seize any American ship trading with France or its allies.

Madison was about to learn how dangerous it had been to make Robert Smith secretary of state. Smith, dealing with Erskine, agreed not to submit the deal-breaking conditions to Madison. They persuaded each other (and themselves) that Canning did not mean for these conditions to be held as essential to the main agreement. Therefore Madison did not need to see them. This suppression of key elements in the instructions was a diplomatic blunder of major proportions. Madison seized at the watered-down offer with relief and pride, interpreting it as a triumph of the Embargo, which had done what he predicted all along — it had reduced proud England to submission. On his own authority, not waiting for congressional approval, he suspended the Non-Intercourse Act.

According to an editor of the Madison papers, "Madison heard what he wanted to hear."[5] He sent word to Jefferson that the Embargo had been successful after all, and that Jefferson was being given the credit denied him in the final days of his presidency (55). Jefferson responded to the news: "I rejoice in it as the triumph of our forbearing and yet persevering system."[6] The *National Intelligencer* wrote: "Thanks [be given] to the sage who now so gloriously reposes in the shades of Monticello!"

(55). When the French minister, Turreau, warned Gallatin that there was something fishy in the offer (54), this was interpreted as sour grapes: "The president and his friends quieted their uneasiness by attributing their triumph to their own statesmanship" (55).

On April 19, Madison lifted the non-intercourse law, to be effective June 10. Ships were immediately fitted out and jumped the date for resumed trade. Congratulations flowed in on Madison. Even the surliest Federalists admitted that he had won a glorious victory. Timothy Pickering, of all people, became a friendly guest in the White House.

> New England quickly turned from revolutionary thoughts while she engaged in money-making; and as though the tide of fortune had at last set in Madison's favor, a stroke of his diplomacy raised the tottering administration to a sudden height of popularity such as Jefferson himself had never reached. (19)

When a special early session of Congress met in May, Madison delivered his annual address early, and could not resist the temptation to crow. England's accommodation was greeted as "corroborating the principles by which the public councils have been guided during a period of the most trying embarrassments" (56). Thus were the sufferings of the Embargo retroactively justified. Congressional response to the annual message was gratifying. "For the moment Madison was the most popular president that ever had met Congress" (58). John Randolph, who had hounded Madison as a "Yazoo man," now praised him as a way of denigrating Jefferson, who left a "calamitous and deplorable" state of things at the end of his term. Luckily, Randolph said, Madison proved "some Joseph to have stepped in and changed the state of things" (57).

Barent Gardinier, a Federalist congressman from New York, took the same tack, saying that poor Madison, previously the victim of Jefferson's attempts to woo France, quickly came to terms with England when given his own way. The Federalists were "praising Madison merely to gratify their antipathy to Jefferson," thus proving "the rule that in public life one could never safely speak well of an opponent" (58). So rosy had relations with Congress become that Madison resubmitted the nomination of a minister to Russia, the very thing that Congress had denied to Jefferson. Now the proposal sailed through easily (62) — thus sending John Quincy Adams off on the journey that Louisa Johnson Adams felt deprived her of her two oldest sons, and sealed their fate.

But Madison's rocket-rise to fame and favor soon sputtered out, as his reputation fell back to earth. Two days after word of suspended non-intercourse reached London, Canning brusquely disavowed the settlement. Not only had Madison not recognized the conditions of the British offer. He had also insulted the King. While accepting the offer of *Chesapeake* reparations, including a discontinuance of further punishment for Admiral Berkeley, Madison wrote that *not* to punish Berkeley would be a stain on the monarch's honor (51). This was not a response by Robert Smith, but by Madison writing for him — and it showed that Madison could use the same kind of intemperate language he had blocked when Jefferson indulged in it. These words alone might have sunk the negotiation, even aside from the neglected conditions. "If he wished a reconciliation, they were worse than useless; but if he wished a quarrel, he chose the right means" (51). Adams writes that Erskine was wrong to accept such an insult to his King, and doubly wrong to transmit it to London.

Erskine, disgraced for misrepresenting his government, was recalled. His replacement was quickly announced, and was a deliberate insult to the United States. The new minister, Francis James Jackson, was a man branded with dishonor for a war atrocity, the shelling of civilians that leveled Copenhagen when it would not surrender its navy to the British for use against Napoleon (70). Gallatin, aware of the crisis this appointment signaled, asked Madison to return at once from his summer break at Montpelier (79) — the American ships that had sailed prematurely, on the announcement that non-intercourse no longer applied, were now all at risk of capture by the British navy (80). But Madison was determined to observe Jefferson's avoidance of the capital during the unhealthy season. That, dangerously, left Robert Smith as the man in place to receive Jackson.

Madison at first hoped that Jackson was coming with an explanation of the misunderstanding that had taken place. When he found that Jackson came simply to insist on Erskine's full and original instructions, the president felt that he had been trapped with an offer England never meant to be acceptable — he said, "Such an outrage on all decency was never before heard of even on the shores of Africa [by Tripolitan pirates]" (81). Jackson, for his part, with no one to greet him but Robert Smith, soon began to assert that Madison was the one who acted in bad faith, seducing Erskine into desertion of his instructions. Vituperation all round replaced the euphoria that had cheered America just weeks before.

For the first time in this contest, Englishmen and Americans could no longer understand each other's meaning. Erskine had so confused every detail with his own ideas, and Canning's course on one side of the Atlantic seemed so little to accord with his tactics on the other, that neither party could longer believe in the other's good faith. Americans were convinced that Canning had offered terms which he intended them to refuse. Englishmen were sure that Madison had precipitated a settlement which he knew could not be carried out. Madison credited Canning with fraud as freely as Canning charged Madison with connivance. (82)

Madison reimposed the Non-Intercourse Act, without constitutional warrant for doing so (81). Congress, in drafting the act, said he could suspend it if a nation ended its trade restrictions, but not that he could put it back in place. When the president returned from Montpelier, Jackson had been in town, fencing with Robert Smith and entertaining Federalist foes of the administration (especially Timothy Pickering). Madison received him with all the formality of a state dinner that Jefferson had abandoned, taking Jackson's wife in to dinner. But he was furious nonetheless. "A man of tact would have seen that from the moment Madison became formal he was dangerous" (88). Soon Madison wrote a letter for Smith to send as his own, telling Jackson that their exchanges were so full of misunderstanding that he must submit anything else he had to say in writing (89). Jackson took that as demeaning to his government, and turned more warmly toward Federalist troublemakers, who toasted him for attacking the Francophile stubbornness of Madison. Jackson appealed to the American people over their government's head, never a good idea, as Citizen Genêt had proved (111). Madison, again through Smith, informed Jackson that he was no longer welcome in the capital (95).

The second session of the Eleventh Congress met in November, after the Erskine-Jackson exchange had occurred. Madison's administration was left with the ineffectual Non-Intercourse Act as the only protest against continued English depredations. That was a sieve through which ships passed continually, with the extra benefit of paying no duties.

> Finally, a law which in the eyes of a community was not respectable was not respected. The community had no other defense against bad legislation; and in a democracy the spirit of personal freedom deserved cultivation to the full as much as that of respect for bad law. The Non-Intercourse Act

was not only a bad law — the result of admitted legislative imbecility — but it had few or no defenders even among those who obeyed it. (118)

Gallatin tried to come up with a measure that would continue the censure of England (and, pro forma, of France) while encouraging some trade on which he could collect customs.

> Gallatin best knew how much the Non-Intercourse Act or any other system of commercial restriction weakened the treasury. He knew that neither the president nor Congress offered the germ of a better plan. He faced an indefinite future of weakness and waste, with a prospect of war at the end; but this was not the worst. His enemies, who were disposed to destroy, were skillful enough to invent the means of destruction. They might deprive him of the United States Bank, his only efficient ally; they might reject every plan, and let the treasury slowly sink into ruin; they might force the country into war for no other object than to gratify their personal jealousies. Gallatin believed them capable of all this, and Madison seemed to share the belief. The treasury, which had till that time sustained the Republican party through all its troubles, stood on the verge of disaster. (118–19)

In the new Congress, Gallatin gave Nathaniel Macon, the chairman of the House Ways and Means Committee, a plan for excluding British and French merchant *ships* but not British and French *products* if carried by American vessels. This would open up some trade and bring more duties in, while still formally objecting to British depredations. Known as Macon's Bill, this plan was debated for months in both houses of the Congress.

> The measure was as mild a protest as human skill could devise if compared with the outrages it retaliated, but it had the merit of striking at the British shipping interest which was chiefly to blame for the conduct of the British government . . . The opposition objected to the new policy for the double reason that it was too strong and too weak . . . According as commerce or passion weighed with the reasoners, the bill was too violent or disgracefully feeble. (130)

When Federalists expressed alarm that the bill would infuriate both the great powers, Macon argued that this would renew the Embargo again, but on the cheap, since others would enforce it for us:

> Macon reflected only the views of Madison and Gallatin when he replied that if England and France should retaliate by excluding American ship-

ping from their ports, they would do what America wanted; for they must then enforce the Non-Intercourse which the United States had found impossible to enforce without their aid. (130)

Senator Samuel Smith denounced this "side-way" of accomplishing "a great national measure" (136). He favored, instead, the arming of commercial vessels and fitting them out with convoys (130). After months of debate, Smith succeeded in killing the bill, for reasons Madison believed were corrupt — part of a scheme between Senator Smith and Secretary Smith to protect the family's business interests (131–32). Yet he kept Secretary Smith in office.

Unable to get even the faulty Macon's Bill through the legislature, the administration fell back on a truly bizarre scheme, once again introduced by Macon, though at Gallatin's prompting, and therefore called Macon's Bill Number 2 (though the first one had never passed). This was the last and weakest plan to use commercial restriction as a coercive policy, "the last stage toward the admitted failure of commercial restrictions as a substitute for war" (137). The bill would throw open all former kinds of trade, but would restore non-intercourse with France if England revoked its Orders in Council, or would impose it on England if France revoked the Berlin and Milan Decrees — this time expressly giving the president discretion in deciding whether and when and to whom the new punishment would be dealt and for how long. The bill's opening effect was decidedly favorable to England, since it was far the greater provider of trade. It would therefore anger Napoleon. "The objections to the bill were overpowering, for its effect was equivalent to alliance with England. Had the United States taken active part in the war against France, they could have done Napoleon no greater injury than by the passage of this act, which invited Great Britain to control American commerce for her military purposes" (138).

Madison's administration, so popular in its first months, had fallen into debility and disunion. It was spending more than the supposedly wastrel Federalist regimes, and getting less in terms of security and prosperity. John Randolph wrote, at the end of the 1810 congressional session:

We adjourned last night a little after twelve, having terminated a session of more than five months by authorizing a loan of as many millions, and — all is told. The incapacity of government has long ceased to be a laughing matter. The cabinet is all to pieces, and the two houses have tumbled about their own ears. (148)

Talk of the cabinet's squabbling was exaggerated, but only because that seemed the only reasonable explanation for its fecklessness. Complaints reached such a pitch that Virginia's congressman Walter Jones pleaded with Jefferson to intervene, as if he alone could restore some semblance of unity to the fractured Republicans:

> I never knew them more disconnected in sentiment and system, as proba-
> bly may have been made manifest to you by the desultory and inconclusive
> work of nearly three months. You will recollect that at the close of the last
> Congress the appearance of umbrage was confined to Mr. Gallatin and Mr.
> R. Smith; indeed, excepting themselves there were no other secretaries ef-
> fectively in office. It is now supposed, and I believe with truth, that the for-
> mer stands alone against the more or less unfriendly dispositions of all the
> rest. Their main abettors of last spring have abated nothing of their strong
> and indecent zeal. (133)

Jones was right. The cabinet's troubles were not confined to Smith's war with Gallatin. Secretary of the Navy Hamilton was incompetent. Secretary of War Eustis could not control General Wilkinson because the latter was under Madison's protection. Gallatin was so perturbed by Wilkinson's meddlesome ways that he warned France's minister against them: "I am specially charged to assure you that whatever proceedings of General Wilkinson may seem to warrant your suspicions must not be attributed to the executive, but solely to the vanity, the indiscretion, and the ordinary inconsistencies of that general, whom you know perhaps as well as we" (30).

Wilkinson had marked the beginning of Madison's administration with a stunning act of disobedience. Ordered to move his military camp in Louisiana out of malarial lowlands, he waited two months before taking action, so that the debilitated men died as much from the delayed move as from their original diseases. Almost half his force of two thousand men was lost (124). The military board set up to investigate this reached an inconclusive verdict, and Madison gave Wilkinson the benefit of the doubt. Robert Rutland, an editor of Madison's papers, says:

> Madison's handling of the Wilkinson case was damaging to his presidency,
> and was probably the worst mistake he made while in the White House.
> Not only did he saddle the country with an incompetent soldier, he also
> kept alive the whitewash started by Jefferson with a military decision made

for political reasons. Once Wilkinson was permitted to keep his command, he was an albatross the Republican presidents thought they had to protect. This was a bad precedent, leading to the further politicalization of the army and navy, with disastrous consequences that would keep cropping up during the Mexican War and would get completely out of hand during the Civil War, when commands were dispensed not for ability but to safeguard party control of the White House. Some of this would undoubtedly have happened even if Madison had done the right thing and sacked Wilkinson when he had the chance. But by dodging this responsibility, Madison harmed the war effort, hurt the army's morale, and in effect became a buck-passer instead of a courageous leader.[7]

Tricked by Napoleon

Adams devotes seven chapters of this volume to Napoleon, since it is his thesis that Napoleon, more than anyone, brought on the War of 1812 — or at least that it was the effect of Napoleon's actions. Most histories told from the American vantage point ignore or minimize Napoleon's agency, treating the lead-up to war as an essentially bipolar transaction, with England and America clashing over neutral trade. Adams argues throughout the first two volumes of his Madisonian history that there was a complex interplay of three actors, and it was the addition of the third agent (Napoleon) that made it impossible to find peace between the other two. A sequence of British navigation acts was matched by Napoleon with a series of "continental" acts — the British trying to isolate Napoleon from useful foreign trade, the French trying to seal England out from European ports.

America's response was an attempt, increasingly hopeless, to find some space between these two systems. It did not seem entirely hopeless at the time, since both the British and French schemes had loopholes in them, some intended, many unintended. Each tried to encourage some trade, useful to itself, and choke off other trade, useful to the enemy. The British would let American vessels reach ports — but only if monitored by them. Napoleon would accept American goods directly from American (or Caribbean) sources — but only if this trade could be kept free of taint by British interference or control. So, with variations from regulation to regulation, what England would condone France condemned, and what France would condone England condemned. Given this impasse, America tried to starve both sides (by Embargo) until one or the other loosened its restrictions, or to flood both sides (Macon's Bill Number 2) till one beat the other in redirecting them.

The chinks in the system were constantly being probed by American vessels, as enterprising captains ducked into the markets of Portugal, Sweden, Holland, or Russia. Even with its vast navy England could not blockade all the ports under Napoleon's sway. And even with his vast armies, Napoleon could not repulse trade in every harbor under his nominal control. The three-part choreography was more complicated than a simple scheme will indicate, but some interlocking high points can be put as symbols of the *motu perpetuo:*

England: Fox (Partial) Blockade (1806)
    France: Berlin Decree (1806)
        America: Non-Importation Act (1806)
England: Orders in Council (1807)
    France: Milan Decree (1807)
        America: Embargo (1807)
England: Orders in Council (1808)
    France: Bayonne Decree (1808)
        America: Enforcement Act (1808)
England: Orders in Council (April, 1809)
    France: Vienna Decree (1809)
        America: Non-Intercourse Act (1809)
England: Orders in Council (May, 1809)
    France: Rambouillet Decree (1810)
        America: Macon Bill Number 2 (1810)

Through all the twists and turns of this process, both European powers said that they were not hostile to America, or even to neutral trade, properly understood. A true neutral, each maintained, would not be helping the other side. But accepting neutrality in the terms defined by England would automatically make any vessel a belligerent in Napoleon's eyes, and vice versa. Each saw its own role as essentially defensive, not offensive. England was staving off Napoleon's imperial designs on its island home. Napoleon was keeping his European realm from strangulation by the British fleet. America was an unfortunate pawn in this interplay between two methods of "self-defense." Jefferson's dream of a perfect neutrality could not exist but by giving up trade altogether.

This triangular conflict was most often interpreted by Madison as a one-on-one clash with England. He thought British acts were not defensively aimed at Napoleon, but offensively aimed at the United States.

When not motivated by greed, they were driven by malice, by resentment at America's rejection of British rule. It was easier for Madison to believe, at least part of the time, Napoleon's claim that he was just protecting the rights of neutrals. After all, Napoleon did not have a fleet that was a constant presence in the Caribbean. He did not stop American vessels for impressments. Admittedly, he seized or burned the ships he stopped, but fewer of these came his way than ran afoul of the British fleet. The Federalists were right that Madison's actions de facto favored Napoleon. But the Republicans were right to say that was not their intent.

The real question was, how long could this process be sustained? Whenever it could not, America would become involved in a war with one or the other side — and most probably with England. Although the British had the "global reach" to inflict damage in the American hemisphere, it also had outposts there that could be damaged in return, especially in Canada or Jamaica. Besides, Madison believed that "the original sin against neutrality lies with Great Britain" (207). As Adams notes, "The theory of original sin led to many conclusions hard to reconcile" (207).

This interplay of the three countries was complicated by internal conflict within each of them. Trade policies were proposed and opposed by shifting factions at home. In America, different sides were taken not only by Federalists and Republicans, but by Federalists disagreeing with other Federalists, Republicans with Republicans. The same was true to an even greater extent in England, where the Tory government Canning spoke for was falling apart in 1810. The situation was particularly murky there because the King was insane, his heirs were disgraced, and both major parties were riven with disputes, so that "every piece on the chessboard stood in the way of its neighbor" (185). Madison was mistaken in seeing some unitary will in the British. Unfortunately, the one point of universal accord in Britain was a matter that Madison considered changeable — the need for impressments in order to maintain the British navy. France did nominally have a single will — Napoleon's — but that will was volatile and unpredictable, and when Napoleon committed conquered realms to his brothers, they proved restive and shattered the united front of French policy.

With the passage of Talleyrand's influence, the new French minister of foreign affairs, Jean-Baptiste de Champagny, tried to open vents to the outer world, as a way of repairing France's economy. Champagny, who was about to become the Duc de Cadore, had allies in the minister of the interior (the Comte de Montalivet), the minister of police (Joseph Fouché), the minister of the treasury (Mollien), the minister of marine (Denis Decres), and Napoleon's brother Louis, the King of Holland. These men were convinced that Napoleon was driving France toward bankruptcy, and they collaborated with powerful local merchants to poke holes in the envelope Napoleon was trying to seal around Europe (157). The American minister in France, John Armstrong, took note of these developments and raised hopes in Washington — "for the fiftieth time" (159) — that Napoleon's punitive attitude toward neutral ships was about to change. A presage of change was also read into the fact that Napoleon recalled Turreau, the military man who had so often delivered bad news to Jefferson and Madison (160).

But when Cadore tried to get Armstrong and Napoleon together to discuss a trade agreement, Napoleon fretted at this effort to alter his policy, and mocked Armstrong's inability to speak French — he said Armstrong should be recalled to America for this deficiency (162). Instead of seeking an accommodation with America, Napoleon pretended that he had just heard of the Non-Intercourse Act, and he reciprocated with the Rambouillet Decree, which ordered the seizure of American ships sequestered in ports under his control (167). When the Emperor's brother Louis tried to resist the confiscations in Holland, he was forced to abdicate (171).

No sooner had Napoleon frothed with spurious indignation at America's Non-Intercourse Act than he was informed of Macon's Bill, which reopened trade everywhere. Macon's Bill, remember, offered to cut off trade with England if France repealed its anti-neutral decrees, or to cut it off with France if England repealed its Orders in Council. Napoleon thought he could finesse this situation, not by repealing his decrees but by offering exemptions from them if American ships were specifically licensed by him (174–75). Furthermore, he said he would suspend his decrees of Berlin and Milan on the condition that America force England to lift its blockade of Europe (180). This proposal was sent to America in what became famous as the Cadore Letter. "The Emperor himself, August 2, dictated the letter — the most important he ever sent to the United States government" (179).

Madison was elated by the missive, as by Erskine's proposal the year before. The earlier one seemed to show that the Embargo had worked. This one, he thought, indicated that the Macon Bill had worked. Jefferson, on reading newspaper reports of the offer, congratulated Madison again and rejoiced "that one power has got out of our way, and left us a clear field with the other."[8] Madison responded that now it would not be enough for Britain to cancel its Orders as they applied to America. It must also lift the blockade of Napoleon, or it would be "perfidious to the other belligerent."[9] Just as he had with Erskine, Madison leaped before looking. He embraced the terms of the Cadore Letter. On November 2, he issued a proclamation saying that the Berlin and Milan Decrees were withdrawn.

In fact, Napoleon promised they *would be* withdrawn *provided* that America not only re-impose a ban on British trade but "cause their [French] rights to be respected by the English" (180). Madison had not considered carefully enough that the Cadore Letter "required the president to enforce his [Napoleon's] rights *before* the Emperor should withdraw his decrees" (209). As Napoleon told his minister of the interior, "It is evident that we commit ourselves to nothing" (184). For the second time, Madison had acted on a deceptive offer from a foreign power, and "made himself a party to Napoleon's fraud" (213). As Robert Rutland puts it:

> To say that Madison jumped the gun is too mild. The president threw away all caution and issued a Proclamation accepting Napoleon's claims at face value. Unless the British made a similar promise to call off the Orders in Council, a clamp-down on American commerce with Britain would begin in February, 1811.[10]

As Madison had informed Jefferson, the happy new situation with regard to France gave him the delusion that France would now support his effort to take the Floridas.

In the summer of 1810, a dissident group of Spanish subjects in West Florida captured the fort at Baton Rouge and declared themselves an independent nation. They petitioned to be admitted to the United States. Madison wanted to act immediately on this opportunity, lest the rebels be tempted to ask another nation to adopt them; but he admitted to Jefferson that there were constitutional objections to an immediate response, throwing into question "the adequacy of the existing laws of the United States for territorial administration" (216). One cannot add territories by executive fiat, without some kind of congressional authorization — and Congress would not be reconvening for another four months. Besides, troops would be needed to support the insurgents, and this, too, required action by Congress. "Madison saw all this, but though aware of his want of authority, felt the strongest impulse to act without it" (215).

He rationalized swift action on the old grounds that West Florida had really been part of the Louisiana Purchase, so he was dealing with what was in fact United States territory, not some foreign domain (217). He moved troops there on October 27; they were in occupation by December 7, and Governor Claiborne in New Orleans governed them as part of Louisiana Territory. A debilitated Spain, still racked by the Peninsular War, could not effectively protest "this filching a petty sand heap in a remote corner of the world" (220).

When the Eleventh Congress opened its second session in December, Madison revealed to it what he had done in Florida. Congress, which could have challenged the legality of Madison's act, decided that it "had best be accepted in silence as plainly beyond the Constitution" (223). Henry Clay of Kentucky raised the old arguments about Florida as already purchased.

> Congress approved this opinion, which was in truth neither weaker nor stronger than the arguments by which the Louisiana Purchase itself had been sustained. Fate willed that every measure connected with that territory should be imbued with the same spirit of force or fraud which tainted its title. The southern states needed the Floridas, and cared little what law might be cited to warrant seizing them; yet a Virginia Republican should have been startled at learning that, after October, 1803 [the Purchase date], every president, past or to come, had the right to march the army or send the navy of the United States at any time to occupy not only West Florida but also Texas and Oregon, as far as the North Pole itself, since they claimed it all, except the Russian possessions, as a part of the Louisiana Purchase, with more reason than they claimed West Florida. (224)

Timothy Pickering, objecting to Clay's argument, cited a letter from Talleyrand asserting in 1804, when the Purchase was negotiated, that France did not include Florida in the transaction. Since this secret letter had never been officially published, Pickering was censured for releasing it, a partisan move he took as a compliment (225). While Congress was still debating what to do with West Florida, Madison sent Congress a secret request for money to acquire East Florida by "a subversion of the Spanish authorities within the territory" (228). He sent two agents to stir up a rebellion that would require America to step in.

Congress also had to back up with law the proclamation accepting the Cadore Letter. Madison's proclamation had declared that Napoleon had repealed the Berlin and Milan Decrees, but by February he had not in fact done so, and John Randolph denounced the "bargain which credulity and imbecility enter into with cunning and power" (239). As rumors reached America of ships still being seized by Napoleon, Madison was in the unenviable position of saying that Napoleon was observing an agreement, against the evidence of his actions. Madison called for patience as he waited, month after month, for Napoleon to make good what he thought had been pledged. On March 18, 1811, he wrote to Jefferson:

> It is, as you remark, difficult to understand the meaning of Bonaparte toward us. There is little doubt that his want of money and his ignorance of commerce have had a material influence. He has also distrusted the stability and efficacy of our pledge to renew the non-intercourse against Great Britain, and has wished to execute his in a manner that would keep pace only with the execution of ours, and at the same time leave no interval for the operation of the British Orders without a counter-operation in either his or our measures. In all this his folly is obvious. (243)

Relying on the naïveté of Napoleon, on "his ignorance of commerce," was never a safe move. "Of all theories on which to found political action, the least reasonable was that of assuming Napoleon to be foolish; yet his 'obvious folly' was Madison's explanation of an ingenious and successful device to enforce the Continental System" (243).

Madison was forced to ask the French minister who had replaced Turreau, Jean-Mathieu-Philibert Sérurier, whether Napoleon had actually canceled his decrees — which was doubly embarrassing, since he was asking to find out if something had occurred after he announced that it had. Robert Smith did nothing but prolong the humiliation when he wrote a letter demanding information from Sérurier.

> Although everyone knew privately that Sérurier would say nothing on the subject, the president could not afford to give the silence official emphasis, and he probably regarded Smith's attempt to do so as a part of his general effort to discredit the whole system of commercial restrictions. The proposed letter to Sérurier could be of no use except to embarrass Congress in legislating against England. (243)

Smith had at last become intolerable. Madison's hope that he could be his own secretary of state, treating Smith as a figurehead, had proved empty. Smith could not be kept entirely out of the way, especially when

Madison was at Montpelier. Foreign ministers dealt with Smith, who invariably complicated (when he did not compromise) their relations with the administration. That was true with Erskine and Jackson from England, with Turreau and Sérurier from France. Within the cabinet, Smith was a constant irritant, since he coordinated his actions with those of his brother Samuel in the Senate, and with other foes of Gallatin. John Randolph deplored the influence of this faction, calling them "the Invisibles" because he suspected that they had more influence than outsiders could see (252). Randolph was back in his role as unwelcome scourge when he described the Smith faction:

> I am satisfied that Mr. Gallatin, by a timely resistance to their schemes, might have defeated them and rendered the whole cabal as important as Nature would seem to have intended them to be; for in point of ability (capacity for intrigue excepted), they are utterly contemptible and insignificant. (252)

By March of 1811, Gallatin had had enough — he offered Madison his resignation. Madison knew the price of firing Smith, and at last realized that Gallatin was worth the price. Gallatin was authorized to sound James Monroe on the idea of replacing Smith as secretary of state.

Monroe had been offended by the rejection of the treaty he negotiated with England, and had let Randolph maneuver him into a bid for the presidency against Madison in 1808. Even after he became governor of Virginia, he wrote that Madison should be left to reap the returns of his own folly (255). But when the secretaryship was offered him, he asked the advice of a Randolph ally, John Taylor of Caroline. Taylor had been so opposed to Madison's succession that he asked Jefferson to seek a third term as a way of blocking it. But now he advised Monroe to join Madison's administration. He foresaw that Napoleon's fraud would soon be discovered, making it necessary to start all over again on foreign policy, for which Monroe should be on hand in Washington (256).

Monroe took the advice, but answered Gallatin's agent that he could join the administration only if Madison were open to a complete change in the course of his foreign dealing (257). Monroe needed a pledge that he would not be a mere figurehead. His questions suggested in an obvious way that Madison's tilt toward France and against England needed correction. Madison needed Monroe, and needed Gallatin even more, so he accepted the implied criticism of his prior actions, and wrote: "I perceive not any commitments, even in the case of the abortive adjustment

with that power [England], that could necessarily embarrass delibera-
tions on a renewal of negotiations" (259).

Once he was assured that he had a replacement, Madison demanded
Smith's resignation. But he still wanted to placate the man's connections, so he offered him the prize post of minister to Russia. Under the
"enlightened" leaders Peter, Catherine, and Alexander, Russia had become an important player in European politics (and was soon to defeat
invasion by Napoleon). The country was a major consumer of American
trade goods. That is why Jefferson had tried and failed to open a diplomatic base there. Then, in the flush early days of Madison's tenure, Congress approved the mission, and John Quincy Adams was sent as the
first minister. Madison, the backstairs arranger of things, thought he
could replace Adams with Smith by appointing Adams to the Supreme
Court — Congress had already confirmed that appointment by the time
Adams heard of it and turned it down. News of that refusal had not
reached Madison when he offered Smith a plum to reconcile him to losing the office at State.

Smith, though angry at his dismissal and calling it unjust, said at first
that he would accept the Russian assignment. But when he talked with
his political friends and supporters, they resisted the idea. With Smith
removed from the country, they would lose one of their agents for domestic mischief. They convinced him that he was being made the victim
of a "shameful intrigue" (261). Smith wrote "An Address to the American
People," denouncing policies he had endorsed, charging that Madison
was a lackey to Napoleon. This confirmed what Federalists believed, but
did not explain why Smith had been part of the Jefferson and Madison
administrations for ten years. Madison encouraged Joel Barlow to write
a response to Smith, but one was hardly needed. The shrewdness of
Madison in getting Monroe as Smith's replacement was vindicated. No
one thought Monroe was too friendly to France, or hostile to England.

It was hard for Madison to keep excusing Napoleon as he stalled on
his pledge to cancel the Berlin and Milan Decrees. Jonathan Russell,
who had become the minister in Paris after Armstrong brought the
Cadore Letter to America, found that he could confirm nothing having
to do with the letter. Five months after it had been sent, all he could report from Paris was this:

No one here except the Emperor knows if the Berlin and Milan Decrees be
absolutely revoked or not; and no one dares inquire of him concerning

them. The general opinion of those with whom I have conversed on the subject is that they are revoked. There are indeed among those who entertain this opinion several counselors of state; but this is of little importance, as the construction which the Emperor may choose to adopt will alone prevail. (265)

Nine days after he wrote those words, he read a statement in a French newspaper that the decrees could not be revoked because the British blockade was still in place.

Napoleon knew how to keep an American president dangling. While he refused definitively to revoke the decrees, he once again assured Madison that "I am no way opposed to the Floridas becoming an American possession" (266). This cajoling alternated with defiance, as on March 17, when he told deputies from the Hanseatic League: "The Decrees of Berlin and Milan, founded on the nature of things, will form the constant public law of my empire during the whole time that England shall maintain her Orders in Council of 1806 and 1807" (275). When Cadore was replaced as foreign minister on April 17, the new man, Hugues-Bernard Maret, showed that he knew the Emperor's purpose by saying that his aim was "to gain time, leaving the principles of the matter a little obscure," until the United States should go to war with England as a way of ending the blockade of Europe (279).

While Madison was still trying to deny the intent of the Emperor, his man in Paris, Jonathan Russell, spelled it out for him:

> It is my conviction, as I before wrote you, that the great object of the actual policy is to entangle us in a war with England. They abstain therefore from doing anything which would furnish clear and unequivocal testimony of the revocation of the Decrees, lest it should induce the extinction of the British Orders and thereby appease our irritation against their enemy. (281)

Napoleon's designs on American shipping, murky in words, were clear in deeds. He demanded that American ships be seized in Denmark, Sweden, and the Russian ports of Archangel and Riga. The wisdom of Jefferson and Madison in seeking representation at the main Baltic power, Russia, became evident at this crisis. Napoleon was angry that "America enjoyed a monopoly of the Baltic trade . . . American vessels swarmed in Russian ports" (292). John Quincy Adams had arrived just when Tsar Alexander I was ready to defy Napoleon's order that this trade be cut off. The new minister was able to help coordinate the united action of the Baltic powers. This is the one place where Henry Adams unequivocally praises his grandfather, calling this diplomatic feat better even than his later creation of the Monroe Doctrine. Because it helped draw Napoleon into his attempt to punish Russia, Adams's quiet work contributed to the Emperor's downfall.

> Adams's diplomatic victory was Napoleonic in its magnitude and completeness. Even Caulaincourt [Napoleon's emissary to St. Petersburg], whom he overthrew, goodnaturedly congratulated him after he had succeeded, against Caulaincourt's utmost efforts, in saving the American ships . . . In this, the most brilliant success of his diplomatic career, he could not be blamed for doubting whether such fortune could last. (290)

Henry Adams no doubt wants us to remember, at this point, that Madison had tried to send Robert Smith to Russia, as a way of getting rid of him. No wonder Adams considered Madison a lucky president.

2

WAR

The *History*, Volume Six

OOKING BACK, the approaches to a war seem obvious. But in 1812 the British were caught unawares. They could not believe, after so many protests and no action, that Americans really cared deeply about restrictions and impressments. New Englanders had profited from England's war, and used more deserters than were ever recovered. America surely could not be asking the British to disable their own navy when it was in a death grip with Napoleon. For that matter, England thought the United States more likely to go to war with France. Bonaparte was not simply pressing men from American ships but destroying those ships, at sea and in Dutch and Spanish harbors. His promise to lift the Berlin and Milan Decrees was such a clear lie that Americans could not keep pretending to believe it.

England was also distracted by its own internal troubles, especially by economic decline verging on crisis (297). The King's madness had at last created a regency for his son, who did not feel confident enough to bring in, as expected, his Whig friends, but retained the embattled Tories, disappointing the most able man in the ministry, Marquis Wellesley. Wellesley was one who could see the gravity of America's pleas, since he appreciated the gravity of the man making them, William Pinkney. The two of them wanted to alert their respective nations of the real shape of events, but neither was being listened to. Their own exchanges were cordial, intelligent — and useless. Each had to wear the mask thrust upon him by his principals — Pinkney maintaining pro forma his country's empty claims that Napoleon had canceled the decrees, and Wellesley fobbing him off, pro forma, with assurances that nothing was really so terrible.

Pinkney was a man with a distinguished career at home and distinguished service abroad — he had been sent on diplomatic missions by Presidents Washington and Jefferson, and he collaborated with Monroe in forming the proposed treaty with England in 1806. He would later become famous as a lawyer in two of the most significant Supreme Court decisions, *McCulloch v. Maryland* (1819) and *Cohens v. Virginia* (1821), prompting a contemporary judgment that "no man has ever appeared at the bar of the Supreme Court who has furnished more light to the judges and received a more undivided hearing from the Court and bar."[1] Maurice Baxter writes: "He became the leading member of the Supreme Court bar: supreme oratory, thorough preparation, supreme confidence, even his dandified appearance, enhanced his reputation."[2] Yet his service as minister to England is counted one of the few failures in a life crowded with achievement. Only Adams, with his vivid memories of how hard it was for his father to deal with the British government during the Civil War, had the expertise to realize that Pinkney's performance was as brilliant as it was ineffectual. He rated him above all other men who held his position, including Charles Francis Adams:

> He had passed there nearly five years of such violent national hostility as no other American minister ever faced during an equal length of time, or defied at last with equal sternness; but his extraordinary abilities and character made him greatly respected and admired while he stayed, and silenced remonstrance when he left. For many years afterward, his successors were mortified by comparisons between his table oratory and theirs. As a writer he was not less distinguished. Canning's impenetrable self-confidence met in him powers that did not yield, even in self-confidence, to his own; and Lord Wellesley's oriental dignity was not a little ruffled by Pinkney's handling. As occasion required, he was patient under irritation that seemed intolerable, as aggressive as Canning himself, or as stately and urbane as Wellesley; and even when he lost his temper, he did so in cold blood, because he saw no other way to break through the obstacles put in his path. America never sent an abler representative to the court of London. (310)

Though Adams is writing a diplomatic history, he is forced — here as in many other places — to point out the incapacity of diplomacy, even of the highest order, to make up for the blunders of rulers. Given a bad case to argue, Pinkney had to come up with all the lawyer's cleverness that would later impress John Marshall on the bench. Trying to make the British lift their Orders in Council, he had first to convince the Regent that Napoleon had lifted his decrees, and for that the only proof he could adduce was a lack of proof:

> On such occasions it is no paradox to say that the want of evidence is itself evidence. That certain decrees are not in force is proved by the absence of such facts as would appear if they were in force. Every motive which can be conjectured to have led to the repeal of the edicts invites to the full execution of that repeal, and no motive can be imagined for a different course. These considerations are alone conclusive. (301)

To the claim that he was advancing Napoleon's argument against the British blockade, he answered with refined legalisms to distinguish his position from the French one (303). When these rarefied arguments did not get the attention of the government, "he had no resource but to lose his temper, which he did with proper self-control" (304). What little he could do he succeeded in doing by employing anger instead of reason:

> Centuries of study at Oxford and Edinburgh, and generations devoted to the logic or rhetoric of Aristotle, Cicero, and Quintilian, had left the most educated classes of Great Britain still in the stage of culture where reasoning, in order to convince, must cease to be reasonable. As Pinkney became positive and arrogant, Wellesley became conciliatory and almost yielding. (304)

Only by threatening to leave did Pinkney finally wrest from Wellesley the fulfillment of his promise to send a new minister to replace the obnoxious Francis Jackson, along with a renewal of the offer to settle the *Chesapeake* matter. Knowing that was the most he could accomplish, he refused an invitation to the Prince Regent's first diplomatic reception and asked only to receive the customary audience for leavetaking.

By the time Jackson's replacement, Augustus Foster, arrived in Washington, the *Chesapeake* controversy was shoved aside by a new clash at sea, in which the United States frigate *President* fired by mistake on the British corvette *Little Belt*, killing nine British seamen (only three Americans had been killed on the *Chesapeake*). Foster was a man far more tactful than Jackson, but his message — that the Orders in Council could not be lifted until the French decrees were — was one that Madison did not want to hear. Even Monroe, who had become secretary of state with a determination to be harsher toward France, had to turn a deaf ear to Foster's strong arguments for that course. He stalled Foster for a while, hoping to hear confirmation of the fact that Napoleon had, indeed, canceled his decrees; but Jonathan Russell could report nothing from Paris but his failure to get from the Duc de Cadore a guarantee that Napoleon would keep his word.

Monroe defended Madison's dogged faith in Napoleon's Cadore Letter with legal hairsplitting to equal Pinkney's in London. Even when it was reported that American cargoes were being confiscated in ports Napoleon controlled, Monroe denied that this proved the decrees were still in effect. The decrees covered only international law, he said, for ships *at sea;* what was done with them after they docked in a foreign land fell under national (municipal) law (325). Foster was justified in saying, however diplomatically, that this was shysterism in the service of a despot. He also protested the seizure of West Florida, suggesting none too subtly that this reflected a payoff from Napoleon for Madison's service to him (321).

It became harder and harder for Monroe to invent quibbles in Napoleon's defense (339). He was reduced to bluster and casuistry, mimicking the treatment that had dismissed him in European courts.

> Under the circumstances, Monroe needed more than common powers in order to play his part. Talleyrand himself would have found his impassive countenance tried by assuring Foster in the morning that the decrees were repealed, and rating [scolding] Sérurier in the afternoon because they were in force. Such conversations, extended over a length of time, might in the end raise doubts of a statesman's veracity; yet this is what Monroe undertook. (341)

Monroe, who had said he came into the government to change its ways, had been reduced to defending its ways, even against his own best instincts. As he later confessed to his old mentor, John Taylor of Caroline:

> I have been afraid to write to you for some time past, because I knew that you expected better things from me than I have been able to perform. You thought that I might contribute to promote a compromise with Great Britain, and thereby prevent a war between that country and the United States; that we might also get rid of our restrictive system. I own to you that I had some hope, though less than some of my friends entertained, that I might aid in promoting that desirable result. This hope has been disappointed. (241)

Taylor was forgiving, but John Randolph felt that his old friend had simply sold out to Madison.

Tripwire

While the politicians were lying to each other, a wire was tripped in a remote spot, the Tippecanoe Creek. Historians compare this backwoods tripwire for international conflict with an earlier one. In 1754, an Indian skirmish far from Europe's power centers had served to ignite the Seven Years War when young George Washington ambushed a French party near Fort Duquesne. In the same way, war with England was hastened on the nation in 1812 by William Henry Harrison's raid on an Indian village. As usual, Adams connects this backcountry affair with world economic conditions. The Indians who lived by trapping and trading for the fur industry had found their market blocked by the combined action of the British Orders in Council, the French decrees, and the American Embargo, "which combined to render their peltry valueless, so that they could scarcely buy the powder and shot to kill their game" (355). The *Chesapeake* affair had also made British Canadians prepare for possible war by seeking out Indian allies. At the same time, the brilliant Shawnee leader Tecumseh was forming a broad alliance of tribes to prevent the further sale of Indian land.[3] William Henry Harrison feared that this alliance would be put at the disposal of the British, and he tried to kill Tecumseh's inspiring brother ("the Prophet") while Tecumseh was making a tour of southern tribes, working to bring them into his coalition.

Harrison, the son of the famous Virginia revolutionary Benjamin Harrison (who chaired the committee that drafted the Declaration of Independence), had been promoted to positions of western influence by his fellow Virginians — Washington as president, and Jefferson as secretary of state. They put him in charge of the Northwest Territory, and allowed him to circumvent the ban on slavery there. Jefferson's benevolence had bowed to the need for adding western territories to the United States. Jefferson allowed that imperative to override his abhorrence of debt, personal and public, and turn debt into a kind of devil's tool for prying land from the Indians. He had written Harrison in 1803:

> To promote this disposition to exchange lands, which they have to spare
> and we want, for necessaries which we have to spare and they want, we
> shall push our trading houses, and be glad to see the good and influential

individuals among them in debt, because we observe that when these debts get beyond what the individual can pay, they become willing to lop them off by a cession of lands. (349)

The same letter goes on:

> I must repeat that this letter is to be considered as private and friendly . . . You will also perceive how sacredly it must be kept within your own breast, and especially how improper to be understood by the Indians. For their interests and their tranquility it is best they should see only the present age of their history.[4]

On the matter of Jefferson's Indian policy, Adams did not approach the *History* with a predisposition hostile to Jefferson, and only came to be critical as he learned more and began to admire more the Shawnee warrior Tecumseh. And even then he did not become as critical of Jefferson as modern scholarship has been.[5] Adams lists three things that prevented peaceful dealings with the Indians — white trespass, forced sale of lands, and trial of Indians by white juries (343–47). All three, along with the white-induced drinking that plagued the tribes, were exacerbated by Jefferson's policy, which was to "gradually circumscribe" the Indians.[6] Adams says that only a buffer zone between the two peoples could have prevented the exploitation of one by the other: "No acid worked more mechanically on a vegetable fiber than the white man acted on the Indian" (343). Jefferson persuaded himself that he was doing the Indians a favor by depriving them of land they were incapable of using fruitfully, and forcing them to learn more economical management of smaller estates:

> His greed for land equaled that of any settler on the border, and his humanity to the Indian suffered the suspicion of having among its motives the purpose of gaining the Indian lands for the whites. Jefferson's policy in practice offered a reward for Indian extinction, since he not only claimed the territory of every extinct tribe on the doctrine of paramount sovereignty, but deliberately ordered his Indian agents to tempt the tribal chiefs into debt in order to oblige them to sell the tribal lands, which did not belong to them but to their tribes . . . No one would have felt more astonishment than Jefferson had some friend told him that this policy, which he believed to be virtuous, was a conspiracy to induce trustees to betray their trusts; and that in morals it was as improper as though it were not virtuously intended. Shocked as he would have been at such a method of obtain-

ing the neighboring estate of any Virginia family, he not only suggested but vigorously carried out the system toward the Indians. (348–49)

Madison inherited the policy of Jefferson, on Indians as on other matters. Harrison was an appropriate instrument of the westward expansion favored by the Jeffersonians. He contravened the Treaty of Greenville — negotiated by Secretary of State Timothy Pickering — which stipulated that no chief could sell his tribe's land without consultation of the whole body of affected Indians. Harrison convened a group of "depraved" chiefs and extracted from them a grant of about three million acres (354). This egregious act made Harrison an involuntary recruiting agent for Tecumseh, who was fighting just this kind of confiscation masked as purchase. Harrison tried to seize on Tecumseh's absence to wipe out the village where his brother was in residence, but his own force was almost wiped out instead.

Harrison advanced on the village in alternating bursts of boldness and hesitancy, seeking an excuse to attack the place by night. Joseph Daveiss, the man who had brought Burr before two grand juries in Kentucky, led a group of that state's militia in Harrison's force. He was a critic of Harrison's cautious advance, on the grounds that it alerted the Indians and gave them time to prepare for attack. When Harrison took up a position near the village, he did not fortify it, claiming that he had too few axes, though he had the resources to build an entire fort only a month earlier on the same march. His lightly guarded camp was invaded before dawn, and 61 of his men were killed, with over 150 wounded — the bodies of 38 Indians were found on the field. When he advanced on the village in the morning it had been deserted, with the Prophet leading the withdrawal.

What had happened? Tecumseh, on his return to the area, said that the "transaction" was the initiative of "a few of our young men at the village" (373): "Those I left at home were (I cannot call them men) a poor set of people, and their scuffle with the Big Knives I compared to a struggle between little children who only scratch each other's faces" (371). Adams says that there was every reason to trust Tecumseh more than the self-justifying and self-contradictory reports that made the "battle" an American victory — a "victory" that Harrison would later ride into the presidency. "Tecumseh commonly told the truth, even with indiscretion" (309). Harrison's blunder had made it certain that Tecumseh would become an extremely effective ally of the British in the impending war, a far more important military figure than Harrison himself — one indeed whom Adams calls "the most powerful American then living" (356). For Adams, Tecumseh was the American Toussaint.

Canada

The West's fear of Tecumseh and the British was pushing the government toward war, but Adams was wrong in accepting the common view that western "warhawks" forced a resisting Madison into battle. Madison was not abandoning his policy of commercial coercion but supplementing it when he decided that he had to deny the British one more essential trade item — Canadian timber.[7] With England's European sources cut off by the interaction of its own blockade and Napoleon's decrees, the British needed timber for their endless fleet construction and repair. Canada was the principal source of this crucial resource. "The increase in Canadian lumber production and exports between 1808 and 1812 was simply astronomical, and it is no exaggeration to say that Canada sustained the Royal Navy for the duration of the war against France."[8] If Madison could take Canada and cut off the lumber lifeline of England's navy, the British would have to lift their Orders in Council and stop pressing men off American ships.

Luckily, taking Canada seemed an easy task. The French Canadians were supposed to be unhappy with British rule, maintained with small contingents of the British army. Seizing the land would require no navy. Land forces could strike at the main forts before the British navy could bring reinforcements to them. Jefferson wrote confidently: "The acquisition of Canada this year [1812], as far as the neighborhood of Quebec, will be a mere matter of marching, and will give us experience for the attack on Halifax the next [year], and the final expulsion of England from the American continent" (528). John C. Calhoun said: "I believe that in four weeks from the time that a declaration of war is heard on our frontiers the whole of Upper and a part of Lower Canada will be in our possession" (440). People began to talk as if the conquest had already been effected. John Randolph mocked the endless iteration of three syllables: "Ever since the report of the Committee of Foreign Relations came into the House, we have heard but one word — like the whippoorwill, but one monotonous note: Canada, Canada, Canada" (395).

Madison knew that there would be resistance to war, and not only in New England. But with Smith gone from the cabinet, he had a secretary of state who would help him orchestrate pressures on Congress. James Monroe was no stranger to war. He had joined the revolutionary army as a teenager, had crossed the Delaware with Washington, been badly wounded at Trenton, endured the winter at Valley Forge, and was promoted to colonel by the time of the Battle of Monmouth. Adams badly misreads the Madison-Monroe dynamic. He thinks that Monroe came into the government with a pro-British bias but that Madison overbore his views: "Monroe was far from easy, but he had accepted, as was his wont, the nearest dominating will, and he drifted without an effort" (378).

But Monroe was not the weakling Adams makes him. He had amply demonstrated his independence in the past — when he openly sided with the French Revolution as Washington's minister to France, when he broke instructions in order to purchase Louisiana as Jefferson's minister to France, and when he broke instructions again as minister to England, signing the draft treaty that Jefferson rejected in 1806. Monroe's resentment of that rejection, with its implied criticism of his conduct, had ended for a while his communications with Jefferson and Madison — that is why Madison sent his offer of the State Department through an intermediary, Virginia senator Richard Brent (254).

Monroe's reply to Brent, saying that he could not simply accept the policies already formulated, was an implicit demand that he be exonerated from the old charge of breaking his instructions. That Madison understood the letter in this sense is clear from a part of his own letter to Monroe not quoted by Adams:

> I perceive not any commitments even in the case of the abortive adjustment with that power [England], that could necessarily embarrass deliberations on a renewal of negotiations, inasmuch as the variance of opinion turned not a little on different understandings of the questions decided, and as the questions more immediately interesting to the harmony of the two countries, namely as in the *Chesapeake,* the Orders in Council, and the blockades, are either of a subsequent date or left without any positive decision.[9]

Madison dismissed, by omission, the principal criticism Jefferson made of the 1806 treaty — its failure to address impressment — and Monroe took this as an apology for past claims that he had been too independent in negotiating the treaty.[10] With that problem cleared up, Monroe was ready to join Madison in preparing for war.

During the August–September vacation in Virginia, Madison and Monroe made preparations for the new Congress the president had summoned to convene a month earlier than usual. Adams thinks Madison was just stalling in this period, hesitating between a discredited acceptance of the Cadore Letter and an unwillingness to do more against England than maintain the feeble non-importation. The address Madison delivered to Congress was, Adams admits, "an invitation to war" (382), but one that balanced criticism of England with criticism of France (381). He thinks Madison was waiting for Congress to take the lead. J.C.A. Stagg more probably argues that the annual message, like the summons for an early meeting of Congress, was part of a concerted effort by Madison and Monroe to bring the Congress to a new belligerency. They were the true war hawks. They had anticipated resistance like that of Giles of Virginia, who tried to make Madison's call for troops feckless by inflating the numbers needed (396).

Henry Clay, the leader of the war party in the House, was not forcing the hand of Madison and Monroe but working with them hand in hand. He coordinated strategy with Monroe for inching Congress toward war.[11] Madison increased the pressure for war in March, when he released inflammatory letters from a spy for Canada, John Henry. He had bought these letters from the fake French "Count de Crillon" with a secret payment of fifty thousand dollars (419).[12] Adams thinks Madison was simply naïve when he bought Henry's documents, but the president and his secretary of state could see that they contained nothing of real use to a foreign government. What they wanted was an indication that Canada had designs on America, justifying a plan to attack it before it could carry out those plans. The same consideration, and not simple naïveté about Napoleon, made them extend their original claim that France was observing the conditions of the Macon Bill. That, too, concentrated all the onus on England, and tamped down any moves toward joining the British in their war against Napoleon, moves prompted by new disclosures of French destruction of American shipping (429). Even after all these efforts, Congress finally voted for war over the objections of a sizable majority. The "warhawk" chamber, the House, carried the motion, 79–49, but it took two weeks of secret sessions for the Senate to reach a 19–13 vote (451). Madison and Monroe had to drag Congress into this commitment. The northern part of the nation did not go along with it at all. "Except Pennsylvania, the entire representation of no northern state declared itself for the war; except Kentucky, every state south of the Potomac and the Ohio voted for the declaration" (451–52).

What made Adams so seriously mistake the role of Madison and Monroe at this juncture? The problem was Adams's general confusion about the real character of Madison, as opposed to his nuanced reading of Jefferson's psychology. Adams disagreed with Jefferson on many things, but took him seriously. Madison's changes in position — fluctuating, for instance, from the nationalism of the Constitution to the states' rights stand of the Kentucky Resolutions and then back to a reluctant nationalism as president — came, Adams thought, from a comparative lack of weightiness. He thought Madison capable of acting in impetuous ways and then clinging to a rash decision out of mere petulance. He attributed more deviousness to him than he possessed. In a paradoxical way, Madison was too simple for Adams to understand him. Adams could explore with great shrewdness complex or theatrical figures like Jefferson, Napoleon, or Canning. He got bored too soon with men who looked as if they had few depths to be plumbed.

Adams does not, in other words, take Madison's mind seriously because it is not his kind of mind. Jefferson's was. Jefferson was a romantic, an enthusiast, an idealist, an inspirer, an aesthete. Madison was altogether a better thinker — more balanced, organized, practical, and self-critical. But he had the failings as well as the strengths of the intellectual. One trait especially betrays the intellectual in politics. In areas he understood thoroughly and in depth, like the structure of the state, Madison could adapt, could take a holiday from theory, could apply counter-measures, be flexible, pragmatic, inconsistent by intention rather than inadvertence. But in an area where he did not have real expertise, he tended to be rigid, doctrinaire, and ideological. Where the professional might relax, the amateur stayed tense.

The areas where Madison was an amateur were foreign policy and economics. He had no experience of the British or French worlds, and Gallatin was a grownup in a playpen when dealing with the financial views of Jefferson and Madison. But Madison tried to compensate for these weaknesses with unearned certitudes. He wrote a short treatise on money to prepare for his first trip to the Continental Congress. He wrote a long book on the legal basis of neutral trade to persuade Congress to impose commercial restrictions. And he bolstered Jefferson's resolve on the Embargo with predictions that England could not afford to lose American products. When England did not crumble under this pressure, he maintained (along with Jefferson) that the Embargo had simply not been enforced long enough or thoroughly enough. That is why the war for Canada was not an abandonment of his peaceful coercion policy but its ultimate application. He wanted to use the war to restrict commerce in Canadian timber, fish, and wheat. Had he succeeded in conquering Canada, the nation would probably not have let him offer it back in return for neutral trade. But he did not think that far ahead. He wanted only to prove his theory, and taking Canada was the one way left for doing that.

In order to silence the considerable minority opposed to the war, the House adopted the British Parliament's way of "calling the previous question" to end debate on a pending motion with an instant vote (245–46). Stanford of North Carolina said that this was as effective at gagging the opposition to government as the Sedition Act had been (395). That is an exaggeration, but Jefferson had become a champion of even more direct repression. He informed Madison that those protesting the war could be silenced by tar and feathers in the South and by lynching in the North — acts he could condone, apparently, because they would be forms of private enterprise rather than government action:

> The Federalists indeed are open-mouthed against the declaration [of war]. But they are poor devils here, not worthy of notice. A barrel of tar to each state south of the Potomac will keep all in order, and that will be freely contributed without troubling government. To the north they will give you more trouble. You may there have to apply the rougher drastics of [ex-] Gov. Wright [of Maryland], hemp and confiscation.[13]

When Congress followed up the war's opening with its 1813 legislation, Adams notes how Republicans continued to centralize the powers of government.

> Madison, Monroe, Gallatin, as well as Jefferson and the whole Republican party, accepted a highly paid mercenary army, a fleet of ships-of-the-line, a great national debt at high interest, and a war of conquest in coincidence with the wars of Napoleon, on ground which fifteen years before had been held by them insufficient to warrant resistance to France. (599)

Do passages like that confirm the common view that Adams was saying the Republicans just became Federalists when power tempted them? On the contrary, the war, which he praises, was carrying Madison beyond both Federalism (which now opposed the war) and Republicanism (whose principles should have forbidden it) into pragmatic new territory where the old ideologies were irrelevant. Though the West did not force Madison into the war against its will, western leaders did support it. These were young men, thinking outside the former categories of North or South. The new leaders in Congress were in their thirties — Clay, the House Speaker, was thirty-four. They were not reversing positions they had been too young to espouse in their own adult years.

> None of the new leaders could remember the colonial epoch, or had taken a share in public life except under the Constitution of 1789, or had been old enough to feel and understand the lessons taught by opposition to the Federalist rule. They knew the Federalists only as a faction, more or less given to treasonable talk, controlling some thirty or forty votes in the House, and proclaiming with tedious iteration opinions no one cared to hear. The young war Republicans, as they were called, felt only contempt for such a party; while, as their acts showed, they were filled with no respect for the technicalities of their executive head, and regarded Gallatin with distrust. Of statesmanship, in the old sense, they took little thought. Bent on war with England, they were willing to face debt and probable bankruptcy on the chance of *creating a nation,* of conquering Canada, and carrying the American flag to Mobile and Key West. After ten years devoted to weakening national energies, such freshness of youth and recklessness of fear had wonderful popular charm. The reaction from Jefferson's system threatened to be more violent than its adoption [emphasis added]. (380)

The Republicans had invited the West into their coalition, and they relinquished, accordingly, some of their control over the party. Power was not returning to the North, to Federalists, but moving to the West, and changing character as it did so.

In opposing the war, Federalists adopted a kind of rule-or-ruin folly which Adams treats as criminal. Some told the British minister they would support the war, but only out of hope that America would lose and the Republicans would be turned out (413). "Their conduct could seldom be explained on rational grounds, but in January, 1812, they seemed to lose reason. Their behavior, contradicting their own principles, embarrassed their friends still more than it confused their enemies" (412).

Here Adams takes an objective and long-range view of what was happening, and introduces an idea that would later be pursued by the Schlesingers, *père et fils* — that politics in America moves by cycles, in bursts of alternating energies (though Adams charts periods of less than half the span favored by the Schlesingers):

> Experience seemed to show that a period of about twelve years measured the beat of the pendulum. After the Declaration of Independence, twelve years had been needed to create an efficient Constitution; another twelve years of energy brought a reaction against the government then created; a third period of twelve was ending in a sweep toward still greater energy; and already a child could calculate the result of a few more such returns. (380–81)

This is not a cyclic view of history of the sort his brother Brooks would win Henry over to in the 1890s. He is not espousing here a doctrine of return, but of forward movement. Progress toward more unified national action may be held up, periodically, for a rest, a regathering of resolve; but then it resumes its course. Going back to Federalism would not move this process on. The Federalists had forfeited the ideal of a national vision, of the West as the future, of the people as a partner in the endeavor, of populist energy as the necessary fuel. In ways both conscious and unconscious the Republicans had fostered all these. They were creating a nation.

In this new situation, however, a hangover of old Republican ideology left the country ill prepared for war. Madison had no real army to take Canada, but the myths of Republican virtue made that unnecessary. The yeomen of the militia, with their own arms and their states' training, could respond like Minutemen to the easy task of taking a country under the deadening weight of an imperial colony. After all, no navy would be needed — just men to cross the border and secure their conquest before British ships could rush new troops to Canada. This view was confirmed by the one piece of primitive intelligence-gathering undertaken before the war. Secretary of War Eustis had sent a secret agent, Benjamin Stickney, into Canada late in December, 1811, and received his report in February, 1812. Stickney, who was the son-in-law of Madison's friend John Stark, had the Republicans' ideological contempt for regular troops, and he dismissed the British regulars at Quebec as "much debilitated by intemperance," easy prey for virtuous freemen.[14]

Jefferson reassured Madison that militias could accomplish the mission. Virginia alone could do it, troops from its southern counties mounting the summer invasion and those from the northern counties taking up winter service. "Governor Barbour will attend to circum-

stances, and so apportion the service among the counties that those ac-
climated by birth or residence may perform the summer tour, and the
winter service be allotted to the upper counties."¹⁵ Jefferson, a man of
airy conjectures, never had an airier one than this of a "summer tour."

War in the West

Since war was declared on June 18, 1812, there was plenty of time, Madison thought, to take Canada, or at least Lower Canada, before winter set
in. (The British had divided the country for administrative purposes
into a western Upper Canada and an eastern Lower Canada.) It was important to take Lower Canada first, since that was the part of the country with greater access to and from the sea, where British reinforcements and naval support had to be anticipated and prevented. Yet the
first strike had to be launched from the West, since Tecumseh's collaboration with the British made American settlements there vulnerable.
The opening assaults were supposed to be simultaneous in the West and
East; but troops proved more difficult to raise and move through the resisting eastern states. So land war began in the West.

The area most at risk was the Michigan Territory, whose governor, a
lawyer named William Hull, had approached Madison for more troops
even before war was declared. As a young Yale graduate, Hull had been a
gallant officer in the Revolution; but at age fifty-nine he no longer had
any military interest or ambition. Madison, however, had few men he
could call on to lead the western forces, and Hull reluctantly agreed to
become brigadier general there. He was ordered to return to Detroit,
taking a group of Ohio volunteers and some regulars back through a wilderness. He reached Detroit just as war was declared, and was ordered
to invade Canada as part of a pincer operation coordinated with invasion of Montreal from the East.

Hull, who thought the Canadians would not support the British
troops or Indians, took his little army over the Detroit River on July 12,
and occupied the unfortified town of Sandwich. He issued a proclamation to the Canadians saying that "no white man found fighting by the
side of an Indian will be taken prisoner; instant death will be his lot"
(503). To begin a bargaining war of atrocity with Tecumseh and his allies was not a wise step. Once on Canadian soil, Hull could not decide
whether to attack the lightly garrisoned Fort Malden. He was worried
about his supply line back through the forest, which was menaced by

Tecumseh's warriors. The Ohio militia had officers who were rebelling against his control, and his mismanagement of communications had let his plans and orders fall into enemy hands (501).

Against Hull's confused and divided and undersupplied men, the advantages of professionalism were demonstrated by the British major general in charge of Canadian defense, Sir Isaac Brock. Though Brock was almost twenty years Hull's junior, he already had a distinguished record fighting in Holland and the Baltics, and he had put down a troop rebellion when he first came to Canada in 1803. He had only 1,500 regular troops to defend a thousand miles of frontier, but he moved quickly to secure both the western and eastern approaches and to keep open rapid communication between them on the Great Lakes. He was the civil governor of Upper Canada, and he dismissed its legislature when it proved obstructive (517), took harsh action against balking militias, and led reinforcements to Fort Malden to rebuff Hull. Above all, he respected and knew how to use his Indian allies, especially Tecumseh. He reported to London from Fort Malden, where he linked up with Tecumseh:

> I found some extraordinary characters. He who attracted most my attention was a Shawnee chief, Tecumseh . . . A more sagacious or more gallant warrior does not, I believe, exist. He was the admiration of everyone who conversed with him. (524)

William Henry Harrison, with his attack on Tecumseh's village, had created a fine fighting instrument for the British.

Hull retreated across the Detroit River and holed up in Fort Detroit, trying to bring up reinforcements by detaching needed troops back along Indian-raided trails. He thought the fort should be abandoned while his men withdrew toward a more secure base of support, but the men of the West threatened to mutiny if he did this (514). "Hull's vacillations and evident alarm disorganized his force. The Ohio colonels were ready to remove him from his command, which they offered to Lieutenant Colonel Miller of the U.S. Fourth Regiment; but Colonel Miller declined this manner of promotion, and Hull retained control" (521). Unable to withdraw himself, Hull dispatched 350 of his sorely needed men to open a route for reinforcements, but they were cut off from returning to him by Tecumseh's braves. Brock moved his mere 350 regulars, with 600 Indian allies, across the river and set up his guns against Detroit.

He answered Hull's threat of atrocity with a proclamation that prisoners would be protected if Hull surrendered, but would be turned over to the Indians if they resisted. At this point, two companies of Michigan militia, Hull's own men, deserted, further weakening the imperiled post (527). Hull's wife and children were with him in the fort, and he could not stand the thought of their being raped and killed by Indians (526). He surrendered.

Jefferson, who said that taking Canada would be a mere march, thought that an American defeat by Canadians could not be explained except by treason. This is another case of naïve optimism recoiling into conspiratorialist suspicion. Jefferson wrote to the editor of the *Aurora,* "The treachery of Hull, like that of Arnold, cannot be a matter of blame to our government" (528). The Michigan Territory was now under British control, "the greatest loss of territory that ever before or since befell the United States" (529).

> If any man in the United States was more responsible than Hull for the results of the campaign, it was Ex-President Jefferson, whose system had shut military efficiency from the scope of American government; but to Jefferson, Hull and his surrender were not the natural products of a system, but objects of hate and examples of perfidy. (528)

This is as harsh a judgment as Adams ever delivered on Jefferson, but it is mild next to what other students of the War of 1812 would conclude. Alfred Thayer Mahan mocked the way Jefferson said he could control the Gulf Stream with his commercial bans and take Canada with a few militiamen:

> Jefferson, with a curious insanity of optimism, had once written, "We begin to broach the idea that we consider the whole Gulf Stream as of our waters . . ." With like blindness to the conditions to which his administration had reduced the nation, he now wrote, "The acquisition of Canada . . . will be a mere matter of marching."[16]

Theodore Roosevelt is even more caustic:

> Twelve years' nerveless reign of the doctrinaire Democracy had left us impotent for attack and almost as feeble for defense. Jefferson, though a man whose views and theories had profound influence upon our national life, was perhaps the most incapable executive that ever filled the presidential chair; being almost purely a visionary, he was utterly unable to grapple

with the slightest actual danger and, not even excepting his successor Madison, it would be difficult to imagine a man less fit to guide the state with honor and safety through the stormy times that marked the opening of the present century. Without the prudence to avoid war or the forethought to prepare for it, the administration drifted helplessly into a conflict in which only the navy prepared by the Federalists twelve years before, and weakened rather than strengthened during the intervening time, saved us from complete and shameful defeat.[17]

War in the East

The armies aimed at Lower Canada in the East, which should have been the first to invade Canada, did not suffer an early disaster like Hull's in the West only because they did not yet exist. Madison had begun a war that required rapid mobilization in and through a region that opposed the war. The man sent there to raise troops was Henry Dearborn, Jefferson's former secretary of war, a revolutionary veteran who had never commanded more than three hundred men in war. Now sixty-one, he was as reluctant to be called back to service as was his partner in the West, William Hull. Madison soon learned what an impossible assignment he had given his general. He wrote to Gallatin: "The militia detachments [in New England] are either obstructed by the disaffected governors or chilled by the Federal spirit diffused throughout the region most convenient to the theater" (529).

As general of the eastern armies, Dearborn was supposed to coordinate his movements with Hull in the West, but he had no secure route for communicating with a man who could not even keep his own lines open to the rear through Tecumseh-ridden territory. Besides, for a former secretary of the army, Dearborn showed an astonishing inability to find out exactly what his jurisdiction was (518). His efforts were further stalled by an unexpected armistice offer from England. The ministry there could not believe that the United States still wanted war after the cancellation of the Orders in Council. The armistice offer was sent through the British minister in Washington, and the governor general of Lower Canada was informed of it. He proposed to Dearborn that there be a cessation of hostilities until the matter could be resolved (519). Dearborn took on himself the political decision to abide by this, and sent word of it to Hull in Detroit. That message was too slow to reach Hull in time, but Brock knew of it through his better communications on the Lakes, and he meant to take Detroit before he could be stopped by such negotiations (524). Madison overruled Dearborn's acceptance of the ceasefire, but only after more delay had been added to the slow gearing up of war in the Northeast.

Deploying troops for the invasion of Niagara, Dearborn established two subordinate units, incompatible in their makeup, one under the Federalist leader of militia, Stephen Van Rensselaer, and the other under a Republican leader in the regular army, Alexander Smyth. They could not settle precedence between them, so they each failed separately — Van Rensselaer first. He invaded the Niagara peninsula on October 12, but when his advance party was surrounded by British forces on Canadian territory, his militia units refused to cross the border to come to their fellows' rescue, saying they had no authority to fight outside the country. A young lieutenant colonel named Winfield Scott resisted bravely in a clash that killed Brock on Canadian territory (543), but the survivors in the American invading band had to surrender.

Then Smyth took his turn at failure. He was an American exception at this stage of the land war, a young man (forty-five) for command — but that was not a virtue in his case. Born in Ireland, he had risen as a florid orator in the Virginia legislature.

> Dearborn, knowing little of Smyth, was glad to entrust the army to a regular officer in whom he felt confidence; yet an Irish temperament with a Virginian education promised the possibility of a campaign which, if not more disastrous than that led by William Hull of Massachusetts, or by Stephen Van Rensselaer of New York, might be equally eccentric. (540)

It was. Smyth took command with a proclamation insulting his predecessors and their troops, and especially denigrating the militia among them:

> The nation has been unfortunate in the selection of some of those who have directed it. One army has been disgracefully surrendered and lost. Another has been sacrificed by a precipitate attempt to pass it over at the strongest point of the enemy's lines with most incompetent means. The cause of these miscarriages is apparent. The commanders were popular men, destitute alike of theory and experience in the art of war. (544)

Smyth, who had written a drill book, strutted about, marching his troops and whipping up their anger at him, issuing bombastic boasts.

He tried two abortive crossings into Canada, then found himself hiding from his own men for fear of assassination.

> Upon this, General Smyth's army dissolved. "A scene of confusion ensued which it is difficult to describe," wrote Peter B. Porter soon afterward — "about four thousand men without order or restraint discharging their muskets in every direction." They showed a preference for General Smyth's tent as their target, which caused the general to shift his quarters repeatedly. (547)

Smyth's performance had been "disgraceful and gasconading" (the words are those of his fellow Virginian Monroe), and he was quietly cashiered (572).

One reason for the dissolution of the eastern army was raging dysentery and other sickness, which disabled half the troops (347). The first mark of undisciplined camps is the lack of hygiene, which can fell an army as effectively as can any foe, a point George Washington had made in contrasting regular with militia encampments. When Dearborn himself took over the remains of the army of the Northeast and tried to advance it to a winter camp in Canada, fulfilling at least that much of the war's original program, his militia refused to go over the line (548). The year that was supposed to end with the conquest of Canada had concluded, instead, with the loss of the Northwest to British dominance.

Factors of Loss

Adams's skill as a military historian shows in the way, without breaking the narrative march of the *History*, he presents all the things that went wrong with the conduct of the war in its early stages — which amounted to all the things that can possibly go wrong in war. The effort failed on point after point of military necessity.

1. *Clarity of Objective.* War was declared with the vague aim of conquering Canada, but there was no setting of priorities, no sense of the necessary steps toward that goal, no weighing of the costs and how to minimize them. As the military historian Russell Weigley says, "There was no strategy for the war beyond general agreement in the government and the War Department that Canada ought to be attacked."[18] This was, Weigley adds, an "incongruously offensive" notion, when the requirements of defense were neither met nor even faced.[19] Adams puts the problem this way:

The seashore was nowhere capable of defense; the Lakes were unguarded; the Indians of the Northwestern Territory were already in arms, and known to be waiting only a word from the Canadian governor-general; while the whole country beyond the Wabash and Maumee rivers stood nearly defenseless. (495)

Because the only thought, if it can be called that, was of invading Canada, no precautions were taken against Canada's invading the States — which it quickly did, seizing effective control of the Michigan Territory when it captured Detroit.

If the overall goal was murky, the instructions to theater commanders were bound to be as well. Dearborn in the East was unsure of his jurisdiction (808). Hull in the West yielded to Madison's urgings that he take command under the impression that he would have a merely defensive role in Detroit. He was surprised when he was told to invade. J.C.A. Stagg notes that such ambiguous commissions were not uncharacteristic of Madison.

> This was not the first occasion on which the President had used ambiguity as a way of advancing his goals, and he probably hoped that when war was declared Hull would respond to orders to enter Upper Canada. The subsequent problems and ultimate failure of the northwestern campaign, however, all originated in the misunderstanding thus created.[20]

2. *Clarity of Command Structure.* The troops Madison sent to Detroit came from different militias and regular detachments, with officers not clearly subordinate to Hull as regional commander in chief. The militia treated Hull with contempt (526), and regulars tried to replace him with an officer they preferred (521). Things were even worse in the East, where Dearborn could not bring into line the Federalist militiaman Van Rensselaer and the Virginia regular Smyth (539–40). Things would get still worse next year, when James Wilkinson was sent north to dispute jurisdictions and drunkenly botch his assignments (748–53).

3. *Integration of Forces.* Militiamen and regular soldiers not only distrusted but sabotaged each other. Regulars hated militias — Winfield Scott thought the latter "vermin." The militias were especially despised in the East, because New England governors, opposed to the war, refused to call most of them to arms. Madison, rather than force the issue to civil war, brought militias up from other states, but they soon claimed that their terms had run out, or obeyed only their own officers, or refused to cross the border into Canada. Regulars saw their troops being

slaughtered on the Canadian side of the border, within eyesight of militias who would not come to their rescue. James Monroe, when he later became secretary of war, described the disintegrating militias:

> It may be stated with confidence that at least three times the force in militia has been employed at our principal cities, along the coast and on the frontier, in marching to and returning thence, than would have been necessary in regular troops, and that the expense attending it has been more than proportionately augmented from the difficulty, if not the impossibility, of preserving the same degree of system in the militia as in the regular service. (1092)

Disease raged in the ill-kept militia camps. Originally thought to provide a cheaper alternative to the regular army, militiamen proved more costly as well as less useful: "Excessively expensive, wasteful, insubordinate, and unsteady, no general dared to depend on them" (570). John Mahon describes the lower fighting readiness of militias in the War of 1812 as compared with those in the Revolution:

> Roughly 398,000 American militiamen served during the war for less than six months, and another 60,000 enrolled for slightly longer terms. This was a more wasteful use of manpower than during the American Revolution, when only 164,000 men had served such short hitches. Long-termers during the Revolution totaled 231,000, but in the War of 1812 only 50,000. Some militiamen are known to have engaged for as many as ten short tours of duty. This kind of coming and going was prodigal of supplies, for short-termers as often as not carried home articles of issue which it was nearly impossible to replace. Blankets were in such short supply that recruits were asked to bring their own. The commissary general issued a greatcoat every two years in lieu of a scarce blanket. Not only did the short-term system increase the cost of supplies, it also vastly enlarged the pension lists for generations in the future.[21]

4. *Professionalism.* Yet even the regular army was hardly professional at the outset of the war. It had not been kept up for war purposes, as the navy had by the Quasi and Tripolitan wars. New recruits were rushed in for the war, whose training was rudimentary or incomplete. Many of the officers were new as well, chosen by political patronage. Winfield Scott described the situation at the beginning of the war:

> Federalists were almost entirely excluded from selection, though great numbers were eager for the field, and in New England and some other states there were very few educated Republicans; hence the selection from

those communities consisted mostly of coarse and ignorant men. In the other states, where there was no lack of educated men in the dominant party, the appointments consisted generally of swaggerers, dependants, decayed gentlemen, and others "fit for nothing," which always turned out utterly unfit for any military purpose whatever. (494)

5. *Intelligence.* There had been no systematic attempt, before the war or in its early stages, to learn the disposition and capacities of Canadian troops, militias, and military posts. The Americans did not have the British skill for using the Indians to collect intelligence. One of the few with Indian connections, because of his fur business, was John Jacob Astor — but the secretary of war made no effort to learn from him (501–2). In the West, no one knew where Tecumseh would strike next, so fear of him was felt everywhere. His Indians, when they took Michilimackinac and sent survivors fleeing into Detroit, added to the panic Hull felt before his surrender (511).

6. *Logistics.* Of all Hull's many failures, logistics was probably the most important. Denied the Great Lakes by British ships on them, his troops from Ohio had to cut a way through overgrown swamps to reach Detroit. This path ran through Indian country and could not be maintained as an open avenue for supplies and reinforcements. When Hull needed help toward the end of his siege, and sent almost half his troops to get it, they were jumped by Indians who were watching the route. There was no secure route for logistical support.

7. *War Finance.* When Gallatin tried to raise taxes for war preparation, Congress not only denied him the taxes but deprived him of the bank from which reasonable loans could be arranged and currency kept stable: "The first and fatal blow to the Treasury was the loss of the Bank of the United States, which left government without financial machinery or a sound bank-note circulation" (886). The most prosperous local banks were in New England, and they refused money to the war effort. Since specie drained to them thanks to the sale of manufactured goods, the currency was destabilized elsewhere, and "nearly one third of the national resources" were denied to the government and its war (886). Congress, though straitened in all these ways, had not only to support the rapidly expanding regular army but the federalized (and inefficient) militias. Even the New England militias, which would not join in the war offensive, mustered for local defensive purposes and demanded pay from the federal government. The enticement, on completion of a year's

service, of 160 acres of land in the West, though it saved money for Congress, did little to excite recruits, since similar bounties had not been honored after the Revolution. "The nation went to war on a financial shoestring, with the inevitable consequence of inadequate logistical support for the armed forces."[22]

8. *Supply.* Troops set off for Canada without the blankets, shoes, coats, and hats needed for winter service (411). They were also lacking doctors and medical supplies. Where there are no competent agents, acting under inspectors general, war profiteering is bound to thrive. Early in the Niagara campaign, Stephen Van Rensselaer described his troops: "Many are without shoes; all clamorous for pay; many are sick . . . I receive no reinforcements of men, no ordnance or munitions of war" (536).

Adams contrasts American conditions with the Canadian response to invasion. Isaac Brock wielded his small body of military men with precision because he had a professional command structure, he ruthlessly subordinated the militia to the regulars, he had rapid intelligence and communication. He was short of supplies, but he supplemented what he had by capture of American posts and depots. Brock simply had no equal on the other side:

> Brock was not only a man of unusual powers, but his powers were also in their prime. Neither physical nor mental fatigue such as followed his rivals' exercises paralyzed his plans. No scruples about bloodshed stopped him midway to victory. He stood alone in his superiority as a soldier. Yet his civil difficulties were as great as his military, for he dealt with a people [in Upper Canada] better disposed toward his enemies than toward himself; and he succeeded in both careers. (515)

Brock was a warrior. The Americans did not know what to do with this man who had faced Napoleon's army. "Brock's energy counterbalanced every American advantage" (517). Critics charged that he used the savagery of Indians as a terrorist weapon — he admitted it. Hull was unstrung when Brock said that he would be unable to control his Indians if Detroit did not surrender (525). When Brock crossed the Detroit River and put his men in range of Hull's guns, he was criticized as foolhardy, but he had good intelligence of conditions from within the fort.

> I got possession of the letters my antagonist addressed to the secretary of war, and also the sentiments which hundreds of his army uttered to their friends. Confidence in their general was gone, and evident despondency

prevailed throughout. I crossed the river contrary to the opinion of Colonel Proctor, etc. It is therefore no wonder that envy should attribute to good fortune what, in justice to my own discernment, I must say proceeded from a cool calculation of the *pours* and *contres*. (124)

Brock wanted to make quick work of Detroit so he could get back to the eastern points of engagement.

Tecumseh could work with such a man. The two made a formidable team. Those Americans who had called for war with Canada rightly said that the United States had more manpower, wealth, and resources than the country to the north. But it was unable to deploy these assets and bring them to bear by military means. Besides, the United States did not have Brock. It did not have Tecumseh. I am reminded of what Fabius Maximus is supposed to have said to his brave companion Giskon, when the latter remarked on the vast army of Hannibal, spread out under the promontory they were standing on. When his friend expressed wonder at the forces arrayed against them, Fabius said, "They do not have Giskon."[23]

Fortunately for the United States, Canada did not have Brock or Tecumseh for long. Both warriors died on the front line. On October 14, 1812, Brock was killed while leading an assault on a hill at Queenston, New York (541). A year later, October 5, 1813, resisting a charge by Richard Mentor Johnson's cavalry at the Battle of the Thames, Tecumseh was killed, "the last Indian leader of international significance" — the heir of Joseph Brant, the ally of Britain, the scourge of America, the champion of his people.[24]

3

NAVAL HISTORY

The *History*, Volume Six

Congress declared war on June 18, 1812. Operations began immediately on both land and sea. Secretary of War William Eustis sent a dispatch on that day telling General William Hull to launch from Detroit an invasion of Canada. Secretary of the Navy Paul Hamilton on the same day ordered his few sea-ready ships to rendezvous at New York (551–52). Adams takes up first the land operations (chapters fourteen to sixteen) before turning to the "Naval Battles" (chapter seventeen). This is understandable, indeed expectable. The war's major events would take place on land, and would engage large numbers of combatants, while the navy was small and its engagements few. Yet it took time for the land armies to be mustered, moved, and brought to bear on the foe — ineffectually at first.

The country's ships, however, what there were of them, sprang into action at once, and they had more immediate success than did the armies. The uniting of the nation, which is Adams's theme, was advanced only after long fumbling on land. Early victories of the navy, by contrast, created a sudden afflatus of national pride. The navy's success was, of necessity, small in scale, since the United States had only seven frigates, and one of these saw no action. The frigates had gun mounts rising to forty-some. Great sea battles in the eighteenth century involved ships of the line, with gun mounts rising to seventy-some. They fought, as their name declares, in line formations, bringing great fire power to bear, deployed by thousands of men. Congress had ruled out a navy on that scale, preventing the construction of American ships of the line. It seemed impossible for the ludicrously small American contingent to pose any challenge to the British navy, which had roughly 200 ships of the line and 250 frigates. Since America had so few ships, the secretary of the navy was at first frantically concerned that he would lose any of them. He warned them to patrol the coast and duck back to safety whenever British ships loomed up on the horizon.

But the commodores had other things in mind. Their ships were small but superb, and they had used them to great effect in the Quasi War and the Tripolitan War. Unlike the army, the navy had kept its men and weaponry in a state of trained readiness. While the militias on land were disobeying orders to avoid combat, the sea captains disobeyed orders to get at the foe — and they did this with stunning early successes that dismayed the enemy and put a fighting spirit in the entire American community. Even the New Englanders who opposed the war were boastful about the navy, since they supplied the nation's seamen.

The improbability of this achievement has led it to be much studied. Naval history in general was getting on a professional footing just as Adams composed the *History*. The book that marks the real dawn of the discipline, Alfred Thayer Mahan's *Influence of Sea Power upon History, 1660–1783*, was published in 1890, when Adams was bringing out his *History*'s final volumes. Mahan is called America's naval Clausewitz, one who integrated the study of economics, politics, and military forces, something Adams did for both the land and sea operations studied in the *History*. Mahan would not get around to writing his own analysis of the War of 1812 until 1905, when he devoted two volumes to *Sea Power in Its Relations to the War of 1812*. But Adams had already by 1891 performed much the same analysis, and reached many of the same conclusions, as Mahan did.

Mahan argues that the War of 1812 could have been prevented or waged successfully (not to a mere stalemate, as happened) by a relatively small earlier investment in naval power. The United States could not have gone head to head with the British fleet. But a few efficiently deployed ships of the line could have made it prohibitively difficult for England to extend itself, beyond its crucial commitment against Napoleon, in an effective war with America:

What had been possible during the decade preceding the war — had the nation so willed — was to place the navy on such a footing, in numbers and constitution, as would have made persistence in the course Great Britain was following impolitic to the verge of madness, because it would add to her war embarrassments the activity of an imposing maritime enemy, at the threshold of her most valuable markets, the West Indies, three thousand miles away from her own shores and from the seat of her principal and necessary warfare.[1]

Adams makes the same case in his account of congressional debates in 1811, where he paraphrases and endorses remarks made in the House by Langdon Cheves of South Carolina:

His argument, as a matter of expediency, was convincing; for every American ship-of-war, even when blockaded in port, would oblige the British to employ three ships of equal or greater size to relieve each other in blockading and watching it. The blockading service of the American station was peculiarly severe. England had no port nearer than Halifax for equipments or repairs; in general all her equipments must be made in Europe, and for only three months' service; in winter she must for months at a time abandon the blockade, and leave the coast free. No method could be devised by which, with so small risk and so little waste of money and life, the resources of England could be so rapidly drained as by the construction of heavy war vessels. Once at sea, an American seventy-four had nothing to fear except a squadron, and even when dismantled in port she required the attention of a hostile fleet. (407)

Mark Russell Shulman contrasts Adams with the men he calls "navalists" because Adams never endorsed the idea of a large navy.[2] But neither did Mahan (despite later misuses of his name for promotion of an omnicompetent navy). Both argued for a navy tailored to a specific political purpose within specific economic and cultural constraints.[3] That is why Mahan says only a few ships of the line would have been sufficient in 1812. He and Adams were Clausewitzians, who thought of war as politics carried on by other means. Mahan's version of the famous maxim of Clausewitz is: "War is simply a political movement, though violent and exceptional in character."[4] Shulman, who quotes mainly from Adams's *Life of Albert Gallatin*, thinks that Adams remained an opponent of the navy all his life; but his changed attitude to the navy is his principal departure from the earlier book. In the biography Adams concluded that "Mr. Gallatin was essentially in the right" on the navy (G 171). He no longer thought that when describing the War of 1812 — and Gallatin no longer thought that when financing the War of 1812.

American resistance to investment in sea power had never been primarily financial, but ideological, from the time when Madison and Gallatin in the House had tried to prevent the construction of the six frigates created by Washington's administration.[5] As Richard Johnson said, in response to Cheves's speech of 1811: "I will refer to Tyre and Sidon, Crete and Rhodes, to Athens and to Carthage . . . Navies have been and always will be engines of power, employed in projects of ambition and war" (407). The same objections, of course, were made to standing armies — and they left the military in a wretched condition for waging the War of 1812. It was the contrast between undisciplined land forces and naval teamwork that impressed Adams, with his admiration for professionalism of every kind.

The difference between the comparative success of the navy in 1812 and the abject failure of the armies in that year is easily stated. Secretary of War Eustis had to put together armies from disparate groups of militias and regulars with poor (when any) training, few qualified leaders, and no logistical infrastructure. Before the war, militia "drill" was largely a social event, with spotty to nonexistent real work on artillery, fortification, and other disciplines. Regular troops maintained some order only on posts engaged with Indian foes. But ships cannot be sailed by weekend warriors. A ship needs constant attention, for what Mahan called "the management under all circumstances of the great machine which a ship is."[6] This is true all the time, and not merely in actual combat. The crew has therefore a vital interest in the ship's continual servicing, in the expertise of its masters, the soundness of its structure, the hygienic conditions on board, the competence of the crew, the reliability of its suppliers. Desertion occurred regularly in all the land fighting in this war, in ways that were more difficult on shipboard. (Where does a deserter at sea go?)

The generals of the land forces were part-time officers, politically appointed, with little or no experience of combat. There had been no call for their use in the Quasi War or the Tripolitan campaigns. What experience they had went back thirty years to the Revolution, since which time they had been in other lines of work, mainly political. The average age of the generals was sixty, while the naval captains were in their thirties (564). The latter were, most of them, men who had been subordinate officers in the Tripolitan and Quasi wars. They had been lieutenants under capable captains at that time, and were now of an age to replace their first masters. A general can conduct war at some distance from the front. A ship's captain is always as close to the combat as any of his sub-

ordinates, and he must be fit and alert if he is to succeed. The competence of naval officers must be demonstrated from the minute they put
to sea, while the incapacity of land commanders can go for long periods
undetected or unremedied. Theodore Roosevelt, in his history of naval
action in the War of 1812, described the young veterans now taking
charge:

> The captain [of 1812] had perhaps been a midshipman under Truxton
> when he took the *Vengeance* [in 1800], and had been sent aboard the cap-
> tured French frigate with the prize-master. The lieutenant had borne a part
> in the various attacks on Tripoli, and had led his men in the desperate
> hand-to-hand fights in which the Yankee cutlass proved an overmatch for
> the Turkish and Moorish scimitars. Nearly every senior officer had extri-
> cated himself by his own prowess or skill from the dangers of battle or
> storm; he owed his rank to the fact that he had proved worthy of it. Thrown
> upon his own resources, he had learned self-reliance; he was a first-rate
> practical seaman, and prided himself on the way his vessel was handled.
> Having reached his rank by hard work, and knowing what real fighting
> meant, he was careful to see that his men were trained in the essentials of
> discipline, and that they knew how to handle the guns in battle as well as
> polish them in peace.[7]

The competitive edge maintained by the naval commanders has provoked some criticism of them, since it gave them a prickly sense of honor
and emulation, leading to jealousy and duels. According to James E.
Valle:

> The Quasi War with France and the War of 1812 had yielded a crop of over-
> whelmingly proud and egotistical young commodores pathologically pre-
> occupied with personal "honor" and incapable of sacrificing private consid-
> erations for the good of the service.[8]

Adams is so approving of the navy that he reports with praise the captains' defiance of orders — "Rodgers and Decatur showed no regard to
the wishes of the government" (553). He does not, for instance, con-
demn Isaac Hull's trick to keep command of the *Constitution* away from
the man scheduled to take charge of the ship, William Bainbridge (556).
This seems inconsistent, since Adams is scathing about the way militiamen ignored orders and took control of their own lives on land. But
those rebellions were against professional standards, and the naval men
were upholding standards not provided by their superiors. The neglect
of the navy by Presidents Jefferson and Madison, and the bungling in-

terference with it by Secretaries of the Navy Robert Smith and Paul Hamilton (the former corrupt, the latter alcoholic), meant that the navy could survive only by sealing itself off to some degree from political hostility to it. Mahan will criticize the captains of this war not for failing to heed Hamilton's land-defense policy, but for not being even more adventurous than they were in hunting out from home.[9] But the frigates would not have succeeded at all unless they had moved partway toward the goal Mahan set for them.

Some attribute this independence to political motives in the officers. Since New Englanders were the men most called to the sea, and New England was the last bastion of Federalism, a fair number of naval officers were Federalists. In the land army, on the contrary, militia officers were appointed by state authorities or elected by their men, and regular officers were appointed by the national authority, with its patronage policy established in the retention of James Wilkinson. The exclusion of most Federalists from army command reduced the size of the already small pool of available talent. When a Federalist officer did serve, like Stephen Van Rensselaer, New York's major general of militia, his loyalty was suspect, and he committed compensatorily rash acts (539).

Adams allows the navy its own method of creating professionalism because it was, in effect, fighting for its life. It had to bring ancillary services up to its standards, or perish from general incompetence. The navy, despite the neglect and opposition begun by Jefferson and continued by Madison, could not sail without prior equipping by foundries that cast cannon, by hemp and canvas producers, by ships' surgery suppliers, by victualers, as well as by the ships' architects and maintenance men. The army, by contrast, had gone for decades without quartermaster activity or logistical networks. Congressmen made fun of Eustis, the secretary of war, as one "who consumes his time in reading advertisements of petty retailing merchants to find where he may purchase one hundred shoes or two hundred hats" (573). But he had to shop on his own, since he had no underlings doing this basic work. The mystique of the Minutemen, who would rally with their own weapons, had prevented the creation of arms depots, supply systems, and military contracts for coordinated action. Eustis's whole War Department was made up, at the outset, of "eight clerks, not one of whom had been twelve months in office" (410).

In the event, the navy played a surprisingly important role, given its size, even when the achievement was only a symbolic one. It sustained national pride when there was little else to base it on. And when, as at Lake Erie and Lake Champlain, army and navy personnel had to collaborate, some of the seamen's professionalism was communicated to the land officers and men. Adams was good at studying these structural elements in warfare. He had become aware of the economic, technological, and supply functions of war while working for his father during the Civil War. That is why he was able to advance beyond the few models provided him for military history, and more especially for naval history.

The originality of Adams as a naval historian can be gauged only if we look at his predecessors in the treatment of the navy's performance in the War of 1812. I have mentioned some ways in which he anticipated Mahan's treatment of the war. But did he advance beyond the level attained by others before him? There had been a good deal written about the navy's performance in the War of 1812, but of serious narrative histories there were only three — by William James (not the American author) in England and, in America, by James Fenimore Cooper and Theodore Roosevelt. These men went beyond the early cult literature that sprang up around the heroes of the war — Captains Lawrence, Hull, Macdonough, Decatur, and (especially) Commodore Oliver Hazard Perry. The captains uttered famous rallying cries — Lawrence's dying "Don't give up the ship," Perry's "We have met the enemy and they are ours" — but they occasioned later controversies as well, libel suits and judicial hearings over disputed actions. The most famous of these involved Commodore Perry's criticism of Captain Jesse Elliott's conduct at the Battle of Lake Erie.

There was also a general interest, served by amateur historians, stemming from the fact that this was the last war fought under sail, one that perfected the art of maneuvering on an unstable sea, through veering winds, to bring guns efficiently to bear on moving targets. There was also a David-against-Goliath fascination with the way a few American ships embarrassed the huge and supposedly invulnerable British fleet. In fact, the first scholarly work devoted to the war, by William James, was written to rescue the British fleet from humiliation.

James argued, in the 1820s, that America had "super frigates," which were not a fair match with British frigates.[10] He claimed, furthermore, that American seamen were not better than, or even as good as, British seamen. Americans did as well as they did only because they had so many British deserters to serve and instruct them. James, who had been a proctor at the vice-admiralty court in Jamaica, was in the United States when the war broke out, and he was imprisoned for several months before escaping to Halifax. His prior office and experience gave him access to admiralty and other records, and his account is generally accurate about naval statistics, chronology, and events, despite the special pleading against American skill and courage.

James's six-volume *Naval History of Great Britain* was answered in 1840 by James Fenimore Cooper's two-volume *History of the Navy of the United States of America*, the second major predecessor to Adams's treatment of the naval war.[11] This book, once popular and now forgotten, will surprise those who know Cooper only as the author of the Leatherstocking Tales. They do not remember what a long association he had with the sea. When, at sixteen, he was expelled from Yale for brawling, he tried to sail with Francisco Miranda's filibustering expedition to liberate Venezuela.[12] Failing that, he sailed before the mast as a merchant shipman while waiting to be old enough to join the navy. He then served over three years in the navy, part of that time on the Great Lakes, part of it on three ships at sea, including a period on the sloop *Wasp*, commanded by James Lawrence, who uttered the famous "Don't give up the ship."[13]

Discouraged by Jefferson's attempts to cut back the navy, Cooper left it to take over his father's estate; but he kept in touch with former comrades as they rose in the service, and he planned for a long time to write a naval history. He was given access to naval records, and he interviewed participants in the battles of the War of 1812, in person or by correspondence. His work is generally well regarded by naval historians, even though he rendered it vulnerable by not citing his sources.[14] His knowledge of ships and sailors is evident in the sea novels he wrote, as the first American to base his fictions on British forebears like Smollett, Scott, and Marryat.

One of Cooper's admirers — both of the naval history and of his sea novels — was Theodore Roosevelt, Adams's third and last important predecessor.[15] As a student at Harvard (class of 1880), Roosevelt began to write a naval history of the War of 1812 after taking out the William James volumes from the Porcellian Club library. His object was to defend American seamen from James's denigration of them. Roosevelt pursued this project intensely while he dabbled in law studies at Columbia and entered New York state politics. In 1882, shortly after being elected to the state assembly, he published *The Naval War of 1812*. He was so successful in his effort at impartiality that the British, when they came to update James's volumes with an extensive new history, asked Roosevelt to contribute the 1812 section to volume six of *The Royal Navy* — while the United States Navy ordered that a copy of the book be placed on every vessel in service.[16] Roosevelt's *Naval War* was a brilliant achievement for a twenty-four-year-old, the most scholarly book of naval history that had appeared in America, with the partial exception of George Emmons's compilation, the *Statistical History of the United States Navy* (1853).

Roosevelt could have been great in any of a number of careers, and history was one of them. He did write later histories, especially his four-volume *Winning of the West,* and he was elected president of the American Historical Association in 1912. But he resembled that other gentleman historian, Henry Cabot Lodge, who never wrote another historical work to rank with his first one, *The Life of George Cabot* (written under Adams's supervision). The two men, distracted by strenuous political careers, descended as historians to writing potboiler biographies (Lodge of Alexander Hamilton and others, Roosevelt of Oliver Cromwell and others). Roosevelt's western volumes borrowed heavily (without attribution) from other authors, especially James Gilmore, and they were tainted with the racism that also appears, though less prominently, in *Naval War.* Yet his later work should not dim the real merits of his first book.

After leaving Harvard, Roosevelt aspired to be another Parkman or Prescott, one of the learned men of leisure whose money and family connections gave them access to precious government documents. For the American side of his book on the War of 1812, he received help from a friend of the family, William Hunt, the secretary of the navy (a post Roosevelt himself and five of his relatives, including cousin Franklin, would later hold). For the British side, he had the help of his uncle James Bulloch, whom we met when Adams was trying to thwart his building of Confederate ships in England. Roosevelt's mother was a Georgian, proud of her warrior family, descended from the revolutionary hero Archibald Bulloch. She clandestinely sent aid to the Confederacy from her New York mansion, and told her children about her stepbrother James's heroic blockade-running during the Civil War. Young Theodore and his sister Anna used to play "Confederate blockade" with toy boats in Central Park.[17] Bulloch, who was not pardoned after the Civil War, stayed on in England and was writing his own naval history — *The*

Secret Service of the Confederate States in Europe, or How the Confederate Cruisers Were Equipped (1883) — when his admiring nephew visited him.

Roosevelt worked hard on his history. He built model ships to familiarize himself with the various riggings of battleships. He laid out the action with the help of these models and large charts. His young and very social wife had trouble pulling him away from his project, complaining once that "we're dining in twenty minutes, and Teedy's drawing little ships."[18] The resulting book provides a judicious weighing of the naval forces deployed at each engagement, but it is going too far to claim that "today *Naval War* remains the definitive work in its field."[19] That title belongs to Mahan's later two volumes. Both Cooper and Roosevelt fail to anticipate the Mahan approach, which Adams did approximate. Roosevelt says nothing about command structure, overall strategy, or coordination with land forces. He never discusses the relations of the captains with the secretary of the navy or — except in the case of Perry and Elliott — with each other. He takes Hull from one adventure on the *Constitution* to the next one without remarking how he stayed with the ship. He makes no comments on the difference between a coastal defense strategy and hunting on the open ocean. He stays with each engagement, one by one, on the tactical level. In this he marks no advance over Cooper, though his description of the battles is more precise and full.

Mahan integrated what was occurring in the land war with his account of naval action. Roosevelt, who intended to write a separate book on the land war, gave up that project, simply adding a quick chronology of its main events as a preface to his third edition, along with a new chapter, at the end of the book, on the siege of New Orleans (which was more a land battle than a naval action). His work is further narrowed by his concentration on proving William James wrong about force levels, crew makeup, seamanship, and courage. The only time he breaks the sober tone of his book is to make satiric comments on the British historian — as when James argues that Americans showed cowardice by donning helmets when they boarded an enemy ship.[20] This kind of correction, thoroughly carried out, had its importance for Roosevelt's day, when James's authority was still great; but such corrective relevance is a wasting asset.

Adams knew all three of his predecessors, though he rarely cites James and uses only tacitly some of Roosevelt's force estimates. Of course, the space he can devote to battles is far more limited than that of the others (James, Cooper, and Roosevelt), who devoted whole books to the sea war. Adams must proportion this part of his history to the rest, which includes political, economic, and diplomatic activity. But this union of the naval war with all the war's other aspects is what makes him anticipate Mahan and fashion a lasting account of the War of 1812.

The Frigates' Moment of Glory

Adams's analysis of the navy begins from an appreciation of its basic equipment, the famous frigates but also the whole range of smaller vessels used as support craft and privateers. Naval architecture was an early American achievement. The frigates were built with compensatorily full armament and crew capacity, to make up for Congress's ban on ships of the line. The brigs, sloops, clippers, and schooners had been designed for speed and maneuverability in smuggling and blockade-running. Even the small warships built for service on the Great Lakes were done with great technical ability. Adams describes with loving care this collection of hornets for stinging His Majesty's ships.

Pride of place went to the frigates built under the Federalist presidents, six by Washington, two by Adams. Only one of these had been lost (in Tripoli) when the War of 1812 began. They had been designed by a genius, Joshua Humphreys, who gave them extra layers of protection (leading one to be called "Old Ironsides" after it weathered broadsides that did not pierce it) and more guns than were carried by other frigates. Yet his ships lost nothing in speed and maneuverability.[21] C. S. Forester, in his history of the naval War of 1812, said that Humphreys "instilled a living force into his fighting machines."[22] But Adams is just as impressed by the smaller craft that darted with insouciance through the lumbering British war vessels.[23] One of the most lyric flights Adams allows himself came when he imagined the British, with their vast military fleet and commercial convoys, wondering at these venturesome boats:

> Already the American ship was far in advance of the British model — a swifter and more economical sailor, more heavily sparred and more daringly handled. In peace, competition had become difficult, until the British ship owner cried for war; yet he already felt, without acknowledging it even to himself, that in war he was likely to enjoy little profit or pleasure on the day when the long, low, black hull of the Yankee privateer, with her tapering, bending spars, her long-range guns, and her sharp-faced captain, should appear on the western horizon, and suddenly, at sight of the heavy-

lumbering British merchantman, should fling out her white wings of canvas, and fly down on her prey. (J 979)

Adams's brother Charles, in the advance copy of the book sent him for marking up, suggested that the final phrase here be changed to "and pounce on her helpless prey," but Henry wisely retained the drama of those six final monosyllables.

Small as the fleet was at any time, it was especially weak when this war was declared — Secretary of the Navy Hamilton had given no previous warning or preparation. The *Constitution* had not mustered a new crew after dismissing its old one. The *Constellation* and the *Chesapeake* were undergoing repair — the *Constellation* never would get to sea, since the British navy sealed it up at Norfolk before it was ready to sail. But in New York Captain John Rodgers was ready to sail, with the frigate *President* and the sloop *Hornet*, while in Norfolk Commodore Stephen Decatur had the frigates *United States* and *Congress*, along with the sloop *Argus*. Hamilton ordered Decatur to join Rodgers at New York, where they could repulse from the coast British ships of their class "and then return immediately to harbor" (552). Hamilton had no confidence in his own forces — he meant "to use the frigates as harbor defenses rather than send them to certain destruction" against a superior foe (553).

Decatur opposed this strategy. He wanted the ships to go out as single hunters (551). But he followed orders so far as to take his ships to New York, where he joined Rodgers in a search for the *Belvidera*, a British ship that had been harassing merchantmen off New England. Their five-ship squadron was the largest American team that would take to the ocean during the war — and it was the last time the frigates hunted in a pack. The squadron quickly found the *Belvidera*, and the *President* fired a broadside that killed nine on the British ship. But when a second broadside was fired, a deck gun on the *President* blew up, killing or wounding sixteen. Rodgers was among the wounded, with a broken leg. The *Belvidera* escaped, and went to Halifax to warn the commanding admiral of the American waters, Henry Sawyer, that there was an American war squadron at sea.

Rodgers, despite his wound, did not turn back to New York. Adams writes: "The secretary [Hamilton] might have spared himself the trouble of giving further orders, for many a week passed before Rodgers and Decatur bethought themselves of his injunction to return immediately into port after striking the *Belvidera*" (552). The ships went to intercept the annual convoy taking specie to England from the West Indies. The clash with the *Belvidera*, with consequent repairs and treatment of wounds, delayed them too long to block the convoy, though they sailed all the way to British waters hoping to catch it. Adams thought it was a mistake to take the few ships away on this wild goose chase (553). Mahan, on the contrary, argued that Rodgers's plan was brilliant, praising "the deterrent effect of Rodgers's invisible command."[24] Rodgers was paradoxically protecting the American shore by leaving it. It was lucky, in this view, that the *Belvidera* escaped and warned Halifax, since Vice Admiral Henry Sawyer had intended to spread his ships along America's eastern seacoast, blocking its harbors, and now he hesitated to disperse them so. C. S. Forester spelt out the implications of Mahan's view.

> Rodgers knew that during these last few weeks, with the imminent approach of war, American merchant vessels had begun to swarm home, and part of his manifold duties was to ensure their safe entry into American harbors, and he had to do this in the face of a manifestly superior force. His disappearance out to sea with his united squadron was the most effective way of ensuring this. No single British cruiser would gladly remain at a focal point off the American coast when the captain was aware that at any moment Rodgers's topsails might appear over the seaward horizon, cutting him off from escape; no British admiral would gladly have his cruisers dispersed in situations inviting their destruction in detail. With Rodgers's departure known, there would be urgent British orders for concentration. The net cast to entrap American shipping would be entirely altered in character; the individual strands would have to be made strong, at the cost of making the holes infinitely larger — so large that in the event the homeward bound shipping made its escape with remarkably small losses. Rodgers's bold decision to take his squadron far out to sea had profound effect on the rest of the war.[25]

But for Rodgers's action, the next naval event, the war's first glorious exploit, might have turned out in a very different way — the overtaxed and staggering *Constitution*, making for Boston, might not have slipped into harbor past stationed British blockaders.

As soon as the *Constitution* was fitted out with a new crew (a Humphreys frigate took up to 450 men), Captain Isaac Hull put out to sea from Norfolk, sailing toward New York. The *Constitution* would become the most famous of the original frigates. It had served well in the Tripolitan and Quasi wars, but its real fame began now, when all it accomplished was an escape — an escape, nonetheless, rated "one of the most exciting and sustained chases recorded in naval history" (555). Hull's ship was sighted, as it moved up the coast, by a major British force — a ship of the line and three frigates — which gave chase to it. Normally, a Humphreys frigate would have no trouble outrunning its pursuers, but there was a dead calm that day (July 17). Since the sails would not work, Captain Hull put out his boats to tow the ship by rowing.

The British imitated this tactic, but with an extra advantage — they could take boats from other ships to tow the one closest to their prey. So Hull had his boats plant kedge anchors, working in relays — as the boat was winched up to one kedge, another was being planted farther out. The British matched that tactic, too; but they could not send out the kedge party too far without bringing it within range of the *Constitution*'s stern guns. For two days and two nights, this heavy labor went on, broken only by intervals when a breeze could be coaxed to move the ship by wetting its sails.

> Then came the lightest of breezes, and Hull set all sail. The most careful organization and good seamanship were required to get in the boats while the ship was under way; with the enemy only half a mile out of range, an accident could be fatal, especially as a pursuer could well, if an opportunity presented itself, leave a boat behind him to be picked up by a following friendly ship . . . Then the breeze died away to nothing, the ships all lying motionless on a glass sea in the growing heat of the July sun. Out went the boats again, and the dreadful toil at the oars recommenced.[26]

For long sleepless hours, Hull had to be alert to every smallest changing factor, spelling his men, timing his relays, putting out sail while pulling in boats. He needed all his stamina and concentration. As Mahan puts it: "Under such circumstance, accurate appreciation of advantages, and unremitting use of small opportunities, are apt to prove decisive."[27]

Fenimore Cooper, with his years of shipboard service, described the intricate choreography of simultaneously raising sail and recalling boats.

> The beautiful manner in which this advantage was improved excited admiration even in the enemy. As the breeze was seen coming, the ships' sails were trimmed, and as soon as she was under command, she was brought close up to the wind, on the larboard tack; the boats were all dropped in alongside; those that belonged to the davits were run up, while the others

were just lifted clear of the water, by purchases on the spare outboard spars, where they were in readiness to be used at a moment's notice.[28]

As the chase went on, Hull lightened his ship by pumping out two thousand tons of drinking water — the British, far from their harbor, could not afford to do that. Hull was not forced to the even greater extremity of jettisoning boats, guns, or other heavy equipment. Still, the *Constitution* did not lose its dogged pursuers until, on the second night of this ordeal, a rain squall came up and let Hull sail free. "Perhaps nothing during the war tested American seamanship more thoroughly than these three days of combined skill and endurance in the face of an irresistible enemy" (555–56).

It was Hull's good fortune that the harbor he was making for was Boston. The *Constitution* had been built there, and the town had a proprietary interest in it. This showed the wisdom of President Washington, who had the original six frigates built in different cities, to create a sense of the whole nation participating in the navy's creation. The *United States*, for instance, was built in Philadelphia, the city of the Constitution, under the personal supervision of Joshua Humphreys. Other cities, using his plans, built "their" component of the fleet — Baltimore, for instance, making the *Constellation*. But Boston had a special tie with its ship. As word spread of what Hull and his crew had done, the city went mad with admiration.

> For once, even the Federalists of New England felt their blood stir; for their own president and their own votes had called these frigates into existence, and a victory won by the *Constitution*, which had been built by their hands, was in their eyes a greater victory over their political opponents than over the British. (556)

Isaac Hull did not go ashore to share the festivities. He knew that incoming ships were cleaned, refitted, and resupplied for a new captain while the incoming officer made his report, underwent an evaluation of his service, and waited for a new assignment. Hull, who had been a lieutenant on the *Constitution* during the Quasi War, wanted to fight his ship, now that he was in command, and not just run with it. He did not, therefore, dock the ship in the inner harbor, but ordered supplies brought out to it. The *Constitution* had not been at sea long enough for her hull to be fouled, and he had no wounded to send ashore. He took the ship out to find prey.

The first one he fell upon was the *Guerrière*, which had been part of the pack chasing him. Its captain, J. R. Dacres, had sent a challenge by way of an American merchantman, saying that any American frigate that wanted the real *Guerrière* ("Warrior") could meet him off Sandy Hook — the British ship *Little Belt* had earlier been fired on at dusk, under the misapprehension that it was the *Guerrière* (556–57). When the *Constitution* met the *Guerrière,* it took a heavy pounding — it was here that it earned the nickname "Old Ironsides" — but in a mere thirty minutes of rapid fire it so riddled the *Guerrière,* killing or wounding seventy-nine, that the injured ship could not be sailed back as prize. After taking off the survivors, Hull blew up the *Guerrière.* Thus, a mere month after coming into Boston as a hero, he returned with another feat to his credit.

> The Sunday silence of the Puritan city broke into excitement as the news passed through the quiet streets that the *Constitution* was below, in the outer harbor, with Dacres and his crew of prisoners on board. No experience of history ever went to the heart of New England more directly than this victory, so peculiarly its own; but the delight was not confined to New England, and extreme though it seemed it was still not extravagant, for however small the affair might appear on the general scale of the world's battles, it raised the United States in one half hour to the rank of a first-class power in the world. (558)

This is a large claim; but Adams is saying no more than Fenimore Cooper had:

> It is not easy, at this distant day, to convey to the reader the full force of the moral impression created in America by this victory of one frigate over another. So deep had been the effect produced on the public mind by the constant accounts of the successes of the English over their enemies at sea, that the opinion, already mentioned, of their invincibility on that element, generally prevailed; and it had been publicly predicted that, before the contest had continued six months, British sloops of war would lie alongside of American frigates with comparative impunity. Perhaps the only portion of even the American population that expected different results was that which composed the little body of officers on whom the trial would fall, and they looked forward to the struggle with a manly resolution rather than with a very confident hope. But the termination of the combat just related far exceeded the expectations of even the most sanguine.[29]

The giddiness was prolonged by a string of victories for other ships. On September 7, the USS *Essex* brought into Delaware the first captured

British warship, HMS *Alert* (560). On October 17, USS *Wasp* defeated HMS *Frolic* — and though the *Wasp* was captured by a ship of the line before it could bring its prize home, "the fight between the *Wasp* and the *Frolic* roused popular enthusiasm to a point where no honors seemed to satisfy their gratitude to Captain Jones and his crew" (562). On October 17, Stephen Decatur, with the *United States*, fought and captured the *Macedonian*, the only British frigate that was to be refitted for use by the American navy. The *United States* had eleven casualties, the *Macedonian* ninety-nine (363). December 13, the *Constitution*, back at sea under command of William Bainbridge, destroyed the frigate *Java*. Though Bainbridge had to blow up his prize, he took the *Constitution* home to more celebration in Boston. The record compiled was astonishing:

> During the six months the war had lasted the little United States navy captured three British frigates, besides the twenty-gun *Alert* and the eighteen-gun *Frolic*, privateers by scores had ravaged British commerce, while the immense British force on the ocean had succeeded only in capturing the little *Nautilus*, the twelve-gun *Vixen*, and the *Wasp*. (565)

Theodore Roosevelt described the first eight months of war:

> To appreciate rightly the exultation Hull's victory caused in the United States, and the intense annoyance it created in England, it must be remembered that during the past twenty years the island power had been at war with almost every state in Europe, at one time or another, and in the course of about two hundred single conflicts between ships of approximately equal force (that is, where the difference was less than one half), waged against French, Spanish, Italian, Turkish, Algerine, Russian, Danish, and Dutch antagonists, her ships had been beaten and captured in but five instances. Then war broke out with America, and in eight months five single-ship actions occurred, in every one of which the British vessel was captured.[30]

The British press denounced the commanders of the Royal Navy for "letting themselves" be humiliated by a tenth-rate power. The reaction in England was as emotional as that in America. The loss of the *Guerrière* was mourned by the *Times* of London:

> Never before in the history of the world did an English frigate strike to an American . . . There are commanders in the English navy who would a thousand times rather have gone down with their colors flying than have set their fellow sailors so fatal an example. (623)

George Canning said in Parliament: "It cannot be too deeply felt that the sacred spell of the invincibility of the British navy was broken by those unfortunate captures" (624). The Humphreys frigates were treated as if they were magic ships, and British frigates were warned in the newspapers that they should not fight with them — only ships of the line could do that (629). It was suggested, in fact, that not even ships of the line could beat them (630). After a third British frigate was captured, England's leading publication devoted to maritime affairs, *The Pilot*, reacted this way:

> Down to this moment not a single American frigate has struck her flag. They insult and laugh at our want of enterprise and vigor. They leave their ports when they please, and return to them when it suits their convenience; they traverse the Atlantic; they beset the West Indies Islands; they advance to the very chops of the Channel; they parade along the coasts of South America; nothing chases, nothing intercepts, nothing engages them but yields them triumph. (631)

(That passage, by the way, shows how diligently Adams had read the newspapers in his long days at the British Museum.) The derring-do of the Humphreys frigates had that air of "the impossible" performed against "the invincible" that has jolted other warring nations — as when John Paul Jones ghosted in and out of British harbors in the spring of 1778, or "Jimmy" Doolittle led an air raid on five Japanese cities in April, 1942. Such feats, of little strategic significance, changed the climate of morale on both sides.

The British had reason to be stunned. They had become complacent about their vast navy, forgetting that it was manned by press gangs and officered by thinning ranks of the privileged; that routine had caused stagnation; that weariness from the war with Napoleon had taken a toll; that past success made it presume new successes rather than earn them. The American crews did not need to be pressed; they were seamen bred, proud of their gunnery, their sailing skills, and the ships they had been given to sail. Theodore Roosevelt exaggerated, but not entirely, when he said that years of defying the superpowers with their illegal trade had made the commercial seamen of America both brave and resourceful:

> Wherever an American seaman went, he not only had to contend with all the legitimate perils of the sea, but he had also to regard almost every stranger as a foe. Whether this foe called himself pirate or privateer mattered but little. French, Spaniards, Algerines, Malays, from all alike our

commerce suffered, and against all our merchants were forced to defend themselves. The effect of such a state of things, which made commerce so remunerative that the bolder spirit could hardly keep out of it, and so hazardous that only the most skillful and daring could succeed in it, was to raise up as fine a set of seamen as ever manned a navy . . . There could not have been better material for a fighting crew than cool, gritty American Jack.[31]

Americans needed all the cheering up they could get from the navy. There was no good news on land. On the very day when Isaac Hull came into Boston harbor with the captive *Guerrière* crew, word reached the city that his uncle, General William Hull, had surrendered Detroit to British siege troops, and that Fort Dearborn at Chicago had been burned down after its capture and the slaughter of its inhabitants.

The naval victories of the summer and autumn of 1812 helped Madison win re-election in November. Victories at sea muted some of the Federalist opposition to the war. The loss of Detroit actually helped Madison in the West, since it roused the war fever there to muster resistance to Indian attack. Unable to come up with their own candidate, the Federalists supported the renegade Republican candidate from New York, DeWitt Clinton, who was being groomed for power by the young political wizard Martin Van Buren. But Clinton could not put together a coherent opposition:

> No canvass for the presidency was ever less creditable than that of De Witt Clinton in 1812. Seeking war votes for the reason that he favored more vigorous prosecution of the war; asking support from peace Republicans because Madison had plunged the country into war without preparation; bargaining for Federalist votes as the price of bringing about peace; or coquetting with all parties in the atmosphere of bribery in bank charters — Clinton strove to make up a majority which had no element of union but himself and money. (581)

Madison beat Clinton, 128 to 89.

4

THE WAR'S SECOND YEAR

The *History,* Volume Seven

O NCE SAFELY RE-ELECTED, Madison could clear his cabinet of its encumbrances. Attorney General Caesar Rodney was incensed at not being chosen to replace Justice Chase (on his death) at the Supreme Court, and Madison appointed William Pinkney, returned from his great if ultimately unsuccessful service in England, to be the attorney general. The president's main goal was to get rid of his secretaries of the army and of the navy, the weak Eustis and the hopeless Hamilton. Over the navy he placed a man who had turned down the post before, William Jones (593). He made John Armstrong of New York the secretary of war, solving one problem with another. In his first term, the cabinet had been divided because the conflict between Gallatin and Robert Smith had envenomed proceedings. In his second term, the rivalry of Armstrong and Monroe would have the same effect.

Madison would have preferred someone other than Armstrong. In fact, he first asked Monroe to serve as both secretary of state and of war. But northern Republicans objected to this, as turning over too many high posts in the government to Virginians. With that plan baffled, Madison looked for someone to hold New York in the party, after the split caused there by DeWitt Clinton's bid for the presidency. Armstrong, too, wanted to be president — which is why Monroe objected to the promotion of a rival to his own candidacy. But he was the only New Yorker of stature outside the Clinton camp. Not for the first time, Madison felt that the only way to be a party uniter was to become a cabinet divider.

Armstrong was the son of a Pennsylvania hero in the French and Indian War. He had served as a young officer in the Revolution, but earned opprobrium by writing the Newburgh Address, voicing officers' dissatisfaction at the end of the Revolution. This, of course, did not bother Jefferson, who made Armstrong his minister to France. But in that role he botched reparations payments under the Louisiana Purchase and enthusiastically backed the Cadore Letter that deceived Madison. For every minus, however, there seemed to be a plus. He had married into the Livingston family in New York, which meant that he opposed DeWitt Clinton's break from the party in the 1812 election. He had military experience. He was not tainted by any of the first year's defeats. In its confirmation proceedings, some in the Senate voiced their dissatisfaction with the choice. Virginia would not vote for a man who might stand in Monroe's way.

> In spite of Armstrong's service, abilities, and experience, something in his character always created distrust. He had every advantage of education, social and political connection, ability, and self-confidence; he was only fifty-four years old, which was also the age of Monroe; but he suffered from the reputations of indolence and intrigue. So strong was the prejudice against him that he obtained only eighteen votes against fifteen in the Senate on his confirmation; and while the two senators from Virginia did not vote at all, the two from Kentucky voted in the negative. Under such circumstances, nothing but military success of the first order would secure a fair field for Monroe's rival. (591)

Armstrong at once became the most important figure in the second year of the war — a useful figure in the West, an ineffective one in the East, and a disastrous one at the defense of Washington.

Western Theater

In the West, Armstrong reined in William Henry Harrison, who had been given authority beyond his talent. As the putative hero of Tippecanoe, he was boosted as the local leader to retake Detroit after its loss. The whole territory looked to him. Though states were touchy about control of their militia, Henry Clay and other Kentuckians turned theirs over to this man from another territory (Indiana). But after claiming that he would retake Detroit in the autumn of 1812, Harrison had to admit in December that he could not manage that — a fact he blamed on his supply train, on "the imbecility and inexperience of the public agents and the villainy of the contractors" (676). He was right about the poor supply system, but he misused the supplies when they reached him.

The logistical problem Harrison faced in getting men and goods to Detroit was horrendous. The first fight occurred in trying to get to the fight. As a military historian, Adams is very good at the gritty details of supply, logistics, payments, hygiene, morale, and discipline. The set-piece battles and the combat heroes are one thing. Here is the underside of war made vivid as Harrison tries to move an army and its support system to the front.

> Throughout the months of October and November Harrison's army stood still, scattered over the state of Ohio, while wagons and packhorses wallowed in mud toward the Maumee Rapids. None arrived. Sometimes the wagons were abandoned in the mud; sometimes the packhorses broke down; sometimes the rivers were too low for boats; then they froze and stopped water transport. Universal confusion, want of oversight and organization, added to physical difficulties, gave play to laziness, incapacity, and dishonesty. No bills of lading were used; no accounts were kept with the wagoners; and the teams were valued so high, on coming into service, that the owners were willing to destroy them for the price to be received. The waste of government funds was appalling, for nothing short of a million rations at the Maumee Rapids could serve Harrison's objects, and after two months of effort not a ration had been carried within fifty miles of the spot. In Winchester's camp at Defiance the men were always on half rations, except when they had none at all. During the greater part of December they had no flour, but lived on poor beef and hickory roots. Typhus swept them away by scores; their numbers were reduced to about one thousand. The exact force which Harrison had in the field was a matter of conjecture, for he sent no return of any description to the adjutant general's office. The government gave him *carte blanche,* and he used it. Chaos and misconduct reigned in every department, while he, floundering through the mud along his line of two hundred miles front, sought in vain for a road. (676)

When his men and material reached him, Harrison decided he could not recapture Detroit after all. He fumbled with the idea of taking Fort Malden, but this plan fell through when the action of a subordinate proved disastrous. Actually, this subordinate — Brigadier General James Winchester — was Harrison's superior in military rank, but had ceded command to Harrison in the rush to create a single force for taking back Detroit. Winchester had moved a forward detachment up to the Maumee River, where he was waiting for Harrison to join him. In that period of waiting, a report came that some French settlers were endangered by Indians, thirty miles away, on the Raisin River. Winchester let a band of volunteers go forward to rescue them. Then, when they were pinned down by enemy fire, he took the rest of his command to their rescue, camping for the night without fortifying his area.

The British commander, Colonel Harry Proctor, brought troops from Fort Malden to the scene, in sufficient numbers to prevail if he had attacked at once. But Proctor, as Adams will amply demonstrate, was a coward and a fool. He would be as much a bane to Canadians in the second year of the war as Isaac Brock was a boon in the first. Proctor thought it safer to bring up field pieces and use artillery on the exposed camp — though Kentucky riflemen picked off Proctor's men as they serviced these guns. Winchester's force could have held out until Harrison came to its rescue if Winchester had provided his men any kind of cover. An outlying unit that included Winchester broke and fled when charged by Proctor's Indian force of six hundred men. The unit was run down as it tried to escape through deep snow. "Nearly a hundred Kentuckians fell almost side by side, and were scalped" (685). Winchester was captured by the Indian chief Round Head and taken to Proctor, at whose prompting Winchester sent an order to the remaining force on the river to surrender.

Had Proctor followed up this conquest by advancing on Harrison, who was now at the Maumee with an advance force of only nine hundred men, he could have taken the leader of the armies assembling against him — Brock would have done that. But Proctor, thinking only of his own safety, hurried back to the fort at Malden, in such haste that he left his wounded prisoners behind, unguarded.

> Nothing excused such conduct, for Proctor knew the fate to which he was exposing the prisoners. That night the Indians, drunk with whiskey and mad with their grievances and losses, returned to Frenchtown and massacred the wounded. About thirty perished, some apparently burned. Fortunately for the United States, the glamour of Proctor's victory hid his true character, and he was made a major general — the most favorable event of the war for the American armies he was to meet, and one which cost Great Britain even more in pride than in power. (686–87)

This episode had cost Harrison nearly a thousand men, killed or captured, and he was as anxious to escape the vicinity as Proctor was. Adams, in one sentence, nicely balances the symmetrical scurrying of these two generals:

> If Proctor was afraid of Harrison, with more military reason Harrison was afraid of Proctor; and while the British colonel, deserting his wounded prisoners, hurried from the field of battle, and felt himself in danger until the next day he was again entrenched at Malden, at the same moment Harrison, burning the post at the Maumee Rapids, and destroying such stores as were collected there, hastened back to the Portage or Carrying River some fifteen miles in the rear. (688)

Harrison then built a fortified camp, Fort Meigs, and asked his superiors in Washington whether he should continue his campaign in the winter snow. "Harrison would not take on himself the disgrace of admitting his inability to recapture Detroit, and the President would not, without his express admission, order him to desist" (679). To save face, Harrison blundered on, collecting four thousand men for a raid on Malden by February 11. But when that date passed without action, the Kentucky and Ohio militias' terms of enlistment ended, and they went home: "Not only had they failed to reoccupy a foot of the ground abandoned by Hull, but they left Harrison almost alone at Fort Meigs, trembling lest the enemy should descend on his rear and destroy his supplies, or force him back to protect them" (689).

Thus far Madison had turned the whole conduct of the war in the West over to Harrison, "for fear of displeasing Kentucky" (690). But when John Armstrong replaced Eustis as secretary of war, he instantly saw the folly of Harrison's endeavor. A successful assault on Detroit could come only after America had gained control of Lake Erie — he soon had men building ships for that effort. Harrison was to maintain a presence in the territory, but not to attack until he had support from the lake. Disgusted that authority had been taken from him, Harrison went off to Cincinnati to raise troops for "maintaining a presence." Only five hundred men were left to hold Fort Meigs, and only scattered bands of militia to guard eight other military posts, built to fend off Indian attacks. Adams continues his ironic description of Proctor as the Americans' secret weapon:

> Then the value of General Proctor to his enemy became immense. Between January 22, when he attacked Winchester, and the end of April, when he moved on Fort Meigs, Proctor molested in no way the weak and isolated American garrisons. With hundreds of scouts and backwoodsmen at his

command, he had not the energy or the knowledge to profit by his opponents' exposed and defenseless condition. He allowed Major Wood to make Fort Meigs capable of standing a siege; he let Harrison, unmolested, pass a month away from his command; he looked on while the Virginia militia marched home, leaving only a handful of sickly men, under a major of artillery, to defend the unfinished fort; he made no attempt to waylay Harrison, who returned with reinforcements by way of the Auglaize River, and not until Harrison had enjoyed all the time necessary to prepare for attack, did Proctor disturb him. (691)

Finally, at the end of April, Proctor began his siege of Fort Meigs, with a thousand of his own men, twelve hundred Indians under Tecumseh, and artillery including two twenty-four-pound guns, along with gunboats on the river. American reinforcements arriving on May 5 captured Proctor's guns but were instantly overwhelmed by the Indians, who slaughtered them while Harrison looked on from Fort Meigs (692). The earthenwork fortifications of Meigs itself, designed by West Point engineer Eleazar Wood, resisted Proctor's guns, and Kentucky riflemen kept up a withering fire from its rampart. Proctor withdrew, baffled.

Summer was at hand, and Proctor decided to go capture the supplies Harrison had built up along the shore of Lake Erie. Proctor wanted these, among other reasons, to feed his Indians, who were growing restive for want of food. He came on a flimsy stockade called Fort Stephenson. Harrison had ordered the man in charge there, a Kentucky regular, Major George Croghan, to abandon and burn the fort, but Croghan refused to flee, and worked to strengthen his stockade. When Proctor tried to storm it, his men were mowed down, so he went back to Malden again, having bungled another mission. Harrison, who had listened to the guns of the battle and done nothing to relieve Croghan, was as discredited as Proctor. Secretary of War Armstrong sounds like Adams himself in his description of the two inept generals' way of fumbling around each other with reciprocating timidities:

> It is worthy of notice that, of those two commanders, always the terror of each other, one [Proctor] was now actually flying from his supposed pursuer; while the other [Harrison] waited only the arrival of Croghan at Seneca to begin a camp-conflagration and flight to Upper Sandusky. (698)

Armstrong meanwhile was hastening construction of the inland navy. He ordered Commodore Oliver Hazard Perry to leave a gunboat at Newport, where he was supervising the city's harbor defense, and take charge of the brigs and schooners being built at Presqu'Isle (now Erie). Perry brought navy discipline to the land war. He came of a naval family. His father, Christopher Raymond Perry, had served on naval vessels and privateers in the Revolution. In the Quasi War, Oliver was a fifteen-year-old midshipman on his father's frigate, the *General Greene,* when it helped Toussaint Louverture defeat his rivals in Saint Domingue. In the Tripolitan War, the twenty-year-old Oliver commanded one of the three sloops that supported William Eaton's triumphant entry into Derna. His younger brother, Commodore Matthew C. Perry, would serve in the Mexican War and achieve the "Open Door" to Japan in 1854. The Perrys were a prominent Rhode Island family — Adams knew their standing well, since, as we saw earlier, one of their descendants was his friend and ex-student Perry Belmont.

At Erie, Oliver Perry, now twenty-eight, found five ships being finished by the master shipbuilder Noah Brown. He got them fitted, manned, and launched by June. They were joined by four other vessels taken from the east end of the lake. After reconnoitering, Perry took his squadron to Detroit, which was being guarded by a British fleet under Robert Barclay. Perry's flagship was called the *Lawrence,* after his friend James Lawrence, who had just died on the *Chesapeake* saying, "Don't give up the ship." Perry had a large blue flag made with those words stitched on it in white letters, which he meant to raise as the signal for attack on Barclay's fleet.

The six British vessels had guns of longer reach than Perry's, so Perry ran in swiftly to use his guns at shorter range. The *Niagara,* commanded by Jesse Elliott, was supposed to provide support for him, but it stood off until the *Lawrence* was riddled and immobilized, all but one of its guns disabled. Perry, taking his blue flag with him, jumped into a skiff and was rowed to the *Niagara,* which had moved up at last. After Perry left the *Lawrence,* the few men still alive on it struck its flag, and the British thought the battle was over. They gave three cheers.[1] But Perry took command from Elliott, ran the *Niagara* through the British line, firing broadsides in opposite directions as he did so, and turned certain defeat into a last-minute victory. His report became immortal: "We have met the enemy and they are ours."

The luck which attended Perry's career on the Lake saved him from injury, when every other officer on the two opposing flagships and four fifths of his crew were killed or wounded, and enabled him to perform a feat almost without parallel in naval warfare, giving him a well-won immortality by means of the disaster unnecessarily incurred. No process of argument or ingenuity of seamanship could deprive Perry of the fame justly given him by the public, or detract from the splendor of his reputation as the hero of the war. More than any other battle of the time, the victory on Lake Erie was won by the courage and obstinacy of a single man. (706)

The reason for Elliott's failure to support the *Lawrence* was bitterly disputed for many years, by the two men and by their partisans. Adams remarks simply that "the *Niagara* was badly managed by Elliott" (705). Theodore Roosevelt grants Elliott's "misconduct," but thinks Perry may not have made his plans well or his signals clear.[2] Fenimore Cooper avoids judgment in his naval history, but he became a fervent champion of Elliott in the newspapers, perhaps from Federalist views he shared with Elliott. Cooper claimed that Elliott had been told to keep his place unless specifically signaled to leave it — a defense that Mahan takes apart in convincing detail.[3]

Now that American forces had control of the lake, Harrison could attack Proctor at Detroit. He had a large force ready, including a new element — cavalry, led by Richard Mentor Johnson, whose horsemen could detect and deter Indian raids (707). Proctor was ready to abandon Detroit, but Tecumseh opposed this, calling him a coward (708). Proctor withdrew nonetheless, not even bothering to destroy the bridge over the Canards River to impede Harrison's pursuit. "This crowning proof of Proctor's incapacity disorganized his force" (709). Others joined Tecumseh in denouncing him. Proctor kept retreating, abandoning supplies and artillery, until the presence of women and children and wounded forced him to make a stand. This is where Johnson's mounted attack took the life of Tecumseh. The British were no longer a force to be reckoned with in the West. They had depended on Tecumseh to eke out their numbers.

Not more than seven or eight hundred British soldiers ever crossed the Detroit River; but the United States raised fully twenty thousand men, and spent at least five million dollars and many lives in expelling them. The Indians alone made this outlay necessary. The campaign of Tippecanoe, the surrender of Detroit and Mackinaw; the massacres at Fort Dearborn, the River Raisin, and Fort Meigs; the murders along the frontier, and the campaign of 1813 were the price paid for the [seizure of] Indian lands in the Wabash Valley. (716)

Eastern Theater

John Armstrong, after arranging things more efficiently in the West, was not so skillful in the East. He formed a sensible plan there but could not get his officers to carry it out. He intended to launch a pincer movement on Montreal, with converging armies coming from Kingston in the West and up Lake Champlain in the East. But Henry Dearborn, considering Kingston too heavily manned to be captured, swerved west to take the militarily insignificant capital of Upper Canada, York (now Toronto). "From the moment Dearborn turned away from the St. Lawrence and carried the war westward, the naval and military movements on Lake Ontario became valuable chiefly as a record of failure" (726).

Dearborn burned York — this destruction of a minor regional capital would be used as a precedent when the British set fire to Washington. The assault on York cost one-fifth of Dearborn's army. Among the fallen was Zebulon Pike, "the best brigadier then in the service" (727). Dearborn, reporting that his men were "very sickly and depressed," was so disanimated that he asked to retire (718).

Armstrong now made the terrible mistake of replacing Dearborn with James Wilkinson, brought up from his old post in the Louisiana Territory. Armstrong was choosing men now for their loyalty to him in the competition with Monroe, and he apparently thought he could rely on Wilkinson to support him, making him another of the many whom Wilkinson disappointed. "This result of Dearborn's removal was incalculably mischievous, for if its effect on Wilkinson's vanity was unfortunate, its influence on the army was fatal. Almost every respectable officer of the old service regarded Wilkinson with antipathy or contempt" (741). No one had more contempt for Wilkinson than the man who was now asked to serve under him, Major General Wade Hampton, a hot-tempered South Carolinian, who threatened to resign rather than take orders from Wilkinson (745). Armstrong, striving to keep Hampton, said that he would give orders directly to him, not going through Wilkinson. But Wilkinson was not one to accept such an arrangement.

Armstrong now decided to go north himself, to oversee operations. Perhaps that eventuality was in his mind when he moved Wilkinson. Monroe was convinced that Armstrong was doing what he had tried to do himself — serve at the front, promoting his campaign for the presidency. But all Armstrong did, in fact, was join in the bickering of Hampton and Wilkinson. When Armstrong proposed an attack on Kingston,

Wilkinson argued for attacking Montreal. Then they switched sides. In the event, Armstrong decided to do neither, and set up a winter camp (in mid-October) without informing Wilkinson (749). Then he withdrew to Albany, leaving it to Wilkinson and Hampton to decide whether they should continue fighting. Each of these two thought that Armstrong was abandoning his responsibility in order to shift blame for the season's loss onto him (750–51). This is one of the few things they agreed on, and one of the few in which they were justified. "Armstrong's reasons for leaving the theater of war have been interpreted in different ways, most of them unfavorable to him."[4]

Wilkinson sent a force to cope with a marauding incursion by the British colonel Joseph Morrison. The British with eight hundred men defeated Wilkinson's detachment of two thousand at Chrysler's Farm (752–54). American casualties were 102 killed (to 22 British), 237 wounded (to British 148), and 100 taken prisoner.[5] "This defeat was the least creditable of the disasters suffered by American arms during the war. No excuse or palliation was ever offered for it" (753). Another installment was being paid on the great expense entailed in Jefferson's and Madison's long-continued protection of Wilkinson.

Wade Hampton, who was waiting for Wilkinson to join him for the assault on Montreal, was forced from his advance position by a buildup of British forces. He wrote an insulting letter to Armstrong implying that the secretary had meant to sacrifice him. Armstrong's actions were themselves too questionable for him to sanction an investigation of his underlings (759). Wilkinson meanwhile wrote to Hampton asking for supplies and reinforcements. Hampton replied that he had neither the one nor the other. Wilkinson accused Hampton of "beastly drunkenness" and demanded his arrest.[6] "Armstrong and Wilkinson made common cause in throwing upon Hampton the blame of failure" (769). In fact, all three men, in shifting combinations, blamed one or both of the others.

While they quarreled, Americans holding two bits of Canada just across the Niagara River — Fort George and the small town of Newark — withdrew from them, burning Newark and nearby Queenston as they retired. British troops crossed onto American soil on December 18, seized Fort Niagara, and torched Buffalo and Black Rock in reprisal. Their fury was reflected in the license given Indians to massacre. The governor general of Canada, George Prevost, said he had been reluctant to pursue "a system of warfare as revolting to his own feelings and so little congenial to the British character," but he decided that the burning of York had to be avenged on both Buffalo and Black Rock (763). The second year of the war ended, in the East, more disastrously than the first one had. In 1812, no Canadian soil was won. In 1813, American territory was seized and held in the East, just as, in the foregoing year, it had been in the West. Fort Niagara remained in British hands for the rest of the war.

Wilkinson's troops went into winter quarters, where their presence was supposed to halt any further advances of the British. The Americans' fighting was now with the weather, and with each other:

> The temperature soon dropped to thirty degrees below zero. Officers who had been appointed through political influence appropriated the pay of the dead, swindled dying soldiers, and sold government stores for personal enrichment. Sensing weakness, the British offered Americans five months' pay with a guarantee that they would not have to serve against the United States if they would desert.[7]

"The only happy result of the campaign was to remove all the older generals — Wilkinson, Hampton, and Morgan Lewis — from active service" (760).

Southern Theater

Winter did not interrupt military operations in the South, where Madison and Monroe wanted to use the war as an excuse for seizing Mobile, Pensacola, and St. Augustine. An order of February 12, 1813, led to the seizure of Mobile (769–70). But Congress balked at the idea of using a war with England as a way of taking Florida away from Spain, and Gallatin persuaded Madison that the hope of Russian mediation to end the war would be dashed if the United States attacked the Tsar's ally, Spain (765–69). Andrew Jackson, who had his Tennessee volunteers ready to swarm into Natchez, was disgusted when he was ordered to disband them (766).

Jackson was able to reassemble his troops for war with the Creek Indians, some of whom had responded to Tecumseh's call for solidarity with the British. A band of these Indians was defeated on July 27, 1813, at Burnt Corn, "about eighty miles north of Pensacola" (780). But when the conquerors withdrew into Fort Mims, they were attacked and massacred on August 30. "Two hundred and fifty scalps became trophies of the Creek warriors — a number such as had been seldom taken by Indians from the white people on a single day" (781).

White retaliation was bound to be massive. The Creeks were few in number and poorly armed. "Four thousand warriors who had never seen a serious war even with their Indian neighbors, and armed for the most part with clubs, or bows and arrows, were not able to resist long the impact of three or four armies, each nearly equal to their whole force, coming from every quarter of the compass" (781). Two of those armies came from Georgia, under Major General Thomas Pinckney and Brigadier General John Floyd. Two others came from Tennessee, one under Andrew Jackson, the other led by Major General John Cocke (781). Jackson set out for the remote asylum of the Creeks, at the Hickory Ground, but he had to turn back in November for want of supplies, and in December his men's term of service ended. He tried to prevent their disbanding, first forcibly, then calling on them to volunteer again, but they rejected his plea (786–87). General Cocke meanwhile massacred some Hillabee Indians who had promised peaceful submission to Jackson (788–89), and Floyd's Georgians defeated a Creek stronghold at Autossee (788–89).

> Thus the year 1813 ended without closing the Creek war. More than seven thousand men had entered the Indian country from four directions, and with a loss of thirty or forty lives had killed, according to their reports, about eight hundred Indians, or one fifth of the hostile Creek warriors; but this carnage had fallen chiefly on towns and villages not responsible for the revolt. (790)

Jackson refused to follow his troops back to Tennessee. Maintaining his advance post at Fort Strother, he forced Tennessee's governor to send new troops or suffer the disgrace of seeing Jackson and his few followers killed for want of support. The first detachment was of six-month militiamen, with whom Jackson made an unsuccessful raid in January of 1814 (791–93). But in February a regiment of regulars joined him. With his hand strengthened, Jackson decided to discipline the refractory militiamen, shooting one for disobedience, calling for the arrest as deserters of any who left before their six months were up, and arresting General Cocke on charges of abetting mutiny (95–96). This was a foretaste of the highhanded but effective measures Jackson would use to impose order in defense of New Orleans (795–96).

With only a month left of his militiamen's term, Jackson pushed frantically into hostile territory and won a battle at the Horse Shoe, a bend in the Tallapoosa River, where almost every Indian warrior was slaughtered (796–98). One man who received an arrow wound in Jackson's army was Sam Houston, who had lived for three years with the Cherokees before joining Jackson's band (798). When the Indians agreed to settle with their conquerors, Jackson offered them a "Capitulation" that took two-thirds of their land as war reparations. Those who refused, he said, could try to withdraw into Spanish territory, but he would probably hunt them down before they got there (798–99). The Indians had to yield to his single-minded determination.

> On 9 August, 1814, on behalf of the United States, he took title in the Treaty of Fort Jackson to twenty million acres of Creek land. Almost as many Creeks had fought on the side of the United States as against them, but Jackson's treaty stripped friend and foe of lands, without discrimination.[8]

War at Sea

Brilliant as was the first year of single-ship engagements at sea, those successes could not be prolonged. Three things brought an abrupt end to America's romance with its frigates. First, the British no longer underestimated the American ships. Second, they had more ships available for use against America after Napoleon's 1812 setback in Russia. And third, they used these ships, including ships of the line, to blockade the American coast, cutting off the frigates' egress and ingress. Only quick-darting privateers could slip through this net thrown up on the Atlantic coast, since they were not worth the heavy investment of catching them with great warships.

The blockade choked off commerce as well as military operations, limiting imports and increasing their price, checking exports and sending *their* prices down. "No ordinary operations of war could affect the United States so severely as this inexorable blockade. Every citizen felt it in every action of his life. The farmer grew crops which he could not sell, while he paid tenfold prices for every necessity" (803). But there was a partial and insulting exception to this action. The British deliberately let New England merchants evade the blockade, encouraging defiance of their own government's war. The most galling use of the blockade occurred within Chesapeake Bay, which became "a British naval station" (804). Rear Admiral Sir George Cockburn terrorized Virginia and

Maryland with land raids from his ships. He sealed up or destroyed Jefferson's useless gunboats in the bay, and kept the frigate *Constellation* immobilized at Norfolk (806–7), though his attempted invasions of Norfolk and Hampton failed (807–12). The conditions for taking and burning Washington had now been established.

The first attempt by frigates to break out from the blockade was made by Stephen Decatur with the USS *United States* and the converted British frigate *Macedonian*. Blocked in New York harbor, he sailed up the East River into Long Island Sound, but a British squadron led by Sir Thomas Hardy, who had fought alongside Nelson, chased him back to New London (813–14). The second attempt at escape proved tragic, since it led to the loss of the only Humphreys frigate destroyed by the British, the *Chesapeake*, which had been the center of controversy ever since the British fired on it six years earlier. It had become known as an unlucky ship ever since, and crews were reluctant to serve on it (822).

When the captain of the HMS *Shannon*, Sir Philip Bowes Vere Broke, saw that the *Chesapeake* seemed rigged to sail, he withdrew in order to tempt it out for combat, and even sent a challenging letter to make it clear that he would let the ship emerge (818). The British navy was still smarting from its defeats in single-ship duels, and meant to prove that the losses had been a fluke.

> The loss of a British frigate mattered little to a government which had more than a hundred such frigates actually at sea, not to speak of heavier ships; but the loss of the *Chesapeake* was equivalent to destroying nearly one fourth of the disposable American navy. Already the *Constellation* was imprisoned at Norfolk; the *United States* and *Macedonian* were blockaded for the war; the *Congress*, though at sea, was unseaworthy and never cruised again; the *Adams* was shut in the Potomac; the *Essex* was in the Pacific. The United States Navy consisted, for active service on the Atlantic, of only the *President*, 44, at sea; the *Constitution*, 44, replacing her masts at the Charlestown navy yard; the *Chesapeake*, 38, ready for sea; and a few sloops of war. (819)

Broke was so eager for the challenge to an American frigate that he refused to take prizes that would remove him from the scene, burning twenty-five captured ships to stay ready for combat.[9]

James Lawrence, the captain of the *Chesapeake*, should not have answered Broke's challenge. "The first duty of a British officer was to take risks; the first duty of an American officer was to avoid them, and to fight only at his own time, on his own terms" (819). As Mahan points out, the task for American frigates, if they could break the blockade, was to interrupt British communications, not to engage in duels. Even if Lawrence had won against the *Shannon,* his real mission would have been delayed, perhaps permanently, since almost always a ship must return to harbor for repairs after battle and Lawrence could not count on the opportunity to get out of harbor a second time.[10] Besides, Lawrence had a raw crew and a team of officers who were strangers to each other, while Broke had an officer team that had served together for seven years and trained rigorously. All Boston had watched Broke engage in frequent gunnery practice just offshore (822). As Mahan says:

> It is possible for an officer to command a ship for seven years, as Broke had, and fail to make of her the admirable pattern of all that a ship of war should be, which he accomplished with the *Shannon;* but no captain can in four weeks make a thoroughly efficient crew out of a crowd of men newly assembled and never out of harbor together.[11]

But if Lawrence was taking out an unlucky ship, he had a sense that his own life was charmed. He had served in the Quasi and Tripolitan wars. He took part, along with Oliver Hazard Perry, in Decatur's raid on Tripoli that destroyed the *Philadelphia.* Then, as captain of his own ship, he had achieved a string of easy victories, including a famous one over HMS *Peacock,* which gave him a low opinion of British naval prowess (819–22). A dashing, charismatic figure, he could not resist the call to a duel. The naval audacity Adams normally praises was here pushed too far. Lawrence was so chivalrous that he refused to rake the *Shannon* when it luffed to let him come up to it. He had the chance to cross its bow and deliver the worst kind of broadside, one that travels the whole length of a deck. Instead, he came alongside, so fast that he had to back the maintopsail to brake his ship, losing crucial seconds.[12]

The battle that followed was surreally intense and brief. Broke's cool veterans wrought havoc systematically, in a whirlwind of destruction. The *Chesapeake's* rigging was destroyed by the second broadside; it veered out of control, unable to bring its guns to bear, swerving backward into the *Shannon,* whose skilled boarders lashed and invaded it. The British historian William James carefully timed the battle from multiple reports, in figures Mahan accepts as accurate — seven minutes of point-blank broadsides, four minutes of lashing and boarding, four minutes to subdue the American combatants.[13] Broke himself led the first boarders, but could not meet his dueling partner in a final struggle, since Lawrence had already been fatally hit by a musket shot from the *Shannon*.

> The disgrace to the Americans did not consist so much in the loss of a ship to one of equal force, as in the shame of suffering capture by a boarding party of [only] fifty men. As Lawrence lay wounded in the cockpit, he saw the rush of his men from the spar deck down the after ladders, and cried out repeatedly and loudly, "Don't give up the ship! Blow her up!" (826)

No one could give up the ship. The sharp blow of the attack left no time for surrender. Before the ship's colors could be struck, a British boarder had hauled them down.

> Few naval battles have been more sanguinary than this. It lasted altogether no more than fifteen minutes, and yet both ships were charnel houses. The *Chesapeake* had 48 men killed and 98 wounded, a large proportion of whom fell by the raking fire of the *Shannon*, after the *Chesapeake* was taken aback, and by the fire of the boarders. The *Shannon* had 23 killed and 56 wounded, principally by the *Chesapeake*'s [opening] broadside. It was impossible for ships of that size to approach so near in tolerably smooth water, and to fire with so much steadiness, without committing great havoc.[14]

Adams, who defended Barron in the old *Chesapeake* controversy, tries to exonerate Lawrence from the charges brought against him, saying that he was just unlucky in the loss of his ship's rigging and the shot that felled him (826–28). He shows a touchingly generous spirit toward the navy, here as elsewhere, but better historical judgment is rendered by Mahan — or by Roosevelt, who wrote: "Hard as it is to breathe a word against such a man as Lawrence, a very Bayard of the sea, who was admired as much for his dauntless bravery as he was loved for his gentleness and uprightness, it must be confessed that he acted rashly."[15]

Six weeks later the British won another important sea battle. The *Argus* was a brig commanded by Captain W. H. Allen, who had been on the *Chesapeake* when it was attacked by the *Leopard*. "Allen was the officer who snatched a coal from the galley and discharged the only gun that was fired that day" (810). Then he had been Decatur's master of gunnery when the *United States* captured the *Macedonian*. In August of 1813 he was harrying enemy ships in the British Channel, where he took twenty-one prizes before letting himself be caught at dawn and defeated by the British *Pelican*. These defeats elated the British and dejected the

Americans almost as much as the feats of the *Constitution* the year before had produced the opposite effects (830, 833).

With the frigates out of action, the United States was not entirely disarmed at sea. Fast smaller ships could get out of port, not only navy sloops of war but private ships commissioned to harass enemy trade. There were 550 such commissions during the war, and the privateers took 1,300 prizes.[16] Adams admires these ships almost as much as the frigates. Built from designs based on the requirements of smuggling, they were fast, maneuverable, and well managed. Sloops, brigs, and schooners, they carried from 80 to 160 men, enough men to board and fight if that was necessary, but in vessels that could carry them nimbly away from danger. "The private armed vessel was built rather to fly than to fight" (839). They were difficult to control, and the British who captured them never quite got the knack of it (840).

The privateers inflicted four times the damage that government vessels did (848). Even when British merchant ships were convoyed by warships, they were not safe from these marauders.

> Two or three such craft hanging about a convoy could commonly cut off some merchantman, no matter how careful the convoying man-of-war might be. By night they could run directly into the fleet and cut out vessels without even giving an alarm, and by day they could pick up any craft that lagged behind or happened to stray too far away [from their protector] . . . At the close of the war, the most efficient vessel afloat was probably the American sloop-of-war, or privateer, of four or five hundred tons, rigged as a ship or brig, and carrying one hundred and fifty or sixty men, with a battery varying according to the ideas of the captain and owners [up to twenty or so guns], but in the case of privateers, almost invariably including one "Long Tom," or pivot-gun. (838)

Adams is positively enchanted by tales of the venturesome privateers, who fought for profit and not from patriotism. They bedeviled the Caribbean islands and harried the coasts of Ireland and Scotland. They put pressure on British merchants to bring about peace.

> In truth the schooner was a wonderful invention. Not her battles, but her escapes won for her the open-mouthed admiration of the British captains, who saw their prize double like a hare and slip through their fingers at the moment when capture was sure. Under any ordinary conditions of wind and weather, with an open sea, the schooner, if only she could get to windward, laughed at a frigate . . . Whether ship, brig, schooner, or sloop,

the American vessel was believed to outsail any other craft on the ocean. (840–41)

But after these effusions of the heart, Adams's head is forced to admit the limitations of a war carried on by privateering — one that Mahan disapproved of as a distraction from the real work of the navy. Reliance on the privateers kept Congress from building its own light boats, which could have done more damage at less cost. Since the aim of the privateer was to get his prize to market rather than to damage the enemy, many of his prizes were recaptured in the attempt to get them through British blockade or patrols. A government vessel would have destroyed the merchandise, to remain dedicated to fighting (850). Besides, the privateers siphoned off seamen from the navy, just as short-term militia enlistments cut the manpower of the regular army.

> Seamen commonly preferred the harder but more profitable and shorter cruise in a privateer, where fighting was not expected or wished, to the strict discipline and murderous battles of government ships, where wages were low and prize money scarce. Of all towns in the United States, Marblehead was probably the most devoted to the sea, but of nine hundred men from Marblehead who took part in the war, fifty-seven served as soldiers, one hundred and twenty entered the navy, while seven hundred and twenty-six went as privateersmen. (852)

In the scramble for elusive riches, privateers took increasing risks until at least half of them ended up captured (846). In the hard account books of war, the privateers were little more than a nuisance to the enemy, although — Adams would insist — a beautiful nuisance.

Peace Overtures

Madison began war in the summer of 1812 expecting an invasion of Canada by the November election and control of that country's eastern part early in 1813 — the conquest had to be swift in order to stop the timber traffic and make England beg humbly for an end to hostilities. Instead, Detroit had fallen in the West by the election date, and American cities had been captured in the East by the beginning of 1813. A failure of nerve was natural in these circumstances, and Madison underwent it. For the first time he backed off from the demand that Britain give up pressing. A hard line on this had sunk Monroe's treaty and stymied a *Chesapeake* settlement. But now Madison offered an "arrangement" that would "suspend the practice." Instead of making demands on England, America would impose demands on itself to make pressing unnecessary. All foreign sailors would be dismissed from American ships. To keep those sailors from taking up American citizenship to continue their service, no one would henceforth be naturalized but on condition of not leaving America for five years (613).

Congress refused to pass a bill so abject. It took away basic rights — of American merchants to employ whom they wished, and of future American citizens to work or travel as they wished. It could lead to the loss of thousands of men already in American crews, causing a sharp dip in American trade. Evasion of the law would be hard to prevent or punish — it was for this reason that Castlereagh rejected the idea from the British side (609). It was a craven measure, reeking of panic.

The same panic made Madison leap at an offer by the Russian Tsar to mediate peace negotiations between two of his trade allies, to strengthen his hand against Napoleon. Madison was so eager for this that he chose and sent off commissioners to the negotiations before England had time to reject the offer. The minister already in Russia, John Quincy Adams, was appointed to lead the peace delegation. A Federalist was also needed, and he appointed James Bayard of Delaware, the man who had ended the House logjam over Jefferson's election in 1801, but who later accused Jefferson of breaking his bargain for that vote, and who had been defeated when Jefferson put up Caesar Rodney to run against him. Madison did not have Jefferson's long memory for grudges, and he knew Bayard as a man who could bargain well. The third member was to be Gallatin, whom Madison asked to go on the mission without surrendering his post at Treasury. There was a precedent for this. John Jay and Oliver Ellsworth had been sent on diplomatic missions while retaining their seats on the Supreme Court (661).

Madison sped Bayard and Gallatin on their way before the Senate could confirm their appointments. But after the two had joined Adams in St. Petersburg, news arrived that the Senate had refused to confirm Gallatin while he remained secretary of the treasury. Castlereagh, moreover, had turned down talks sponsored by the Tsar. He would discuss peace, but not through intermediaries. For these direct talks Madison appointed two new commissioners to join Adams and Bayard — Henry Clay and Jonathan Russell. He also appointed a new secretary of the treasury, George Washington Campbell, so that the Senate could confirm Gallatin as a fifth member of the commission, its last to be appointed and so the least in seniority. They were all to meet with the British negotiators in Gothenburg, Sweden (later changed to Ghent in the Netherlands). The Americans would soon learn that the British were proposing to end a war disastrous to America with a peace even more disastrous.

5

THE WAR'S THIRD YEAR

The *History*, Volume Eight

A DOUBLE ACTION gives the eighth volume its extraordinary interest, the blend of tragedy and hope. There is a descending arc of civil ineptitude and shame, crossed by a rising arc of military courage and pride. In the downward plunge of civil incompetence, the cabinet performs ill, the Congress not at all, the peace commission in fits and starts, and New England perniciously. In the upward surge of military glory, the army finally becomes professional, its infantry efficient, its artillery and fortification superb. In the contest to see which of these tendencies would cancel the other, the military vigor prevailed over the civil lassitude, but it was a close race.

Adams's admiration for the army's new fighting spirit makes his description of their feats vivid. By the third year of fighting, the superannuated leaders from the revolutionary era had been winnowed out, to be replaced by young men who had seen what was wrong in the earlier campaigns and meant to remedy it — men like Winfield Scott, Eleazar Ripley, and Jacob Brown. Scott had used the months in winter quarters (1813–1814) to drill his men with new discipline. "Three months of instruction converted the raw troops into soldiers" (926). Ripley proved in the North what Andrew Jackson did in the South — that even militiamen could be made to fight when they had tough and inspiring leadership. Brown resembled the old general in Evelyn Waugh's *Sword of Honor*, whose code was simply "Biff! Biff!" "Wherever Brown went, fighting followed" (925). "Among all the American major generals, he alone made raw troops as steady as grenadiers, and caused militia to storm entrenched lines held by British regulars" (955). The preceding volume of the *History* was notably lacking in heroes. This book has a galaxy of them. The army's new men resembled the captains who took out the frigates in 1812 — they *sought* battle where the Hulls and Dearborns had shied from it. The balance of 1812 had been reversed, with the army now rebuking the navy for timidity on Lake Erie (929).

The army's great opportunity came in July, at Chippawa River near Niagara Falls, where a victory gave the land forces an elating experience such as the navy had enjoyed when the *Constitution* sank the *Guerrière* (937). Scott's and Ripley's men first captured Fort Erie, taking 170 prisoners (933). Then for twelve long hours they pursued retreating British troops who tore up bridges as they crossed them. The British troops were joined by Major General Phineas Riall's force, rushing to their rescue from Fort George. Riall too was a fighter, and he surprised the Americans with an aggressive attack across the river. Scott was forced to withdraw across Street's Creek and draw up his lines there (935–36). Then, on July 6, "Scott tempted destruction by leaving his secure position behind the creek" (937). He crossed the creek under withering fire and broke the British lines in less than an hour — though he was outnumbered in men and guns. Only in regular troops were the two sides equal:

> The number of Riall's men killed was nearly three times the number of Scott's killed, and proved that the battle was decided by the superior accuracy or rapidity of the musketry and artillery fire, other military qualities being assumed to be equal. The battle of Chippawa was the only occasion during the war when equal bodies of regular troops met face to face, in extended lines on an open plain in broad daylight, without advantage of position; and never again after that combat was an army of American regulars beaten by British troops. Small as the affair was, and unimportant in military results, it gave to the United States army a character and pride it had never before possessed. (938)

After the battle, Jacob Brown's troops pursued the remains of Riall's army until they reached Fort George. There Riall acquired enough reinforcements to make Brown retire to the scene of earlier battle at Chippawa. Riall had now become the pursuer. They met once again on July 26. Riall had been joined by Lieutenant General Gordon Drummond, like Brock a veteran of battle with Napoleon's armies. Drummond had already destroyed Buffalo, and was "regarded as the ablest military officer in Canada" (940). Brown ordered Winfield Scott to deploy his troops defensively to the north, where he stumbled unexpectedly upon the British left, drawn up by Drummond along Lundy's Lane. Though it was late in the afternoon, Scott attacked instantly. Major Thomas Jessup joined his troops with Scott's in assailing the left, where they drove in the British line and captured a wounded Riall (943).

But the center of the British line could not be taken, since it was covered by guns too high for American artillery to reach. At nine P.M., Brown ordered Lieutenant Colonel James Miller to storm the hill and capture the guns. Under cover of darkness, with under five hundred men, Miller approached close enough unseen to rush on the guns, "bayoneting the artillery men where they stood," which Adams calls a "superb feat of arms" (945). For the next three hours, the British tried to recapture their guns, but were beaten back every time by Miller's small band. "Perhaps this feat was more remarkable than the surprise of the battery" (946). Meanwhile, the Americans stayed on the attack, firing at the enemy's musket flashes in the dark. Finally Miller, about to be overwhelmed, had to withdraw. The night battle, lasting five hours, had pitted two thousand Americans against three thousand British, and it was fought to a draw.

Scott and Brown were wounded on the American side, and Riall and Drummond on the British. Brown from his bed gave orders to renew the attack in the morning, but so many officers and men had been killed or seriously wounded that the army could not be reassembled by that time. Actually, the British should have attacked, but "Chippawa and Lundy's Lane had already produced an effect on the British army" (914). It had a new wariness of American fighting strength. A letter in the Halifax newspaper registered the impact of these battles on the British:

> The officers of the army from Spain who have been engaged in Upper Canada have acknowledged that they never saw such determined charges as were made by the Americans in the late actions . . . In the action of the 25th July, the Americans charged to the very muzzles of our cannon, and actually bayoneted the artillery men who were at their guns. Their charges were not once or twice only, but repeated and long, and the steadiness of the British soldiers alone could have withstood them. (951)

Drummond let the Americans withdraw to Fort Erie, an unfinished site that Ripley's troops began frantically to fortify. Drummond should have attacked them while they were at these labors (956), but he delayed, waiting for reinforcements. He wanted heavy siege guns, which would not have been needed in the first days of his attack, before the redoubt was strengthened. He did not bombard the fort until August 13, and he loosed his men on it the next day, in two columns, 2,400 men storming the objective, while 1,000 were held in reserve (959). When his men seized an outer bastion of the fort, he failed to send the reserve to protect them and advance their assault, and they succumbed to an explosion of munitions where they were stalled (963). In the resulting panic, the British lost 905 men, the Americans 84.

> General Drummond was excessively mortified by his failure, in truth the severest blow that British arms could suffer at that moment. For the fourth time in six weeks, a large body of British troops met a bloody and unparalleled check, if not rout, from an inferior force. (964)

Now the Americans besieged their besiegers. Drummond did not have animals to draw his great guns away; his troops were sick; the heavy rain demoralized them. Ripley took his men out of the fort and attacked the British lines. In the fighting that ensued, the Americans lost a quarter of their men (tragically including Ripley), while the British lost a third of their larger number.

> The next day Drummond issued a general order claiming a victory over an American force of "not less than five thousand men [it was half that number], including militia"; but his situation, untenable before the sorties, became impossible after it. Three out of six battering cannon were disabled, he had lost six hundred men in battle, and his losses by sickness were becoming enormous. (971)

Drummond wrote the Canadian governor that he could no longer hold his position against "so vastly superior and increasing a force of the enemy" (971).

Lake Champlain

If things were looking up in the region of Niagara, they were not so promising to the east. With Napoleon in exile, England was free to send larger numbers of crack troops to settle the American irritation. By September they were ranging freely through Maine, destroying ships and cargo at Bangor, extracting oaths of allegiance to the King, laying the groundwork for annexation of American territory at the conclusion of the war (976). "One hundred miles of Massachusetts sea coast passed quietly under the dominion of the King of England" (975). Even more disturbing, the British had prepared a great army and navy to seize Lake Champlain, reaching deep into American territory. That is the route that Americans should have secured from the outset of the war, as the direct path to Montreal; but the leadership in Washington had continually put off this first requisite, and now the British were on the verge of closing the avenue for good. They were sending a land army of eleven thousand men, led by Canada's governor himself, to attack the American position at Plattsburg, the point American generals had chosen for control of the lake (979). "Great Britain had never sent to America so formidable an armament. Neither Wolfe nor Amherst, neither Burgoyne nor Cornwallis, had led so large or so fine an army as was under the command of Sir George Prevost" (978).

They were sending, as well, a navy flotilla to make an attack on Plattsburg from the lake, coordinated with the assault on its land side by the army. This was commanded by George Downie, whose fleet was made up of the thirty-one-gun *Confiance* (crew of 300), along with three smaller ships and twelve gunboats. The American squadron, led by Commander Thomas Macdonough, was made up of the twenty-six-gun *Saratoga* (crew of 240), three smaller ships, and ten gunboats. The greatest disparity was in the type of guns brought to bear by either side. The British squadron had sixty long-range pieces to Macdonough's forty-five.

> If Downie chose his own distance beyond range of the thirty-two-pound carronades, and fought only his long guns, nothing could save Macdonough except extreme good fortune, for he had but fourteen twenty-four-pound guns against Downie's thirty-four. Firing by broadsides, Downie could throw from his single ship, the *Confiance*, sixteen twenty-four-pound shot, to which Macdonough could reply only with eight, even if he used all his long guns on the same side. (982)

Macdonough could prevail over firepower only by forethought. The British army marched to Plattsburg — so confident as not to break column when harassed along the way — and waited for the sound of Downie's ship guns to attack the town. Secretary of War Armstrong had yielded once again to the urge to move the war westward by sending most of Plattsburg's defending troops, led by General Izard, off to join Brown near Niagara. Since Izard arrived too late to help Brown,

Armstrong had taken him out of effective action in both crucial theaters:

> At one end of the line Sir George Prevost retreated from Plattsburg September 12; at the other end, Lieutenant General Drummond retreated from Fort Erie September 21; and Izard's force, constituting the largest body of [American] regular troops in the field, had been placed where it could possibly affect neither result. (989)

Luckily, Plattsburg was well fortified by the engineer to whom Izard had given that task, Joseph Gilbert Totten (984), and the fifteen hundred men holding it under Brigadier General Alexander Macomb were up to their assignment.

But, for all their efforts, the fort would have fallen had not Macdonough won his battle on the water. Thomas Macdonough came from fighting stock. His brother James had served on the *Constellation* when it defeated *L'Insurgente* in the Quasi War. Thomas himself had been with Perry and Lawrence in Stephen Decatur's raid into Tripoli harbor to destroy the captured *Philadelphia*. Macdonough knew something about unconventional war, and he proved it by both the strategy and the tactics he used at Plattsburg. In terms of strategy, he chose his fighting area well. Tactically, he rigged his ship for a special purpose.

The bay of Plattsburg has an island (Crab Island) almost in the middle of its mouth. Macdonough drew up his line of ships and anchored them just inside the broader of the inlets around Crab Island — the one Downie had to use if he were to get within gun range of Plattsburg. This meant that Downie had to file his ships in single line past the gauntlet Macdonough had created, and that he could not use his long guns from a distance. The *Confiance* had to maneuver slowly under shifting winds, which let Macdonough's ships fire raking shots as it approached. Then Downie had to anchor his flotilla in order to stay in position for firing broadsides against the anchored American squadron. Downie was killed early in the battle, when one of his own guns jumped its carriage and crushed him, but the *Confiance* fired rapidly and well, eventually disabling all the guns on the *Saratoga's* starboard side.

At this point, Macdonough executed a planned maneuver, difficult enough to pull off even when not receiving a hail of cannonballs. Besides his regular anchors, Macdonough had planted kedge anchors in such a configuration that he could winch the ship clear around without fouling the anchor lines (if all went well). Adams rightly refers to Fenimore

Cooper's description of this exercise, since Cooper loved to describe the details he knew about from his midshipman days. Cooper describes the close call:

> The stream anchor, suspended astern, was let go accordingly. The men then clapped on the hawser that led to the starboard quarter, and brought the ship's stern over the kedge, but here she hung, there not being sufficient wind, or current, to force her bows round. A line had been bent to a bight in the stream cable, with a view to help wind the ship, and she now rode by the kedge and this line, with her stern under the raking broadside of the *Linnet*, which brig kept up a steady and well-directed fire. The larboard batteries having been manned and got ready, Captain Macdonough ordered all the men from the guns, where they were uselessly suffering, telling them to go forward. By rowsing on the line, the ship was at length got so far round, that the aftermost gun would bear on the *Confiance*, when it was instantly manned, and began to play. The next gun was used in the same manner, but it was apparent that the ship could be got no farther round, for she was now nearly end on to the wind. At this critical moment, Mr. Brum, the [sailing] master, bethought him of the hawser that had led to the larboard quarter. It was got forward under the bows, and passed aft to the starboard quarter, when the ship's stern was immediately sprung to the westward, so as to bring all her larboard guns to bear on the English ship, with fatal effect.[1]

As Adams says, this trick gave the *Saratoga* a second fighting life, after the *Confiance* was all but fought out (984).

Theodore Roosevelt claims that Macdonough's feat on Lake Champlain was far greater than that of Perry on Lake Erie. He says that Perry had an initial superiority over his foe, and rescued the situation only after squandering that advantage. Macdonough was fighting a greater force than his own, and he prevailed only by forethought, use of the fighting space, technological ingenuity, quick thinking, and courage. "Down to the time of the Civil War, he is the greatest figure in our naval history."[2]

Capture of Washington

Though for most of 1814 the military and civil authorities were pulling in opposite directions, in one case they worked together, and the result was the fall of the capital through joint civil-military bungling. John Armstrong, as secretary of war, continued his conflict with Monroe.

When Monroe criticized Armstrong for not fortifying Washington, Armstrong resented this intrusion into his sphere of military authority. He became more stubborn in maintaining that defenses were not necessary. Baltimore, he said, was the only sensible strategic target for the British fleet in Chesapeake Bay. Adams says of Armstrong: "Probably he was right, and the British would have gone first to Baltimore had his negligence not invited them to Washington" (996).

Besides Armstrong's conflict with Monroe, he clashed directly with Madison over the defense of Washington. The secretary of war had suggested that this be an assignment for Brigadier General Moses Porter; but the president overruled him, preferring Colonel William Winder, since he was the cousin of Levin Winder, Maryland's governor, and Madison thought the Winders would give him greater support from the nearby Maryland militia if one of them was in charge (996). Armstrong took this rebuff to his choice as a further sign of Monroe's meddling, and he found confirmation in the fact that Monroe rode out to scout the approaches of any troops toward the city. From that time, Armstrong let Monroe, Madison, and Winder bear the brunt of failure.

Winder, like Monroe, began personally to scout the area, neglecting to make preparations while performing a task that properly belonged to a subaltern (1002). Scouts and pickets had not been established to track enemy action, so no obstacle was thrown in the way of the perambulating enemy:

> For five days, from August 18 to August 21, a British army, which though small was larger than any single body of American regulars then in the field, marched in a leisurely manner through a long-settled country, and met no show of resistance before coming within sight of the Capitol. Such an adventure resembled the stories of Cortez and De Soto [marching right up to Inca and Aztec towns]; and the conduct of the United States government offered no contradiction to the resemblance. (1002)

The British wondered at this lack of obstacles to their advance, and rightly blamed it on a failure of American intelligence. One of the British officers, referring to Americans as a generic "Jonathan," wrote in his journal: "Jonathan is so confounded that he does not know when or where to look for us, and I do believe that he is at this moment so undecided and unprepared that it would require little force to burn Washington."[3]

When Winder at last deployed his militia, it was at Old Fields, on the line of march toward Washington from the south. But when he spied the British, he withdrew to the Washington Navy Yard, thinking to defend that rather than intercept the British (1005). Informed of this by Armstrong, Madison ordered Winder back into action against the British at Bladensburg. Winder hastily moved his troops in that direction. He was about to leave behind a set of five artillery pieces, with four hundred trained men to service them, under the command of Commodore Joshua Barney. They had been brought to the navy yard from gunboats on the Patuxent River. Since the boats had been sealed up in the river by British ships on Chesapeake Bay, Barney scuttled them and took his guns to the defense of the capital. Barney now protested Winder's attempt to leave him behind, and the secretary of the navy, with Madison's approval, said they must be taken to Bladensburg, where they alone would end up resisting the British (1007).

As the troops were being posted at the Bladensburg Road, Madison asked Armstrong, who had been conspicuously passive during this whole operation, if he had conferred with Winder on tactics. When Armstrong answered no, Madison said they should discuss the matter. Armstrong rode over toward Winder, and Madison tried to follow, but he temporarily lost control of a horse he was not used to and could not get there before the brief conversation ended. When Madison reached Armstrong and asked if any improvements had been made, Armstrong answered that things were being managed.[4] Robert Rutland thinks this is the moment when Madison finally saw through Armstrong: "Whether he realized it or not, Armstrong's goose was cooked."[5] Madison had criticized Armstrong in the past, diffidently, but let him continue doing what he criticized.[6] Now that day was over, too late to protect Washington.

Monroe, who had no military rank, was the first cabinet member to reach Bladensburg, and he rearranged the militia that had arrived (1010). But most of the militia were coming as the attack began, and they took up their positions haphazardly. "Although some seven thousand men were present, nothing deserving the name of an army existed" (1011). Winder's delay in getting them to Bladensburg had rendered them almost useless. The British had only four thousand to the Americans' seven thousand, but their attack instantly scattered the defenders. Alfred Thayer Mahan, who tells this story of the land war because Barney's naval men were engaged in it, describes the disgrace:

In the defenders of Bladensburg was realized Jefferson's ideal of a citizen soldiery, unskilled but strong in their love of home, flying to arms to oppose an invader; and they had every inspiring incentive to tenacity, for they and they only stood between the enemy and the center and heart of national life. The position they occupied, though unfortified, had many natural advantages, while the enemy had to cross a river which, while in part fordable, was nevertheless an obstacle to rapid action, especially when confronted by the superior artillery the Americans had.[7]

The artillery Mahan refers to was Barney's battery. The guns did not arrive until the battle had begun, but Barney set them up on a rise and began rapid fire at the advancing enemy. The British flowed around and behind this small band, and Barney's marines fought them off with bayonets while the gunners kept firing. For half an hour they stood their ground. Adams quotes the British naval historian William James:

> Not only did they serve their guns with a quickness and precision that astonished their assailants, but they stood till some of them were actually bayoneted with fuses in their hands, nor was it till their leader was wounded and taken, and they saw themselves deserted on all sides by the [militia] soldiers, that they left the field. (1012)

The British, admiring Barney's gallantry, "greeted him with a marked respect."[8] This was gallantry indeed, since Barney's men caused or made possible most of the 250 British casualties.

The battle on Bladensburg Road was over by four in the afternoon. The British regrouped and rested for two hours, then moved on toward Washington. The main body camped at eight P.M., a quarter of a mile from the Capitol, while an advance team was sent to burn down the Capitol. General Robert Ross and Admiral George Cockburn, with two hundred men, destroyed the White House. At the same time, the Americans burned the navy yard, with any vessels there — the fire blazed throughout the night (1013). The French minister Sérurier, from his home in the Octagon House near the White House, reported to Talleyrand: "I never saw a scene at once more terrible and more magnificent" (1013).

Adams's mordant comment: "In truth, a government which showed so little capacity to defend its capital could hardly wonder at whatever treatment it received" (1014). The next day, in a thunderstorm, other public buildings were destroyed, and Admiral Cockburn smashed all the type cases of a newspaper that had vilified him: "Be sure that all the C's are destroyed, so that the rascals cannot any longer abuse my name" (1015). The British invaders were later rebuked by their government for not causing more destruction. They were ordered, at the next assault, to "make its inhabitants feel a little more the effects of your visit . . . make the portion of the American people experience the consequences of the war, who have most contributed to its continuance" (1128–29).

Winder had been among the first to flee the field at Bladensburg. Adams finds it difficult to find a bottom to Winder's ignorance and incompetence:

> In the brief moment of his preparations on the field at Bladensburg, he found time to give the characteristic order to his artillery: "When you retreat, take notice that you must retreat by the Georgetown road." When he left the field of Bladensburg, he rode past Barney's sailors, at their guns, and sent his aide to Colonel Bell, on the hill covering Barney's right, with an order to retreat. "After accompanying the retreating army within two miles of the Capitol, I rode forward for the purpose of selecting a position." He reached the Capitol first, and was presently joined there by Monroe and Armstrong. Having decided not to fight at the Capitol, or at any point between the Capitol and Georgetown, he rode to Georgetown. Behind Rock Creek his army would have been safe, and he could certainly have rallied for that [purpose] a thousand men to stop the panic; but he thought a farther retreat necessary, and went on to the heights. On the heights, nothing could reach him without hours of warning, but he rode three miles farther to Tenallytown. At Tenallytown his exhausted men stopped a moment from inability to run farther, yet he seemed angry at their fatigue. Struck by a fresh panic at the glare of the burning city, he pressed his men on at midnight. "After waiting in this position [Tenallytown] until I supposed I collected all the force that could be gathered, I proceeded about five miles farther on the river road, which leads a little wide to the left of Montgomery Court House, and in the morning gave orders for the whole to assemble at Montgomery Court House." The river road was the road that led farthest from the enemy westward, when every motive required retreat toward Baltimore, if anywhere. The next morning Winder returned to the Rockville road, till he reached Rockville, or Montgomery Court House, sixteen miles from Washington, where at last he paused . . . Neither William Hull, Alexander Smyth, Dearborn, Wilkinson, nor Winchester showed such incapacity as Winder, whether to organize, fortify, fight, or escape. When he might have prepared defenses, he acted as scout; when he might have fought, he

still scouted; when he retreated, he retreated in the wrong direction; when he fought, he thought only of retreat; and whether scouting, retreating, or fighting, he never betrayed an idea. (1018–19)

Adams, who is generally good on the terrain of battles, is especially knowledgeable here. He liked to explore surrounding countryside on horseback, whether in Scotland or in Rome, and down through the years he had ridden all over the Washington area. When he says that Winder would have been safe behind Rock Creek, he knows what he is talking about. That is where he regularly rode with Clover, during her lifetime, and where Carrington and Sybil ride in his novel *Democracy*. One of the points of special interest in that long passage on Winder is its contrast with the coolness and courage of Madison, who went out to strengthen and dispose the army as the British approached. This man of fragile health, who had lain at death's door from illness the preceding winter, lived on horseback day after day, borrowing strange mounts when his own was tired.

Adams admires what Madison did, as the enemy moved on his capital, from August 22 to August 24. Two days before the British entered Washington, Madison rode out to the first encampment of the army at Old Fields, four miles south of Bladensburg, midway between it and the navy yard (Winder had not decided yet which approach to guard). Madison stayed the night there, discussed tactics, and reviewed the troops in the morning (1004). When he left, Winder went off to Bladensburg to bring up some militia himself, and while he was gone the British began to march on Old Fields, coming up from the south on the Bladensburg Road. The army in panic sent its supplies off to Washington, ready to retreat but not knowing where — until Winder returned and moved them to the navy yard (rather than to Bladensburg, the more obvious choice). At dawn, he still had time to move the army to Bladensburg, where he had superior numbers to check the British advance, but he had sent word to Armstrong that he would defend the yard, rather than attack the foe.

Armstrong passed this message to Madison, who was disturbed by it. He rode with Armstrong, at eight o'clock in the morning, to move Winder to Bladensburg. By noon the troops were arriving at Bladensburg, and Madison, as we have seen, rode around with Armstrong, trying to make him intervene more effectively in troop placement. "The president, with two or three of his cabinet officers, considerably in advance of all their own troops, nearly rode across the bridge into the British line, when a volunteer scout warned them of their danger" (1010). Madison stayed, making what suggestions he could, until almost the moment of the British attack, when he went back to see to his wife's safety and make sure documents had been removed from the White House. The following passage should be contrasted with the one on Winder's retreats — in it, one gets the feeling, almost, that Adams was riding with Madison in these hectic days.

> The President left Bladensburg battlefield toward two o'clock. He had already ridden in the early morning from the White House to the navy yard, and thence to Bladensburg — a distance of eight miles at the least. He had six miles to ride, on a very hot August day, over a road encumbered by fugitives. He was sixty-three years old, and had that day already been in the saddle since eight o'clock in the morning, probably without food. Soon after three o'clock he reached the White House, where all was confusion and flight. He had agreed with the cabinet, in case of disaster, to meet them at Frederick in Maryland, fifty miles away, but he did not go toward Frederick. Before six o'clock he crossed the Potomac in a boat from the White House grounds, and started by carriage westward, apparently intending to join his wife and accompany her to his residence at Montpelier in Loudon County, adjoining Frederick County, on the south side of the Potomac. Secretary Jones, Attorney General Rush, and one or two other gentlemen accompanied him. In the midst of a troop of fugitives, they traveled till dark, and went about ten miles, passing the night at a house "a few miles above the lower falls" . . . Of all the rulers, monarchical or republican, whose capitals were occupied by hostile armies in the Napoleonic wars, Madison was personally the most roughly treated. (1016–17)

The next morning, he found his wife, and instead of going to Montpelier, he tried to send her there while he sought Winder, to make sure the troops were moving to the defense of Baltimore, the obvious next target for the British. He followed Winder's course until assured that he was in fact bound for Baltimore, then sent word to members of his scattered cabinet that they should return to Washington (1021). He had intelligence that the British had withdrawn from the capital, but there was no assurance that the fleet on the Potomac would not hit it from the west, following up the land attack from the east — or that the two forces would not make a joint assault. It would have been justifiable to assemble the government elsewhere — that had happened in the Revolution, when Philadelphia was taken by the British. But he was determined to restore order at the center, and Dolley insisted on returning with him. It was perhaps their finest hour.

The first order of business, in the ravaged capital, was to set up the defenses that should have been there before. Armstrong was now disqualified for the task — some troops had already sent word to the president that they would not obey Armstrong's orders (1023). In the circumstances, Madison did not have the luxury of putting down this mutiny — instead, he put Monroe in charge, as acting secretary of war as well as secretary of state. This was the "usurpation" Armstrong had feared, and when Madison asked him to step down temporarily, he of course resigned. The cabinet impasse was working itself out by attrition. Madison would ask Governor Daniel Tompkins of New York to become secretary of state; but when he declined, Monroe was kept in both offices (1023).

The government had to be re-established, the capital protected, direction of the war in the North resumed, and Baltimore defended. Luckily Baltimore, seeing what had happened to Washington, undertook its own defense. It had begun the fortification of the city with entrenchments and batteries on the land approaches, and with sunken ships to block access to the harbor. It had skilled artillerymen at Fort McHenry to fire upon ships trying to get across the sunken obstacles. Madison's old enemy Samuel Smith was the head of the Maryland militia, and he refused to recognize the authority of Winder to take command of the city. Winder appealed to his cousin the governor, and to President Madison and Secretary Monroe; but no one trusted federal direction anymore. It was *sauve qui peut*, and Baltimore *peut*. Militia skirmishers not only checked General Ross's approach but shot him dead on the land, while — in the outer harbor — Admiral Cockburn's guns, lighting up the night for Francis Scott Key's edification, never got close enough to hit the city. Despite the requisitioning of supplies from Alexandria, and more harassing of the bay's shoreline, Britain's Chesapeake campaign was over.

6

SHAME AND GLORY

The *History*, Volume Eight

W HILE, IN THE WAR'S third year, the army was pulling itself together, the government was coming apart. The success of the former was continually imperiled by the failure of the latter, as the army called for men and money that the Treasury and Congress could not supply. The symbol of the government's plight was the ruinous state of Washington after the British torched it. William Wirt, visiting the city two months after the attack, called it a "mournful monument of American imbecility and improvidence" (1070). The government that returned there at the end of August, 1814, was homeless. The Madisons would never again live in the blackened White House — the French minister Sérurier kindly moved out of the Octagon House so they could camp there. Congress had lost its Capitol chambers. It fit itself into disjunct spaces of the Post Office and Patent Office. John Randolph said that unthinkable alternatives were the only things keeping Madison in office:

> Nothing less than the shameful conduct of the enemy [in burning the government buildings] and the complexion of certain occurrences to the eastward [New England separatism] could have sustained Mr. Madison after the disgraceful affair at Washington. The public indignation would have overwhelmed in one common ruin himself and his hireling newspapers. (1070)

In fact, there would be some calls for Madison's resignation over the next several months, especially after the punitive terms for a peace settlement were issued by the British in Ghent. Rumors of the proposed demands had reached Washington even before it was taken by the British, but their full horror was not formally announced till October. The British said they would not make peace unless America would cede territory for an Indian state in the Northwest, surrender parts of Maine, and give up rights to the Great Lakes and the Newfoundland fisheries. The public mood in London was for vengeance against Madison's aid to Bonaparte. "Next to Napoleon, the chief victim of English hatred was Madison" (1180). Various Federalists said that only the president's removal would make the British bargain for peace in a less vindictive way (1121–23).

Jefferson tried to console Madison with the thought that he was not to blame for his subordinates' bungling. "Every reasonable man must be sensible that all you can do is to order — that execution must depend on others, and failures to be imputed to them alone" (1071). He expressed the same thought to Monroe: "I never doubted that the plans of the President were wise and sufficient. Their failure we all impute 1) to the insubordinate temper of Armstrong, and 2) to the indecision of Winder" (1071). But it can hardly have escaped Madison's own consciousness that he had first appointed these men, and then kept them at their posts.

As soon as Congress reassembled, it heard the gloomy news from Secretary of the Treasury George Campbell that the government had run out of money for conducting hostilities, and had no prospect of raising it. In a confession of inadequacy before this problem, Campbell resigned (1058–61). At the same time, Secretary of War James Monroe reported that the ranks of troops were not being filled, and there was no prospect of filling them. The problem was simply put — no money to pay, and no men to be paid. A. J. Dallas, who replaced Campbell at Treasury, came up with a desperate attempt to raise money — which his own president vetoed. Secretary Monroe came up with a desperate attempt to provide troops — which Congress rejected.

Dallas said that he had nothing but "the fragment of an authority to borrow money when nobody was disposed to lend, and to issue treasury notes which none but necessitous creditors or contractors in distress . . . seemed willing to accept" (1079). He argued that taxes must be doubled — but those (mainly in New England) able to pay such taxes were unwilling, and those (mainly in the South) willing to pay were unable. The South's plight was described by Jefferson:

All markets abroad and all at home are shut to us . . . We can make indeed enough to eat, drink and clothe ourselves, but nothing for our salt, iron, groceries, and taxes which must be paid in money. For what can we raise for the market? Wheat? — we only give it to our horses, as we have been doing ever since harvest. Tobacco? — it is not worth the pipe it is smoked in. (1082, 1224)

Besides, the tax issue had to wait on the prior matter of a currency. Paying taxes in a depreciating currency was inequitable as well as ineffectual. Why should the North, which had specie, use it when the South was using state notes of debased value? Virginians turned to Jefferson for suggestions in this quandary, and he went against everything he had ever believed in his attempt to help Madison through the crisis. He, the advocate of state sovereignty, who had opposed the centralization of finance in the Bank of the United States, now said the federal government should monopolize the issuance of paper money, not only denying the power of the states to issue their own notes but compelling the government's creditors (including the states) to accept what it issued: "The state legislatures should be immediately urged to relinquish the right of establishing banks of discount. Most of them will comply on patriotic principles, under the convictions of the moment, and the non-complying may be crowded into concurrence by legitimate devices" (1080–81). Jefferson did not say what such legitimate devices might be, and Dallas knew that the states would never accept such an arrangement — the North out of self-interest, the South out of Jefferson's former principles.

Dallas proposed, instead, the chartering of a new bank to stabilize the currency (1083). It would have some of Jefferson's newly suggested coercive power, but in a disguised way. It would be a private bank, but the government would reserve to itself the right to suspend payments in specie during a crisis. John C. Calhoun opposed this on traditional southern grounds, saying the government should not control the bank, and any bank should be required to have at least ten percent of its credit in specie (1085). But there was no sense requiring what could not be had. Bolling Hall of Georgia said the government should just pass a legal tender act making paper money a valid currency. This would only accelerate downward the depreciation that was already taking place. Congress, after searching for some other alternative and coming up with none, had to consider Dallas's plan, though Daniel Webster attacked it with wittily pointed rhetoric:

> This is indeed a wonderful scheme of finance. The government is to grow
> rich because it is to borrow without the obligation of repaying, and is to
> borrow of a bank which issues paper without the liability to redeem it . . .
> They found their bank in the first place on the discredit of the government,
> and then hope to enrich government out of the insolvency of the bank.
> (1089)

Congress, reluctantly and after long struggle, passed the Dallas proposal. Madison — who was presumably regretting his failure to support
Gallatin on renewal of the bank when there was sufficient credit to give
it a foundation — vetoed the bill. It was in effect a prolongation of the
present ineffectual system, since it could only "keep the institution alive
by limited and local [state] transactions" (1090). A real bank would
have to wait upon the peace, when specie would again become available.
That seemed to be a confession that the war could not be sustained, and
that peace would have to be sought on any terms. Dallas interpreted it
that way, and told Congress that the government was bankrupt. When
Jefferson's son-in-law, John Eppes, the chairman of the Ways and Means
Committee, read this message to his committee, he threw it on the table
in disgust and asked a Federalist member: "Well, sir, will your party take
the government if we will give it up to them?" The Federalist answered:
"No, sir! Not unless you will give it to us as we gave it to you!" (1091).

The prospects were so dark that there was an effort to prevent the reporting of congressional debate. This could only give aid and comfort to
the enemy. Why should England desist from war, or grant peace without
extravagant conditions, after it learned how helpless was its foe? The
Federal Republican, published in Washington, editorialized:

> The interest upon the public debt remains unpaid, and there exists not the
> means, without making the most ruinous sacrifices, to pay it. The govern-
> ment is in arrears to the army upward of nine million dollars; to the navy,
> about four millions . . . The condition of our finances is known to the en-
> emy; and is it possible he will be such a fool as to give us peace, after the
> mortal blow we aimed at him, when he knows we cannot pay the interest
> on the public debt, that we cannot pay our army or our navy, and when he
> finds us unable to defend any part of the country at which he strikes? (1121)

Adams's brilliant treatment of the finances of the war is another ex-
ample of the way his prior experience had equipped him for writing the
History. The problems of financing the Civil War had made him study
Britain's use of legal tender before and after this War of 1812 — and he

makes a glancing reference to England's practice in the *History* (1089). The *History* is, throughout, an economic history and not merely a diplomatic or military one.

So much for the shortage of money, addressed by Dallas. How about the shortage of men, which had to be addressed by Monroe, now the secretary of war as well as of state? The latter was facing "a task beyond the powers of any man" (1025). Neither the regulars nor the militias were replenishing their ranks. Many who enlisted in the militias stayed for short terms, refused service outside the state (or inside it, in the case of New England) or across the Canadian border. They cost more than regulars while doing less, and made the recruiting of regulars almost impossible by offering an easier and more lucrative alternative. Even with these easier alternatives to regular service, the states had trouble filling their musters, and each incentive they invented to make up for this — shorter terms, easier exemptions, bounties in the form of land grants — just further diminished the pool for regulars.

The expense of the militias mounted inexorably. Their lack of hygienic discipline made them prone to all kinds of diseases. "The mortality when compared with that of the regular service was enormous; five men sickened and died where one regular soldier suffered" (1062).

> Besides its military disadvantages, the militia service was tainted with fraud. Habitually and notoriously in New England and New York, the militiamen, when called out, attended muster, served a few days in order to get their names on the payroll, and then went home. The United States government wasted millions of dollars in pay and pensions for such men. Another source of waste was in the time required to place them in the field [and bring them back after short terms]. The government struggled to avoid a call of militia, even though risking great disasters by the neglect. (1062–63)

Yet the states clung to the militia system — for one thing, they had patronage power over the appointment of officers; for another, they wanted power to keep men at home for local defense, no matter where the regulars were fighting. Yet Jefferson continued to claim that militia alone were to be relied on. He wrote Monroe on October 16, 1814:

> We must prepare for interminable war. To this end we should put our house in order by providing men and money to an indefinite extent. The former may be done by classifying our militia, and urging each class to the description of duties for which it is fit. It is nonsense to talk of regulars.

They are not to be had among a people so easy and happy at home as ours.
We might as well rely on calling down an army of angels from heaven.
(1092)

Monroe could not have disagreed more. Militias were the bane of his
life. On the very day when Jefferson wrote to him, he was reporting to
Congress that the militias were a useless drain on the government, and
that a regular army must be supplied by the only means left — a draft
(1092–93). Republicans opposed this, on the grounds that it would
make them so unpopular as to drive them from power. Federalists opposed it, since they were against the war in the first place. Senator
Daggert of Connecticut compared Monroe's draft to the *levée en masse*
of Napoleon: "In atrocity it exceeds that adopted by the late Emperor of
France for the subjugation of Europe" (1097).

If Congress would not support an outright draft for the regular army,
Monroe proposed a draft for militiamen to serve two years (instead of
six-month or nine-month terms), in effect making the militia more like
the regular army. Failing that, he proposed to exempt any five militiamen who would hire one man for the regulars (1094). Congress resisted
both of these schemes. The government's own talk of insolvency and
lack of manpower made it seem that it was too inept to be relied on, so
the states must shift for themselves. Jeremiah Mason of New Hampshire voiced a thought that others were entertaining:

> Should the national defense be abandoned by the general government, I
> trust the people, if still retaining a good portion of their resources [i.e., not
> paying taxes to the general government], may rally under their [state] gov-
> ernments against foreign invasion, and rely with confidence on their own
> courage and virtue. (1097–98)

It was suggested that indentured servants be freed on condition of their
joining the army. Daniel Webster warned southerners that if indentured
servants could be freed for military service, so could their slaves (1100).

The Connecticut legislature passed an unconstitutional bill refusing
the federal government the right to use its militia. Robert Stockton of
New Jersey endorsed that move: "This [Monroe] bill also attacks the
right and sovereignty of the state governments. Congress is about to
usurp their undoubted rights — to take from them their militia" (1102).
The response to Monroe's bill proves that Adams was not exaggerating
when he said: "The militia began by rendering a proper army impossible, and ended by making government a form" (1065). Monroe's propos-

als were beaten back. All that was done for the army was to lower the recruiting age from twenty-one to eighteen, double land bounties, and exempt a militiaman who could provide a substitute to the regulars. As Adams says, this would not even meet the troops' replacement rate, much less add to their number.

But in one sense that did not matter. Monroe had no money to pay extra troops if they were given him. In the forlorn hope of securing loans, he trudged around to the Washington banks himself, offering his personal guaranty as security. "At no time of his life were Monroe's means sufficient to supply his private needs, and nothing could express so strongly his sense of national bankruptcy as the assertion that his credit was required to support that of the United States" (1106). The government itself seemed to be disappearing before one's eyes. Senator Gore of Massachusetts said: "These appear to me the spasms of a dying government" (1106). Congressman Joseph Hopkinson of Pennsylvania said: "The federal government was at the last gasp of existence" (1107).

New England

In the general breakdown of the war's support system, New Englanders were most at fault, in ways Adams considers little short of treason. They had begun as war profiteers and ended toying with the idea of breaking out of the Union. As long as the British refrained from enforcing their blockade in the North, merchants there engaged in trade with the enemy, both abroad and in Canada. The ban on trade that hurt the rest of the nation was a blessing to them. "New England was pleased at the contrast between her own prosperity and the sufferings of her neighbors. The blockade and the embargo brought wealth to her alone. The farming and manufacturing industries of New England never grew more rapidly than in the midst of war and commercial restrictions" (916). American major general George Izard, charged with the defense of Lake Champlain, complained of the products streaming past him into Canada, while he had insufficient forces to stop them:

> From the St. Lawrence to the ocean, an open disregard prevails for the laws prohibiting intercourse with the enemy. The road to St. Regis is covered with droves of cattle, and the river with rafts destined for the enemy. The revenue officers see these things, but acknowledge their inability to put a stop to such outrageous proceedings. On the eastern side of Lake Cham-

plain the high roads are found insufficient for the supplies of cattle which are pouring into Canada. Like herds of buffaloes they press through the forest, making paths for themselves. (973)

Madison wisely decided not to start a civil war within the foreign war by trying to crack down on New England. He saw how feckless had been the effort to enforce Jefferson's Embargo there. The war with Canada had to be waged, in the East, across a buffer zone of resistance.

But the resistance increased and soured in April of 1814, when England began to enforce the blockade there. The British aim had been to spur the North's separation from the South; but since the loophole gave New England such rewards, there was no motive to disturb the status quo. "New England thus made profits from both sides, and knew not what to do with the specie that flowed into her banks" (917). The British, when they realized that they were pressuring New England to stay in such a lucrative position, removed the exemption from blockade, causing a panic in the North. Hitherto it had been to the merchants' advantage to keep up the war. Now they became desperate to end it. Townships fired off end-the-war petitions to the Massachusetts General Court. The committee formed to present these resolutions clearly had some members who knew that Madison wrote the Virginia Resolutions of 1798, since it used his language of interposition:

> Whenever the national compact is violated and the citizens of the state are oppressed by cruel and unauthorized laws, the legislature is bound to *interpose* its power, and wrest from the oppressor his victim. This is the spirit of our Union, and thus it has been explained by the very man who sets at defiance all the principles of his early political life [emphasis added]. (911)

The committee had clearly done its homework on the president's writing, since it referred as well to Madison as the author of *Federalist* No. 46, which says that a state may invite other states to convene for the common good. "This was the mode proposed by Mr. Madison in answer to objections made as to the tendency of the general government to usurp upon that of the states" (912).

This was bad enough in Adams's eyes; but when the states proposed an anti-war convention to be held in secret at Hartford, he was sure that the aim was secession. He admits that this plan was thwarted by the choice of moderate delegates to the meeting (1112). But Adams is right in thinking that Madison had reason to distrust New England in general and to fear what might go on in the Hartford Convention. The revival of Federalism, deliberately undermining the war effort, Madison saw as a return to what Jefferson had called "the time of the witches." He wrote:

> The greater part of the people in that quarter have been brought by their leaders, aided by their priests, under a delusion scarcely exceeded by that recorded in the period of witchcraft, and the leaders are becoming daily more desperate in the use they make of it.[1]

While the convention was in preparation, William Wirt found Madison obsessed with it:

> He looks miserably shattered and woebegone. In short, he looked heartbroken. His mind is full of the New England sedition. He introduced the subject and continued to press it, painful as it obviously was to him. I denied the probability, even the possibility, that the yeomanry of the North could be induced to place themselves under the power and protection of England, and diverted the conversation to another topic, but he took the first opportunity to return to it, and convinced me that his heart and mind were painfully full of the subject. (1070)

When delegates from Hartford took their amendment petitions to Washington, they found the city rejoicing at the news of peace from Ghent. Madison no longer saw any reason even to discuss what the New Englanders had brought him. Harrison Gray Otis, their leader, growled: "We have received no invitation from Madison — what a mean and contemptible little blackguard."[2] The time of shame was over. It was a time for glory — since another piece of news reached Washington, along with the tidings from Hartford and Ghent. This came from New Orleans.

Glory

The peace agreement, already signed, was not known in America when the last great battle of the war was fought, one that cast a retrospective glamour over all the military wins and losses that preceded it, and made the peace a triumph, not merely an accommodation. Great Britain had planned a major assault on New Orleans for the summer of 1814. It was to be launched from Jamaica, after a huge task force had assembled there. The aim was not to conquer and hold Louisiana for England — territorial additions made sense only in the North, for the Indian allies and to extend Canadian control over the Great Lakes. Holding a province as far from Canada as Louisiana would not be worth the effort. This invasion had different goals. It could draw American troops away from the northern theater, sapping America's war-making capacity. It could make New Orleans a bargaining chip at the peace table, inducing Americans to acquiesce in the loss of land to Canada if this were returned to them. And it could bring Spain back into play as a check on American ambitions. In line with this latter goal, the invaders were ordered not to encourage old French or Spanish inhabitants to think of union with England, but rather of renewed ties to Spain (1127–28). Also, no slaves were to be freed in Louisiana — that could give wrong ideas to the British slaves in Jamaica (1129).

In anticipation of an invasion of New Orleans, Andrew Jackson, having successfully completed his Creek Indian war, was ordered to take up James Wilkinson's old command of the Louisiana Territory. Jackson, like Wilkinson before him, was slow to move toward New Orleans. First he wanted to complete the formal capitulation of the Creeks, with the seizure of their land. Then he meant to seize Mobile and absorb East Florida into the United States, a longtime goal for Jackson's Tennesseans, but one for which Madison had temporarily lost his enthusiasm, given the exigency of ending the war. Seizing Florida would complicate the diplomacy of peace-making with England, Spain's ally.

Nonetheless, Jackson proceeded to Mobile, since "the defense of New Orleans was not in his mind" (1131). Madison's government was too distracted, with invasion and secession and insolvency, to curb Jackson's insubordination.

> At the same moment government was brought to a standstill at Washington by the appearance of General Ross's army in the Patuxent, and the raids on Washington and Baltimore. Between August 20 and September 25, the War Department could do little more than attend to its own pressing dangers. Jackson was left independent, substantially dictator over the Southwest. If New England carried out its intentions, and the government sank, as seemed probable, into helplessness, his dictatorship was likely to be permanent. (1130)

George Bancroft, the admirer (and appointee) of Jackson, did not like this part of the *History,* as he signaled in his marginal notations on the preliminary copy sent him.

Jackson justified his action in Florida on the grounds that the British had sent help to the Creek Indians there. He issued a bombastic proclamation to the region:

> The base, the perfidious Britons have attempted to invade your country. They had the temerity to attack Fort Bowyer [at Mobile] with their incongruous horde of Indians and Negro assassins . . . Have they not made offers to the pirates of Barataria to join them and their holy cause? And have they not dared to insult you by calling on you to associate as brethren with them and this hellish banditti? (1138)

By this time Monroe was learning, from Halifax and Bermuda, how imminent was the attack on New Orleans. He told Jackson on October 21 that he must give up his Florida obsession: "I hasten to communicate to you the directions of the President that you should at present take no measures which would involve the government in a contest with Spain" (1138). Jackson ignored that order, too, and marched four thousand men to occupy Pensacola on November 7. Even John Armstrong, Jackson's patron when Madison had opposed promoting him, criticized this action: "The general's attack and capture of the town on the 7th of November, 1814, was to say the least of it decidedly ill-judged, involving at once an offense to a neutral power, and probably a misapplication of both time and force as regarded the defense of New Orleans" (1139).

Finally, on December 2, Jackson reached New Orleans, after spending three months in useless (and forbidden) campaigning in Florida (1132). There he found a defenseless town under panicked and disconsolate leadership. Advancing on it was the greatest fleet that had so far crossed the ocean — sixty vessels, led by the eighty-gun ship of the line *Tonnant* ("Thunderer"). The fleet bore over a thousand cannon, ten thousand seasoned troops, and a superb team of leaders.[3]

> Hitherto the frequent British disasters — at Plattsburg, Hackett's Harbor, Fort Erie, and the Moravian towns — had been attributed to their generals. Sir George Prevost, Major Generals Drummond and Riall, and Major General Proctor were not officers of Wellington's army. The British government, in appointing Sir Edward Pakenham to command at New Orleans, meant to send the ablest officer at their disposal. Pakenham was not only one of Wellington's best generals, but stood in the close relation of his brother-in-law, Pakenham's sister being Wellington's wife. In every military

respect Sir Edward Pakenham might consider himself the superior of Andrew Jackson. He was in the prime of life and strength, thirty-eight years of age, while Jackson, nearly ten years older, was broken in health and weak in strength. Pakenham had learned the art of war from Wellington, in the best school in Europe. He was supported by an efficient staff and a military system as perfect as experience and expenditure could make it, and he commanded as fine an army as England could produce, consisting largely of Peninsula veterans. (1157–58)

Adams makes an extended comparison between the assault on New Orleans and that on Washington. There are some key similarities, which make the differences even more startling. Both towns were unfortified and unprepared. Both had poor intelligence of the enemy's approach. Both had divided leadership, civil and military — at least until, at the last moment, Jackson arrived. But the conflicts in Washington between Winder, Armstrong, Monroe, and Madison were not repeated in New Orleans. As soon as Jackson saw the dithery state of things there, he gathered all power — civil and military — into his own hands.

He issued a proclamation to the people of the city, in which he threatened them with punishment if they were not unanimous, and at the same time he recommended the legislature to suspend the writ of habeas corpus. Finding the legislature hesitant, Jackson declared martial law by proclamation the same day, December 10, and assumed dictatorial powers. (1146)

Yet, until the enemy was upon him, Jackson imitated Winder and Monroe, scouting all around New Orleans without ever finding the enemy. Not until six American gunboats, stationed as pickets, were captured and destroyed by an advance party of British ships did the city realize how close the British were (1143). That was on December 14. During the night of December 18, British reconnoiterers reached a Spanish fishing village at the head of Bayou Bienvenue, fifteen miles from New Orleans. They received information on the best line of advance, and took back with them fishermen to pilot their boats. Two days later, an American picket force of nine men was sent to the village without learning anything of the British visit or the fishermen who had gone off to guide them. Two days after that, the picket was suddenly taken by a force of seventeen hundred men (1147). The British went on to surprise American militiamen at a plantation seven miles from New Orleans.

The record of American generalship offered many examples of misfortune, but none so complete as this. Neither Hull nor Harrison, neither Winder nor Samuel Smith, had allowed a large British army, heralded long in advance, to arrive within seven miles unseen and unsuspected, and without so much as an earthwork, a man, or a gun between them and their object. The disaster was unprecedented, and could be repaired only by desperate measures. (1147)

But this is where the difference between Winder and Jackson becomes apparent. Surprised thus, Jackson did not panic or withdraw. When the British camped for the night, preparing to advance at dawn, Jackson attacked *them:*

> If until the moment of the enemy's appearance Jackson showed no more military capacity than was shown by Winder, his conduct thenceforward offered a contrast the more striking because it proved how Washington might have been saved. Winder lost his head when he saw an enemy. Jackson needed to see his enemy in order to act; he thought rightly only at the moment when he struck. (1149)

Jackson quickly moved one of his two warships on the Mississippi, the schooner *Carolina,* to a point where it could shell the British, while he attacked by land from two directions. The battle was a standoff, but it came as a shock to the British and checked their advance. This gave Jackson breathing space for what he needed most — fortification. Outnumbered two to one in men, he needed every advantage of position and cover. By attacking at the first chance, Jackson purchased his all-important second chance. "Brilliant as the affair was, its moral effect was greater than the material injury inflicted" (1106). This would later be known as the First Battle of New Orleans (December 23).

Withdrawing two miles from the enemy, Jackson chose well a spot five miles below the city for defense of it. This is where his dictatorial reign proved its worth. He had dragooned the whole population into service, and now teams worked feverishly — soldiers, sailors, French, Spanish, Creoles, blacks, Indians — to build earthworks, and to widen and deepen the trenches before them. In one day and night, enough progress had been made to keep the British from attacking before their whole force arrived. Then a further wait ensued as British artillery was trundled laboriously through bayou and swamp. Jackson's defenses were meanwhile extended and deepened — providing a redoubt high enough to require scaling ladders, and slick with mud that gave little purchase for anyone hoping to climb it.

In the Second Battle of New Orleans (December 28), the British made their first charge on the redoubt, four thousand men attacking three thousand defenders. Their cannon had destroyed the *Carolina* on the preceding day (1164), but Jackson had moved up his other sloop, the *Louisiana,* to a position where it could riddle the attackers (1160). The charge was repulsed. Pakenham decided that, before his next assault, he must mount a major artillery barrage to open a breach in the earthworks and/or to disable the American guns.

This great cannonade opened on New Year's Day (the Third Battle of New Orleans), preparing for the major engagement of January 8. Pakenham had twenty-four guns to Jackson's twenty, throwing 350 pounds at a discharge to his 224. But Jackson's guns were well placed, and their firing was rapid and accurate. The sailors had brought their guns off the destroyed *Carolina* and the idle *Louisiana.* Jean Lafitte's pirates had joined the defense, and put their artillery skills to good use. For a whole chapter, Adams celebrates the American gunnery.

> The artillery battle of January 1, 1815, offered the best test furnished during the war of relative skill in the use of that arm. The attack had every advantage over the defense. The British could concentrate their fire to effect a breach for their troops to enter; the Americans were obliged to disperse their fire on eight points. The American platforms, being elevated, offered a better target than was afforded by the low British batteries, and certainly were no better protected ... No other battle of the war except that at Chrysler's Farm left the defeated party with so little excuse for its inferiority. (1165)

Since the British barrage had not succeeded in either of its goals, breaching the wall or crippling the guns, their charge on January 8 (the Fourth Battle of New Orleans) was made against a murderous fire. The British plan was to turn Jackson's right flank (by crossing a river) and charge his middle. They succeeded in turning his flank and capturing a battery of guns. Jackson blamed this on the cowardice of the Kentucky troops at that position, but Adams argues that they were exposed, poorly reinforced, outnumbered, and that they put up a brave resistance — inflicting casualties on 43 soldiers and 20 sailors attacking them, and wounding both detachments' leaders (1179). The Kentuckians properly spiked their guns before retiring. If the British who captured this flank had pressed on to New Orleans, the city lay exposed to it; but they would have lacked support from their main force, which was being mowed down before Jackson's redoubt. They wisely withdrew.

The defeat was almost miraculous. Adams gives the total casualties (killed, wounded, missing) of January 8 as 2,036 British to 71 Americans. Later and better figures are still astonishing. On January 8, 192 British were killed to only 13 Americans. Among the British dead were Pakenham and three of his four major generals, along with many other officers. Counting all four engagements at New Orleans, the total casualties were 2,444 British to 336 Americans, "a ratio of about 7 to 1."[4] Even though this great battle was fought after the peace treaty with England was signed at Ghent, it had a tremendous effect on the American spirit. The nation had not gained any of the five aims articulated by Madison at the outset of the war, yet it felt victorious. This one event colored the way Americans looked back on the war, as a thing to take pride in. It added one more to the gallery of heroes cherished in the aftermath of a struggle that had, for much of its course, been ignominious.

Even Timothy Pickering, who expected Jackson to lose and would have welcomed the loss of the West, found himself elated by the victory.[5] It reminded him of the days when he had fought against England under Washington, and made him a patriot again. Other Federalists also became more reconciled to the war and its outcome. In one sense, they had to — their sympathizers in England, who had expressed discontent with the idea that Americans "got off easy" in the peace settlement, changed their tune when news of New Orleans reached them. They realized, after this loss of a powerful army, that they had not been in a position to dictate terms after all. This, and the fact that Napoleon had just escaped from Elba, gave the British more urgent tasks than thinking of revenge against America (1221). In that sense, the Battle of New Orleans was not a post-war and irrelevant event. It validated the peace terms.

Since this is the culminating battle of the war, to which Adams devotes the closing chapters of volume eight (as he had closed volume two with the glorious exploits of the Tripolitan War), it is useful to look here at a technique Adams uses throughout his treatment of military engagements. It has already been noticed that he runs a detailed comparison between the battles for Washington and New Orleans. He makes a shorter comparison of December 23 events at New Orleans with the Battle of Lundy's Lane, since they were both night battles (1156). He makes another comparison, of Pakenham's frontal charge at New Orleans with Drummond's at Fort Erie. Drummond was more successful with fewer means because he attacked at night (1180–81). Adams thinks that Pakenham's daylight attack gave too visible a target to Jackson's deadly gunners.

It is part of Adams's technique as a military historian to make these analytical comparisons wherever he finds them useful. He probably developed the approach from his reading of the naval historians (James and Cooper and Roosevelt). It was accepted practice in naval history to make comparisons of sea engagements, according to settled and detailed criteria. These included:

Type, dimensions, rigging, and weight of vessel.

Type, number, and throw-weight of guns.

Type and number of combatants (sailors, marines, soldiers).

Weather, time of day, visibility, wind, and positions (leeward or windward).

Number and type of supporting or opposing vessels (if any), in line, squadron, or convoy.

Type and result of combat (mutual disengagement, flight, boarding, striking, capture, destruction).

Numbers and rank of enemy prisoners and wounded.

Estimated worth of prize (if any).

Conduct of ship, officers, crew.

Number and severity of casualties to men, damages to ship.

These factors were calibrated with legal precision, because they were the basis for rewarding or punishing officers, for keeping ships' records, and for reparation claims in courts of admiralty. They were needed for making complex assessments. How, for instance, might one judge an engagement in which one ship strikes but the other one sinks (as happened with the *Bonhomme Richard* in the Revolution)? Adams follows this procedure in his discussion of naval battles all through the *History*. What is interesting is to see how he applies similar tests to land battles, using sometimes the same criteria, sometimes analogous ones. The number, type, and throw-weight of field guns, for example, can be judged in much the same way as ship guns were, with only minor differences — pivot guns being used at sea, mortars on land, etc. Elements like weather, time of day, or visibility are also comparable. Adams pays special attention to fighting in fog or smoke as well as at night (1154, 1179). But the advantages of field terrain are only partly analogous to positions at sea (leeward, windward, etc.). And the numbers and types of combatants are more varied on land than on sea, comprising forces like regulars, militia, cavalry, infantry, artillery, scouts, Indians, etc.

This kind of analysis can become fairly mechanical — it makes for numbed reading in (for instance) Roosevelt's exhaustive lists of ship specifications. But Adams is flexible — he uses the appropriate criteria only when it helps understand the battle at hand. And his quantitative military analyses have not been much noticed by those who want to talk of Adams as a scientific historian. They should be. This final volume of the war is full of vivid descriptions of individual acts of courage. But it is not merely anecdotal. It is analytical throughout.

7

PEACE AND NATIONALISM

The *History*, Volume Nine

T HOUGH THE BATTLE of New Orleans took place after peace terms were settled at Ghent, Adams saves the peace commission's work for his last volume, to be considered with the conditions it set for Madison's last year as president, when nationalizing pressures caused him to leave office on a triumphant note. This had the air of a last-minute rescue. For months the news from Ghent had been terrifying, with the prospect of prolonged war depressing the nation. The simultaneous arrival of the three pieces of news already mentioned had a magic effect. The threat of northern secession disappeared like a popped balloon, the bearable terms from Ghent looked like an escape from the gallows, and the victory in New Orleans changed the whole air of the war. The capital was dizzy with relief and pride, and Madison's stock soared.

Gallatin first joined his fellow delegates to Ghent with bad news from his stay in London, where he had heard the British howling for revenge. The *Times* of London was especially vociferous:

Having disposed of all our enemies in Europe, let us have no cant of moderation. There is no public feeling in the country stronger than that of indignation against the Americans . . . As we urged the principle, No peace with Bonaparte! so we must maintain the doctrine of, No peace with Madison! . . . With Madison and his perjured set no treaty can be made, for no oath can bind them . . . Our demands may be couched in a single word — Submission!! (1186–87)

This and other papers called not only for cessions of territory to the Indians and Canada, but for repair of the "swindle" by which Napoleon and Jefferson stole Louisiana from Spain: "We shall inquire a little into the American title to Louisiana, and we shall not permit the base attack on Florida to go unpunished" (1186, 1188).

The British commissioners were forbidden to discuss the grievances which had led America to declare war — impressments, or trade restrictions, or Canadian alliances with the Indians. Instead, they proposed a settlement on the basis of *uti possidetis* ("state of possession" at the time of the treaty), since they were expecting to hear any moment that British troops had taken much of New York, Maine, and Louisiana. With this territory in hand, they could barter for what they wanted — an Indian nation carved out of the Northwest, with British access to the Mississippi; a buffer around the Great Lakes that would allow no American forts on their shores, no American navy on their waters; incorporation of half of Maine into Canada; and denial of American fishing rights at Newfoundland.

The Americans were instructed to propose terms equally unacceptable to the other side — for example, to insure peace in North America by incorporating Canada into the United States. This was a demand so preposterous that the Americans did not have the nerve even to submit it (1192). Instead, Gallatin wrote an eloquent reply to the British proposal, subtly representing the British as waging a war of conquest for territory. Prime Minister Castlereagh recognized the cleverness of his adversary. He was at the Congress of Vienna, working out the terms of European settlement after the Napoleonic Wars, and he did not want England to be seen as an aggressor nation. He decided that the British negotiators were off on the wrong tack. He wrote to Lord Bathurst, who was directing the negotiations from London in his absence, that "the territorial questions might be reserved for ulterior discussion" (1220).

Lord Liverpool agreed with this point, and said that such humbling demands would simply harden American support for Madison, positioning him as the leader in a war of national survival. Liverpool added that "it is very material to throw the rupture of the negotiations, if it is to take place, upon the Americans" — and that was not easy to do if the talks broke down because Britain wanted large chunks of the American continent. Gallatin was playing for time to let such considerations take hold. J. Q. Adams wanted to break off talks over the demand for an Indian nation, but Gallatin dissuaded him. Here, as in the Gallatin biography, Henry Adams makes it clear that his grandfather was incapable of leading the talks.

> All Gallatin's abilities were needed to fill the place [of J. Q. Adams, the delegation's leader]. In his entire public life he had never been required to manage so unruly a set of men. The British commissioners were trying, and especially Goulburn was aggressive in temper and domineering in tone; but with them Gallatin had little trouble. Adams and Clay were persons of a different type, as far removed from British heaviness as they were from the Virginian ease of temper which marked the cabinet of Jefferson, or the incompetence which characterized that of Madison. Gallatin was obliged to exert all his faculties to control his colleagues; but whenever he succeeded, he enjoyed the satisfaction of feeling that he had colleagues worth controlling. They were bent on combat, if not with the British, at all events with each other; and Gallatin was partly amused and partly annoyed by the unnecessary energy of their attitude. (1203)

Gallatin's stalling for time was met, on the other side, by an equal willingness to wait for news of further victories. But this hopeful mood was shattered by reports that Drummond had been bloodily repulsed at Fort Erie and Cockburn had failed to take Baltimore (1207). This changed the factors in play. "Castlereagh at Vienna found himself unable to make the full influence of England felt, so long as such mortifying disasters by land and sea proved her inability to deal with an enemy she persisted in calling contemptible" (1208). Castlereagh was growing impatient with what he called "the millstone of an American war."[1]

In this new situation, when *uti possidetis* seemed less promising to England, Gallatin worked to substitute the principle of *status quo ante* (the situation before), conditions as they had existed on the eve of the war. Madison was naturally unhappy with this. It renounced everything he had gone to war for, suggesting that so much effort and treasure and lives had been spent for nothing. But Gallatin knew this was the best that could be won — *if* it could be won. The British were especially intransigent on two conditions — their own Mississippi navigation rights and exclusion of America from the Newfoundland fisheries. As it happens, those were exactly the points on which two of the American commissioners would not yield. For the westerner Clay, American control of the Mississippi was non-negotiable. For Adams, the fisheries were not only a vital part of the New England economy but a matter of family pride, since his father had secured them in the treaty that ended the Revolution.

There seemed no way to break this impasse until Lord Wellington came to the rescue. The victor of Napoleon was asked, on November 4, 1814, to take command of the British forces in Canada and bring the war to a swift and favorable conclusion, seizing what territories England thought essential for a stable peace. Replying on November 9, Wellington renounced the whole principle of *uti possidetis* as a basis for ending the war:

> I confess that I think you have no right, from the state of the war, to demand any concession of territory from America . . . You have not been able to carry it into the enemy's territory, notwithstanding your military success and now undoubted military superiority, and have not even cleared our own territory on the point of attack. You cannot on any principle of equality in negotiation claim a cession of territory excepting in exchange for other advantages which you have in your power . . . Then if this reasoning be true, why stipulate for the *uti possidetis?* You can get no territory; indeed, the state of your military operations, however creditable, does not entitle you to demand any. (1211–12)

This was a crushing reply from the government's own principal expert on war. "After inviting and receiving so decided an opinion from so high an authority, the government could not easily reject it . . . The British ministry had no choice but to abandon its claim for territory" (1211–12). Wellington said that if he went to Canada, it would be only "to sign a peace which might as well be signed now."[2]

With *uti possidetis* thus abruptly removed from consideration, that left only *status quo ante* as a principle for settlement. When this was understood on both sides, the Mississippi and fishery points could be fudged. Lord Bathurst ordered his negotiators to set aside those issues for future negotiations and make a general peace settlement. Gallatin brought his refractory fellows to agree with this (1216–17). Neither the British nor the Americans had any longer a stake in the war worth its continuance. Principle lapsed on both sides into a simple willingness to stop fighting.

The news of peace did not reach America in time to prevent the Battle of New Orleans — which turned out to be fortunate for America. But other clashes also occurred, and were not as pleasant. Admiral Cockburn continued his raids in the South, seizing Cumberland Island on the coast of Georgia as a first step toward marching on Savannah (1225). Worse than that, the Humphreys frigate *President* was lost on January

15, when Stephen Decatur struck its flag. He had been chased by a British squadron made up of the fifty-six-gun *Majestic* and three frigates, including the forty-six-gun *Endymion*. Only the *Endymion* was fast enough to catch the *President,* but their two-and-a-half-hour battle crippled the *President* enough that, when the other frigates came up, and the *Pomone* fired a broadside into the *President,* Decatur struck his flag.

The action was controversial. It was disappointing that a hero of the first year of the war, when Decatur in the *United States* had captured the *Macedonian,* should lose the war's last sea battle. A court-martial not only cleared but praised Decatur, yet Adams is more judgmental: "Anxious to escape rather than to fight, Decatur in consequence failed either to escape or resist with effect . . . Decatur was doubtless justified in striking when he did; but his apparent readiness to do so hardly accorded with the popular conception of his character" (1229, 1231). Adams seems to have had it in for Decatur since the time when Decatur righteously condemned Captain Barron for striking the *Chesapeake's* flag (J 944).

Yet these bits of bad news were absorbed in the almost eerie euphoria that hit the nation after the war. Only weeks before the peace treaty was signed, it looked as if the British were going to exact a terrible price for Madison's attack on them. Yet he was now treated as a victor. Why? A confluence of factors, some superficial, some profound, made this possible. The profound factors Adams will explore in his final chapters on nation-making. But the more superficial were, in themselves, important enough to brighten the peace. For one thing, the very fact that England's draconian terms were not exacted brought a tremendous feeling of relief. "Not an inch ceded or lost!" was now the boast (1237). For another, the victories of the last year of the war had given the nation a new sense of unity and pride, a pride that broke all bounds when Jackson won the Battle of New Orleans. A more important factor in play was the economic surge that followed on the treaty. Upon a parched nation, a refreshing shower of goods and money seemed to be released. Two years of American harvests sailed off at once to a Europe begging to buy grain and goods.

Seven years of combined embargo and blockade had delivered staggering blows to the economy. Though the "bounce" now given it was simply a matter of catching up on long-stalled commercial action, it felt like a reward for the effort of the war and it held commercial promise for the future. Luckily for Madison, the section of the country that most quickly rebounded was the part that had suffered most — his own region, the South.

> Of fifty millions received from abroad in payment for domestic produce within seven or eight months after the peace, the slave states probably took nearly two thirds, though the white population of the states south of the Potomac was less than half the white population of the Union. The stimulus thus given to the slave system was violent, and was most plainly shown in the cotton states, where at least twenty million dollars were distributed in the year 1815 among a white population hardly exceeding half a million in all, while the larger portion fell to the share of a few slave owners. (1246)

Adams misses none of the ironies here. Madison had based his whole diplomacy on the belief that Europe needed trade more than America did, and that the American character could put up with the forgoing of luxuries. It was now proved, almost deliriously, how much America needed foreign trade — and Madison, of all people, was the beneficiary of this discovery.

It was gratifying to some (and Adams shares the feeling) that the region suffering most from the peace was New England. This was the part of the country that resented and resisted the war. Yet it was the region that profited from the war and was stricken by the peace. It now lost the domestic monopoly on sales of its burgeoning factories. It lost the covert shipping to foreign competitors. It lost the double market of supply to both sides in the Niagara and Champlain areas. It lost the near monopoly on specie, as it had to pay out now as well as collect. Between February and June of 1815, the hard money held in Massachusetts banks fell by a half, and within a year that was down to a quarter (1248).

Secretary of the Treasury Dallas contributed to this drain on New England banks by demanding from its states payment of taxes in specie, though he accepted local currencies from other regions (1249–50). This was not simply a punitive measure for New England's conduct in the war (though that was a bonus) — it reflected Dallas's determination to make specie circulate more briskly so that paper money could be phased out. Adams, who worked so hard for the same result after the Civil War, admires the way Dallas used the national bank (restored on April 19, 1815) to discipline local banks (1271–72). He also admits that Dallas was wise in using the national debt, as Hamilton had, rather than trying to erase it, as Gallatin had (1271–72).

This change in Adams's own position is one of the major developments in his thinking. Gallatin, too, had been a convert to the bank, but he never reconciled himself to the debt. Adams sees the new credit system as one of the changes he traces in the *History.* "A surplus of more than $20,000,000 was likely to accumulate in the Treasury before the close of the year [1816]. Old ideas of economy and strict restraints on expenditure could no long maintain themselves in the presence of such an income" (1277). Adams also sees merit in Dallas's protectionism for infant manufactures, as opposed to the strict free trade values of his own reform days (1254, 1257–58).

As the war ended Madison had, for the first time, a loyal and cooperative cabinet. The administration proposed, and Congress acted on, very energetic government measures during his last year in office. Secretary of the Treasury Dallas promoted the national bank, the debt, and hard currency. Secretary of the Navy Benjamin Crowninshield sold off the useless gunboats to help build ships of the line (1241–42). Secretary of War Monroe called for a peacetime army of twenty thousand men (1239). Madison, reverting to original Republican principles, balked at only one thing: when Congress gave him an internal improvements bill, he vetoed it, holding that a constitutional amendment was needed before Congress could build roads and canals in peacetime (1284). There was still some distance between what he had thought and what he had wrought.

These initiatives — centralized financial planning, a standing army and permanent navy, internal improvements — show how far the country had moved from the original principles of Virginia. Madison backed Monroe's army proposal in the message to Congress that he sent along with the Treaty of Ghent. A peacetime army, he argued, is a deterrent to war (1238–39). That was the old Federalist position — old Republicans held that it was a provocation to war. Congressman Joseph Desha of Kentucky was still a Republican of the ancient school — he demanded that Monroe's army be cut from twenty thousand to six thousand men. Armies, he reminded his fellows, give birth to big government, with all its attendant evils: "The advocates of a perpetual system of taxation discover that if they cannot retain a considerable standing army, they will have no good pleas of riveting the present taxes on the people" (1241). After extended debate, the size of the army was set at ten thousand, still too much for Desha and his fellow purists, and not enough for Monroe. But Monroe could afford to bide his time. He was about to become president for eight years. Never again would the nation be without a standing army.

On internal improvements, Madison was out of step with his own party and his own region. The South needed improvement more than most areas. Even Republicans like Henry Clay and John C. Calhoun argued strenuously for the improvements bill. Calhoun said, "If we are restricted in the use of our money to the enumerated powers, on what principle can the purchase of Louisiana be justified?" (1283). The war had taught the nation how necessary were rapid communication and transportation. Generals Hull and Harrison had failed because logistical lines were lacking or exiguous — a situation that could be remedied only by gaining control of the Great Lakes. Improvement would now mean, among other things, federal lighthouses on the lakes that had been preserved from British designs on them.

The explosion of population westward showed that new territories needed development. They needed roads, water sources, postal stations, the support of army posts. Prior actions of the government — not only the Louisiana Purchase referred to by Calhoun, but the restored bank, the Embargo and its enforcement acts, the government erected in New Orleans, the seizure of West Florida — had changed the standards of constitutionality in many people's eyes (1281). Adams says that the debates over the improvements bill no longer turned on the Constitution. Those objecting to it were more concerned with costs, with increased taxes, with the challenge to local commercial interests, than with the Constitution (1283–84).

Virginia legislators, unlike those of Kentucky and South Carolina, voted against the internal improvements bill, and soon regretted it. A committee of the legislature in 1816 reported:

> While many other states have been advancing in wealth and numbers with a rapidity which has astonished themselves, the ancient Dominion and elder sister of the Union has remained stationary. A very large proportion of her western territory is yet unimproved. (1294)

It was the South that was soon "clamorous for roads, canals, and banks" (1294). Another Virginia committee said that the state must have credit and commerce in order to compete with other regions.

> A prejudice has gone abroad . . . that the policy of Virginia is essentially hostile to commerce and to the rights of commercial men. Upon the removal of this prejudice must depend the future contributions of the Com-

monwealth toward the prosperity and glory if not the happiness and safety of *the United States* . . . Without foreign commerce there can exist neither ships, seamen, nor a navy; and a tremendous lesson has taught Virginians that without a navy she can have no security for her repose [emphasis added]. (1295)

The South paid for Madison's veto. New York built the Erie Canal, and Pennsylvania the Cumberland Road, without federal help. But if the improvements bill had gone through, Gallatin's hope for canals from the Chesapeake to the Ohio and from the Santee to the Tennessee River might have been realized (1297). Madison's gesture of consistency was at odds with the energies he had himself unleashed.

Despite this one point on which he was out of step with the nation and his state, Madison left office more popular than he had been when he entered it. The nation was contented, and was grateful to him, for what it had done to itself. That, at least, was in accord with Republican principles — that people themselves should accomplish their own goals. Adams treats the forces of nationalization in three special areas — geographic, economic, and military.

Geographic Nationalization

Adams measures the demographic changes that had occurred since his description of the nation in 1800. In sixteen years, the population of the country had almost doubled, but its distribution was radically different. In 1800, two-thirds of the population lived within fifty miles of the Atlantic coast, and all the important cities were expanding there. Only a tenth of the population lived west of the mountains, where it was largely cut off from the East. By 1817, the population of the northern and southern states had grown by about a quarter, the middle states had doubled their population, but the three western states had quadrupled their numbers, and the territory was booming (1287). The drive to the West was not only quantitatively stunning. It was different in quality from the first settlements in the East. The people moving west in this period left behind many of the ideals, but also the mental confines, of the first colonies. As he put it proleptically in his first volume: "In the early days of colonization, every new settlement represented an idea and proclaimed a mission" (J 121), whether an errand into the wilderness or a political scheme of free government. The Americans described at the end of Madison's second term have little time or use for mission or utopia —

and that is what he admires about them. "From Lake Erie to Florida, in a long unbroken line, pioneers were at work, cutting into the forests with the energy of so many beavers, and with no more express moral purpose than the beavers they drove away" (J 121). The new immigrants into the West came not on a divine errand but for work (J 116).

The apparent dispersal of population westward was, paradoxically, a unifying force for the whole nation. The farther one went off from the center, the more the center had to make sure it would hold. Jefferson *nationalized* the West — not merely by the Louisiana Purchase, but even more by the governance act that he passed in order to incorporate the new territory into a vision controlled from Washington. This governance violated every principle of *both* the old parties, as one can see in its being denounced by John Quincy Adams from Massachusetts and John Randolph from Virginia. Jefferson brushed aside the division of government into mutually checking elements — he appointed, without congressional approval, the executive, the legislative, and the judiciary officials, all accountable only to him. In the northern part of the new territory, he defied the separation of civil from military responsibility, blending them both in General Wilkinson.

Many treat this as an anomaly, just a momentary lapse in Republican principle, a temporary necessity to be forgiven because of no lasting importance. Adams sees it as a necessary part of the nationalizing effort. In the old leftist phrase, "Who says A must say B." Adams's view of the West is more sophisticated than Frederick Jackson Turner's. In the Turner view, and in popular sentiment, the West exercises a kind of automatic magnetism, drawing people to new frontiers, providing a vent from the crowded cities, democratizing the settler in the mere process of removal. Adams's view is in accord with that of modern historians of the West. Far from acting as a separate principle, on its own, at odds with the East, the West was driven by forces from the East.

That would notoriously be so in the Gilded Age, when money and politics in Washington created the territorial rules, the state incorporation acts, the railroads, the river rights, the telegraph communication, the cavalry, the postal routes, the land grants. Eastern money controlled the cattle drives, the stage and steam companies, the Indian removal, the army posts that became the support or the site of towns and cities (Fort Wayne, Fort Worth, Fort Apache, Fort Bend, etc.). These are what made the West possible, and bound it into the national life. And all that began with Jefferson's nationalizing of the West. When his control of the

West was threatened, or seemed to be, by Aaron Burr, Jefferson again stretched every constitutional principle in his effort to bring Burr to the gallows and keep the West nationalized.

Deplorable as Jefferson's nationalizing power may have been in terms of his own earlier principles, it was part of the sequence that Adams finds inevitable and mainly beneficial. National expansion requires national energy. Adams does not think in static terms of two different entities, the East and the West, but in dialectical terms of their interplay. In fact, the failure of the Federalists came from their refusal to accept an interplay with any opposite or complement. They were incapable of making a nation because they were self-satisfied in their sectionalism. They hoped for little from change, and clung to a belief that stability must rest on privilege. That the privilege was often illusory just made them dishonest as well as ineffectual.

The Republicans, by contrast, were optimistic about change, hopeful about the capacity of the American people. They welcomed western expansion, where the Federalists resented or resisted it. Republicans also knew that they had to reach outside their region if they were to protect its vulnerable system of slavery (which they prettified as "agrarian virtue"). They needed an alliance, initially with Pennsylvania and New York, to make up for the fact that they would be a minority region if forced to stand alone. Federalists felt that they could stand apart and just watch the democratic experiment disintegrate for lack of sound roots in the past. The virtuous and learned would pick up the pieces after the dissolute and ignorant had made a wreck of things. The Federalists did not feel a need for compromise — which is just as well, since they were incapable of it. Jefferson wanted a national party, wanted it enough to violate his own principles in order to get it. He opposed patronage, for instance, but his dependence on office-hungry Pennsylvanians and New Yorkers made him not only practice it, but practice it energetically and well. For Federalists, no such problem arose in principle — one rewarded one's own because one's own were the only people worthy of reward.

The simplistic view of Federalists and Republicans is that one stood for centralization of authority and power, and the other for decentralization. But reality cannot be sorted neatly into such nice compartments. The center and the periphery must always interact. In fact, they are defined *only* by their relationship to each other — the center is central to what, the periphery is peripheral to what? Federalists refused to recognize this reality, or to do so with consistency. They wanted to protect, and therefore to contract, their hold on ancient values. They were not static (no one can be). They were centripetal. Republicanism was centrifugal, expanding out toward new constituents, new spaces, new opportunities. It was optimistic that it could do so and retain its identity.

But optimism is a force for change, and change alters identity. A centrifugal process must generate ever new energies at the center to radiate outward to the periphery — otherwise, expansion becomes mere accretion of disjunct parts. Power must permeate growth. The branch flourishes only when connected with the life of the trunk. That is why the Republican rhetoric condemning power could not survive the requirements of expansion. This does not mean — as some people say Adams means — that Republicans *became* Federalists once they achieved power. That is what John Taylor of Caroline claimed, and Adams considers him a prisoner of the past, an anachronism, an irrelevance (1315). Adams believes that the Republicans transcended both parties, and party ideology itself, to become that most American of things — pragmatic. Geography made them do it. Adams is right to say that Jefferson represents the best of the American people, since they are a pragmatic people. "A people which had in 1787 been indifferent or hostile to roads, banks, funded debt, and nationality, had become in 1815 habituated to ideas and machinery of the sort on a great scale" (1214). That is what Adams meant by calling Jefferson a subject for comedy. He kept failing to be as idealistic and single-minded, as ideological and pure, as he thought he should be or would be — "and a good thing, too," as the British say.

Economic Nationalization

Though population grew in the time Adams describes, wealth grew faster, and it was widely distributed. All parts of society with the exception of slaves had some share in the rewards of a growing economy. This no doubt contributed to the good cheer at the war's end and to the optimism that sapped any gloom the Federalists still hoped to peddle: "Prosperity put an end to faction" (1245). New England suffered setbacks at the peace, but it was best able to sustain them, since its hypertrophy during the war was pathological — it drained the rest of the country to profit from the hostilities it denounced. As Adams predicted in his first social history, the middle states proved the most promising and progressive region. Now he says, "The middle states were far in advance of the eastern and southern in opening communications with the West" (1297). They used new technologies better than other regions. New York was the pioneer in transportation, with the Erie Canal and steamboats, since its fertile expanse was "nowhere fifty miles from navigable water" (1296). Pennsylvania was also a leader in steam technology: "In 1811, a boat of four hundred tons was built at Pittsburgh and sent down the river to New Orleans, where it plied between New Orleans and Natchez. Two were built at the same place in 1813" (1299). Adams notes that if Jackson had gone earlier to New Orleans (as he was ordered), he could have used steamboats to bring men and supplies to the city's defense (1148).

The South was finally able to share the national prosperity. The upper tier of southern states increased its domestic production by forty percent more than the year of Jefferson's inauguration. "The net revenue collected in Virginia increased nearly seventy percent, comparing the year 1815 with the average of the five years 1800–1804; while that collected in North Carolina more than doubled" (1292). The lower tier of the South had even faster growth, thanks in part to technology (the cotton gin). "The domestic exports of Georgia and Louisiana trebled in value" (1268). Those who claimed that the slave economy was not efficient were, tragically, wrong. If anything, this new period of prosperity in the South temporarily made unthinkable any challenge to the slave system. Abolitionism was forced into abeyance — but even that had the immediate effect of contributing to the country's overall self-satisfaction, its escape from controversy, from the ideological wars of the past.

The financial problems of the war made it clear to many that a centralized credit and banking apparatus was necessary. This nationalized the economy under Dallas's system. A general credit apparatus would be used for railroads. Inventions had been stimulated by the war. Engineering took giant strides:

> Another significant result of the war was the sudden development of scientific engineering in the United States. This branch of the military service owed its efficiency and almost its existence to the military school at West Point, established in 1802. The school was at first much neglected by government. The number of graduates before the year 1812 was very small; but at the outbreak of the war the corps of engineers was already efficient. Its chief was Colonel Joseph Garner Swift, of Massachusetts, the first graduate of the academy; Colonel Swift planned the defenses of New York harbor. The lieutenant colonel in 1812 was Walker Keith Armistead, of Virginia —

the third graduate, who planned the defenses of Norfolk. Major William McRee, of North Carolina, became chief engineer to General Brown, and constructed the fortifications at Fort Erie, which cost the British General Gordon Drummond the loss of half his army, besides the mortification of defeat. Captain Eleazar Derby Wood, of New York, constructed Fort Meigs, which enabled Harrison to defeat the attack of Proctor in May, 1813. Captain Joseph Gilbert Totten, of New York, was chief engineer to General Izard at Plattsburg, where he directed the fortifications that stopped the advance of Prevost's great army. None of the works constructed by a graduate of West Point was captured by the enemy; and had an engineer been employed at Washington by Armstrong and Winder, the city would have been easily saved . . . During the critical campaign of 1814, the West Point engineers doubled the capacity of the little American army for resistance, and introduced a new and scientific character into American life. (1342)

Military Nationalization

The country went into the War of 1812 still in thrall to the ideology of militias. Unlike standing armies, militias were not supposed to be either corrupt or stagnant. Since they were under state control, they would not tempt the federal government to use them for international adventurism. Militias were "closer to the people," with all the virtues of amateurism. They would fight with "yeoman virtue," taking Canada (in Jefferson's illusion) by a summer's march. Experience in the war undercut all these assumptions. Too many times the militias not only failed in themselves but crippled the regular army's performance and endangered the national effort.

State control made the militias the playthings of party and patronage deals. New England's refusal to release militias into national service was naturally resented by the regulars and by other militias. The refusal of some militias to cross their own state line was a grievance to neighboring states. The refusal of others to cross the Canadian border made Jefferson's summer stroll a somber jest. Militias were not truly independent. They needed federal pay, pensions, weapons, uniforms, supplies, transportation, and channels of communication. But they liked to think of themselves as independent of these things they both needed and failed to use efficiently. The superiority of professionalism to amateur war-making was illustrated dramatically in the contrast between the trained seamen and the untrained land forces (both regular and militia) at the war's inception. That became more gradually evident as the regulars were professionalized over the course of the war. By its end, the militias were a source of dismay to Madison, of fury to Monroe, and of disgust to the regulars. Never again would militias be called on to play the lead role in national defense. That would seriously affect the way people thought about the relation of the states to the national government. From now on, wars would be waged primarily by regulars, more and more of them under the command of officers trained at West Point. The Indian wars, the Mexican War, the suppression of John Brown, the Civil War — all were to be conducted by West Point officers (fighting, in the last case, on both sides).

Jefferson, who said "peace is my passion," disliked military glory. He denigrated the Society of the Cincinnati. He wanted to disband the navy and reduce the army. The nation shared some of that feeling before 1812. But the war introduced military pride as a force for *national* unity. The revolutionary generation had passed, but a new line of heroes or presumed heroes was glorified during and after the war — Oliver Hazard Perry, Stephen Decatur, Winfield Scott. The fame of some was quick to fade, though they had their moment of deserved renown — Isaac Hull (hero of the *Constitution*), Jacob Brown (hero of Lundy's Lane), Thomas Macdonough (hero of Plattsburg), Joshua Barney (hero of Bladensburg). Five veterans of the war would become president — James Monroe (commanding officer at Washington), Andrew Jackson (hero of New Orleans), William Henry Harrison (supposed hero of Tippecanoe), John Tyler (captain of a Richmond brigade), and Zachary Taylor (hero of Fort Harrison). The pacific Jeffersonians had ended up fostering a militarism that would be essential in extending and controlling the West, and very useful in making a nation. Adams approved.

8

─────◄◆►─────

NATION-MAKING

The *History*, Volume Nine

ADAMS HAS TOLD a dramatic story in his nine volumes — how a nation stagnating at the end of Federalist rule shook itself awake and struck off boldly in new directions in the first sixteen years of the Jeffersonians' rule. In one way, this picture corresponds with accepted notions. Jefferson had, after all, promised a "second revolution." But his aim was initially a conservative one — to return to the original Revolution, which had been betrayed by the Federalists. He would draw back from the world, hobble federal power, let states and merchants conduct their own affairs. He promised to be even more wary of foreign entanglements than President Washington had been. He would recall embassies, put the navy to sleep, get rid of all taxes but customs duties, and give himself little to do.

Adams agrees that there was, indeed, a second revolution — just not the one Jefferson thought he would be conducting. Yet he gives Jefferson the credit for aspiring to a new revolution, whatever its shape. Jefferson did not betray his principles in riding these new energies. It just proved impossible to return to the days of the first revolution, whether that was conceived in Federalist or Republican terms.

In the brief space of thirty years, between 1787 and 1817 — a short generation — no great people ever grew more rapidly and became more mature in so short a time. The idioms of 1787 were antiquated in 1815, and lingered only in districts remote from active movement. The subsidence of interest in political theories was a measure of the change, marking the general drift of society toward practical devices for popular use, within popular intelligence. (1314)

Insofar as the second revolution had ties with the first one, it went beyond it — by completing it. The Revolution broke formal ties of subordination to England. The War of 1812 broke a cultural thralldom. After the first revolution, there remained a psychological sense of dependence on England, or inferiority to it, that had to be broken. The second war broke it:

> Had a village rustic, with one hand tied behind his back, challenged the champion of the prize ring, and in three or four rounds obliged him to draw the stakes, the result would have been little more surprising than the result of the American campaign of 1814. The most intelligent and best educated part of society, both in the United States and in Great Britain, could not believe it, and the true causes of British defeat [as it was called] remained a subject of conjecture and angry dispute. The enemies of the war admitted only that peace had saved Madison; but this single concession, which included many far-reaching consequences, was granted instantly, and from that moment the *national* government triumphed over all its immediate dangers [emphasis added]. (1238)

This psychological declaration of independence went beyond the nationalizing factors considered in my previous chapter — the measurable changes in the country's demography, economy, and military establishment. It changed the whole national ethos, the character and identity of the United States. Adams knew how hard it is to go beyond quantitative statistics to qualitative alterations in a culture — to move from the material base of life to its cultural superstructure. It is worth repeating here a sentence earlier cited: "The growth of character, social and national — the formation of men's minds, more interesting than any territorial or industrial growth — defied the tests of censuses and surveys" (J 31). Yet Adams devised approaches to social history that met the difficulty he identified — both in the opening social history and in these concluding chapters of volume nine. He explored the changed political, legal, religious, intellectual, and artistic atmosphere of 1817.

1. *The Political Atmosphere.* The War of 1812 remade American politics by finally discrediting New England Federalism. Jefferson had advanced that process during and after his own terms in office, but the war completed it. It dispelled any yearnings back toward England as a deter-

minative factor in the political life of the nation. There had been a partial revival of Federalism during the Embargo, when New England felt its old vigor returning — but it was being emboldened to rush on its own destruction during the war, when its trading with the enemy, its refusal to release militias for national service, its resistance to taxes, its religious denunciations of the war, its convention at Hartford, all made it an object of revulsion to the rest of the nation. The Congregationalist churches were severely damaged by their sympathy with England and their railing at "Jacobin" enemies. The attendants at the Hartford Convention could only with difficulty live down, later, their association with it — and some never did. Massachusetts and Connecticut tried to forget that they had encouraged separatism, but others would not let them.

Much of early American political history had revolved around the poles of Anglophile or Francophile attraction. The Francophiles were discredited by Napoleon's despotism, and many Republicans tried to forget or deny they ever entertained a predilection for France; but that became a dead issue after 1817. By contrast, the Federalist discredit lasted. That some Americans wanted to return to a monarchy had been a real if exaggerated fear among Jeffersonians. That ceased to be even a remote problem after the war, when sympathy with England lost its respectability. With the removal of the old Anglophile-Francophile polarity, clear-cut ideological lines became confused. They no longer made sense.

Most Federalists did not want to renew that fight, which had become an embarrassment to them, and the few Republicans who wanted to reassert their first ideology looked out of date. When John Taylor of Caroline tried to restate the Republican orthodoxy in 1814, he did it by going back twenty-five years to argue with John Adams's 1789 *Defence of the Constitutions.* He was living in an intellectual "twilight zone" with the dead. "Political philosophers of all ages were fond of devising systems for imaginary Republics, Utopias and Oceanas, where practical difficulties could not stand in their way. Taylor was a political philosopher of the same school, and his Oceana on the banks of the Rappahannock was a reflection of his own virtues" (1315–16).

Politics had moved on. Old political alignments no longer applied when the New Englander John Quincy Adams was serving as secretary of state to the Virginia president James Monroe, and when a Connecticut Supreme Court justice like Joseph Story wrote opinions indistinguishable from those of the Virginia chief justice John Marshall (1277, 1311). New issues, new categories for dealing with them, had broken down the compartments of earlier theory.

2. *The Legal Atmosphere.* During Jefferson's two terms, the courts were on the defensive. The most that John Marshall could do was check the aggressions of the victorious Republicans. Unlike Justice Chase, he did not try to oppose the repeal of the Judiciary Act. He made a stunning gesture in *Marbury v. Madison,* but did not press the matter to any immediate action. He resisted the pressures to execute Burr by executive direction. But in these acts he was moving cautiously, fending off a hostility to the courts felt by a respectable portion of the community. In Madison's administration, however, Marshall began to find more support for decisions that favored the nation over the states, holding legislatures to their own contracts — in the Olmstead case of 1809 and the Yazoo lands case of 1810. Then, in the glow of the war's ending, he could turn over to his associate, Joseph Story, a case (*Martin v. Hunter's Lessee*) that denied the whole Republican principle of state sovereignty. Legal nationalism could not go further than Story did in his opinion:

> The Constitution of the United States was ordained and established not by the states in their sovereign capacities but emphatically, as the preamble of the Constitution declared, by "the people of the United States." It is a mistake [to say] that the Constitution was not designed to operate upon states in their corporate capacity. It is crowded with provisions which restrain or annul the sovereignty of the state in some of the highest branches of their prerogative . . . The states are stripped of some of the highest attributes of sovereignty and the same are given to the United States. (1312)

3. *The Religious Atmosphere.* Adams recognized that religion was still the dominant intellectual force in American life, but it changed its character drastically during the first two decades of the nineteenth century. In the opening chapters of the *History,* he described the established churches in New England and the South as clinging to their old authority over the community, and by that very fact losing their hold on it. Repeated formulae rather than new thinking had deadened the pulpits. Anglicans in Virginia were beginning to listen to Baptists and Presbyterians. Congregationalists in Massachusetts were beginning to listen to Unitarians and Universalists. In 1800, the bans on theater and Sunday travel were already gone, the enrollment at Harvard and William and

Mary was down, the recruiting of clergy to the established churches had stalled.

It was with relief that Boston welcomed into its pulpits, at the outset of the new century, the fresh faces and ideas of Unitarians. Young preachers of a deeper faith were called to major parishes in the city — William Ellery Channing in 1803 when he was twenty-three, Joseph Stevens Buckminster in 1805 when he was twenty-one, Samuel Cooper Thatcher in 1811 when he was twenty-five (1302–3). There was a new electricity in what had been the stagnant air of New England's churches: "No such display of fresh and winning genius had yet been seen in America as was offered by the genial outburst of intellectual activity in the early days of the Unitarian schism" (1206). This was a first springtime for what became a more famous American movement, the offspring of this one, Transcendentalism.

This shift in the theological climate was academically ratified in 1805, when the Unitarian Henry Ware was appointed Hollis Professor of Theology at Harvard (1301). The Calvinists, forced from their ancient stronghold, had to set up an orthodoxy in exile at Andover Academy (1302). This shaking of the nearest thing America had to an established religion showed just how far the country was from real establishment, and how open it was to change even in its deepest and oldest religious traditions: "In religion, the Unitarian movement of Boston and Harvard College would never have been possible in England, where the defection of Oxford or Cambridge, and the best educated society in the United Kingdom, would have shaken Church and State to their foundations" (1343).

The Unitarians did not so much set up new doctrine, at least at first, as they opposed all doctrine, claiming that it tried to define the indefinable. In religion as in politics, the old polarities and hard lines of theory were being treated not merely as wrong but as outdated. Religion, like politics, was broadened by optimism and prosperity. Channing himself wrote:

> In our judgment of professed Christians, we are guided more by their temper and lives than by any peculiarities of opinion. We lay it down as a great and indisputable opinion, clear as the sun at noonday, that the great end for which Christian truth is revealed is the sanctification of the soul, the formation of the Christian character, and wherever we see the marks of this character displayed in a professed disciple of Jesus, we hope, and rejoice to

hope, that he has received all the truth which is necessary to his salvation. (1305)

Channing voiced a national, not just a New England, sentiment. The emotional revivals of the Second Great Awakening proclaimed holiness more important than learning. Campbellites rebelled against Presbyterian orthodoxy, just as Unitarians repudiated the niceties of New England's creed. Thomas Campbell said his followers must turn from what he called the "jarrings and janglings" of doctrinal controversy to "Christ and his simple word" (1307). The Campbellites were populist mystics, just as the Unitarians were elitist mystics. Both were theologically liberal in the sense John Henry Newman gave to liberalism — "the anti-dogmatic principle." Where the old pulpit had thundered with demand and threat, the new one comforted. "The church then charmed" (1306).

> The Unitarian and Universalist movements marked the beginning of an epoch when ethical and humanitarian ideas took the place of metaphysics, and even New England turned from contemplating the omnipotence of the Deity in order to praise the perfections of his creatures. The spread of great popular sects like the Universalists and Campbellites, founded on assumptions such as no orthodox theology could tolerate, showed a growing tendency to relaxation of thought in that direction. The struggle of existence was already mitigated, and the first effect of the change was seen in the increasing cheerfulness of religion. (1144)

Threats of hellfire, sermons on "sinners in the hands of an angry God," had lost their earlier power to hypnotize whole congregations. "Between the theology of Jonathan Edwards and that of William Ellery Channing was an enormous gap, not only in doctrines but also in methods" (1342).

It must be repeated that Adams did not see this as a change happening only in New England but throughout the nation, as religion became more humanitarian. Standards of democracy were undermining the old monarchical model of religion, with human dignity and human rights demanding moral recognition on their own, despite traditional formulae: "For the first time in history, great bodies of men turned away from their old religion, giving no better reason than that it required them to believe in a cruel Divinity, and rejected necessary conclusions of theology because they were inconsistent with human self-esteem" (1344).

In New England, these religious changes were rapidly advanced during the War of 1812, when the established clergy disgraced itself by its sympathy with England.

Driven to bay by the deistic and utilitarian principles of Jefferson's democracy, they fell into the worldly error of defying the national instinct, pressing their resistance to the war until it amounted to treasonable conspiracy. The sudden peace swept away much that was respectable in the old society of America, but perhaps its noblest victim was the unity of the New England Church. (1309)

4. *The Intellectual Atmosphere.* Harvard, no longer training mainly for the ministry, enjoyed a leap in enrollment in the war years (1322). Like the Boston pulpits, it felt the relief of escape from doctrinal constraints. History, in particular, was no longer the applied theology of Cotton Mather's chronicles. The sense of national destiny, encouraged by the outcome of the War of 1812, would soon be reflected in the epic tales of America's past considered earlier (in part one, chapter two). In fact, many of Adams's historical predecessors were attending Harvard at this time — Prescott, Bancroft, Everett, Ticknor, along with Emerson and Palfrey (1322). When these men looked for models, they would no longer turn to England but to Germany. And when they produced their volumes, Prescott, Parkman, and Bancroft would be addressing a national (not a local) audience.

In 1805, secular learning and sophistication took a major step forward with the founding of the *Monthly Anthology and Boston Review.* This would later develop into Adams's own journal, the *North American Review.* Its first editors were still Anglophiles in style, but they had broken with the religious past. They were Unitarians, and they would soon be Transcendentalists.

5. *The Aesthetic Atmosphere.* The literature Adams described in the *History*'s opening chapters combined the theological world of Cotton Mather with the poetic forms of Alexander Pope, lacking the one man's fire and the other's genius. The Connecticut Wits produced a pallid simulacrum of an Augustanism no longer current even in England. But the new century led to attempts at distinctive American patterns. These still drew part of their inspiration from England, but from the fresh springs of the Romantic movement. They took on the feel for nature that would soon breathe through Transcendentalism and the Hudson River School. This break from a stiff Augustan aesthetic was like the religious break from dogma or the political break from ideology. What was being written stood in relation to the Connecticut Wits rather as a sermon by William Ellery Channing stood to one by Jonathan Edwards.

Adams's prime example of the new American spirit in literature is the genial satire of Washington Irving's Knickerbocker Tales. Irving was not a savage critic like Pope or Swift, but an amused ironist, a mental attitude Adams was quick to sympathize with and respond to. Irving was able "to burlesque without vulgarizing, and to satirize without malignity" — as in his gently pointed mockery of Jefferson as Wilhelmus Kieft, who replaces war with the more powerful weapon of a proclamation (1324–25). The bitter old Federalist-Republican debates are no more welcome here than is Calvinist catechesis. The *Monthly Anthology and Boston Review* printed some of the new work of American writers, including in an 1817 issue William Cullen Bryant's "Thanatopsis," which treated the whole universe as a romantic Wordsworthian ruin (1323–24).

The American painters of 1800 were trained by Benjamin West at the Royal Academy, except for the provincial Charles Willson Peale. But in the new century, Washington Allston came back to America to try something different in subject and style. Adams puts him among those he finds expressive of a national ethos. "The poetry of Bryant, the humor of Irving, the sermons of Channing, and the painting of Allston were the object of permanent approval to the *national* mind" (1330, emphasis added).

Adams's Originality

What sets Adams's *History* apart, in its own time and in ours? There are a number of original features. It turns upside down the previous consensus on the period covered, so drastically that many have missed the point of the *History* entirely — which is not that Republicans became Federalists in office, but that they led a breakout from both ideologies. Adams brings to bear on his daring thesis many kinds of evidence, archival and cultural, that had not before been so deftly interwoven. The book also *thinks internationally* while telling a national tale. No other general account of the Jeffersonians' achievement tracks so carefully the international events that were affecting and being affected by what went on within the borders of the United States.[1] Adams was bucking an American tendency of long standing — the sense that America's special destiny could be worked out without foreign aid or hindrance.

People even now who spend some time in Europe and follow international affairs in the papers there are given a jolt when they return to

America and find whole chains of events around the world neglected or barely reported in our best papers and journals. Some of this can be explained by the lack of a declared imperialism in our past. England and France, Germany and Italy, have memories of colonial life on other continents — "Uncle Henry lived or ruled there." Foreign names, geography, history, and languages are at least dimly familiar to some part of the home population. By contrast, Americans are notoriously poor in learning other languages, and American history as taught in the schools is narrowly conceived in American terms.

Even scholarly history can suffer this defect. You can search the indexes to Dumas Malone's six-volume *Jefferson and His Time* and find not a single reference to Manuel Godoy, despite his importance to America's dealings with New Orleans, the Louisiana Territory, and the Floridas. To this tendency Adams was in decided opposition. His theme is the making of the American nation, and he knew that nations are forged on the anvil of other nations. If one were to ask for the two leading figures in American history during the first sixteen years of the nineteenth century, the normal answer might be Jefferson and Madison. Adams, on the other hand, thinks they were Jefferson and Napoleon. Jefferson's actions were taken in the context of endless joustings with Bonaparte, or attempts to distance himself from him, or to escape the shadow of alleged collaboration with him. Even in electoral politics, he had always to cope with the charge of Francophile leanings toward Napoleon. The fate of Louisiana and the Floridas was dependent on Bonaparte. The War of 1812 was in large part prompted by his maneuverings to pit the Anglophone nations against each other. His power was continually felt or feared or flattered by the Jeffersonians. He, more than anyone or anything, forced Jefferson out of his original plan of disengagement from the world.

To emphasize from the outset the importance of Napoleon to the Jeffersonian administrations, Adams introduces him in the *History*'s first volume with a Miltonic flourish: "Most picturesque of all figures in modern history, Napoleon Bonaparte, like Milton's Satan on his throne of state, although surrounded by a group of figures little less striking than himself, sat unapproachable on his bad eminence; or, when he moved, the dusky air felt an unusual weight" (227). To tell the story of these years without an awareness of Napoleon's role — or, for that matter, of the role of the British ministers, the Russian Tsar, the Spanish King — is like describing a boxing match in which only one fighter is visible. The most accurate depiction of what he is doing with his hands and body will not convey *why* he is parrying so, losing balance, striking the air, falling down, getting up again.

To say that Jefferson and Napoleon are the contending giants in Adams's *History* is not, oddly enough, to say that he is writing "great man" history. These two are like Napoleon and his Russian rival, General Kutuzov, in *War and Peace*, men doing they knew not what, borne along by their people, by their foes, by accident or by concatenating factors seen and unseen — so that they accomplish very often the exact opposite of what they intended. Napoleon abets or baffles Jefferson into policies that succeed despite Jefferson's will. But Napoleon, too, is baffled over and over while he acts with an illusion of control — in Egypt, in Saint Domingue, in Spain, in Russia, at the English Channel. Adams and Tolstoy — contemporaries who were writing about the same Napoleonic years — are the supreme ironists of their subject.[2] While working on the *History* in 1883, Adams reflected on how his leading figures were being led:

> In regard to them I am incessantly forced to devise excuses and apologies or to admit that no excuse will avail. I am at times almost sorry that I ever undertook to write their history, for they appear like mere grasshoppers, kicking and gesticulating in the middle of the Mississippi River. There is no possibility of reconciling their theories with their acts, or their extraordinary foreign policy with dignity . . . My own conclusion is that history is simply social development along the lines of weakest resistance, and that in most cases the line of weakest resistance is found as unconsciously by society as by water. (L 2.491)

Over and over Tolstoy shows his characters carried along by actions they thought they were guiding — Pierre into a marriage forced on him, Napoleon into an invasion forced on him by "an unseen hand."[3] To attribute large events to a great man, he said, is like thinking that the hand on the face of a clock moves the hidden clockworks behind the face, rather than vice versa.[4] We are all in the plight of General Weierother, who thought he was in charge at the Battle of Austerlitz:

> He was like a horse in harness running downhill with a heavy load behind him. Whether he were pulling it or it were pushing him, he could not have said, but he was flying along at full speed with no time to consider where this swift motion would land him.[5]

Why, with this view of things, do Adams and Tolstoy dwell on their respective leading figures? Tolstoy answers that some men are better fitted to be the instruments of "the unseen hand" of history. They are used because they are usable. Napoleon was a force field in which all the hopes and angers and fears of the French Revolution, and resistance to it, and its aftermath, played themselves out. Men followed or resisted him because the same electrical currents were running through them, not because he was giving them the energies they lent him. In the same way, Adams's Jefferson is the only vehicle for a national vision of any sort in America. He offered "the line of least resistance" to forces breaking out of the old ideologies, out of the material constraints and mental blinders of the past.

The passage about grasshoppers kicking and gesticulating on the Mississippi is most often quoted by people reading the *History* backward from the *Education*. To them, it is an early statement of the determinism, even defeatism, of Adams's pessimistic final years. But Adams rightly insisted he was writing a comedy. History can use its puppets for a happy outcome as well as a tragic one — and Adams thought the outcome of his narrative was a very happy one. Tolstoy, too, was no pessimist. When forced back on his own deepest feelings, which were religious, he called the "unseen hand" what he really meant — Providence.

> Consciously a man lives on his own account in freedom of will, but he serves as an unconscious instrument in bringing about the historical ends of humanity. An act he has once committed is irrevocable, and that act of his, combining in time with millions of acts of others, has an historical value. The higher a man's place in the social scale, the more connection he has with others, and the more power he has over them, the more conspicuous is the inevitability and predestination of every act he commits. "The hearts of kings are in the hand of God." The king is the slave of history.[6]

Providence, not Kutuzov, saved Russia from Napoleon. Kutuzov was a fool, like Napoleon, but a religious fool (at least in Tolstoy's version of him). He, too, did not know what he was doing. But where Napoleon had an illusion of control, Kutuzov had a resignation to the loss of control, letting the people wage their "war of the cudgel."[7]

Adams's Jefferson has his own equivalent of Kutuzov's trust in Providence. It is his optimistic trust in the people and in the future. That brought about a resignation to what the people were doing to and through him, beyond his original conception. By trusting that the outcome would be glorious, he became the transmitter of forces that would make the outcome glorious — and would make him accept it almost despite himself. Adams identified this source of strength in his earliest descriptions of Jefferson. "He wished to begin a new era" (J 101). "Jefferson's personality during these eight years appeared to be the government, and impressed itself, like that of Bonaparte, although by a different process, on the mind of the nation" (J 127).

Even when they understand it (which few have taken the trouble to do), some will not like Adams's *History*. I can think of three main groups in this category. First, the pacifists. Adams thought war a necessary instrument for making a nation amid nations; he believed the War of 1812 should have begun earlier. He admits, however, that what was done while the war was being put off — the concentration of executive power by the Embargo, the temporary seizure of West Florida, the influx of western members into Congress — helped bring on and manage the war. Adams's own experience of the Civil War made him think of that conflict as a remaking of the Union, a necessary and noble task. He is harsh toward New England for not supporting the War of 1812 in exactly the same way he was harsh on the Confederacy for what he called its "treason" in 1861.

A second group may object to the fact that Adams says practically nothing about the effect of slavery on Jefferson, on his allies, and on his policies. Adams opposed slavery, but the racism of his time — with regard to Jews, blacks, and people of color generally — had infected him. It was noted earlier that he opposed the Fourteenth and Fifteenth Amendments giving blacks legal status and the vote. In this area he was *too* favorable to Jefferson. To emphasize his great theme, the making of the nation, he is willing to downplay the factor that would almost unmake it. The West was, in the *History,* a unifying force. It would later become the source of division as states fought over the admission or exclusion of slavery in its territories.

A third group that could object to the forging of a national unity is made up of those who do not want one of the perquisites of that, a strong federal government. These may be the most vociferous of all, since they think of themselves as Jeffersonian in a sense that denies all but local authority. They may feel betrayed, like the crestfallen fan: "Say it ain't so, Joe." Jefferson is not supposed to have done what he did. That was, in fact, John Randolph's refrain much of the time. But Jefferson's large vision could not be contained in the little boxes of his first commitment. The finally liberating thing about Jefferson is that he was not a Jeffersonian in that initial (one may call it that Albert Jay Nock) sense. Like most great figures, he was larger than his devotees would like.

But whatever one thinks of Adams's own views, anyone can learn from the construction of the *History* how to study the interplay of the many factors — national and international interests, personal and impersonal influences, planned and unplanned events — that go into a period of great social change. Why and how did the Jeffersonians make a nation? Because they *had* to. They could not make or maintain a government fitted to their time without doing so. Their own acts and those prompting or responding to their acts insensibly but irresistibly bore them along. That is why Adams is right to see continuity between the Jefferson and the Madison administrations, all of it the work of the Jeffersonians. Party-making (with patronage, the Twelfth Amendment, the war on the judiciary), war-making (with Tripoli or with England), the supplanting of state militias with a standing professional army, territorial expansion achieved or attempted (in Louisiana, Florida, or Canada), a vigorous campaign of internal improvements, a central financial system, intellectual and technological innovations, a religious tolerance across regional boundaries — all these worked together in nation-making. But literally uncountable agencies were also necessary to the unforeseen result. To identify many of these factors is not to know them all or have one binding explanation for the outcome. Tolstoy's novel moves on many levels, with a highly personal story to tell, but it reminds us that much will never be told because much will never be known:

> The more deeply we search out the causes [of a war], the more of them we discover; and every cause, and even a whole class of causes taken separately, strikes us as being equally true in itself, and equally deceptive through its insignificance in comparison with the immensity of the result, and its inability to produce (without all the other causes that concurred with it) the effect that followed.[8]

This is the irony of history as Adams traces it. It tells us how the Jeffersonians wrought better than they knew while they thought they were doing something else. In the end, they made a nation.

EPILOGUE

T HE WISDOM OF Adams's *History* has not been generally as-
similated, mainly because it is read (if at all) through lenses
and filters of false preconception. But even those who have
read through the whole nine volumes can misrepresent it to
themselves by trivializing it. Their reasoning goes this way. Jefferson
came into office promising to decentralize government and he centralized it — but why should this surprise us? Don't many politicians go
back on their campaign promises? Franklin Roosevelt promised in 1932
that he would balance the national budget. Instead, he undertook the
unparalleled peacetime expenditures of the New Deal. Woodrow Wilson
was re-elected in 1916 on the slogan "He Kept Us Out of War" — then he
deftly maneuvered his way into the European conflict.

But Jefferson's small-government principles were not a campaign
promise. They were part of a founding ideology, one that some people
think is *the* founding ideology. Others think that the founding ideology
was Hamilton's. The first group believes that Jefferson's ideology won
out in the end. We are a democracy, not a monarchy or an oligarchy. Lincoln advanced the cause of human equality by returning to Jefferson's
great declaration that "all men are created equal." The suspicion of government has survived — has survived even Jefferson's lapses from it
while he was in power. The agrarian economy of "yeomen" is long gone,
but "the family farm" survives as a symbol of many moral attitudes. It is
a sacred symbol, even when the symbol covers large agribusiness combines.

Others think that the clash between reality and symbol in this case proves that Hamilton won. Even the rural mask now covers a capitalist face. Hamilton thought that the nation must become great and imperial, and could do so only on a bustling commercial basis. According to Calvin Coolidge, "The chief business of the American people is business." Our government by corporate lobbyists, our politics of money, seem to confirm that view. It is not accidental that "the Free World" and "the free market" are used interchangeably.

Which side is right? And why does it have to be proved right by appeal to one or more of the Founders? (Hamiltonians recruit Washington, Franklin, and John Marshall; Jeffersonians recruit Madison, Mason, and Patrick Henry.) Henry Adams questioned all such attempts. It made no sense, he thought, to see all later history of the United States as the continuation of an eighteenth-century feud. The idea that Americans can be neatly sorted into Jeffersonians or Hamiltonians brings to mind the W. S. Gilbert lyric in *Iolanthe:*

> I often think it's comical
> How Nature always does contrive
> That every boy and every gal
> That's born into the world alive
> Is either a little Liberal
> Or else a little Conservative.

Yet Americans continue to think we must get right with the Founders. Early in the twenty-first century there was a wave of best-selling books about John Adams, Benjamin Franklin, Alexander Hamilton, and Thomas Jefferson. The authors out on book tour for these works were asked to explain this sudden interest in the Founders. But this was part of a recurring phenomenon. There has always been a fascination bordering on the worshipful with what Catherine Drinker Bowen called, in her own bestseller, "the miracle of Philadelphia." President Kennedy famously asked how such a collection of talent could have come together in the formation of our government. The Founders have the air of demigods. Such piety has, of course, prompted revisionist attempts to bring the idols back down to our level, but they float magically back up again.

This should not be surprising. Ours is not only the world's oldest democracy (it can even be argued that we are the first real democracy), but one of the few governments not to have been overthrown by revolution or conquest. We are the standing refutation of the classical political theory that democracies are by nature unstable. Next to other governments in the West, we seem ageless. England underwent its two overthrows in the seventeenth century, and its government has evolved under a mystically "unwritten" constitution. France's great revolution of 1789 was followed by a chain of mini-restorations and mini-revolutions. Germany has fluctuated to include or exclude interchangeable parts, by conquest or imposed peace. Middle Europeans have seen their borders redrawn by outsiders or reclaimed by insiders, changing "owners" as frequently as Poland did. Russia had its revolution of 1918 reversed in the 1990s. Italy is a mosaic of parts accumulated by interacting revolutions, bargains, and confiscation, and it is now ruled by revolving-door governments.

Against this backdrop, the United States is paradoxically "the New World" with the oldest settled constitution. It is a place that has changed frenetically, claiming ever to be young, yet it is proud of its ancient settlement, an eighteenth-century document that still rules our lives. This raises an interesting question. What is it to have that new-old thing, a "revolutionary tradition"? If it is a tradition, it should preclude or evade the need for revolution. If it is still revolutionary, it should be fundamentally remaking itself on a continuing basis. The poles of this expression can lead not only to contradiction but to accusation. Those stressing revolution can be called "Bolshevik" by the traditionalists. Those stressing tradition can be branded as "betraying the revolution" on which we were founded.

Some think this problem is solved by the fact that America's basic values are capitalistic, and capitalism is itself a blend of revolutionary mobility and traditional stability. As Joseph Schumpeter demonstrated, there is nothing less rooted to the past — more ready for gambles on the future and risk in the present — than capitalism. It professes to remake anything and everything at the whim of the market. Yet those with the biggest stake in the profits of the system are determined to hold on to the power they wield, resisting at least one kind of change, that which would replace them. There, then, you have a revolutionary tradition.

Yet where is this to be found in the Constitution? The capitalist system is no more present there than is the political party system. Protection of property and trade is there. But that is not the same thing as the capitalist system. Almost every government guarantees contracts, thus protecting property and commerce. Yet Jefferson, for one, would have challenged the idea that a Hamiltonian world is spelled out in the Constitution. In the same way, elections are guaranteed in the Constitution, but that is not the same thing as the two-party system we have developed. Nonetheless, some of those defending the capitalist system insist that is not only in the Constitution but in the "original intent" of the Founders. That is the seal of approval endlessly sought. We feel that we not only honor but need the Founding Fathers. Without them we become illegitimate children.

Yet we know what was in the mind of one Founder, probably the most important one when it comes to constitutional exegesis. Madison, who drew up the rough draft of the document but disagreed with key portions of its final promulgation, said that it was a first effort that should be "liquidated" (clarified) in practice. It was like a blueprint that should be a guide but not a prison to contractors working from it. In *Federalist* No. 37, he criticizes what we know as "fundamentalist" readings of the Bible to attack fundamentalist readings of the Constitution:

All new laws, though penned with the greatest technical skill, and passed on the fullest and most mature deliberation, are considered as more or less obscure and equivocal, until their meaning be liquidated and ascertained by a series of particular discussions and adjudications. Besides, the obscurity arising from the complexity of objects, and the imperfection of the human faculties, the medium through which the conceptions of men are conveyed to each other, adds a fresh embarrassment [obstacle]. The use of words is to express ideas. Perspecuity therefore requires not only that the ideas should be distinctly formed, but that they should be expressed by words distinctly and exclusively appropriated to them. But no language is so copious as to supply words and phrases for every complex idea, or so correct as not to include many equivocally denoting different ideas. Hence it must happen that, however accurately objects may be discriminated in themselves, and however accurately the discrimination may be considered, the definition of them may be rendered inaccurate by the inaccuracy of the terms in which it is delivered. And its unavoidable inaccuracy must be greater or less, according to the complexity and novelty of the objects defined. When the Almighty himself condescends to address mankind in their own language, his meaning, luminous as it must be, is rendered dim and doubtful, by the cloudy medium through which it is communicated. Here then are three causes of vague and incorrect definitions: indistinctness of the object, imperfection of the organ of conception, inadequateness of the vehicle of ideas. Any one of these must produce a certain degree of obscurity. The convention, in delineating the boundary between the Federal and State jurisdictions, must have experienced the full effect of them all.

Madison says in the same *Federalist* that the inexactness of the boundary between state and federal powers is just as evident in the separation between the three departments of government — and, by analogy, with all the other constitutional limits marked in the document. There could not be a better statement of the problems with "strict construction" and "original intent." As "Thomas Jefferson" says in a Jon Stewart comedy skit, "If we had wanted the Constitution written in stone, we would have written it in stone."

But there is a problem, of course. This eighteenth-century document is still the law of the land, and it must be construed as such. How can it give us infallible guidance if it is fallible? The answer is obvious, though unacceptable to some. It must be treated as what it is, as a fallible thing. It is a great human achievement, but it reflects a society that was deeply flawed (as all societies must be). The idea of human dignity in that society was very far from ours. It denied basic human rights not only to slaves, but to women, to Native Americans, to recent and propertyless immigrants. Yet some would reimpose the norms of that society on our time — for instance, in the constitutional definition of "cruel and unusual punishment." The eighteenth century routinely practiced things we now consider barbaric — public lashing, for instance, judicial mutilation, punitive treatment of the insane, public execution, capital punishment for minor felonies. Thomas Jefferson proposed the *lex talionis* for the state of Virginia. Here is his prescription for sexual offenses:

> Whosoever shall be guilty of rape, polygamy, or sodomy with man or woman shall be punished, if a man, by castration, if a woman, by cutting through the cartilage of her nose a hole of one half inch diameter at the least. (JP 2.497)

Since he proposed these punishments, he obviously did not think them cruel or unusual. To say that we are bound by the view of his society is to deny all possibility of moral progress.

But how are we to preserve the Constitution once we have become critical of its assumptions? There are two ways: by amending it, if necessary, or by seeing that a term like "cruel and unusual punishment" expressed a desirable norm only approximated in the eighteenth century and more fully realizable now. We have a model for construing the Constitution this way if we look at how Lincoln construed the Declaration of Independence. In his debates with Stephen Douglas, Lincoln said that Jefferson's statement that "all men are created equal" should mean that blacks are the equal of whites. But it did not mean that to Jefferson. That was not his "original intent," and Lincoln was not giving his words a "strict construction."

For Jefferson, in this context "man" had its eighteenth-century meaning, *homo politicus,* man capable of self-government. That excluded not only slaves but others in a state of radical dependency on the *homines politici* — women, for instance, or the entirely propertyless. That women were not included is proved by Jefferson's other statement in the Declaration, that *homines politici,* when they become unhappy with their government, have a right to change it. But women had no such right to participate in the changes of the Revolution. They could not vote for change or have any legal say in drafting the new form of government, promulgating its plan, ratifying its acceptance, or holding office in it after its acceptance. That right belonged to "all men," in Jefferson's sense. It did not belong to any women. Even Lincoln, four score and seven years after Jefferson wrote, did not think it belonged to women.

Then why, if Lincoln did not think the Declaration's statement extended to women, did he think that it extended to slaves? He did not think it extended fully even to them. He did not, at the time of the debates with Douglas, think it included a right to vote or have a social equality with whites (especially any right to marry them).

> I will say then that I am not, nor ever have been, in favor of bringing about *in any way* the social and political equality of the white and black races, that I am not nor ever have been in favor of making voters or jurors of Negroes, nor of qualifying them to hold office, nor to intermarry with white people; and I will say in addition to this that there is a physical difference between the white and black races which I believe will *forever* forbid the two races living together on terms of social and political equality. And inasmuch as they cannot so live, while they do remain together there must be the position of superior and inferior, and I *as much as any other man* am in favor of having the superior position assigned to the white race. [emphasis added][1]

Lincoln still in that sense denied that they were *homines politici.* But he found it wrong, in the improved moral climate of his time, to deny that they were *homines,* as opposed to a species of property. He simply denied the right of one man to own another. Developments in the course of the nineteenth century had made it impossible to think that "all men are created equal" could have any content at all if it countenanced chattel slavery: "I do not understand that because I do not want a Negro woman for a slave I must necessarily want her for a wife."[2] If this is a "creative misreading" of Jefferson, it is one that we have continued to employ. Lincoln saw what Jefferson did not, that "all men are created equal" must *at least* mean that there should be no slaves. Moral progress since Lincoln's time has made us see what he did not, that social equality is not only possible but desirable, for blacks but also for other minorities and for women.

Of course, Lincoln's reading of the Declaration did not become operative until the Thirteenth Amendment was ratified. And since then we have seen radical changes in meaning adopted without such violence. But that amendment was made possible only by a grueling and bloody war. We have tacitly accepted his principle of creative misreading. It is now settled law, for instance, that the Constitution is egalitarian in ways that were never imagined at the time of its adoption. We can change our conceptions without either war or amendment. After all, the constitutional term "we the people" has undergone a metamorphosis exactly like that of "all men" in the Declaration. The "people" proposing, ratifying, and administering the Constitution were, in 1789, the same *homines politici* Jefferson referred to. Yet very few American citizens would read that meaning into the term "the people" in our day, or would want to return to it.

One assumption underlying the creative-misreading approach may be that the Founders, or at least the most intelligent and morally sensitive ones, if they could be resurrected in our world, would accept our sense of "men" or "people" or "cruel" or "unusual," rather than their own original sense of their meanings. This seems an arrogant assumption to many. Who are we to feel superior to such great men, or to demand their acceptance of our view if they want to continue being considered great? Those who judge the Founders this way are often accused of "presentism," the imposition of anachronistic norms on the past. They are said to be condescending to our moral superiors just because they lived in the eighteenth century, and are accused of being arrogant, of refusing to learn from the past. But why should we not accept present norms if they are better? Non-slavery is better than slavery. Women's equality is better than their suppression. Incarceration is better than castration. Anyone who denies this is the moral relativist.

We often hear attacks on presentism without the acknowledgment that there can be such a thing as pastism — the belief that the past is beyond our challenge or judgment. This is a recurrent historical phenomenon. Many cultures hold that they are descended from a heroic time, a golden age. This was the basis of New England ministers' "jeremiads," arguing that the sons of the Puritan fathers had stumbled down a slope into moral lethargy. For us to apply such pastism to the Founders is natural because there is such continuity in our government, with no entire break from their time to ours. It has only once been tragically disturbed — by the Civil War, which nonetheless caused no overthrow at the center. This brings the Founders closer to us than a mere count of years would indicate. We are still in their world, we believe or hope.

That is why some take it as an affront to say that the Founders were flawed. This is revisionism. Textbooks that notice past mistreatment of slaves or Native Americans or women are called revisionist by conservatives like Lynne Cheney and some local education boards. They are condemned as un-American or anti-American. People once fought over the removal of Washington's "I cannot tell a lie" from schoolbooks.

Even if the Founders were flawed, at was assumed or asserted, we should not say so in front of the children. This encourages disrespect and therefore undermines the law. Take the cherry tree from Washington and the republic is at risk. There is a kind of infantilism in American attitudes toward the Founders. This is not confined to trivial things in grade school. It is seen whenever the founding ideologies are invoked as if they can be traced in a straight line from then to now — as if Hamiltonism or Jeffersonianism were things readily identifiable today. This is where Adams becomes so useful. He tells us that those ideologies were not in effect even when Madison left office.

The Jeffersonians helped bring about a country different from the one they had to deal with in 1800. The very terms used to describe it had changed radically in meaning. "Nation" no longer referred to a collection of states. This new country envisaged things the old one had not — projection of American power abroad, an energetic adoption of the means of western expansion, greater hesitancy to punish "heresy," a governmental patronage of science. These could not be crammed back into the old straitjackets of prior ideology. Attempting to do that is what has made people misread the *History*, thinking Jefferson, if he stopped acting like a Republican in the John Randolph mode, had to become a Federalist in the Hamilton mode, as if there were no alternatives to the one or the other. This or that. Either-or. Adams says both-neither. History is far more complex than the interplay of two (or many) ideologies. Chance, mistakes, opportunism, progress, reassessments, forgetfulness — all of them and more concatenate something less neat than anyone envisaged.

There was no going back to Jefferson's or Hamilton's "original intent." Jefferson's "agrarian virtue" was inextricably entangled in slavery. Hamilton's commercial elitism was at odds with the populist direction of the country. Some analogues or extensions of what they said can be found — just as broadening of constitutional meanings can — but constantly trying to revalidate what was time-bound as if it were eternal leads to quibbling and waste of intellectual energy. It diverts attention from what is really happening in the world. It constantly cycles back to childish illusions.

Does this mean that the past has nothing to say to us? Certainly not. Lincoln learned from the Declaration without being slavish toward it. The founding achievement is rich with lessons, of problems overcome, of ways to address obstacles, or brave first attempts at what was insoluble in the Founders' time but not necessarily in ours. Henry Adams gives us sound guidance in the choice he made of a Founder to admire, not ideologically but pragmatically — Washington was his special hero.[3] The most practical and realistic of the Founders were Franklin and Washington — and of the two, Washington had the more important role, military and civilian, in the new government. He had the most hands-on experience of the possibilities and difficulties of the people he was dealing with — in the day-to-day efforts of the war, in the resistance to greater central authority, in the pitfalls of setting up a new government and keeping it on course, in the problem of freeing slaves in his will and providing for their support long after he died. He is often confined to the Federalist side of the ledger, since he supported Hamilton's financial program and John Marshall celebrated him in a biography weighted toward the Federalists. But he was free of the ideological underpinnings of either side — the Francophile-Anglophobe tilt of Jefferson, the Anglophile-Francophobe bias of Hamilton. His neutrality policy escaped both traps.

Washington is the least studied Founder in terms of what he thought, as opposed to what he did — as if he had no intellectual legacy because he had no (or little) ideology. But Edmund Morgan shows how profound were his views on the role of America in the world, on the need to avoid international conflict long enough to establish a republican ethos.[4] Joseph Ellis writes that, though Washington increasingly opposed slavery, he knew that it could only be politically opposed in the 1790s by an extension of federal authority, and that would undermine the loyalty of states' rightists, which would endanger (if not bring down) the fragile new government.[5]

As Washington had a "Fabian strategy" forced on him, against his temperament, in the war, so he conducted a Fabian presidency, knowing what could and could not be accomplished, abandoning impracticable efforts, even when that made him contravene his own best instincts and hopes (as with his abandonment of a plan for Native American "homelands").[6] He could not yet use national powers that would become available, not long after, to the Jeffersonians. Intellectuals do not much study Washington because he was not an intellectual himself. But he had a profounder understanding of what was needed and how to supply it than anyone else in the early period.

> Whatever minor missteps he made along the way, his judgment on all the major political and military questions invariably proved prescient, as if he had known where history was headed; or, perhaps, as if the future had felt compelled to align itself with his choices. He was the rarest of men, a supremely realistic visionary, a prudent prophet.[7]

There is much to be learned from the past — but it is better learned from the pragmatists than from the ideologues. Washington would have been the least surprised or disoriented to see what the nation looked like after the Jeffersonians had made it.

NOTES

Introduction: Reading Henry Adams Forward

1. Richard Hofstadter, *The Progressive Historians: Turner, Beard, Parrington* (Alfred A. Knopf, 1968), p. 30.

2. Noble E. Cunningham, *The United States in 1800: Henry Adams Revisited* (University Press of Virginia, 1988).

3. Hofstadter, op. cit., p. 30.

4. Ruth Lassow Barolsky, "A Study of Henry Adams's *History of the United States*," History Ph.D. dissertation, University of Virginia, 1965, reflecting the views of her director, Merrill Peterson.

5. William Dusinberre, *Henry Adams: The Myth of Failure* (University Press of Virginia, 1980), p. 32.

6. Henry Adams, critique of Brooks Adams's manuscript life of John Quincy Adams, Houghton Library, Harvard, in "Brooks Adams Letters to Henry Adams" (MS AM 1751).

7. Edward Chalfant, "Henry Adams and History," American Civilization Ph.D. dissertation, University of Pennsylvania, 1954.

8. Barolsky (op. cit.), despite her title, limits herself to the first four (Jeffersonian) volumes, and concentrates on only two episodes in that span — the Louisiana Purchase and the Embargo. William Jordy, in *Henry Adams: Scientific Historian* (Yale University Press, 1952), treats the *History* in the light of Adams's later history-as-physics views, which he had not yet adopted. Jordy also finds the influence of Comte and Tocqueville in the *History*, though Adams had disowned them well before he wrote it (*North American Review* 120 [April, 1875], pp. 120, 281, and part 2, chap. 1, below).

PART ONE: THE MAKING OF AN HISTORIAN

1. Grandmother Louisa and the South

1. Manuscript commentary on Brooks Adams's life of John Quincy Adams, Houghton Library, Harvard, keyed to pages of the biography — here p. 5.

2. Ibid., p. 289.

3. So unreasoning is the prejudice that Adams wrote for his family that Earl Harbert and William Dusinberre claim that the *History* was written as a defense of John Quincy Adams! See Harbert, *The Force So Much Closer Home: Henry Adams and the Adams Family* (New York University Press, 1977), pp. 90–99, and Dusinberre, *Henry Adams: The Myth of Failure* (University Press of Virginia, 1980), pp. 26–33.

4. Commentary on Brooks Adams's manuscript, on p. 429.

5. Ibid.

6. Joan R. Challinor, "Louisa Catherine Johnson Adams: The Price of Ambition," Ph.D. dissertation, American University, 1982, pp. 592–93.

7. Catherine A. Allgor, "Adams, Louisa Catherine Johnson," *American National Biography* (Oxford University Press, 1999), p. 113.

8. Ibid., and Challinor, op. cit., and Challinor, "The Mis-Education of Louisa Catherine Johnson," in *Proceedings of the Massachusetts Historical Society* 95 (1986), pp. 21–48, and Katherine T. Corbett, "Louisa Catherine Adams: The Anguished 'Adventures of a Nobody,'" in Mary Kelley, editor, *Woman's Being, Woman's Place: Female Identity and Vocation in American History* (Hall, 1979), pp. 67–84. Some feminists may be hesitant about Louisa Adams's importance because she challenges feminists' investment in Abigail Adams as their heroine.

9. Paul C. Nagel, *John Quincy Adams* (Harvard University Press, 1997), p. 67.

10. "Record of a Life" (A 265). See Jack Shepherd, *Cannibals of the Heart: A Personal Biography of Louisa Catherine and John Quincy Adams* (McGraw-Hill, 1980), pp. 63–64.

11. L. H. Butterfield, "Taming a Dragon-Killer: Notes for the Biographer of Mrs. John Quincy Adams," *Proceedings of the American Philosophical Society* 188 (1974), p. 166.

12. "Record of a Life" (A 265). Paul Nagel says "she never forgave this snub." *The Adams Women: Abigail and Louisa Adams, Their Sisters and Daughters* (Oxford University Press, 1987), p. 168.

13. Challinor, "Louisa Catherine Johnson Adams," p. 109. The letter is in Richard Alan Ryerson et al., editors, *Adams Family Correspondence*, Vol. 3 (Harvard University Press, 1993), pp. 37–39, where it is called "the first extant letter from a famous mother to a famous son."

14. Ibid., Vol. 5, p. 310.

15. Ibid., p. 38.

16. Abigail Adams to Thomas Boylston Adams, cited in Paul C. Nagel, *Descent from Glory: Four Generations of the John Adams Family* (Oxford University Press, 1983), p. 86.

17. Charles Francis Adams, *Letters of Mrs. Adams*, Vol. 2 (Little, Brown, 1840), p. 146.

18. I cite from the unpaginated manuscript of Adams's projected edition in the Houghton Library at Harvard.

19. Abigail Adams to Thomas Boylston Adams, July 12, 1801.

20. John Quincy Adams to Thomas Boylston Adams, July 21, 1801. J. Q.'s regret was not a familial one, but this: "I know not whether upon rigorous philosophical principles it be wise to give a great and venerable name to such a lottery ticket as a new-born infant." This misgiving would make sense when George Washington Adams committed suicide.

21. Henry Adams, Louisa manuscript, "Quincy, 1801."

22. "Adventures of a Nobody" (A 269). The manuscript has been inconsistently paginated by a later hand, and these quotes come from p. 121.

23. Ibid., p. 122.

24. "Adventures of a Nobody," entry for July 4, 1809.

25. Henry Adams, Louisa manuscript, "St. Petersburg, 1809."

26. This seems to be the source for the scurrilous charges against J. Q. Adams, when he ran for re-election as president in 1828, that he had "pimped" for the Tsar in Russia. Nagel, op. cit., p. 317.

27. Ryerson et al., op. cit., p. 273.

28. Abigail Adams Smith, *Journal and Correspondence of Miss Adams* (Wiley & Putnam, 1841), p. 30.

29. Charles Francis Adams II, *Autobiography* (Houghton Mifflin, 1916), pp. 11–12. Abigail's management of her children's lives led her to interfere with marriage prospects she considered unworthy. Not only had she prevented John Quincy from continuing his courtship of Mary Frazier — she did the same thing when her daughter Abigail (Nabby) was drawn to a man called Royall Tyler. Abigail (then in England) told John Quincy to spy on the lovers and report to her in secret: "Cover [address] those letters which you wish *me only* to see to Col. Smith, but do not address them in your handwriting. I will some time or other take occasion to mention to him that if he should receive any letter addressed to me to give it me alone." Ryerson et al., op. cit., Vol. 6, p. 196. Ironically, Nabby was saved from this suitor only to marry a faithless man who was in and out of debtors' prison. Nabby begged John Quincy to take the wastrel son of this wastrel husband to Russia with him, where he impregnated Louisa's sister and had to marry her in haste.

30. John Adams to Abigail Adams, Oct. 12, 1799.

31. Detached sheet in A 265.

32. Butterfield, op. cit., p. 175.

33. Shepherd, op. cit., p. 302.

34. Ibid.

35. Louisa Adams to her son John, Nov. 14, 1830.

36. Louisa Adams to Charles Francis Adams, Feb. 7, 1838.

37. Louisa Adams to Charles Francis Adams, Aug. 19, 1827.

38. Sarah Grimké to Louisa Adams, Feb. 25, April 13, Nov. 12.

39. Shepherd, op. cit., p. 384.

40. Ibid., p. 369.

41. Ibid., p. 409.

42. Jefferson to the Marquis de Chastellux, Sept. 2, 1785 (JP 8.468).

43. Henry Adams, manuscript critique of Brooks Adams's life of John Quincy Adams, Houghton Library, Harvard, on p. 429 of the manuscript.

2. Boston Historians

1. F. L. Mott, "One Hundred and Twenty Years," *North American Review* 240 (1935), p. 144ff. Frank Otto Gatell, *John Gorham Palfrey and the New England Conscience* (Harvard University Press, 1963), chap. 6, "The *North American*," pp. 78–90.

2. Hans Rudolf Guggisberg, *Das europäische Mittelalter im amerikanischen Geschichtsdenken des 19. und des frühen 20. Jahrhunderts* (Verlag von Helbing & Lichtenhahn, 1964), p. 68.

3. Lord Acton, "The Study of History" (Cambridge Inaugural Lecture as Regius Professor of Modern History), in J. Rufus Fears, editor, *Selected Writings of Lord Acton*, Vol. 2 (Liberty Classics, 1984), p. 530.

4. Edward Gibbon, *The History of the Decline and Fall of the Roman Empire*, edited by J. B. Bury (Methuen, 1909), Vol. 2, chap. 15, p. 5.

5. J.G.A. Pocock, *Barbarism and Religion*, Vol. 2 (Cambridge University Press, 1999), pp. 310–18.

6. Ibid., Vol. 1, chap. 10, p. 256.

7. Ibid., Vol. 2, chap. 15, pp. 33–34.

8. Ibid., Vol. 1, p. 156: "De Pouilly had contended that early Roman history was a tissue of heroic fictions."

9. Ronald L. Meek, the editor of Adam Smith's works, gives Smith credit for being the first of the Scots to use the four-stage framework of social development: *Social Science and the Ignoble Savage* (Cambridge University Press, 1976), pp. 99–130.

10. Aristotle, *Rhetoric* 1402b, 1376a.

11. Pocock, op cit., Vol. 1, p. 156.

12. Acton, in Fears, op. cit., Vol. 2, p. 528.

13. Dirus S. Goldstein, "History at Oxford and Cambridge: Professionalization and the Influence of Ranke," in Georg G. Iggers and James M. Powell,

Leopold von Ranke and the Shaping of the Historical Discipline (Syracuse University Press, 1990), p. 141.

14. Acton, in Fears, op. cit., Vol. 3, p. 678.

15. G. P. Gooch, *History and Historians in the Nineteenth Century* (Longmans, Gree, 1913), p. 406. The vast archival material Bancroft collected for his last volumes is in the New York Public Library.

16. George Bancroft, *History of the United States of America,* rev. ed., Vol. 5 (Little, Brown, 1865), pp. 230–43.

17. Hildreth wrote of Bentham: "In moral sciences, and especially in legislation, the principle of utility is the only certain guide, and in the estimation of an impartial posterity, Bentham will rank with Bacon as an original genius of the first order." Introduction to Hildreth's translation from the French of Étienne Dumont's précis of Bentham, *The Theory of Legislation* (Little, Brown, 1840), p. iii.

18. Hildreth had great fun with this sentence of Bancroft: "As the fleets and armies of England went forth to consolidate arbitrary power, the sound of war everywhere else on earth died away." With mock admiration, Hildreth wrote: "To establish the fact of absolute cessation of war on the earth must have taken years of research among the barbarous tribes." See Donald G. Darnell, *William Hickling Prescott* (Twayne Publishers, 1975), pp. 31–32.

19. Michael Kraus and Davis D. Joyce, *The Writing of American History,* rev. ed., (University of Oklahoma Press, 1928), p. 114.

20. Thucydides, *His Accounts* 1.1, 22.

21. George M. Marsden, *Jonathan Edwards* (Yale University Press, 2003), pp. 335–40.

22. *Monthly Anthology,* July, 1805, p. 541.

23. See Louis Leonard Tucker, *The Massachusetts Historical Society* (Northeastern University Press, 1995), p. 178ff.

24. Samuel Eliot Morison, Introduction to William Bradford, *Of Plymouth Plantation* (Alfred A. Knopf, 1963), p. xxxii.

25. A good account of Deane's many contributions to New England history is Justin Winsor's "Memoir of Charles Deane, LL.D.," *Proceedings of the Massachusetts Historical Society,* 1891, pp. 45–89.

26. Charles Deane, editor, "*A Discourse of Virginia* by Edward Maria Wingfield," *Transactions and Collections of the American Antiquarian Society* 4 (1860), p. 94.

27. Some later confusion came from a failure of Adams's memory in the *Education,* where he says that Palfrey brought up Pocahontas not at this Boston meeting but during Palfrey's later visit to London "after the war" (E 923–24).

28. John Gorham Palfrey, *History of New England During the Stuart Dynasty* (Little, Brown, 1858), p. 89: "That he [Smith] was not himself proof against a traveler's temptation to exaggerate is rendered but too probable by the engravings which illustrate his books, and which it is natural to suppose he must, if

anything, have passed under his eye. Among their other remarkable representations, those which exhibit him as taking the kings of Pamunkee and Paspahagh with his own arm show those monarchs as taller than himself by more than a head. He seizes the giants by their long hair, which he is scarcely able to reach."

29. Winsor, op. cit., pp. 63–67.

30. Henry Adams, "Captain John Smith," NAR 104 (Jan., 1867), p. 14.

31. The editor cut the last paragraph of the article, which survives in manuscript at Harvard's Houghton Library. Adams defended the right to make unpopular discoveries, since "the one great literary triumph of our century has been its bold and brilliant application of the laws of criticism to historical composition." It was presumably thought that this was at once too apologetic and too boastful.

32. Bradford Smith, *Captain John Smith: His Life and Legend* (J. B. Lippincott, 1953), p. 301.

33. Ibid., p. 116.

34. J. A. Leo Lemay, *Did Pocahontas Rescue John Smith?* (University of Georgia Press, 1992), p. 25.

35. John Smith, Dedication to *The General History*, in *The Complete Works of John Smith*, Vol. 2, edited by Philip Barbour (University of North Carolina Press, 1986), pp. 41–42.

36. Lemay, op. cit., p. 26.

37. Ibid., p. 27.

38. Smith, op. cit., pp. 41–42.

39. Philip Barbour, *The Three Worlds of Captain John Smith* (Houghton Mifflin, 1964), pp. 24, 258; Smith, op. cit., Vol. 1, pp. 10–13.

40. Lemay, op. cit., p. 24.

41. Ibid., p. 27.

3. Civil War Politics

1. Sumner's emotional yearning for companionship is well traced by Frederick J. Blue, "The Poet and the Reformer: Longfellow, Sumner, and the Bonds of Male Friendship, 1837–1874," *Journal of the Early Republic* 15 (1995), pp. 273–97.

2. David Donald, *Charles Sumner and the Coming of the Civil War* (Alfred A. Knopf, 1960), p. 286.

3. Ibid., p. 287.

4. Ibid., p. 294–95.

5. The flood of angry newspaper reports, speeches, and pamphlets is recorded in June Crutchfield, "The Northern Reaction to the Sumner-Brooks Affair," Ph.D. dissertation, University of Chicago, 1950, pp. 45–67.

6. Henry's brother Charles, who was in Washington too, saw clearly that Sum-

ner was at odds with his father because he counted him one of the "compromisers" on slavery. *Charles Francis Adams, 1835–1915: An Autobiography* (Houghton Mifflin, 1916), pp. 80, 84, 88.

7. "The Great Secession Winter of 1860–1861" was not published until 1910, when Henry's brother Charles released it in the *Proceedings of the Massachusetts Historical Society,* of which Charles was president.

8. Charles Francis Adams, *An Address on the Life, Character, and Services of William Henry Seward* (Weed, Parsons, 1873), p. 48. Adams's father was still voicing his "disgust at the management contrived to defeat his [Seward's] nomination" in favor of "a person selected partly on account of the absence of positive qualities, so far as known to the public, and absolutely without the advantage of any experience in national affairs beyond the little that can be learned by an occupation for two years of a seat in the House of Representatives" (pp. 42, 47). This posthumous attack was so distressing to Lincoln's former secretary of the navy, Gideon Welles, that he wrote a 215-page book to refute it by drawing on the cabinet notes in his diaries: *Lincoln and Seward* (Sheldon, 1874). But Henry's brother Charles repeated his father's criticisms of Lincoln in even stronger terms, attacking "Lincoln's folly" in his autobiography and saying that when Lincoln at last left Springfield he lost time "perambulating the country, kissing little girls and growing whiskers," instead of rushing to Seward's assistance. *Charles Francis Adams,* pp. 77, 82. Henry alone of his family came to recognize the greatness of Lincoln.

9. Charles Francis Adams, *Diary,* March 28, 1861. Charles Francis's interpretation of this interview was repeated in exaggerated form in his son's biography, and was adopted by Ernest Samuels (S 1.95–96). But Charles Francis's misunderstanding of the situation is well explained by Mark Neely, "Abraham Lincoln and the Adams Family Myth," *Lincoln Lore* 1167 (Jan., 1970), pp. 1–4.

10. Norman B. Ferris, *Desperate Diplomacy: William H. Seward's Foreign Policy, 1861* (University of Tennessee Press, 1976), pp. 22–23.

11. Richard N. Current, *Lincoln and the First Shot* (J. B. Lippincott, 1963), pp. 103–10.

12. *Charles Francis Adams,* p. 89.

13. David Donald, *Charles Sumner and the Rights of Man* (Alfred A. Knopf, 1970), p. 25.

14. Ibid.

15. Norman B. Ferris, *The Trent Affair: A Diplomatic Crisis* (University of Tennessee Press, 1977), pp. 171–81.

16. Ibid., pp. 184–86.

17. Ibid., p. 102.

18. On Feb. 14, 1862, Henry wrote Seward's son, who was his assistant at the State Department, asking for diplomatic correspondence on the Declaration of Paris (L 1.283). He also consulted Weed about publishing a paper on the Decla-

ration (L 1.273–74). It was this project that evidently prompted the treatise on the Declaration. He no doubt reworked it for publication in 1891, but the basic text would have been written in 1862.

19. A courier from Charleston was arrested in New York with letters revealing negotiations with the South over the Declaration of Paris. Ferris, op. cit., pp. 112–14.

20. Ibid., pp. 173–74.

21. Charles Gayson Summersell, *CSS Alabama: Builder, Captain, and Plans* (University of Alabama Press, 1985), pp. 8–20. For more on Bulloch, see part two, chap. 3, below.

22. When Adams knew them, in the 1860s, Palmerston was prime minister and Russell was foreign secretary, but in the 1840s their roles had been the reverse — Russell as prime minister and Palmerston as foreign secretary; and Russell had dismissed Palmerston from office.

4. Postwar Politics

1. Adams, "American Finances, 1865–1869," *Edinburgh Review* 129 (April, 1869), p. 507.

2. Ibid., pp. 504–33.

3. Adams, "The Session," NAR 108 (April, 1869), pp. 610–11.

4. Adams, "Civil Service Reform," NAR 109 (Oct., 1869), p. 454.

5. Mark Twain and Charles Dudley Warner, *The Gilded Age* (Oxford University Press, 1996), p. 357.

6. Ibid., pp. 399–400.

7. Adams, "The Session," p. 515.

8. James Gallatin was dead by the time his younger brother, Albert Rolaz Gallatin, commissioned Adams's life of their father.

9. Adams, "Civil Service Reform," pp. 414–15.

10. Charles Francis Adams, "A Chapter of Erie," NAR 109 (July, 1869), and Henry Adams, "The New York Gold Conspiracy," NAR 109 (Oct., 1870).

11. Jean Edward Smith, *Grant* (Simon & Schuster, 2001), p. 483.

12. Henry and Charles Adams, "The Independents in the Canvass," NAR 123 (Oct., 1868), pp. 426–65.

13. He actually edited only five years of issues, since guest editors filled in for him during the year he spent in Europe after his wedding.

14. He hoped to include a seventh essay, on the state of literature in America, but when James Russell Lowell, his colleague on the Harvard faculty, turned him down, he called on Thomas Lounsbery of Yale, who did not deliver the piece (L 2.237–38).

15. NAR 122 (Jan., 1876), p. 39.

16. Richard Hofstadter, *Social Darwinism in American Thought* (Beacon Press, 1955), p. 53.

Notes❖413

17. NAR 122, p. 58.
18. Ibid., p. 78.
19. Ibid., pp. 90–91.
20. Adams, NAR 123 (Oct., 1876), p. 361.

5. Historical Method

1. Doris S. Goldstein, "History at Oxford and Cambridge: Professionalization and the Influence of Ranke," in Georg G. Iggers and James M. Powell, editors, *Leopold von Ranke and the Shaping of the Historical Discipline* (Syracuse University Press, 1990), p. 143.

2. For one of the great British archival publication projects, dating from 1858, the so-called Rolls Series (*Chronicles and Memorials of Great Britain and Ireland During the Middle Ages*), see David Knowles, "The Rolls Series," in *Great Historical Enterprises* (Thomas Nelson and Sons, 1963), pp. 101–34, and Philippa Levine, *The Amateur and the Professional: Antiquarians, Historians, and Archaeologists in Victorian England, 1838-1886* (Cambridge University Press, 1986), pp. 115–18. Levine notes how important was the Public Record Office Act of 1838, which began the process of consolidating previously scattered archives in a new building opened in 1861. Ibid., pp. 101–4.

3. Ibid., pp. 143, 157–62. T. H. Heyck, *The Transformation of Intellectual Life in Victorian England* (Croom Helm, 1982), pp. 147–48.

4. Noel Annan, *The Dons: Mentors, Eccentrics, and Geniuses* (University of Chicago Press, 1999), p. 88.

5. All these terms were used by Adams and students in their joint publication of his graduate students' work, *Essays in Anglo-Saxon Law* (Little, Brown, 1876).

6. Levine, op. cit., p. 79.

7. Annan, op. cit., p. 95.

8. Adams, review of J. R. Green, *A Short History of the English People*, NAR 121 (July, 1875), p. 219.

9. Knowles, op. cit., p. 103.

10. Henry Cabot Lodge, *Early Memories* (Charles Scribner's Sons, 1913), pp. 186–87.

11. Stewart Mitchell, "Henry Adams and Some of His Students," *Proceedings of the Massachusetts Historical Society* 66 (1936–1941), p. 299.

12. Ibid.

13. Lindsay Swift, "A Course in History at Harvard College of the Seventies," *Proceedings of the Massachusetts Historical Society* 52 (1918–1919), pp. 75–76.

14. In the *Education* and elsewhere, Adams refers to his time at Harvard and at the *North American Review* as seven years, counting the sabbatical he spent in Europe after the first two years at each institution.

15. For the importance of *Essays in Anglo-Saxon Law*, see Hans Rudolf

Guggisberg, *Das europäisch Mittelalter im amerikanischen Geschichtsdenken des 19. und des frühen 20. Jahrhunderts* (Verlag von Helbing & Lichtenhahn, 1964), pp. 71–75.

16. Swift, op. cit., p. 75.

17. Jefferson to John Cartwright, June 5, 1824.

18. Jefferson, "Report of the Commissioners for the University of Virginia," in Merrill D. Peterson, editor, *Thomas Jefferson: Writings* (Library of America, 1984), p. 466.

19. Oscar Cargill, "The Medievalism of Henry Adams," in *Essays and Studies in Honor of Carleton Brown* (New York University Press, 1940), pp. 325–26.

20. Henry Adams, "The Anglo-Saxon Courts of Law," in *Essays on Anglo-Saxon Law*, p. 52.

21. Guggisberg, op. cit., pp. 73–75, 237.

22. Adams, review of Stubbs's *Constitutional History of England*, NAR 119 (July, 1874), pp. 237–40. Adams prefers to Stubbs's view that of another Germanist, Rudolph Sohm.

23. Adams, review of Henry Maine, *Village Communities*, NAR 114 (Jan., 1872), p. 198.

24. Adams, "The Anglo-Saxon Courts," p. 1.

25. Adams, NAR 120 (April 1875), p. 434.

26. Ernest Young, "The Family Law of the Anglo-Saxons," in *Essays on Anglo-Saxon Law*, p. 177.

27. Ibid., p. 150.

28. Adams, "The Anglo-Saxon Courts," pp. 36–37.

29. It is of interest that Adams criticized a book attacking coeducation in the NAR (Jan., 1874, pp. 140–52). The physician author of the book claimed that equal education would put too much strain on the female body and intellect. Adams, who admired his grandmother's expertly managed travel through a warring Europe, and her shrewd judgments of politicians, could not agree with either of the doctor's judgments. Adams answered that, in fact, girls show earlier and more intense curiosity for study than boys, and to stifle that would be to divert women into more trivial pursuits, fulfilling prophecies of their lesser capacity: "The facility she shows, and which is generally so much greater than that of her brother, who very often does not begin fairly to work for some years later, often until he is busy with professional study, is to be found connected with her greater interest in her studies" (p. 143). This part of the review probably reflects appreciation of the intense education Clover received at the Agassiz School (this was just two years after their marriage). Adams does criticize, though, the early debut of girls into society and their reading of frivolous French novels.

30. Swift, op. cit., p. 75.

31. The Essex Junto was largely a matter of John Quincy's imagination, as David Hackett Fischer has demonstrated: "The Myth of the Essex Junto," *William and Mary Quarterly* 21 (1964), pp. 181–235.

32. William Branch Giles had written Jefferson, before his death, for information he could use against Adams in the forthcoming contest with Andrew Jackson. Jefferson confused some dates in response, which muddied the waters.

33. Adams, "Lodge's Cabot," *The Nation* 627 (July 3, 1877), and Lodge, "New England Federalism," *The Nation* 653 (Jan. 3, 1878).

34. *The Nation* 138 (1879), Aug. 21, pp. 128–29, and Aug. 28, pp. 144–45.

35. Adams always differed from Lodge over Hamilton. Though he printed Lodge's admiring essay on the man in the *North American Review*, he removed some gibes at Jefferson (L 2.273), and later pretended not to have read Lodge's Hamilton biography, to avoid arguing on the subject — he said "the subject repels me more than my regard for you attracts" (L 2.476).

36. In the notebook, Adams lets his patriotism and Anglophobia show in ways he did not allow himself in the *History*, branding articles as "disingenuous" or saying this one "raves" while that one emits a "wild wail."

6. Historical Artistry

1. For formal experiment in the novels, see Garry Wills, "Henry Adams: The Historian as Novelist," in Grethe B. Patterson, editor, *The Tanner Lectures on Human Values* (University of Utah Press, 2004), pp. 579–615.

2. John T. Morse, Jr., "Incidents Connected with the American Statesmen Series," *Proceedings of the Massachusetts Historical Society* 64 (1930), pp. 370–88.

3. Milton Cantor, Introduction to *John Randolph* (Peter Smith, 1969), pp. ix, xiii.

4. Robert McColley, Introduction to *John Randolph: A Biography* (M. E. Sharpe, 1996), p. 4.

5. Robert Dawidoff, "Randolph, John," in *American National Biography*, Vol. 18 (Oxford University Press, 1999), p. 129.

6. For the rest of the chapter, simple page numbers will refer to the *Randolph*.

7. McColley, op. cit., p. 8.

8. Adams had acquired access to many of Randolph's letters and papers (L 2.339), along with court records and personal details from the 1857 two-volume biography of Randolph by Hugh A. Garland that Adams had at his fingertips (L 2.321, 479).

9. Charles T. Cullen et al., editors, *The Papers of John Marshall*, Vol. 2 (University of North Carolina Press, 1977), p. 168.

10. See ibid., pp. 161–78, for an excellent account of the evidence in the case. In 2004 an opera (*Nancy*) was made from this lurid material by composer-librettist Garrison Hull. See Jonathan Padget, "The Scarlet Libretto," *Washington Post*, May 13, 2004, p. C-05.

11. Leonard Baker, *John Marshall: A Life in Law* (Macmillan, 1974), p. 153.

12. The letter, with Nancy's long response, is printed in William Cabell Bruce,

John Randolph of Roanoke, 1773–1833, Vol. 2 (G. P. Putnam's Sons, 1922), p. 334.

13. Dawidoff, op. cit., p. 131.

14. Paul C. Nagel, *Descent from Glory: Four Generations of the John Adams Family* (Oxford University Press, 1983), p. 50.

15. Henry Adams, manuscript edition of Louisa Adams's diary, Houghton Library, Harvard.

16. Bruce, op. cit., Vol. 1, p. 510.

17. Ibid., Vol. 2, p. 8.

18. Hugh A. Garland, *The Life of John Randolph*, 11th ed., Vol. 2 (D. Appleton, 1857), p. 344.

19. John Hay, quoted in Edward Chalfant, *Better in Darkness* (Archon Books, 1993), pp. 440, 448, 452.

20. Ward Thoron, editor, *The Letters of Mrs. Henry Adams, 1865–1883* (Little, Brown, 1936), p. 405.

21. Worthington C. Ford, editor, *Letters of Henry Adams*, Vol. 1 (Houghton Mifflin, 1930), p. 342.

22. Morse, op. cit., p. 386.

23. Chalfant, op. cit., p. 452.

PART TWO: THE MAKING OF A NATION

I. JEFFERSON'S TWO TERMS

1. A People's History

1. Harvey Wish, *The American Historian: A Social-Intellectual History of the Writing of the American Past* (Oxford University Press, 1960), pp. 133–57.

2. *Cornelii Taciti De Origine et Situ Germanorum*, edited by F.G.C. Anderson (Oxford University Press, 1938).

3. Ibid., Introduction, p. xxvii.

4. Ibid., p. xvi.

5. Lindsay Swift, "A Course in History at Harvard College in the Seventies," *Massachusetts Historical Society* 52 (1918–1919), p. 71.

6. I subtract from Adams's page count for space at the chapter breaks, and count Macaulay at approximately 330 words per page, Adams at 400.

7. Macaulay planned at first to make his history cover a century and a half of English life, but was detained in his efforts at completion.

8. David Hume, *The History of England from the Invasion of Julius Caesar to the Revolution in 1688*, Vol. 6 (1778 ed. in Liberty Classics, 1983), p. 140.

9. Ibid., p. 533.

10. Ibid., Vol. 5, p. 133; Vol. 6, p. 142.

11. Ibid., Vol. 6, p. 148.

12. Ibid., p. 543; Thomas Babington Macaulay, *History of England*, Vol. 2 (Houghton Mifflin, 1900), p. 111.

13. Ibid., p. 124.

14. Hume, op. cit., Vol. 6, p. 542; Macaulay, op. cit., Vol. 2, p. 130.

15. Ibid., pp. 91–92.

16. Ibid., p. 95.

17. Ibid., p. 92.

18. Ibid., p. 106.

19. Ibid., pp. 56–90.

20. Ibid., p. 69.

21. Ibid., pp. 40–45.

22. Ibid., pp. 110–112.

23. Here and in the immediately following chapters, simple page numbers will refer to *The History of the United States of America During the Administrations of Thomas Jefferson.*

2. Jefferson's Success

1. Gordon Wood, *The Creation of the American Republic, 1776–1787* (University of North Carolina Press, 1969), p. 78.

2. Though Jefferson claimed he had no connection with the *Aurora*'s content, when he wanted to make a response to a critic of his social conduct in the White House, he penned it himself and had Duane run it as, presumably, his own editorial comment (DM 4.386). This was a risky procedure, as Jefferson should have learned from his dealings with James Callender — he opened himself to blackmail if Duane wanted to produce letters contradicting his claim to have no influence on the *Aurora*.

3. On the false statistics submitted by Jefferson, see Richard E. Ellis, *The Jeffersonian Crisis: Courts and Politics in the Young Republic* (W. W. Norton & Company, 1971), p. 41.

4. Henry Adams, editor, *The Writings of Albert Gallatin*, Vol. 4 (J. B. Lippincott, 1879), p. 425.

5. This is one French document Adams did not find during his stay in Paris. It emerged later (DM 4.252).

3. Reaching Out

1. Louis H. Pollak, "*Marbury v. Madison:* What Did John Marshall Decide and Why?" *Proceedings of the American Philosophical Society* 148 (2004), p. 8.

2. There is now a "revisionist" school of *Marbury*ists who claim that Marshall (for some reason) actually *limited* the scope of judicial review rather than *asserting* it by saying that he gave the Court no power beyond that of self-protection

when the other branches encroached on it. A good statement of this assault on the "conventional" view is James Étienne Viator's "*Marbury* and History: What Do We Really Know About What Really Happened?" *Revue Juridique Thémis* 37 (2003), pp. 329–61. But a more persuasive reassertion of the conventional view is Noah Feldman's "The Voidness of Repugnant Statutes: Another Look at the Meaning of *Marbury,*" *Proceedings of the American Philosophical Society* 148 (2002), pp. 27–37.

3. Wilkinson's appointment was made just after the trial, but it was known to be in the works beforehand. Jefferson had previously turned him down for exactly the same position, on the republican grounds that military should not be combined with civil office. He overcame scruple in the new situation.

4. The words in quotation marks are taken from John Quincy's diary for the day of the speech. Dumas Malone therefore says that Adams was being unfair to Randolph by following the tradition of "the Adams family" (DM 4.478); but Adams is just quoting the words of an eyewitness on the day of the event, words that did not misrepresent the facts (as other accounts confirm). There was no family bias in play.

5. Malone thinks Adams "does considerable violence" to a sentence in Pichon's report by translating *éclats* as "scandals" instead of "uproars," and by omitting a continuation of the sentence in which Merry and Yrujo are also criticized. Malone devotes a whole Appendix to this quibble (DM 4.498–99). Adams's omission is not a crucial one, and an omission of something is not a denial of it. As for *éclats,* Adams's long immersion in early-nineteenth-century documents gave him a very good feel for the nuances of diplomatic language. The only apparent error of French translation in the *History* is the repeated use of "actual" instead of "current" to translate *actuel* (at, e.g., 571, 660, 703); but even that criticism is not warranted. The *OED* shows that the English word still had the French meaning in the nineteenth century.

4. Three Foes

1. William H. Masterson, *William Blount* (Louisiana State University Press, 1954), pp. 309, 342–43.

2. Leonard W. Levy, *Jefferson and Civil Liberties: The Darker Side* (Harvard University Press, 1963), p. 70.

3. President Nixon would have the same problem when he pronounced Lieutenant Calley guilty of war crimes in Vietnam before he was tried.

4. Levy, op. cit., pp. 72–73.

5. For the dinner party at John Wickham's house, described by Henry St. George Tucker, who was present at it, see Leonard Baker, *John Marshall: A Life in Law* (Macmillan, 1974), pp. 467–69.

6. Ibid., pp. 478–79.

7. Malone thought that this second subpoena was served on the president, but

in my review of his biography I argued that it went to Hay. Malone granted my "impressive detective work," and no longer said that he could claim that the second subpoena went to Jefferson. He thought the matter irrelevant, nonetheless, since he still believed there was some privilege involved in Marshall's response to Jefferson. See Wills, "The Strange Case of Jefferson's Subpoena," and Malone, "Executive Privilege: Jefferson and Burr and Nixon and Ehrlichman," *New York Review of Books*, May 2, 1974, pp. 15–19, and July 18, 1974, pp. 56–59.

8. David Robertson, *Reports of the Trials of Colonel Aaron Burr*, Vol. 1 (Philadelphia, 1808), p. 182.

9. Jefferson to Hay, Aug. 7, 1807.

10. Baker, op. cit., p. 507. Burr expressed his gratitude toward Martin in 1823, when he took the great lawyer into his home and cared for him, after a stroke, until his death three years later.

11. Charles T. Cullen, editor, *The Papers of John Marshall*, Vol. 6 (University of North Carolina Press, 1977), p. 488.

12. Jefferson to Madison, Oct. 15, 1810.

13. R. Kent Newmyer, *John Marshall and the Heroic Age of the Supreme Court* (Louisiana State University Press, 2001), p. 202.

14. Jefferson to J. B. Colvin, Sept. 20, 1810.

15. Jefferson to James Brown, Oct. 27, 1808.

16. Everett Somerville Brown, editor, *William Plumer's Memorandum of Proceedings in the United States Senate, 1803–1807* (Macmillan, 1923), pp. 618–19.

5. Anything but War

1. In fact, the British would later say that the captain of the *Leopard* was not following Admiral Berkeley's orders, issued from Halifax, since they did not specify the use of deadly force to effect a search. Adams thinks this excuse lame, since the *Leopard* was Berkeley's own flagship, sent out on this mission with its captain presumably informed of his superior's intentions.

2. Bancroft thought that the poor maintenance facilities at the Eastern Branch naval yard did not excuse Barron's taking a vessel to sea before it was in fighting condition. One reason Barron could not quickly ready his guns was that spare lumber was still encumbering the deck. In the margin where Adams defends Captain Barron (942), Bancroft wrote: "On this point Commodore [erased word], well acquainted with the officers, did not agree with you. You are in the wrong according to his judgment. The fault of putting to sea unprepared for fight was Barron's fault."

3. Merrill D. Peterson, *Thomas Jefferson and the New Nation* (Oxford University Press, 1970), p. 910.

4. Noble E. Cunningham, Jr., *In Pursuit of Reason: The Life of Thomas Jefferson* (Louisiana State University Press, 1987), p. 319.

5. Leonard D. White, *The Jeffersonians* (Free Press, 1951), p. 7.

6. Robert M. Johnstone, Jr., *Jefferson and the Presidency: Leadership in the Young Republic* (Cornell University Press, 1978), p. 287.

7. R. Kent Newmyer, *Supreme Court Justice Joseph Story: Statesman of the Old Republic* (University of North Carolina Press, 1985), p. 62.

8. Peterson, op. cit., p. 915.

9. Ibid., pp. 912–17.

10. Jefferson to Madison, Oct. 15, 1810.

II. MADISON'S TWO TERMS

1. False Dawn

1. Page numbers standing alone in this section refer to M.

2. Henry D. Gilpin, editor, *The Papers of James Madison* (Langtree & O'Sullivan, 1849).

3. Jack N. Rakove, editor, *James Madison: Writings* (Library of America, 1999).

4. J.C.A. Stagg, *Mr. Madison's War: Politics, Diplomacy, and Warfare in the Early American Republic, 1783–1830* (Princeton University Press, 1983), p. 506.

5. Robert Allen Rutland, *The Presidency of James Madison* (University Press of Kansas, 1990), pp. 39–40.

6. Jefferson to Madison, April 27, 1809.

7. Rutland, op. cit., p. 56.

8. Jefferson to Madison, Oct. 15, 1810.

9. Madison to Jefferson, Oct. 19, 1810.

10. Rutland, op. cit., p. 64.

2. War

1. David L. Sterling, "Pinkney, William," *American National Biography*, Vol. 17 (Oxford University Press, 1999), p. 549.

2. Maurice Baxter, "Pinkney, William," in Kermit L. Hall et al., editors, *The Oxford Companion to the Supreme Court of the United States* (Oxford University Press, 1992), p. 635.

3. Adams is right in saying that "Tecumthe" is a better transliteration of the warrior's name than "Tecumseh," though modern scholars prefer "Tecumtha." The general usage is, however, so familiar that I follow it.

4. Merrill D. Peterson, editor, *Thomas Jefferson: Writings* (Library of America, 1984), p. 1120. See also Jefferson's letter to Henry Dearborn, Dec. 29, 1802.

5. See, for instance, Anthony J. C. Wallace, *Jefferson and the Indians* (Harvard University Press, 1999), especially pp. 220–26.

6. Peterson, op. cit., p. 1118.

7. This is the thesis brilliantly argued by one of the editors of Madison's pa-

pers, J.C.A. Stagg, in *Mr. Madison's War: Politics, Diplomacy, and Warfare in the Early American Republic, 1783–1830* (Princeton University Press, 1983), pp. 39–40.

8. Ibid.

9. Madison to Monroe, March 26, 1811, cited in Harry Ammon, *James Monroe: The Quest for National Identity* (University Press of Virginia, 1990), p. 287.

10. Ibid.

11. Stagg, op. cit., pp. 95–96.

12. John Henry had been commissioned by the governor of Canada, Sir George Prevost, to get information on New England's discontent with the Embargo. When Henry turned up no solid information, the governor refused to reward him and Henry tried to peddle his reports in England. Failing there, too, he brought the letters to America and collaborated with the spurious Count de Crillon in selling them to Madison. After the first edition of the *History*, Adams uncovered more facts about the Count, who was in fact Paul-Émile Soubiran. He corrected the text of his *History*, and published an article, "Count Edward de Crillon," in the first issue of the journal of the American Historical Association, as a favor to the journal's editor, John Franklin Jameson (L 4.286). See "Count Edward de Crillon," *American Historical Review* (Oct., 1895), pp. 51–69, and Samuel Eliot Morison, "The Henry-Crillon Affair," *Proceedings* MHS 69 (1960), pp. 207–31.

13. Jefferson to Madison, June 29, 1912, in J.C.A. Stagg, editor, *The Papers of James Madison*, Vol. 4 (University Press of Virginia, 1984), p. 519.

14. Stagg, *Mr. Madison's War*, pp. 228–29.

15. Jefferson to Madison, June 29, 1812, in Stagg, *Papers*, Vol. 4, p. 520.

16. Alfred Thayer Mahan, *Sea Power in Its Relations to the War of 1812*, Vol. 1 (Little, Brown, 1905), p. 291.

17. Theodore Roosevelt, *The Naval War of 1812* (Modern Library reprint, 1999), p. 251.

18. Russell F. Weigley, *The American Way of War: A History of United States Military Strategy and Policy* (Indiana University Press, 1973), p. 47.

19. Ibid., p. 46.

20. Stagg, *Mr. Madison's War*, p. 193.

21. John K. Mahon, *The War of 1812* (University of Florida, 1972), p. 384.

22. Allan R. Millett and Peter Maslowski, *For the Common Defense: A Military History of the United States of America* (Free Press, 1984), p. 104.

23. Plutarch, *Fabius Maximus* 15.2.

24. John Sugden, "Tecumseh," *American National Biography*, p. 424.

3. Naval History

1. Alfred Thayer Mahan, *Sea Power in Its Relations to the War of 1812*, Vol. 2 (Little, Brown, 1905), pp. 208–9.

2. Mark Russell Shulman, "The Influence of History upon Sea Power: The Navalist Reinterpretation of the War of 1812," *Journal of Military History* (April, 1992), p. 203.

3. Mahan wrote, against those who thought only in terms of large navies: "Because America could not possibly put afloat the hundred — or two hundred — ships of the line which Great Britain had in commission, therefore, many argued, as many do today, that it was vain to have any navy" (op. cit., Vol. 1, p. 71). Mahan is often lumped with "big navy" men like President Theodore Roosevelt, though he criticized Roosevelt's naval expansionism. See Richard W. Turk, *The Ambiguous Relationship: Theodore Roosevelt and Alfred Thayer Mahan* (Greenwood Press, 1987), pp. 57–62. Mahan believed a large navy was needed for the imperial tasks of the United States at the end of the nineteenth century; but he never wanted a navy that starved the other military arms, or that could not be supported by a nation's economic base, or that was disproportionate to the goals usefully to be pursued.

4. Alfred Thayer Mahan, *The Interest of America in Sea Power, Present and Future* (Little, Brown, 1897), p. 177. Clausewitz called war "a continuation of political intercourse carried on with other means" (*On War* 1.24, in the Michael Howard and Peter Paret translation, Princeton University Press, 1976, p. 87).

5. Thomas Mason et al., editors, *The Papers of James Madison*, Vol. 15 (University Press of Virginia, 1985), pp. 530–31.

6. Alfred Thayer Mahan, "Naval Education," *United States Naval Institute Proceedings* 5 (1879), p. 353.

7. Theodore Roosevelt, *The Naval War of 1812* (Modern Library reprint, 1999), p. 17.

8. James E. Valle, *Rocks and Shoals: Order and Discipline in the Old Navy, 1800–1861* (Naval Institute Press, 1980), p. 24.

9. Mahan, *Sea Power*, Vol. 2, p. 216. On the other hand, Mahan believed in concentration of force, and found single-frigate victories strategically inconsequential. The only part of the 1812 naval war he fully approved of was the coordinated action on the Great Lakes. Ibid., Vol. 1, pp. 289–90; Vol. 2, p. 101.

10. William James, *The Naval History of Great Britain*, 5 vols. (Baldwin, Craduck, and Joy, 1822–1824). A sixth volume was added to the 1826 edition.

11. James Fenimore Cooper, *History of the Navy of the United States of America* (Lea and Blanchard, 1840). Cooper, for the most part, contradicts James without naming him in the *History*, but he wrote a detailed critique of him in two parts for the *United States Magazine and Democratic Review* 19 (1842), pp. 411–35, 515–41.

12. This is one of the many fascinating new items of information turned up by Alan Taylor in *William Cooper's Town* (Alfred A. Knopf, 1995), pp. 342–43. He also proves that Cooper's father was not, as all biographers had been claiming, murdered by a political opponent.

13. Walter Muir Whitehill, "Cooper as a Naval Historian," in Mary E. Cun-

ningham, editor, *James Fenimore Cooper: A Re-Appraisal* (New York State Historical Association, 1954), p. 470.

14. William S. Dudley, senior historian at the Naval Historical Center, wrote in 1991: "James Fenimore Cooper was the first and in some ways the best of the nineteenth-century historians of the U.S. Navy. Before him came some men who scribbled, cut, and pasted, but none before him had created a comprehensive and coherent portrait of the American navies from 1775 to 1815." Dudley, "Alfred Thayer Mahan on the War of 1812," in John Hattendorf, editor, *The Influence of History on Mahan* (Naval War College Press, 1991), pp. 1411–42.

15. Roosevelt, op. cit., p. 13: "To get an idea of the American seamen of that time, Cooper's novels, *Miles Wallingford, Home as Found,* and *The Pilot,* are far better than any history. In *The Two Admirals,* the description of the fleet maneuvering is unrivaled."

16. Sir William Laird Clowes, editor, *The Royal Navy: A History from the Earliest Times to the Present,* Vol. 6 (S. Low, Marston, 1901).

17. Kathleen Dalton, *Theodore Roosevelt: A Strenuous Life* (Alfred A. Knopf, 2002), p. 31.

18. John Allen Gable, Introduction to Roosevelt, op. cit., p. xii.

19. Edmund Morris, *The Rise of Theodore Roosevelt* (Coward, McCann & Geoghegan, 1979), p. 154.

20. Roosevelt, op. cit., p. 184.

21. A good study of Humphreys's importance is chap. 1, "Mr. Humphreys's Frigates," in Geoffrey M. Footner, *U.S.S. Constellation: From Frigate to Sloop of War* (Naval Institute Press, 2003), pp. 1–31.

22. C. S. Forester, *The Naval War of 1812* (Michael Joseph, 1957), p. 38.

23. Footner, op. cit., pp. 16–17.

24. Mahan, *Sea Power,* Vol. 1, pp. 322–29.

25. Forester, op. cit., pp. 24–25.

26. Ibid., pp. 41–42.

27. Mahan, *Sea Power,* p. 329.

28. Cooper, op. cit., p. 72.

29. Ibid., p. 85.

30. Roosevelt, op. cit., p. 57.

31. Ibid., p. 19.

4. The War's Second Year

1. James Fenimore Cooper, *History of the Navy of the United States of America,* Vol. 2 (Lea and Blanchard, 1840), p. 310.

2. Theodore Roosevelt, *The Naval War of 1812* (Modern Library reprint, 1999), p. 151.

3. Alfred Thayer Mahan, *Sea Power in Its Relations to the War of 1812,* Vol. 2 (Little, Brown, 1905), pp. 83–89.

4. John K. Mahon, *The War of 1812* (University of Florida Press, 1972), p. 209.

5. Ibid., p. 213.

6. J.C.A. Stagg, *Mr. Madison's War: Politics, Diplomacy, and Warfare in the Early American Republic, 1783–1830* (Princeton University Press, 1983), p. 346.

7. Mahon, op. cit., p. 215.

8. Ibid., p. 244.

9. Ibid., pp. 123–24.

10. Mahan, op. cit., p. 132.

11. Ibid., p. 140.

12. Ibid., p. 136.

13. William James, *The Naval History of Great Britain*, Vol. 5 (Baldwin, Craddock, and Joy, 1824), pp. 382–87. Adams claims, it is not clear on what evidence, that the *Shannon* fired broadsides for eleven or twelve minutes (828).

14. Cooper, op. cit., Vol. 2, p. 164.

15. Roosevelt, op. cit., p. 107.

16. Allan R. Millett and Peter Maslowski, *For the Common Defense: A Military History of the United States of America* (Free Press, 1984), p. 107.

5. The War's Third Year

1. James Fenimore Cooper, *History of the Navy of the United States of America*, Vol. 2 (Lea and Blanchard, 1840), p. 352. Theodore Roosevelt, the landlubber, quotes (without credit) and paraphrases this description, while Mahan, the strategic thinker, just says Macdonough "winded" the boat.

2. Theodore Roosevelt, *The Naval War of 1812* (Modern Library reprint, 1999), p. 219.

3. Donald R. Hickey, *The War of 1812: A Forgotten Conflict* (University of Illinois Press, 1990), p. 197.

4. Irving Brant, *James Madison*, Vol. 6 (Bobbs-Merrill, 1961), p. 300.

5. Robert Allen Rutland, *The Presidency of James Madison* (University Press of Kansas, 1990), pp. 161–62.

6. J.C.A. Stagg, *Mr. Madison's War: Politics, Diplomacy, and Warfare in the Early American Republic, 1783–1830* (Princeton University Press, 1983), pp. 99, 405.

7. Alfred Thayer Mahan, *Sea Power in Its Relations to the War of 1812*, Vol. 2 (Little, Brown, 1905), pp. 349–50.

8. Ibid., p. 48.

6. Shame and Glory

1. Madison to W. C. Nicholas, Nov. 25, 1814.

2. Ralph Ketcham, *James Madison* (University Press of Virginia, 1990), p. 597.

3. Robert V. Remini, *The Battle of New Orleans* (Viking, 1999), p. 40.

4. John K. Mahon, *The War of 1812* (University of Florida Press, 1972), p. 368.

5. Papers of Timothy Pickering, MHS, Vol. 16, p. 225.

7. Peace and Nationalism

1. Bradford Perkins, *Castlereagh and Adams: England and the United States, 1812-1832* (University of California Press, 1964), p. 132.

2. Ibid., p. 109.

8. Nation-Making

1. By using the term "general history," I mean to preclude specialist diplomatic histories in the tradition of Samuel Flagg Bemis.

2. Adams owned a French translation of *War and Peace* (without its historical appendix), published in 1884, after he had published the first volumes of the *History* (S 2.349). But it is not known when he bought it or when (if at all) he read it. He made no marks in the margins, as with books he read.

3. Leo Tolstoy, *War and Peace*, translated by Constance Garnett (Modern Library, 1994), p. 1294.

4. Ibid., p. 286.

5. Ibid., p. 289.

6. Ibid., pp. 689–90.

7. Ibid., p. 1175.

8. Ibid., p. 688.

Epilogue

1. Don E. Fehrenbacher, editor, *The Writings of Abraham Lincoln*, Vol. 1 (Library of America, 1989), p. 636.

2. Ibid.

3. Adams was free of his family's bias even in this. The patriarch John Adams and most of his descendants resented "the General." It will be remembered that Abigail loathed the choice of George Washington Adams as the name of John Quincy's son. As David Hackett Fischer notes, "the Adams family . . . deeply resented the adulation of George Washington." *Washington's Crossing* (New York: Oxford University Press, 2004), p. 443.

4. Edmund S. Morgan, *The Genius of George Washington* (New York: W. W. Norton, 1980).

5. Joseph J. Ellis, *His Excellency: George Washington* (Alfred A. Knopf, 2004), pp. 202–3.

6. Ibid., pp. 211–14.

7. Ibid., p. 271.

ACKNOWLEDGMENTS

My first debt of gratitude is to the great treasury of Adams papers, the Massachusetts Historical Society, to its director William Fowler and its research librarian Peter Drummey. Then to the Houghton Library of Harvard University for Adams's handwritten copy of his grandmother Louisa's writings and his commentary on his brother Brooks's life of their grandfather, John Quincy Adams. My gratitude also goes to the Library of Congress for the mass of archival material Henry Adams brought back from Europe for the preparation of his *History*. I appreciate deeply the care with which Douglas Wilson read the entire manuscript and offered very helpful suggestions. Additional help was given me on specific topics by Thomas William Heyck, Robert Lerner, Irwin Weil, and David Van Zanten.

Sections of part one, chapter three, were delivered as the Richard Nelson Current Award lecture. Adams's critique of the Grant administration was dealt with in my Tanner Lectures at Yale, "The Novels of Henry Adams."

At Houghton Mifflin, I thank the editor who bought the book, Eric Chinski, the editor who saw it through, Eamon Dolan, the manuscript editor Larry Cooper, and the publicist Walter Vatter. A special and recurring debt is to my agent, Andrew Wylie.

INDEX

Abolitionism, 52
Acton, Lord, 34, 36, 37, 40
Adams (U.S. warship), 328
Adams, Abigail, 12
  and J. Q. Adams
    hypercritical injunctions addressed
      to, 19–20
    and marriage to Louisa, 11, 17, 18–
      19, 20, 21–23
  burial crypt of, 27
  and daughter's suitors, 407n.29
  and feminists, 27, 406n.8
  and presidential blazonry, 109
  sons/grandsons broken by, 24, 27
Adams, Abigail (Nabby) (daughter),
    407n.29
Adams, Brooks
  HA letter to, 50
  and Adams memorabilia, 43
  and Louisa Adams's "Narrative," 15
Adams, Charles (son of John Adams),
    25
Adams, Charles (brother of HA)
  HA's biography of Gallatin attacked
    by, 99
  HA's letters to, 12, 25, 33, 40, 57–58,
    62, 74
  on HA's use of "vindictive" in *History*,
    223
  book of on J. Q. Adams, 5
  in Civil War, 49
  and father's coldness, 24

on Lincoln, 411n.8
and Macaulay's *History*, 125–26
as Massachusetts Historical Society
    president, 43
as reformer with HA, 78
as Seward campaigner, 51
on Seward's policies, 63
Adams, Charles Francis (father of HA)
  and HA, 52
  and Louisa Adams, 17
  book of on Charles Francis Adams,
    5
  on childhood travels across Europe,
    24
  on compromise, 53
  first presidential library built by, 43
  and Free Soil party, 51, 52–53
  on Lincoln, 60
  and Macaulay's *History*, 125–26
  as minister to England, 44, 51, 61–70,
    74
  and mother's feminism, 27
  and parents' conflict, 26
  and Pinkney, 272
  pre–Civil War efforts of, 56, 57
    HA on, 59
  Seward wants as secretary of treasury,
    58
  and son Charles's life, 24
  and Sumner, 53, 58
Adams, Charles Francis (uncle of HA),
    21

Adams, George Washington (uncle
   of HA), 21, 23, 24, 25–26,
   407n.20
   suicide of, 25
Adams, Henry Baxter, 34
Adams, Henry (HA)
   career of as historian
      and access to foreign sources, 37,
         38
      analytic comparisons in, 364–65
      experiences of as training for writ-
         ing *History*, 7, 71, 352–53
      and Gallatin biography, 104, 106
      Germanic influence in, 39, 40
      and Harvard teaching, 33–34, 87–
         92 (*see also under* Harvard Col-
         lege and University)
      learned journalism as aim, 40–41
      as military historian, 317
      and narrative strategy in Burr biog-
         raphy, 118
      as New England writer, 33
      new generation trained by, 33–34
      as *North American Review* editor,
         33, 40
      personal wealth as support of, 37
      Pocahontas essay, 37, 38, 41, 44,
         45–48, 101
      and reporting in Civil War period,
         49–50, 61, 70–71
      research in European venues, 45,
         101–3, 130, 313
      and research on Gallatin, 97–101
      research related to New England
         Federalism, 96–97
      and romanticism, 42–43
      "what really happened" as goal of,
         36
   and Civil War period
      in London, 6, 44–45, 49–50, 51, 61–
         71, 182
      and Sumner-Seward conflict, 50,
         51, 71
   economic program of, 73–74, 77, 83
   family of, 11, 12
      and uncle's suicide, 25
      see also individual family members
   on Hamilton, 4, 29
   and Gallatin, 100

   and Jefferson, 3, 29–30, 136, 150, 281,
      381–82
   on Madison, 7–8, 281
      and cabinet, 60
   married to Marion ("Clover"), 99, 116,
      131, 346, 414n.29
      on honeymoon, 80, 91
   nationalism and proto-imperialism
      of, 2
   and navy, 298, 302, 305–6
   and politics, 30
   in post–Civil War period
      annual reports on legislation, 77
      on Grant and cabinet, 76–77
      and Andrew Johnson, 74, 75, 76
      and Legal Tender Act, 77–78
      muckraking reform, 7, 78–79, 80
      and Reconstruction Amendments,
         75–76
   as proto-feminist, 17
   on Randolph, 111, 198
   on role of individual in history, 390,
      391
      and Jefferson, 391–92
   secession hated by, 133, 392
   and social history, 3, 123, 126, 382
   and South, 11–12, 17, 28–29, 30–31
   and terrain of Washington area, 346
   and Transcendentalism, 39
   and Washington, 403
   on wedding rings as slavery badge, 27
   see also History of the United States
      (Adams)
Adams, John
   HA on, 12, 96
      sees as demagogue, 4, 29
      and HA on needed leadership, 139
      HA on U.S. under, 3
   and Louisa Adams, 22
   and Blount secession plot, 203
   books on, 396
   cabinet of, 143
   and Daveiss, 204
   death of, 12
   and decisions made between election
      and inauguration, 237–38
   Defence of the Constitutions, 383
   and emergency session of Congress,
      144

and "family feud" thesis, 4
Gallatin on, 100
and "midnight judges," 148–49
and Quasi War, 153, 161
Randolph's opposition to, 105–6
and son Charles, 25
and Washington, 425n.3
Adams administration, frigates built under, 306
Adams, John (brother of Charles Francis Adams), 21, 23, 24, 26, 26–27
Adams, John (son of Charles Francis Adams), 61
Adams, John Quincy, 12–14
and Abigail Adams, 19–20
Brooks Adams's book on, 5, 13
HA on, 4, 15, 31
in biography of Gallatin, 99, 100
and "Essex Junto," 96, 414–15n.31
as peace delegate, 367–68
and Burr, 118
on diplomatic assignment in Prussia, 17, 19
Embargo defended by, 23, 227, 228
and "Essex Junto," 96
and "family feud" thesis, 4
in House of Representatives, 26
and Jefferson, 112–13
on Jefferson's attitude on Embargo, 236
on Jefferson's submission to France, 195
on Louisiana governance, 375
marriage of, 11, 14, 15, 16, 18–19, 20–24, 26–27, 28
and Abigail Adams, 11, 17, 18–19, 20, 21–23
and delay on arriving in London, 19
as minister to Russia, 23–24, 254, 268
in peace mission, 333, 367–68, 368
in thwarting of Napoleon's trade restrictions, 269–70
wearing of sword required, 177–78
in Paris with father, 24
on Pickering case, 165
and Randolph, 112
as secretary of state to Monroe, 383
as senator, 22, 23, 227, 228

and slavery, 28
strong attachments avoided by, 19
and Sumner, 52
Adams, John Quincy (son of Charles Quincy Adams), 21
Adams, Louisa Johnson (grandmother of HA), 11, 12, 14–18
and HA on coeducation, 414n.29
HA's editing papers of, 7
and HA's *History*, 31–32, 106
HA's proposed book on, 14
and HA on subjugation of women, 95
and HA's view of J. Q. Adams, 14
burial of, 27
on Burr, 117–18
on diplomatic formality, 177–78
and feminists, 406n.8
as feminist and abolitionist, 27–28
on Gallatin, 100
on Jefferson, 136–37, 176
on Jefferson's New Year's reception, 180
marriage of to J. Q. Adams, 11, 14, 15, 16, 18–19, 20–24, 26–27, 28
and Abigail Adams, 11, 17, 18–19, 20, 21–23
and delay on arriving in London, 19
Washington home of, 17
and Moore, 134
poetry of, 26
on Randolph, 109–10, 174
and Randolph/Burr biographies, 104–5, 106
and son George, 25–26
sons "deserted" by, 23, 254
Adams, Marion ("Clover") (wife of HA), 99, 116, 131, 346, 414n.29
Adams, Thomas (brother of J. Q. Adams), 18, 21, 23
Addington, Edward, 72, 175, 182, 187
"Address to the American People" (Smith), 268
"Adventures of a Nobody" (Louisa Johnson Adams), 16
Aesthetic atmosphere, 1817 changes in, 387
"Agrarian virtue"
Republicans' disregard for, 145
and slavery, 403

Alabama (Confederate warship), 66–67, 68

Alert, HMS, 312

Alexander I (tsar of Russia), 268, 269, 333

Alfred (king of Wessex), 88, 93

Alien Act, 206

Alien and Sedition Acts
  HA on, 4
  Gallatin on, 100
  and Henry's defense of Federalists, 109
  and Randolph's opposition to John Adams, 106

Allen, W. H., 330

Allgor, Catherine, 16

Allston, Washington, 388

"American Finances, 1865–1869" (HA), 74

"American History Through Literature" series, 105

American Indians. *See* Indians, American

"American Statesman" series, 105, 116

Ames, Fisher, 131

Andover Academy, 385

Anglophiles vs. Francophiles, 383

"Anglo-Saxon Family Law" (Young), 95

Anglo-Saxons and Anglo-Saxon language
  and HA at Harvard, 88, 94–95
  Jefferson as advocate of, 93
  see also Teutonism

Anti-Corn-Law League, 73

Anti-Masons party, 52

April Fool's Letter, 63, 65

Argus (U.S. sloop), 307, 330

Aristotle, on probability, 35

Armistead, Walker Keith, 378

Armstrong, John, 316
  and Andrew Jackson, 359
  as minister to France, 168, 187, 193, 231, 263, 316
  on seizure of Texas, 191
  as secretary of war, 315, 316, 319
  and engineers, 379
  and Great Lakes navy, 320
  Jefferson on, 350
  and Monroe, 315, 323, 341–42, 348

  in War of 1812, 319, 323–24, 339–40, 343, 345, 346, 348, 360

Army, U.S.
  officer selection in, 301
  politicization of, 260
  professionalism lacking in, 292
  regulars replacing militias in, 380
  standing army established, 372–73
  in War of 1812, 299
    fighting in collaboration with navy, 301
    see also War of 1812
  West Point engineers in, 378–79
  see also Militias, American

Arnold, Benedict, Hull compared to (Jefferson), 287

Artistic interests
  of HA and Jefferson, 30
  J. Q. Adams's lack of, 15

Aryans, HA on, 94

Astor, John Jacob, 293

Augustine, Saint, 54

Aurora, Philadelphia, 134, 146, 147, 179, 192, 287, 417n.2

Bacon, Ezekiel, 240, 241, 242, 244

Bagehot, Walter, 40

Bainbridge, William, 300, 312

Baker, Ray Stannard, 78

Baltimore, defense of (War of 1812), 348

Bancroft, George, 33, 38, 39, 40, 42, 43, 46, 80, 218, 358, 387

"Bank of England Restriction, The," 72–73

Bank of the United States, 112, 251, 257, 293, 351

Barbary pirates, 217. *See also* Tripolitan War

Barbour, James, 284–85

Barbour, Philip, 48

Barclay, Robert, 321

Barlow, Joel, 132, 268

Barney, Joshua, 343, 344, 345, 380

Barron, James, 217–18, 226, 330, 370, 419n.2

Bartlett, John Russell, 98

Bathurst, Lord, 367, 369

Battle of Bladensburg, 7, 343–44, 380

Battle of Chippewa, 336, 337

Battle of Lake Erie, 302
Battle of Lundy's Lane, 337, 363, 380
Battle of New Orleans, 357–64
  and peace treaty, 363, 366, 369
  pride from, 363, 366, 370
  stages of
    First Battle, 361
    Second Battle, 362
    Third Battle, 362
    Fourth Battle, 362
  and steamboat use, 378
Battle of the Thames, Tecumseh killed
  at, 295
Baxter, Maurice, 272
Bayard, James, 333
Bayes, Thomas, 35
Bayonne Decree of Napoleon (1808),
  233, 234, 261
Beaumarchais, Pierre-Augustin, 8, 150,
  198
Beaumont, Gustave Auguste de la
  Bonnière de, 37
Bell (colonel at Battle of Bladensburg),
  345
Belmont, Perry, 90, 321
Belvidera (British warship), 307–8
Bentham, Jeremy, 39, 409n.17
Benton, Thomas Hart, 164–65
Berkeley, George (British admiral), 216,
  220, 221, 225–26, 253, 255,
  419n.1
Berlin
  HA in, 56
  J. Q. Adams on diplomatic mission in,
    17, 19
  see also Germany
Berlin Decree (1806), 222–23, 226–27,
  231, 232, 258, 261
  Napoleon's offer to suspend, 263, 271
  proclamation of suspension of (Madi-
    son), 264, 266
  suspension of uncertain in U.S., 268–
    69
Bermuda (southern blockade runner),
  68
Berthier, Louis Alexandre, 153
Bispham, George Tucker, 84
Black Rock, British torching of, 324
Bladensburg, Battle of, 7, 343–44, 380
Blenerhassett's Island, 208, 212

Blockade
  and HA on hypothetical seizing of
    Texas, 191
  by Britain of American coast (War of
    1812), 327
    New England exempted, gains
      profit from, 327, 355–56
    New England exemption removed
      for, 356
  by Britain of European continent,
    195, 235, 261, 269
  by Napoleon and in American Civil
    War, 71
  during War of 1812
  see also Neutral trade restrictions
Blount, William, 203
Bollman, Eric, 207, 208, 212
Bonaparte, Jérôme, 181
Bonaparte, Joseph, 162, 232
Bonaparte, Louis, 263
Bonaparte, Lucien, 154, 162–63
Bonaparte, Napoleon. *See* Napoleon
  Bonaparte
Bonaparte, Paulina, 154
Bonapartes, correspondence of, 36
Bonhomme Richard (U.S. warship),
  364
Boston *Daily Advertiser*, 40, 57, 58, 81
Boston *Daily Courier*, 40
Boston *Post*, 81
Boston Review, 387, 388
Boutwell, George, 76
Bowdoin, James, 188, 193
Bowen, Catherine Drinker, 396
Boylston family, 12
Brackenridge, Hugh Henry, 134
Bradford, William, 44
Brant, Joseph, 295
Breckinridge, John, 164, 204, 207
Brent, Richard, 279
Bright, John, 65–66, 72, 73, 79
Britain. *See* England; London
"British Finance in 1816" (HA), 46, 72
British House of Lords, and Senate im-
  peachment of Chase, 173
British Museum, HA research in, 45,
  101, 313
Brock, Sir Isaac, 286–87, 288–89, 294–
  95
  vs. Proctor, 318

Broke, Sir Philip Bowes Vere, 328, 329
"Broken voyage" rule for neutral trade,
    187, 189. *See also Essex* decision
Brooks, Preston, 55, 56
Brooks family, 12
Brown, Charles Brockden, 134
Brown, Jacob, 335–36, 337, 339, 379,
    380
Brown, James, 173
Brown, Noah, 321
Bruce, William Cabell, 114–15
Brum (sailing master on *Saratoga*), 341
Bryant, William Cullen, 133, 388
Buchanan, James, 61
Buckminster, Joseph Stevens, 385
Buffalo, N.Y., British torching of, 324,
    336
Bulloch, Archibald, 304
Bulloch, James, 68, 304
Burke, Edmund, 173
Burnet, Gilbert, 36
Burr, Aaron
    HA's biography of, 1, 104, 116–17, 118
    Louisa Adams on, 117–18
    and British minister Merry, 183
    and Chase trial, 172–73
    and Gallatin, 71, 117
    and Hamilton, 112, 117, 147, 172
    and hypothetical seizure of Texas, 192
    and Jefferson, 140
    and Louisiana Purchase, 165
    and Marshall, 140
    Martin's defense of, 174–75
    as New Yorker, 133
    and New York patronage battles, 145,
        146–47
    ostracism of, 147, 172
    and Randolph, 112
Burr conspiracy, 7, 103, 117, 118, 201–8
    grand jury dismissals of, 104, 107
    and Jefferson's defense of Wilkinson,
        213, 214–15
    trial for, 201, 208–13
        and Jefferson's continued efforts,
            213–14
        and Marshall, 201, 208–9, 210, 211,
            212–14, 215, 384
        and subpoena to Jefferson, 209–11
Butler, Andrew, 54–55
Butterfield, Lyman, 25–26, 27

Cabot, George, 96, 165, 304
Cadore, Duc de, 262–63, 269, 274
Cadore Letter, 263–64, 266, 268–69,
    274, 280
    and Armstrong, 316
Calhoun, John C., 115, 116, 137, 278, 351,
    373
Callender, James, 7, 417n.2
Cameron, Elizabeth Sherman, 16
Campana, Madame, 36
Campbell, Alexander, 106
Campbell, George Washington, 333–34,
    350
Campbell, Thomas, 386
Campbellites, 386
Canada
    British vulnerability in, 262
    and Embargo, 229
    as England's timber producer, 278
    goods from New England shipped to,
        355–56
    Jefferson's thoughts of seizing, 220–
        21
    Seward's bellicosities toward, 63–64
    and War of 1812, 278, 285
        invasion(s) of, 285–95, 296, 314,
            316–20, 322, 323–25, 336–38,
            379
Canning, George, 221–22
    and HA's experience of politics, 71
    and *Chesapeake* affair, 219, 220, 222
    and Embargo, 235, 244, 252–53
    and Embargo settlement, 255, 256
    in line of prime ministers, 175
    on naval defeats to U.S., 313
    as opponent, 150
    vs. Pinkney, 272
    Tory government of, 262
"Canons of Etiquette to Be Observed by
    the Executive" (Jefferson), 179
Cantor, Milton, 105
Capitalism, as basic American value,
    397–98
Carlos IV (king of Spain), 152, 153, 157,
    158, 162
    class pose of, 177
    and Napoleon's invasion, 231
Carlyle, Thomas
    and HA's interest in monasteries, 88
    and HA's muckraking, 78–79

Carolina (U.S. schooner), 361, 362
Casa Yrujo, Marqués de, 101
Castlereagh, Lord, 71, 234–35, 253, 333, 367, 368
Catherine the Great (empress of Russia), 268
Caulaincourt, Armand-Augustin-Louis de, 270
Cevallos, Don Pedro de, 187
Chalfant, Edward, 5
Challinor, Joan, 16, 17, 19
Champagny, Jean-Baptiste de, 262–63. *See also* Cadore Letter
Champlain, Lake, fighting at, 302, 323, 339–41
Channing, Edward, 33–34
Channing, William Ellery, 135, 385–86, 387, 388
Chanoyes, Madam, 48
Chapters of Erie (HA), 46
Character traits, Jefferson's geographic chart of, 30–31
Charleston, in 1800 (HA's *History*), 138
Chartres, as "female," 30
Chase, Salmon P., 61
   as HA father figure, 74
   and Legal Tender Act, 77, 78
Chase, Samuel, 110
   death of, 315
   impeachment of, 110, 171, 172–75
   and Hay in Burr trial, 211–12
   as Jefferson loss, 201
   and repeal of Judiciary Act, 169, 384
Chastellux, François-Jean, Marquis de, 35
Cheetham, James, 147
Cheney, Lynne, 402
Chesapeake (U.S. warship), 307, 321, 328–30, 370
Chesapeake affair, 61, 216–22
   vs. fatalities on *Little Belt*, 273
   and hard line on impressments, 333
   in Madison letter to Monroe, 279
   and readiness for War of 1812, 275
   reparations commission (Rose mission) on, 224, 225–27
   reparations offer for renewed, 253, 255
   settlement offer renewed, 273
Chesapeake Bay, 134

British blockade of, 327–28
British campaign around, 342–48
Cheves, Langdon, 298, 299
Chippewa River, battle at, 336, 337
Christophe, Henri, 159, 162
Chrysler's Farm, Battle of, 324, 362
Church-state separation, *North American Review* essays favor, 85
Citizen Genêt, 149, 167, 256
Civil Service Reform (HA), 77
Civil War
   HA with father in England during, 61–70
   HA records onset of, 40–41
   and HA as reporter, 49–50
   HA's diplomatic experience during, 70–71
   HA's experience of, 7
   and HA's hatred of secession, 133
      Confederacy seen as treason, 392
   and HA on South, 28–29
   as disturbance of continuity, 402
   and politicization of military, 260
   as remaking of Union, 392
Claiborne, William, 165, 265
Clausewitz, Carl von, and Mahan, 297, 298
Clay, Henry
   and Florida, 265
   and Harrison as militia leader, 316
   for improvements bill, 373
   on list of western plotters (Burr conspiracy), 207
   and Randolph, 113
   and War of 1812, 280, 283
      as peace delegate, 333, 368
   as young congressional leader, 283
Clinton, DeWitt, 147, 236, 251, 314, 315, 316
Clinton, George, 145, 146, 147, 236, 251
Cobbett, William, 134
Cobden, Richard, 65–66, 72, 73, 79
Cockburn, Sir George, 327–28, 344–45, 348, 368, 369
Cocke, John, 326
Coeducation, HA on, 414n.29
Cogswell, Joseph, 39
Cohens v. Virginia, 272
Comedy, HA as writing, 391
Commager, Henry Steele, 3

Command structure, as fault in 1812 invasion of Canada, 291
Compromise of 1850, 53
Confessions of Saint Augustine, 54
Confiance (British warship), 339, 340, 341
Congress (U.S. frigate), 307, 328
Congress of Vienna, and British position in War of 1812 negotiations, 367
Connecticut, HA's *History* on, 137
Connecticut Wits, 132, 134, 387
"Conscience Whigs," 53
Conservatism
of America vs. Europe (HA in *History*), 138
of Canning, 221
Constellation (U.S. frigate), 206, 307, 310, 328, 340
Constitution, U.S.
HA on, 6, 85–86
and Calhoun on enumerated powers, 373
and capitalist system, 397–98
and internal improvements, 373
interpretation of, 398–401
and Founding Fathers, 401–2
and Louisiana Purchase, 164
in *Marbury v. Madison*, 169–71
and Louisiana governance system, 165
as oldest settled constitution, 397
and state sovereignty (Story), 384
Constitution, USS
Isaac Hull as commander of, 300
as hero, 380
and Roosevelt's accounts, 305
in Tripolitan War, 184
in War of 1812, 307, 308–11, 312, 328, 331, 336
Coolidge, Calvin, 396
Cooper, James Fenimore
as naval historian, 302, 303, 309–10, 423n.14
and HA, 306, 364
on American victories, 311
and Elliott, 322
on Macdonough's victory, 340–41
and Mahan, 305
and New York cultural history, 133
Corbin, Abel, 79

Cortez, and ease of British march on Washington, 342
Cotton gin, 378
"Cotton Whigs," 53
Court packing, by Grant, 78
Courts
Jefferson's against power of, 209, 214
see also Judiciary Act; Supreme Court
Cranch, Mary, 23
Crawford, William H., 98
Creative misreading, 401
Creek Indians and Creek War, 325–27, 358
Crillon, Count de, 280, 421n.12
"Crime Against Kansas, The" (Sumner), 54
Crittenden, John, 55
Croghan, George, 320
Cromwell, Oliver, TR biography of, 304
Crowninshield, Benjamin, 372
Crowninshield, Jacob, 240, 241
Cuba, Jefferson offers aid against Spain for, 232
Cultural anthropology, by HA's contemporaries, 125
Cumberland Road, 374
Cunningham, Noble, 4, 238, 241
Currency, War of 1812 crisis over, 351–52
Curtius, Ernst, 91

Dacres, J. R., 311
Daggett, David (Connecticut senator), 354
Dallas, Alexander (A. J.), 146, 350, 351–52, 353, 371, 372, 378
Dana, Richard Henry, 52
Daveiss, Joseph, 204, 205, 206–7, 277
Davis, Jefferson, 67
Davis, Wilson, 57, 59
Dawidoff, Robert, 105
Dayton, Jonathan, 213
Deane, Charles, 43–44, 45, 46, 48
Dearborn, Henry, 31–32
army's new officers contrasted with, 336
as secretary of war, 31–32, 144, 288
in War of 1812, 288, 289, 290, 291, 323
Winder compared to, 345

Decatur, Stephen, 184, 300, 302, 307, 312, 328, 340, 369–70, 380
Declaration of Independence
and equality as applied to slaves et al., 399–400
and Lincoln, 399–400, 403
Declaration of Paris, 66–68, 69
Decline and Fall of the Roman Empire, The (Gibbon), 8
Decres, Denis, 263
Defence of the Constitutions (Adams), 383
Democracy
HA on, 2. 6
and Germanic peoples, 93
Jefferson vs. Hamilton on, 3, 29
and religious change, 386
Democracy (HA novel), 16, 28, 60, 74, 79, 104, 143
and Belmont, 90
and Rock Creek, 346
Dennie, Joseph, 134
Desha, Joseph, 372
De Soto, Hernando, and ease of British march on Washington, 342
Dessalines, Jean-Jacques, 159, 162
Diman, Jeremiah, 82
Diplomacy
in addressing of immediate grievances, 219–20
and Jefferson's rejection of conventional etiquette, 175–83
as overridden by rulers' blunders, 272
and personal trust, 70
symbolic language of, 181
Dissent, Jefferson on silencing of (1812), 282
Documents Related to New England Federalism, 1800–1815 (HA), 96, 165
Donald, David, 65
Don Quixote, Randolph compared to, 110, 115
"Don't give up the ship!," 321, 330
Doolittle, "Jimmy," 313
"Dos de Maio" (second of May), 231, 232
Dos de Maio, El (Goya painting), 231
Douglas, Stephen, 54, 399
Downie, George, 339, 340

Draft military, Madison's suggestion of, 354
Dred Scott decision, and slave power, 114
Drummond, Gordon, 336, 337–38, 340, 359, 363–64, 368, 379
Dryden, John, 127
Duane, William, 134
and HA's muckraking, 7
on Burr in prison, 209
vs. Burr, 147
and Gallatin, 146, 250
Jefferson's editorials run by, 179, 417n.2
and Pennsylvania patronage, 145, 146
Dunbar, Franklin, 84
Dupont de Nemours, Pierre Samuel, 155, 157

Eaton, William, 184, 205, 206, 207, 321
Economic nationalization, 377–79
Economics
HA's doctrine in, 73–74, 77, 83
centenary view of (*North American Review*), 84
see also Finance
Edinburgh Review, 74
Education, centenary view of (*North American Review*), 84–85
Education of Henry Adams, The
on Charles Francis Adams's thwarting of Confederate naval plans, 69
and HA's grandmother, 15
and HA's mother, 13
on HA's teaching career, 90
and British stance during Civil War, 69, 70
cheap pessimism in, 70
on disagreement between Sumner and Charles Francis Adams, 58–59
and Grant, 79
on Grant's cabinet, 76
and *History*, 5–6, 391
and Lincoln-Seward conflict, 60
and *Mont Saint Michel and Chartres*, 130
pessimism of attributed to *History*, 5–6
Saint Augustine passage in, 54

Education of Henry Adams, The (*cont.*)
  Seward described in, 57
  on Sumner rift, 59
  and Sumner's checking of Seward, 65
  and Sumner's election as senator, 53
  and Teutonic thesis, 93
  and Washington experience, 50
Edward the Confessor, 93
Edwards, Jonathan, 41–42, 131, 386, 387
Eggleston, Edward, 123
Eldon, Lord, 72
Election of 1800, 140, 144, 160, 333
Election of 1804, 183
Election of 1808, 236–37
Elliott, Jesse, 302, 305, 321, 322
Ellis, Billy (slave), 107
Ellis, Joseph, 403
Ellsworth, Oliver, 333
Embargo (1807), 223–25, 234–36, 261
  acts to supplement, 227
  HA on, 96–97
  and HA on J. Q. Adams, 13
  and HA on Jefferson, 4
  J. Q. Adams support for, 23
  American manufacturers blessed by, 252
  as bargaining chip against Orders in Council, 235, 240
  and 1808 election, 237
  executive power concentrated from, 392
  Gallatin's enforcement ad absurdum of (Enforcement Act), 241–42, 243–44
  Indians harmed by, 275
  Jefferson's conspiratorial explanation for failure of, 240–41, 242
  Jefferson's loss of self-confidence over, 239, 240
  and Jefferson's post-election torpor, 237
  and Macon's Bill, 257
  Madison on, 281–82
  and Madison's forbearance toward New England, 356
  Napoleon aided by, 233
  nationalizing effect of, 216
  New England resistance to, 227–30, 242, 243
  Randolph's early version of, 196
  repeal of, 244, 251
    Congressional debate on, 242–43
    Turreau on, 252
  Republican coalition unraveling under, 250
  seen as success (1809), 253, 254
  and slave power, 114
  and U.S. impasse in French-British conflict, 260–61
Emerson, Ralph Waldo
  at Harvard, 387
  journal of, 39
  and Sumner, 52
Emerson, William, 42
Eminent Victorians (Lytton Strachey), 99
Emmons, George, 304
Endymion (British frigate), 370
Enforcement Act (1808), 241–42, 243–44, 261
England (Britain)
  and Burr conspiracy, 202
  Canadian timber needed by, 278
  Chesapeake affair hatred in, 221 (*see also Chesapeake* affair)
  considered as possible ally, 150, 155, 158, 176, 188–90, 198, 199, 233
  discord in (1810), 262
  and Federalism, 383
  and Floridas
    ceded to Spain, 166
    and Monroe in London, 187, 188
    and Napoleon's aims, 153–54
    U.S. seizure of West Florida protested, 274, 367
    see also Floridas
  and Jeffersonians, 175–76
  Jefferson welcomes trouble with, 220
  Madison sparring with over trade and reparations, 252–57
  and neutral trade, 195–96, 222–23, 260–62
  and *Essex* decision, 187, 189, 193, 194, 195–96, 200, 222
  and impressments, 195–96, 200 (*see also* Impressment)
  and Macon's Bills, 257–58
  and Madison on Britain's "original sin," 262

negotiation efforts, 198–201, 224, 225–27, 253–56, 271–74
one-sided impact of, 194–95
Orders in Council, 223, 235, 253, 261, 288 (*see also* Orders in Council)
Stephen's book on, 193–95, 221
revolutions in, 397
see also London
Enlightenment
and historical method, 34, 35–36, 41
Scottish, 35, 126, 132
"Entangling alliances," Jefferson's renunciation of, 142–43, 381
Enterprise, USS, 184
Entropy, historical, 130
Enumerated powers, Calhoun on, 373
Eppes, John, 352
Erie, Lake, War of 1812 on, 319, 320–22, 336
Erie Canal, 374, 378
Erie Railroad takeover, 78, 79
Erskine, David, 218–19, 253, 255–56, 263, 264, 267
Essays in Anglo-Saxon Law (HA et al.), 88, 91, 92
Essex, USS, 311–12, 328
Essex decision, 187, 189, 193, 194, 195–96, 200, 222
"Essex Junto," 96, 414–15n.31
Esther (HA novel), 39, 104, 131
Eustis, William, 251, 259, 296, 299, 301, 315, 319
Evarts, William, 74, 76, 101
Everett, Edward, 33, 38, 39, 387
Examination of the British Doctrine Which Subjects to Capture a Neutral Trade Not Open in Time of Peace (Madison), 194

Fabius Maximus, 295
"Family farm" as symbol, 395
"Family feud" thesis
of the *History*, 4–5
on Randolph biography, 105
Federalist, The, and Madison, 197, 250
    Federalist No. 37, 398
    Federalist No. 46, 356
Federalists and Federalism, 376–77
    HA on, 4, 5

and British monarchy, 175
and Burr conspiracy, 204, 209, 210
and 1808 election(s), 236, 237
and 1817 political atmosphere, 382–83
and Embargo, 230, 233, 251–52
Hildreth as defender of, 40
and Jackson (English emissary), 256
vs. Jefferson, 137
and Jefferson's first inaugural, 141, 142
Madison's removal suggested by, 350
national vision forfeited by, 284
naval officers as, 301
navy prepared by (TR), 288
and neutral-trade conflicts, 262
on peacetime army, 372
and prosperity, 377
and religion, 131
in resistance to 1802 closure of New Orleans, 156
revival of (War of 1812), 357
William Graham Sumner for, 83
and War of 1812, 282, 283, 310
    and Battle of New Orleans, 363
    and DeWitt Clinton's candidacy, 314
    and draft, 354
    and young war Republicans, 283
Federal Republican, 352
Feminism, of Abigail and Louisa Adams, 27, 406n.8
Fernando (son of Carlos IV of Spain), 231
Fielding, Henry, 113
Fifteenth Amendment, HA's opposition to, 75, 392
Finance
    Dallas's postwar demand for payment in specie, 371
    new credit system, 372
    War of 1812 brings crisis of, 350–52
    and Monroe's desperation, 355
    as War of 1812 fault, 293–94
Fingal (southern blockade runner), 68
First Battle of New Orleans, 361
First Embargo Supplementary Act, 227
Fisk, Jim, 78, 79
Fiske, John, 123
Florida (Confederate warship), 68

Floridas, 166–69, 176
and British peace treaty ambitions, 367
Clay on rights to, 265
and Godoy, 389
Jackson aims to conquer, 358–59
and Jefferson's cultivation of Napoleon, 195, 233
and attitude toward England, 220
and Jefferson on Spain's attitude, 188
and Jefferson on Spain's overthrow, 232
and Jefferson on war with Britain, 221–22
and Louisiana intrigues, 153–54, 157–58
and Madison administration
Madison's hopes for, 264
Napoleon seen as key to acquisition of, 253
U.S. attempt to start rebellion in, 265
and War of 1812, 325
and Monroe in Spain, 186
and Napoleon, 389
and Berlin Decree, 222
offer of, 231, 234
proposal for handover of (1805), 190–93, 197
spurning of overtures on, 236
on U.S. acquisition of, 269
and neutral-trade negotiations, 199
West Florida, 157–58, 162
rebellion in and U.S. seizure of, 264–65, 274, 373, 392
Floyd, John, 326
Ford, Worthington, 117
Foreign policy under Jefferson administration, 149–52, 160
and *Chesapeake* affair, 216–22
and disregard of diplomatic etiquette, 175–83
and "double messages" to Congress, 193
Embargo, 223–25, 234–36, 261
and Enforcement Act, 241–42, 243–44
in post-election period, 237, 240–41, 242–43
repeal of, 244, 251

seen as success (1809), 253, 254
see also Embargo
and Floridas, 166–69, 176, 186
and Louisiana/Florida intrigues, 152–59
Louisiana Purchase, 162–66
and Napoleon's invasion of Spain, 231–34
negotiations with France/Spain/England over Florida and other issues (1805), 186–93
and neutral trade, 193–201, 222–27
Tripolitan War, 148, 161, 183–85
Foreign policy under Madison administration
and Floridas
attempt to stir up East Florida, 265
West Florida seized after rebellion, 264–65
and neutral trade, 253–56, 260–62, 273–75
see also War of 1812
Forester, C. S., 306, 308
"Forest mysticism," 124
Fort Bowyer, 354
Fort Dearborn, 314, 322
Fort Erie, 336, 337, 379
Fort George, 324, 336
Fort Malden, 317–18, 319
Fort McHenry, 348
Fort Meigs, 319, 320, 322, 379
Fort Mims, 325–26
Fort Niagara, 324–25
Fort Stephenson, 320
Foster, Augustus, 273–74
Fouché, Joseph, 263
Founding Fathers
legitimacy from, 398
and pastism, 402
in present-day world, 401
worshipful attitude toward, 396, 402
Fourteenth Amendment, HA's opposition to, 75, 392
Fourth Battle of New Orleans, 362
Fox, Charles James, 175, 198, 261
France
HA research in, 101, 102
disunity in, 262
England's trade measures against, 260–62

and Floridas
  and Jefferson on Spanish aggres-
    sions, 192
  and Monroe mission, 186
  proposal for $10 million handover,
    190–91
  and U.S. designs on, 158
  and U.S.-England conflict, 220
  see also Floridas
Jefferson as fearful toward, 176
Jefferson sees as ally against England,
  199
and Louisiana, 166
  and closing of New Orleans ship-
    ping deposits, 156
  retrocession of, 152–53
  see also Louisiana Purchase; Loui-
    siana Territory
Monroe in, 157, 162, 163–64, 188
and neutral trade, 194, 195 (*see also*
  Neutral trade restrictions)
revolutionary past of, 397
and U.S. attempts to acquire Florida
  and Texas (1805), 187, 188–93
see also Napoleon Bonaparte
Francophiles vs. Anglophiles, 383
Franklin, Benjamin
  books on, 396
  and Hamiltonians, 396
  as practical economist, 84
  as practical and realistic, 403
Frazier, Mary, 16, 18, 21–22, 407n.29
Freeman, Edward A., 87, 88
Free Soil party, 51, 52
French and Indian War, memories of,
  188
French Revolution
  and Monroe, 279
  and Napoleon, 391
  and Republican-Federalist conflict,
    142
Fries, John, 212
Frigates of U.S. Navy, 184, 185, 225, 296,
  301, 302, 306–14, 327, 331. *See
  also specific vessels*
Frolic, HMS, 312
Frontiers, Turner's view of, 375
Fugitive Slave Law, and slave power,
  114
Fulton, Robert, 132

Fundamentalism, and Madison on Constitution, 398

Galileo, and stolen Vatican archives, 36
Gallatin, Albert, 100–101
  and HA, 3, 11–12, 78, 97
    HA's "Life" of, 1, 29, 97–101
    HA's work on economic reform, 7
    "as Virginian," 12, 28, 100, 133
  and Burr, 117
  and impeachment of Chase, 173
  and Burr vs. Jefferson, 71
  canal system as hope of, 374
  and *Chesapeake* affair, 216, 218, 219
  Duane's attacks on, 146
  in 1805 diplomatic crisis, 189
  on Embargo, 224, 237
  and Embargo implementation, 228,
    229, 243
  and England, 175
  and financial views of Jefferson and
    Madison, 281
  foes of
    "the Invisibles," 267
    in Pennsylvania, 134
  and foreign affairs role, 149
  and Jefferson as diplomat, 150
  and Jefferson's post-election torpor,
    238
  and Macon's Bill, 257–58
  Madison's abortive effort to make sec-
    retary of state, 250
  and negotiations over attempts to ac-
    quire Florida and Texas, 189, 193
  and navy, 298
  on new credit system, 372
  on peace mission, 333, 367–68, 369
  as practical economist, 84
  and Randolph, 197
  Rose informed of war threat by, 227
  as secretary of treasury, 144, 146
    distress of, 257
    and England's appointment of
      Jackson, 255
    and Jones on cabinet, 259
    Madison's struggle to reappoint,
      251
    and patronage, 145–46, 147
    resignation offered, 267
    vs. Smith, 315

Gallatin, Albert (*cont.*)
  and taxes against public debt, 147–48
  tenure ended, 333–34
  and War of 1812, 293, 298
  U.S. improved under, 4
  and war coming with Britain (1808–1809), 224, 229, 242
  and proposal to reinstate gunboats, 243–44
  and War of 1812, 3, 282
    Madison letter to, 288
    and plan for attacking Florida, 325
  and Whiskey Rebellion, 134
  wife of, 31
  on Wilkinson, 203, 206
  and Yazoo issue, 111
  and young war Republicans, 283
Gallatin, James, 78
Gardinier, Barent, 254
Garibaldi, Giuseppe, HA interview with, 40, 41
Garland, Hamlin, 115
Gaskell, Charles Milnes, 88
  HA letters to, 5, 14, 89
  Essays in Anglo-Saxon Law to, 92
General Greene (U.S. frigate), 321
General History (Smith), 45, 46, 48
Genêt, Citizen, 149, 167, 256
Geographic nationalization, 374–77
Geography of eastern U.S.
  HA on mountains as divisive, 128–29
  HA on Pennsylvania-Virginia affinity, 134–35
  and Mississippi as West's avenue to outside world, 203
George III (king of England)
  class pose of, 177
  Napoleon equated with, 232
Germanic peoples. *See* Teutonism
Germans' Rise and Territory, The (Tacitus), 124
Germany
  HA in, 33, 39, 40, 50
  American historians studying in, 39
  and Bancroft, 38
  changing boundaries of, 397
  historical models sought in, 387

  state-subsidized research programs in, 37
  see also Berlin
Ghent, peace negotiations in, 334, 357, 366
Gibbon, Edward, 6, 8, 33, 34–35, 36
Gilbert, W. S. (*Iolanthe*), on political categorization, 396
Gilded Age, 74, 375
Gilded Age, The (Twain), 77
Giles, William Branch, 71, 98, 149, 170, 171, 209, 214, 250, 280
Gilman, Daniel Coit, 84–85, 90
Gilmore, James, 304
Giskon, 295
Gladiator (southern blockade runner), 68
Glorious Revolution, Macaulay on, 93, 126
Gneist, Rudolf von, 91
Godkin, E. L., 85, 99–100
Godoy, Manuel
  and HA's archival material, 103, 150
  finesse and force for, 193
  and *History*, 8
  and hypothesis of U.S. seizure of Texas, 191
  and Louisiana proposal from France, 152, 153–54
  Malone's neglect of, 389
  and Mobile Act, 167, 168
  and Monroe's mission, 187
  and Napoleon, 158, 161, 162, 231
  and New Orleans closing, 156
  as opponent, 150, 190
Goethe, Johann Wolfgang von 39, 88
Goodrich, Elizur, 145
Gore, Christopher (senator from Massachusetts), 355
Gothenburg, Sweden, peace negotiations proposed for, 334
Goulburn, Henry, 368
Gould, Jay, 78, 79
Governance act for Louisiana, 164–65, 375
Governmental powers, transportation improvement as (Macaulay), 128
Graham, John, 207
Granger, Gideon, 145, 174

Grant, Ulysses S.
  HA and cabinet choices of, 60, 76–77, 143
  and Jefferson's or Madison's advisers, 7
  HA's hopes for, 76
  court packing by, 78
  and gold conspiracy, 79
Grant, Ulysses S., Jr., 90
Grant, Virginia, 79
Graybell (rumor-monger against Martin), 210
Great Britain. *See* England; London
Great Lakes
  warships built for service on, 306
  see also Lake Erie, War of 1812 on
"Great man" theory of history, as different from HA's history, 390
"Great Secession Winter, The" (HA), 41, 59
Greece, freedom championed for, 232
Green, John Richard, 87, 91, 123
Grigsby, Hugh Blair, 97, 98
Grimké, Angelina and Sarah, 27–28
Griswold, Roger, 183
Grote, George, 37
Grotius, Hugo, 194
Grzanowski, Ernst, 91
Guerrière (British warship), 310–11, 312, 314, 336
Guggisberg, Hans Rudolf, 93–94
Guides, Philosophers, Friends (Thwing), 90
Gulf Stream, Jefferson's claim on, 287
Gunboats
  artillery pieces from (Battle of Bladensburg), 343
  in Chesapeake Bay (War of 1812), 328
  in Embargo implementation, 224
  Jefferson's program for, 225
  at New Orleans, 360
  proposal to rehabilitate, 243–44
  sold off, 372
Gurney, Edward, 33
Gurney, Ephraim, 79–80

Habeas corpus
  and Burr conspiracy, 207, 208

Jackson recommends New Orleans suspension of, 360
Haiti. *See* Saint Domingue
Hall, Bolling, 351
Hamilton, Alexander
  HA on, 4, 29
  and Gallatin, 100
  and Lodge, 415n.35
  and HA on Embargo, 13
  Anglophile-Francophobe bias of, 403
  books on, 396
  and Burr, 112, 117, 147, 172
  and excise on grain alcohol, 147
  and Gallatin, 144
  and hypothetical seizure of Texas by force, 192
  and Jefferson, 239, 395–96
  Lodge biography of, 304
  and national debt, 371
  vs. populism of U.S., 403
  as practical economist, 84
  and public debt, 147
  Talleyrand on, 151
Hamilton, Paul, 251, 259, 296, 301, 307, 315
Hamiltonians or Hamiltonianism
  and Jeffersonians, 3
  and today's situation, 402
Hamlet, quoted, 150
Hampton, Wade, 323–24, 325
Hannibal, Fabius Maximus remark on army of, 295
Hardy, Sir Thomas, 328
Harper's, Nast satire in, 79
Harrison, Benjamin, 275
Harrison, William Henry, 275, 277, 286, 316–20, 322
  Jackson's unpreparedness compared with, 361
  and logistical lines, 373
  as veteran becomes president, 380
  and Wood's engineering, 379
Harrowby, Lord, 187
Hartford Convention, 356–57, 383
Harvard College and University
  HA teaches at, 11, 87–92
    editing of Gallatin papers, 97
    Gallatin biography, 97–101, 104

Harvard College and University (*cont.*)
  Germanic influence celebrated, 39, 40
  graduate seminars introduced by, 37
  historians trained, 33–34
  and historical method, 7
  refusal of offer and acceptance, 80
  research on J. Q. Adams and "Essex Junto," 96–97
  and romanticism, 42–43
  and southern position, 29
  and Teutonism, 92–95, 124
John Adams younger expelled from, 26
J. Q. Adams as professor at, 13
and changed religious atmosphere, 384–85
decline of (1800), 131, 132
and Hildreth, 40
during War of 1812, 387
Hastings, Warren, 173
Hawthorne, Nathaniel, 38
Hay, George, 209, 210–12, 213, 214
Hay, John, 59, 60, 88, 116, 117
Hayes, Rutherford, 81
Hengist (Saxon chief proposed for national seal), 93
Henry, John, 280, 421n.12
Henry, Patrick
  and Gallatin, 100
  and Jeffersonians, 396
  papers of tracked down, 98
  Randolph's challenge to, 109
Hepburn v. Griswold, 78
Herodotus, 124
Hildreth, Richard, 39–40
Hillabee Indians, 326
Historical entropy, 130
Historical Essays (HA), 46, 67, 95
Historical research and methodology
  HA on, 91–92
  by HA on American documents, 96, 97
  by HA in Europe, 101–3, 130
    in British Museum, 45, 101, 313
  by HA on Gallatin, 97–98
  HA learns at Harvard, 87 (*see also under* Harvard College and University)

HA's refinement of views on, 7
and HA's work on Pocahontas story, 48
by gentlemen historians, 37–38
Germanists in, 39
history of, 34–37
  conjectural approach, 34–35
  turn to archival approach, 35–37
Macaulay's history from below, 126
and New England archivists, 41–42, 43
19th-century archival revolution in, 34, 36–37, 130
of Tacitus, 124
History
  HA's forward-movement view of, 284
  at postwar Harvard, 387
  role of individual in, 390–92
  see also Naval history
History of England (Macaulay), 125, 126–27
History of the Navy of the United States of America (Cooper), 303
History of the United States (Adams)
  (combined histories on Jefferson and Madison years), 1–2, 8
  and HA's diplomatic experience, 70
  and Louisa Adams, 31–32, 106
  Bancroft on treatment of Jackson in, 358
  beginning of (survey of national condition in 1800), 81, 123
    vs. end, 3–4, 123–24
  hope for future in, 138–39
  and Macaulay, 125–30
  on major regions, 130–38
  and Teutonists, 124, 125, 126
  Burr in, 117, 118
  on Burr conspiracy and trial, 201, 202, 203–4, 205–7, 209
  on cabinets of Jefferson and Madison, 60–61
  on *Chesapeake* affair, 218
  Cunningham on, 4
  and *Education* effect, 5–6, 391
  on Embargo effect, 230
  enemies of, 392–93
  "family feud" thesis on, 4–5
  and "force of the national movement," 86

and Gallatin research, 98
and Germanic influence, 39
and grandmother Louisa, 31–32
Hofstadter on, 2
vs. ideological straitjackets, 402–3
Jefferson in, 136
on Jefferson administration
  and 1800 election, 140
  and European experience vs. Jeffer-
    sonian innocence, 151
  Indian policy of, 276
  and Jefferson's post-election torpor,
    238, 239
  and Jefferson as strong executive,
    61
  turnabout from founding ideology,
    395
  see also Jefferson administration
and Madison, 188 (*see also* Madison
    administration)
naval battles in, 364
neglect of, 7
on new credit system, 372
originality of, 388
political season as time-unit of,
    140
on Randolph, 173–74, 198, 204
and slavery vs. states' rights, 113
and social change, 393
and Sumner on Jefferson, 83
style of, 8
Thucydides as model for, 41
tragic figures in, 198 (*see also*
    Randolph, John; Tecumseh;
    Toussaint Louverture)
and War of 1812, 50
  finances, 352–53
  on flaws in early stages of, 290
  see also War of 1812
and Washington experience, 50
world context of, 231, 388–89
  and trade measures during Napole-
    onic conflict, 260
  see also Adams, Henry
*History of the United States of America
    During the Administration of
    Thomas Jefferson* (Adams), 1
*History of the United States of America
    During the Administrations of
    James Madison* (Adams), 1

History of the United States (Bancroft),
    46
History of the United States (Hildreth),
    39
History of the United States (Holst),
    85
Hoar, E. Rockwood, 76
Hofstadter, Richard, 2–4, 138
Holst, H. von, 85
Homines politici, 400–401
Hopkins, Samuel, 131
Hopkinson, Joseph, 355
Hornet (U.S. sloop), 307
Horsa (Saxon chief proposed for na-
    tional seal), 93
Houghton, Henry, 116–17
Houston, Sam, 327
Howells, William Dean, 116
Hudson River School, 387
Hull, Isaac, 300, 302, 305, 308–11, 312,
    314, 380
Hull, William, 285–87, 291, 294, 296,
    314, 319
  army's new officers contrasted with,
    336
  Jackson's unpreparedness compared
    with, 361
  and logistical lines, 373
  Smyth compared to, 289
  Winder compared to, 345
Humanitarian causes, in Pennsylvania,
    134
Hume, David, 34, 35, 36, 126–27
Humphreys, Joshua, 184, 306, 310, 313,
    369
Hunt, William, 304

Ideology
  1817 confusion of, 383
  of Jefferson, 395
  and Jefferson on partnership with
    other countries, 142
  pragmatic transcending of, 377, 383–
    84, 402–3
Impeachment
  and Blount, 203
  of Samuel Chase as justice, 110, 171,
    172–75
    and Hay in Burr trial, 211–12
    as Jefferson loss, 201

Impeachment (*cont.*)
  under Jefferson administration, 169–75
  Marshall considered for, 209, 211, 214
Imperialism, in European past, 389
Impressment, 195, 200
  and HA on hypothetical seizing of Texas, 191
  British see U.S. as indifferent toward, 271
  British unanimity over, 262
  and French vs. British behavior, 262
  Madison's proposed arrangement on, 332–33
  and Monroe's 1806 draft treaty, 279
  and peace negotiation, 367
  reaffirmation of right of, 223
  and Rose mission, 226
  and settlement of *Chesapeake* grievance, 220
Inaugural address of Jefferson (first), 141–44, 249
Inaugural address of Jefferson (second), 192, 249
Inaugural address of Madison (first), 249
Indians, American
  HA on, 94
  in Battle of Tippecanoe, 275, 277–78
  and Constitution, 399
  Creek Indians and Creek War, 325–27, 358
  Embargo harmful to, 275
  Jefferson's policies toward, 276–77
  Napoleon calls for alliance with, 161
  and War of 1812, 285, 286, 291, 293, 294, 318, 320
    fear of helps Madison's re-election, 314
    in Florida, 325–27
    and peace negotiations, 367
  Washington's plan on homelands for, 404
  see also Tecumseh
Influence of Sea Power upon History, 1660-1783 (Mahan), 297
Intellectual atmosphere, 1817 changes in, 387
Intelligence, as War of 1812 flaw, 293
  vs. British intelligence, 294–95

Internal improvements
  Madison's stand against, 372, 373, 374
  as nation-making, 393
  need for, 373–74
International trade
  and Jefferson's tax policy, 147–48
  see also Neutral trade restrictions
Interposition
  and New England opposition to Enforcement Act, 243
  and New England opposition to War of 1812, 356
Intrepid, USS, 184
"Invisibles, the" (foes of Gallatin), 267
Iolanthe (Gilbert lyric), on political categorization, 396
Irony of history, nation-making as, 393
Irving, Washington, 38, 42, 125, 133, 388
Ivanhoe (Scott), 42–43
Izard, George, 339–40, 355, 379

Jackson, Andrew, 203
  in Battle of New Orleans, 359–66
  and Creek War, 325–27, 358
  Florida as objective of, 358
  Louisiana Territory under command of, 358
  and militia, 335
  as veteran becomes president, 380
Jackson, Francis James, 255, 256, 267, 273
James, Henry, 30, 151
James, William, HA letter to, 30
James, William (British historian), 302–3, 305, 306, 329, 344, 364
Java (British frigate), 312
Jay, John, 333
Jay-Gardoqui Treaty, 156, 157, 203
Jay's Treaty, 199
Jefferson, Martha (daughter), 106, 107
Jefferson, Thomas
  HA on, 3, 29–30, 136, 281
  and Beaumarchais, 8
  and Burr conspiracy, 7
  and cabinet, 60
  and democracy, 29
  and Madison, 8
  and new revolution, 381–82

and relations with advisers, 7
and research on Gallatin, 98
and strong executive, 61
wishful thinking observed, 188
and HA on Embargo, 13
and J. Q. Adams, 112–13
on American Revolution as recovery of Saxon freedoms, 93
and Armstrong, 316
and *Aurora*, 146, 179, 417n.2
and Barlow, 132
and Bayard in 1800 election, 333
books about, 396
and Burr, 140, 147
on citizen soldiery, 344
clothes of, 176–77, 178, 182
creative misreading of, 401
cruel and unusual punishments proposed by, 399
in 1805 diplomatic crisis, 189
and England, 175
and equality as applied to slaves (Declaration of Independence), 399–400, 401
Francophile-Anglophobe tilt of, 403
and Gallatin, 71, 101
and Germanic democracy, 92–93
and Hamilton, 239, 395–96
and William Henry Harrison, 275
Irving's mockery of, 388
Madison compared with, 281
Madison consoled by (1814), 350
Madison letter to, 266
and Marshall, 140, 201, 214
Jefferson seen as Napoleon's collaborator, 233
on militia, 284–85, 287, 353–54
and Napoleon, 150, 176, 389–90, 391, 392
seen as Napoleon's lackey, 130, 233
on Napoleon's offer to Madison, 263–64
and national vision, 391
and neutral-trade negotiations, 199
in *North American Review* centennial issue, 83
optimistic trust of, 391–92
and Pinkney, 272
as pliant and conciliatory, 198

popular support all-important for, 239
portrait of, 178
and pragmatism, 377
on prying land from Indians, 275–76
and Randolph, 106, 109, 110, 112, 254, 392
and religion, 82, 131
Theodore Roosevelt on, 287–88
and secession, 136
and "second revolution," 381
as secretary of state, 239
on silencing of dissent (1812), 282
small-government principles of, 395
as southerner (HA's *History*), 135
and strong federal government, 392–93
stubbornness of, 224
on "time of witches," 357
on travel difficulties, 128
U.S. improved under, 4
as Virginia governor during Revolution, 238–39
on war, 216
and War of 1812, 278, 282, 379
and financial crisis, 351
sees militias as triumphant, 284–85, 287
and West Florida, 166
and Wilkinson, 213, 214–15, 259–60, 418n.3
and Yazoo issue, 111
Jefferson administration
and Burr conspiracy, 201–8
and Marshall, 201, 208–9, 210, 211, 212–14, 215
trial for and aftermath, 208–15
cabinet of (first), 143–44
HA on, 368
as continuous with Madison, 393
and 1800 election, 140
Federalism discredited by, 382
and foreign relations, 149–52, 160
and *Chesapeake* affair, 216–22
and disregard of diplomatic etiquette, 175–83
and "double messages" to Congress, 193
Embargo, 223–25, 241–42, 243, 244 (*see also* Embargo)

Jefferson administration (*cont.*)
  and Floridas, 166–69, 176, 186 (*see also* Floridas)
  and Louisiana/Florida intrigues, 152–59
  Louisiana Purchase, 161–66 (*see also* Louisiana Purchase; Louisiana Territory)
  and Napoleon's invasion of Spain, 231–34
  negotiations with France/Spain/England over Florida and other issues (1805), 186–93
  and neutral trade, 193–201, 222–27 (*see also* Neutral trade restrictions)
  Tripolitan War, 148, 161, 183–85
  impeachments under, 169–75
  Inaugural address (first), 141–43
  and "midnight judges," 148–49
  navy neglected under, 300, 301
  and Cooper, 303
  paradoxical outcomes of, 244–45
  and patronage, 144–48, 376
  post-election paralysis of (1808–1809), 237–45
  and Embargo, 237, 240–41, 242–44
  and religious atmosphere, 384
  second term of, 186
  and War of 1812
    historians' condemnation of, 287–88
    and Hull's surrender, 287
  West nationalized by, 375–76
Jefferson and His Time (Malone), 389
Jeffersonianism
  historians on, 3
  and today's situation, 402
Jeffersonians
  HA on, 2, 5, 8
  and HA's reform efforts, 7
  and HA's study of Gallatin, 101
  and *Education*, 6
  and federal power, 113–14
  and foreign policy, 150
  and Gallatin's papers, 97
  and Hamiltonians, 3
  history as governing, 393
  Jefferson as departing from original spirit of, 393

  militarism fostered by, 380
  and Napoleon, 389
  transformation of country under, 402
  U.S. improved under, 4
Jefferson-Madison-Gallatin "triumvirate," 97
  HA on, 3
  and negotiations over U.S. demand for Florida and other issues, 188–89, 190
"Jefferson rule" on presidential subpoena, 210, 211
Jessup, Thomas, 337
John Randolph (Adams), 1, 105–6
Johns Hopkins University, 84–85
  HA invited to, 85, 90–91
  HA's influence at, 34
Johnson, Andrew, 29, 74, 75, 76
  impeachment of, 76–77
Johnson, Catherine (sister of Louisa Adams), 23
Johnson, Joshua (father of Louisa Adams), 17–18
Johnson, Louisa, 11. *See also* Adams, Louisa Johnson
Johnson, Nancy (sister of Louisa Adams), 18
Johnson, Richard, 299
Johnson, Richard Mentor, 295, 322
Johnstone, Robert, 239
Jones, John Paul, 313
Jones, Walter, 259
Jones, William, 312, 315, 347
Journalism
  by HA from England, 62
  by HA in post–Civil War period, 51
    annual reports on legislation, 77
  by HA in pre–Civil War Washington, 49
  HA's ambitions in, 40–41
Judicial independence, Jefferson's opposition to, 209
Judiciary Act (1801), 169, 171
  repeal of, 171, 201, 208
  and Chase, 169, 384
  and Marshall, 169, 384
Julia (slave helped to freedom by Louisa), 28
Julius Caesar (Shakespeare), quoted, 150

Jurisprudence, centenary view of (*North American Review*), 84

Kant, Immanuel, 39
Kedge anchors, 304, 340–41
Keitt, Lawrence, 55
Kennedy, John F., on Constitutional Convention, 396
Kentucky Resolutions, 281
Kentucky and Virginia Resolutions, 164, 243
Key, Francis Scott, 348
Key West, as young war Republicans target, 283
King, Clarence, 84
King, Rufus, 14, 154, 168, 176, 179, 236
Knox v. Lee, 78
Kutuzov, General (*War and Peace*), 390, 391

Lafitte, Jean, 362
Lake Champlain, fighting at, 302, 323, 339–41
Lake Erie, War of 1812 on, 319, 320–22, 336
Lake Ontario, in War of 1812, 323
Lamar, Lucius, 29, 47
Latin America, Randolph opposes representatives to, 113
Latrobe, Benjamin, 249
Laussat, Pierre-Clément de, 165
Lawrence (Perry flagship), 321
Lawrence, James, 301, 303, 321, 328–30, 340
Leclerc, Victor-Emmanuel, 154, 155, 159, 162, 176
Lectures on the Early History of Institutions (Maine), 95
Lee, Madeleine (HA heroine), 16, 17
Lee, Robert E., 59
  son of, 12
Legal atmosphere, 1817 change in, 384
Legal Tender Act (1862), 74, 76, 77
Leib, Michael, 146, 250
Lemay, J. A. Leo, 48
Leopard (British frigate), 216, 219, 220, 225–26, 330, 419n.1
Levy, Leonard, 204–5
Lewis, Morgan, 325
Liancourt, Duc de, 136

Library of Congress, HA's researches in, 102–3
Life of Albert Gallatin, The (Adams), 1, 29, 97–101
  pedestrian formality of, 104, 106
  as Shulman source, 298
Life of George Cabot, The (Lodge), 304
Lincoln, Abraham
  Adamses' opinion of, 62
  Charles Francis Adams on, 60, 61, 411n.8
  and HA on president's advisers, 7
  and HA's journalism, 49
  HA votes for, 50
  HA on wartime powers of, 61
  and Declaration of Independence, 399–400, 403
  and Jefferson's notion of equality, 395
  and secession crisis
    HA's reporting on, 40, 59–60
    and Seward, 57, 58
  and Seward's dispatch to Charles Francis Adams, 63
  Seward's plans for manipulation, 51
  and Seward-Sumner relationship, 51, 65
Lincoln, Levi, 111, 144, 145, 238
Linnet (British warship), 341
L'Insurgente (French warship), 340
Little Belt (British corvette), 273, 311
Liverpool, Lord, 367
Livingston, Edward, 163, 164
Livingston, Robert, 147, 151, 154, 157, 163, 166, 168, 189, 199
Livingston family, 316
Livy, 35
Lodge, George ("Bay") Cabot, 90
Lodge, Henry Cabot, 7, 29, 33, 89–90, 91, 96, 165, 304
Logistics, as fault in 1812 invasion of Canada, 293, 294
London
  HA's experience with legation in, 6, 49–50, 51, 61–71, 74, 88
  HA research in, 101–2, 313
  Macaulay on size of, 129
  see also England
Longfellow, Henry Wadsworth, and Sumner, 52

Louis XVI (king of France), Napoleon
equated with, 232
Louisiana (U.S. sloop), 362
Louisiana Government Act, 183
Louisiana Purchase, 161, 163–66
and Armstrong, 316
as based on misunderstanding, 157
and British peace treaty ambitions,
367
Clay on assumed claims implied by,
265
and difficulties of Napoleon in New
World, 162
and enumerated powers (Calhoun),
373
and "explosion of April," 162–63
and Florida, 153, 157, 166
and Madison on West Florida, 265
and Monroe's independence, 279
as nationalizing the West, 375
Randolph's authorizing of, 110
and slave power, 114
unclear boundaries of, 189
Louisiana Territory (pre-Purchase)
and Godoy, 389
intrigues over retrocession of, 152–59
and role of Toussaint's rebellion,
154, 155, 157, 159, 162
and Napoleon, 389
intent to occupy, 161–62, 176
Louisiana Territory (post-Purchase)
governance of, 164–65, 173, 375
Jackson in command of, 358
Wilkinson as governor of, 165, 173,
202, 203, 259–60, 375, 418n.3
Lowell, James Russell, 80, 101
Luisa (queen of Spain), 152–53, 158
Lundy's Lane, Battle of, 337, 363, 380
Lynching, Jefferson's recommendation
of (1812), 282
Lyons, Lord, 63, 65, 67

Macaulay, Thomas Babington, 36, 40,
93, 125–30
Macdonough, James, 340
Macdonough, Thomas, 302, 339–41,
380
Macedonian (British frigate), 312, 328,
330, 370

Macomb, Alexander, 340
Macon, Nathaniel, 98, 109, 138, 242,
257
Macon's Bills, 257–58, 263, 280
and Napoleon's letter, 263
Macon's Bill Number 2, 258, 261
Madison, Dolley, 31, 179, 180, 347,
348
Madison, James, 281–82
HA on, 7–8, 281
and cabinet, 60
J. Q. Adams rewarded by, 23
ambiguity characteristic of, 291
and British occupation of Washington, 342, 343, 346–48
and Burr, 147
and impeachment of Chase, 173
and decisions made between election
and inauguration, 237–38
Duane's attacks on, 146
in 1805 diplomatic crisis, 189
election of as president, 236
for second term, 314
and Embargo, 224
and England, 175
and Gallatin, 101
Jefferson compared with, 281
and Jefferson as diplomat, 150
and Jeffersonians, 396
and Jefferson's post-election torpor,
238
and Louisiana Territory governance,
164–65
and Macon on 1808–1809 plans,
242
and militia, 380
and Mobile River rights, 188
and Monroe in Paris, 200
as Napoleon's lackey, 130, 268
on neutral trade (book), 194
on patronage removals, 145
political style of, 250
and Randolph, 112, 197–98, 254
and War of 1812 debacles, 349
and Randolph on Monroe, 199
on relations of with advisers, 7
and Theodore Roosevelt on Jefferson,
288
and secession, 136

as secretary of state, 144
  in absence of previous foreign
    travel, 149
  on British relaxation of blockade,
    235
  and diplomatic courtesy, 182
  and Embargo, 229, 235, 237
  vs. European opponents, 150–51
  and "midnight appointment" of
    Marbury, 170
  and Napoleon's Bayonne Decree, 233
  and patronage, 146
  and prospect of war (*Chesapeake*
    affair), 218
  and Rose mission, 226, 227
  and Turreau, 182
as southerner (HA's *History*), 135
and Story as Supreme Court justice,
  242
U.S. improved under, 4
in War of 1812
  British hatred toward, 350
  British occupation of Washington,
    342, 343, 346–48, 361
  and Washington conflicts, 360
and West Florida, 166, 167
wife of, 188
and Yazoo issue, 111
Madison administration
  cabinet of, 250–51, 259, 315–16
  HA on, 368
  and Gallatin, 146
  postwar soundness of, 372
  Smith replaced by Monroe as secre-
    tary of state, 266–68
  as continuous with Jefferson, 393
  and Florida, 358
  foreign policy of
    and Floridas, 264–65, 325 (*see also*
      Floridas)
    and neutral trade, 253–56, 260–64,
      273–75 (*see also* Neutral trade re-
      strictions)
  and internal improvements, 372–74
  and Jefferson's policy on Indians, 277
  and nationalization, 245
  navy neglected under, 300–301
  and religious atmosphere, 384
  troubles of, 258–59

War of 1812
  advent of, 271, 275, 277–78, 280–
    81, 282, 296
  Battle of New Orleans, 357–64
  British ravaging of New England,
    338–39
  and Creek War, 325
  and end of Napoleon's reign, 338
  financial crisis, 350–52, 355
  Lake Champlain battles, 339–41
  on Lake Erie, 319, 320–22
  military manpower crisis, 353–55
  and navy, 296–97, 300–302, 306–
    14, 327–32
  New England opposition to (Hart-
    ford Convention), 355–57, 383,
    392
  operations against Canada (first
    year), 285–95, 314
  operations against Canada (second
    year), 316–20, 322, 323–25
  operations against Canada (third
    year), 336–38
  peace negotiations, 349, 352, 367–
    69
  plan to attack Florida, 325
  third-year changes, 335–36
  Washington captured and burned,
    341–48, 349
  see also War of 1812
  and Wilkinson, 215, 259–60
  writings produced during, 249–50
Mahan, Alfred Thayer, 297, 305
  and HA, 302, 305, 306
  on Battle of Bladensburg, 343–44
  on *Chesapeake* vs. *Shannon*, 329,
    330
  on Elliott's misconduct, 322
  on Hull's seamanship, 309
  on Jefferson's excessive optimism, 287
  and large navies, 422n.3
  on privateering, 332
  on Rodgers, 308
  on single-frigate victories, 422n.9
  War of 1812 criticisms by, 301
Mahon, John, 292
Maine, Sir Henry, 91, 94–95
Maitland, Frederic, 88
Majestic (British warship), 370

Malone, Dumas, 145, 149, 150, 172, 173, 178–79, 192, 197, 210–11, 233, 238

Jefferson and His Time, 389

Marblehead, Mass., War of 1812 seamen from, 332

Marbury, William, 170

Marbury v. Madison, 169–71, 201, 384, 417–18n.2

Maret, Hugues-Bernard, 269

Marriage, under Anglo-Saxon law, 95

Marryat, Edward, 303

Marshall, John
  and HA, 3, 7, 11–12, 169
  and Burr, 140
  and Burr conspiracy trial(s), 201, 208–9, 210, 211, 212–14, 215, 384
  and change in legal atmosphere, 384
  and Daveiss, 204, 206
  on Embargo, 236
  and Gallatin, 100
  and Hamiltonians, 396
  and Jefferson, 140, 201, 214
    seen as Napoleon's collaborator, 233
  and *Marbury v. Madison,* 169–71
  and Pinkney, 272–73
  and Randolph scandal, 106–7
  and repeal of Judiciary Act, 169
  as southerner (HA's *History*), 135
  and Story, 383–84
  Washington biography by, 403

Martin, Luther, 110, 174–75, 207–8, 210, 212

Martinez Yrujo. *See* Yrujo, Don Carlos Martinez

Martin v. Hunter's Lessee, 384

Mason, George, 135, 396

Mason, James, 64, 65–66

Mason, Jeremiah, 354

Massachusetts
  HA's disdain for, 11, 80
  and states' rights, 114
  see also New England

Massachusetts Historical Society, 43, 96, 103, 117

Mather, Cotton, 41, 387

McClure's, 78

McColley, Robert, 105

McCulloch v. Maryland, 272

McCullough, Hugh, 74, 76

McKean, Thomas, 145, 156, 167, 180

McMaster, John Bach, 123

McRee, William, 379

Mead, Cowles, 204

Medieval history, at Harvard, 87–89

Mediterranean Fund, 148

Memorial and Remonstrance (Madison), 250

Merry, Anthony, 176, 177–78, 179, 180, 181, 182, 183, 189, 190, 201, 218

Merry, Mrs. Anthony (wife of British minister), 32, 179, 180, 182

Mexican War, and politicization of military, 260

Mexico
  and Burr conspiracy, 202
  Jefferson offers aid against Spain for, 232
  and proposal to seize Texas, 191

Middle Europe, changing boundaries of, 397

Middle states
  HA's *History* on, 132–34
  economic progressiveness of, 377–78

"Midnight judges," 148–49, 169
  and Marbury, 170

Milan Decree (1807), 258, 261
  Napoleon's offer to suspend, 263, 271
  proclamation of suspension of (Madison), 264, 266
  suspension of uncertain in U.S., 268–69

Military nationalization, 379–80

Militias, American, 379–80
  Jefferson's faith in, 284–85, 287, 353–54
  officers of, 301
  privateers compared with, 332
  reasons for continuation of, 353
  regulars as replacing, 380, 393
  shortcomings of, 290, 299, 353, 379
  and War of 1812
    in Chesapeake campaign, 348
    in defense of Washington, 342, 343, 344
    at end of enlistment term, 319
    and faults in 1812 invasion, 291–92, 293
    under Jackson, 326, 335

and manpower crisis, 354–55
and myth of republican virtue, 284
New England's refusal to provide,
288, 291, 383
under Ripley, 335
Smyth's insulting of, 289
Miller (U.S. lieutenant colonel), 286
Miller, James, 337
Mills (Massachusetts senator), 250
Minuteman, mystique of, 301
Miracles, Hume's essay on, 34
Miranda, Francisco, 303
Misreading, creative, 401
Mississippi River
in War of 1812 peace negotiations,
368, 369
western transportation on, 129, 203
and navigation rights, 156
and West Florida, 157–58
Missouri Compromise, 14
Mobile
and HA on Jefferson's aims, 188
Jackson's march on, 358
and Mississippi trade, 158
War of 1812 as excuse for seizing, 325
as young-war-Republicans' target,
283
Mobile Act, 167–68
Mobile River, navigation rights on, 188
Modern Chivalry (Brackenridge), 134
Mollien, François-Nicolas, 263
Mommsen, Theodor, 91
Monarchy, desire to return to (among
Federalists), 383
Monopolies, during Madison administration, 252
Monroe, James
and HA on J. Q. Adams, 13
as 1808 candidate, 112, 236, 267
as emissary in England, 168, 187–88,
196, 198–99, 200, 219–20
Chesapeake affair demands submitted, 219–20
and *Essex* decision, 187–88
Jefferson letter to, 232
treaty negotiated and rejected
(1806), 200–201, 219, 267, 272,
279, 332
as emissary in France, 157, 162, 163–
64, 168, 188

and Florida deal, 191
Louisiana Purchase accepted, 163–
64
Louisiana Purchase boundaries
unspecified, 189
seizing of Florida urged by, 191
as emissary in Spain, 186–87
Jefferson to on Madison's performance, 350
and Randolph, 112, 193, 196, 199,
236, 267, 275
Revolutionary War experience of, 279
as secretary of state, 267
and Armstrong, 315, 323, 341–42,
348
on militias in 1812 debacles, 292
negotiations over British trade restrictions, 273–75
and past independence as emissary,
279
and War of 1812, 278–81, 282, 342,
345
as secretary of war, 348
calls for peacetime army, 372–73
and militias, 380
and shortage of military manpower,
350, 353
and shortage of money for military,
355
on Smyth's performance (War of
1812), 290
as veteran becomes president, 380
in War of 1812 political conflicts, 360
and West Florida, 166
Monroe administration
J. Q. Adams in, 383
and Floridas, 169
Monroe Doctrine, and J. Q. Adams's
success in Russia, 270
Montalivet, Comte de, 263
Montesquieu, as conjectural historian,
34
Monthly Anthology, 387, 388
Monticello, 136
dinner protocol at, 179
Jefferson driven from during Revolution, 239
as summertime residence, 218
Montpelier, 255, 256, 267, 347
Mont-Saint-Michel, as "male," 30

Mont Saint Michel and Chartres (Adams), 43, 88
    and HA's *Education*, 130
Moore, Tom, 134
Morales, Don Juan Ventura, 156
Moral leadership, Jefferson's forfeiting of (1808), 191–92, 233
Moral progress, and constitutional interpretation, 399
Morfontaine, Treaty of, 153, 154
Morgan, Edmund, 402
Morgan, Edwin, 55
Morgan, George, 206
Morgan, John, 134
Morgan, Lewis Henry, 98
Morison, Samuel Eliot, 44
Morning Post (English newspaper), 221
Morris, Gouverneur, 107
Morrison, Joseph, 324
Morse, John T., 105, 106, 116–17
Motley, John Lothrop, 33, 38, 39, 125
Mount Vernon Street, and HA, 28
Muckraking, by HA, 7, 78–79
    and *North American Review*, 80
Mulgrave, Lord, 187
Murat, General, 231
Murray, Ambrose, 55

Nagle, Paul, 24
Napoleon, Prince (cousin of Napoleon III), 65
Napoleon Bonaparte
    in HA's archival material, 103
    and HA's experience in London, 70
    in HA's *History*, 8, 151
        appreciation of, 389–390
        as adversary, 151, 190, 389–90
    Americans seen as cowards by, 223
    and Barlow, 132
    British see American demands as serving, 221
    conquered realms under brothers of, 262
    defeat of, 327, 338
    escape of from Elba, 363
    finesse and force for, 193
    as First Consul, 152
    and Florida, 166, 176, 190–91
    formal courtesies dismissed by, 181
Jefferson compared with, 391
    Jefferson's deference to and consequences, 176, 192
    Jefferson seen as collaborator or lackey of, 130, 233
    as Jefferson's opponent, 150, 176, 389–90
    and Jefferson on strength of government (HA's *History*), 143
    levée en masse of, 354
    and Louisiana Purchase, 161–63, 176
    and Louisiana Territory, 152–53, 154–55, 157, 158
    Madison seen as lackey of, 130, 268, 350
    Malone on military action against, 192
    and military draft, 354
    Monroe sees peril of for England, 200
    and neutral trade, 263
        Berlin Decree of, 222–23, 226–27, 261 (*see also* Berlin Decree)
        Cadore Letter, 263–64, 266, 268–69, 274, 280, 316
        on Embargo, 234
        and Embargo repeal, 252
        and Macon's Bill Number 2, 258
        Milan Decree, 258, 261, 263, 264, 266, 268–69, 271
        and Non-Intercourse Act, 263
        Rambouillet Decree, 261, 263
        Russia's defiance of, 269–70
        Taylor on, 267
    and Peninsular War, 231
    and role of individual in history, 391
    and Saint Domingue revolt, 159 (*see also* Saint Domingue)
    and Talleyrand, 151–52, 163, 181
        and Caribbean cul-de-sac, 162
        and New World operations, 154
        and sale of Louisiana, 163
        and War of 1812, 260
    see also France
"Narrative of a Journey from Russia to France, 1815" (Louisa Johnson Adams), 15
Nast, Thomas, 79
"Nation," change in meaning of, 402

Nation, The, 97, 99
National destiny, new postwar sense of, 387
National identity, and Jeffersonians, 2
National Intelligencer, 253
Nationalism, of Adams, 2
Nationalization (nation-making)
  and HA on Napoleon's role, 389
  complex causation of, 383
  economic, 377–79
  through Embargo, 216
  geographic, 374–77
  as irony of history, 393
  Jefferson administration results in, 245
  and Louisiana Purchase, 161
  military, 379–80
  and national party, 147, 161, 393
  and opponents of strong federal government, 392–93
  through patronage, 144, 147
  and pragmatic transcending of party ideology, 377
  through protection of trade, 148
  and Tripolitan War, 161, 185
  through Twelfth Amendment, 160
  through War of 1812, 296
  and Washington's vision, 404
  young Republicans for, 283, 284
Native American party, 52
Native Americans. *See* Indians, American
Nautilus (U.S. warship), 312
Naval architecture, 306
Naval history, 297–98, 302–6
  analytical comparisons in, 364
  see also individual historians
Naval History of Great Britain (James), 303
Naval War of 1812, The (TR), 303–4, 305
Navy, British
  complacency over, 313
  size of, 297
  subsequent dominance of, 327
Navy, U.S.
  foreign commerce dependent on, 374
  as frigates not ships of the line, 296
  (*see also* Frigates of U.S. Navy)

and Jefferson
  in drydock, 143, 217
  and need for trade protection, 148
  opposition to, 225
  seen as invitation to attack, 218
  plans for expansion of (1805), 189
  politicization of, 260
  in Tripolitan War, 184–85
  and War of 1812, 296–97, 300–302, 306–14, 327–31
  considered unnecessary, 278, 284
  historians on, 288, 302–6
  performance of army contrasted with, 299–300, 301
  and privateers, 327, 331–32
  and young commodores, 148, 300
Neutral trade restrictions, 222–223, 260–61
  and HA on hypothetical seizing of Texas, 191
  American seamen made bold and resourceful by, 313–14
  books on, 193–95, 221
  of Madison, 194, 281
  British policy on, 195, 222
  and *Essex* decision, 187, 189, 193, 194, 195–96, 200, 222
  Orders in Council, 223, 235, 253, 261, 288 (*see also* Orders in Council)
  Congressional ultimatums on, 196
  and Embargo, 223–25, 227, 234–36, 241–42, 261 (*see also* Embargo)
  and impressments, 195–96, 200 (*see also* Impressment)
  and Macon's Bills, 257–58
  Madison on, 261–62
  and Britain's "original sin," 262
  and Napoleon, 263
  Bayonne Decree, 233, 234
  Berlin Decree, 222–23, 226–27, 261 (*see also* Berlin Decree)
  Cadore Letter, 263–64, 266, 268–69, 274, 280, 316
  on Embargo, 234
  and Embargo repeal, 252
  and Macon's Bill Number 2, 258
  Milan Decree, 258, 261, 263, 264, 266, 268–69, 271

Neutral trade restrictions (*cont.*)
  and Non-Intercourse Act, 263
  Rambouillet Decree, 261, 263
  Russia's defiance of, 269–70
  negotiation efforts
    Monroe/Pinkney mission (1806),
      198–201
    Rose mission (1807), 224, 225–27
    Pinkney in London, 271–73
    Foster mission, 273–74
  and Non-Intercourse Act, 253–54,
    256–57, 258, 261, 263
  and one-sided impact of neutral
    trade, 194–95
  and Randolph's critique (HA), 197–98
  Russia's defiance of Napoleon's order
    on, 269–70
  and War of 1812, 260
Newburgh Address, 316
Newcomb, Simon, 83–84
New England
  HA's *History* on, 131–32
  archivists in, 41–42, 43
  delinquent militias of, 353
  and Embargo
    and moral leadership, 233
    resisted, 227–30, 242, 243
    return of vigor from, 383
  England's war profitable to, 271
  Jefferson on (HA *History*), 142
  moral stumbling decried in, 402
  religious changes in, 385, 386–87
  after suspension of Non-Intercourse
    Act, 254
  and War of 1812
    British allow evasion of blockade,
      327, 355
    British halt evasion of blockade,
      356
    British ravaging of (third year),
      338–39
    disadvantages of peace for, 371
    and navy, 297, 301, 310, 312
    opposition to, 278, 288, 291, 293,
      350, 355–57, 383, 392
    profit from, 355, 371, 377
    and religious change, 386–87
    and separatism, 349, 355–57
    in third year, 335

Newman, John Henry, 386
New Orleans
  Battle of, 357–64
    and peace treaty, 363, 366, 369
    pride from, 363, 366, 370
    and steamboat use, 378
  as Burr conspiracy target, 203
  closing of to U.S. shipping deposits
    (1802), 156, 190
  and Godoy, 389
  Napoleon on possession of, 161
  protests by delegates from, 183, 203
  as westerners' port, 156, 203
Newton, Sir Isaac, 127
New York
  delinquent militias of, 353
  in 1800 (HA's *History*), 132–33, 137
  patronage battles in, 145, 146–47
  transportation systems of, 378
    Erie Canal, 374, 378
  see also Middle states
"New York Gold Conspiracy, The," (HA),
  79
New York *Times,* HA's dispatches to, 62
Niagara (U.S. warship), 321, 322
Nicholas, Wilson Cary, 98, 236, 250
Nicholson, Joseph H., 110, 172
Niles, Mr. (reporter for Senate), 115–16
Nixon, Richard M., 205, 210, 211
Nock, Albert Jay, 393
Non-Importation Act (1806), 197, 199,
  200, 261
Non-importation bill, 223
Non-Intercourse Act (1809), 254, 256–
  57, 261
  and Macon's Bill, 258
  Madison's lifting of, 254, 255
  Madison's reimposition of, 256
  and Napoleon, 263
  in offer for lifting of Orders in Coun-
    cil, 253
  suspension of, 253–54
Norman Conquest, Macaulay on, 93
North American Review, 33, 46, 72, 79–
  81
  HA as editor of, 33, 40, 80, 81
  and HA on Oxford School, 93
  "Bank of England Restriction" in, 72–
    73

and *Boston Review,* 387
centennial issue of, 81–85, 125
Civil Service Reform in, 77
corruption articles in, 78
and Houghton, 116–17
Osgood as publisher of, 117
and Tilden endorsement, 81
North Carolina, HA's *History* on, 138
Nullification, and New England opposition to Enforcement Act, 243

Octagon House, 349
Of Plymouth Plantation (Bradford), 44
"Old Ironsides," 306
Olmsted case, 384
On the Equality of the Sexes and the Condition of Women (Grimké), 27
Ontario, Lake, in War of 1812, 323
Orders in Council, 222, 223, 261
and American Indians, 275
and Cadore Letter, 264
cancellation of, 288
and Embargo, 235, 240
Gallatin's warning on, 227
and Macon's Bill Number 2, 258, 263
in Madison letter to Monroe, 279
and Napoleon's decrees, 269, 273
offer to rescind, 253
relaxation of (Sweden and West Indies), 235
timber cutoff seen as forcing suspension of, 278
Oriental religions, HA's admiration of, 39
"Original intent," 398, 399, 400, 403
Osgood, James, 81, 117
Otis, Harrison Gray, 357
Oxford School of medievalists, 87, 92, 93

Pacifists, as critics of HA's *History,* 392
Pakenham, Sir Edward, 359–60, 362, 363–64
Palfrey, John Gorham, 33, 42, 43, 44, 45, 46, 47, 48, 52, 387
Palgrave, Francis, 88
Palgrave, Francis, Jr., 88
Pallavicino, Pietro, 36

Palmerston, Lord, 50, 62, 69–70, 71, 412n.22
Parkman, Francis, 33, 37, 39, 43, 94, 125, 304, 387
Parties, political
and pragmatic transcending of party ideology, 377, 383–84, 402–3
see also Federalists and Federalism; Republicans
Party-making, and nation-making, 147, 161, 393
Pastism, 401–2
Past and Present (Carlyle), 88
"Patriarchal Theory, The" (Young), 95
Patriarchy, HA vs. Maine on, 94–95
Patronage
HA's opposition to, 77
in appointment of army officers, 301
and Jefferson administration, 144–48, 376
and militia system, 353
Peacock, HMS, 329
Peale, Charles Willson, 388
Pelican (British warship), 330
Peninsular War, 231, 265
veterans of in army attacking New Orleans, 360
Pennsylvania
Cumberland Road of, 374
in 1800 (HA's *History*), 133–34, 137
Jefferson's need of, 146
and steam technology, 378
see also Middle states
Pensacola
and HA on Jefferson's aims, 188
Jackson's occupation of, 359
and Mississippi trade, 158
War of 1812 as excuse for seizing, 325
People's history, 123
Perceval, Spencer, 72, 221, 222
Perry, Christopher Raymond, 321
Perry, Matthew C., 321
Perry, Oliver Hazard, 302, 305, 320–22, 329, 340, 341, 380
Perst, George H., 91
Peter the Great (tsar of Russia), 268
Peterson, Merrill, 3, 237
Petty, William, 127
Philadelphia (frigate), 184, 329, 340

Philip II (king of Spain), 177
Physick, Philip Syng, 134, 188
Pichon, Louis-André, 149, 176, 178–79, 180
Pickering, John, 169, 170, 171–72, 201
Pickering, Timothy
  and Embargo repeal, 244
  and Florida, 265
  and Francis James Jackson, 256
  and Merry, 183
  and neutral trade's apparent success, 254
  and New Orleans victory, 363
  and northern secession, 165–66
  papers of, 96
  and Rose, 226, 227
  Treaty of Greenville negotiated by, 277
Pierce, Franklin, 67
Pike, Zebulon, 323
Pilot, The (English maritime publication), 313
Pinckney, Charles, 168, 186
Pinckney, Thomas, 326
Pinkney, William, 198–99, 200, 271–72, 274, 315
Pitt, William, 72–73, 143, 150, 158, 175, 182, 187, 190, 194, 197
Plattsburg, 339–40, 380
Plumer, William, 176, 182, 194, 215
Pocahontas, HA's essay on, 37, 38, 41, 44, 45–47, 48
  and British Museum, 45, 101, 313
  and revisionists, 47–48
Pocock, J.G.A., 36
Poland, changing boundaries of, 397
Police state, and Gallatin warning about Embargo, 229
Political atmosphere, at War of 1812 end, 382–84
Political parties
  and pragmatic transcending of party ideology, 377, 383–84, 402–3
  see also Federalists and Federalism; Republicans
Political seasons, as units of time for HA, 140
Political theories, as giving way to practicality, 381–82
Politics
  of HA (radical and socialist), 95

and HA's description of legislative process, 74–75
  HA's and Jefferson's dislike of, 30
  HA views as corrupt and degraded, 54
  centenary view of (*North American Review*), 82–83
  cyclical progress of (HA), 283–84
  New York electioneering, 132–33
  and patronage (Jefferson administration), 145–47
  and Twelfth Amendment, 160
Polk, James Knox, and Mexican War, 114
Pomone (British frigate), 370
Pope, Alexander, 387
Poplar Forest, 239
Population, changes in (1800–1816), 374
Porcupine's Gazette, 134
Porter, Moses, 342
Porter, Peter B., 290
Portfolio (publication), 134
Portland, Duke of, 221, 222
Power, Jefferson's new concept of, 143
Pragmatism of American people, 377
  and transcending of party ideology, 377, 383–84, 402–3
Preble, Edward, 184
Prescott, William Hickling, 33, 37, 38, 42, 125, 304, 387
Presentism, 401
President (U.S. frigate), 273, 307, 328, 369–70
Pressing. *See* Impressment
Prevost, Sir George, 324–25, 339, 340, 359, 379, 421n.12
Prevost, J. B., 173
"Primitive Rights of Women" (Young), 95
Privateering
  Confederate government's use of, 67
  and Declaration of Paris, 67
  in War of 1812, 327, 331–32
Proceedings of the Massachusetts Historical Society, 43, 44
Proctor, Harry, 295, 318–20, 359, 379
Professionalism
  HA's admiration for, 299
  of British in War of 1812, 286

superiority of, 379–80
U.S. Army's lack of, 292–93
in U.S. Navy, 301, 302
"Prophet, the" (brother of Tecumseh),
275, 277
Protectionism, HA and Dallas on, 372
Prussia. *See* Berlin; Germany
Psychological declaration of indepen-
dence, War of 1812 as, 382
Public debt
Jefferson's policy on, 147–48
and War of 1812 financial crisis, 352
Pufendorf, Samuel von, 194

Quasi War, 153
army not used in, 299
navy used in, 292, 297
Constitution in, 308
and Lawrence, 329
and Macdonough, 340
and Perry, 321
and Truxton, 206
and young commodores, 300
pride and professionalism from, 161
Quentin Durward (Scott), 42
Quincy, Josiah, 242
Quincy, Mass.
HA's liking for, 30, 108
Louisa Adams on, 22, 26
first presidential library in, 43
Quincy family, 12

Racism
of HA, 75, 392
of William Graham Sumner, 83
Raisin River, battle at, 318, 322
Rambouillet Decree (1810), 261, 263
Randolph, Edmund, 109
Randolph, John, 31, 32, 105–16
HA on, 111, 198
HA biography of, 1, 104, 105–6
Louisa Adams on, 109–10, 174
and Burr conspiracy, 204, 205, 208,
209, 213
in Chase trial, 173–74, 212
on district court elimination, 149
on Embargo, 230
on England vs. Napoleon, 196
and family scandal, 106–7
on invasion of Canada, 278

on "the Invisibles" (foes of Gallatin),
267
and Jefferson, 106, 109, 110, 112,
254
as betraying original purpose, 392
on Jefferson's plan for Florida, 192,
196
on Louisiana governance, 375
and Madison, 112, 197–98, 254
and War of 1812 crises, 349
on Madison administration flaws,
258–59
as mad truth-teller, 204
on mistaken proclamation on Berlin
and Milan decrees, 266
and Monroe, 112, 193, 196, 199, 236,
267, 275
papers of, 98
physical impairment of, 107–8
and Pocahontas essay, 47
on program to restore neutral trade,
196
as prototypical Republican, 402
shoddy clothing of, 177
and states' rights vs. slavery, 113–14
Randolph, Nancy, 106–7
Randolph, Richard, 106–7
Randolph, Theodorick, 107
Randolph, Thomas M., 215
Ranke, Leopold von, 36
Reconstruction, HA against, 28–29
"Record of a Life, or My Story" (Louisa
Johnson Adams), 15–16
Religion
HA and Macaulay on, 129
centenary view of (*North American
Review*), 82
changes in atmosphere of (1817),
384–87
in 1800 (HA's *History*), 131, 132
in New England historical narratives,
42
tolerance in as nation-building, 393
Report (defending Virginia Resolu-
tions), 250
Republicanism
and Jefferson's dinner table, 179
religion as check on, 131
and War of 1812, 282–83
and war-peace decisions, 201

Republicans
 vs. federal judiciary, 169
 and Jefferson's first inaugural, 141
 and Louisiana Purchase, 164
 and neutral-trade conflicts, 262
 optimism of, 376–77
 transforming pragmatism of, 377
 and War of 1812, 282–83
 young generation of, 283, 284
Republican virtue
 and invasion of Canada, 284
 Randolph bewails loss of, 112
Revisionism
 accounts of Founders' flaws as, 402
 on *Marbury*, 417–18n.2
"Revolutionary tradition," 397
Riall, Phineas, 336, 337, 359
Ripley, Eleazar, 335, 338
Rise of Silas Lapham (Howells), 116
Rochambeau, Comte de, 162
Rodgers, John, 300, 307–8
Rodney, Caesar A., 110, 210, 315, 333
Rolfe, John, 45
Romanticism
 of HA, 42–43
 in 1817 aesthetic atmosphere, 387
 and Oxford School of medievalists, 92
Rome, HA in, 33
Roosevelt, Franklin
 early death of, 238
 as secretary of navy, 304
 unkept promises of, 395
Roosevelt, Theodore
 as "big navy" man, 422n.3
 as naval historian, 302, 303–5
 and analytical comparisons, 364, 365
 on War of 1812, 306, 312, 313
 and lack of preparedness, 287–88
 naval warfare in, 300, 322, 330, 341
Rose, George, 224, 225
Rose mission, 225–27
Ross, Robert, 344, 348, 358
Roth, Paul, 92
Round Head (Indian chief), 318
Royal Navy, The, 304
Rush, Benjamin, 134
Rush, Richard, 347

Ruskin, John
 and HA's muckraking, 78–79
 HA's reading of, 89
 romantic medievalism of, 88
Russell, Jonathan, 268, 269, 274, 333
Russell, Lord John, 50, 67, 68, 69–70, 71, 412n.22
Russia
 J. Q. Adams as minister to, 14, 23–24
 and Baltic trade, 269
 defiance of Napoleon's order against, 269–70
 Motley as secretary of legation in, 38
 and Napoleon's illusion of control, 390
 revolution in, 397
 Smith offered post as minister to, 268
 War of 1812 mediation offered by, 325, 333
Rutland, Robert, 259–60, 264, 343

Saint Augustine, 54
St. Augustine, Florida, War of 1812 as excuse for seizing, 325
Saint Domingue (St. Domingo; Haiti), 154, 155, 159, 161, 162, 176, 192, 390. *See also* Toussaint Louverture
Sainte-Beuve, Charles-Augustin, 126
Samuels, Ernest, 6
San Jacinto (Union ship), 64
Saratoga (U.S. warship), 339, 340–41
Sarpi, Fra Paolo, 36
Savannah, and War of 1812, 369
Sawyer, Henry, 307, 308
Saxons. *See* Anglo-Saxons and Anglo-Saxon language; Teutonism
Schlesingers, on cyclical progress in political history, 282–83
Schumpeter, Joseph, 397
Schurz, Carl, 81
Science, centenary view of (*North American Review*), 83–84
Scott, Walter, 42, 88, 92, 303
Scott, Sir William, 187, 194
Scott, Winfield, 289, 291, 292, 335, 337, 380
Scottish Enlightenment, 35, 126, 132
Sea Power in Its Relations to the War of 1812 (Mahan), 297

Secession
  HA's hatred of, 133
  Confederacy viewed as treason, 392
  of New England
    and Hartford Convention, 356–57, 383
    peace news removes threat of, 366
    Pickering's attempt, 96, 165
    South and North in flirtations with (1798, 1804), 133, 136
    westerners' attempt at, 203
    westerners' threat of, 156
  see also Civil War; Separatism
Second Battle of New Orleans, 362
Second Embargo Supplementary Act, 227
Second Great Awakening, 386
Second of May ("Dos de Maio"), 231, 232
Secret Service of the Confederate States in Europe, or How the Confederate Cruisers Were Equipped (Bulloch), 304–5
Sectionalism, of Federalists, 376
Sedition Act, 174, 214, 282. *See also* Alien and Sedition Acts
Senate, HA on, 76
Separation of church and state, *North American Review* essays favor, 85
Separatism
  of New England (War of 1812), 383
  of Pickering and Griswold, 183
  see also Secession
Sérurier, Jean-Mathieu-Philibert, 266, 267, 274, 344, 349
Seven Years War, igniting of, 275
Seward, William, 50, 51, 56–61, 62–66, 71
  and Charles Francis Adams's mission to England, 62
  as HA father figure, 74
  and HA's journalism, 49
  HA as supporter of, 50
Shakespeare, William, quoted, 150
Shannon, HMS, 328–30
Shendandoah (Confederate warship), 68
Sherman, John, 59
Shippen, William, 134

Short, William, 244
Short History of the English People (Green), 123
Shulman, Mark Russell, 298
Sidmouth, Lord, 72
Slave power, centralized government allied with, 113–14
Slavery
  and HA on Jefferson, 392
  HA's opposition to, 75
  J. Q. Adams's stand against, 14, 28
    HA on, 14
  and Louisa Johnson Adams, 27–28
  and "agrarian virtue," 403
  and British plans for Louisiana, 358
  and conditions in South (HA's *History*), 135, 136, 138
  and Constitution, 399
  and Harrison in Northwest Territory, 275
  in Louisiana Purchase, 166
  and postwar economic boom, 371
  and Randolph, 113
  Republicans' protection of, 376
  and South's prosperity, 378
  and suggested freeing of indentured servants, 354
  Sumner opposes, 54
  and Washington, 403–4
Slidell, John, 64, 65–66, 72
Smirke, Sir Robert, 132
Smith, Bradford, 47
Smith, John, and HA's essay on Pocahontas, 43, 44, 45, 46–48
Smith, Robert
  vs. Gallatin, 259, 315
  post of minister to Russia offered to, 268, 270
  as secretary of navy, 217, 301
    and gunboat proposal, 244
    profiteering from, 251
    and Rose mission, 226
  as secretary of state, 250–51, 253, 266–67
    and Jackson, 256
    and Macon's Bill, 258
    Madison paper issued in name of, 249
    Madison writes response to Canning for, 255

Smith, Samuel, 196, 197, 198, 201, 250,
251, 258, 267, 348, 361
Smith, William, 250
Smiths of Maryland, 7
Smollett, Tobias George, 303
Smyth, Alexander, 289–90, 291, 345
Social change, complex variety of factors
in, 393
Social Darwinism, of William Graham
Sumner, 82–83
Social history
of HA, 382
and opening chapters of *History*, 3,
123, 126
"people's history" as, 123
Society of the Cincinnati, and Jefferson,
380
Sohm, Rudolph, 92
Soubiran, Paul-Émile, 421n.12
South
HA's fondness for, 11–12, 17, 28–29,
30–31
HA's *History* on, 134–38
internal improvements needed in,
373–74
plight of during War of 1812 (Jefferson), 350–51
postwar prosperity of, 371, 38
see also Virginia
South Carolina, HA's *History* on, 137–38
Spain
HA research in, 101, 102
and British designs on New Orleans,
358
and Burr conspiracy, 202, 203, 204
as England's new ally, 252
and Floridas
acquisition of, 166
controversy over ownership of,
166–68
Jefferson on, 188, 192
and Monroe mission, 186, 188
and Napoleon's aims, 153–54
and Napoleon's offer, 190
and unclear Louisiana Purchase
boundaries, 189
see also Floridas
Jefferson sees as ally against England,
199

and Louisiana, 152–54, 156, 157, 158,
163 (*see also* Louisiana Purchase)
Napoleon's invasion of, 231–34, 390
and Jefferson's deference, 192
and neutral trade, 194
and U.S. attempts to acquire Florida
and Texas (1805), 186–93, 358
Sparks, Jared, 33, 42
Spaulding, Elbridge G., 77–78
"Spirit of '63," 188, 190
Stagg, J.C.A., 280, 291
Stark, John, 284
States' rights
and Jefferson administration, 245
and Louisiana Purchase, 164
and militias, 354
and Randolph on Yazoo issue, 110
slave power as opposing, 113–14
and Story's denial of state sovereignty,
384
and Washington on slavery, 404
*Statistical History of the United States
Navy* (Emmons), 304
Steffens, Lincoln, 78
Stephen, James, 194, 221
Stevens, Thaddeus, 71, 77
Stewart, Jon, 399
Stickney, Benjamin, 284
Stockton, Robert, 354
Story, Joseph, 52, 240–41, 242, 244,
383–84
Strachey, Lytton, 99
"Strict construction," 399, 400
and Louisiana Purchase, 164
Stuarts (kings of England), Hume and
Macaulay on literature under, 127
Stubbs, William, 87, 88, 91, 94
Subpoena, to Jefferson, 209–11
Sullivan, James, 227, 228, 229
Sumner, Charles, 50, 51–56, 71
as HA father figure, 74
and HA's journalism, 49
and Civil War diplomacy toward Eng-
land, 65–66
and *Trent* affair, 65
diplomatic assignment from, 40
in growing dispute with Charles Francis Adams, 58–59
and Reconstruction, 29, 47

Sumner, William Graham, 82–83
Supply, as War of 1812 fault, 294
and Harrison campaign, 317
Supreme Court
J. Q. Adams offered appointment to, 268
and impeachment of Chase, 172–75
and Legal Tender Act, 77–78
suspended session of, 144
Swartout, Samuel, 207, 208, 212
Swift, Joseph Garner, 378
Sword of Honor (Waugh), 335
Sybel, Heinrich von, 91

Tacitus, Cornelius, 124, 124–25, 126
Talleyrand (Charles-Maurice de Talleyrand-Périgord)
as adversary, 150–51, 190
in archival material of HA, 103
and *Chesapeake* affair reports, 218
on England-U.S. alliance, 231
finesse and force for, 193
and Florida, 157, 166, 167, 168, 186, 190–91, 192, 197
and Godoy (HA), 158
Jefferson messages to, 142, 155
and Louisiana, 157, 265
and non-alienation pledge, 154, 163, 168
and Monroe, 187
and Louisiana Purchase treaty, 168
and Monroe's duplicity, 274
and Napoleon, 151–52, 163, 181
and Caribbean cul-de-sac, 162
and New World operations, 154
and sale of Louisiana, 163
on "non-intervention," 172
Sérurier letter to on White House burning, 344
successor to, (Champagny), 262
and XYZ affair, 155
Tammany organization, 133
Tarbell, Ida, 78
Taxes, Jefferson's policy on, 147–48
Taylor, Henry Osborne, 34
Taylor, John, 164, 267, 274–75, 377, 383
Taylor, Zachary, 380
Tecumseh, 8, 275, 276, 277–78, 293, 295

and American settlements in West, 285
Brock on, 286
and Creek Indians, 325
death of, 295, 322
and invasions of Canada, 285–86, 320, 322
as tragic figure, 198
Territorial administration, U.S. laws on, 264. *See also* Governance act for Louisiana
Teutonism, 92–95
and first part of HA's *History*, 124, 125, 126
Texas
and HA on Jefferson's aims, 188
annexation of, 114
and Louisiana Purchase
and demand for surrender of, 186
proposal to seize by force, 188, 191
"Thanatopsis" (Bryant), 388
Thatcher, Samuel Cooper, 385
Thiers, Louis-Adolphe, 36
Third Battle of New Orleans, 362
Thirteenth Amendment, 401
Adams support for, 75
Thomas Watson (southern blockade runner), 68
Thoreau, Henry David, 39
Thornton, Edward, 176
Thucydides, 6, 40–41, 140, 230
Thwing, Charles Franklin, 90
Ticknor, George, 39, 387
Tilden, Samuel, 81, 97
Times (London), 312, 366
Tippecanoe Creek, Battle of, 275, 277–78, 316, 322
Harrison as supposed hero of, 380
Tocqueville, Alexis de, 37
Tolstoy, Leo, *War and Peace*, 2
and historical causation, 390–91, 393
Tom Jones (Fielding), 113
Tomkins, Daniel, 229, 348
Tonnant (British warship), 359
Toombs, Robert, 55
Totten, Joseph Gilbert, 340, 379
Toussaint Louverture, 8, 103, 150, 153, 154, 157, 159, 162, 233, 278

Toussaint Louverture (*cont.*)
  Perry's services in aid of, 321
  as tragic figure, 198
Trade, international
  and Jefferson's tax policy, 147–48
  see also Neutral trade restrictions
Tragic figures, in HA's *History*, 198. *See also* Randolph, John; Tecumseh; Toussaint Louverture
Transactions and Collections of the American Antiquarian Society, 43, 44
Transcendentalism, 39, 385, 387
  and Sumner, 52
Transportation
  HA and Macaulay on, 128–29
  on Mississippi, 129, 156, 203
  New York as pioneer in, 378
Treason
  HA sees Confederacy as, 392
  constitutional definition of, 209, 213
Treaty of Fort Jackson, 327
Treaty of Ghent, 372
Treaty of Greenville, 277
Treaty of Morfontaine, 153, 154
Treaty of Paris, 152
Trent affair, 64
Tres de Maio, El (Goya painting), 231
Tripolitan War, 148, 161, 183–85, 255, 292, 363
  army not used in, 299
  navy used in, 297
    Constitution in, 308
    and Lawrence, 329
    and Macdonough, 340
    and Perry, 321
  and TR on experience of naval officers, 300
Triumvirate. *See* Jefferson-Madison-Gallatin "triumvirate"
True Relation of Virginia (Smith), 45, 46
Truxton, Thomas, 205, 206, 300
Tucker, Henry St. George, 113
Tucker, St. George, 108, 114
Turner, Frederick Jackson, 47, 375
Turreau, Louis-Marie, 182
  on Burr conspiracy, 201
  on Embargo, 252
  on English offer, 254

in exchange with Madison on Florida and Louisiana, 167
  and Jefferson on Embargo, 234
  on Jefferson's isolation, 183
  on prospects of war, 218, 220–21
  recall of, 263
  and Smith, 267
Twain, Mark, *The Gilded Age*, 77
Twelfth Amendment, 160
Two Million Act, 193, 196
Tyler, John, as veteran becomes president, 380
Tyler, Royall, 407n.29

Unitarians, 384–386, 387
United States
  as oldest democracy, 396
  and "revolutionary tradition," 397
  sense of special destiny for, 388
United States (frigate), 307, 310, 312, 328, 330, 370
United States Bank, 112, 251, 257, 293, 351

Valle, James E., 300
Van Buren, Martin, 314
Vanity Fair, 58
Van Rensselaer, Stephen, 289, 291, 294, 301
Vansittart, Nicholas, 72
Vengeance (French frigate), 300
Victor, Marshal, 161
Vienna Decree (1809), 261
Viollet-le-Duc, Eugène-Emmanuel, 89
Virginia
  HA's *History* on, 135–36, 137, 138
  hospitality of, 179
  internal improvements needed in, 373–74
  see also South
Virginia dynasty, Clinton's wish to displace, 251
Virginia and Kentucky Resolutions, 137
Virginia Resolutions (1798), 197, 250, 356
Vixen (U.S. warship), 312
Voltaire, 34, 35, 99

Wagner, Richard, 88
Walpole, Horace, 40

War
  and *Chesapeake* affair, 218, 219
    Gallatin on prospect of, 219
  commercial restrictions as substitute
    for, 258, 278
  Jefferson's attitude toward, 216
  and nationalization, 245
  vs. permanent embargo (Gallatin),
    224
*War in Disguise, or the Frauds of the
    Neutral Flags* (Stephen), 194
War of 1812
  and HA, 2–3, 7, 8
    approval of, 392
    Civil War experiences, 71
    study of British economic condi-
      tions, 50
  J. Q. Adams's negotiation of end to,
    24
  advent of
    and Battle of Tippecanoe, 275, 277–
      78
    congressional declaration of war,
      280–81, 282, 296
    as unexpected, 271
  armistice offer by England, 288
  Battle of New Orleans, 357–64
  as breaking psychological/cultural de-
    pendence on England, 382
  crises springing from
    financial, 350–52, 355
    of military manpower, 353–55
  and Embargo, 241
  and end of Napoleon's reign, 327, 338
  invasion of Canada
    in East, 288–89
    in East (second year), 323–25
    in East (third year), 336–38
    expectations for, 278, 332, 379
    and Lake Erie battles, 319, 320–22
    reasons for defeat in, 290–95
    and "Upper" vs. "Lower" Canada,
      285
    in West, 285–88, 314
    in West (retaking of Detroit), 316–
      20, 322
  lack of preparedness for, 284–85, 299
  Lake Champlain fighting (third year),
    339–41
  Mahan on, 297–98
  and Monroe, 279–81, 282, 342, 345
  and Napoleon, 260, 389
  and navy, 296–97, 300–302, 306–14,
    327–32
    against British blockade, 327–28,
      329
    considered unnecessary, 278, 284
    historians on, 288, 302–6
    last sea fight, 369–70
    performance of army contrasted
      with, 299–300, 301
    and privateers, 327, 331–32
    and young commodores, 148, 300
  and New England
    British allow evasion of blockade,
      327, 355
    British halt evasion of blockade,
      356
    British ravaging of (third year),
      338–39
    disadvantages of peace for, 371
    and navy, 297, 301, 310, 312
    opposition to, 278, 288, 291, 293,
      350, 355–57, 383, 392
    profit from, 355, 371, 377
    and religious change, 386–87
    and separatism, 349, 355–57
    in third year, 335
  peace negotiations, 333–35, 367–69
    and Battle of New Orleans, 363
    and Britain's knowledge of U.S.
      plight, 352
    Britain's original demands, 349–50,
      367
    original U.S. position, 367
    and revengeful British public opin-
      ion, 366–67
    settlement, 357
    and *uti possidetis* principle, 367,
      368, 369
  political atmosphere changed by,
    382–83
  and postwar euphoria, 370–71
  prevention of (Malone on Jefferson),
    192
  purpose of, 278, 282
  Randolph's opposition to, 112
  and Republicans' stance, 282–83
  seizure of Florida as obviating, 233
  and slave power, 114

War of 1812 *(cont.)*
  in South
    and Creek War, 325–27
    plan to take Florida, 325
  third-year changes in, 335–36
  veterans of as president, 380
  Washington captured and burned,
    328, 341–48
    aftermath of, 349
    Jackson's lesson on, 361
  and Wilkinson, 215
War finance, as 1812 fault, 293–94
War and Peace (Tolstoy), 2, 390–91, 393
Washington, D.C.
  HA's preference for, 11, 31
  British capture and burning of, 341–
    48
    aftermath of, 349
    burning of York as precedent for,
      323
    Jackson's lesson on, 361
Washington, George, 403–4
  and HA, 3, 11–12, 403
  on U. S. Grant, 76
  and Adams family, 425n.3
  as childless, 25
  and "entangling alliances," 142–43,
    381
  Fabian presidency of, 404
  and Hamilton, 396
  and William Henry Harrison, 275
  in igniting of Seven Years War, 275
  and Jefferson's plea to rescue Virginia,
    238–39
  and nationalization, 404
  on need for hygiene in military, 290
  and Pinkney, 272
  on slavery, 136
  as southerner (HA's *History*), 135
Washington administration, frigates
    built during, 299, 306, 310
Wasp (U.S. sloop), 303, 312
Watchtower (Cheetham publication),
    147
Waugh, Evelyn, 335
Webster, Daniel, 53, 351–52, 354
Weed, Thurlow, 50, 56–57, 58, 66, 74
"We have met the enemy and they are
    ours," 321
Weigley, Russell, 290

Weld, Theodore, 28
Wellesley, Arthur (Duke of Wellington),
    235, 360
  and Pakenham, 360
  and peace negotiations, 369
Wellesley, Marquis of, 271–72, 273
Wells, David, 74
West (U.S.)
  growth of, 374
  Mississippi as avenue for, 203
    and navigation rights, 156
  nationalizing of, 375–76
  pioneer pragmatism in, 374–75
  as unifying force (*History*), 392
West, Benjamin, 388
West Florida, 157–58, 162
  rebellion in and U.S. seizure of, 264–
    65, 373, 392
    British protest against, 274
  see also Floridas
West Point
  increasing numbers of officers from,
    380
  military engineers from, 378–79
Whig party, 52–53
Whiskey Rebellion, 133, 134, 147, 203
White, Horace, 81
White, Leonard, 239
White House, burning of, 344, 347
Wilkinson, James, 165
  and Burr conspiracy, 165, 203–4, 205,
    206, 207, 208, 213, 215
    and Randolph, 112
  and Jefferson, 213, 214–15, 259–60,
    418n.3
  letter(s) of, 209, 211
  as Louisiana Territory governor, 165,
    173, 202, 203, 259–60, 375,
    418n.3
  and Madison, 259, 260
    and Eustis as secretary of army,
      251
  and patronage, 301
  in War of 1812, 291, 323–25
  Winder compared to, 345
William and Mary, College of, 135, 384–
    85
Wilson, Joseph, 53
Wilson, Woodrow, unkept promises of,
    395

Winchester, James, 317–18, 345
Winder, Levin, 342, 348
Winder, William, 342, 343, 345–46,
    347, 348, 350, 360
  and engineers, 379
  Jackson's unpreparedness compared
    with, 361
Wingfield, Edward, 44
Winning of the West (TR), 304
Wirt, William, 349, 357
Wistar, Caspar, 134
Women
  and HA on coeducation, 414n.29
  HA on subjugation of, 95
  as excluded from political life, 400
  in Germanic tribes, 124
Wood, Eleazar Derby, 320, 379
Worcester, Marquis of, 128

Wright, Robert, 282
Writings of Albert Gallatin, The (Ad-
    ams), 1
Wythe, George, 135

XYZ affair, 155

Yazoo issue, 110–11, 158
  and Marshall, 384
  and Randolph, 110–12, 174, 193, 196–
    97
York (now Toronto), seizure and burn-
    ing of in War of 1812, 323
Young, Ernest, 95
Yrujo, Don Carlos Martinez, Marqués de
    Casa, 101, 156, 167, 179, 180, 182,
    202
  wife of, 179